Encyclopedia of the Great Depression and the New Deal

Volume Two

James Ciment, Editor

 SHARPE REFERENCE

An imprint of M. E. Sharpe, INC.

SHARPE REFERENCE

Sharpe Reference is an imprint of M.E.Sharpe INC.

M.E.Sharpe INC.
80 Business Park Drive
Armonk, NY 10504

Library of Congress Cataloging-in-Publication Data

Ciment, James.
Encyclopedia of the Great Depression and the New Deal / James Ciment
p. cm.
Includes bibliographical references and index.
ISBN 0-7656-8033-5 (set; alk. paper)
1. United States–History–1933-1945–Encyclopedias. 2. Depressions–1929–United States–Encyclopedias. 3. New Deal, 1933-1939–Encyclopedias. I. Title.
E806.C543 2000
973.917'03–dc21   00-056285
CIP

Printed and bound in the United States of America

The paper used in this publication meets the minimum requirements of American National Standard for Information Sciences—Permanence of Paper for Printed Library Materials,
ANSI Z 39.48.1984.

(BM) 10 9 8 7 6 5 4 3 2 1

CONTENTS

PART V
BIOGRAPHIES

INTRODUCTION TO PART V

Section V of the *Encyclopedia of the Great Depression and the New Deal* includes over 250 biographies of major personalities of the Great Depression era. A person familiar with the names in the Table of Contents will immediately notice two obvious characteristics about the list: the vast majority of the personalities on it are white and most of them are male. (And the vast majority are American, though a few key foreign leaders from Canada, China, France, Germany, Great Britain, Italy, Mexico, and the Soviet Union are included.)

For the most part, African Americans were excluded from participating in the nation's politics and governance during the Great Depression, although the administration of President Franklin D. Roosevelt did take the first tentative steps toward racial inclusion in its appointments. Congress and the courts, of course, were almost fully the white man's preserve. Business and even union leadership—with the notable exception of A. Philip Randolph and his Brotherhood of Sleeping Car Porters—was equally closed off to African Americans. For women, the picture was no less bleak. True, Roosevelt appointed the first female cabinet member in American history—Labor Secretary Frances Perkins—but that bold choice was a rare one. And as for Congress and the courts, they remained as male as they were white.

The vast majority of entries fall into three general categories: politics, business and labor, and culture. In the first are key congressmen (no significant congress-women emerged in the period); top officials in the administrations of Presidents Herbert Hoover and Franklin Delano Roosevelt; virtually all of the Supreme Court justices; and several important personages in local and state government.

As this was an era in which government service and labor unions eclipsed business as the arena of change, business figures are fewer in this volume than they would be in an encyclopedia about other eras, such as, for instance, the 1920s. Still, the biographies of several key corporate leaders are included here. (It is interesting to note that high-profile gangsters figure in the history of the Great Depression more prominently than businesspersons.) More numerous are the profiles of the era's militant and high-profile union leaders.

Roughly half of the people included in this biography section are cultural figures. They include writers, artists, musicians, intellectuals, and athletes, as well as film, radio, and theatrical personalities. Despite—or, perhaps, because of—the bleak economic times, popular culture was at the center of American life. Both talking films and radio, although introduced before the stock market crash, came into their own during the Great Depression. And, of course, it is in the realm of culture—both so-called high culture (literature, art) and low (media, sports)—that African Americans and women feature most prominently, in one of the few truly meritocratic arenas of public life in the pre–civil rights and pre–women's liberation era.

ABBOTT (BUD) AND COSTELLO (LOU)

A popular radio, Broadway, and film comedy duo, William "Bud" Abbott and Louis "Lou" Costello made their radio debut in 1938, with Costello playing the buffoon and Abbot acting the straight man.

Abbott was born in Asbury Park, New Jersey, in 1896 and Costello in Paterson, New Jersey, in 1908. Abbott, who came from a theatrical family, worked odd jobs in the theater as a young man, while Costello had been a prizefighter, stuntman, and actor. In 1929, Costello was doing a vaudeville act at the Empire Theater in New York when his regular straight man fell ill. Abbot, working in the box office, agreed to go on with him.

For the next nine years, the two performed their comedy skits on stages around the country, until they debuted on the radio in 1938 and then on Broadway—in *The Streets of Paris*—in 1939. Two years later, they made *Buck Privates*, the first of many films they did together. Costello died in 1959, and Abbott in 1974.

See also: films, feature; radio.

Bibliography

Dunning, John. *On the Air: The Encyclopedia of Old-Time Radio.* New York: Oxford University Press, 1998.

Thomas, Bob. *Bud & Lou: The Abbott & Costello Story.* Philadelphia: Lippincott, 1977.

ACE, GOODMAN AND JANE

One of the most prolific and popular radio writing and entertaining teams of the 1930s, Goodman and Jane Ace wrote and performed together on the radio show *Easy Aces* from 1928 to 1945.

Goodman, born in 1899, and Jane, in 1905, met while working on his high school newspaper in Kansas City, Missouri. Goodman, a reporter for the Kansas City *Post*, was the first to enter radio when he took a job on a local radio station hosting a fifteen-minute daily program commenting on daily life and current events.

Soon he brought his wife into the act, and their natural, conversational style won a devoted following in Kansas City and, through syndication, nationally.

The show was known for its wry humor and Jane's many malapropisms. While a later effort to put the show on television failed, Goodman became a comedy writer for TV personalities Milton Berle, Sid Caesar, and others. Jane and Goodman died in 1974 and 1982, respectively.

See also: radio.

Bibliography

Dunning, John. *On the Air: The Encyclopedia of Old-Time Radio.* New York: Oxford University Press, 1998.

Hilmes, Michele. *Radio Voices: American Broadcasting, 1922–1952.* Minneapolis: University of Minnesota Press, 1997.

ACUFF, ROY

Called the "King of Country Music" in the 1930s, Roy Acuff is best known for reviving the musical traditions of rural southern whites. A singer, songwriter, and fiddle player, he became nationally famous through radio broadcasts from the "Grand Ole Opry" theater in Nashville.

Acuff was born in Maynardsville, Tennessee, in 1903. As he grew up, he listened to what was called at the time "hillbilly" music, since referred to as "bluegrass." Along with his backup, the Smoky Mountain Boys, Acuff wrote and performed such hit songs of the Great Depression era as "The Great Speckled Bird" and "The Wabash Cannonball," which became his theme song.

Acuff later entered politics, though his bid to become Tennessee's governor in 1948 fell short. He continued to record country music in the 1950s and 1960s, and died in 1992.

See also: music; radio.

Bibliography

Dunning, John. *On the Air: The Encyclopedia of Old-Time Radio.* New York: Oxford University Press, 1998.

Hilmes, Michele. *Radio Voices: American Broadcasting, 1922–1952.* Minneapolis: University of Minnesota Press, 1997.

ADAMIC, LOUIS

A journalist, novelist, and social essayist, Louis Adamic is best known for his 1938 book *My America*, a combination autobiography and utopian essay on the importance of unity among the American people.

Born in 1899 in Slovenia, then part of the Austro-Hungarian Empire, Adamic came to the United States in 1913 and became a citizen five years later. As a journalist, Adamic wrote about immigrant issues and explored the failure of the immigration assimilation model in his book *Laughing in the Jungle* in 1932. Returning to Yugoslavia in 1934—of which Slovenia was then a part—Adamic wrote a series of novels about a man who tries to return to his peasant roots.

In *My America*, Adamic explored the issues of ethnic and racial diversity in America and lamented that the country would never fulfill its dream and potential unless divisions among the nation's peoples were overcome. Beginning in 1940, he served as editor of the journal *Common Ground*, which also explored racial and cultural issues.

Adamic became a supporter of Yugoslav communist leader Josip Broz Tito in the post–World War II era. When Adamic died of a gunshot wound in 1951, political foul play was suspected, but authorities ruled his death a suicide.

See also: African Americans; literature; newspapers and magazines.

Bibliography

Adamic, Louis. *Laughing in the Jungle.* New York: Arno Press, 1969 (reprint).

————. *My America, 1928–1938.* New York: Da Capo Press, 1976 (reprint).

McWilliams, Carey. *Louis Adamic and Shadow-America.* Los Angeles: A. Whipple, 1935.

AGEE, JAMES

Among the most widely read and influential film critics of the 1930s and 1940s, James Agee is probably best known to history for *Let Us Now Praise Famous Men* (1941), a book he collaborated on with photographer Walker Evans on impoverished sharecroppers in the Great Depression.

Agee was born in Tennessee in 1909. After attending Harvard, he became a critic, writing for *Fortune* and *Time* under the pseudonym "In the Nation." In 1936, *Fortune* sent Evans and him to Alabama for six weeks to chronicle sharecropper life. The article never appeared, but five years later he turned his magazine accounts into the lyrical prose that filled the book *Let Us Now Praise Famous Men.*

In the 1940s and 1950s, Agee turned to screenwriting (*The African Queen* and *The Night of the Hunter*) and fiction, with his most famous novel, *A Death in the Family*, published posthumously in 1957, two years after his death.

See also: *Let Us Now Praise Famous Men;* literature; newspapers and magazines; Evans, Walker.

Bibliography

Bergreen, Laurence. *James Agee: A Life.* New York: Dutton, 1984.

Maharidge, Dale. *And Their Children After Them: The Legacy* of Let Us Now Praise Famous Men: *James Agee, Walker Evans, and the Rise and Fall of Cotton in the South.* New York: Pantheon, 1989.

ALEXANDER, WILL

A liberal southerner and agricultural expert, Will Alexander played a critical role in the shaping of the Bankhead-Jones Farm Tenancy Act, the legislation that created the Farm Security Administration (FSA). Then, as head of the FSA, Alexander, though white himself, made sure the agency helped the poorest sharecroppers—regardless of race—and provided government loans to more than 50,000 black farm families.

Alexander was born in rural Missouri in 1884, receiving his bachelor of arts from Scarritt-Morrisville College and, in 1912, a bachelor of divinity degree from Vanderbilt University. After serving as a minister in various southern cities, including a stint in Nashville, working with the unemployed, Alexander founded the Commission on Inter-racial Cooperation in Atlanta, which he headed from 1919 to 1944. He was also involved in a number of other organizations promoting racial equality and harmony and served on the boards of a number of black colleges around the South.

Best known for his work on behalf of southern sharecroppers—he coauthored a book on the subject, *The Collapse of Cotton Tenancy*, in 1935—Alexander was appointed assistant head of the Resettlement Administration by its director, Rexford Tugwell, in 1935. At the same time, he was a member of President Franklin D. Roosevelt's Commission on Farm Tenancy. There, he helped shaped the FSA and was then appointed to direct it. Alexander was instrumental in keeping the FSA vital and active in the face of growing opposition from conservatives in Congress.

Aside from helping sharecroppers with loans, Alexander commissioned filmmaker Paul Lorentz to make two documentaries on rural America and its troubles—*The River* (about the Mississippi and its flooding problems) and *The Plow That Broke the Plains* (concerning the poor farming practices that had led to soil erosion). In addition, Alexander hired a number of photographers—including Walker Evans, Dorothea Lange, and Gordon Parks—to document farm poverty, in order to stir up concern among the public and government officials.

Alexander resigned from the FSA in 1940. During World War II, he worked with various manpower agencies to make sure that hiring programs were racially blind. He then worked in various philanthropic agencies. Alexander died in 1956.

See also: agriculture; films, documentary and newsreel; photography; Southern Tenant Farmers Union; Farm Security Administration; Resettlement Administration; Evans, Walker, Lange, Dorothea; Tugwell, Rexford.

Bibliography

Dykeman, Wilma. *Seeds of Southern Change: The Life of Will Alexander.* New York: Norton, 1976.

Johnson, Charles S., Will Alexander, and Edward R. Embree. *The Collapse of Cotton Tenancy.* Chapel Hill: University of North Carolina Press, 1935.

ANDERSON, MARIAN

Marian Anderson was an African-American opera singer who was refused the right to sing at Constitution Hall in Washington, D.C., in 1939 by the Daughters of the American Revolution, a women's patriotic group. In response, First Lady Eleanor Roosevelt invited Anderson to perform at the Lincoln Memorial, where a mixed-race audience listened to her lilting contralto voice.

Born in poverty in Philadelphia in 1897, Anderson received her first musical training in the choir of the Union Baptist Church. Accepted into training by the New York Philharmonic Orchestra in 1925, Anderson then moved to Europe, where she performed until 1935.

After the 1939 episode in Washington, she was asked to perform at the White House and became the first African American to sing with the Metropolitan Opera in New York in 1955. Anderson died in 1993.

See also: African Americans; music; Roosevelt, Eleanor.

Bibliography

Anderson, Marian. *My Lord, What a Morning: An Autobiography.* Madison: University of Wisconsin Press, 1992.

Keiler, Allan. *Marian Anderson: A Singer's Journey.* New York: Scribner, 2000.

Marian Anderson sings "The Star Spangled Banner" on Easter Sunday 1939, commemorating the first anniversary of her memorable concert on the steps of the Lincoln Memorial. After the Daughters of the American Revolution refused to allow the African-American contralto to sing at their Constitution Hall, First Lady Eleanor Roosevelt arranged the Lincoln Memorial concert. *(Library of Congress)*

ARMSTRONG, LOUIS

One of the greatest jazz musicians of all time, Louis Armstrong established his reputation as a consummate trumpet-player in the 1920s and, in the 1930s, went on to become a bandleader, vocalist, film star, and comedian.

Born in New Orleans in 1901, Armstrong was drawn to music at a young age, following the city's various marching bands as a boy and joining some of them as a trumpeter in his teens. In 1922, he was made second trumpet in the famed band of King Oliver, the Creole Jazz Band, where Armstrong made some of his first recordings.

As leader of his own Hot Five and Hot Seven ensembles, Armstrong—also known as Satchmo—redefined New Orleans jazz in several key recordings between 1925 and 1928, with "Savoy Blues" and "West End Blues." With them, Armstrong helped usher in the age of the virtuoso jazz solo within an ensemble piece.

Around the same time, Armstrong was also developing the innovative "scat" style of singing, which strung together nonsensical syllables as if the voice itself was a musical instrument. This style of singing would soon be picked up by Ella Fitzgerald and others.

In the 1930s, Armstrong became a national celebrity, not only with hits like "Wild Man Blues" and "Gut Bucket Blues" but also as a comic film actor in movies like *She Done Him Wrong* (1933), starring Mae West. In the years to come, Armstrong would continue to record and act in films. He also became something of a goodwill ambassador for the United States after World War II. Armstrong died in 1971.

See also: films, feature; music; West, Mae.

One of the great innovators in the history of jazz, trumpeter Louis Armstrong had numerous hits in the 1930s, including "Wild Man Blues" and "Gut Bucket Blues." *(Brown Brothers)*

Bibliography

Armstrong, Louis. *Satchmo: My Life in New Orleans*. New York: Prentice-Hall, 1954.

Storb, Ilse. *Louis Armstrong: The Definitive Biography*. New York: Peter Lang, 1999.

ARNOLD, THURMAN

An important legal thinker whose ideas about an expansive regulatory state influenced many New Dealers, Thurman Arnold was head of the Department of Justice's antitrust division, which he expanded and energized dramatically, from 1937 to 1943.

Born to a well-to-do family in Laramie, Wyoming, in 1891, Arnold graduated Phi Beta Kappa from Princeton in 1911 and received his law degree from Harvard in 1914. He opened his own law firm in Chicago in 1916. Shortly thereafter, his National Guard unit was sent on an expedition to Mexico against revolutionary Pancho Villa; from 1917 to 1918, Arnold served in the artillery in World War I.

Returning to Wyoming after the war, he practiced law with his father and went into politics, serving in the state legislature and as mayor of Laramie. In 1927, he was appointed dean of the West Virginia University Law School, where he helped reform the state's legal system. In 1930, he joined the faculty of the Yale Law School, where he taught until 1937 and published several critical political and legal texts, including *The Symbols of Government* (1935) and *The Folklore of Capitalism* (1937), dealing with the importance of popular symbols, stories, and myths in formulating effective policy.

The texts were influential with many New Dealers and led Attorney General Robert Jackson to appoint Arnold assistant attorney general for the antitrust division. Arnold set himself three goals to revitalize the division: a well-publicized, consistent policy; an expansion of staff; and an end to partisan politics within the division.

Indeed, Arnold increased staff from several dozen to over 300 lawyers and launched 215 investigations, leading to ninety-three suits. But Arnold was less interested in breaking up companies than he was in making sure that they knew that he was keeping a close eye on their activities and that he would intervene unless they pursued nonmonopolistic, fair business practices.

With the onset of World War II, however, the Franklin D. Roosevelt administration became less interested in controlling big business than in harnessing it to the war effort. Arnold grew disgusted at the limitations he was placed under and resigned his post in 1943. Roosevelt then appointed him to the Court of Appeals for the District of Columbia, where he served until 1945, before going into private practice.

After the war, Arnold worked on several high-profile cases defending persons charged with communist espionage. He died in 1969.

See also: New Deal, first; New Deal, second.

Bibliography

Arnold, Thurman. *The Symbols of Government*. New Haven: Yale University Press, 1935.

Arnold, Thurman. *The Folklore of Capitalism*. New Haven: Yale University Press, 1937.

Edwards, Corwin. "Thurman Arnold and the Anti-Trust Laws." *Political Science Quarterly* 42 (September 1943): 143–55.

ASTAIRE, FRED AND ROGERS, GINGER

The most renowned and accomplished dancing couple in American cinematic history, Fred Astaire and Ginger Rogers starred together in several popular films in the 1930s, including *Flying Down to Rio* (1933), *The Gay Divorcee* (1934), *Top Hat* (1935), and *Swing Time* (1936).

Astaire was born in Omaha in 1899 and studied dance from the age of four. By 1906, he was dancing with his sister Adele on the vaudeville stage, breaking onto Broadway in 1917. The two achieved world renown with such stage hits as *For Goodness Sake* (1922), *Funny Face* (1927), and *The Band Wagon* (1931). In 1932, Adele retired and Fred began looking for a new dance partner, whom he found in Ginger Rogers.

Born Virginia Katherine McMath in Independence, Missouri, in 1911, Rogers also began her dancing career on the vaudeville stage, before going on to Broadway in 1929. Her big break there came in George Gershwin's *Girl Crazy* in 1930. The following year, she moved on to Hollywood, where she hooked up with Astaire in 1933.

As a team, they were known for their perfect coordination of movement and the lightness and elegance of their steps. Most of their movies were in the highly sophisticated style of the musical comedies of the day. But Astaire and Rogers films were also appreciated by critics for their ability to mesh plot and song effortlessly.

For all her grace on the dance floor, Rogers preferred dramatic acting and starred in a number of films. In 1940, she won a best actress Academy Award for playing the title role in *Kitty Foyle*. She continued to star in films and on the stage through the 1970s. Rogers died in 1995.

Astaire, meanwhile, went on to dance with numerous other partners, including Rita Hayworth, Judy Garland, Cyd Charisse, and Audrey Hepburn. He was awarded a special Academy Award in 1949 for his contributions to movie musicals. Astaire continued to star on film and in television until his death in 1987.

See also: films, feature; music; Gershwin, George.

Bibliography

Croce, Arlene. *The Fred Astaire & Ginger Rogers Book*. New York: Vintage Books, 1977.

Dickens, Homer. *The Films of Ginger Rogers*. Secaucus, NJ: Citadel Press, 1975.

Mueller, John E. *Astaire Dancing: The Musical Films*. New York: Knopf, 1985.

AUTRY, GENE

Among the most popular and lasting of the "singing cowboys" of the 1930s, Gene Autry became the premier star of the so-called B, or low-budget, westerns of the era, playing in both movie serials and feature films.

Born in Texas in 1907, Autry moved to Oklahoma as a teenager and became a railroad telegraph operator. Autry was also singing, playing guitar, and composing songs. In 1929, he had his first hit record with "That Silver-Haired Daddy of Mine," which sold over half a million copies.

In 1930, he began his own radio show in Oklahoma where he developed his signature yodeling style of country music vocals, earning himself the sobriquet "Oklahoma's Yodeling Cowboy." Signed to Columbia Records that same year, he recorded a number of hits in the 1930s, including "A Gangster's Warning," "My Old Pal of Yesterday," and the labor song "The Death of Mother Jones."

Referred to in publicity releases as a "tuneful cowpuncher," Autry made a singing appearance in his first film, *In Old Santa Fe*, in 1934, which led to his starring role in a thirteen-part series called *Phantom Empire*. His first lead role in a feature film came in *Tumbleweeds* in 1935, followed by *The Singing Cowboy* (1937) and *Back in the Saddle* (1941). In his films, Autry always played upstanding, moral characters who never drank or swore.

Autry served in the Army Air Corps during World War II and starred in two television shows in the 1950s. He was inducted into the Country Music Hall of Fame in 1969. Financially savvy, Autry accrued a fortune from his music and films and became owner of the California Angels baseball franchise. He died in 1998.

See also: films, feature; music; radio.

Bibliography

Autry, Gene, and Mickey Herskowitz. *Back in the Saddle.* Garden City, NY: Doubleday, 1978.

Rothel, David. *The Gene Autry Book.* Madison, WI: Empire Publishing, 1988.

BAILEY, JOSIAH

A conservative Democratic senator from North Carolina, Josiah Bailey is best remembered for his 1937 "conservative manifesto," a petition he circulated among other conservatives in Congress to combat what they considered to be the liberal excesses of the New Deal.

Born the son of a minister in small-town North Carolina in 1873, Bailey graduated from Wake Forest College in 1893 and then helped his father edit the *Biblical Recorder*, a Baptist weekly newspaper that was the state's second largest periodical. He became sole editor upon his father's death in 1895. As an important opinion-maker in the state, Bailey was recruited by the dominant Democratic Party in its efforts to promote the "white supremacy" gubernatorial campaign of 1895, which effectively ended the fusion government of blacks, poor whites, and populists.

Dissatisfied with journalism, Bailey began studying law in 1905 and began practicing after passing the bar in 1908. Soon Bailey was involving himself in politics, as an unsuccessful candidate for the Democratic gubernatorial nomination in 1914. For the next sixteen years, he practiced law and worked on the campaigns of others, finally winning the Democratic nomination for senator in an upset victory in 1930. In the heavily Democratic state, this was tantamount to winning the office itself and, indeed, Bailey easily defeated his Republican opponent in the general election.

Believing that the country needed a change in the early years of the Depression, Bailey supported Franklin D. Roosevelt's presidential bid in 1932 and backed some of the early New Deal legislation designed to get business back on its feet. But by 1934, he had become increasingly suspicious of the expanding federal bureaucracy and began to speak out for a return to voluntary, private enterprise initiatives to end the economic hard times. Still, as a pragmatic politician, he supported the popular Roosevelt's reelection bid in 1936; Bailey also won reelection in the Democratic landslide that year.

Angered when Roosevelt tried to pack the Supreme Court with liberal justices in 1937, Bailey issued his "conservative manifesto," formally called "An Address to the People of the United States." He spoke out against the "collectivism" of the New Deal and called on his fellow congressmen to turn away from the New Deal and support a balanced budget, lower taxes, states' rights, and local initiatives for unemployment relief.

In 1938, Bailey became head of the powerful Senate Commerce Committee, where, surprisingly, he dropped his former isolationist stance and helped the Roosevelt administration pass the Lend-Lease Act and repeal the Neutrality Act of 1939. During World War II, Bailey was an outspoken opponent of labor's right to strike, but also a supporter of the United Nations. He won reelection in 1942 and died in office in 1946.

See also: court-packing plan; New Deal, first; New Deal, second; Lend-Lease Act; neutrality acts.

Bibliography

Moore, John Robert. *Senator Josiah William Bailey of North Carolina.* Durham, NC: Duke University Press, 1968.

Patterson, James T. *Congressional Conservatism and the New Deal, 1933–1939.* Lexington: University of Kentucky Press, 1967.

BALDWIN, STANLEY

Prime minister of Great Britain in the mid-1930s, Stanley Baldwin presided over the country during the Italian invasion of Ethiopia, the German reoccupation of the Rhineland, and the Italian-German intervention in the Spanish Civil War, three events that helped usher in World War II. A Conservative Party politician, Baldwin downplayed the importance of these aggressive acts while, at the same time, beginning the rearmament of Great Britain.

Baldwin was born in 1867 and educated at Cambridge University. Upon graduation, he helped manage his father's many industrial concerns. In 1908, he entered politics as a member of the House of Commons, serving there through 1917. From 1917 to 1921, he was financial secretary of the British treasury, and he became chancellor of the exchequer in 1922. He served as prime minister from 1923 to 1929, with a short break in 1924, and from June 7, 1935 to May 28, 1937.

Resigning from his third term as prime minister in May 1937, he was replaced by Neville Chamberlain and died in 1947.

See also: Great Britain; Ethiopian war; Rhineland, reoccupation of; Chamberlain, Neville.

Bibliography

Jenkins, Roy. *Baldwin*. London: Collins, 1987.

Williamson, Philip. *Stanley Baldwin: Conservative Leadership and National Values*. New York: Cambridge University Press, 1999.

BARKLEY, ALBEN

One of the strongest supporters of the New Deal, Democratic senator Alben Barkley of Kentucky was also responsible for one of the largest political setbacks of the Franklin D. Roosevelt administration, when the senator was accused of using Works Progress Administration (WPA) personnel and money for his reelection campaign in 1939.

Barkley was born in rural Kentucky in 1877 and began practicing law there in 1898. He was elected to the House of Representatives in 1912, where he served until 1926. From that year until 1947, he remained a member of the Senate, where he served on the powerful finance and foreign affairs committees. In 1937, he was chosen to replace the recently deceased Joseph Robinson as Senate majority leader.

While the 1939 WPA scandal did not significantly damage Barkley's career, it resulted in congressional cutbacks in WPA funding, as well as the passage of the Hatch Act, which banned political activism and financial contributions by federal workers. He was elected vice president under Harry Truman in 1948, but failed to win the Democratic presidential nomination in 1952. Reelected to the Senate in 1952, he served there until his death in 1956.

See also: Democratic Party; Hatch Act; Works Progress Administration; Robinson, Joseph; Document: Hatch Act, August 2, 1939.

Bibliography

Barkley, Alben William. *That Reminds Me*. Garden City, NY: Doubleday, 1954.

Davis, Polly Ann. *Alben W. Barkley: Senate Majority Leader and Vice President*. New York: Garland, 1979.

BARUCH, BERNARD M.

The so-called *éminence grise*, or behind-the-scenes power, of the Democratic Party in the 1930s, industrialist Bernard M. Baruch attempted to push the Franklin D. Roosevelt administration and the New Deal into a more conservative direction.

Baruch was born in 1870 in Camden, South Carolina. He graduated from the City College of New York in 1889 and worked himself from office boy to major Wall Street financier by the early 1900s. In 1917, President Woodrow Wilson appointed Baruch to head the War Industries Board, which coordinated industry during World War I. He also served as a major economic adviser at the Versailles peace conference in 1919.

While Baruch supported the conservative John Nance Garner for the 1932 Democratic nomination for president, he backed Roosevelt after the latter won the nomination, and he tried to bring fellow conservative Democrats, like John Raskob and Al Smith, on board the Roosevelt campaign.

Widely credited as one of the authors of the National Recovery Administration, he was the political mentor of Hugh Johnson, who was appointed to run it, though Baruch had reservations about Johnson's character. Throughout the 1930s, Baruch tried to steer New Dealers away from pursuing inflationary policies.

During World War II, Baruch served as an unofficial adviser to the Roosevelt administration on industrial mobilization, and he was a key player on early Cold War atomic policy. Baruch died in 1965.

See also: banking; New Deal, first; New Deal, second; National Recovery Administration; Johnson, Hugh; Roosevelt, Franklin D.; Document: National Industrial Recovary Act, June 16, 1933.

Bibliography

Baruch, Bernard Mannes. *Baruch*. New York: Holt, 1957–1960.

Schwarz, Jordan. *The Speculator: Bernard M. Baruch in Washington, 1917–1965*. Chapel Hill: University of North Carolina Press, 1981.

BASIE, WILLIAM "COUNT"

One of the best known and most musically influential proponents of the jazz style known as "swing," William "Count" Basie was a composer and bandleader in Kansas City and Chicago during the 1930s.

Born in New Jersey in 1904, Basie studied music with his mother and learned to play the organ from the legendary musician "Fats" Waller. Traveling the country as a musician, Basie found himself stranded in Kansas City in 1927 and soon became leader of his own nine-piece band. Broadcasting on the radio—where local announcers dubbed him "Count," in competition with "Duke" Ellington—he came to the attention of jazz impresarios who brought him to Chicago in 1935.

Basie's band, which featured topflight soloists like trumpeter Thad Jones and saxophonist Lester Young, was famous for its syncopated chording, popularly called "comping." Basie and his band had numerous national hit compositions, including "One O'Clock Jump" and "Jumpin' at the Woodside." He died in 1984.

See also: music; radio; Ellington, Edward Kennedy "Duke."

Bibliography

Basie, Count. *Good Morning Blues: The Autobiography of Count Basie*. New York: Random House, 1985.

Dance, Stanley. *The World of Count Basie*. New York: Charles Scribner's Sons, 1980.

BENNETT, HARRY

Personal assistant to Ford Motor Company president Henry Ford and unofficial head of the company's security division, Harry Bennett is best known for organizing the armed and violent resistance to unionizing efforts by Ford workers in the early and middle 1930s.

Born in Ann Arbor, Michigan, in 1892, Bennett studied to be a commercial artist at Detroit Fine Arts Academy, but domestic violence caused him to run away at age seventeen and join the navy, where he became an expert boxer. After his enlistment ended in 1916, Bennett drifted to New York, where he and a navy friend got into a fistfight with some customhouse workers. The fight was witnessed by a journalist who brought the young Bennett to Henry Ford's attention. At the time, Ford was building his massive River Rouge plant in Detroit and looking for toughs to maintain order among the hardfisted workers.

Like most of the company's officials, Bennett had no formal title but was put to work hiring security guards for the plant and for the Ford family. He also engaged in detective work and served as a liaison between the Ford family and the press. In March 1932, Bennett was in charge of the security force charged with confronting several thousand demonstrators participating in a hunger march organized by the communist-led Detroit Unemployed Council. While Bennett tried to calm the situation, Ford security men or local Dearborn police—it is not certain which—opened fire on the crowd, killing four. Bennett was knocked unconscious by rocks and hospitalized.

In May 1937, Bennett organized the company's resistance to unionization efforts by the United Automobile Workers (UAW). Just three months earlier, the UAW had won a major victory at General Motors, forcing the auto giant to recognize the union after a six-week sit-down strike. But Ford had no intention of dealing with unions and told Bennett to do whatever was necessary to stop the UAW from organizing workers. When union officials tried to leaflet at the River Rouge plant, Bennett had his security men attack them.

The workers and the UAW took their case to the National Labor Relations Board—established under the National Labor Relations Act of 1935—which ruled in favor of the workers, forcing Bennett, as head of security, to pay damages. Still, the company was able to avoid recognizing the UAW until a 1941 strike shut the River Rouge plant down.

In 1943, Ford appointed Bennett to the company's board of directors, where he was put in charge of all personnel decisions. He left the company in 1945 and retired to a ranch in California. He died in 1979.

See also: Ford Motor Company; General Motors; hunger marches; strikes, sit-down; Unemployed Councils; unions and union organizing; United Automobile Workers; National Labor Relations Act.

Bibliography

Bennett, Harry. *Ford: We Never Called Him Henry*. New York: Tom Doherty Associates, 1951.

Bernstein, Irving. *The Turbulent Years: A History of the American Worker, 1933–1941*. Boston: Houghton Mifflin, 1970.

Bryan, Ford R. *Henry's Lieutenants*. Detroit: Wayne State University Press, 1993.

BENNETT, RICHARD BEDFORD

Conservative Party prime minister of Canada from 1930 to 1935, Richard Bedford Bennett presided over the dramatic collapse of his country's economy following the U.S. stock market of 1929. While Bennett had promised voters to fight the Depression with vigor, he did little in his first four years in office to alleviate unemployment and stagnation, although he did introduce a New Deal-like set of programs in 1935.

Bennett was born in New Brunswick in 1870 and practiced law there from 1893 to 1897, when he moved to Alberta. In 1911, he joined the House of Commons, representing Calgary, and later served as minister of justice and leader of the Conservative Party in the 1920s.

Upon taking office in 1930, Bennett underestimated the depth of the Depression, although Canada, dependent on exports of natural resources, was devastated by the collapse of the industrial economies of Europe and the United States. As farmers lost their land and workers were laid off, Bennett offered little more than modest employment programs and higher tariffs.

Bennett's anti–Depression proposal of 1935 advocated nationalization of primary industries, such as banking and transportation, and even of land itself. In addition, the program included child and female labor laws, a social welfare system, and vastly expanded labor rights, the latter leading to a vast expansion of Canadian unions. However, much of the program was ruled unconstitutional by the Canadian Supreme Court.

The lingering Depression led to popular anger with Bennett and the Conservatives, leading to an overwhelming victory for the Liberal Party in 1935, headed by MacKenzie King. Still, Bennett remained head of his party through 1938. The following year, he moved to England, where he was made a viscount. Bennett died there in 1947.

See also: Canada; King, William Lyon MacKenzie.

Bibliography

Glassford, Larry A. *Reaction and Reform: The Politics of the Conservative Party Under R. B. Bennett, 1927–1938.* Toronto: University of Toronto Press, 1992.

Neatby, H. Blair. *The Politics of Chaos: Canada in the Thirties.* Toronto: Copp Clark Pitman, 1986.

BENTON, THOMAS HART

A painter and muralist associated with the American regionalist school of the 1930s, Thomas Hart Benton idealized rural, frontier, and small-town life in his numerous public and private artworks of the Great Depression era. This regional art style, say art historians, was characteristic of American arts and letters during the period, which tried to discover and revive native themes and imagery.

Benton was born in Neosho, Missouri in 1889 and attended the Art Institute of Chicago and the Académie Julian in Paris. He began his career as a cartoonist for a Missouri newspaper in 1906. Critics point out that the features of his later art—including stylized figures and vigorous movement—were influenced by the cartoons he drew and admired in his early career. Along with Grant Wood, John Sloan, and others, Benton rejected American artists' dependence on French and European styles.

Among his more famous works are murals for the New School for Social Research (1931) and the Whitney Museum (1932), both in New York City. In 1933, Benton received a commission to paint for the federal Public Works of Art Project.

Although a strong believer in mid-American values and isolationism, Benton displayed a consistent interest in social causes. In the mid-1930s, he contributed art to an antilynching show in Manhattan. Benton taught at the Art Students League in New York and the Art

Institute and the School of Design in Kansas City. He died in 1975.

See also: arts, fine; Public Works of Art Project; Sloan, John; Wood, Grant.

Bibliography

Adams, Henry. *Thomas Hart Benton: An American Original.* New York: Knopf, 1989.

Benton, Thomas Hart. *An Artist in America.* Columbia: University of Missouri Press, 1983.

BERGEN, EDGAR

One of the most popular radio and stage stars of the 1930s, Edgar Bergen was best known for his ventriloquist act, featuring the wisecracking dummy Charlie McCarthy and the slow-witted Mortimer Snerd.

Bergen was born to Swedish immigrant parents in Chicago in 1903 and lived in Sweden with his family for several years as a child. In later years, he would use Swedish in his act. While in school in Chicago, he learned the various vocal tricks he would come to use in his ventriloquist act and modeled the dummy Charlie McCarthy. He paid his way through Northwestern University by doing ventriloquist and magic acts on stage.

Touring on the vaudeville stage in the early 1930s with his increasingly popular ventriloquist act, Bergen broke into radio with *The Edgar Bergen–Charlie McCarthy Show* in 1937. For the rest of the decade, it would be rated the most popular show on the airwaves. He continued with the show through 1957 and then guest-starred on various television shows through much of the rest of his life. Bergen died in 1978.

See also: radio.

Bibliography

Dunning, John. *On the Air: The Encyclopedia of Old-Time Radio.* New York: Oxford University Press, 1998.

Hilmes, Michele. *Radio Voices: American Broadcasting 1922–1952.* Minneapolis: University of Minnesota Press, 1997.

BERKELEY, WILLIAM "BUSBY"

A movie director and choreographer, William "Busby" Berkeley is best known for his Great Depression-era musical extravaganzas, including *Gold Diggers of 1933* (1933) and *Footlight Parade* (1933), which he directed, and *42nd Street* (1933), which he produced.

Berkeley was born in Los Angeles in 1895. From a family of actors, Berkeley worked on the stage from the age of five, doing comedy acting and dancing in musicals. As a young adult, he became a choreographer on Broadway and was brought to Hollywood by film producer Samuel Goldwyn in 1930.

But it was as a director of musicals for rival Warner Brothers that he became famous. Many of his films took place backstage in a theater and, in the spirit of the escapist entertainment of the day, involved actors and acting companies who overcame poverty through talent, hard work, and a stroke of good luck. Among the stars Berkeley directed were Joan Blondell, James Cagney, Ruby Keeler, Dick Powell, and Ginger Rogers.

With the decline of movie musicals in the 1940s, Berkeley's career went into an eclipse, although he briefly returned to direct a musical on Broadway in 1970. Berkeley died in 1976.

See also: films, feature; *Footlight Parade*; *Gold Diggers of 1933*; Cagney, James; Astaire and Rogers.

Bibliography

Pike, Bob. *The Genius of Busby Berkeley.* Reseda, CA: CFS Books, 1973.

Rubin, Martin. *Busby Berkeley and the Tradition of Spectacle.* New York: Columbia University Press, 1993.

BERLE, ADOLF A., JR.

One of the members of the so-called Brain Trust that advised Franklin D. Roosevelt during the 1932 campaign and through the first years of the administration, Adolf A. Berle Jr. was the architect of the critical speech at the Commonwealth Club of San Francisco in September 1932 in which Roosevelt laid out plans for the early New Deal.

Berle was born in Brighton, Massachusetts, in 1895, the son of a Congregational minister. A child prodigy, Berle graduated from Harvard at the age of eighteen and received his law degree from the university's law school at twenty-one. Heavily influenced by his parents' Social Gospel ideology, in which Christians were called upon to do social work, Berle got his first legal job with the firm of Louis Brandeis, a future reformist justice of the Supreme Court.

After two years in army intelligence during World War I and at the postwar Versailles peace conference, Berle worked for several years at the Henry Street Settlement House on New York's Lower East Side before forming his corporate law firm in 1933. Meanwhile, he began teaching corporate law at Columbia in the mid-1920s.

In 1933, Berle published the influential book *The Modern Corporation and Private Property*, which warned about the dangers of corporate consolidation and wealth concentration. The book and Berle's position at Columbia brought him to the attention of Raymond Moley, an adviser to Roosevelt, then governor of New York.

After advising Roosevelt during the 1932 campaign, Berle did the same for New York mayoral candidate Fiorello La Guardia in 1933. After La Guardia's election, Berle was put to work devising an ultimately successful plan to rescue the finances of the nearly bankrupt city government.

In 1938, Roosevelt appointed Berle assistant secretary of state, with a specialty in economic affairs. Berle became especially interested in Latin America and helped shape the hemispheric response to the rise of fascism in Europe and Japan in the late 1930s and early 1940s.

During World War II, Berle was put in charge of the State Department's international intelligence network and was an early critic of the Soviet Union. After the war, he worked occasionally for the Central Intelligence Agency and the Twentieth Century Fund, an early think tank. Berle died in 1971.

See also: Brain Trust; Commonwealth Club speech; New Deal, first; World War II, early history of; La Guardia, Fiorello; Moley, Raymond; Roosevelt, Franklin D.

Bibliography

Berle, Adolf A. *The Modern Corporation and Private Property.* New York: Macmillan, 1933.

Schwarz, Jordan. *Liberal: Adolf A. Berle and the Vision of an American Era.* New York: Free Press, 1987.

BERLIN, IRVING

One of the most prolific and popular American songwriters of the twentieth century, Irving Berlin wrote music for the Broadway musical *Face the Music* (1932) and the score for the Fred Astaire and Ginger Rogers hit movie *Top Hat* (1935).

Born Israel Baline in Mogilyov, Russia (now Belarus), in 1888, Berlin came from a long line of Jewish cantors, or singers of liturgical music in synagogues. He immigrated to New York City with his family in

1893. With little formal education, Berlin went to work as a street singer and singing waiter while still a teen. He also began writing songs, publishing his first, "Marie from Sunny Italy," in 1907. When the publisher misspelled his last name as "Berlin," the young composer stuck with it.

In 1911, he had his first hit, "Alexander's Ragtime Band," which became a kind of anthem of ragtime music. He soon began writing scores for Broadway shows, including Florenz Ziegfeld's *Follies*. In 1919, Berlin formed the Irving Berlin Music Corporation to publish his own tunes.

Over the course of his career, Berlin wrote over 800 songs, as well as scores for nineteen Broadway shows and eighteen movies. One of his most memorable tunes, "God Bless America," written during World War I, was first performed by Kate Smith in 1938, becoming an alternative national anthem for the United States.

Berlin continued to write music during and after World War II, turning out hits such as "White Christmas" (1942) and "There's No Business Like Show Business" (1946). He died in 1989 at the age of 101.

See also: films, feature; music; Smith, Kate.

Bibliography

Bergreen, Laurence. *As Thousands Cheer: The Life of Irving Berlin*. New York: Viking Penguin, 1990.

Freedland, Michael. *Irving Berlin*. New York: Stein and Day, 1974.

BETHUNE, MARY McLEOD

Director of the National Youth Administration's (NYA) Division of Negro Affairs from 1936 through 1944, Mary McLeod Bethune was the most important adviser to Eleanor Roosevelt and the Franklin D. Roosevelt administration on racial issues during the New Deal.

Bethune was born in Mayesville, South Carolina, in 1875, and attended missionary schools there and in

Director of the National Youth Administration's (NYA) Division of Negro Affairs, Mary McLeod Bethune (*left*) meets with First Lady Eleanor Roosevelt and NYA Executive Director Aubrey Williams at the National Conference on Problems of the Negro and Negro Youth, held in Washington in January 1937. (*Corbis*)

North Carolina and Georgia. In 1904, she moved to Daytona, Florida, where she founded a school for African-American girls. In 1929, the school was merged with another institute to form Bethune-Cookman College.

A founder of the National Council of Negro Women (NCNW) in 1935, Bethune was then recruited into the Roosevelt administration. There she became the mentor for a group of black federal officials, who set up an unofficial association that they called the Federal Council on Negro Affairs, but was more popularly known as the "black cabinet."

As head of this informal group and through her position at the NYA—which placed her among the highest-ranking black officials in America—Bethune pushed hard to get blacks included in New Deal public works programs and is widely credited with the modest inclusionary racial practices of some New Deal agencies.

During World War II, she helped select African-American candidates for the Women's Army Auxiliary Corps. In 1945, she served as a State Department official at the formation of the United Nations. Bethune died in 1955.

See also: African Americans; women; "black cabinet"; National Youth Administration.

Bibliography

Holt, Rackham. *Mary McLeod Bethune: A Biography*. Garden City, NY: Doubleday, 1964.

McCluskey, Audrey Thomas, and Elaine M. Smith, eds. *Mary McLeod Bethune: Building a Better World: Essays and Selected Documents*. Bloomington: Indiana University Press, 1999.

BILBO, THEODORE

Among the most conservative and reactionary members of Congress, Democratic senator Theodore Bilbo of Mississippi was one of the principal figures in the defeat of antilynching legislation in the 1930s.

Born to poverty near Poplarville, Mississippi, in 1877, Bilbo attended the University of Nashville and studied law at Vanderbilt University. As a populist and white supremacist, he won his first election to the Mississippi state senate in 1907. Four years later, he was elected lieutenant governor and, in 1916, governor. He tried to win a congressional seat in 1920 and the governorship in 1924, but lost both times. On a strong white supremacist platform, he returned to the gubernatorial mansion in 1928 and won a U.S. Senate seat in 1934.

At first a strong supporter of President Franklin D. Roosevelt and the New Deal, Bilbo turned against both after a few years, viewing them as dangerously socialistic. He then became a key member of a group of conservative southern Democrats whom Roosevelt had to placate in order to get his reform legislation through Congress.

An advocate of sending blacks "back" to Africa, Bilbo proved influential in the defeats of several antilynching bills introduced into Congress in the middle and late 1930s. Later in the decade, he even had praise for the racial policies of Fascist Italy and Nazi Germany.

Despite a scandal surrounding influence peddling, Bilbo remained in the Senate until his death in 1947.

See also: Democratic Party; lynching.

Bibliography

Green, Adwin Wigfall. *The Man Bilbo*. Baton Rouge: Louisiana State University Press, 1963.

Morgan, Chester M. *Redneck Liberal: Theodore G. Bilbo and the New Deal*. Baton Rouge: Louisiana State University Press, 1985.

BLACK, HUGO

A liberal, pro–New Deal senator from Alabama and later a Franklin D. Roosevelt appointee to the Supreme Court, Hugo Black's most important contribution to the history of the Great Depression was his introduction of a thirty-hour-per-week bill in March 1933 that prompted the formation of the National Recovery Administration later that year.

Black was born in Harlan, Alabama, in 1886, studied law at the University of Alabama, and opened a law office in Birmingham in 1906, where he practiced for twenty years. In 1926, he ran for elective office for the first time, winning a U.S. Senate seat.

As a liberal Democrat, Black sponsored a bill in the first weeks of the Roosevelt administration that would have banned from interstate commerce anything manufactured in a factory where workers labored for more than thirty hours a week. The purpose of the bill was to spread out work to as many people as possible; Black estimated it would create 6 million jobs.

Although the bill passed the Senate, the Roosevelt administration opposed it as both too inflexible a tool for fighting the Depression and likely to be ruled unconstitutional by the Supreme Court. Roosevelt's opposition killed the bill in the House. Instead, Roosevelt proposed the far more more ambitious National Industrial Recovery Act, which did pass in 1933.

Four years later, Roosevelt appointed Hugo Black to serve on the Supreme Court. As part of the growing Roosevelt-appointed liberal majority, Black was a critical vote in reversing the Court's propensity to strike down New Deal legislation as unconstitutional. In later years, Black would become well-known for his liberal support of federal powers and civil rights; he was the author of the judicial doctrine that used the Fourteenth Amendment to restrict the power of states to pass legislation undermining the Bill of Rights. Black served on the Court until his death in 1971.

A former Democratic senator from Alabama, the liberal Hugo Black was appointed to the Supreme Court by President Franklin Roosevelt in 1937. *(Library of Congress)*

See also: National Recovery Administration; Supreme Court; Document: National Industrial Recovery Act, June 16, 1933.

Bibliography

Black, Hugo Lafayette. *A Constitutional Faith*. New York: Knopf, 1969.

Newman, Roger K. *Hugo Black: A Biography*. New York: Pantheon Books, 1994.

BLITZSTEIN, MARC

A pianist, composer, and playwright, Marc Blitzstein is best known for his controversial 1937 dramatic opera *The Cradle Will Rock*, which was closed down by authorities as subversive.

Born in Philadelphia in 1905, Blitzstein was considered a child prodigy who was invited to play as a soloist with the Philadelphia Orchestra at the age of fifteen. He then went on to study piano and musical composition in Paris and Berlin in the 1920s.

A strident antifascist in the 1930s, Blitzstein wrote his opera *The Cradle Will Rock* as a condemnation of the union-busting tactics of capitalists. A product of his belief that fascist thinking could be exposed and fought with art, the piece is considered a classic work of 1930s agit-prop, or agitational propaganda theater.

The piece was condemned by conservatives, who were able to get local police to prevent its staging at a New York City theater on opening night. So Blitzstein and director Orson Welles led the audience and players to another theater where the cast performed the opera without props or costumes. Blitzstein continued to write operas until his death in 1964.

See also: music; Federal Theater Project; Welles, Orson.

Bibliography

Gordon, Eric A. *Mark the Music: The Life and Work of Marc Blitzstein*. New York: St. Martin's, 1989.

Welles, Orson. *The Cradle Will Rock: An Original Screenplay*. Santa Barbara, CA: Santa Teresa Press, 1994.

BLUM, LÉON

S ocialist premier of France in 1936 and 1937, Léon Blum presided over a Popular Front government that unified all parties of the Left in an effort to combat the effects of the Great Depression, ward off fascism in France, and prepare the country's defense against Nazi Germany and Fascist Italy.

Blum, the first Jewish premier in French history, was born in 1872 in Alsace, France, near the German border. He was educated at the prestigious École Normale Supérieure and studied law at the Sorbonne, where he received the highest honors in his class. Following the anti-Semitic Dreyfus affair, he became a member of the Socialist Party in 1904 and was first elected to the Chamber of Deputies, France's legislature, in 1919.

After a split with the Communists in 1920, Blum helped rebuild the Socialist Party and edited its journal *Le Populaire*. Defeated in the election of 1928, he returned to the Chamber of Deputies in 1932.

With the rise of the Right in France in the early 1930s, Blum worked hard to build a coalition between Socialists, Radicals, and other liberal democratic opponents of fascism, which led in 1936 to the triumph of the Popular Front and Blum's election as premier.

Faced with massive sit-down strikes—which helped inspire those at General Motors in the United States—Blum's government introduced the forty-hour workweek and the right to collective bargaining for workers. In addition, the Popular Front coalition nationalized defense industries and the Bank of France. Partly intended to prepare the country to defend itself against the Rome-Berlin Axis, the measures antagonized business and the Right. When conservative forces in the legislature refused to grant him emergency powers to fight the Depression, Blum resigned.

After the German invasion of France in 1940, Blum was indicted by the pro-Nazi Vichy government for "war guilt," but was exonerated. Imprisoned in a German concentration camp, he was liberated by American troops in 1945. A venerated elder statesman after the war, Blum died in 1950.

See also: Popular Front; strikes, sit-down; France.

Bibliography

Blum, Léon. *For All Mankind*. New York: Viking, 1946.

Colton, Joel. *Léon Blum: Humanist in Politics*. New York: Knopf, 1966.

BOGART, HUMPHREY

A theater and film actor known for his "hard-boiled" image as a gruff, plainspoken individualist and adventurer, Humphrey Bogart first came to widespread public attention playing a murderer in both the Broadway theatrical and Hollywood film productions of *The Petrified Forest* in 1935 and 1936, respectively.

The son of a prominent surgeon, Bogart was born in New York City on December 25, 1899, and served in the navy during World War I, where an accident left his upper lip stiffened, which became his facial trademark.

Bogart went on to play largely gangster roles in a number of less-than-memorable films in the late 1930s, before starring in two major hits in 1941: *High Sierra* and *The Maltese Falcon*. He later starred in a series of American film classics, including *Casablanca*, (1942), *The Big Sleep*, (1946), *Key Largo*, (1948), and *The African Queen*, (1951), the latter earning him an Academy Award for best actor. Bogart died in 1957.

See also: films, feature.

Bibliography

McCarty, Clifford. *The Complete Films of Humphrey Bogart*. Secaucus, NJ: Carol Publishing Group, 1995.

Sperber, Ann M. *Bogart*. New York: William Morrow, 1997.

One of the new "hard-boiled" stars of the 1930s was Humphrey Bogart, shown here at his Beverly Hills home. *(Brown Brothers)*

BONNIE (PARKER) AND CLYDE (BARROW)

A mong the most famous and notorious of the gangsters created by the raw conditions of the Great Depression, Bonnie Parker and Clyde Barrow became a media sensation after robbing a series of small-town banks in the southern Great Plains between 1932 and 1934.

Barrow was the older of the two and the more experienced as a criminal. Born in small-town Texas in 1909, he began his criminal career as a teenager spending several years in jail, before meeting Parker in 1930. Shortly thereafter, he spent two more years in prison for robbery. Parker was born in Louisiana in 1911 and had no criminal record before she met Barrow in 1930.

After Barrow's release from prison in the summer of 1932, the two went on a twenty-one-month spree robbing banks, gas stations, restaurants, and businesses, mostly in Missouri, New Mexico, Oklahoma, and Texas. They were often joined in these criminal activities by a small gang of criminals, which included Clyde's brother Buck and his wife, Blanche, Ray Hamilton, and W. D. Jones.

While never able to get more than $1,500 in a take, they earned national notoriety and press attention for

Bonnie Parker, shown above with gun and cigar, was the female half of the most notorious criminal duo of the Great Depression-era. Along with her partner Clyde Barrow, Parker died in a hail of police bullets in May 1934. *(Brown Brothers)*

their numerous shoot-outs with police, the last of which—outside Gibsland, Louisiana—resulted in their deaths in May 1934.

See also: crime; Federal Bureau of Investigation; "Pretty Boy" Floyd; Capone, Al.

Bibliography

Milner, E. R. *The Lives and Times of Bonnie and Clyde.* Carbondale: Southern Illinois University Press, 1996.

BOURKE-WHITE, MARGARET

One of the pioneering photo journalists of the 1930s, Margaret Bourke-White is best known for a 1937 collaborative book of essays and photos on southern sharecroppers she did with writer Erskine Caldwell.

Born into a middle-class family in New York City in 1906, Bourke-White (she took her mother's maiden name Bourke after she was briefly married in the mid-1920s) attended several universities, including Columbia, Michigan, Western Reserve (now Case Western Re-

serve), and Cornell in the 1920s, where she studied photography.

Specializing in architectural photography, she was hired in 1929 by publisher Henry Luce for his new magazine, *Fortune.* Among her assignments were photo-essays on the Krupp Iron Works in Germany and various projects of the Five-Year Plan in the Soviet Union. In 1934, she teamed up with essayist James Agee on a piece about drought conditions in America that Agee would later expand, with photographer

Walker Evans, into the book *Let Us Now Praise Famous Men.*

The following year she again teamed up with a famous writer, playwright Erskine Caldwell, a collaboration that resulted in the photo and essay book *You Have Seen Their Faces.* She and Caldwell—who were married from 1939 to 1942—also worked together on books about Czechoslovakia before the Nazi takeover and a panorama of America. In 1936, Bourke-White became one of the first four staff photographers to work for Luce's new photo-essay magazine, *Life,* and her photograph of the Fort Peck dam graced the cover of the magazine's premier issue.

During World War II, Bourke-White became the first woman photographer attached to the U.S. Army, covering military action in the Atlantic, North Africa, and Europe. Although struck with Parkinson's disease in 1952, she continued to photograph and write until her death in 1971.

See also: *Let Us Now Praise Famous Men;* magazines and newspapers; photography; *You Have Seen Their Faces;* Agee, James; Caldwell, Erskine; Evans, Walker; Luce, Henry.

Bibliography

Caldwell, Erskine. *You Have Seen Their Faces.* Athens: University of Georgia Press, 1995 (reprint).

Goldberg, Vicki. *Margaret Bourke-White: A Biography.* New York: Harper & Row, 1986.

BRANDEIS, LOUIS

One of the most liberal justices on the United States Supreme Court in the 1930s, Louis Brandeis was a strong supporter of the New Deal, frequently voting to uphold the constitutionality of various legislative acts that created New Deal programs and agencies during the Great Depression.

Born in Louisville, Kentucky, to a German-speaking Jewish family in 1856, Brandeis was educated in Germany and the United States before attending Harvard Law School, where he graduated first in his class in 1877. He soon set up a thriving legal practice in Boston and earned a reputation as a defender of laws that regulated work conditions and as a supporter of trust-busting legislation. His efforts on these issues won him the respect of President Woodrow Wilson, who appointed him to the Supreme Court in 1916, despite being strongly opposed by conservatives and business groups.

A defender of civil liberties, Brandeis was also a strong supporter of much of the New Deal legislation emerging from the White House and Congress in the early and middle 1930s, although he voted with the majority in the *Schechter Poultry Corporation v. United States* ruling, which struck down the National Industrial Recovery Act in 1935. Later, however, Brandeis voted with the majority on decisions upholding the Wagner Act (National Labor Relations Act) and the Social Security Act.

When President Franklin D. Roosevelt introduced his so-called court-packing plan of 1937—adding one new justice for every sitting justice over the age of seventy, in an attempt to get a more liberal, pro–New Deal court—Brandeis, the oldest of the justices at eighty-one, vehemently opposed him. Still, old age and infirmity forced Brandeis to retire two years later. He died in 1941.

See also: court-packing plan; National Labor Relations Act; Social Security Act; *Schechter Poultry Corporation v. United States;* Supreme Court; Documents: National Labor Relations Act, July 5, 1935; Social Security Acts, August 15, 1935; *Schechter Poultry Corporation v. United States.*

Bibliography

Baker, Leonard. *Brandeis and Frankfurter: A Dual Biography.* New York: New York University Press, 1986.

Urofsky, Melvin I., and David M. Levy, eds. *Letters of Louis D. Brandeis.* Albany: State University of New York Press, 1971–1978.

Urofsky, Melvin I. *Louis D. Brandeis and the Progressive Tradition.* Boston: Little, Brown, 1981.

BRIDGES, HARRY

Chairman of the Joint Marine Strike Committee, Harry Bridges was the leader of the July 1934 longshoremen's strike in San Francisco. When police attacked picketers, the labor protest turned into a general strike that shut down the city for several days.

Born in Australia in 1901, Bridges became a merchant seaman as a teenager and immigrated to the United States in 1920, where he worked as both a seaman and a dockworker. Settling in San Francisco in 1922, Bridges became active in the local chapter of the International Longshoremen's Association (ILA) and joined its radical "Albion Hall" wing, named after its meeting place. In 1933, the radicals organized a wildcat, or unauthorized, strike against the so-called Blue Book union, which was controlled by the Waterfront Employers Association (WEA), a trade group.

Still, the major issue angering dockworkers in the early 1930s was the "shape-up," the daily morning ritual whereby longshoremen were assigned, or not assigned, to various docks for work. Humiliating and unpredictable, it was also succeptible to corruption and favoritism, as foremen—who often accepted bribes—chose compliant men.

By early 1934, Bridges and the Albion wing had used the problems associated with the Blue Book and the shape-up to place themselves on top of the San Francisco ILA branch. When the WEA refused to negotiate with them, the ILA convinced more than 12,000 dockworkers to walk off the job in every West Coast port except Los Angeles in early May.

By early July, virtually the entire West Coast shipping industry was shut down, and employers were looking to end the strike. On July 5, the San Francisco police attacked the strikers, who fought back in running battles along the waterfront. That night, the governor called in 1,700 National Guardsmen to secure the city. On July 16, the ILA convinced other unions to organize a general strike, which shut the city down for four days.

Eventually, the Joint Marine Strike Committee, under pressure from the American Federation of Labor, called an end to the strike. This angered Bridges and the ILA, though on July 26 they won all of their demands from the WEA.

In 1937, Bridges led the Pacific Coast division of the ILA out of the union, to form the more radical International Longshoremen's and Warehousemen's Union (ILWU), which affiliated itself with the Congress of Industrial Organizations. Bridges served as the ILWU's president from 1937 to 1977.

Throughout his career, Bridges was dogged with charges that he was a Communist. Although he denied them, he refused to denounce Communists in his union, saying they were some of the most dedicated and active organizers. Although he became a citizen in 1945, the American government had tried to deport him as a Communist in the late 1940s. Bridges died in 1990.

See also: American Federation of Labor; Congress of Industrial Organizations; strikes, general; unions and union organizing.

Bibliography

Larrowe, Charles P. *Harry Bridges: The Rise and Fall of Radical Labor in the United States.* New York: Lawrence Hill, 1972.

Nelson, Bruce. *Workers on the Waterfront: Seamen, Longshoremen, and Unionism in the 1930s.* Urbana: University of Illinois Press, 1988.

BROUN, HEYWOOD

One of the most influential liberal newspaper columnists of the 1930s, Heywood Broun is also remembered as one of the principal founders of the American Newspaper Guild, a union of newspaper reporters.

Born in Brooklyn in 1888, Broun attended Harvard University for several years but never graduated. He began his reportorial career covering the baseball scene in New York for the *Morning Telegraph*. In 1912, he moved to the *Tribune*, where he started his popular and influential column "It Seems to Me." He took the column with him when he went to work for the *World* in 1921.

During the 1920s, he had a number of differences with his editors over controversial issues, and was fired at one point for a column he wrote in *The Nation*, a leftist journal, in which he called the *World* a "pseudo-liberal" newspaper. When the *World* merged with the *Telegram* in 1931, Broun went back to work writing his column for the new newspaper until 1939. He also wrote a column for the liberal magazine *The New Republic* after 1935.

Always interested in politics and labor issues, Broun ran a losing campaign for Congress on the Socialist ticket in 1930 and, in 1933, helped found the American Newspaper Guild and served as its president until his death in 1939. During those years, Broun organized and participated in a number of strikes against newspapers around the country.

See also: American Newspaper Guild; newspapers and magazines; *Nation, The;* unions and union organizing.

Bibliography

Broun, Heywood Hale, ed. *Collected Edition of Heywood Broun.* New York: Harcourt, Brace, 1941.

O'Connor, Richard. *Heywood Broun: A Biography.* New York: Putnam, 1975.

BROWDER, EARL

Secretary-general of the Communist Party of the United States during its peak years in the Great Depression, Earl Browder was its presidential candidate in the 1936 and 1940 elections.

Browder was born to a family of radicals in Wichita, Kansas, in 1891; his father was an active member of both the Populist Party in the late nineteenth century and the Socialist Party in the early twentieth century. Young Browder joined the Socialist Party in 1907 but left five years later because he found their critique of the existing capitalist order too mild. Instead, he became affiliated with anarcho-syndicalists, or radical unionists. An opponent of United States participation in World War I, he was jailed briefly in 1919 and 1920 and became a member of the newly formed Communist Party in 1921. In 1930, he was elected its secretary-general.

As the Great Depression deepened in the early 1930s, the party began to organize the jobless into Unemployed Councils, conducting so-called hunger marches and demonstrations demanding that Congress pass the Workers Unemployment Insurance Bill. Although these marches became a model for the Bonus Army of 1932, which came to Washington demanding relief for World War I veterans, Browder had mixed feelings about the issue of government relief. The main concern of the party, he believed, should be not relief, but the overthrow of the existing economic system.

Browder was highly critical of President Franklin D. Roosevelt's New Deal policies, seeing them as little more than a desperate effort to save capitalism. But the Communist Party leader was an obedient servant of Moscow, and when the Soviet-directed Communist International (Comintern)—the organization of communist parties worldwide—called for a Popular Front of all liberal and leftist forces in Western democracies in order to stave off fascism, Browder went along.

In 1936, Browder replaced William Z. Foster as the

Party's candidate for the presidency; Foster had suffered a near fatal heart attack during the 1932 campaign and, for a variety of political reasons, had fallen out of favor with Moscow. For all his talk of overthrowing capitalism, Browder proved more amenable than Foster in his actions to the idea of working within the democratic system, which jibed with the Comintern's Popular Front strategy.

As presidential candidate in 1936 and 1940, Browder did poorly, winning well under 100,000 votes in each election. Also in 1940, he was temporarily imprisoned for problems with his passport. But his real problems were with Moscow. By the middle of World War II, the Soviets had decided that the American Communists should take a harder line against the existing government in Washington, and Browder, who argued that peaceful coexistence between capitalism and socialism was possible, fell out of favor. He was dismissed from the party hierarchy in 1944 and thrown out of the party in 1946.

He wrote several books on communism in his later years and died in 1973.

See also: Communist Party; hunger marches; Popular Front; Unemployed Councils; Soviet Union; Foster, William Z.

Bibliography

Browder, Earl. *The People's Front.* New York: International Publishers, 1938.

Ryan, James G. *Earl Browder: The Failure of American Communism.* Tuscaloosa: University of Alabama Press, 1997.

BRUNDAGE, AVERY

President of the United States Olympic Committee (USOC) and a member of the International Olympic Committee (IOC) in 1936, Avery Brundage supported American participation in the Berlin Olympics of that year, dismissing efforts to boycott the Nazi-run event.

Born in Detroit in 1887, Brundage was a pentathlon and decathlon competitor in the 1912 Stockholm Olympics and was U.S. all-round amateur sports champion in 1914, 1916, and 1918. Brundage then went on to found a construction company, which made him extraordinarily wealthy.

In 1928, he was elected president of the Amateur Athletic Union, where he served off and on until 1935. In 1929, he was appointed to the U.S. Olympic Association, serving there until 1953.

A strong believer in the need to keep amateur athletics and professional sports distinct, Brundage spoke out adamantly against Jewish and other groups who argued that the United States should not participate in the 1936 Berlin Olympics, which many believed were being used as a showcase for Nazi racial ideology. Brundage was also criticized for remarks he made that were viewed as sympathetic to the Nazis.

Despite his controversial stand and statements about Nazi Germany and the Berlin Olympics, Brudnage went on to become vice president and president of the IOC from 1945 to 1952 and from 1952 to 1972, respectively. In the final year of his administration, Brundage was widely criticized for insisting that the 1972 Munich Olympic Games continue after Palestinian terrorists murdered eleven Israeli athletes. Brundage died in 1975 in West Germany.

See also: sports; Nazi Germany; Olympic Games (Berlin 1936).

Bibliography

Guttmann, Allen. *The Games Must Go On: Avery Brundage and the Olympic Movement.* New York: Columbia University Press, 1984.

Mandell, Richard D. *The Nazi Olympics.* New York: Macmillan, 1971.

BUCK, PEARL

Author of *The Good Earth*, one of the best-selling novels of the Depression era, Pearl Buck heavily influenced American views of China, convincing many that the United States should support that country in its struggle against the invading Japanese in the 1930s.

Born Pearl Sydenstricker in West Virginia in 1892, Buck passed her youth as the child of Presbyterian missionaries in China and received her primary schooling in Shanghai. During a stint back in the United States, she graduated from Randolph-Macon Woman's College in Virginia in 1914. Returning to China soon after, she became a college professor in Nanjing and married a missionary named John Buck. Beginning in 1923, she wrote journalistic pieces about life in China for the American press.

The Good Earth (1931), a somewhat sentimentalized view of Chinese peasant life, was an immediate hit and was followed by *Sons* (1932) and *A House Divided* (1935), which composed a trilogy.

In 1934, she divorced Buck and the following year married American publisher Richard Walsh, returning permanently to live in the United States. The film version of *The Good Earth* appeared, coincidently, in 1937, the same year Japan invaded China. The film, highly sympathetic to the Chinese, touched the hearts of many Americans, although it failed to bring immediate American military support for their cause. In 1938, Buck won the Nobel Prize for Literature.

After World War II, Buck established a foundation to aid the illegitimate children of Asian women and American servicemen. She continued to write novels, biographies, and an autobiography until her death in 1973.

See also: films, feature; *Good Earth, The*; literature; China; Japan.

Bibliography

Buck, Pearl. *My Several Worlds: A Personal Record*. New York: Day, 1954.

Conn, Peter J. *Pearl S. Buck: A Cultural Biography*. New York: Cambridge University Press, 1996.

BURNS (GEORGE) AND ALLEN (GRACIE)

George Burns and Gracie Allen were among the most popular radio and movie personalities of the 1930s. A husband-and-wife comedy team, they hosted a hit radio show from 1933 to 1950 and starred in three popular movies between 1932 and 1941.

Burns was born Nathan Birnbaum in New York City in 1896, and Allen, originally Grace Ethel Cecile Rosalie Allen, was born in San Francisco in 1902. Both came from theatrical families, going on stage for the first time in their early teens, Burns as a singer and Allen as a member of a vaudeville team with her sisters.

The couple, who married in 1926, began their domestic comedy routines on the stage before adapting them to radio, with Burns as the straight man and Allen as an eccentric comedienne prone to humorous malapropisms.

Their Hollywood debut came in *The Big Broadcast* of 1932. Other Burns and Allen films of the Depression era included *International House* (1933), *Love in Bloom* (1935), and *College Swing* (1938). Allen also starred in several films without Burns, including *The Gracie Allen Murder Case* (1939) and *Mr. and Mrs. North* (1941).

In 1950, the two transferred their radio show to television and continued in that medium until 1958. After Allen's death in 1964, Burns went into retirement, reemerging to make a series of hit films in the 1970s, including *The Sunshine Boys* (1975), for which he won an Academy Award for best supporting actor. Burns died at the age of 100 in 1996.

See also: films, feature; radio.

The most popular husband-and-wife comedy team of the 1930s, George Burns and Gracie Allen hosted a hit radio show from 1933 to 1950 and starred in three box-office-hit films during the Great Depression. *(Brown Brothers)*

Bibliography

Clements, Cynthia. *George Burns and Gracie Allen: A Bio-Bibliography*. Westport, CT: Greenwood Press, 1996.

Gottfried, Martin. *George Burns and the Hundred-Year Dash*. New York: Simon & Schuster, 1996.

BUTLER, PIERCE

Along with several other Supreme Court justices appointed by Republican presidents in the first two decades of the twentieth century, Pierce Butler was part of a conservative coalition that ruled a number of critical pieces of New Deal legislation unconstitutional in the early and mid-1930s.

Butler was born near Northfield, Minnesota, in 1866 and was admitted to that state's bar in 1888. After a stint as county attorney in St. Paul, Butler opened a law firm that came to specialize in railway law. He worked on antitrust cases during the administration of President William Howard Taft and was picked for the Supreme Court in 1922 by President Warren G. Harding, on then-Chief Justice William Howard Taft's advice.

Opposed by liberals from the beginning, Butler became known as one of the "four horsemen" or "battalion of death," names given to the four most conservative Supreme Court justices by New Deal supporters. The others were James McReynolds, George Sutherland, and Willis Van Devanter.

As a strict constitutional constructionist, Butler opposed most extensions of federal government power. A supporter of business and states' rights, he ruled with the majority against the National Industrial Recovery Act in 1935 and the Agricultural Adjustment Act in 1936. However, he was in the minority in the 1937 *NLRB v. Jones & Laughlin Steel Corporation*, which ruled the National Labor Relations Act constitutional.

Butler served on the Supreme Court until his death in 1939 and was replaced by liberal justice William O. Douglas.

See also: Agricultural Adjustment Act; National Labor Relations Act; National Recovery Administration; *NLRB v. Jones and Laughlin*; *Schechter v. United States*; *United States v. Butler et al.*; Supreme Court; Douglas, William O.; McReynolds, James; Sutherland, George; Van Devanter, Willis.

Bibliography

Brown, Francis Joseph. *The Social and Economic Philosophy of Pierce Butler*. Washington, DC: The Catholic University of America Press, 1945.

Leuchtenburg, William E. *The Supreme Court Reborn: The Constitutional Revolution in the Age of Roosevelt*. New York: Oxford University Press, 1995.

BYRNES, JAMES F.

A Democratic South Carolina senator during the first two Franklin D. Roosevelt adminstrations, James F. "Jimmy" Byrnes was a moderate supporter of much New Deal legislation, but an ardent opponent of African-American civil rights.

Born in Charleston in 1879, shortly after the collapse of the radical Reconstruction government in South Carolina, Byrnes was a self-educated lawyer first elected to the House of Representatives in 1911, where he served until 1925. Elected to the Senate in 1931, Byrnes was considered a member of Roosevelt's group of unofficial assistants, popularly known as the Brain Trust, and was influential in steering critical New Deal legislation through the Congress.

Like other moderates, however, Byrnes became increasingly alienated from the New Deal during Roosevelt's second administration. Believing that the Depression was largely over in 1937, he urged the president to cut back on public works projects and other inflationary programs. Byrnes also participated in the filibuster organized by southern conservatives in the Senate against antilynching legislation in 1938. Later, as governor of South Carolina in the early 1950s, Byrnes became an outspoken opponent of school integration.

In 1941, Roosevelt appointed Byrnes to the Supreme Court, where he served for little more than a year before being tapped to head the Office of War Mobilization from 1942 to 1945. Secretary of state under Harry Truman from 1945 to 1947, he was an advocate of strong Cold War measures against the Soviets. Byrnes retired from public life in 1955 and died in 1972.

See also: Brain Trust; lynching; New Deal, first; New Deal, second; Supreme Court.

Bibliography

Byrnes, James F. *All in One Lifetime*. New York: Harper, 1958.

Robertson, David. *Sly and Able: A Political Biography of James F. Byrnes*. New York: W. W. Norton, 1994.

CAGNEY, JAMES

One of the most popular film actors of the 1930s, James Cagney was best known in that decade for his gangster roles in films like *Public Enemy* (1931).

Cagney was born in 1899 and grew up in the immigrant neighborhoods of New York City's Lower East Side, where he picked up his trademark tough-guy staccato accent. He became a vaudeville singer and dancer who starred on stage with his wife Frances in the 1920s.

His big breakthrough came in 1929 in the Broadway musical *Penny Arcade;* he also starred in the film version—renamed *Sinner's Holiday*—the following year. But his most memorable role was that of a gangster or criminal. After *Public Enemy*, he starred in *Angels with Dirty Faces* (1938), *Each Day I Die* (1939), and *The Roaring Twenties* (1939). Cagney was also an accomplished dancer, who won a best actor Academy Award for *Yankee Doodle Dandy* in 1942.

Cagney was a strong supporter of liberal and leftist causes in the 1930s and was one of the few Hollywood actors to openly support Upton Sinclair's End Poverty in California gubernatorial campaign in 1934.

Cagney continued to star in a variety of dramatic, musical, and comedic film roles until the early 1980s, despite an "official" retirement from the entertainment business in 1961. Cagney died in 1986.

See also: End Poverty in California; films, feature; *Public Enemy;* Sinclair, Upton.

With his boxer's face and machine-gun-style verbal delivery, James Cagney became a popular star of 1930s-era gangster films, including the 1938 *Angels with Dirty Faces,* which this publicity still advertised. *(Brown Brothers)*

Bibliography

McCabe, John. *Cagney*. New York: Knopf, 1997.

Warren, Doug. *James Cagney: The Authorized Biography*. New York: St. Martin's, 1983.

CAIN, JAMES M.

A writer of the so-called hard-boiled school of fiction writing, James M. Cain is best remembered for a series of fast-paced novels filled with violence and sex, including *The Postman Always Rings Twice* (1934), *Double Indemnity* (1936), and *Mildred Pierce* (1941).

Cain was born in Annapolis, Maryland, in 1892 and graduated from Washington College in 1910. He edited an army newspaper while serving overseas in World War I. After the war, he returned to Washington College and earned his master's degree. He then became a journalist, writing for both the Baltimore *American* and the Baltimore *Sun*. In 1923 and 1924, he taught journalism at St. John's College in Annapolis, before moving to New York City to work as an editorial writer at the *World* from 1924 to 1931. He was also briefly the managing editor at the *New Yorker*.

Postman, his first novel, was a huge success, with its low-life characters, nasty scheming, and explicit sexuality. It would be made into a stage play in 1936 and filmed in 1946 and again in 1981. *Serenade*, written in 1937, dealt with the then taboo subject of bisexuality. It was followed by *Double Indemnity*, about a staged murder and a botched life insurance scam, which made it to the screen in 1944. Cain's last best-seller of the Great Depression was the creepy mother-daughter story of *Mildred Pierce*, turned into a film in 1945.

Cain continued to write novels during and after World War II, though none had the edginess or success of his 1930s-era efforts.

See also: films, feature; literature.

Bibliography

Hoopes, Roy. *Cain*. New York: Holt, Rinehart & Winston, 1982.

Skenazy, Paul. *James M. Cain*. New York: Ungar, 1989.

CALDWELL, ERSKINE

A mong the most popular novelists and acclaimed essayists of the Great Depression era, Erskine Caldwell is best known for *Tobacco Road* (1932) and *God's Little Acre* (1933), best-selling novels about rural southern poverty, and *You Have Seen Their Faces* (1937), a collaborative collection of essays and photographs he worked on with his future wife, Margaret Bourke-White.

Born in rural Georgia in 1903, Caldwell moved about frequently as his missionary father preached at churches around the state. Caldwell later credited his ability to understand and portray rural poverty to these early days on the road. He attended, but did not graduate from, the University of Virginia.

Settling in Maine in 1926, he set to work on *Tobacco Road*, which became an immediate and controversial (for its faithfulness to the crude language and customs of the rural South) best-seller. The novel was later turned into a successful Broadway production. He followed up this success with another, *God's Little Acre*.

In 1935, joining Bourke-White as she photographed impoverished southern sharecroppers, Caldwell wrote the essays for their book *You Have Seen Their Faces*. The two were married in 1939 and worked on photo-essay books about Europe until their divorce in 1942.

Caldwell worked as a correspondent in World War II. After the war, he wrote Hollywood screenplays and more works of fiction, but none of the latter attracted much popular or critical attention. He died in 1987.

See also: literature; photography; *Tobacco Road*; Bourke-White, Margaret.

Bibliography

Caldwell, Erskine. *God's Little Acre*. Athens: University of Georgia Press, 1995 (reprint).

———. *Tobacco Road*. Athens: University of Georgia Press, 1995 (reprint).

———. *You Have Seen Their Faces*. Athens: University of Georgia Press, 1995 (reprint).

Cook, Sylvia Jenkins. *Erskine Caldwell and the Fiction of Poverty: The Flesh and the Spirit*. Baton Rouge: Louisiana State University Press, 1991.

Miller, Dan B. *Erskine Caldwell: The Journey from Tobacco Road: A Biography*. New York: Knopf, 1995.

CALLOWAY, CAB

Although not among the great jazz innovators, Cab Calloway was nevertheless one of the most popular singers and bandleaders of the Great Depression era, most notably for his 1931 hit "Minnie the Moocher."

Calloway, born Cabell Calloway III, in Rochester, New York, in 1907, briefly attended law school in Chicago, but was drawn to nightclub singing. In 1928, he began conducting a band and moved to New York City the following year. There, he performed in the all-black musical *Ain't Misbehavin'*, featuring the music of jazz and blues great Fats Waller.

Soon a top bandleader and singer at Harlem's fabled Cotton Club, Calloway became best known for his scat style of singing, which featured nonsensical lyrics that mimicked instruments. Indeed, one of his favorite scat lines—"hi-de-hi, hi-de-hi-do"—earned him his nickname, the "King of Hi-de-ho." Calloway later starred in all-black films and musicals, including *Stormy Weather* (1943) and a revival *Porgy and Bess* (1935). Calloway died in 1994.

See also: music; *Porgy and Bess*.

Bibliography

Calloway, Cab. *Of Minnie the Moocher & Me*. New York: Crowell, 1976.

Dunning, John. *On the Air: The Encyclopedia of Old-Time Radio*. New York: Oxford University Press, 1998.

A bandleader and singer at Harlem's famed Cotton Club, Cab Calloway was best known for his scat-style singing and his flamboyant performances. *(Brown Brothers)*

CAPONE, AL

While better known for his exploits as a Prohibition-era gangster of the 1920s, Alphonse "Al" Capone was indicted for federal income tax invasion in June 1931. His conviction in October of that year is often viewed by historians as one of the events marking the end of the gangster era of the 1920s.

Capone was born in Brooklyn, the son of Neapolitan immigrants, in 1899. Dropping out of primary school, he joined a gang of young criminals in lower Manhattan, where he got the razor slash across his left cheek that earned him the nickname "Scarface."

With the advent of Prohibition, Capone's criminal career went into high gear and, by 1925, he had become the number one gangster in Chicago. Able to escape prosecution for violent crimes, he was indicted for tax evasion in 1931 and sentenced to eleven years in prison, first in Atlanta and then at Alcatraz, the notorious prison in San Francisco Bay. Suffering from advanced syphilis, he was released from prison in 1939 and died in obscurity in Florida in 1947.

See also: crime; Prohibition.

Bibliography

Bergreen, Laurence. *Capone: The Man and the Era.* New York: Simon & Schuster, 1994.

Kobler, John. *Capone: The Life and World of Al Capone.* New York: Putnam, 1971.

One of the most notorious gangsters of the Prohibition era, Al Capone was eventually brought down on more prosaic charges—he was sentenced to eleven years imprisonment for tax evasion in 1931. *(Brown Brothers)*

CAPRA, FRANK

Best known for his screwball comedies of the early 1930s and his film paeans to small-town American life and American values, Frank Capra became one of the most popular and critically acclaimed Hollywood directors of the Great Depression era with such films as *It Happened One Night* (1934) and *Mr. Smith Goes to Washington* (1939).

Born in Palermo, Sicily, in 1897, Capra immigrated with his family to Los Angeles in 1903 and graduated from the California Institute of Technology in 1918. After a stint as an engineering instructor for the army, Capra began working in Hollywood, doing a host of tasks including writing, editing, and directing silent shorts for Mack Sennett. His major breakthrough as a director came with *That Certain Thing* in 1928.

It Happened One Night was Capra's great contribution to the screwball genre, which usually portrayed upper-class people in preposterous situations, with scripts that moved the dialogue along at breakneck speed. In the film, a poor reporter—played by Clark Gable—is sent to follow a runaway heiress—played by Claudette Colbert—and the two fall in love, highlighting the American possibility for bridging social classes.

In *Mr. Deeds Goes to Town* (1936), Gary Cooper plays a country bumpkin who outwits slick city lawyers trying to settle a rich uncle's will, demonstrating the basic common sense and goodwill of small-town Americans. *It Happened, Mr. Deeds*, and a third comedy, *You Can't Take It With You*, earned Capra an unprecedented three Academy Awards for best director. Later, in *Meet John Doe* (1941), Capra offered a somewhat darker vision of a small-town hero—again played by Gary Cooper—who outwits an industrialist attempting a fascist takeover of the United States.

During World War II, Capra was recruited to direct a series of propaganda films for the U.S. military entitled *Why We Fight*. After the war, Capra continued to direct hit comedies, including *It's a Wonderful Life* (1946), *State of the Union* (1948), and *Pocketful of Miracles* (1961). Capra died in 1991.

See also: films, feature; Colbert, Claudette; Cooper, Gary; Gable, Clark.

Bibliography

Capra, Frank. *The Name Above the Title: An Autobiography*. New York: Macmillan, 1971.

Maland, Charles J. *Frank Capra*. New York: Twayne, 1995.

CÁRDENAS, LÁZARO

President of Mexico from 1934 to 1940, Lázaro Cárdenas was a liberal reformer whose boldest move was to nationalize the foreign oil interests in the country in 1938, turning them over to the state-run Petróleos Mexicanos, or Pemex, which continues to enjoy a monopoly over the Mexican petroleum business to this day.

Born Lázaro Cárdenas del Río in Jiquilpan, Mexico, in 1895, the future president was of Indian descent and received a very basic education. A local public official in his home state of Michoacán at eighteen, Cárdenas soon joined up with the rebel army of Venustiano Carranza during the Mexican Revolution in 1913. Cárdenas rose through the ranks to become general, the highest rank in the Mexican army, after Carranza took power in 1917.

A politician as much as a military leader, Cárdenas was elected governor of Michoacán in 1928 and was a key figure in the formation of what would become the Institutional Revolutionary Party, better known by its Spanish acronym PRI, in 1929. During the early 1930s, Cárdenas helped shape the PRI into a unified national force and was briefly minister of the interior and minister of war and the marines. He retired from the latter position in 1934 to run for president.

Although his election was virtually guaranteed by the PRI's lock on power, Cárdenas nevertheless campaigned vigorously throughout Mexico, promising land reform and industrialization programs. Once elected, however, he moved cautiously on these reforms until he could consolidate his hold on the government and the PRI.

By 1936, he felt confident enough to begin an aggressive reform program and, by the end of his administration in 1940, he had distributed twice as much land to the peasantry as all his predecessors combined. He also expanded government banks so that peasants could borrow money, created the Confederación Nacional Campesina (National Peasant Confederation), and formed the Confederación de Trabajadores de Mexico (Confederation of Mexican Workers), a national trade union federation. All of these organizations helped solidify his political base.

Among Cárdenas's boldest moves was his expropriation of foreign-owned industries, including the powerful oil industry, much of it owned by American companies. At first, he turned the industries over to the trade unions, but then made them into autonomous public corporations that acted much like private ones.

In the PRI tradition, Cárdenas handpicked his successor General Manuel Ávila Camacho, in 1940. After a brief retirement, Cárdenas returned to government as minister of national defense from 1943 to 1945. He continued to play a role as governmental adviser for much of the rest of his life. Cárdenas died in 1970. His son Cuauhtemoc was also an important Mexican politician, becoming mayor of Mexico City and nearly winning the presidency in 1988 on an anti-PRI ticket.

See also: Mexico.

Bibliography

Ashby, Joe C. *Organized Labor and the Mexican Revolution under Lázaro Cárdenas.* Chapel Hill: University of North Carolina Press, 1967.

Becker, Marjorie. *Setting the Virgin on Fire: Lázaro Cárdenas, Michoacán Peasants, and the Redemption of the Mexican Revolution.* Berkeley: University of California Press, 1995.

Weyl, Nathaniel. *The Reconquest of Mexico: The Years of Lázaro Cárdenas.* New York: Oxford University Press, 1939.

CARDOZO, BENJAMIN

Among the more liberal justices of the Supreme Court in the New Deal era, Benjamin Cardozo was part of the majority that rendered decisions declaring the National Labor Relations and the Social Security Acts constitutional.

Born in New York City in 1870, Cardozo was the son of Sephardic Jews. His father, Albert Jacob, a member of the New York Supreme Court, had to resign in a corruption scandal in 1872. Benjamin was admitted to the New York bar in 1891 and was elected to the state Supreme Court on a reformist ticket in 1913. Promoted soon after to the Court of Appeals, he rendered a number of judgments, including one that helped to establish modern consumer protection laws.

In 1932, President Herbert Hoover appointed Cardozo to the U.S. Supreme Court. Although voting with the majority against the National Recovery Administration (NRA) in the noted *Schechter v. United States* decision in 1935—Cardozo declared the law that created the NRA to be "delegation run riot," in that it usurped legislative authority and gave it to an executive branch agency—Cardozo was considered part of the court's liberal wing, along with Louis Brandeis and Harlan Stone, voting to support the acts, creating the National Labor Relations Board and the Social Security system. A moderate supporter of civil rights and the federal government's authority to enforce them, Cardozo served on the Court until his death in 1938.

See also: National Recovery Administration; National Labor Relations Act; Social Security Act; Supreme Court; Brandeis, Louis; Stone, Harlan.

Bibliography

Kaufman, Andrew L. *Cardozo.* Cambridge: Harvard University Press, 1998.

Levy, Beryl Harold. *Cardozo and The Frontiers of Legal Thinking, with Selected Opinions.* Cleveland: Case Western Reserve University Press, 1969.

CARNEGIE, DALE

Author of the best-selling nonfiction book of the Great Depression era—*How to Win Friends and Influence People* (1936)—Dale Carnegie emphasized that even in the midst of economic hard times people with the right attitude about success could still improve their lives financially and in other ways.

Carnegie, born Dale Carnegey, was born on a poverty-stricken farm in Missouri in 1888, but was able to make it through high school and college, where he became an expert debater. First a salesman in the Midwest and then an actor in New York, Carnegie began teaching classes at the YMCA in the 1920s.

With his classes attracting record numbers of students, Carnegie decided to put down in words what he was lecturing about. The result was *Public Speaking: A Practical Course for Business Men*, published in 1926. But it was *How to Win Friends*, with its upbeat tone and pop psychology truths, that made Carnegie a national celebrity. He went on to publish another best-selling success book, *How to Stop Worrying and Start Living*, in 1948. Carnegie died in 1955, a very wealthy man.

See also: *How to Win Friends and Influence People;* literature.

Bibliography

Carnegie, Dale. *How to Win Friends and Influence People.* New York: Pocket Books, 1982.

Kemp, Giles. *Dale Carnegie: The Man Who Influenced Millions.* New York: St. Martin's, 1989.

CHAMBERLAIN, (ARTHUR) NEVILLE

Conservative Party prime minister of Great Britain from 1937 to 1940, Neville Chamberlain governed at a time of growing tensions in Europe. A strong believer in the policy of appeasement, whereby concessions to German dictator Adolf Hitler were supposed to avoid a war, Chamberlain has gone down in history as the man who sacrificed the freedom of Czechoslovakia at the infamous Munich conference of 1938.

Born in Birmingham, England, in 1869 to a family of landowners, industrialists, and statesmen, Chamberlain helped managed his father's estates in the Bahamas before becoming an executive in Birmingham's metalworking industry in the late 1800s and early 1900s.

His political career began as lord mayor of Birmingham, an appointed position, in 1915. Briefly a member of Liberal Party Prime Minister David Lloyd George's World War I–era coalition government, Chamberlain was elected to the House of Commons in 1918. After a series of appointments running various departments of the government in the early 1920s, Chamberlain served as chancellor of the exchequer, or finance minister, from 1931 to 1937. He was elected prime minister in May 1937, replacing Stanley Baldwin.

Immediately upon coming to office, Chamberlain was faced with a series of international crises. To break apart the alliance between Fascist Italy and Nazi Germany, he recognized the former's brutal takeover of Ethiopia, and he maintained British neutrality in the Spanish Civil War, even though the Italians and Germans actively supported the fascist forces seeking to overthrow the legitimately elected republican government in Spain in the late 1930s.

In 1938, Chamberlain traveled three times to Germany, hoping to appease Hitler by allowing him to take over the Sudetenland, a German-speaking enclave within Czechoslovakia. After the final meeting at Munich in September, Chamberlain returned to England proclaiming he had achieved "peace in our time," a statement mocked by Germany's invasion of the rest of Czechoslovakia in March 1939. The Nazi nonaggression pact with the Soviet Union, signed in August 1939, undercut Chamberlain's efforts to build an anti-German alliance with the Russians.

When the Germans invaded Poland in September 1939, Chamberlain declared war on the Nazi state. Some historians have argued that Chamberlain's willingness to appease the Nazis reinforced U.S. isolationist sentiment and undermined Washington's support for Britain, even after London declared war on Germany.

From the fall of 1939 through the early spring of 1940, the prime minister presided over the "phony war," a quiescent lull broken in the spring of 1940 by the German invasion of Norway, the Low Countries, and France. Indeed, it was Britain's failed expedition to Norway in April that finally undermined his political authority, leading to his resignation and replacement by Winston Churchill in May. Chamberlain remained in the government through September, when ill health forced him to resign. He died in November 1940.

See also: Great Britain; Ethiopian War; fascism, Italy; Munich Conference; Nazi Germany; Nazi-Soviet nonaggression pact; Spanish Civil War; World War II, early history of; Baldwin, Stanley; Churchill, Winston.

Bibliography

Fuchser, Larry William. *Neville Chamberlain and Appeasement: A Study in the Politics of History.* New York: Norton, 1982.

McDonough, Frank. *Neville Chamberlain: Appeasement and the British Road to War.* New York: St. Martin's, 1998.

Rock, William R. *Chamberlain and Roosevelt: British Foreign Policy and the United States, 1937–1940.* Columbus: Ohio State University Press, 1988.

CHANDLER, RAYMOND

Among the most popular detective writers in American history, Raymond Chandler made a name for himself in the 1930s penning stories for pulp magazines and publishing mystery classics like *The Big Sleep* (1939) and *Farewell My Lovely* (1940).

Born in Chicago in 1888, Chandler spent most of his youth and early adulthood in England with his Irish-born mother. In 1914, he joined the Canadian army and British Royal Flying Corps (later the Royal Air Force) to fight in World War I. He moved to California in 1919 and became an executive with an oil company. But when the Great Depression hit the industry hard, Chandler turned to fiction writing to support himself. His first short story—"Black Mask"—was published in 1933.

Developing his uniquely dark view of southern California's underlife and the cool, cynical dialogue that was his trademark, Chandler published a series of novels in the 1930s, 1940s, and 1950s, most of which featured his private investigator protagonist, Philip Marlowe. During and after World War II, Chandler turned to screenwriting, penning such movie classics as *Double Indemnity* (1944) and *The Blue Dahlia* (1946). Chandler continued to turn out fiction until his death in 1959.

See also: films, feature; literature; Documents: Lend-Lease Act, March 11, 1941; Atlantic Charter, August 14, 1941.

Bibliography

Chandler, Raymond. *The Big Sleep & Farewell, My Lovely.* New York: Modern Library, 1995.

Marling, William. *Raymond Chandler.* Boston: Twayne, 1986.

CHIANG KAI-SHEK

Head of the Nationalist Chinese government on the mainland from 1928 to 1949 and leader of the Nationalist government in exile on the island of Taiwan from 1949 until his death in 1975, Chiang Kai-shek presided over China during the most tumultuous period in its modern history.

Chiang was born into a middle-class family in the province of Chekiang in 1887 and educated at military academies in China and Japan. He even served in the Japanese military from 1909 to 1911. He returned to his homeland when the revolution against the Manchu dynasty began in 1911 and from 1913 to 1916 fought to prevent the seating of a new emperor.

After a brief return to private life, Chiang joined the Kuomintang, or Nationalist Party of Chinese revolutionary leader Sun Yat-sen, who wanted to unify the country under a central republican government. Several years of fighting against warlords, however, proved unsuccessful, and Chiang went to study communist institutions in the Soviet Union in 1923. Despite this training, Chiang remained an ardent anti-Communist.

After Sun Yat-sen's death in 1925, the Chinese Communists—with the help of the Soviet Union—made a push for power. But Chiang, at the head of the Nationalist army, drove them into the mountains of southeastern China in 1927. Then Chiang turned his army against the warlords of the northern part of the country. Although he took Beijing in 1928, he was never able to fully quell their activity. In 1930, Chiang was converted to Christianity by the family of his second wife, Soong Mei-ling.

As nominal head of China, Chiang spoke of land and other reforms, but was able to accomplish little, as provincial leaders, warlords, and Communists still controlled much of the country. Making things even more precarious for the Nationalist government, Japan invaded and annexed the northern province of Manchuria in 1931, turning it into the puppet state of Manchukuo in 1933. Chiang, however, chose to ignore the Japanese, launching an offensive against the Communists in the southeast instead, forcing them—under the leadership of Mao Zedong—to make the so-called long march to a remote region in northwestern China in 1934.

Leader of the Nationalist Chinese forces during the 1930s, Chiang Kai-Shek fought a two-front war against Chinese communist forces and Japanese invaders. *(Brown Brothers)*

Meanwhile, the Japanese were consolidating their control over Manchuria and threatening the rest of China. And although Chiang wanted to continue to fight against the Communists, he was threatened with overthrow if he did not unite with them against the Japanese, which he reluctantly agreed to do in 1936. The following year, the Japanese launched a massive invasion of central and eastern China. For four years, Chiang and the Communists fought desperately against the militarily superior Japanese, with only a minimum amount of aid from the United States after about 1940. The Chinese forces were able to keep the Japanese largely confined to the cities, the most populous areas, and along key lines of communication. The countryside belonged to the Nationalist and Communist resistance forces.

From 1941 to 1945, the Chinese were aided in their struggle by massive amounts of aid from the United States and, at the very end of the war with Japan, by an invading Soviet army. In the four years that followed the end of World War II, Chiang led his forces in a bitter civil war against Mao and the Communists. The Nationalists lost the war and were forced into exile on the island of Taiwan, where they established the quasi-independent Republic of China. Chiang Kai-shek ruled the island in dictatorial fashion until his death in 1975.

See also: China; Japan; Soviet Union; World War II, early history of; Mao Zedong.

Bibliography

Crozier, Brian. *The Man Who Lost China: The First Full Biography of Chiang Kai-shek.* New York: Scribner, 1976.

Furuya, Keiji. *Chiang Kai-shek: His Life and Times.* New York: St. John's University Press, 1981.

Morwood, William. *Duel for the Middle Kingdom: The Struggle Between Chiang Kai-shek and Mao Tse-tung for Control of China.* New York: Everest, 1980.

CHURCHILL, WINSTON

Conservative Party British prime minister from 1940 to 1945, Sir Winston Churchill presided over his country's difficult but ultimately successful war against Nazi Germany and Fascist Italy during World War II. Churchill's inspired rhetoric and willingness to stand up to German dictator Adolf Hitler in the early years of the war helped convince an isolationist America that its national security was tied up with Britain's and that America should support the British in their struggle against Nazi Germany.

Born in 1874 to the powerful Conservative politician Lord Randolph Churchill and Jennie Jerome, the daughter of a New York financier, Winston was educated at Sandhurst, Britain's premier military academy, and served with the British army in India and Africa in the 1890s.

Entering politics in the early 1900s, Churchill served in Parliament and a number of other positions in the government, including head of the admiralty during World War I. In and out of office in the 1920s and 1930s, Churchill became a prolific essayist. By the late 1930s, he had become increasingly vocal in his criticism of the appeasement policy of Prime Minister Neville Chamberlain, who believed that giving Hitler what he wanted on the Continent would allow Europe to escape another world war. Churchill labeled the Munich conference of March 1938, where Chamberlain acceded to the German dictator's demands for a part of Czechoslovakia, "a total and unmitigated defeat."

Opinions like this galvanized that part of the Conservative Party leadership who believed that war with Nazi Germany was inevitable and that Britain should do everything it could to prepare for it. The rhetoric thrust Churchill into the leadership position of this group. When Chamberlain resigned in April 1940, Churchill became prime minister.

Despite the fall of France in June and the disaster of Dunkirk, where hundreds of thousands of British troops barely escaped entrapment by the Germans through a mass evacuation across the English Channel, Churchill remained adamant in his belief that Britain must never surrender to the Nazis.

Recognizing that Britain could not continue to fight alone, Churchill did everything in his power to bring the Americans into the war. His inspiring rhetoric—after Chamberlain's language of appeasement—convinced many Americans that Britain had to be defended at all costs, short of actual military participation by the United States. To achieve such aid, Churchill cultivated a friendship with President Franklin D. Roosevelt that helped secure U.S. support, first in the form of military surplus matériel, old destroyers, and—through the 1941 Lend-Lease Act—massive military aid.

In August 1941, Churchill sailed to North America to meet with Roosevelt off the coast of Newfoundland, where the two issued the Atlantic Charter, setting out the goals of democracy and freedom for a war that the United States was on the brink of joining in full. After Pearl Harbor and America's entry into World War II, Churchill worked closely with Roosevelt to coordinate action against the Nazis, although the two had strong disagreements about an invasion of the European continent itself and the future status of the British empire, which Churchill wanted to retain and Roosevelt believed had to be granted independence.

In July 1945, shortly after victory over the Nazis, the British electorate voted Churchill out of office,

Prime Minister of Great Britain from 1940 to 1945, Winston Churchill was instrumental in winning American military and economic aid for his country before American entry into World War II. *(Brown Brothers)*

believing that the postwar era required Labour Party leadership. Briefly reelected prime minister in the mid-1950s, Churchill spent most of his long postwar retirement writing his memoirs and a series of magisterial books on the history World War II. He died in 1965.

See also: Atlantic Charter; Great Britain; Lend-Lease Act; Munich Conference; Nazi Germany; World War II, early history of; Chamberlain, Neville; Roosevelt, Franklin D.

Bibliography

Cannadine, David, ed. *Blood, Toil, Tears, and Sweat: The Speeches of Winston Churchill.* Boston: Houghton Mifflin, 1989.

Churchill, Winson. *While England Slept: A Survey of World Affairs, 1932–1938.* New York: G. P. Putnam's Sons, 1938.

Gilbert, Martin. *Churchill: A Life.* New York: Holt, 1991.

Kimball, Warren F., ed. *Churchill & Roosevelt: The Complete Correspondence.* Princeton: Princeton University Press, 1984.

COHEN, BENJAMIN V.

One of the top legal minds of his era and a protégé of Supreme Court Justices Louis Brandeis and Felix Frankfurter, Benjamin V. Cohen is best known as one of the chief architects of the Securities Exchange Act of 1934, which created the Securities and Exchange Commission, and the Public Utilities Holding Act of 1935.

Born in Muncie, Indiana, in 1894 to a well-to-do immigrant family, Cohen received his law degree from the University of Chicago in 1915 and a specialized law degree from Harvard University a year later. At Harvard, the brilliant Cohen came to the attention of Professor Felix Frankfurter, himself the protégé of Louis Brandeis. When Brandeis and Frankfurter were asked by President Woodrow Wilson to recruit the best legal minds for government work, they convinced Wilson to make Cohen the attorney for the U.S. Shipping Board from 1917 to 1919.

At the Versailles peace conference in 1919, Cohen helped negotiate Britain's Palestine Mandate, with part of its mission being to create a Jewish homeland there, and from 1919 to 1921, he worked as legal counsel for the American Zionist movement. From 1922 through 1933, Cohen worked as a lawyer on Wall Street, focusing on securities issues, but also did *pro bono* work for the National Consumers' League.

In 1933, Frankfurter, an adviser to Franklin D. Roosevelt, and Brandeis brought Cohen to the attention of the president, who assigned Cohen the task of writing securities reform legislation along with presidential adviser Thomas G. Corcoran. At the same time, Cohen was given the title of associate general counsel of the Public Works Administration. Cohen and Corcoran worked on other key pieces of New Deal legislation, including the Public Utilities Holding Act, the Rural Electrification Act of 1935, and the Fair Labor Standards Act of 1938.

By 1940, Cohen—a strong interventionist—was advising Roosevelt on the best way to make aid available to Britain and was instrumental in shaping the executive order issued by the president making American destroyers available to the British. Cohen also helped draft the Lend-Lease Act of 1941. During the war, he served as counsel to the American ambassador in London and, from 1943 to 1945, as general counsel to the Office of War Mobilization. Cohen was also one of the architects of the Dumbarton Oaks agreement of 1945 that established the United Nations.

After the war, Cohen advised several administrations on domestic and foreign policy issues. He died in 1983.

See also: New Deal, first; Fair Labor Standards Act; Public Utilities Holding Act; Rural Electrification Administration; Securities and Exchange Commission; Lend-Lease Act; Brandeis, Louis; Corcoran, Thomas G.; Frankfurter, Felix.

Bibliography

Lash, Joseph P. *Dealers and Dreamers: A New Look at the New Deal.* New York: Doubleday, 1988.

Parrish, Michael E. *Securities Regulation and the New Deal.* New Haven: Yale University Press, 1970.

COOPER, GARY

The quintessential all-American male film lead and Hollywood star of the 1930s, Gary Cooper starred in a number of comedy classics directed by Frank Capra, including *Mr. Deeds Goes to Town* (1936) and *Meet John Doe* (1941), as well as other box office hits like *The Plainsman* (1937) and *Sergeant York* (1941).

Born Frank James Cooper in Helena, Montana, in 1901—the son of a Montana Supreme Court justice—Cooper dropped out of Grinnell College in Iowa to go to Hollywood in 1924. Initially a stunt man, he acted and then starred in a number of silent westerns in the 1920s. His big breakthrough came in *The Virginian* (1929), one of the first Hollywood talkies. His handsome looks and easygoing acting style earned him fame

as a sometimes taciturn and sometimes plainspoken man in films like *A Farewell to Arms* (1932), *Beau Geste* (1939), and *The Westerner* (1940). Cooper continued to make films during and after the war, including the 1952 *High Noon*, considered one of the finest westerns ever made. Cooper died in 1961.

See also: films, feature; Capra, Frank; *Sergeant York.*

Bibliography

Dickens, Homer. *The Films of Gary Cooper.* New York: Citadel Press, 1970.

Meyers, Jeffrey. *Gary Cooper: American Hero.* New York: William Morrow, 1998.

COPLAND, AARON

Among the most popular American composers of the twentieth century, Aaron Copland infused classical music with a modernist style and folk rhythms to create a uniquely American musical idiom. While Copland began composing music in the 1920s, some of his most enduring pieces date from the Great Depression era, including orchestral works such as *El Salón México* (1936) and the ballet *Billy the Kid* (1938).

Copland was born the son of Jewish immigrants in New York City in 1900 and was taught the piano by

an older sister. Taking advantage of a new and uniquely American form of education at the time, Copland learned composition and harmony through a correspondence course. In 1921, he traveled to France and studied under the influential Nadia Boulanger. Three years later, he returned to New York and began writing compositions for the New York Symphony.

Influenced by European modernism, American folk music, and jazz, he composed a series of ballets, including *Billy the Kid* and later *Rodeo* (1942) and

One of the great composers of the twentieth century, Aaron Copland wrote *El Salón México* of 1936 and the the music for the 1938 ballet "Billy the Kid." *(Brown Brothers)*

Appalachian Spring (1944). During the 1930s, he also wrote two orchestral pieces designed for young people's orchestras—*Second Hurricane* (1937) and *An Outdoor Adventure* (1938). Copland also composed music scores for two Depression-era films, *Of Mice and Men* (1939) and *Our Town* (1940). He continued to create music for films and orchestras through the 1940s, 1950s, and 1960s, going into virtual retirement in 1970. Copland died in 1990.

See also: films, feature; music.

Bibliography

Copland, Aaron. *Copland on Music.* Garden City, NY: Double-day, 1960.

Pollack, Howard. *Aaron Copland: The Life and Work of an Un-common Man.* New York: Henry Holt, 1999.

CORCORAN, THOMAS G.

One of the most brilliant legal minds of his generation and a protégé of Supreme Court Justice Felix Frankfurter, Thomas G. Corcoran was a key architect of several critical pieces of New Deal legislation, including the 1933 Securities Exchange Act, which created the Securities and Exchange Commission, the 1933 Tennessee Valley Authority Act, the 1935 Public Utilities Holding Company Act, and the Fair Labor Standards Act of 1938.

Born in Pawtucket, Rhode Island, in 1900 to an upper-class Irish-American family with political connections, Corcoran attended Brown University, where he was valedictorian, and received his law degree from Harvard University in 1926. At Harvard, his quick intellect made him law review editor and brought him to

the attention of Professor Frankfurter, who got him a one-year clerkship with Supreme Court Justice Oliver Wendell Holmes.

Corcoran then spent the next five years working at a Wall Street legal firm where he became an expert in securities law. In March 1932, he went to work on the legal staff of the Reconstruction Finance Corporation (RFC), a public corporation established by the Herbert Hoover administration to revive the nation's businesses and financial institutions. Corcoran remained at the RFC almost continuously through 1940.

But like other key figures in the new Franklin D. Roosevelt administration, Corcoran's relatively minor position belied his importance. In fact, Corcoran, via Frankfurter, who was a close adviser to Roosevelt, had been picked to help write the critical securities legislation that the president was contemplating. In this task, he was accompanied by another Frankfurter protégé, Benjamin V. Cohen.

At the same time, Corcoran was establishing a close personal and political relationship with the president, who relied on Corcoran to help write some of his speeches. Corcoran also orchestrated the president's generally unsuccessful campaign to rid the Senate of its more conservative members, by campaigning against them in the 1938 election. Because of this, Corcoran was much disliked by congressional conservatives, leading Roosevelt to dismiss him from the administration after the 1940 elections.

He returned to private law practice, but was brought before a congressional committee investigating influence peddling in 1941. No charges were ever brought, but the cloud remained over Corcoran's name for the rest of his life. Corcoran died in 1981.

See also: election of 1938; Fair Labor Standards Act; Public Utilities Holding Company Act; Reconstruction Finance Corporation; Securities and Exchange Commission; Tennessee Valley Authority; Cohen, Benjamin V.; Frankfurter, Felix; Roosevelt, Franklin D.

Bibliography

Lash, Joseph P. *Dealers and Dreamers: A New Look at the New Deal.* New York: Doubleday, 1988.

Parrish, Michael E. *Securities Regulation and the New Deal.* New Haven: Yale University Press, 1970.

COUGHLIN, FATHER CHARLES

A Roman Catholic priest who capitalized on the new medium of radio to spread his spiritual and political message, Father Charles Coughlin was an early supporter of President Franklin D. Roosevelt and the New Deal. But Coughlin turned against the New Deal in the mid-1930s. With populist rhetoric that often contradicted itself, Coughlin came to believe at once that Roosevelt's programs were both too socialistic and that his administration was too beholden to Wall Street bankers and wealthy Jews.

Coughlin was born in Canada in 1891 and educated at St. Michael's College in Toronto. While he briefly flirted with the idea of a political career when he was young, he decided to join the priesthood instead and was ordained in Detroit in 1923. Three years after that, he was appointed pastor of the tiny congregation of the Shrine of the Little Flower Church in the lower-middle-class Detroit suburb of Royal Oak.

From the very beginning of his pastorate, Coughlin experimented with radio, offering his Sunday sermons to a small listening public over Detroit station WJR. But his gift for language and mellifluous voice—described by one listener as "a voice made for promises"—soon attracted a larger audience, and by the time the Depression began Coughlin was being listened to by people as far afield as Chicago and Cincinnati.

Even as his listenership expanded, so did his repertoire of themes, as Coughlin soon began to weigh in on political issues across the ideological spectrum. He attacked communism on the one hand, but on the other he turned increasingly against President Herbert Hoover, whom he accused of being a stooge for international bankers. He denounced the gold standard and called for inflationary financial policies that he said would lift the threat of poverty from his working-and middle-class audience. By 1932, Coughlin was the most listened-to man in America, needing a staff of more than a hundred to deal with the torrents of appreciative mail he received every week.

Hoover detested the man, but Roosevelt appreciated Coughlin's power—indeed, it is said that Roosevelt's own mastery of radio was partly learned from listening to Coughlin's sermons—and cultivated the radio preacher's support. The attention worked as Coughlin bitterly attacked Hoover throughout the 1932 campaign as a tool of Wall Street. And when Roosevelt announced his New Deal, Coughlin proclaimed, "the New Deal is Christ's deal." The choice that year, Coughlin preached, was "Roosevelt or ruin."

But within two years of Roosevelt's coming to power, Coughlin had turned against the president and the New Deal. The radio preacher was particularly upset about the administration's unwillingness to pursue strong enough inflationary policies like jobs programs and massive public spending. With a not very subtle anti-Semitic message, Coughlin began accusing the president of being in league with Jewish bankers and

Father Charles Coughlin, a radio preacher in Michigan, was among the most influential and listened-to broadcast personalities of the 1930s. *(Brown Brothers)*

financiers who wanted to prolong the Depression for their own economic interests.

Now receiving more mail than anyone in the United States—including the president—Coughlin launched a political organization he called the National Union for Social Justice (NUSJ) in 1934. With its "Sixteen Principles"—which, among other things, called for the predictable inflationary policies, but also for the nationalization of the nation's heavy industries—the NUSJ grew rapidly to an estimated 8 million members strong. The group lacked a real national organizational structure, however, and it was questionable how much political power the NUSJ could bring to bear on the electoral process.

Still, the potency of Coughlin and the NUSJ was not to be dismissed easily. When Roosevelt proposed U.S. membership in the World Court in 1935, the isolationist Coughlin and the NUSJ were able to generate so much anti–World Court mail that Congress refused

to ratify the treaty. The World Court vote represented the first major legislative defeat Roosevelt faced in his first term in office.

Indeed, most historians believe that pressure from Coughlin and other populist spokespersons, like Louisiana senator Huey P. Long and his Share Our Wealth movement and old-age pension advocate Francis Townsend, pushed Roosevelt to adopt the more radical measures of the so-called Second New Deal, including the Social Security Act, the National Labor Relations Act, and the failed "soak the rich" tax bill.

In 1936, Coughlin, Townsend, and Gerald L. K. Smith, successor to the assassinated Long as head of the Share Our Wealth movement, formed the Union Party, nominating Representative William Lemke (R-ND) as their presidential candidate. Coughlin claimed he would win 10 million votes for Lemke, but Lemke got less than a tenth of that. By stealing their political thunder, Roosevelt won in a landslide.

The 1936 election did not end Coughlin's career nor his influence, but it sharply delineated their limits. While still listened to by millions, Coughlin's increasingly bitter and anti-Semitic rhetoric relegated him to the political fringes by the late 1930s. With America's entry into World War II in 1941, Coughlin came under government scrutiny and his magazine, *Social Justice*, was banned from the mails. That same year, the American Catholic hierarchy ordered him to stop his broadcasts. Coughlin remained pastor of the Shrine of the Little Flower until he retired in 1966. He died in 1979.

See also: banking; National Union for Social Justice; New Deal, second; Share Our Wealth Society; Townsend Plan; Union Party; Lemke, William; Long, Huey P.; Roosevelt, Franklin D.; Townsend, Francis.

Bibliography

Brinkley, Alan. *Voices of Protest: Huey Long, Father Coughlin, and the Great Depression*. New York: Knopf, 1982.

Coughlin, Charles Edward. *The New Deal in Money*. Royal Oak, MI: The Radio League of the Little Flower, 1933.

Lee, Alfred McClung, and Elizabeth Briant Lee, eds. *The Fine Art of Propaganda: A Study of Father Coughlin's Speeches*. New York: Harcourt Brace, 1939.

Sheldon, Marcus. *Father Coughlin: The Tumultuous Life of the Priest of the Little Flower*. Boston: Little, Brown, 1973.

Tull, Charles J. *Father Coughlin and the New Deal*. Syracuse, NY: Syracuse University Press, 1965.

COWLEY, MALCOLM

As a leftist intellectual and editor of the liberal journal *The New Republic* from 1929 through 1944, Malcolm Cowley was at the center of many of the political, intellectual, and literary debates during the Great Depression era.

Cowley was born in small-town Pennsylvania in 1898 and grew up in Pittsburgh. He dropped out of Harvard to serve with the American Ambulance Service in France during World War I, but finished his degree in 1920. During the early 1920s, he joined other American literary figures as part of the "lost generation" in Paris and wrote a collection of essays about his experiences there.

Taking over at *The New Republic* in 1929, Cowley soon shifted the magazine further to the Left, and, in September 1932, he joined more than fifty prominent writers and intellectuals in signing a letter supporting the presidential candidacy of Communist Party leader William Z. Foster.

Cowley continued to write and edit articles about the role of intellectuals, writers, and artists in society, debating the issue of aesthetics and social involvement. In the 1940s, Cowley was instrumental in the revival of William Faulkner's literary reputation. He also published a series of books on writing and American literature through the 1970s. Cowley died in 1989.

See also: literature; *New Republic, The*; newspapers and magazines; Faulkner, William.

Bibliography

Cowley, Malcolm. *The Dream of the Golden Mountains: Remembering the 1930s.* New York: Penguin Books, 1981.

Kempf, James Michael. *The Early Career of Malcolm Cowley: A Humanist Among the Moderns.* Baton Rouge: Louisiana State University Press, 1985.

DALADIER, ÉDOUARD

Among the most prominent politicians of France in the Great Depression, Édouard Daladier led his Radical Party into the leftist Popular Front coalition with Premier Léon Blum's Socialist Party, as well as the Communist Party, in 1935. As premier in the late 1930s, Daladier joined with British prime minister Neville Chamberlain in signing the Munich Pact, handing over part of Czechoslovakia to Nazi Germany and helping to usher in World War II.

Daladier was born in Carpentras, France, in 1884 and joined the Chamber of Deputies in 1919. He was appointed minister of colonies in 1924 and served as minister of war, minister of public instruction, and minister of public works at various times in the late 1920s and early 1930s. He was briefly elected premier in 1933, but his government collapsed the following year.

As partner in the Popular Front government, Daladier supported workers' rights legislation and other left-wing programs and policies. When the coalition collapsed and Blum resigned, Daladier took over the reins of government and was premier of France during the country's takeover by Nazi Germany in June 1940. During the invasion, Daladier tried to escape to North Africa to set up a government-in-exile, but was arrested by the pro-Nazi Vichy government, convicted on trumped-up charges of failing to prepare France militarily for war, and handed over to the Germans, who imprisoned him for the duration of World War II.

Following the war, he was elected to the Chamber of Deputies from 1946 through the collapse of the Fourth Republic in 1958, when he retired from politics. Daladier died in 1970.

See also: France; Munich Conference; Nazi Germany; World War II, early history of; Blum, Léon; Chamberlain, Neville.

Bibliography

Géraud, André. *The Gravediggers of France: Gamelin, Daladier, Reynaud, Pétain, and Laval: Military Defeat, Armistice, Counter-Revolution.* Indianapolis: Bobbs-Merrill, 1940.

DAWES, CHARLES G.

Charles G. Dawes, a banker who had helped create a plan that reorganized German finances in the mid-1920s, was the person chosen by President Herbert Hoover in 1932 to preside over the Reconstruction Finance Corporation (RFC), the administration's largest program for fighting the economic effects of the Great Depression.

Dawes was born in Marietta, Ohio, in 1865. He attended Marietta College and studied law in Cincinnati before starting a practice in Lincoln, Nebraska, in 1887. He served as U.S. comptroller of the currency from 1897 to 1902 and organized the Central Trust Company of Chicago after that. Head of supply procurement for the American Expeditionary Force in World War I, he became the first director of the budget in 1921.

During the German financial crisis of 1923, Dawes was called upon to establish a system—the so-called Dawes plan—whereby that country could effectively pay its World War I reparations to the Allies through the loans from the United States. The plan is widely seen as saving the European financial system in the 1920s and earned Dawes a Nobel Peace Prize in 1925.

Vice president under Calvin Coolidge from 1925 to 1929, Dawes then served as ambassador to Great Britain from 1929 to 1932, when he was called back to run the newly formed RFC. Designed to provide finan-

cial aid to big business and, later, agriculture, it was also expanded to fund public works and employment projects, though Dawes was reluctant to use all of the resources and power that had been granted the RFC.

In June 1932, Dawes suddenly resigned from the RFC to devote all his time to rescuing his financially troubled Central Trust Company, which was saved only through a massive infusion of cash from the RFC he had just left. While some critics saw favoritism in the plan, most economists argued that the collapse of the Central Trust Company would have sent devastating shock waves through the financial system. As it was, Dawes's precipitous resignation from the RFC to save his bank was seen by many as a sign of the depths to which the country's financial system had sunk. Dawes spent the latter years of the Depression writing a memoir and died in 1951.

See also: banking; Reconstruction Finance Corporation.

Bibliography

Dawes. Charles G. *How Long Prosperity?* Chicago: A. N. Marquis, 1937.

Olson, James S. *Herbert Hoover and the Reconstruction Finance Corporation, 1931–1933.* Ames: Iowa State University Press, 1977.

DEWEY, THOMAS E.

Perhaps the best-known prosecutor in America during the Great Depression, Thomas E. Dewey earned a reputation investigating and prosecuting organized crime in New York City that would propel him into the governor's office and to the head of the Republican national ticket in 1944 and 1948.

Born in Owosso, Michigan in 1902, Dewey graduated from the University of Michigan in 1925 and Columbia University Law School in 1928. In 1931, he became chief assistant to the U.S. attorney for the southern district of New York. Four years later, he was appointed special prosecutor where he obtained

seventy-two convictions out of seventy-three prosecutions of crime figures for racketeering and other organized crime. In 1937, he was elected district attorney for New York and made an unsuccessful bid for governor in 1938, nearly upsetting the very popular Herbert Lehman.

Running again in 1942, Dewey was elected. He ran for president and lost against Franklin D. Roosevelt in 1944 and against Harry Truman in 1948. After leaving the governor's office in 1955, Dewey returned to his private law practice. He died in 1971.

See also: crime; Republican Party; Lehman, Herbert.

Bibliography

Dewey, Thomas. *The Case Against the New Deal.* New York: Harper and Brothers, 1940.

Stolberg, Mary M. *Fighting Organized Crime: Politics, Justice, and the Legacy of Thomas E. Dewey.* Boston: Northeastern University Press, 1995.

DIDRIKSON, MILDRED "BABE"

One of the most gifted and versatile athletes of the Depression era, or any other time, Babe Didrikson was an Olympic gold medalist in track and field, a semiprofessional basketball player, and one of the most successful woman golfers in the history of the sport.

Born Mildred Didrikson to a working-class family in Beaumont, Texas, in 1914, the future sportswoman excelled in athletics from a young age, racing street cars to improve her running ability and leaving high school to play semiprofessional basketball.

In 1932, Didrikson came to the attention of the American public with a string of extraordinary athletic accomplishments. She was made an All-American in basketball and competed in eight track-and-field events at the annual Amateur Athletic Union competition, winning six of them and setting world records for the high jump, javelin throw, and eighty-meter hurdles. She was declared the meet's overall champion. At the 1932 Olympic Games in Los Angeles, she won gold medals in the javelin and eighty-meter hurdles and would have won one in the high jump if she had not been disqualified when her head went over the bar before her feet did (this has since become the standard form of high jumping).

Always an excellent amateur golfer, Didrikson turned professional in 1935 and became a champion almost immediately. Over the course of her career, she would win fifty-five tournaments, including an impressive seventeen in a row, and she often beat men's scores. Didrikson was a favorite with many fans not just for her athletic skills but her demeanor. She loved to joke and wisecrack, shaking up the rather staid world of professional athletics at the time. In 1938, she married professional wrestler George Zaharias and was thereafter known as Babe Didrikson Zaharias.

In 1949, Didrikson helped found the Ladies Professional Golfers Association (LPGA). Plagued with colon cancer since 1941, she died in 1956 at the age of 45.

The most accomplished female athlete of her generation, Mildred "Babe" Didrikson won two gold medals in track and field at the 1932 Olympic in Los Angeles, before going on to become a champion golfer. *(Brown Brothers)*

See also: sports.

Bibliography

Cayleff, Susan E. *Babe: The Life and Legend of Babe Didrikson Zaharias.* Urbana: University of Illinois Press, 1995.

Knudson, R. Rozanne. *Babe Didrikson: Athlete of the Century.* New York: Viking Kestrel, 1985.

DIES, MARTIN, JR.

As chairman of the House Committee for the Investigation of Un-American Activities (later the House Un-American Activities Committee, HUAC), Democratic representative Martin Dies Jr. of Texas was instrumental in the late 1930s in the defunding and dismantling of a number of New Deal agencies, most notably, the Federal Theater Project.

Dies was born in Colorado, Texas, in 1901. After receiving his undergraduate education at the University of Texas, Dies graduated from the law school of the National University in Washington in 1920. Opening a law practice in Texas, he quickly became involved in politics, winning election to the House of Representatives in 1931. He made an early name for himself blaming alien workers for the growing unemployment in the country, a position that led the Immigration and Naturalization Service to cut back the number of legal immigrants from Mexico to less than 2,000 annually.

A conservative southerner, Dies nevertheless supported Franklin D. Roosevelt and the early New Deal. Like many other southern Democrats, however, Dies turned against Roosevelt in the president's second term, feeling that the New Deal had veered off into socialism.

In 1938, Dies convinced the House of Representatives to establish the Committee for the Investigation of Un-American Activities, ostensibly to investigate both fascistic and communistic influences in American government and society. In fact, however, the committee soon turned to investigate leftist influences in labor unions and New Deal agencies.

In 1939, these investigations were critical in the destruction of the Federal Theater Project, which Dies claimed was supporting communist and anti-American artists and their endeavors. The committee also investigated charges that workers in the Works Progress Administration were being forced to donate money and time to the campaigns of liberal Democratic Party candidates, most notably, Senator Alben Barkley of Kentucky. The result was the Hatch Act of 1939, banning the involvement of federal workers in electoral activities.

Dies resigned from office in 1945 and went back to practicing law in Texas. He returned to the House from 1953 to 1959 and then returned once again to his private law practice. Dies died in 1972.

See also: Communist Party; unions and union organizing; Federal Theater Project; Hatch Act; House Un-American Affairs Committee; Works Progress Administration; Barkley, Alben.

Bibliography

Dies, Martin. *The Trojan Horse in America*. New York: Dodd, Mead, 1940.

Gellermann, William. *Martin Dies*. New York: John Day, 1944.

Ogden, August Raymond. *The Dies Committee: A Study of the Special House Committee for the Investigation of Un-American Activities, 1938–1944*. Washington, DC: The Catholic University of America Press, 1945.

DIETRICH, MARLENE

With her sophistication and sensuality, German-born actress Marlene Dietrich was one of the top box office stars of the 1930s, playing dangerously seductive women in such films as *Blonde Venus* (1932) and *The Devil Is a Woman* (1935).

Born in Berlin in 1901, Dietrich studied both violin and theater as a young woman. Beginning in the early 1920s, she played a number of small movie parts for the burgeoning film industry of Weimar Republic–era Germany. Her thrust into stardom came in 1930, when she played a seductive but world-weary cabaret artist in Josef von Sternberg's *The Blue Angel*. The movie—a hit around the world—captured the attention of Hollywood. That same year, she starred in the American film *Morocco*, then went on to star in *Dishonored* (1931), *Shanghai Express* (1932), and *The Scarlet Empress* (1934). A surprisingly effective comedienne, she played opposite Gary Cooper in *Desire* (1936) and Jimmy Stewart in *Destry Rides Again* (1939).

During World War II, Dietrich made hundreds of appearances at U.S. and allied army outposts. She continued to star in films in the 1950s, 1960s, and 1970s, as well as performing in nightclubs. She went into retirement in 1978 and died in Paris in 1992.

See also: films, feature.

Bibliography

Dietrich, Marlene. *Marlene.* New York: Grove Press, 1989.

Spoto, Donald. *Blue Angel: The Life of Marlene Dietrich.* New York: Doubleday, 1992.

German-born actress Marlene Dietrich became an international star in the 1932 German film *Blonde Venus* before moving to Hollywood. *(Brown Brothers)*

DILLINGER, JOHN

One of the most notorious gangsters of the Great Depression era, John Dillinger earned a reputation as a dapper and well-dressed bank robber before being gunned down in a famous showdown with the Federal Bureau of Investigation (FBI) outside a Chicago movie theater in 1934.

Born in Indianapolis in either 1902 or 1903—the record is unclear—Dillinger joined the U.S. navy in 1923, but deserted after a few months. A year later, he was arrested in a foiled robbery of a grocery store near the Indiana farm where he grew up. A nine-year stint in the Indiana state prison brought the young Dillinger into contact with professional bank robbers who apparently taught him their illegal trade.

Upon receiving parole in May 1933, Dillinger went on a bank-robbing spree across Indiana and Ohio. Handsome and expensively attired, he earned a reputation as a criminal ladies' man and received great media attention. After a brief capture in Ohio in September, Dillinger escaped with the help of five former convict friends. This gang then conducted a series of bank robberies in Indiana and Wisconsin before fleeing to Tucson. Captured once again and extradited to Indiana, he made yet another daring escape in March 1934.

More bank robberies and close escapes from police capture ensued in Minnesota and Wisconsin. Finally, the FBI and Indiana police—working with a brothel owner friend of Dillinger's named Anna Sage, the famous "lady in red"—tracked Dillinger down and shot

Among the most violent of Great Depression-era gangsters, John Dillinger was captured and escaped twice during the 1930s. Here, at center, he is shown handcuffed to an arresting officer (*left*) and with his defense attorney. (*Brown Brothers*)

him at Chicago's Biograph Theatre on the evening of July 22, 1934, although some people insist that Dillinger was not there and that the FBI killed the wrong man.

See also: crime; Federal Bureau of Investigation.

Bibliography

Girardin, G. Russell. *Dillinger: The Untold Story*. Bloomington: Indiana University Press, 1994.

DiMAGGIO, JOE

Arguably the greatest hitter in the history of baseball, Joseph Paul DiMaggio—also known as Joltin' Joe and the Yankee Clipper—played outfield for the New York Yankees between 1936 and 1951. His fifty-six-game hitting streak in the final season of the Great Depression in 1941 is considered by many sports aficionados to be the greatest record in professional baseball.

DiMaggio was born in California's Bay Area in 1914 and played minor-league baseball in San Francisco before being drafted by the Yankees for the 1936 season. Over the next sixteen years, he helped lead the team to ten American League championships and nine World Series crowns. DiMaggio also spent several years in the military during World War II, most playing exhibition ball.

Yankees outfielder and hitter Joe DiMaggio was one of the greatest baseball players of all time. His fifty-six-game hitting streak in the last season of the Great Depression in 1941 is considered by many to have been the greatest accomplishment in baseball history. *(Brown Brothers)*

Voted Most Valuable Player in the American League in 1939, 1941, and 1947, DiMaggio had a lifetime batting average of .325. After retiring from baseball, DiMaggio was married briefly to film legend Marilyn Monroe in 1954 and was voted into baseball's Hall of Fame in 1955. He later went on to enjoy great wealth as an executive and TV spokesperson. DiMaggio died in 1999.

See also: sports.

Bibliography

Chadwin, Dean. *Those Damn Yankees: The Secret Life of America's Greatest Franchise.* New York: Verso, 1999.

Cramer, Richard Ben. *Joe DiMaggio: The Hero's Life.* New York: Simon & Schuster, 2000.

DISNEY, WALT

America's most popular and successful animator, Walter Elias "Walt" Disney produced a number of hit cartoon films in the 1930s, including the short subject *The Three Little Pigs* (1933). The film included the song "Who's Afraid of the Big Bad Wolf," which became an optimistic anthem for a nation experiencing the depths of the Great Depression.

Disney—whose father was an unsuccessful carpenter-farmer and whose mother was a former schoolteacher—was born into genteel poverty in Chicago in 1901, but his family moved to a small town in Missouri when he was still an infant. His father soon gave up farming and the family moved to Kansas City, where Walt eventually attended the Kansas City Art Institute and School of Design.

Moving back to Chicago at sixteen, Walt continued to draw and take photographs while he finished high school. A truck driver for the American Red Cross in Europe during World War I, Disney returned to Kansas City in 1919 and became a commercial artist. But he also began making short animated advertising films with his brother Roy, who handled the business end of things and remained Walt's main financial adviser throughout Walt's life, taking over the Disney business empire upon his death.

Disney drew his first Mickey Mouse cartoon in 1927 and produced the first animated talkie—*Steamboat Willie*—in 1928. A huge hit, it was followed by other films in the early 1930s, from which Roy soon spun off lucrative product franchises. In 1935, Disney began his lifelong career of adapting classic fairy tales to the animated screen with the popular *Snow White and the Seven Dwarfs*.

While increasingly conservative, anti–New Deal, and anti-labor in his political outlook, Disney was not above picking up on the success of the Federal Theater Project's adaptation of *Pinocchio*, which he turned into another successful fairy tale animated film in 1940. Other popular Depression-era films of Disney's include the comedy *Dumbo* and the surrealistic *Fantasia*, both coming out in 1940, with the latter attracting some controversy when Igor Stravinsky, composer of the symphony *The Rite of Spring*, complained that he was not paid by Disney for the use of the music in the film. That same year, Disney opened a huge new animation studio in Burbank, California.

During the war, the Disney studio produced work for the military and government. After the war, it continued to create animated, live-action, and mixed animation/live-action films—as well as TV programs and an amusement park in southern California. Walt Disney died in 1966. Disney's plans for a much larger amusement park and planned community in Florida were realized by his company after his death.

See also: films, feature; music; Federal Theater Project.

Bibliography

Mosley, Leonard. *Disney's World: A Biography.* New York: Stein and Day, 1985.

Schickel, Richard. *The Disney Version: The Life, Times, Art, and Commerce of Walt Disney.* New York: Simon & Schuster, 1985.

DIVINE, FATHER (GEORGE BAKER)

With his Peace Mission Movement church, Father Divine—also called "The Messenger" by his hundreds of thousands of followers—was the most popular and influential African-American minister of the Great Depression era.

Born outside Savannah, probably in 1877, Divine—originally, George Baker—was the son of a day laborer and a domestic servant. Of his young life, little is known. In the late 1890s, he moved to Baltimore and became a Baptist minister, traveling and preaching throughout the South.

After a period in southern California, where he participated in the birth of the Pentecostal Church, he moved to Harlem in 1915 with a small group of followers to found the Peace Mission Movement. In 1919, he moved his church to semirural Sayville, Long Island, where he attracted thousands of worshiping blacks until frightened local white residents had him arrested on charges of creating a public nuisance in 1931.

Controversy continued to surround Divine when the judge who sentenced him to a year in jail died of a heart attack shortly after the trial and Divine allegedly said, "I hated to do it." This supposed mystical power only enhanced his reputation and following. Again headquartered in Harlem, the Peace Mission expanded from religious activities to provide employment and social services for the community. A believer in the power of the human mind and the importance of language—he refused to use racial categories like "Negro" or "black"—Divine claimed that he himself had transcended race and that his success derived from these teachings.

Divine continued to preach and run his church organization until his death in 1965, when it was turned over to his young white wife whom followers called "Mother Divine."

See also: African Americans; charity and philanthropy.

A popular African-American minister of the 1930s, Father Divine (George Baker) told his audiences to "transcend" racial thinking. A wealthy man, Divine established a Peace Mission in Harlem in the 1930s that provided employment and social services. *(Brown Brothers)*

Bibliography

Weisbrot, Robert. *Father Divine and the Struggle for Racial Equality.* Urbana: University of Illinois Press, 1983.

Wolters, Raymond. *Negroes and the Great Depression: The Problem of Economic Recovery.* Westport, CT: Greenwood Press, 1970.

DOS PASSOS, JOHN

An author with leftist political leanings and a newsreel-influenced, modernist style of writing, John Dos Passos is best known for his fictionalized trilogy on twentieth-century American history, entitled *U.S.A.*

Dos Passos was born the son of wealthy lawyer in Chicago in 1896 and graduated from Harvard University in 1916. During World War I, he served as an ambulance driver in Europe. He published his first book, *Three Soldiers*, an antiwar novel, in 1921, followed by *Manhattan Transfer* in 1925, a novel about the people who ride the subways of New York.

Dos Passos claimed he was turned into a radical by the executions of anarchists Nicola Sacco and Bartolomeo Vanzetti in 1927 and decided to write about America as "two nations"—that is, one nation of the wealthy and another of the poor and dispossessed.

Using a documentary style that incorporated bits of newspaper stories and popular songs, Dos Passos then wrote *The 42nd Parallel* (1930), covering American history from 1900 through the beginning of World War I; *1919*, about the war and the Versailles peace conference (1932); and *The Big Money*, dealing with the 1920s and early 1930s (1936).

Later works by Dos Passos—including *District of Columbia* (1939), *Number One* (1943), and *The Grand Design* (1949)—displayed his growing disenchantment with radical politics and unionism. Increasingly conservative, Dos Passos grew out of favor with readers and critics in later years. He died in 1970.

See also: films, documentary and newsreel; literature.

Bibliography

Dos Passos, John. *U.S.A.* New York: Modern Library, 1937.

Landsberg, Melvin. *Dos Passos' Path to U.S.A.: A Political Biography, 1912–1936*. Boulder, CO: Associated University Press, 1972.

DOUGLAS, WILLIAM O.

Chairman of the Securities and Exchange Commission (SEC) from 1937 to 1939, William O. Douglas helped to reorganize America's discredited stock exchanges and went on to become Franklin D. Roosevelt's fourth Supreme Court justice appointee in 1939.

Douglas was born the son of a Presbyterian minister in Maine, Minnesota, in 1898 and moved first to California and then Washington state as a boy. His childhood was a difficult one. His father died when Douglas was young and he contracted polio, although he escaped paralysis. In 1920, he graduated from Whitman College and and taught school for a short time. In 1922, he enrolled at Columbia University Law School, where he edited the law review and graduated in 1925.

Briefly a corporate lawyer, he returned to Columbia as a law professor before moving on to Yale, where he was a professor until 1936. While there, he assisted the Commerce Department in a massive study of bankruptcies, which brought him to Roosevelt's attention. In 1936, the president appointed Douglas to the SEC and made him chairman the following year.

A close friend of Roosevelt's by this time, he was appointed to replace Louis Brandeis on the Supreme Court in 1939. While he had little time on the Court to effect much Depression-era adjudication, he went on to become one of the Court's more liberal members, signing on to Chief Justice Earl Warren's court decisions advancing civil rights and criminal rights protections in the 1950s and 1960s. He also became famous for his early environmental advocacy.

Debilitated by a stroke, Douglas retired from the Court in 1975 and died in 1980.

See also: Securities and Exchange Commission; Supreme Court; Roosevelt, Franklin D.

Bibliography

Douglas, William O. *Go East, Young Man: The Early Years: The Autobiography of William O. Douglas.* New York: Random House, 1974.

Simon, James F. *Independent Journey: The Life of William O. Douglas.* New York: Harper & Row, 1980.

DUBINSKY, DAVID

President of the International Ladies' Garment Workers' Union (ILGWU), David Dubinsky was one of the labor leaders who joined with John L. Lewis of the United Mine Workers to found the Committee for Industrial Organization (CIO)—later the Congress of Industrial Organizations—in 1935, an industrially based competitor to the craft-oriented American Federation of Labor (AFL).

Born in czarist Russia in 1892, Dubinsky became a union organizer as a teenager and was sentenced to a Siberian labor camp for his pro-labor activities in 1908. Escaping in 1911, he made his way to the United States, where he worked in the New York garment industry as a cutter and went back to labor organizing. From 1921 to 1929, he was manager-secretary of the critical New York Local 10 of the ILGWU, before going on to become secretary-treasurer of the national ILGWU. In 1932, he was elected president of the union.

A dynamic leader, he quickly unified the faction-divided and nearly bankrupt union and helped increase its membership by a factor of ten, to 450,000 members by the late 1930s. At the 1935 annual meeting of the AFL—of which the ILGWU was a member union—Dubinsky joined with Lewis and other industrially oriented labor leaders like Amalgamated Clothing Workers of America president Sidney Hillman to form the CIO.

Within a few years, the CIO had organized millions of workers in mass industries like textiles, steel, and automobiles. But by the late 1930s, growing rifts developed between Dubinsky and Lewis. A socialist by political orientation, Dubinsky did not like the presence of communists in leadership roles of many CIO unions. When Lewis dismissed Dubinsky's concerns—saying that the communists were among the best organizers—Dubinsky refused to participate in the CIO's official 1938 decision to formalize the break made with the AFL three years earlier.

Dubinsky remained head of the ILGWU and an important leader in the AFL until his retirement in 1966, playing a key role in the merger of the AFL and the CIO in 1955. Dubinsky died in 1982.

See also: American Federation of Labor; Congress of Industrial Organizations; International Ladies' Garment Workers' Union; unions and union organizing; Hillman, Sidney; Lewis, John L.

Bibliography

Danish, Max. *The World of David Dubinsky.* Cleveland: World Publishing Co., 1957.

Dubinsky, David. *David Dubinsky: A Life with Labor.* New York: Simon & Schuster, 1977.

EARHART, AMELIA

The world's most famous aviatrix, Amelia Earhart became the first woman to fly solo across the Atlantic Ocean and the first person to fly solo from California to Hawaii, before disappearing in the South Pacific during an around-the-world flight in 1937.

Born in Atchison, Kansas, in 1897, Earhart moved with her family to Chicago as a girl and graduated from high school there in 1916. She worked in Canada as a nurse in the military during World War I and came back to the United States to do social work at the Denison House, a settlement house in Boston.

Always interested in flight, Earhart learned to fly in the early 1920s and bought her first plane in 1922. Six years later, she became the first woman to fly the Atlantic, albeit as a passenger. In 1932, however, she did it as a pilot, alone, and in the record time of under fifteen hours, beating Charles A. Lindbergh. An instant celebrity, she capitalized on her fame with the book *The Fun of It* (1932) and then went on a series of highly publicized flights around the United States.

Determined to set more aviation records, she flew from California to Hawaii, a route longer than the Atlantic, and then, in 1937, launched her around-the-world flight in a twin-engine Lockheed Electra, with navigator Fred Noonan. The two had made it about two-thirds of the way when they disappeared in early July near the international date line several thousand miles southwest of Hawaii. Ever since, rumors have persisted that Earhart and Noonan did not crash but were captured by the Japanese, although no physical evidence has ever been found to support that hypothesis.

See also: Lindbergh, Charles A.

Bibliography

Earhart, Amelia. *The Fun of It: Random Records of My Own Flying and of Women in Aviation*. New York: Brewer, Warren & Putnam, 1932.

Lovell, Mary S. *The Sound of Wings: The Life of Amelia Earhart*. New York: St. Martin's, 1989.

Although she usually piloted her own aircraft, famed aviator Amelia Earhart is shown here as a passenger on a flight from California to New York in December 1935. She disappeared over the Pacific in July 1937, during a round-the-world trip. *(Brown Brothers)*

ECCLES, MARRINER

Appointed by President Franklin D. Roosevelt to the Federal Reserve Board in 1934, Marriner Eccles was a private banker and an assistant treasury secretary who helped write and promote some of the key banking legislation of the New Deal, including the Emergency Banking Act of 1933 and the Banking Act of 1935.

Eccles was born in Logan, Utah, in 1890 to a wealthy Mormon convert family and graduated from Brigham Young College in 1909. In the tradition of his church, Eccles then went to Scotland as a missionary for several years. Upon his return, he took over control of his late father's holdings (the father died in 1912), including a number of banks and manufacturing companies. When the Depression set off depositor runs on banks, Eccles saved his institutions with a simple but ingenious idea: he had his tellers dispense money as physically slowly as possible.

Despite his position as one of the West's biggest bankers, Eccles was far from conservative. Indeed, he believed that people's poverty was generally not of their own doing, but was caused by an economic system that did not distribute its wealth equitably. Influenced by English economist John Maynard Keynes, he believed that the immediate cause of the Depression was underconsumption and that the federal government should spend money to pump up the economy, even if it caused deficits.

Eccles' ideas and banking skills brought him to the attention of the new Roosevelt administration, which recruited him to the Treasury Department to work on the Emergency Banking Act and the Federal Deposit Insurance Act of 1933. Eccles was also one of the architects of the Federal Housing Act of 1934, which established the Federal Housing Administration.

In 1934, Roosevelt appointed Eccles to the Federal Reserve Board, where he backed the Banking Act of 1935, which changed the reserve requirements that private banks needed to meet to secure Reserve Board loans, thereby expanding the money supply and promoting inflation, a needed antidote to the monetary contraction of the Great Depression. Despite his own riches, Eccles also supported higher taxes on the upper classes and corporations in order to redistribute wealth downward.

During the so-called Roosevelt recession of 1937 and 1938, Eccles disagreed with Treasury Secretary Henry Morgenthau's prescription of a balanced budget and cutbacks in federal government spending. Instead, Eccles—in lines with Keynes—said that the government should pursue countercyclical measures, running a deficit to pump money into an economy that was shrinking.

A consistent believer in countercyclical deficit spending, Eccles drew the wrath of conservatives in Congress and, in 1948, President Harry Truman decided not to reappoint him to the Federal Reserve Board. Upon leaving public service, he returned to running his family's business empire. He died in 1977.

See also: Keynesian Economics; Emergency Banking Act; Federal Deposit Insurance Corporation; Federal Housing Administration; Federal Reserve Bank; Morgenthau, Henry, Jr.

Bibliography

Eccles, Marriner. *Beckoning Frontiers: Public and Personal Recollections.* New York: Knopf, 1951.

Hyman, Sidney. *Marriner S. Eccles: Private Entrepreneur and Public Servant.* Stanford, CA: Graduate School of Business, Stanford University, 1976.

EINSTEIN, ALBERT

Author of special and general theories of relativity and winner of the Nobel Prize in Physics, Albert Einstein was a refugee from Nazi Germany working at Princeton University in New Jersey after 1933. In the fall of 1939, he wrote a letter to President Franklin D. Roosevelt about the potential for an atomic weapon, which eventually set in motion the atomic bomb-building Manhattan Project of World War II.

Born in Ulm, Germany, in 1879, Einstein did poorly in the highly regimented school system of his day, but eventually graduated from the renowned Federal Polytechnic Academy in Zurich, Switzerland. In 1900, he took a job in the Swiss patent office in Bern while studying theoretical physics at the University of Zurich. In 1905, he published his Ph.D. thesis and a number of other papers that laid out his pathbreaking theories on relativity.

In 1919, he received international acclaim when a British expedition to study a solar eclipse in the South Pacific provided experimental proof of his theories. He was awarded the Nobel Prize in physics two years later. During the 1920s, he continued to work in theoretical physics, teaching at various European universities and going on speaking tours around the world.

With the rise to power of Adolf Hitler and the anti-Semitic Nazi Party in Germany, the Jewish Einstein renounced his German citizenship and accepted a research position at the new Institute for Advanced Study at Princeton University in 1933. With his knowledge of the German physics program—then the most advanced in the world—Einstein became convinced that the Nazis would try—and might succeed at—building an atomic bomb. This belief was shared by other key physicists, many of whom had fled Europe for America. In 1939, they convinced Einstein to contact Roosevelt and share this information with him. Einstein then wrote his famous letter on the subject and met with the president.

While Einstein did not directly work on the Manhattan Project during the war, he was consulted by scientists working there. After the war, Einstein continued his ultimately unsuccessful search for a unified theory

Jewish physicist Albert Einstein fled to the United States after Adolf Hitler and the Nazis took power in Germany in 1933. Einstein proved influential in Franklin D. Roosevelt's decision to build the atom bomb during World War II. *(Brown Brothers)*

of physics and spoke out against nuclear weapons. He died in 1955.

See also: Nazi Germany; refugees; World War II, early history of.

Bibliography

Brian, Denis. *Einstein: A Life.* New York: John Wiley, 1996.

White, Michael, and John Gribbin. *Einstein: A Life in Science.* New York: Dutton, 1994.

ELLINGTON, EDWARD KENNEDY "DUKE"

One of the most important innovators in the history of jazz music, Duke Ellington was a key figure in the development of the popular swing style of big band dance music in the 1930s, along with Fletcher Henderson and Don Redman.

Born Edward Kennedy Ellington in Washington, D.C., in 1899, the future bandleader and composer began studying the piano at the age of seven and was heavily influenced by the new ragtime piano sound of the first decades of the twentieth century. Playing professionally by age seventeen, Ellington turned away from the classical music career his parents wanted for him and took up the new jazz rhythms pulsating out of the American South.

He began his bandleading career at the Kentucky Club in New York City in 1923, where he developed the so-called jungle style in tunes like "Black and Tan Fantasy." As his band grew, it came to include such greats as saxophonist Johnny Hodges, bass player Jimmy Blanton, trumpeter Bubber Miley, and trombonist Tricky Sam Nanton.

An experimental composer all of his life, Ellington mixed the different instruments in his band in new and innovative ways, expanding the limits of the jazz sound with compositions like "Mood Indigo" (1930). He also became known for creating complicated symphonic jazz compositions and infusing black folk rhythms into his music. An accomplished pianist as well, Ellington is credited by music critics as having influenced almost all subsequent jazz piano players.

Among Ellington's major compositions of the 1930s were "Creole Rhapsody" (1931), "It Don't Mean a Thing If It Ain't Got that Swing" (1932), "Sophisticated Lady" (1933), "Symphony in Black" (1935), and "In a Sentimental Mood" (1935).

Ellington continued to compose and lead his big band through 1973, when he contracted lung cancer. He died in 1974.

See also: music; Henderson, Fletcher; Redman, Don.

Bibliography

Collier, James Lincoln. *Duke Ellington*. New York: Oxford University Press, 1987.

Ellington, Duke. *Music Is My Mistress*. Garden City, NY: Doubleday, 1973.

Ellington, Mercer. *Duke Ellington in Person: An Intimate Memoir*. New York: Da Capo, 1978.

EVANS, WALKER

A photographer whose stripped-down, black-and-white compositions have become the quintessential images of the Great Depression, Walker Evans remains one of the most influential artists in the history of American photography.

Born in St. Louis in 1903, Evans was heavily influenced by the documentary photography of Frenchman Eugène Atget. By 1930, Evans was already leaning toward the architectural photography that would become his hallmark in a series of photos he did in New England, which became part of the first one-man photography show ever curated by New York's Museum of Modern Art.

In 1935, Evans was hired by the Resettlement Administration—renamed the Farm Security Administration (FSA) in 1937—to photograph the impact of the Great Depression on impoverished farmers in the South. While Evans took many portraits and landscapes, he also continued his architectural photography. Even at the time, critics lauded his work for imbuing the mundane realities of everyday life and architecture with a historical classicism.

In 1936, Evans took a leave of absence from the FSA to work with essayist James Agee, documenting the lives of sharecroppers for *Fortune* magazine. Never printed in the magazine, the photos and essays would eventually be published as a book—*Let Us Now Praise Famous Men*—in 1941.

Evans continued to work as a photographer and editor for *Fortune* until 1965 and taught graphic design at Yale from 1965 to 1974. He died the following year.

See also: photography; Farm Security Administration; Resettlement Administration; Agee, James.

Bibliography

Agee, James. *Let Us Now Praise Famous Men: Three Tenant Families.* Boston: Houghton Mifflin, 1941.

Maharidge, Dale. *And Their Children After Them: The Legacy of Let Us Now Praise Famous Men: James Agee, Walker Evans, and the Rise and Fall of Cotton in the South.* New York: Pantheon, 1989.

Mora, Gilles. *Walker Evans: The Hungry Eye.* New York: Abrams, 1993.

FARLEY, JAMES

Political strategist and campaign manager for Franklin D. Roosevelt's gubernatorial and presidential runs, James Farley was rewarded with the position of postmaster general in the administration, which, given its immense patronage possibilities, was a critical post for building a political base in support of the administration and the New Deal.

Farley was born in upstate New York in 1888 and moved to New York City in 1905, where he later studied accounting. Returning to the upstate region where he grew up, Farley served as a clerk in the small upstate town of Stony Point from 1912 to 1919. A gifted political strategist, he soon attracted the attention of state Democratic Party leaders and was rewarded for his efforts with the position of warden of the port of New York in 1919 by newly elected governor Alfred Smith, a position that was abolished the following year.

Farley served a single term in the state legislature in 1923–24—the only elective office he ever held—and was then appointed by Smith to the state's athletic commission in 1924. In 1926, he started his own business but was then chosen secretary of the New York State Democratic Committee, where he organized Roosevelt's successful runs for governor in 1928 and 1930.

Instrumental in winning Roosevelt the Democratic presidential nomination in 1932, Farley arranged a key deal whereby an important Roosevelt competitor—House Speaker John Nance Garner of Texas—was given the vice presidential nomination. Postmaster general through Roosevelt's first two terms, Farley also organized the president's successful reelection campaign in 1936.

A moderate liberal, Farley was one of the figures urging Roosevelt to balance the federal budget and cut back on public works programs early in the second administration. Although Roosevelt took this advice, a rift grew between Farley and the president, as it became clear that both wanted to seek the Democratic Party nomination in 1940. That year, Farley—angry at Roosevelt's third-term aspirations—resigned from the cabinet and, indeed, put his name in contention, though he lost by a vote of 946 to 72 delegates at the convention.

As head of the New York State Democratic Committee, Farley opposed Roosevelt once again in 1944. When his efforts to block the president's renomination failed, Farley left politics to run his business. He retired in 1973 and died in 1976.

See also: Democratic Party; election of 1932; election of 1936; election of 1940; Garner, John Nance; Roosevelt, Franklin D.

Bibliography

Barber, James G. *Portraits from the New Deal.* Washington, DC: Smithsonian Institution Press, 1983.

Farley, James A. *Jim Farley's Story: The Roosevelt Years.* New York: Whittlesey House, 1948.

FAULKNER, WILLIAM

One of the towering figures of twentieth-century American fiction, William Faulkner wrote complex and often difficult short stories and novels that dealt with the tortured lives of southern blacks and whites, creating a fictional world parallel to his small-town Mississippi roots that he called Yoknapatawpha County.

Born in New Albany, Mississippi, in 1897, Faulkner was the descendant of an old Mississippi family, his great-grandfather having served as an officer in the Confederate army. While he was still a child, his family moved to Oxford, where his father became business manager of the University of Mississippi.

In 1918, Faulkner enlisted in Britain's Royal Air Force, but was still in flying school in Canada when World War I ended. Returning to Oxford, he studied for a while at the university and wrote poetry and short fiction. In 1925, he spent six months in Paris.

His first novel—*Soldier's Pay*—was published in 1926, followed by *Mosquitoes* in 1927, both set in the South, if not Mississippi. Both were unsuccessful critically and commercially. In 1929, he wrote *Sartoris*, his first novel set in Yoknapatawpha County. But it was with *The Sound and the Fury*—also published in 1929—that Faulkner began experimenting with the complex time-frames and narrative viewpoints that would characterize most of his later fiction. The book also dealt with southern history and the convoluted racial relations of the region, themes that would permeate virtually all of his subsequent literary output.

In 1929, Faulkner married and settled in a run-down, pre–Civil War mansion on the outskirts of Oxford, where he lived on and off for much of the rest of his life. During the Great Depression era, Faulkner wrote a number of novels that have become classics of American fiction, including *As I Lay Dying* (1930), *Sanctuary* (1931), *Light in August* (1932), *Absalom, Absalom!* (1936), *The Unvanquished* (1938), *The Wild Palms* (1939), and *The Hamlet* (1940). A successful, if somewhat dispiriting, stint as a screenwriter in Hollywood in the 1930s made Faulkner a small fortune. Continuing to write during and after World War II, Faulkner won the Nobel Prize for literature in 1948 and died in 1962.

See also: literature.

Among the greatest fiction writers in American letters, William Faulkner established his reputation in the 1920s and 1930s with a series of novels about southern life, including *The Sound and the Fury, As I Lay Dying,* and *Absalom, Absalom! (Library of Congress)*

Bibliography

Blotner, Joseph. *Faulkner: A Biography*. 2 vol. New York: Random House, 1974.

Gresset, Michel. *A Faulkner Chronology*. Jackson: University of Mississippi Press, 1985.

Minter, David. *William Faulkner: His Life and Work*. Baltimore: Johns Hopkins University Press, 1980.

FIELDS, W. C.

One of the most popular film comedians of all time, W. C. Fields played his trademark hard-drinking, wisecracking, misanthropic characters in a number of movies during the later years of the Great Depression, including *You Can't Cheat an Honest Man* (1939), *My Little Chickadee* (1940), *The Bank Dick* (1940), and *Never Give a Sucker an Even Break* (1941).

Born William Claude Dukenfield in Philadelphia in 1880, Fields left home at age eleven to escape a violent father. By thirteen, he supported himself juggling and pool-hustling and, by twenty-one, was a popular figure on the vaudeville stage circuit. He toured Europe and America and, from 1915 to 1921, performed with the Ziegfeld Follies.

Fields starred in a number of silent films, including the classic *It's the Old Army Game* (1927). But with his sarcastic, nasal voice and caustic verbal humor, he easily made the transition to the talkies, starring in a number of short films in the early 1930s. He played Humpty-Dumpty in the all-star film version of *Alice in Wonderland* in 1933 and Micawber in the 1935 adaptation of *David Copperfield*. But Fields's best claim to film immortality was in a series of hit comedies during the late 1930s and early 1940s. Fields died in 1946; his tombstone reads: "All things considered, I'd rather be in Philadelphia."

See also: films, feature.

In the 1932 comedy *If I Had a Million*, actor W. C. Fields plays a millionaire who decides to give away his money. *(Brown Brothers)*

Bibliography

Deschner, Donald. *The Complete Films of W. C. Fields*. Secaucus, NJ: Citadel Press, 1989.

Louvish, Samuel. *Man on the Flying Trapeze: The Life and Times of W. C. Fields*. New York: W. W. Norton, 1997.

FLOYD, CHARLES ARTHUR "PRETTY BOY"

One of most notorious bank robbers of the 1930s, "Pretty Boy" Floyd became a national celebrity through newspaper accounts that highlighted his good looks, his criminal exploits, and a Robin Hood reputation for stealing from banks and giving to poor farmers. Indeed, Floyd was one of a host of gangsters that appealed to Depression-era readers both excited and horrified by those who escaped the collapsing economic system through violence.

Born Charles Arthur Floyd in a small town in Oklahoma in 1901, the future gangster started out life as a farmer until driven to crime by his inability to raise himself out of poverty. After a failed payroll robbery in 1925, Floyd spent four years in a Missouri prison. Upon his release, he met with other gangsters in Kansas City, where he took up the machine gun as his weapon of choice.

Engaging in a series of bank robberies in the Midwest in the late 1920s, Floyd was captured in 1930 but escaped. Moving back to Oklahoma, he continued robbing banks for several years. He became an almost beloved folk hero for his practice of destroying mortgage papers of impoverished dust bowl farmers at the banks he robbed, prompting composer Woody Guthrie to pen "The Ballad of Pretty Boy Floyd."

> There's many a starving farmer
>   the same old story told
> How the outlaw paid their mortgage and
>   saved their little home.

Floyd's criminal career ended in a hail of FBI gunfire in an Ohio field on October 22, 1934.

See also: crime; dust bowl; Guthrie, Woody.

Although a notorious bank robber, Charles Arthur "Pretty Boy" Floyd earned a reputation as a Depression-era Robin Hood for giving money to the poor and destroying mortgages at the banks he held up. *(Brown Brothers)*

Bibliography

Ruth, David E. *Inventing the Public Enemy: The Gangster in American Culture, 1918–1934.* Chicago: University of Chicago Press, 1996.

FLYNN, ERROL

One of the top leading-man movie stars in Depression-era Hollywood, Errol Flynn was best known for his swashbuckling role as the title character in *The Adventures of Robin Hood* (1938) and as the quintessential movie star, famous more for his looks than for his acting abilities.

Born into a middle-class family in the Australian state of Tasmania in 1909, Flynn was kicked out of a number of private schools for causing trouble. At fifteen, he went to work as a shipping clerk and, six years later, sailed to New Guinea, where he worked as a reporter for an Australian newspaper.

After returning to Sydney, the handsome Flynn began acting and soon moved to England to work in theater. In 1935, he moved to Hollywood, where he played adventuresome characters in a number of low-budget films including *Captain Blood* (1935). His breakthrough into top-flight feature films came in the Crimean war picture *The Charge of the Light Brigade* (1936).

During the next five years, Flynn would become one of the highest-grossing stars in Hollywood with films like *The Prince and the Pauper* (1937), *Another Dawn* (1937), *The Adventures of Robin Hood*, *The Dawn Patrol* (1938), *Dodge City* (1939), *Dive Bomber* (1941), and *They Died with Their Boots On* (1941).

During and immediately after World War II, Flynn acted in a number of hit films, usually adventure stories. But he was having serious problems in his private life, being tried—though acquitted—for the rape of two teen-age girls in 1942. He was drinking heavily, his career went into a tailspin in the 1950s, and he died in 1959.

See also: films, feature.

Bibliography

Flynn, Errol. *My Wicked, Wicked Ways*. London: Heinemann, 1960.

Godfrey, Lionel. *The Life and Crimes of Errol Flynn*. New York: St. Martin's, 1977.

FORD, HENRY

Founder of the Ford Motor Company and one of the business heroes of the 1920s, Henry Ford was vilified during the Great Depression for his harsh anti–organized labor beliefs and practices, in the kind of quintessential fall from public grace that marked the careers of many industrialists in America in the 1930s.

Born on a farm near Dearborn, Michigan, in 1863, Ford turned away from the farming career of his father, moving to Detroit at age sixteen to become a mechanic. After work at a number of industrial plants, including the Detroit Edison Company, Ford began building automobiles and founded the Detroit Automobile Company in 1899. Nine years later, he introduced the Model T, of which he eventually sold over 15 million, making himself one of the richest industrialists in America.

In 1914, Ford introduced the unprecedented five-dollar-a-day wage, which made him a hero to many workers and the public at large. So great was his reputation that he was seriously considered as a candidate for the presidency in the 1920s.

But with the stock market crash of 1929 and the subsequent Depression, Ford was forced to lay off thousands of workers, cutting back on wages and speeding up his famous assembly line for those who remained on the payroll. With organized labor stretching its muscles in the mid-1930s, Ford reacted with bloody attacks by his security men. When General Motors, hit by sit-down strikes in 1937, caved in and recognized the United Auto Workers, Ford refused, unwilling to accept organized labor until war contracts in 1941 made doing so critical for profits.

In 1936, Ford established the Ford Foundation, as a way of keeping the family in control of the company. While Ford had relinquished nominal control over the company to his son Edsel in the 1920s, he returned to full control upon Edsel's death in 1943. Ford retired in 1945, turning over the presidency of the company to his grandson Henry II, and died in 1947.

See also: auto industry; Ford Motor Company; sit-down strikes; United Automobile Workers.

Bibliography

Bryan, Ford R. *Henry's Lieutenants*. Detroit: Wayne State University Press, 1993.

Collier, Peter. *The Fords: An American Epic*. New York: Summit Books, 1987.

Lacey, Robert. *Ford, the Men and the Machine*. Boston: Little, Brown, 1986.

A great innovator in mass production, Henry Ford was unpopular in the 1930s because of his adamant opposition to workers' rights at his company's automobile plants. *(Library of Congress)*

FORD, JOHN

One of the most accomplished and critically acclaimed film directors in the history of Hollywood, John Ford made a name for himself as perhaps the greatest visionary of the movie western with his film *Stagecoach* (1939), which was also the breakthrough movie for western star John Wayne.

Born Sean Aloysius O'Feeney in rural Maine in 1895, Ford followed his brother Francis to Hollywood in 1914, taking a job as property man. He soon changed his name and became a director of short silent films, particularly in the western genre. His first box-office success came with *The Iron Horse* (1924), arguably the first big-budget Hollywood western. Crit-

ical as well as popular success came to Ford with *The Informer* (1935), which depicted events during the Irish rebellion of the early part of the twentieth century.

With *Stagecoach*, Ford established the western as a genre capable of capturing the fundamental moral issues facing humanity, set amidst the spectacular landscape of Monument Valley, to which he would return again and again. The film, which depicts a motley collection of travelers aboard a stagecoach in the Old West, speaks to issues of prejudice and tolerance in American society.

In the final years of the Depression, Ford directed two other cinematic classics: *The Grapes of Wrath*

(1940), based on John Steinbeck's novel of Okies in California, and *How Green Was My Valley* (1941), about a mining town in Wales.

Postwar films by Ford include *My Darling Clementine* (1946), *The Searchers* (1956), considered one of the finest westerns of all time, and *How the West Was Won* (1962). Ford died in 1973.

See also: films, feature; *Grapes of Wrath, The*; Okies; Steinbeck, John.

Bibliography

Bogdanovich, Peter. *John Ford*. Berkeley: University of California Press, 1968.

Sinclair, Andrew. *John Ford*. New York: Dial Press, 1979.

FOSTER, WILLIAM Z.

Longtime communist organizer and activist, William Z. Foster was the presidential candidate of the Communist Party of the United States in the elections of 1924, 1928, and 1932, winning approximately 100,000 votes in the latter.

Born in the industrial town of Taunton, Massachusetts, in 1881, Foster became a labor organizer at the age of thirteen and joined the radical Industrial Workers of the World at eighteen. His rise to national prominence in the union movement came through his role as an American Federation of Labor (AFL) leader during the violent post–World War I steel strike of 1919.

Following the strike and influenced by the communist revolution in Russia, he left the AFL to form the Trade Union Educational League (TUEL) as a communist-influenced competitor to the more established AFL. In 1921, the Moscow-led international communist trade union movement, Profintern, chose the TUEL as its branch in the United States.

As leader of the Communist Party, Foster was picked to head its presidential ticket in 1924 and 1928, but the Party did poorly in the relatively prosperous and conservative 1920s. With the onset of the Great Depression, the Party gained thousands of supporters, and Foster's campaign for president in 1932 gained unprecedented attention in the press.

During the campaign, however, Foster suffered a near-fatal heart attack and, while he continued to run, the party leadership soon deposed him, replacing him with Earl Browder. But Foster recovered and, in 1945, when Browder fell out of favor with the Soviet leadership, Foster was put back in charge of the Communist Party. Following the repudiation of Russian dictator Joseph Stalin—one of Foster's supporters—by new Russian premier Nikita Khrushchev in 1956, Foster went into semiretirement. He died in Russia in 1961.

See also: Communist Party; election of 1932; Browder, Earl.

Bibliography

Foster, William Z. *History of the Communist Party of the United States*. New York: International Publishers, 1952.

Johanningsmeir, Edward P. *Forging American Communism: The Life of William Z. Foster*. Princeton: Princeton University Press, 1994.

FRANCO, FRANCISCO

A Spanish military leader, General Francisco Franco—also known as *El Caudillo*—was head of the Nationalist forces that overthrew the legally elected government of the Spanish republic in a civil war that lasted from 1936 to 1939 and led to the death of nearly 1 million Spaniards on both sides.

Born Francisco Paulino Hermenegildo Teódulo Franco Bahamonde in the province of Galicia in northwestern Spain in 1892, Franco enrolled at the Infantry Academy in Toledo in 1907 and graduated in 1910. At the age of nineteen, he volunteered to fight in Spain's colonial campaigns in North Africa and was promoted to lieutenant of an elite cavalry unit. In 1915, he became the youngest captain in the Spanish army.

A hero in putting down a revolt in Spanish-held parts of Morocco in the 1920s, Franco was promoted to brigadier general in 1926 and became head of the General Military Academy of Spain two years later. But with the end of the monarchy in 1931 and the rise of the antimilitary Spanish republic, funding for the army was cut and Franco was placed on the inactive list. Returned to active duty in 1934 to put down a miners' strike, he was appointed in the following year as chief of staff of the Spanish army.

Divisive elections in 1936 led to a victory of leftist forces, but also plunged the country into a political crisis. With Spain descending into anarchy, Franco issued a manifesto on July 18 from the Spanish-held Canary Islands calling for a conservative uprising within Spain itself. Then, in Morocco and Spain, he raised an army to overthrow the government in Madrid, but was met with unexpected resistance by popular forces on the city's outskirts. In October, he was declared head of a nationalist regime, which claimed to be the real government of Spain. The following March, he organized the Falange, or Spanish Fascist Party, as the political movement of the new regime.

Receiving massive aid from Fascist Italy and Nazi Germany in the form of weaponry and personnel, Franco fought the republican government—which received aid from the Soviet Union and drew antifascist volunteers from around the world—in a brutal civil war that left much of the country in ruins.

With total victory achieved by April 1939, Franco became the unquestioned dictator of Spain, keeping the country technically neutral during World War II, though secretly pro-Axis. After the war, Franco presided over a modest economic modernization program, but kept the country outside the European community and closed off to democratic ideas. Franco died after a long illness in 1975, and his authoritarian regime died with him.

See also: fascism, Italy; Nazi Germany; Soviet Union; Spanish Civil War; World War II, early history of.

Bibliography

Preston, Paul. *Franco: A Biography.* New York: Basic Books, 1994.

Snellgrove, Laurence Ernest. *Franco and the Spanish Civil War.* New York: McGraw-Hill, 1968.

FRANKFURTER, FELIX

A member of the unofficial Brain Trust advisory council during the early Franklin D. Roosevelt administration and the mentor to a host of New Deal appointees, Felix Frankfurter was also Roosevelt's third appointment to the Surpeme Court.

Born in Vienna, Austria, in 1882, Frankfurter moved to the United States as a boy and attended both the City College of New York and Harvard Law School, where he taught from 1914 until his appointment to the Supreme Court in 1939. Before that, he was an assistant to Henry Stimson, during the latter's stint as U.S. attorney for the Southern District Court of New York from 1906 to 1909 and secretary of war from 1911 to 1913.

While a law professor at Harvard, Frankfurter was influenced by Supreme Court Justice Louis Brandeis's legal doctrine of antitrust governmental activism, which would allow for the promotion of more free enterprise, a doctrine that influenced President Woodrow Wilson. Frankfurter served as an adviser to Wilson at the Versailles peace conference in 1919 and was a cofounder of the American Civil Liberties Union in 1920.

Frankfurter was a close confidant of Roosevelt during the latter's time as governor of New York from 1929 to 1933 and then advised him on New Deal legislation and appointments. Frankfurter is considered to have been especially influential in the development of the legislation connected with the so-called Second New Deal of 1935–36, which saw the creation of the National Labor Relations Act and the Social Security Act.

Roosevelt appointed Frankfurter to the Supreme Court in 1939. Although Frankfurter came on to the Court too late to have much influence on New Deal legislation, he became one of the stronger supporters of the concept of judicial restraint, whereby justices avoided trying to legislate through their decisions.

Frankfurter remained on the Court until his resignation in 1962. He died in 1965.

See also: Brain Trust; New Deal, second; National Labor Relations Act; Social Security Act; Supreme Court; Brandeis, Louis; Roosevelt, Franklin D.

One of the most influential legal minds of twentieth-century American jurisprudence, Felix Frankfurter was appointed by President Franklin D. Roosevelt to the Supreme Court in 1939. (*Library of Congress*)

Bibliography

Freedman, Max, ed. *Roosevelt and Frankfurter: Their Correspondence, 1928–1945.* Boston: Little, Brown, 1968.

Parrish, Michael E. *Felix Frankfurter and His Times.* New York: Free Press, 1982.

GABLE, CLARK

One of Hollywood's top leading men in the 1930s, Clark Gable starred in a number of box-office hits through the course of the decade, culminating in his role as Rhett Butler in the top grossing film of the Great Depression, *Gone With the Wind* (1939).

Born William Clark Gable in a small town in Ohio in 1901, Gable worked at a series of odd jobs during his younger years before joining the Ed Lilly theatrical company. During the 1920s, Gable worked on both coasts, playing bit parts in silent films in Hollywood and performing in the experimental Broadway play *Machinal* in 1928.

In 1930, he moved to Hollywood for good, beginning as a gangster star before turning to his signature roles as a comedic, romantic lead in films like *It Happened One Night* (1934), for which he won an Academy Award for best actor. He was also nominated for an Oscar for his performance in *Mutiny on the Bounty* (1935). But it was his role as the roguishly handsome and virile Butler in *Gone With the Wind* that established Gable as a film icon of the twentieth century.

Enlisting in the Army Air Corps in 1942, after the death of his third wife Carole Lombard, he won the Air Medal and became a major. After the war, he starred in a number of movies, including *The Misfits* (1961), which finished filming two weeks before his death in 1960.

See also: films, feature; *Gone With the Wind;* Lombard, Carole.

Bibliography

Jordan, Rene. *Clark Gable.* New York: Galahad Books, 1973.

Tornabene, Lyn. *Long Live the King: A Biography of Clark Gable.* New York: Putnam, 1976.

GARBO, GRETA

Among the most glamorous stars and biggest box-office draws of the 1920s and 1930s, Swedish-born Greta Garbo was known for her sultry voice and exquisite good looks, which she took extra care to have lighted properly.

Born Greta Lovisa Gustafsson in Stockholm in 1905, she grew up in impoverished circumstances, becoming a department store clerk and then a model. She studied at the Royal Dramatic Theater in Stockholm and starred in several Swedish silent films. In 1925, she moved to the United States and went under contract to Metro-Goldwyn-Mayer Studios. After several silent films in the 1920s, she starred in *Anna Christie* (1930), *Mata Hari* (1932), *Grand Hotel* (1932), *Anna Karenina* (1935), and *Camille* (1936), though perhaps her most famous, and surprising, role was as a Russian diplomat in the romantic comedy *Ninotchka* (1939), for which she was nominated for an Academy Award. She also won Academy Award nominations for *Anna Karenina* and *Camille.* She was finally awarded a lifetime achievement Academy Award in 1954.

In 1941, she retired from the film business, becoming a virtual recluse in New York City until her death in 1990.

See also: films, feature.

Bibliography

Paris, Barry. *Garbo: A Biography.* New York: Random House, 1995.

Swenson, Karen. *Greta Garbo: A Life Apart.* New York: Scribner, 1997.

Swedish-born actress Greta Garbo moved to Hollywood in 1925 and starred in such memorable 1930s films as *Mata Hari, Grand Hotel,* and *Ninotchka.* She won two Academy Awards for her performances in *Anna Karenina* (1935) and *Camille* (1936). *(Brown Brothers)*

GARNER, JOHN NANCE

A conservative Texas Democrat and speaker of the house from 1931 to 1933, John Nance Garner was picked to be Franklin D. Roosevelt's first vice president in a 1932 convention deal that sealed Roosevelt's presidential nomination. Garner, a conservative dissenter to much of the New Deal legislation of the Roosevelt administration, was dropped by Roosevelt from the ticket in 1940, and replaced by liberal Henry A. Wallace.

Garner, popularly known as "Cactus Jack," was born in rural Texas in 1868. He studied law and was admitted to the Texas bar in 1890. He served in the state legislature from 1898 to 1902, when he was elected to the U.S. House of Representatives. He served there until becoming vice president in 1933.

An expert political and legislative strategist, Garner helped to pass the graduated income tax and the federal reserve system in the second decade of the twentieth century. He went on to become Democratic whip and then speaker of the house in 1931. Fearful of the growing federal deficit in the early Depression, Garner favored a sales tax to balance the budget.

A favorite with southern conservative Democrats, Garner was a top contender for the Democratic nomination in 1932. His acceptance of the vice presidential nomination secured southern support for Roosevelt's nomination.

Never comfortable in the liberal climate of the New Deal, Garner openly opposed Roosevelt's attempts to pack the Supreme Court in 1937 with liberal justices. For that, Roosevelt never forgave him, dropping him from the ticket in 1940. Garner retired to his ranch in Texas where he remained until his death in 1967, just weeks before his ninety-ninth birthday.

See also: court-packing plan; Democratic Party; election of 1932; election of 1940; Roosevelt, Franklin D.; Wallace, Henry A.

Bibliography

Marquis, James. *Mr. Garner of Texas*. Indianapolis: Bobbs-Merrill, 1939.

Timmons, Bascom Nolly. *Garner of Texas: A Personal History*. New York: Harper, 1948.

GEHRIG, LOU

Known as the "iron horse" for having appeared in 2,130 consecutive games, a record unbroken until 1995, Lou Gehrig played first base for the New York Yankees, where he achieved a career batting average of .340.

Born Henry Louis Gehrig in New York City in 1903, Gehrig attended Columbia University before signing with the Yankees in 1924. Aside from his appearance in 2,130 consecutive games from June 1, 1925, to May 2, 1939—a record which endured until the 1990s—Gehrig had many outstanding baseball accomplishments. He hit over 150 runs batted in (RBIs) in seven seasons, including 184 in 1931, still an American League record. On June 3, 1932, he hit four home runs in a single game and, in 1934, led the American League in hitting, home runs, and RBIs.

Over the course of his career, Gehrig played in thirty-four World Series games, where he established a batting average of .361. But for all his achievements, Gehrig may best be remembered for the way he left baseball. Diagnosed with amyotrophic lateral sclerosis, a degenerative disease that would later bear his name, Gehrig retired in an emotional ceremony at Yankee Stadium in 1939 and was elected to the Hall of Fame that same year. He died two years later.

See also: sports.

Bibliography

Chadwin, Dean. *Those Damn Yankees: The Secret Life of America's Greatest Franchise*. New York: Verso, 1999.

Honig, Donald. *The New York Yankees: An Illustrated History*. New York: Crown, 1987.

Lou Gehrig set numerous hitting records as a New York Yankee first baseman before succumbing in 1941 to amyotrophic lateral sclerosis, now widely known as "Lou Gehrig's disease." *(Library of Congress)*

GERSHWIN, GEORGE AND IRA

George and Ira Gershwin were brothers who formed one of the most successful and innovative composer-lyricist teams in American music. They worked together on the scores and books of more than twenty Broadway shows and movies from 1916 until the death of George in 1937, with their best-received collaboration being the 1935 opera *Porgy and Bess*.

Sons of Russian Jewish immigrants, Ira (originally Israel Gershvin) and George (originally Jacob Gershvin) were born in New York City in 1896 and 1898, respectively. Ira attended City College from 1914 to 1916 and then took odd jobs until joining up with his brother, who had already established himself as a child prodigy on the piano and a performer who publicized songs for the Jerome Remick music-publishing company.

In 1916, George wrote his first published song, "When You Want 'Em You Can't Get 'Em," but his first big hit was "Swanee," performed by singer Al Jolson in the musical *Sinbad* in 1919. Meanwhile, George and Ira collaborated on their first tune, "The Real American Folk Song," for the 1918 show *Ladies First*.

From 1920 to 1924, George wrote numerous songs for the yearly production of the show *Scandals*. In 1924, he composed the American classic "Rhapsody in Blue" and the score for the hit Broadway show *Lady, Be Good!*, which included a number of songs with lyrics by Ira, including "Fascinating Rhythm" and "Oh, Lady, Be Good!"

For the next decade, the two were the hottest musical-writing team on Broadway, collaborating on a series of hit shows that included *Strike Up the Band* (1927), *Funny Face* (1927), *Girl Crazy* (1930), the political satire *Of Thee I Sing* (1931), which became the first musical to win a Pulitzer Prize for drama, and *Let 'Em Eat Cake* (1933). Their efforts culminated in *Porgy and Bess*, which contributed to the American song library such classics as "Summertime," "I Got Plenty o' Nuttin'," and "It Ain't Necessarily So."

George also wrote the scores for several motion pictures in the 1930s, including *Delicious* (1931) and *Shall We Dance* (1937). After George died of a brain tumor in 1937, Ira went on to write lyrics for music composed by Moss Hart, Kurt Weill, and Jerome Kern, as well as to work on several Gershwin revivals. Ira died in 1983.

See also: films, feature; music; Hart, Moss; Kern, Jerome; Weill, Kurt.

Bibliography

Furia, Philip. *Ira Gershwin: The Art of the Lyricist*. New York: Oxford University Press, 1996.

Kendall, Alan. *George Gershwin: A Biography*. New York: Universe Books, 1987.

Rosenberg, Deena. *Fascinating Rhythm: The Collaboration of George and Ira Gershwin*. New York: Dutton, 1991.

GLASS, CARTER

A conservative Democratic senator from Virginia who largely opposed Franklin D. Roosevelt's New Deal legislation, Carter Glass was the author of two critical banking acts of the Great Depression, including the Glass-Steagall Banking Act of 1933, which prohibited commercial banks from using depositors' money to invest in speculative securities.

Born in Lynchburg, Virginia, in 1858, Glass had little formal education, although he followed in his father's footsteps and became a journalist, eventually taking over as publisher of the *Lynchburg Daily News* and the *Daily Advance*. In 1902, Glass was elected to the U.S. House of Representatives, where he served until 1918. During that time, he became an expert in banking issues and was the main architect of the Federal Reserve Act of 1913. In 1918, President Woodrow Wilson appointed Glass secretary of the treasury.

Appointed an interim senator from Virginia in

1920, Glass went on to win his seat electorally and served in the Senate through the 1940s. In 1932, he sponsored the Glass-Steagall Act (not to be confused with the Glass-Steagall Banking Act of the following year), which expanded the definition of acceptable collateral that commercial banks could use to secure loans from the Federal Reserve Bank, which helped expand the monetary supply and produce Depression-fighting inflation.

Still, as a member of the conservative southern wing of the Democratic Party, Glass opposed Roosevelt's nomination for the presidency in 1932 and spoke out strongly against most New Deal legislation. In fact, he was so opposed to Roosevelt that he refused a cabinet appointment in the new administration.

In 1933, he sponsored the Glass-Steagall Banking Act separating commercial and investment banking, a bulwark against commercial bank speculation that lasted until the 1990s. He was also one of the architects of legislation creating the Federal Deposit Insurance Corporation, which offered federal protection for depositors' money. During the second Roosevelt administration, Glass was one of the most vocal opponents of the president's efforts to pack the Supreme Court with liberal justices. Glass died in 1946.

See also: banking; court-packing plan; Federal Deposit Insurance Corporation; Federal Reserve Bank; Glass-Steagall Banking Act; Roosevelt, Franklin D.

Bibliography

Smith, Rixey. *Carter Glass: A Biography*. New York: Longmans, 1939.

Heinemann, Ronald. *Depression and New Deal in Virginia: The Enduring Dominion*. Charlottesville: University Press of Virginia, 1983.

GOLDWYN, SAMUEL

A pioneer of the Hollywood film industry and a cofounder of the Metro-Goldwyn-Mayer (MGM) studios, Samuel Goldwyn was a producer who specialized during the Great Depression era in high-quality films, often with a literary source, including *Dodsworth* (1936), *Wuthering Heights* (1939), and *The Little Foxes* (1941).

Born Schmuel Gelbgisz—and later known as Samuel Goldfish—in Warsaw, Poland, in 1879, Goldwyn emigrated to England as a child, where he was orphaned. He emigrated once again, in his teens, to upstate New York. First a worker in a glove factory and then a top glove salesman, he went into the film business in the early 1900s. Working with director Cecil B. DeMille, he produced *Squaw Man* (1913), an early feature-length film.

In 1917, he founded Goldwyn Pictures Corporation, which merged with two other studios to form MGM in 1924. Goldwyn then became an independent producer who distributed his films through United Artists and RKO. After a series of hit films in the 1930s, Goldwyn continued to produce movies in the 1940s and 1950s. He died in 1974.

See also: films, feature; Mayer, Louis B.

Bibliography

Berg, A. Scott. *Goldwyn: A Biography*. New York: Knopf, 1989.

Marx, Arthur. *Goldwyn: A Biography of the Man Behind the Myth*. New York: W. W. Norton, 1976.

GOODMAN, BENJAMIN DAVID "BENNY"

A topflight clarinet player, a popular bandleader of the 1930s, and a pioneer of the big band "swing" sound, Benny Goodman—known as the "King of Swing"—is often credited with popularizing jazz music among white audiences in Depression-era America.

Born Benjamin David Goodman in Chicago in 1909, the future bandleader joined his first jazz band at the age of nineteen. Moving to New York in 1929, Goodman put together an orchestra in 1933 that became one of the hottest swing bands of the Great Depression. Goodman broke down racial barriers by including black musicians in his band, including pianist Teddy Wilson and vibraphonist Lionel Hampton. Other band members included trumpeter Harry James and drummer Gene Krupa.

Goodman also founded several small bands in the middle and late 1930s in which he tried to return jazz to its pre-swing, pre–big band roots. He continued to lead his big and small bands through the 1970s. Goodman died in 1986.

See also: music.

Bibliography

Firestone, Ross. *Swing, Swing, Swing: The Life and Times of Benny Goodman.* New York: W. W. Norton, 1939.

Goodman, Benny. *The Kingdom of Swing.* New York: Stackpole Sons, 1939.

GRANT, CARY

O ne of the most popular leading men in Hollywood during the 1930s, Cary Grant made a name for himself in a series of slapstick romantic comedies dubbed screwball movies.

Born Archibald Alexander Leach in Bristol, England, in 1904, Grant began his show-business career as part of an acrobatic troupe. When the group toured the United States in 1920, Grant decided to stay and began performing in musical comedies for the stage. He was discovered by actress Mae West and cast opposite her in the 1933 comedy *She Done Him Wrong.*

His debonair good looks, ease with witty repartee, and distinctive intonation soon made him a favorite of the film-going public. He capitalized on his popularity in films like *Topper* (1937), *The Awful Truth* (1937), *Bringing Up Baby* (1938), *Holiday* (1938), *His Girl Friday* (1940), and *The Philadelphia Story* (1940).

Grant continued to act through the 1960s, including four films with Alfred Hitchcock. He received a special career Academy Award in 1970 and died in 1986.

See also: films, feature; Hitchcock, Alfred; West, Mae.

Bibliography

Nelson, Nancy, ed. *Evenings with Cary Grant: Recollections in His Own Words and by Those Who Knew Him Best.* New York: William Morrow, 1991.

McCann, Graham. *Cary Grant: A Class Apart.* New York: Columbia University Press, 1996.

GREEN, WILLIAM

Heir to American Federation of Labor (AFL) founder Samuel Gompers, William Green presided over the organization during the Great Depression. A conservative, craft-oriented unionist, Green long resisted efforts to establish industrial-based unions, leading to a split in the AFL when United Mine Workers (UMW) president John L. Lewis formed the rival Committee for Industrial Organization (CIO) in 1935.

Born in a mining town in Ohio in 1873, Green dropped out of school to become a coal miner at age sixteen. Active in union politics from a young age, he became a local leader within the UMW in 1900, going on to serve as secretary-treasurer of the national UMW from 1913 to 1924. At the same time, he was appointed to serve on the executive council of the AFL, being elected its president in 1924, upon the death of Gompers.

With the onset of the Great Depression, Green warned politicians that the American working classes were becoming increasingly restive. Still, he did little to capitalize on this anger against employers and resisted calls to organize—on an industry-wide basis—the masses of semi-and unskilled workers in the steel, automobile, and other large-scale industries, even after passage of the union-friendly National Labor Relations Act of 1935.

In 1935, Green had a falling-out with Lewis, who then organized the Committee for Industrial Organization within the AFL. In 1936, Green ordered the expulsion of the committee from the federation. But the establishment of the CIO and the independent Congress of Industrial Organizations that grew out of it inspired the AFL to begin its own organizing efforts in the mass industries of the Great Depression, and it soon outstripped the CIO in its industrial membership.

During World War II, Green worked closely with business and governmental leaders to prevent strikes and keep war production going, denouncing the more obstreperous Lewis, who called a miners' strike during the war. Green remained president of the AFL until his death in 1952.

See also: American Federation of Labor; Congress of Industrial Organizations; United Mine Workers; unions and union organizing; National Labor Relations Act; Lewis, John L.

Bibliography

Green, William. *Labor and Democracy*. Princeton: Princeton University Press, 1939.

Phelan, Craig. *William Green: Biography of a Labor Leader*. Albany: State University of New York Press, 1989.

GREENBERG, HANK

One of the greatest baseball stars of the Great Depression era, Hank Greenberg was best known as a pathbreaking Jewish player who, with his quiet dignity, stood up to the anti-Semitic taunts of fans and opposing players. In doing so, he became an athletic role model for Jewish children and adults alike.

Born in the Bronx borough of New York City in 1911, Greenberg played baseball in high school and was recruited by the Detroit Tigers of the American League in 1930. First assigned to outfield, he made a name for himself as the team's star first baseman from 1933 to 1946.

Greenberg became the first player to earn $100,000 a season. Slugging fifty-eight home runs in 1938, he was the first to seriously challenge Babe Ruth's season home-run record of sixty-one. Other Greenberg baseball accomplishments included a series of Detroit records, including most runs batted in and extra-base hits in a season (183 and 103 respectively, both in the 1937 season). Greenberg retired from professional baseball in 1947 and died in 1986.

See also: sports.

Bibliography

Greenberg, Hank, and Ira Berkow. *Hank Greenberg: The Story of My Life*. New York: Times Books, 1989.

Star first baseman for the Detroit Tigers from 1933 to 1946, Hank Greenberg became one of the first Jewish baseball players in the major leagues. (*Brown Brothers*)

GUTHRIE, WOODROW WILSON "WOODY"

A popular balladeer who rode the rails during the Great Depression, Woody Guthrie turned his experiences into some of the most enduring and popular folk songs in American history.

Woodrow Wilson Guthrie was born in Okemah, Oklahoma, in 1912. As a boy, he took up the guitar and harmonica. At the age of fifteen, he ran away from home and began traveling the country. When the Great Depression hit, he lived among the hoboes and migrant workers, where his musical gifts won him warm receptions.

A radical spokesman for labor and leftist political causes, he wrote such ballads as "Union Maid" and "Tom Joad," the latter inspired by the hero of John Steinbeck's novel *The Grapes of Wrath*. Other tunes captured the hard times of hoboes during the Great Depression, including "So Long (It's Been Good to Know Yuh)," "Hard Traveling," and "Blowing Down This Dusty Road." Guthrie also wrote a paean to gangster "Pretty Boy" Floyd, praising the outlaw as a Robin Hood who helped out impoverished farmers with money he stole from banks. Of the more than 1,000 songs Guthrie wrote, however, the most popular is probably "This Land Is Your Land," which became an anthem of the protest movements of the 1960s.

In the late 1930s, Guthrie settled in New York City, where he joined fellow folk singer Pete Seeger to form the Almanac Singers. Guthrie continued to sing and write songs until stricken with Huntington's disease. He died in 1967.

See also: *Grapes of Wrath, The*; music; Floyd, "Pretty Boy."

Bibliography

Guthrie, Woody. *Bound for Glory*. New York: E. P. Dutton, 1943.

Klein, Joe. *Woody Guthrie: A Life*. New York: Knopf, 1980.

An itinerant composer and musician, Woody Guthrie entertained Depression-era audiences with tunes like "This Land is Your Land" and "So Long (It's Been Good to Know Yuh)." *(Corbis)*

Santelli, Robert, and Emily Davidson, eds. *Hard Travelin': The Life and Legacy of Woody Guthrie*. Hanover, NH: University Press of New England, 1999.

HAMMETT, DASHIELL

Stephen Dashiell Hammett, born in Maryland on May 27, 1894, almost single-handedly created the American genre of the "hard-boiled" detective story.

Hammett left school at the age of fourteen, then spent a number of years working a variety of unskilled jobs. He then stumbled into the employ of the Pinkerton Detective Agency, one of the largest detective agencies in America. He found the work interesting, and it would serve as a useful source of material in his future career as a writer. In 1921, ill health forced Hammett to leave Pinkerton's. He used the opportunity to try his hand at writing. He was an immediate success.

Basing his writing on his experiences at Pinkerton's, Hammett wrote detective stories. But they were not the genteel puzzle mysteries made popular by English writers like Dorothy Sayers. Hammett's stories were grittily realistic, with tough guy detectives facing just as tough crooks. Unlike the typical restrained, upper-class British detective hero, Hammett's characters spoke a rough American slang and were quick to use their guns. Throughout the 1920s, Hammett wrote short stories for the then popular pulp magazines (so named because of the cheap paper they used).

In 1929, Hammett wrote his first novel, *Red Harvest*, following it up with four more in rapid succession: *The Dain Curse* (1929), *The Maltese Falcon* (1930), *The Glass Key* (1931), and *The Thin Man* (1934). The success of these novels made him a celebrity. He was hired by Hollywood to write original screenplays as well as movie adaptations of his work—the most successful were *The Thin Man* (1934) and *The Maltese Falcon* (1941)—that entertained Depression-era movie goers. It was during this period that he met and became the lifelong companion of writer Lillian Hellman.

At the peak of his career, Hammett had burned out; he drank more and wrote less. Serving in the army during World War II stalled this decline, but Hammett's life spiraled into obscurity after his discharge. He spent the rest of his life suffering from ill health and pursued by bad debts and congressional committees: Hammett was targeted because of his left-wing sympathies—he had joined the Communist Party in 1937—and in 1951 was hauled before the House Un-American Activities Committee. He died January 10, 1961, in New York City.

Hammett's fiction, like that of fellow American crime writers James M. Cain and Raymond Chandler, expressed something uniquely American. The worlds they created were grim—appropriately so in those dark Depression years—but their work was also infused by a touch of idealism. Hammett protagonists like the Continental Op [Operative] (*Red Harvest, The Dain Curse*), trusted little on faith, doubted the inherent goodness of man, and were willing to use questionable methods, even conniving at murder, to achieve their goals. Yet they still believed in something. They had a personal code of honor that made them get the bad guys, even if they knew that some of the good guys were not much better. It was this morally ambiguous, but not completely hopeless point of view that gave Hammett's fiction its complexity and strength. It was also these elements that made Hammett a central inspiration to the *film noir* genre of cinema that became popular in the 1940s and 1950s.

CARL SKUTSCH

See also: films, feature; literature.

Bibliography

Johnson, Diane. *Dashiell Hammett: A Life.* New York: Random House, 1983.

Layman, Richard. *Shadow Man: The Life of Dashiell Hammett.* New York: Bruccoli Clark Layman, 1981.

HASTIE, WILLIAM

One of the highest-ranking African-American officials in the administration of President Franklin D. Roosevelt, William Hastie fought racist policies within the government as assistant solicitor at the Department of the Interior. He was also appointed by Roosevelt to a judgeship, the first African American to serve on the federal bench.

Hastie was born to a lower-middle-class family in Philadelphia in 1904 and graduated class valedictorian from Amherst College in 1925. He taught school for two years and then went to Harvard, where he earned his law degree in 1930. He then practiced law in Washington, D.C. with his father and taught night courses at the Howard University Law School, where one of his students was Thurgood Marshall.

In 1933, Hastie was picked by Secretary of the Interior Harold Ickes, a well-known civil rights activist, to serve in the assistant solicitor position. One of his tasks was to reorganize the government of the U.S. Virgin Islands, where he served as federal district judge from 1937 to 1939. Upon his return to the mainland, he was appointed dean of Howard University and became involved in the March on Washington Movement to end discrimination in the armed forces.

After the war, he served as governor of the Virgin Islands and as a judge on the federal Third District Court of Appeals until his retirement in 1971. Hastie died in 1976.

See also: African Americans; March on Washington Movement; Ickes, Harold.

Bibliography

Kirby, John B. *Black Americans in the Roosevelt Era: Liberalism and Race.* Knoxville: University of Tennessee Press, 1980.

Ware, Gilbert. *William Hastie: Grace Under Pressure.* New York: Oxford University Press, 1984.

HAWKS, HOWARD

One of the most versatile and talented film directors in Hollywood history, Howard Hawks created movies during the Great Depression era in a variety of genres, from screwball comedies to gangster films to adventure movies.

Born in Goshen, Indiana, in 1896, Hawks became a professional race car driver before moving to Hollywood in 1922 to become a director. His first major film was *A Girl in Every Port* (1928). This was followed by a string of box-office and critical successes in the 1930s and early 1940s, including adventure films like *The Dawn Patrol* (1930) and *Only Angels Have Wings* (1939); romantic comedies such as *Twentieth Century* (1934), *Bringing Up Baby* (1938), and *His Girl Friday* (1940); and the classic gangster film *Scarface* (1932).

Hawks continued to make films during and after World War II, including several classic westerns—*Red River* (1948) and *Rio Bravo* (1959). He retired from the cinema in the late 1960s and died in 1977.

See also: films, feature; *Scarface.*

Bibliography

McBride, Joseph, ed. *Hawks on Hawks: Discussions.* Berkeley: University of California Press, 1982.

McCarthy, Todd. *Howard Hawks: The Grey Fox of Hollywood.* New York: Grove Press, 1997.

HAYS, WILL H.

President of the Motion Picture Producers and Distributors of America (MPPDA, later the Motion Picture Association of America, MPAA) from the early 1920s to the mid-1940s, Will H. Hays was one of the architects of the 1930 Production Code, which laid out a series of rules for what was morally permissible in Hollywood films.

Hays was born in rural Indiana in 1879 and became a lawyer. Drawn to politics, he rose up the ranks of the Republican Party, becoming chairman of the National Committee in 1918. Responsible for the successful presidential campaign of Warren G. Harding in 1920, Hays was rewarded with the position of postmaster general.

As a prominent political figure with an untarnished reputation for religious rectitude—he was an elder in the Presbyterian Church—Hays was picked by a group of producers, who were worried that a string of recent scandals had sullied the film industry's reputation, to run the newly established MPPDA and clean up Hollywood or, at least, create the appearance of a cleaned-up Hollywood. To most people in Hollywood and America at large, Hays *was* the MPPDA, which was popularly called the Hays Office.

Hays, taking his task seriously, established the practice of putting morality clauses in actors' contracts. Those who would not sign were blacklisted. Hays, however, was unable to tame the racier themes in many Hollywood movies. The explicit (for the time) sexuality in many movies led to protests by the Catholic Church and other groups, prompting Hays to establish the Production Code of 1930, which stayed in effect until 1966. Hays retired from the MPPDA in 1945, worked on his memoirs, and died in 1954.

See also: films, feature; Motion Picture Production Code/Production Code Administration.

Bibliography

Baxter, John. *Hollywood in the Thirties*. New York: Barnes & Noble, 1968.

Hays, Will H. *Memoirs*. Garden City, NY: Doubleday, 1955.

Moley, Raymond. *The Hays Office*. Indianapolis: Bobbs-Merrill Company, 1945.

HEARST, WILLIAM RANDOLPH

Owner of a chain of newspapers and an ambitious but ultimately unsuccessful politician, William Randolph Hearst was an archisolationist in the 1930s who used his control of the press to try to keep the United States out of World War II. He was also an early, albeit reluctant, supporter of Franklin D. Roosevelt, but quickly turned against the president once the New Deal got under way.

Hearst, the son of a wealthy mine owner, was born in San Francisco in 1863 and attended Harvard College for two years before being expelled. In 1887, he took over his father's newspaper in San Francisco and revived its sales and reputation through tough investigative reporting and sensational storytelling. He soon moved into the New York newspaper market and went head-to-head against newspaper magnate Joseph Pulitzer through "yellow journalism," or exaggerated reporting. Hearst's newspapers, say many historians, were partly responsible for a U.S. declaration of war against Spain in 1898.

In the early 1900s, Hearst ran unsuccessfully for governor of New York state and mayor of New York City. At the same time, he expanded his newspaper empire to include publications throughout the United States. Increasingly isolationist, he used his chain of newspapers to oppose U.S. entry into World War I and U.S. membership in the postwar League of Nations.

With the onset of the Great Depression, Hearst's empire began to experience a financial crisis, partly caused by Hearst's own extravagant spending, including the construction of his gigantic mansion in San Simeon, along California's coast. To combat the Depression, Hearst supported the conservative measure of a national sales tax, in order to alleviate the growing federal deficit that many orthodox economists said was at the root of the continuing economic malaise.

Ever more conservative in his political outlook during the 1920s and early 1930s, Hearst backed the conservative speaker of the house, Texan John Nance Garner, for the Democratic presidential ticket in 1932. But when that support backfired and appeared to give the nomination to the internationalist former Secretary of War Newton Baker, Hearst agreed to accept Roosevelt as the nominee.

Although Hearst lined up his newspapers behind Roosevelt, he soon turned against both the president and his New Deal legislation, most especially the National Industrial Recovery Act. In 1934, Hearst's Cosmopolitan Studios produced the film *Gabriel Over the White House*, in which a dictator takes over the White House and saves the country through the establishment of a police state. At the same time, Hearst published *The Red Network*, a book that argued that Communists permeated the Roosevelt administration and various New Deal agencies.

Even as he was denouncing Roosevelt's domestic programs, Hearst was joining with conservative and even profascist forces within the country to prevent any U.S. aid to Britain and others opposing Nazi Germany. But Hearst's influence was waning by the middle to late 1930s, as his fortune dissipated and he was forced to sell much of his valuable art collection.

By 1940, he had lost control of most of his newspapers and in 1941 was unable to block the release of Orson Welles's scathing fictionalized biography of Hearst, *Citizen Kane*. By the late 1940s, Hearst had largely disappeared from the national political and journalistic scene. He died in 1951.

See also: *Citizen Kane*; election of 1932; New Deal, first; newspapers and magazines; National Recovery Administration; Garner, John Nance; Welles, Orson.

Bibliography

Nasaw, David. *The Chief: The Life of William Randolph Hearst.* Boston: Houghton Mifflin, 2000.

Swanberg, W. A. *Citizen Hearst: A Biography of William Randolph Hearst.* New York: Scribner, 1961.

HENIE, SONJA

A Norwegian championship figure skater who captured the hearts of millions of Americans through her Olympic wins and winning good looks, Sonja Henie was also an astute self-promoter who parlayed her athletic fame into a lucrative career as a movie star in Hollywood.

Henie was born in Kristiania, Norway, in 1912. Trained originally in ballet, she used much of her dance experience in her skating routines, which incorporated a theatricality not seen before in the sport. Amateur world champion for ten years in a row between 1927 and 1936, she also won gold medals in figure skating at the 1928, 1932, and 1936 Olympic winter games.

After 1936, she went on a tour in the Ice Revues and then starred in ten Hollywood box office hit films between 1937 and 1945. After the war, Henie became a producer of ice shows and a collector of modern art, founding a museum dedicated to the genre outside Oslo, Norway. Henie died in a plane crash in 1969.

After winning gold medals at three Olympics from 1928 to 1936 for her native Norway, Sonja Henie starred in several popular Hollywood films in the late 1930s. *(Brown Brothers)*

See also: films, feature; sports.

Bibliography

Guttmann, Allen. *The Olympics: A History of the Modern Games.* Urbana: University of Illinois Press, 1992.

Henie, Sonja. *Wings on My Feet.* New York: Prentice-Hall, 1940.

HEMINGWAY, ERNEST

Known for spare, journalistic-style fiction and adventurous, masculine themes, novelist and short-story writer Ernest Hemingway was a critically acclaimed and popular writer by the 1930s, having established his reputation with his novels about American expatriates in Europe—*The Sun Also Rises* (1925)—and World War I—*A Farewell to Arms* (1929). Hemingway would go on to fight in the Spanish Civil War in the late 1930s and write down his experiences in the novel *For Whom the Bell Tolls* (1940).

Born in the upper-middle-class community of Oak Park, Illinois, in 1899, the son of a doctor, Hemingway began writing in high school. Upon graduation in 1917, he worked as a reporter in Kansas City before enlisting as an ambulance driver for the Red Cross during World War I. Injured during fighting in Italy, he returned to Oak Park to recover before heading to France as a correspondent for a Canadian newspaper. There, he fell in with the so-called lost generation of American intellectuals and writers who made their home in Paris during the 1920s.

After *The Sun Also Rises* was published, Hemingway continued to write fiction, including numerous short stories, even as he lived the adventurous life of bullfighting, safari hunting, and traveling that he wrote about in his books. During the 1930s, he wrote *Death in the Afternoon* (1933), a novel about Spain and bullfighting, and *The Green Hills of Africa* (1935), a book dealing with African safaris. After buying a house in Key West, Florida, Hemingway wrote *To Have and Have Not* (1937), a novel concerning a gangster who hides in the Florida Keys.

But it was Spain to which he seemed most attached, making several trips there to cover the civil war for American newspapers and magazines and raising funds for the republican government. He also wrote a play about the war entitled *The Fifth Column*, in 1938. After the war, he bought a home outside Havana, Cuba, but then went off to cover the Japanese invasion of China.

Ernest Hemingway was hailed by literary critics and the general reading public for such Depression-era books as *Death in the Afternoon, To Have and Have Not,* and *For Whom the Bell Tolls,* the last based on his experiences in the Spanish Civil War. *(Brown Brothers)*

During World War II, Hemingway served as a correspondent in London and flew several missions for the British Royal Air Force. Afterward, he settled in Cuba and continued to write novels and short stories, winning the Nobel Prize for literature in 1954. In 1960, he fled the communist revolution in Cuba and settled in Idaho. Hemingway died by suicide the following year.

See also: literature; newspapers and magazines; Spanish Civil War.

Bibliography

Burgess, Anthony. *Ernest Hemingway and His World*. New York: Scribner, 1978.

Lynn, Kenneth Schuyler. *Hemingway*. New York: Simon & Schuster, 1987.

Reynolds, Michael S. *Hemingway: The American Homecoming*. Cambridge, MA: Blackwell, 1992.

HEPBURN, KATHARINE

Known for her clipped New England accent, willowy good looks, and on-screen elegance, Katharine Hepburn became a Hollywood star in the 1930s in such films as *Little Women* (1933) and *Bringing Up Baby* (1938), although her career far outlasted the decade.

Born to an upper-class family in Hartford, Connecticut, in 1907, Hepburn began her acting career on the stage at Bryn Mawr College, which she attended from 1924 to 1928. She made her professional stage debut in 1928 and soon became a star on Broadway. Her first film—*A Bill of Divorcement* (1932)—made her an instant movie star. She followed that up with *Morning Glory* (1933), for which she won a best actress Academy Award, and *Little Women* (1933).

She proved she could play comedy as adeptly as drama in the Howard Hawks screwball comedy *Bringing Up Baby,* opposite Cary Grant, and in the 1939 Broadway stage and 1940 film production of *The Philadelphia Story*, the movie version cast with Cary Grant again. Hepburn continued to star in films through the 1980s, winning another three Academy Awards. Hepburn now lives in retirement.

See also: films, feature; Grant, Cary; Hawks, Howard.

Bibliography

Britton, Andrew. *Katharine Hepburn: Star as Feminist*. New York: Continuum, 1995.

Hepburn, Katharine. *Me: Stories of My Life*. New York: Knopf, 1991.

HICKOK, LORENA

A former journalist and a confidante of Eleanor Roosevelt, Lorena Hickok is best known for her fact-finding missions and investigative reports on poverty around the United States conducted between 1933 and 1936 for Harry Hopkins, head of the Federal Emergency Relief Administration and the Works Progress Administration.

Hickok was born in a small town in Wisconsin in 1893 and grew up in a household with an abusive father, whose violent outbursts forced the family to move around the upper Midwest during her childhood. She left home at fourteen to work as a maid and lived with ten separate families by the time she was eighteen. She attended Lawrence College in Wisconsin for a year, but dropped out after classmates ridiculed her because of her weight problem. From 1913 until 1933, she worked mostly as a journalist and was the first woman reporter hired by the Associated Press, which assigned her to cover Eleanor Roosevelt during the campaign of 1932.

The two hit it off immediately and Hickok soon resigned her post to serve as an adviser to the First Lady; Hickok believed that their friendship compromised her own objectivity as a reporter. Hickok is considered by Eleanor Roosevelt biographers to have been instrumental in steering the First Lady toward a more activist role.

In 1933, Hickok was hired by Hopkins to assess the level of poverty in urban and rural areas around the country, and Hickok set out in a car to do just that. Her reports, offering a dismal picture of American life in the depths of the Depression, are filled with both wonderment at Americans' political passivity about their problems and warnings about potential unrest.

In 1937, Hickok left government to work as a publicist for the New York World's Fair until its final year in 1940 and then, in 1941, became a publicist for the Democratic National Committee and executive secretary of its Women's Division until 1945. During those years, Hickok lived at the White House with the Roosevelts, leading to rumors—never proved—that she and Eleanor Roosevelt were lovers.

Hickok continued to work in Democratic Party politics after the war, as well as writing biographies. She died in 1968.

See also: Democratic Party; world's fairs; Federal Emergency Relief Administration; Works Progress Administration; Hopkins, Harry; Roosevelt, Eleanor.

Bibliography

Faber, Doris. *The Life of Lorena Hickok: E. R.'s Friend.* New York: William Morrow, 1980.

Hickok, Lorena A. *One-Third of a Nation: Lorena Hickok Reports on the Great Depression.* Urbana: University of Illinois Press, 1981 (reprint).

Rodger Streitmatter, ed. *Empty Without You: The Intimate Letters of Eleanor Roosevelt and Lorena Hickok.* New York: Free Press, 1998.

HICKS, GRANVILLE

Literary editor of the leftist magazine *New Masses* and one of the most controversial intellectuals of the Great Depression era, Granville Hicks became the center of a major struggle over academic freedom when he was dismissed from his professorship at Rensselaer Polytechnic Institute in 1935 for his outspoken communist politics.

Born in Exeter, New Hampshire, in 1901, Hicks graduated from Harvard and then spent two years in seminary school. Increasingly radical as the 1920s gave way to the Great Depression, Hicks published *The Great Tradition* in 1933, a collection of Marxist-influenced essays on American literature. In 1934, Hicks joined the Communist Party and was dismissed from his teaching post the following year. He became an outspoken supporter of the Republican government in Spain during its struggle with fascist forces in that country's civil war between 1936 and 1939.

By the end of the decade, however, Hicks, like many other American Communists, was growing disillusioned with the Party, especially after the Soviet Union signed a nonaggression pact with Germany in 1939. He broke with the Communist Party that same year.

Hicks continued to write essays and books through most of the rest of his life. He died in 1974.

See also: Communist Party; literature; newspapers and magazines; Nazi-Soviet nonaggression pact; Spanish Civil War.

Bibliography

Hicks, Granville. *Part of the Truth: An Autobiography.* New York: Harcourt, Brace & World, 1965.

Levenson, Leah. *Granville Hicks: The Intellectual in Mass Society.* Philadelphia: Temple University Press, 1993.

Robbins, Jack Alan, ed. *Granville Hicks in the New Masses.* Port Washington, NY: Kennikat Press, 1974.

HILLMAN, SIDNEY

President of the Amalgamated Clothing Workers of America (ACWA) union and a top labor adviser to the administration of Franklin D. Roosevelt, Sidney Hillman was one of the key founders of the Congress of Industrial Organizations in 1935.

Born Simcha Hillman in Lithuania in 1887, the future labor leader was trained to be a rabbi and a worker in a Russian chemical laboratory. After being jailed by the czarist police for labor activism, Hillman emigrated first to England and then, in 1907, to the United States.

He first settled in Chicago and was a leader in a garment workers' strike there in 1909. He soon moved to New York City and was elected president of the ACWA. During his tenure, the union's numbers grew and Hillman was able to win its members unemployment insurance. In addition, under Hillman's leadership, the union established its own housing projects and banks for its members, the latter actually loaning money to several garment firms to keep them financially afloat during the Great Depression.

Hillman was an outspoken critic of President Herbert Hoover's early efforts to end the Depression through voluntary measures by industry. Although a member of the Socialist Party, Hillman worked with the early Roosevelt adminstration, becoming chairman of the Labor Advisory Board of the National Recovery Administration (NRA) in 1933. Section 7 of the NIRA act, which guaranteed certain protections to unions trying to organize, helped double membership in the ACWA to 120,000 by 1934.

Although president of a member union of the American Federation of Labor, Hillman was disenchanted with the conservatism of the federation and its unwillingness to take advantage of the National Labor Relations Act to organize mass industries like steel, textiles, and automobiles.

Along with John L. Lewis of the United Mine Workers and David Dubinsky of the International Ladies' Garment Workers' Union, Hillman was critical in the formation of the Committee for Industrial Organization at the annual AFL meeting in 1935. The Committee would eventually be expelled from the AFL and

President of the Amalgamated Clothing Workers of America, Sidney Hillman was also one of the founders of the Congress of Industrial Organizations. *(Library of Congress)*

become the Congress of Industrial Organizations (CIO).

In 1936, Hillman broke away from the Socialist Party to back Roosevelt's reelection bid for the presidency, a move that many historians say helped consign the Socialist Party to political obscurity. Four years later, Hillman accepted, along with General Motors chairman William Knudsen, a position as cochairman of the Office of Production Management (OPM), an agency established by the Roosevelt administration to coordinate the incipient World War II defense industry establishment. But the differing agenda of the two chairmen hampered the effectiveness of the OPM.

During the war, Hillman took over as head of the Non-Partisan League, the CIO's pioneering labor political action committee, which worked hard to reelect Roosevelt. In 1945, Hillman was picked to head the World Federation of Trade Unions, but died a year later.

See also: American Federation of Labor; Congress of Industrial Organizations; National Labor Relations Act; National Recovery Administration; Section 7 (National Industrial Recovery Act); Office of Production Management; Dubinsky, David; Lewis, John L; Document: National Industrial Recovery Act, June 16, 1933.

Bibliography

Fraser, Steve. *Labor Will Rule: Sidney Hillman and the Rise of American Labor.* Ithaca, NY: Cornell University Press, 1993.

Josephson, Matthew. *Sidney Hillman: Statesman of American Labor.* Garden City, NY: Doubleday, 1952.

HITLER, ADOLF

Arguably the most influential and certainly the most notorious political figure of the twentieth century, Adolf Hitler created the National Socialist (Nazi) Party in the 1920s and led it to power in Germany in 1933. As *führer,* or dictator, of Nazi Germany from 1933 to 1945, Hitler first led the country out of the Depression and then plunged it, and much of Europe and America, into World War II, murdering millions of Jews, Gypsies, homosexuals, disabled persons, and Communists along the way.

Hitler was born in Austria in 1889 and studied art as a boy and young man in Linz and Vienna, where he absorbed the pervasive anti-Semitism of that time. Largely a failure in art, he moved to Munich in 1913 and volunteered for the German army in World War I. Wounded in a gas attack in 1916, he spent the rest of the war in a hospital.

Like many in Germany, Hitler was disillusioned by the nation's sudden surrender in 1918 and blamed the country's Jews for the disaster. He first became involved in politics as army political agent for a minor right-wing party in 1919. Put in charge of the party's propaganda division in 1920, he renamed it the National Socialist German Workers Party, better known as the Nazis.

With the German economy in ruins in 1923, Hitler led his Nazi storm troopers in a failed coup in Munich. Convicted to a five-year sentence, Hitler used what turned out to be a nine-month stint in jail to write his political agenda, *Mein Kampf* ("My Struggle") in 1924.

During the middle and late 1920s, Hitler continued as leader of the Nazi Party, building its membership manyfold, denouncing the corruption and libertinism of the interwar German Weimar Republic, calling for strong-arm tactics to rule Germany, and blaming the Jews for all the problems besetting the country.

With the onset of the Great Depression, which hit highly industrialized Germany particularly hard, the Nazi party grew in membership and power, winning more than 6 million votes in the 1930 elections. Running for president against the ancient war hero Paul von Hindenburg in 1932, Hitler won more than a third of the vote, placing second. With the country in continuing economic and political turmoil—much of it sparked by Nazi agitation and violence—Hindenburg appointed Hitler as chancellor, the German equivalent of prime minister, in January 1933.

On February 27, 1933, the German Reichstag, or parliament building, was burned, allegedly by a Communist. Hitler used this event to abrogate most freedoms in Germany and launch a campaign of violence against the rival Communists. In elections in March, the Nazis won a plurality of the vote and Hindenburg soon issued a decree granting full government powers to Hitler, which was ratified by all nonleftist parties in the Reichstag.

In total control of the German state, Hitler continued to abrogate civil rights, launch attacks on Communists, and consolidate Nazi power over all institutions of the state and society. In 1934, Hitler launched an attack against his rivals within the Nazi power, establishing his full control over the organization. Improved economic conditions, mass propaganda, and antileftist terrorism helped Hitler win 90 percent of the vote in a plebiscite to ratify his new and virtually dictatorial government power.

Now in total control of the German state, Hitler and the Nazis began a massive remilitarization program that helped relieve unemployment but was also in violation of the Versailles Peace Treaty of 1919. In 1935, Hitler ordered the reoccupation of the Saarland, an industrial region near France that had been declared neutral territory at Versailles. A year later, Hitler remilitarized the Rhineland, another industrial region along the French border, again in violation of Versailles. At the same time, he established an alliance with Benito Mussolini, the dictator of Fascist Italy, and the militarists who controlled the government of imperial Japan.

In February 1938, Hitler initiated the *Anschluss*, or connection, with Austria and, at the Munich Conference in September, negotiated with Britain and France to accept a German takeover of the German-speaking Sudetenland region of Czechoslovakia. Six months later, Hitler moved German troops into the rest of Czechoslovakia. Contemptuous of the United States as a racially "mongrel" state, he dismissed American government protests of the takeover.

In August 1939, Hitler signed a nonaggression pact with the Soviet Union, even though he had made it clear in *Mein Kampf* that he hoped to conquer the Slavic regions of Eastern Europe and the Soviet Union to create *lebensraum*, or "living space," for the superior Aryan people, Aryan being a pseudoscientific racial category encompassing the peoples of Germany and northern Europe.

On the first of September, Hitler launched an invasion of Poland that triggered a declaration of war against Germany by France and England, marking the beginning of World War II. Within another year, Hitler conquered France, Scandinavia, and the Low Countries and launched a massive, though ultimately unsuccessful, air attack against Great Britain. In June 1941, Hitler unleashed the *Wehrmacht*, or German army, in the greatest invasion in history against the Soviet Union. On December 11, four days after its ally Japan attacked Pearl Harbor, Hitler declared war on the United States.

During all of this remilitarization and conquest, Hitler was also undertaking a massive repression campaign against Communists, Gypsies, and, most infamously, Jews. Campaigning for power, Hitler had made it clear in the 1920s and early 1930s that he blamed the Jews not only for Germany's loss in World War I, but also for the economic problems associated with the Great Depression. In contradictory fashion, he argued that the Jews were both the bankers who manipulated the economy and the Communists who were trying to destroy the German race in the name of international working-class solidarity.

Upon taking power, Hitler initiated a series of rulings—including the notorious Nuremburg laws of 1935—that denied civil rights to Jews and ousted them from all government and professional positions. Following the assassination of a German official in Paris in 1938, Hitler's Nazi forces launched a coordinated attack on Jewish businesses, homes, and synagogues throughout the country, which came to be called *kristallnacht*, or "night of broken glass." All of this was prelude to a master plan—laid out in 1942—for the annihilation of all the Jews of Germany and Europe. Euphemistically called the "final solution," it ultimately led to the Holocaust, the murder of some 6 million Jews and millions of other people whom Hitler had declared either inferior or a threat to the German people, including Communists, Gypsies, disabled people, and homosexuals.

While Hitler declared that his Third Reich, or empire, would last a thousand years, it was crushed in a brutal six-year war fought against the United States, Britain, and the Soviet Union from 1939 to 1945. The struggle resulted in the virtual destruction of the German nation, the elimination of the Nazi Party, and Hitler's own suicide on April 30, 1945, in his bomb shelter in Berlin, even as Soviet troops were fighting a street-to-street battle for control of the Nazi capital. A week later, Germany surrendered.

See also: Munich conference; Nazi Germany; Nazi-Soviet nonaggression pact; Rhineland, reoccupation of; Soviet Union; World War II, early history of; Mussolini, Benito; Document: State Department Report on Nazi Germany, April 17, 1934.

Bibliography

Davidson, Eugene. *The Making of Adolf Hitler: The Birth and Rise of Nazism*. Columbia: University of Missouri Press, 1997.

Hitler, Adolf. *Mein Kampf*. Trans. Ralph Manheim. Boston: Houghton Mifflin, 1999.

Lukacs, John. *The Hitler of History*. New York: Knopf, 1997.

Shirer, William. *The Rise and Fall of the Third Reich: A History of Nazi Germany*. New York: Simon & Schuster, 1990.

Speer, Albert. *Inside the Third Reich: Memoirs*. Trans. by Richard Winston and Clara Winston. New York: Simon & Schuster, 1997.

HOLIDAY, BILLIE

One of America's most beloved jazz singers, known for the dramatic intensity of her voice and idiosyncratic phrasing, Billie Holiday established her reputation in the songs she performed and recorded with her partner, saxophonist Lester Young, in the late 1930s and early 1940s.

Billie Holiday, originally Eleanora Fagan, was born in Baltimore in 1915, the daughter of a musician father. Working as an errand girl at a local house of prostitution, Holiday was introduced to the jazz sound that was growing in popularity in the 1920s, especially the recordings of blues singer Bessie Smith.

Holiday made her singing debut at a Harlem nightclub in 1931; she recorded her first record in 1933. But she worked largely in obscurity until she went on tour with the Count Basie and Artie Shaw orchestras in 1935. Most jazz aficionados argue that her greatest recordings were made with Young—who gave her the enduring nickname "Lady Day"—during the last years of the Great Depression and the first years of World War II.

Holiday's final years were marked by a difficult and ultimately losing struggle with a heroin addiction, which eventually contributed to her premature death in 1959.

See also: music; Count Basie.

Bibliography

Clarke, Donald. *Wishing on the Moon: The Life and Times of Billie Holiday.* New York: Viking, 1994.

Holiday, Billie. *Lady Sings the Blues.* Garden City, NY: Doubleday, 1956.

HOOK, SIDNEY

One of the leading leftist intellectuals of the Great Depression era and a professor at New York University, Sidney Hook was part of a group of thinkers and philosophers who tried to reconcile Marxist theory with the American liberal tradition.

Born in New York City in 1902, Hook received his doctorate in philosophy from Columbia University in 1927, taking up a teaching post at New York University that he held until 1969. Always interested in historical theory and the development of American democracy, Hook emphasized a socialism that encompassed American individualist values. In his numerous books—including *Towards the Understanding of Karl Marx: A Revolutionary Interpretation* (1933)—he argued for collectivist solutions that would free the individual to realize his or her full social and intellectual potential. Marxism, he wrote in 1936, "is hostile to individualism as a social theory, not to individuality as a social value."

Denouncing capitalism—which, he said, had made "egoistic man," not "social man," the basis of society— he supported the 1932 Communist Party candidacy of William Z. Foster for president. But Hook was also wary of totalitarianism and those who wholeheartedly supported the Soviet Union in the late 1930s.

Becoming increasingly conservative as he grew older, Hook continued to do research and writing after he left New York University and joined the Hoover Institution on War, Revolution, and Peace at Stanford University in 1973. He died in 1989.

See also: Communist Party; Foster, William Z.

Bibliography

Hook, Sidney. *Out of Step: An Unquiet Life in the 20th Century.* New York: Harper & Row, 1987.

Hook, Sidney. *Towards the Understanding of Karl Marx: A Revolutionary Interpretation.* New York: John Day Co., 1933.

Phelps, Christopher. *Young Sidney Hook: Marxist and Pragmatist.* Ithaca, NY: Cornell University Press, 1997.

HOOVER, HERBERT

Perhaps no president entered office more popular, and left more despised, than the thirty-first president, Herbert Clark Hoover. When he was elected to succeed Calvin Coolidge in the Oval Office, the national mood was brimming with confidence. Within the first year of his administration, however, the country found itself in the midst of the worst economic crisis in its history. Hoover's inability to guide the country out of the Great Depression would lead to his electoral defeat in 1932 at the hands of Franklin D. Roosevelt.

HOOVER'S RISE TO PROMINENCE

Herbert Hoover was born in the rural Quaker community of West Branch, Iowa, in 1874. Orphaned at a young age, he eventually worked his way through the recently founded Stanford University, where he earned a degree in geology. It was there that he met his future wife, Lou Henrys, the only female geology student at Stanford. They married in 1899 and remained together until her death in 1944.

After graduation, Hoover made a fortune in mining, developing successful gold, silver, lead, zinc, and copper mines in Australia, China, Burma, and Russia. By 1914 he was a millionaire at the age of forty, operating a consulting firm with offices in London, New York, and San Francisco. However, it was during World War I that he earned a truly global reputation. As chairman of the U.S. Commission for Relief in Belgium, a post that he held from 1915 to 1919, he oversaw the shipment of millions of tons of food to starving people in war-torn Europe. After the United States entered the war, President Woodrow Wilson, recognizing Hoover's considerable administrative talents, appointed him to the chairmanship of the Inter-Allied Food Council. His skill in these posts brought him to the attention of the world. By 1919 he was, next to Wilson himself, the best-known American in Europe and was tremendously popular at home as well.

As the 1920 presidential election neared, members of both parties approached him to consider running for the office; even his future nemesis Franklin D. Roosevelt expressed hope that he would do so. Eventually he did stand for election in a few Republican primaries, but he refused to campaign actively. When Warren G. Harding ended up occupying the White House, Hoover instead accepted the new president's offer of the post of secretary of commerce. In a decade in which most cabinet departments saw their staffs and budgets slashed, Hoover's Commerce Department actually grew. He applied his administrative talents to what he saw as the most serious problems of the U.S. economy. He appointed special commissions to investigate unemployment and the business cycle. He brought several other agencies—such as the Bureau of Mines and the Patent Office—under his jurisdiction. He encouraged businesses to avoid "wasteful competition" and promoted simplification and standardization of production.

ELECTION AND EARLY PRESIDENCY

By 1928 Hoover was well known as a liberal Republican and a competent manager, so when Calvin Coolidge announced that he would not be a candidate for president, Hoover was widely seen as his natural successor. During the campaign he managed to attract considerable support from Democrats and Republicans alike, and he clearly benefited from the economic prosperity of the late 1920s. Ultimately Hoover defeated his Democratic opponent, New York Governor Alfred E. Smith, by an overwhelming electoral vote.

Hoover entered the White House during a time of tremendous national confidence. The economy was booming like never before, and millions of Americans expected that the "Great Engineer" would solve the country's lingering problems—in particular, rural poverty. Hoover himself was confident; in his campaign speeches, he claimed that America was closer than ever to eliminating the problem of poverty once and for all.

Hoover's first priority was the farm crisis. Millions of American farmers had not shared in the prosperity of the 1920s, since overproduction and foreign competition had led to steadily falling prices for agricultural goods. Congress therefore passed his proposed Agricultural Adjustment Act, which created a Federal Farm Board to assist in the stabilization of prices. By the summer of 1929, farm prices had already begun to rise.

With equal vigor Hoover embraced disarmament. In the final years of the Coolidge administration, a naval arms race had developed among the United States, Great Britain, and Japan. That summer the president

Although an able administrator, Republican president Herbert Hoover was widely blamed for the Great Depression, which began during his administration. In the 1932 presidential election he was defeated in a landslide by Democratic candidate Franklin D. Roosevelt. *(Brown Brothers)*

hosted the British prime minister, Ramsay MacDonald, and their talks paved the way for a new disarmament conference that was eventually held in London in 1930.

HOOVER AND THE GREAT DEPRESSION

But the true test of Hoover's leadership came in October 1929, when the booming economy of the 1920s came to a dramatic halt. The stock market faltered in late October and plummeted on Thursday, October 24. Over the next several years, the economy was in free fall. The stocks of such major corporations as U.S. Steel and General Motors lost 90 percent of their value, and businesses across the country struggled to stay afloat by canceling orders and laying off workers; the Great Depression had begun.

Hoover used all the resources at the government's command to cope with the crisis. His main concern was that wages remain high. As long as ordinary people could afford to buy things, the president reasoned, the economy would have to improve. To that end he held a series of conferences with corporate leaders who promised that they would not reduce wages. Hoover pushed through Congress legislation creating the Reconstruction Finance Corporation (RFC), which was authorized to make emergency loans to struggling banks and corporations. The result was an unprecedented growth in government spending and a federal deficit that reached $2.2 billion by 1931.

The president believed that the Depression had originated in Europe. In an effort to protect American businesses from falling global prices, he signed the

Smoot-Hawley Act, which increased import duties to their highest levels in U.S. history. He also believed that the international system of war debts and reparations, which had been a feature of the global economy since the end of World War I, was partially to blame for the economic crisis. He therefore proposed a one-year moratorium on all such payments.

In spite of this unprecedented activity at the federal level, the economy continued its downward spiral. By March 1933, industrial production was less than half what it had been in August 1929. The Smoot-Hawley tariff effectively destroyed American exports, as foreign countries retaliated by raising their rates. The crisis quickly spread to the banking system; in 1931 and 1932, over 5,000 banks closed their doors, and by the end of Hoover's presidency, American banking was in ruins. And although real wages actually increased, thanks to Hoover's agreements with business leaders, this made little difference to the millions of Americans who were unemployed—roughly one in four by 1933.

HOOVER'S SAGGING POPULARITY

Later on Hoover would be remembered less for what he did to fight the Depression than for what he refused to do. In the midterm elections of 1930, Democrats regained control of the House of Representatives for the first time in ten years and made considerable gains in the Senate as well. The new Congress passed a great deal of legislation, much of which Hoover vetoed. In 1931, he vetoed the Muscle Shoals joint resolution, which would have involved the government in the provision of electricity to thousands of households in the rural South. The president argued that while the federal government should do all it could to aid private corporations in promoting recovery, it should not set itself up in competition with private power companies. He also vetoed bills that would have provided direct relief to the unemployed, contending that such expenditures would unbalance the budget while having little effect on the economy.

Because of his opposition to such congressional initiatives, Hoover was accused of being a do-nothing president who was content to let the economy—and the American people—fend for themselves. In fact, this was anything but the case. Hoover was the first president who believed that the government had a responsibility to maintain a healthy economy. By the time he left office, he had spent billions in federal funds in an attempt to end the Depression. Institutions such as the Federal Farm Board and the Reconstruction Finance Corporation would remain important government agencies for

years to come. Indeed, in many ways, Roosevelt's own New Deal would be modeled on Hoover's efforts.

However, this is not the image that most Americans had of Herbert Hoover in the early 1930s. His ongoing battle with the Democratic Congress led to virtual gridlock. His opponents in both parties managed to use even his positive accomplishments against him, such as the war debt moratorium and the Reconstruction Finance Corporation. Hoover, they claimed, was more concerned with bailing out foreign countries and big banks and corporations than he was in relieving the distress of ordinary people.

By 1932 the president had become one of the most hated men in the country. Empty pockets turned inside out were called "Hoover flags." Newspapers used by homeless people to cover their bodies were "Hoover blankets." Shantytowns that popped up on the edges of many American cities were called "Hoovervilles." In Washington, members of the administration and other visitors to the White House reported that a feeling of gloom pervaded the whole place. In a sense, the president had become the personification of the Depression.

Although the Republican Party dutifully nominated Hoover to a second term in the summer of 1932, there was little enthusiasm for his candidacy. During that summer, 20,000 army veterans descended on Washington and set up a massive Hooverville in the middle of the city. Hoover ordered them to disperse in late July, and when they refused the U.S. Army forcibly evicted them. For weeks newsreels and journalistic accounts told stories, often wildly exaggerated, of helpless and unarmed men, women, and children being brutalized by soldiers allegedly acting under the president's orders. Hoover's public image, already tarnished in the eyes of most Americans, fell to a new low. The November elections would establish what everyone already knew—that Hoover had lost the confidence of the American people. Franklin D. Roosevelt won in a landslide even greater than the one that had brought Hoover to office four years earlier.

POST-PRESIDENTIAL CAREER

After his retirement from politics, Hoover continued to make public statements. He was a persistent and severe critic of the New Deal, accusing Roosevelt of trying to impose "regimentation" on the economy and even of aspiring to be a dictator. Hoover's 1934 book, *The Challenge to Liberty*, was one of the most widely read attacks on the administration's policies. However, the former president declined an invitation to join the anti-Roosevelt American Liberty League, a group that he denounced as reactionary. In 1940, he became increasingly concerned about the president's foreign policy, fearing that the United States might be drawn into a foreign war in which no vital national interest was at stake. He would go on to question the early Cold War policies of Harry Truman.

Yet Hoover did more than criticize; he remained an important adviser to the Republican Party well into the 1950s. During and after World War II he addressed the daunting question of feeding Europe, thus returning to the issue that had first brought him to prominence a generation earlier. Later, President Truman appointed the former president to form a commission to examine the organization of the executive branch.

Hoover lived his final years in the Waldorf-Astoria Towers in New York City. From 1940 on he wrote no less than nineteen books, many of which were collections of his own essays and speeches. He remained active in Republican politics, delivering addresses at every Republican National Convention through 1960. He died in 1964, at the age of ninety.

JOHN MOSER

See also: Bonus Army; election of 1932; Bonus bill; Norris-La Guardia Anti-Injunction Act; President's Organization of Unemployment Relief; Reconstruction Finance Corporation; Smoot-Hawley tariff; Documents: Hoover Appeal to Governors for Stimulation of State Public Works, November 23, 1929; Hoover's Veto of Muscle Shoals Bill, March 3, 1931; Hoover's Outline of Program to Secure Cooperation of Bankers to Relieve Financial Difficulties, October 6, 1931; Hoover's "Rugged Individualism" speech, October 22, 1928; Hoover's speech warning on deficit spending, February 25, 1930; Hoover campaign speech, October 31, 1932.

Bibliography

Burner, David. *Herbert Hoover: A Public Life*. New York: Knopf, 1979.

Fausold, Martin L. *The Presidency of Herbert C. Hoover*. Lawrence: University Press of Kansas, 1985.

Ferrell, Robert H. *American Diplomacy in the Great Depression: Hoover-Stimson Diplomacy, 1929–1933*. New Haven: Yale University Press, 1957.

Wilson, Joan Hoff. *Herbert Hoover: Forgotten Progressive*. New York: HarperCollins, 1975.

HOOVER, J. EDGAR

Director of the Federal Bureau of Investigation (FBI) from 1924 until his death in 1972, J. (John) Edgar Hoover greatly enhanced the reputation of the bureau in the 1930s through highly publicized crusades against the gangsters and bank robbers of the era.

Hoover was born in Washington, D.C., in 1895 and studied law at George Washington University. He joined the Justice Department as a file reviewer in 1917 and was put in charge of the roundup and deportations of suspected Communists during the post–World War I "red scare." Made director of the FBI in 1924, he inherited an agency rife with corruption and professionalized it by improving the standards of agent hiring and training. At the same time, he added fingerprinting files, a criminal science laboratory, and other modern innovations.

To build up the agency's reputation and budget, Hoover played upon the heavy media coverage given to the numerous gangsters and bank robbers of the early 1930s and made sure that the FBI got credit for the hunting down—and even killing—of such well-publicized outlaws as John Dillinger and "Pretty Boy"

Floyd. In the process, he coined the term "G-Man," or government man, to describe his agents, who he insisted should dress in suits and be immaculately groomed.

With heightening world tensions in the late 1930s, Hoover was given authority to investigate spies and espionage within the United States; he also made sure the bureau kept track of alleged domestic fascists and communists.

In the years after the war, Hoover's fear and hatred of anybody he deemed subversive led him to investigate, infiltrate, and disparage a variety of dissenting individuals and groups, including Martin Luther King Jr. and anti–Vietnam war organizations.

See also: crime; Federal Bureau of Investigation; Dillinger, John; Floyd, "Pretty Boy."

Bibliography

Potter, Claire Bond. *War on Crime: Bandits, G-Men, and the Politics of Mass Culture*. New Brunswick, NJ: Rutgers University Press, 1998.

Powers, Richard Gid. *G-Men: Hoover's FBI in American Popular Culture*. Carbondale: Southern Illinois University Press, 1983.

Head of the Federal Bureau of Investigation from 1924 until his death in 1972, J. Edgar Hoover made catching high-profile gangsters the top priority of his agency in the early 1930s. *(Brown Brothers)*

HOPKINS, HARRY

Akey administrator during the New Deal who advocated a vast expansion of the government's role in providing aid and jobs to unemployed workers, Harry Hopkins headed the Federal Emergency Relief Administration (FERA), the Civil Works Administration (CWA), and the Works Progress Administration (WPA).

Born in Sioux City, Iowa, in 1890, Hopkins was a believer in the Social Gospel, a philosophy that called for religious faith to be expressed by providing social services to the less fortunate. To realize this ideal, Hopkins became a social worker in the 1910s and worked at the Christadora Settlement House on New York City's Lower East Side in the 1920s.

Becoming an adviser to Governor Franklin D. Roosevelt after the Great Depression began, Hopkins headed the state's Temporary Emergency Relief Administration, a model for the federal relief agencies that would be created when Roosevelt went to Washington in 1933.

In May 1933, Hopkins became the first director of the FERA and immediately went to work spending vast sums of money providing outright grants and then work to some 2 million unemployed laborers. He spent

A former social worker, Harry Hopkins wore many hats during the New Deal, as head of the Federal Emergency Relief Administration, the Civil Works Administration, and the Works Progress Administration. *(Library of Congress)*

about $5 billion during the two-year life of the agency and its successor, the CWA, which Hopkins also headed after its creation in November 1933. With the Democratic election sweep in 1934, Hopkins felt even more emboldened to expand jobs programs and argued against all critics, including conservatives in Congress, who claimed that these were make-work programs that would render people too dependent on government aid.

In 1935, Hopkins urged Roosevelt both to expand jobs programs and to build more substantial projects. In response, the Roosevelt administration established the WPA and appointed Hopkins to run it. With an initial outlay of nearly $5 billion, Hopkins put millions to work constructing buildings, highways, and other public infrastructure projects. When a new recession hit the country after federal spending cuts in 1937 and 1938, Hopkins got another $3 billion to expand the WPA. Altogether, by the end of 1938, Hopkins and the WPA had spent $8.5 billion and provided relief to some 15 million persons.

As the chief administrator of the largest public works agency of the New Deal, Hopkins fought on many fronts for his ideal of federal aid to all unemployed and impoverished Americans. He argued with conservatives in the Congress and the press; he criticized Harold Ickes—head of the rival Public Works Administration—for a too-parsimonious distribution of federal funds; and he worked with Mary McLeod

Bethune and other black officials in the Roosevelt administration to include African Americans equally in all the public works projects, despite resistance to this inclusion by southerners.

Along with the FERA, the CWA, and the WPA, Hopkins served on the President's Drought Committee, the Committee on Economic Security, the National Emergency Council, the National Resources Planning Board, and the Federal Surplus Relief Corporation. Meanwhile, Hopkins became increasingly involved in politics, helping Roosevelt in his 1936 reelection campaign. In 1938, this activity would come back to haunt him through congressional investigations of electoral activity by and contributions from WPA workers in liberal Democrats' campaigns, a scandal that led to the passage of the 1939 Hatch Act, banning such involvement. Hopkins, however, was never directly implicated by these investigations. In 1938, Hopkins was appointed secretary of commerce.

A political adviser to Roosevelt at the 1940 Democratic National Convention, Hopkins soon became the president's liaison to world leaders as World War II began, making trips to London and Moscow to distribute lend-lease aid. A member of the War Production Board that regulated the wartime economy, Hopkins continued to serve as a close personal adviser to Roosevelt throughout the war. A sickly man much of his life, Hopkins died at the relatively young age of 55 in 1946.

See also: election of 1936; election of 1940; Civil Works Administration; Federal Emergency Relief Administration; Federal Surplus Relief Corporation; Hatch Act; Public Works Administration; Temporary Emergency Relief Administration; Works Progress Administration; Lend-Lease Act; World War II, early history of; Bethune, Mary McLeod; Ickes, Harold; Roosevelt, Franklin D.; Documents: Fireside Chat on work relief programs, April 28, 1935; Lend Lease Act, March 11, 1941.

Bibliography

Aams, Henry H. *Harry Hopkins: A Biography*. New York: Putnam, 1977.

Hopkins, Harry Lloyd. *Spending to Save: The Complete Story of Relief*. New York: W. W. Norton, 1936.

Hopkins, June. *Harry Hopkins: Sudden Hero, Brash Reformer*. New York: St. Martin's, 1999.

Sherwood, Robert Emmet. *Roosevelt and Hopkins: An Intimate History*. New York: Harper, 1950.

HOPPER, HEDDA

An unsuccessful movie actress in Hollywood from the early 1920s to early 1930s, Hedda Hopper turned to writing, becoming—along with Louella Parsons—the most influential gossip columnist in America by the end of the Great Depression era.

Born Elda Furry in small-town Pennsylvania in 1890, she studied music in Pittsburgh before running away from her disapproving Quaker family to become a chorus girl on Broadway in 1909. She began to appear in stage productions with comic actor DeWolf Hopper, whom she married in 1913. They divorced in 1922.

Hopper moved to Hollywood, where she made her debut in *The Battle of Hearts* (1916). She acted in over 100 films over the next thirty years, but was never able to become star. Instead, she used her idiosyncratic sense of style (her large, wild hats became her trademark) to win a job as a radio fashion commentator. In 1937, the Esquire Feature Syndicate company hired her to do a Hollywood column. After it appeared in the *Los Angeles Times*, Hopper's status and influence grew immensely. She was soon syndicated in over eighty-five major metropolitan dailies.

While she could be nasty in tone, she was generally more forgiving of the foibles of Hollywood personalities than her archrival, Parsons. Hopper continued to write through most of the rest of her life and died in 1966.

See also: films, feature; newspapers and magazines; Parsons, Louella.

Bibliography

Eells, George. *Hedda and Louella.* New York: Putnam, 1972.

Hopper, Hedda. *From Under My Hat.* Garden City, NY: Doubleday, 1952.

HOWE, LOUIS M.

One of Franklin D. Roosevelt's longest serving advisers and closest friends, Louis M. Howe was a confidant of the future president as far back as the latter's days in the New York state legislature in the second decade of the twentieth century. During the early years of the Roosevelt presidency, Howe worked as his secretary and was known to be the only person who dared to call the president "a fool" to his face.

Howe was born the son of a struggling businessman in Indianapolis in 1871. Short and of slight build, he was sent to a seminary in upstate New York for high school because his parents felt he was not strong enough for public school. Howe never went to college, becoming a newspaper reporter instead. From 1906 on, he covered the New York state legislature for the New York *Herald*.

In 1912, Franklin D. Roosevelt, running for his first reelection to the legislature, fell ill with typhoid and asked Howe to run his campaign. Howe did so, believing that Roosevelt, with his name, charm, and ambition, was likely to move on to higher office. Howe even jokingly called him "Beloved and Revered Future President." When Roosevelt was appointed assistant secretary of the navy in 1913, Howe served as his chief of staff. In 1920, Howe served as Roosevelt's campaign manager in an unsuccessful run for the vice presidency.

After the loss, Howe planned on returning to private life, but felt compelled to stay with Roosevelt after the latter was paralyzed by polio in 1921. While Roosevelt convalesced over the next seven years, Howe kept his name alive by writing articles with a Roosevelt byline and issuing press releases. In 1928, he again worked as a top political aide to Roosevelt in his run for the governor's office of New York. Then, over the next four years, he worked with Roosevelt, planning a possible run for the White House.

When Roosevelt moved to Washington in 1933, Howe became his personal secretary and was said to have more access to the president than any other person. But over the next few years, Howe's influence waned as Roosevelt brought in new advisers. Generally conservative, Howe's opinions were often overridden by the liberal New Dealers surrounding the president. By the time of his death in early 1936, Howe—while still a close friend of Roosevelt's—had been eclipsed as an adviser.

See also: Democratic Party; election of 1932; Roosevelt, Franklin D.

Bibliography

Rollins, Alfred Brooks. *Roosevelt and Howe*. New York: Knopf, 1962.

Stiles, Lela Mae. *The Man Behind Roosevelt: The Story of Louis McHenry Howe*. Cleveland: World Publishing Company, 1954.

HUGHES, CHARLES EVANS

Chief Justice of the Supreme Court from 1930 to 1941, Charles Evans Hughes was an early opponent of expansive New Deal programs like the National Recovery Administration—which he ruled against in the 1935 *Schechter v. United States* decision—but made an ideological shift thereafter and supported the constitutionality of minimum wage legislation and the National Labor Relations Act.

Hughes was born in Glens Falls, New York in 1862. Trained in law, he joined an important New York City law firm in the late nineteenth century and, in 1905, became counsel for the New York state legislature in its investigations of insurance companies and utilities. These investigations gained Hughes a national reputation as a reformer.

The following year, Hughes defeated William Randolph Hearst to become governor of New York state on the Republican ticket. In 1908, he was appointed to the Supreme Court, but resigned in 1916 to run for the presidency, which he lost narrowly to Woodrow Wilson. Appointed secretary of state by President Warren G. Harding, he tried unsuccessfully, after Wilson had already failed, to get the United States into the League of Nations. In 1925, he returned to his private law practice and then returned to the Supreme Court as chief justice in 1930.

While generally a believer in expansive governmental powers, Hughes nevertheless felt that Congress had delegated too much of its legislative power to the executive branch by establishing the economic regulatory agency, the National Recovery Administration. Over the next two years, however, Hughes shifted ideologically somewhat to accept an executive department agency's powers to arbitrate labor disputes implicit in the National Labor Relations Act. This action was effected in the 1937 *NLRB v. Jones and Laughlin* decision. That same year, he backed the constitutionality of minimum wage laws in *West Coast Hotel v. Parrish*.

But Hughes had a major falling-out with Franklin D. Roosevelt after the president offered a plan to add one Supreme Court justice for every sitting justice over the age of seventy. Hughes, like many other critics of the so-called court-packing plan, felt this was an unacceptable and unconstitutional disruption of the checks and balances in the Constitution.

Hughes, citing his old age of 79, resigned from the Court in 1941 and died in 1948.

See also: court-packing plan; National Labor Relations Act; *NLRB v. Jones and Laughlin*; National Recovery Administration; *Schechter Poultry Corporation v. United States*; *West Coast Hotel v. Parrish*; Supreme Court; Documents: Reform of the Federal Judiciary, 1937; Adverse Report on Reform of the Federal Judiciary from the Senate Committee on the Judiciary, June 7, 1937; *Schechter Poultry Corporation v. United States*, 1935; *United States v. Butler et al.*, 1936; *Ashwander v. Tennessee Valley Authority*, 1936; *National Labor Relations Board v. Jones & Laughlin Steel Corporation*, 1937; *West Coast Hotel Company v. Oregon*, 1937; Chief Justice Charles Evans Hughes' Opinion on Admission of a Negro Student to the University of Missouri Law School, 1938.

Bibliography

Danelski, David, and Joseph S. Tulchin, eds. *The Autobiographical Notes of Charles Evans Hughes*. Cambridge: Harvard University Press, 1973.

Pusey, Merlo John. *Charles Evans Hughes*. New York: Macmillan, 1951.

HUGHES, HOWARD

Film producer, millionaire, aviation engineer, and flyer, Howard Hughes turned his family fortune into an aviation and film empire that made him one of the most famous men of the Great Depression era and of twentieth-century American history.

Hughes was born in Houston in 1905. His father had invented a revolutionary drilling bit for the oil industry that made him a wealthy man. More interested in the film than the oil business, Hughes began producing pictures in Hollywood in the mid-1920s, leading up to the epic *Hell's Angels* of 1930, a movie about World War I flying aces that starred the then unknown Jean Harlow. Hughes also produced several other major films in the early 1930s, including *The Front Page* (1931) and the classic gangster story *Scarface* (1932).

Hughes then turned to aviation, which he had been fascinated with since he was a teenager. To learn the business from the ground up, he worked as a baggage handler for American Airlines. When he was discovered working there, it made national headlines. He founded Hughes Aviation and embarked on a series of record-breaking flights during the middle and late 1930s, culminating in a highly publicized round-the-world flight in under four days in 1938. While working on the planes that carried him on these flights, Hughes and his engineers developed several key innovations in airplane technology, including retractable landing gear.

During this period, Hughes was developing a reputation as the country's most eligible bachelor and was involved with film stars Ginger Rogers and Katharine Hepburn, among others. In 1941, he turned his attention to a new star, Jane Russell, for whose buxom chest he engineered a bra using technology developed in the aviation business. The showcase film he produced for her—*The Outlaw* (1943)—was not as successful as the undergarment and was panned by critics and the public alike.

After World War II, Hughes continued to work in film and aviation, as well as becoming involved in the Las Vegas casino industry. But he also grew increasingly eccentric, becoming a total recluse living in one of his Las Vegas hotels until his death in 1976.

See also: films, feature; Astaire and Rogers; Hepburn, Katharine.

Bibliography

Bartlett, Donald L., and James B. Steele. *Empire: The Life, Legend and Madness of Howard Hughes.* New York: W. W. Norton, 1979.

Brown, Peter Harry, and Pat H. Broeskie. *Howard Hughes: The Untold Story.* New York: Dutton, 1996.

HUGHES, LANGSTON

A poet and one of the principal figures of the Harlem Renaissance circle of African-American intellectuals, artists, and writers in the 1920s, Langston Hughes continued to write poetry during the Great Depression era, though the subject matter of his poetry and other writings became increasingly politicized.

James Mercer Langston Hughes was born in Joplin, Missouri, in 1902. Raised by his aunt and his mother in Kansas, Illinois, and Ohio, Hughes wrote poetry in high school and had a poem—"The Negro Speaks in Rivers," which has become his most-anthologized piece—published in the *Crisis*, the official journal of the National Association for the Advancement of Colored People, in 1921.

Hughes enrolled at Columbia University in 1921 but dropped out after a year, preferring to explore the cultural and artistic scene in nearby Harlem, then the unofficial capital of black America. He then traveled to Africa and Europe, returning to the United States in 1924 and winning the top prize in the poetry contest sponsored by the the National Urban League's journal *Opportunity*, which further established his reputation as an important American literary figure. In 1926, he published his first collection of poetry, *The Weary Blues*. Like much of his writing, it was heavily influenced by the rhythms of jazz and the African-American patois.

Hughes then enrolled at Lincoln University in Pennsylvania in 1927 and graduated two years later. In 1930, he published his first book of prose, *Not Without Laughter*, and began publishing in the Communist Party journal *New Masses*. During the early 1930s, he also traveled to California, where he wrote *The Ways of White Folks* (1934), Haiti, and Russia.

Much of his writing during this time was radical in tone and dealt with the harsh social realities of African Americans and working-class people in the Great Depression. Indeed, Hughes signed a petition with a number of other intellectuals endorsing the Communist Party candidacy of William Z. Foster for president in 1932. During the mid-1930s, Hughes turned to playwriting. His 1935 *Mulatto* became a long-running Broadway show.

Hughes continued to write essays, poetry, and plays until his death in 1967.

See also: African Americans; Communist Party; literature; National Association for the Advancement of Colored People; National Urban League; *New Masses*.

Bibliography

Haskins, James. *Always Movin' On: The Life of Langston Hughes.* Trenton, NJ: Africa World Press, 1993.

Hughes, Langston. *The Big Sea: An Autobiography.* New York: Hill and Wang, 1993.

Rampersad, Arnold. *The Life of Langston Hughes.* 2 vols. New York: Oxford University Press, 1986.

A central figure in the Harlem Renaissance, Langston Hughes wrote numerous books and plays during the 1930s, including the long-running Broadway hit, *Mulatto*. (*Library of Congress*)

HULL, CORDELL

Secretary of state through the first three administrations of President Franklin D. Roosevelt, Cordell Hull was a strong believer in free trade and an internationalist foreign policy for the United States. He worked hand-in-hand with the president to try to lift restrictions on U.S. military aid to Britain in the late 1930s and early 1940s when the latter faced the threat of Nazi hegemony in Europe.

Born in rural Tennessee in 1871, Hull was trained as a lawyer and served in Congress as a Democratic representative from Tennessee almost continuously from 1907 to 1931, when he was elected to the Senate.

Although somewhat conservative and opposed to Roosevelt's more radical campaign rhetoric about reining in the power of big business, Hull nevertheless accepted the appointment as secretary of state.

Believing that free trade was essential to U.S. and world economic recovery, Hull went to work immediately to reduce the high tariffs established under the previous Republican administrations in the 1920s and early 1930s. He was critical in getting the Reciprocal Trade Agreements Act of 1934 passed, which helped lower tariffs and set a precedent for post–World War II trading pacts like the General Agreement on

Tariffs and Trade. Hull was also instrumental in blocking efforts to dump U.S. agricultural surpluses abroad, fearing other nations might do the same in the U.S. market.

On relations with Latin America, Hull was a key figure in creating the so-called Good Neighbor policy, which discouraged unilateral U.S. intervention in other Western Hemisphere countries, and helped pull U.S. troops out of Nicaragua. At the same time, he worked to negotiate hemisphere-wide defense arrangements at the Havana foreign ministers' conference of 1940.

But his most important work in the late 1930s was in easing U.S. isolationism, getting around the various neutrality acts, and getting much-needed U.S. military aid to Britain and other countries fighting Nazi Germany and imperial Japan. He worked with Roosevelt to get destroyers to Britain and to get the Lend-Lease Act passed by Congress. At the same time, Hull made a point of strongly denouncing German and Japanese aggression in Europe and China.

During the war, Hull was instrumental in maintaining the Grand Alliance with Britain and the Soviet Union and was a key figure in the negotiations designed to create a postwar world order. He won a Nobel Peace Prize in 1945 for his efforts to establish the United Nations, even though he had resigned shortly after the 1944 elections. Retired, he turned to writing his memoirs. Hull died in 1955.

See also: Good Neighbor policy; Lend-Lease Act; neutrality acts; World War II, early history of; Documents: Roosevelt on Good Neighbor Policy, December 1, 1936; Act of Havana on Hemispheric Defense, July 29, 1940; Lend-Lease Act, March 11, 1941.

Bibliography

Butler, Michael A. *Cautious Visionary: Cordell Hull and Trade Reform, 1933–1937*. Kent, Ohio: Kent State University Press, 1998.

Hull, Cordell. *The Memoirs of Cordell Hull*. New York: Macmillan, 1948.

Pratt, Julius William. *Cordell Hull, 1933–1944*. New York: Cooper Square Publishers, 1964.

HURSTON, ZORA NEALE

An anthropologist and a pioneer collector of African-American folklore, Zora Neale Hurston was one of the few black women hired by the Federal Writers' Project (FWP), though her work for the FWP on the African-American culture of her native Florida was never published.

It is unclear when and where Hurston was born. She herself claimed to have been born in Eatonville, Florida, in either 1901 or 1910, but recent research indicates that she was born in Alabama in 1891. Whatever the case, she received her high school diploma in 1918 in Baltimore and then attended Howard University, where she also wrote fiction, off and on until 1922.

In 1925, she came to Harlem, writing fiction, and was adopted into the literary circles of the Harlem Renaissance. That same year, she received a scholarship to Columbia University and studied anthropology under the legendary Franz Boas. After graduation in 1928, she did field research, collecting the folklore of Haiti and Jamaica.

Returning to New York, she collaborated on the play *Mule Bone* with Langston Hughes in 1931. Her interest in black folklore took her to Florida and led her to publish her findings in *Mules and Men* (1935). She also did research on the voodoo religion of the Caribbean and published her work in *Tell My Horse* (1938). Hurston, however, is best known for her novel *Their Eyes Were Watching God* (1937).

Both her anthropological studies and her fiction came under some criticism from other black intellectuals, who disliked her argument that the self-contained African-American communities of the American South and the Caribbean were a model for black culture, rather than the integrationist approach then favored by most black literary figures and political leaders.

Falling out of favor with critics in the 1940s, Hurston returned to the South in poverty, working at odd jobs until her death in 1960. She published her autobiography, *Dust Tracks on a Road*, in 1942. An anthology of her writing, *I Love Myself When I Am Laughing and Then Again When I Am Looking Mean and Impressive*, was published posthumously in 1979.

See also: African Americans; literature; Hughes, Langston.

Bibliography

Howard, Lillie P. *Zora Neale Hurston*. Boston: Twayne, 1980.

Hurston, Zora Neale. *Dust Tracks on a Road*. New York: Harper Perennial, 1996.

———. *Folklore, Memoirs, and Other Writings*. New York: Library of America, 1995.

ICKES, HAROLD L.

A progressive Republican and secretary of the interior through all four administrations of Franklin D. Roosevelt, Harold L. Ickes is better known for his leadership at the Public Works Administration (PWA), which, though slow in getting started, eventually spent some $5 billion dollars in public works projects.

Born in Frankstown Township, Pennsylvania in 1874, Ickes studied law and passed the bar in Illinois in 1907. Strongly moved by the Social Gospel movement of service to the community, Ickes volunteered in settlement houses and often handled civil liberties cases *pro bono*. He also worked on cleaning up municipal governments and brought several cases against utility companies.

These activities earned Ickes a national reputation as a reformer, and when Roosevelt was picking his first cabinet—and looking to include liberal Republicans—he chose Ickes to run the Interior Department. There, Ickes helped administer legislation that restricted grazing on public lands—to raise the price of livestock—and worked on pricing and distribution arrangements for petroleum under the National Recovery Administration. Ickes was also chosen to head the PWA, one of the first major unemployment initiatives of the New Deal.

A meticulous administrator who wanted to prevent graft at all cost, Ickes moved extremely slowly in dispersing funds for projects, raising complaints among other members of the Roosevelt administration, most notably the heavy-spending Harry Hopkins, who ran the Civil Works Administration and the Works Progress Administration (WPA). Nevertheless, Ickes remained in charge of the agency until it was joined with the WPA to form the Works Projects Administration in 1939.

Over his years in the administration, Ickes grew quite close to Roosevelt and defended him against his political opponents. Indeed, Ickes earned a reputation as the president's "hatchet man" for the harsh attacks

Secretary of the Interior from 1933 to 1945, Harold L. Ickes was one of the strongest proponents of the New Deal and a staunch defender of President Franklin D. Roosevelt. (*Library of Congress*)

he launched against anyone who criticized Roosevelt or the New Deal.

Ickes was also known as one of the strongest supporters of African-American inclusion in the dispersion of New Deal aid and in the hiring for public works programs. He also helped Eleanor Roosevelt arrange a concert for black opera singer Marian Anderson at the Lincoln Memorial in 1939, after the latter was refused the right to sing at a concert hall run by the Daughters of the American Revolution.

A supporter of Roosevelt's efforts to break U.S. isolationism on the eve of World War II, he remained a close confidant of the president during the war. Ickes resigned from his post at the Interior Department in 1946 and died in 1952.

See also: African Americans; Civil Works Administration; National Recovery Administration; Public Works Administration; Works Progress Administration; Anderson, Marian; Hopkins, Harry; Roosevelt, Eleanor; Roosevelt, Franklin D.; Documents: National Industrial Recovery Act, June 16, 1933; Fireside Chat on work relief programs, April 28, 1935.

Bibliography

Clark, Jeanne N. *Roosevelt's Warrior: Harold L. Ickes and the New Deal.* Baltimore: Johns Hopkins University Press, 1996.

Ickes, Harold L. *The Autobiography of a Curmudgeon.* New York: Reynal and Hitchcock, 1943.

Watkins, T. H. *Righteous Pilgrim: The Life and Times of Harold L. Ickes, 1874–1952.* New York: Henry Holt, 1990.

INSULL, SAMUEL

Owner of a utility holding company whose financial excesses in the 1920s led to several trials for embezzlement and fraud in the 1930s, Samuel Insull seemed to many Americans the very incarnation of the corrupt business executive whose greed had led the country into the Great Depression.

Born in London in 1859, Insull worked as a British representative for Thomas Edison before immigrating to the United States in 1881, where he became Edison's private secretary. He was made a vice president of the Edison General Electric Company (now General Electric) upon its founding in 1889 and, three years later, became president of the Chicago Edison Company.

Insull made his real fortune—estimated at $150 million in 1929—by creating elaborate holding structures for multitudes of private utility companies across the country. Financed by stock speculation and loans from gullible bankers, Insull put together the largest holding company in the country in the late 1920s.

But with the stock market crash in 1929, Insull's fortune rapidly disappeared and his elaborate holding company—known as Commonwealth Edison Company—could not finance the enormous debt it had accumulated buying up smaller utility companies. As his company went into bankruptcy in 1932, Insull fled to Europe to escape trial for fraud, embezzlement, and violation of bankruptcy law. After two years of fighting extradition, he was brought back to the United States and put on trial. Three attempts to convict him, however, failed, and Insull returned to Europe, where he died in 1938.

The excesses of his financial dealing and the collapse of the elaborate and precarious holding company he created were partly responsible for passage of the Public Utility Holdings Act of 1935.

See also: utilites; Public Utilities Holding Act.

Bibliography

Hawes, Douglas W. *Utility Holding Companies.* New York: Clark, Boardman Co., 1987.

McDonald, Forrest. *Insull.* Chicago: University of Chicago Press, 1962.

JOHNSON, HIRAM

A progressive Republican senator from California and a strong supporter of many New Deal inflationary and public works programs, Hiram Johnson is best known for his sponsorship of legislation that attempted to prevent U.S. involvement in international affairs in the middle and late 1930s.

Born in Sacramento in 1866, Johnson was trained in the law and earned a statewide reputation as a tough prosecuting attorney in San Francisco in the early twentieth century. Elected governor of California in 1910, Johnson was a reformer who worked assiduously to break the control that the Southern Pacific Railroad had over state politics.

In 1912, Johnson joined with Theodore Roosevelt to form the Progressive, or Bull Moose, Party, and was its vice presidential nominee. The ticket lost to Democrat Woodrow Wilson. Johnson moved on from governor to the U.S. Senate in 1917 and, even during the conservative 1920s, backed a host of reform bills, especially for agriculture.

In the 1930s, although a Republican, Johnson was one of President Franklin D. Roosevelt's closest supporters in the Senate and voted for almost all of the major pieces of New Deal legislation designed to alleviate the plight of farmers and unemployed workers. At the same time, Johnson—as one of the Senate's

most vociferous isolationists—strongly opposed Roosevelt's efforts to provide military aid to countries fighting against Nazi Germany and militarist Japan in the middle and late 1930s. In 1934, Johnson sponsored legislation that prevented the United States from lending money to countries that had defaulted on their World War I loans, thereby excluding all European nations except Finland. The California senator also backed all of the neutrality acts and fought against lend-lease and all other efforts to aid Britain and other future allies of the United States in World War II. During the war, Johnson also opposed the formation of the United Nations.

Johnson died on August 6, 1945, the day the United States dropped the atomic bomb on Hiroshima.

See also: Lend-Lease Act; neutrality acts; World War II, early history of. Document: Lend-Lease Act, March 11, 1941.

Bibliography

Lower, Richard Coke. *A Bloc of One: The Political Career of Hiram W. Johnson.* Stanford, CA: Stanford University Press, 1993.

Weatherson, Michael A. *Hiram Johnson: A Bio-Bibliography.* Westport, CT: Greenwood Press, 1988.

JOHNSON, HUGH

One of the most colorful and outspoken figures of the Great Depression era, Hugh Johnson was a former military officer and businessman appointed to head the signature early New Deal economic recovery program, the National Recovery Administration (NRA) in 1933.

Born in frontier Oklahoma in 1882, Johnson attended West Point and rose to the rank of brigadier general in the U.S. Army. During World War I, he was put in charge of the Purchase and Supply Board of the War Industries Board (WIB), the latter being the agency assigned to regulate the American economy during the war. The WIB—headed by financier Ber-

nard Baruch, who became Johnson's business partner during the 1920s—would serve as a model for Johnson in running the NRA more than a decade later.

In 1919, Johnson retired from the military and went into private business, in which he was engaged during the 1920s and early 1930s. Before and after Franklin D. Roosevelt's 1932 election as president, Johnson was part of the so-called Brain Trust in charge of developing ideas to fight the Depression once the president-elect took office. When the Roosevelt administration established the NRA in June 1933, it was Baruch who suggested that the brash, energetic, blunt-speaking, hard-drinking Johnson be put in command.

The NRA was supposed to establish sets of codes to regulate the way industry produced and distributed goods, in order to prevent cutthroat competition that lowered prices and wages and contributed to the ongoing Depression. Johnson went at the task of bringing sometimes recalcitrant industry leaders on board with his characteristic fervor. It was also Johnson who came up with the NRA's Blue Eagle symbol that companies could display to show they were working with the government; Johnson pressed hard on businesses large and small to adopt the symbol and the program that the symbol represented.

At the same time, Roosevelt was careful not to give the headstrong Johnson control of the Public Works Administration—the employment side of the recovery program—for fear he would spend money too easily and without enough controls to prevent graft. Instead, the president chose the cautious Secretary of the Interior Harold L. Ickes for this task.

Johnson also had difficulties with the labor side of the NRA. Under the legislation that created the program, Section 7 stipulated federal government support for union organizing. To fulfill the mission of Section 7, Johnson created the National Labor Board (NLB) in August 1933 to deal with the growing number of conflicts between employers and workers.

The NLB quickly established rules by which workers could pick representatives for collective bargaining with employers. The Reading Formula, as it was called, declared that a majority of employees in a workplace could determine who their bargaining agent would be, leading to widespread hopes for a mass organizing of industries across the country. But Johnson—not a strong supporter of unions—demurred, replacing the Reading Formula with a policy effectively giving the decision to recognize the workers' bargaining agent to the employers. This inevitably led to the establishment of company unions that divided workers.

Just as Johnson's strong-arm tactics to get businesses signed on to the NRA angered employers, so his interpretation of Section 7 upset employees. Faced with a growing number of complaints from both parties, Johnson began to make himself scarce at the offices of the NRA, going on drunken benders for days at a time. Ultimately, Roosevelt was forced to ask for his resignation in October 1934.

Historians have largely judged Johnson's tenure at the NRA a failure, though they note that Ickes's parsimonious distribution of public works money also contributed to the fact that these early New Deal measures did little to alleviate the effects of the Depression.

Upon retirement, Johnson returned to private business, becoming an isolationist critic of Roosevelt's foreign policy in the late 1930s. Johnson died in 1942.

See also: Brain Trust; New Deal, first; National Recovery Administration; Public Works Administration; Section 7; Baruch, Bernard; Ickes, Harold; Documents: National Industrial Recovery Act, June 16, 1933; Fireside Chat on the National Recovery Administration, July 24, 1933.

Bibliography

Johnson, Hugh Samuel. *The Blue Eagle: From Egg to Earth.* Garden City, NY: Doubleday, Doran & Co., 1935.

Ohl, John Kennedy. *Hugh Johnson and the New Deal.* Dekalb: Northern Illinois University Press, 1985.

KENNEDY, JOSEPH P.

A financier who played a critical role in both the domestic and foreign policy initiatives of the Franklin D. Roosevelt administration, Joseph P. Kennedy served as the first chairman of the Securities and Exchange Commission in the mid-1930s and then as America's ambassador to Great Britain as storm clouds built over Europe in the late 1930s.

The grandson of Irish immigrants and the son of a prominent local politician in Boston, Kennedy was born in 1888 and graduated from Harvard University in 1912. A brilliant financier, he was head of a local bank by the age of twenty-five. Having made millions, he invested his money in Hollywood films, shipbuilding, and Democratic Party politics. During the 1920s, he increased his fortune immensely by manipulating stock prices on Wall Street, retiring, opportunely, in 1929.

With the establishment of the Securities and Exchange Commission in 1934—an agency given the task of cleaning up the corrupt trading practices in the stock market—Franklin D. Roosevelt sought out someone who understood the markets and had the confidence of other financiers. But choosing Kennedy, critics argued, was putting the fox in charge of the chicken coop. Still, the former stock manipulator took his reformist role seriously and established a number of rules that outlawed the techniques he himself had used to grow rich. Many of them are still in operation in one form or another.

After an appointment as head of the United States Maritime Commission, Kennedy was appointed ambassador to London. As the government of Neville Chamberlain—with its appeasement policy—caved in to Adolf Hitler's demands, Kennedy issued a series of increasingly pessimistic reports about the situation in Europe and Great Britain's unwillingness to fight against Nazi Germany. Even after Chamberlain's government gave way to Winston Churchill's—which vowed to fight on regardless of the costs in lives and fortune—Kennedy continued to argue that Nazi Germany was likely to win the war and that the United States should maintain its isolationist stance.

In November 1940, in the midst of Hitler's aerial attack on Britain—the Battle of Britain—Kennedy resigned and returned to the United States, where he continued to argue against U.S. involvement in the war.

After the war, Kennedy put his energy and fortune into the political career of his oldest surviving son, John Fitzgerald, who was elected the thirty-fifth president of the United States in 1960. The elder Kennedy died in 1969, six years after the assassination of John.

See also: stock market; Securities and Exchange Commission; Great Britain; World War II, early history of; Chamberlain, Neville; Churchill, Winston.

Bibliography

Beschloss, Michael R. *Kennedy and Roosevelt: The Uneasy Alliance.* New York: W.W. Norton, 1980.

Koskoff, David E. *Joseph P. Kennedy: A Life and Times.* Englewood Cliffs, NJ: Prentice-Hall, 1974.

Whalen, Richard J. *The Founding Father: The Story of Joseph P. Kennedy.* New York: New American Library, 1964.

KING, WILLIAM LYON MACKENZIE

Liberal Party prime minister of Canada from 1921 to 1930 and 1935 to 1948, William Lyon Mackenzie King was elected the second time due to disaffection with the Conservative administration of Richard Bedford Bennett, but did little to ease the continuing economic depression gripping the country.

King was born in small-town Ontario in 1874. An academic who taught at universities in both Canada and the United States, King also did a stint as a volunteer social worker at Jane Addams's Hull House in Chicago. Always interested in labor issues, King became deputy minister of labor in 1900. Eight years later, he was elected to the Canadian Parliament and became minister of labor in 1909.

In 1911, the Liberals lost power and King went to work for the Rockefeller Foundation, researching labor issues. Maintaining his involvement in politics, he became head of the Liberal Party in 1919. King was then elected prime minister in 1921 and served in that post almost continuously until 1930, when the Liberals lost to the Conservatives in the first year of the Depression.

Leader of the opposition during the first five years of the Depression, King was returned to the prime minister's office in 1935, determined that the country's path out of the economic hard times would come through expanding international trade, especially with the United States. In 1938, he successfully negotiated a more open trade agreement with Washington. King also nationalized the Bank of Canada and strengthened the power of the federal government, creating a system for the redistribution of funds from rich to poor provinces.

Conservative on inflationary policies, the King government ended the programs of public work camps established by the Bennett government. In addition, the government failed to initiate much in the way of New Deal-like social legislation. King was also leader of Canada during World War II, committing the country to the defense of Great Britain in 1939. King retired as prime minister in 1948 and died in 1950.

See also: Canada.

Bibliography

Dawson, Robert M. *William Lyon Mackenzie King: A Political Biography.* Toronto: University of Toronto Press, 1958.

Teatero, William. *Mackenzie King: Man of Mission.* Don Mills, Ontario: T. Nelson & Sons, 1979.

KNOX, FRANK

One of the leading figures in Republican politics in the 1930s and a vice presidential candidate in the 1936 election, Frank Knox was appointed by Franklin D. Roosevelt to serve as secretary of the navy in 1940. This action lent a bipartisan cover to the president's effort to mobilize support for U.S. aid to Britain and intervention against Nazi Germany in the waning years of the Great Depression.

Born William Franklin Knox in Boston in 1874, the future politician attended Alma College in the 1890s and fought in the Spanish-American War in Theodore Roosevelt's Rough Rider cavalry. After the war, Knox went into journalism and, in 1912, co-founded the *Manchester Leader* in New Hampshire, where he pushed for U.S. intervention in World War I. Hired by William Randolph Hearst in 1927 as general manager of his newspaper chain, Knox resigned to become publisher of the ailing Chicago *Daily News*, which he helped turn around financially in the early 1930s, crusading against Prohibition-era gangsters and the corrupt Democratic political machine.

During these years, Knox was involved in the progressive wing of the Republican party. In 1924, he made an unsuccessful bid for the party's nomination for governor of New Hampshire. By the 1930s, however, Knox had become more conservative, openly denouncing New Deal programs, claiming they placed an undue regulatory burden on private enterprise and were socialistic. Knox sought the Republican nomination in 1936 but lost to Alfred Landon of Kansas and was forced to settle for the vice presidential spot on a ticket that went down to a landslide defeat.

Always a strong internationalist, Knox was tapped to be secretary of the navy by Roosevelt at the same time another interventionist, Republican Henry L. Stimson, was chosen to be secretary of war. Knox backed Roosevelt's efforts to provide destroyers to Britain in 1940 and helped get the Lend-Lease Act—freeing up aid to countries fighting Nazi Germany and militarist Japan—passed in 1941. Until his death in early 1944, Knox presided over the greatest expansion in the navy's history.

See also: Lend-Lease Act; World War II, early history of; Stimson, Henry L.

Bibliography

Beasley, Norman. *Frank Knox, American: A Short Biography.* Garden City, NY: Doubleday, Doran & Company, 1936.

Hobdell, George H. "Frank Knox, 11 July 1940–28 April 1944." In *American Secretaries of the Navy*, ed. Paolo Coletta. Vol. 2. Annapolis, MD: Naval Institute Press, 1980.

LA FOLLETTE BROTHERS

The sons of Robert M. La Follette, a founder of Wisconsin progressivism and the Progressive Party candidate for president in 1924, Philip and Robert La Follette Jr. were governor and senator, respectively, of Wisconsin during the 1930s. Both formulated state anti-Depression programs and liberal policies that served as models for many pieces of New Deal legislation.

After the elder La Follette's death in 1925, the two sons assumed his mantle of leadership of Wisconsin progressivism. Robert Jr., born in 1895, won a special election in 1925 and took over his father's U.S. Senate seat, winning reelection as a Republican in 1928. He won as a Progressive in 1934, lost in 1940, and won again in 1946. In the Senate, Robert supported most New Deal legislation, but criticized President Franklin D. Roosevelt for not going far enough to create a more just and equitable economic order.

Philip, born in 1897, was first elected as a Republican to the governor's office of Wisconsin in 1930. During his first two-year term in office, Philip remained highly critical of Republican president Herbert Hoover and his limited efforts to fight the Depression. In comparison, the Wisconsin governor promoted an unemployment compensation program and a loan program for farmers facing mortgage foreclosures, both of which would be modified on a national level by the Roosevelt administration through the Social Security Act and various farm credit agencies, respectively.

In 1932, Philip was defeated in the Republican Party primary. Two years later, he joined with his brother to form the Progressive Party of Wisconsin. Criticizing the capitalist system, with its "cruelty and stupidity," Philip saw his Democratic opponent backed by Roosevelt. Yet he won in an upset and remained governor through 1938, when he was finally defeated by a Republican. After this, he returned to his private law practice and died in 1965.

Robert, meanwhile, continued in the Senate. With a rising post–World War II conservatism, he decided to disband the Progressive Party and run as a Republican, but lost to Joseph McCarthy in the primary. He died in 1953.

See also: Wisconsin Progressive Party; Social Security Act.

Bibliography

Doan, Edward N. *The La Follettes and the Wisconsin Idea.* New York: Rinehart, 1947.

Maney, Patrick J. *"Young Bob" La Follette: A Biography of Robert M. La Follette, Jr., 1895–1953.* Columbia: University of Missouri Press, 1978.

Miller, John E. *Governor Philip F. La Follette, the Wisconsin Progressives, and the New Deal.* Columbia: University of Missouri Press, 1982.

Young, Donald, ed. *Adventure in Politics: The Memoirs of Philip Lafollette.* New York: Holt, Rinehart, and Winston, 1970.

LA GUARDIA, FIORELLO H.

Fiorello Henry La Guardia, U.S. representative and mayor of New York City, was born to immigrants Achille Luigi Carlo La Guardia and Irene Luzzato-Coen on December 11, 1882, in New York City's Greenwich Village. In 1885, his father, a bandleader in the Eleventh U.S. Infantry Regiment, relocated the family first to Fort Sully, South Dakota, and later, in 1889, to Prescott, Arizona, where Fiorello La Guardia attended grammar and high school. During the Spanish-American War, La Guardia followed his father's regiment to Tampa, Florida, as a war correspondent for the *St. Louis* (Missouri) *Post-Dispatch*. After the war, La Guardia, a student of German, Italian, and Croatian, found employment as a clerk at the U.S. consulate in Budapest, Austria-Hungary. By 1904, he headed the Budapest consulate's office at the port of Fiume, where he reformed the local health certification procedures applying to emigrants bound for the United States. Frustrated with diplomacy, La Guardia returned in 1906 to New York City, where he worked as an interpreter at Ellis Island while studying law at New York University. He received his L.L.B. in 1910, passed the bar examination, and began a modest legal practice in New York City with a small clientele of immigrants referred to him by his Ellis Island contacts. La Guardia soon earned a reputation as an effective and ethical defender of workers' rights. His circle of acquaintances included the Syndicalist poet Arturo Giovannitti, Progressive journalist Fannie Hurst, and Socialist leader Jacob Panken.

LA GUARDIA IN CONGRESS

In 1914, local Republicans nominated La Guardia as Representative of the Fourteenth New York district, territory dominated by the Tammany Democrats. Although he lost this election, his aggressive campaign attracted the attention of New York governor Charles S. Whitman, who appointed La Guardia deputy attorney-general of New York state in 1915. In 1916, the Fourteenth district elected La Guardia to Congress, where he took his seat on March 4, 1917, at a special session called by President Woodrow Wilson to declare war against Germany. La Guardia voted for war and the draft act, having pledged, along with four other representatives, to confirm his position by volunteering for military combat service. In July 1917, La Guardia joined the Aviation Section of the U.S. Signal Corps. Commissioned as a lieutenant, he was promoted to captain in October 1917 and placed second in command at the Eighth Aviation Center in Foggia, Italy, where he supervised training, commanded the American Combat Division, flew in bombing raids over enemy territory, and, at the request of the American ambassador, participated in diplomacy. In recognition of La Guardia's service, he was promoted to the rank

Popular mayor of New York City from 1933 to 1945, Fiorello La Guardia was the architect of numerous public works and relief programs for the city during the Great Depression. *(Brown Brothers)*

of major, appointed to the Order of the Crown of Italy, and personally awarded the Italian War Cross by King Victor Emmanuel III of Italy. La Guardia returned to New York City in 1918 and was reelected to Congress as a Republican, defeating Socialist Scott Nearing. The following year he married Thea Almerigotti, a garment worker whom he had met on a picket line in 1913. Within three years, both his wife and their newborn daughter, Fioretta, died of tuberculosis.

La Guardia resigned from Congress in 1919 to take Alfred E. Smith's vacant position as president of the New York City Board of Aldermen, Smith having been elected governor of New York. In 1922, the Twentieth New York district voted La Guardia to Congress, again as a Republican. His progressive views and confrontational style, however, soon alienated the more conser-

vative Republican leadership, prompting him to run as a Socialist in 1924. Reelected continuously until 1932, La Guardia aggressively opposed Prohibition and immigration restriction laws while advocating increased veteran's benefits, rent control, and child labor legislation. During the Depression, he denounced President Herbert Hoover's proposed sales taxes, government layoffs and salary reductions, loans to distressed businesses and banks, and federally guaranteed home mortgages. Alternatively, La Guardia, with the support of Senator Robert Wagner, urged the government to directly assist the impoverished through unemployment insurance, job training, farm relief, loans to individual families, regulation of interest rates, and Red Cross distributions of food and finished goods. "The word 'dole' doesn't scare me," La Guardia declared in 1931. He continued to promote labor reforms and coordinate union lobbying at the Capitol. The Norris-La Guardia Anti-Injunction Act (1932), which La Guardia co-authored with Senator George Norris of Nebraska, limited the courts' ability to halt or otherwise restrict strike activities.

LA GUARDIA AS MAYOR

In 1933, La Guardia was elected mayor of New York City as a fusion candidate; he would be reelected in 1937 and 1941, becoming the first New York City mayor to serve three consecutive terms. La Guardia's accomplishments as mayor, many financed by the Roosevelt administration's New Deal expenditures, included the replacement of dilapidated tenements with new, low-rent public housing; the building of the Triborough Bridge, Lincoln Tunnel, and Henry Hudson Parkway; the unification of the rapid transit system under city ownership; the creation of new public parks, playgrounds, zoos, and other recreational facilities; the building of new public libraries and school buildings, including the establishment of a high school devoted to art and music education; and the construction of an international airport. La Guardia also improved the city government's day-to-day operations by eliminating graft in the awarding of municipal contracts, balancing the city budget, reforming civil service policies, and appointing public officials based on expertise rather than party connections. Under his first administration, New York City adopted a new charter, replacing the unwieldy Board of Aldermen with a smaller, more efficient City Council. La Guardia presided over the United States Conference of Mayors from 1935 to 1945. While mayor of New York, he also served as director of the U.S. Office of Civilian Defense (1941–42) and as a chairman of the joint Board of Defense of the United States and Canada (1940–47).

After leaving office in 1946, La Guardia traveled widely, visiting Brazil as a special U.S. ambassador and investigating postwar conditions in Europe as director of the United Nations Relief and Rehabilitation Administration. He died in New York City on September 20, 1947.

RAE M. SIKULA

See also: Harlem riot (1935); Norris-La Guardia Anti-Injunction Act; Document: Norris-La Guardia Anti Injunction Bill, March 20, 1932.

Bibliography

Kessner, Thomas. *Fiorello La Guardia and the Making of Modern New York*. New York: McGraw-Hill, 1989.

La Guardia, Fiorello. *The Making of an Insurgent*. Philadelphia: Lippincott and Crowell, 1948.

Mann, Arthur. *La Guardia: A Fighter Against His Times*. Philadelphia: J. B. Lippincott, 1959.

LANDON, ALFRED "ALF"

A moderately progressive governor of Kansas from 1933 to 1937, Alfred "Alf" Landon was the presidential nominee of the Republican Party in 1936 who lost in an overwhelming landslide to Franklin D. Roosevelt.

Landon was born in small-town Pennsylvania in 1887 and moved with his family to Independence, Kansas, at the age of 17. He received a law degree from the University of Kansas in 1908 and went into the petroleum business four years later. Progressive in his politics, he supported the Bull Moose candidacy of Theodore Roosevelt for president in 1912 and became active in Kansas politics. During World War I, he served in the army's chemical warfare division.

During the 1920s and early 1930s, Landon continued to work in both the oil industry and Kansas politics, running successfully for governor in 1932. His win that year and his reelection in 1934—the only Republican governor to buck the Democratic landslide—made him a national figure in the depleted ranks of the Republican Party leadership.

In 1936, Landon was picked to be the Republican nominee for president. With his progressive background, Landon at first supported much of the New Deal and campaigned on a platform of making the Roosevelt programs more cost-effective. He also cited his own ability to keep his state's budget balanced through the Depression years. But more conservative forces in the Republican Party soon convinced him to switch tactics and attack the New Deal, which Landon did. Denouncing Social Security and accusing the Roosevelt administration of harboring Communists, Landon was supported by William Randolph Hearst, the Liberty League, and other elements of the far Right.

While the Republicans spent lavishly on his campaign—the $14 million price tag was the highest amount spent on any campaign in American history up to that time—Landon was swamped in a Roosevelt landslide, losing by 10 million popular votes and 523 to 8 in the electoral college. He won only two states—Vermont and Maine.

Landon largely retired from national public life after his defeat, although he did speak out against the isolationists in his party in the late 1930s. He died in 1987, shortly after his one hundredth birthday. His daughter, Nancy Landon Kassebaum, went on to become a prominent Republican senator from Kansas.

See also: election of 1936; Liberty League; Republican Party; Roosevelt, Franklin D.; Document: Republican party platform, 1936.

Bibliography

McCoy, Donald R. *Landon of Kansas.* Lincoln: University of Nebraska Press, 1966.

Palmer, Frederick. *This Man Landon: The Record and Career of Governor Alfred M. Landon of Kansas.* New York: Dodd Mead, 1936.

After surviving the 1934 Democratic landslides of 1932 and 1934, Kansas Governor Alfred Landon was chosen to head the national Republican ticket in 1936, when he was defeated by President Franklin D. Roosevelt. *(Library of Congress)*

LANGE, DOROTHEA

A photographer whose highly individualized portraits of Americans captured the despair of Depression-era America, Dorothea Lange was hired by the Resettlement Administration (later the Farm Security Adminstration) to chronicle the miseries of the poor and bring them to public attention in the hopes of building political support for various antipoverty New Deal programs.

Born in Hoboken, New Jersey, in 1895, Lange studied photography in her teens and traveled the United States at age twenty, selling photographs to pay her way. Settling in San Francisco, she became a portrait photographer during the 1920s. A famed photograph, "White Angel Breadline" (1932), which depicted an old man in a breadline, brought Lange national attention when it was published in the magazine *Survey Graphic.*

In 1935, she was hired by the California State Emergency Relief Administration to chronicle the lives of migrant farmers, or Okies, in their camps around the Central Valley and elsewhere in the state. Later that year, she went to work for the Resettlement Administration, photographing the poor around the country.

Lange also continued to take photographs commercially for newspapers and magazines. One of these photos—"Migrant Mother" (1936), depicting a gaunt, haunted-looking woman with an infant on her lap, published in the magazine *Midweek Pictorial*—has become one of the best known images of the Great Depression.

An American Exodus: A Record of Human Erosion in the Thirties was a collection of Lange's photographs published in 1939. In the early World War II period, Lange photographed the mass internment of Japanese.

After the war, she did photo-essays for *Life* magazine. Lange died in 1965.

See also: newspapers and magazines; Okies; photography; Farm Security Adminstration; Resettlement Administration.

Bibliography

Lange, Dorothea. *An American Exodus: A Record of Human Erosion in the Thirties*. New Haven: Yale University Press, 1969.

Meltzer, Milton. *Dorothea Lange: A Photographer's Life*. Syracuse: Syracuse University Press, 2000.

LEDBETTER, HUDSON WILLIAM "LEADBELLY"

Legendary blues guitarist and composer Hudson William Ledbetter, shown here with his wife, was better known by his stage name "Leadbelly." *(Corbis)*

A blues composer who wandered the country as an itinerant musician from the 1910s to the 1940s, William Hudson Ledbetter—better known by his nickname "Leadbelly"—wrote some of his classic tunes during the 1930s, including "Scottsboro Boys" and "Bourgeois Blues."

Born the son of sharecroppers in Mooringsport, Louisiana in 1885, Ledbetter moved to Texas with his family and, from a young age, showed great musical talent, mastering the twelve-string guitar. After playing for a time in brothels, Ledbetter began the travels that would continue through the rest of his life.

Aside from earning money from his guitar-playing and singing, Ledbetter also got in trouble with the law, being in prison from 1918 to 1925 for murder and 1930 to 1934 for attempted murder. On both occasions, however, he won release through his music, the first time by writing a tune for the warden and the second time upon the request of music collector John A. Lomax.

Lomax then hired Ledbetter as his chauffeur and took him on a tour that introduced the guitarist and blues man to white audiences during the late 1930s and early 1940s. At the same time, he also recorded many of his compositions, including "Goodnight Irene" and "Rock Island Line." Aside from guitar, Ledbetter also played the accordion, harmonica, mandolin, and piano. Although Ledbetter died in 1949, his music is considered by music experts to be critical to the development of folk, rhythm and blues, and rock and roll.

See also: music.

Bibliography

Garvin, Richard M. *The Midnight Special: The Legend of Leadbelly.* New York: Bernard Geis Associates, 1971.

Wolfe, Charles K. *The Life and Legend of Leadbelly.* New York: HarperCollins, 1992.

LEMKE, WILLIAM

The chief ideologue of North Dakota's progressive, pro–small farmer Non Partisan League and one of the state's two representatives in Congress between 1933 and 1941, William Lemke ran as the presidential candidate of the populist, anti–New Deal Union Party in 1936, founded by radio priest Father Charles Coughlin and Huey P. Long's successor as head of the Share Our Wealth movement, Gerald L. K. Smith.

Born in Minnesota in 1878, Lemke graduated from the University of North Dakota in 1902 and received his law degree from Yale in 1905. A proponent of a utopian socialist community in Mexico, Lemke purchased land for that purpose. But his plan was disappointed by President Woodrow Wilson's hostility to the Mexican administration of Victoriano Huerta.

By 1915, Lemke had become the chief attorney for the Equity Cooperative Exchange, an agrarian advocacy organization. Chairman of the Republican state committee from 1916 to 1920, Lemke was also a member of the Non Partisan League's executive committee from 1917 to 1921. He is credited as the initiator of much of the league's legislative agenda, including the implementation of the state-owned Bank of North Dakota, a state grain elevator, the Workmen's Compensation Bureau, and agencies to provide low-cost credit and home loans to farmers.

Lemke was elected North Dakota's state attorney general in 1920 but lost the governor's race in 1922 and a race for the U.S. Senate as a member of the Farmer-Labor Party, an offshoot of the League, in 1926. Elected to the House of Representatives in 1932, he helped push through bankruptcy and mortgage acts designed to help economically troubled farmers and small businesspersons.

While Lemke generally supported Franklin D. Roosevelt and the New Deal, he reluctantly accepted the presidential nomination of the Union Party in 1936. But Coughlin's promise to galvanize 20 percent of the nation through his broadcasts failed and Lemke received about one-tenth that number of votes.

Except for a single term from 1941 to 1943, Lemke continued to serve in the House of Representatives until his death in 1950.

See also: election of 1936; Farmer-Labor Party; Share Our Wealth Society; Union Party; Coughlin, Father Charles; Long, Huey P.; Smith, Gerald L. K.

Bibliography

Bennett, Davis H. *Demagogues in the Depression: American Radicals and the Union Party, 1932–1936.* New Brunswick, NJ: Rutgers University Press, 1969.

Blackorby, Edward C. *Prairie Rebel: The Public Life of William Lemke.* Lincoln: University of Nebraska Press, 1963.

LEWIS, JOHN L.

John Llewellyn Lewis was born on February 12, 1880, in Lucas, Iowa, the son of a Welsh immigrant coal miner. After completing the seventh grade, he dropped out of school and became a coal miner himself, first in Lucas and from 1907 to 1909 in Panama, Illinois. While in Panama, he was elected president of the local United Mine Workers of America (UMW) organization and, in 1909, was elected by District 12 of the UMW to lobby as a legislative representative for state mine safety legislation in Illinois. Lewis served as a field and legislative representative for the American Federation of Labor (AFL) from 1910 to 1916 and, in 1917, was appointed chief statistician for the UMW and business manager for the *United Mine Workers Journal*. He was named UMW international vice president in 1917, acting UMW president in 1919, and international president in 1920, a post he held until his retirement in 1960.

With a membership of 700,000 in 1920, the UMW was the largest union affiliated with the AFL. During the 1920s, Lewis waged a series of bitter organizational battles within the UMW to centralize administrative and collective bargaining powers under his control, even as membership in the UMW dwindled to just 75,000 at the end of the decade. In 1926, he defeated a rival's bid for the UMW presidency amid charges of electoral fraud and, in the years that followed, successfully purged the organization of Communists and many of his opponents while fighting off challenges from rival unions such as the National Miners Union and the West Virginia Mine Workers.

In 1933, Lewis and UMW economist William Jett Lauck were instrumental in the passage of Section 7 of the National Industrial Recovery Act (NIRA), a key component of the Franklin D. Roosevelt administration's New Deal, and within three months more than 90 percent of U.S. coal miners had been organized under the federal relief program.

In 1934 and 1935, Lewis spearheaded efforts within the AFL to expand union organization efforts among mass-production and nonskilled workers, groups that had long been largely ignored by the AFL. While older, more established unions within the AFL had been organized along craft lines, New Deal programs such as the NIRA encouraged the establishment of new industrial unions that would organize all workers, regardless of specialty, within particular industries. Subsequently, Lewis and his allies within the AFL proposed the establishment of broad-based industrial unions that would encompass all employees, skilled and unskilled, in the steel, auto, and rubber industries.

When these initiatives were rebuffed by AFL president William Green, Lewis, frustrated with Green's cautious and conservative leadership, established the Committee for Industrial Organization (CIO) in 1935. By mid-1936, the CIO consisted of thirteen labor unions representing approximately 1,500,000 workers. The AFL executive council expelled the CIO unions, including the UMW, from its organization later that year, and Lewis's movement reorganized as the Congress of Industrial Organizations (CIO) in 1938.

The CIO quickly won contracts with the United States Steel Corporation, Goodyear Rubber Corporation, and General Motors Corporation, and by the end of 1937 CIO unions had a larger membership than did the AFL affiliates. Hundreds of thousands of previously nonunionized workers in mass-production industries had been organized into CIO-affiliated unions by the late 1930s, including thousands of African-American industrial workers.

A lifelong Republican, Lewis was nevertheless an early supporter of the Roosevelt administration, and in 1936 the CIO contributed $500,000 to the president's successful reelection campaign. However, disillusionment with the Roosevelt administration's handling of the "little steel" strike of 1937, failure to sufficiently curb unemployment, and interventionist foreign policy led Lewis to break with the president. By the late 1930s, Lewis had become the administration's most prominent and vocal labor critic, and in 1940 he endorsed the Republican presidential candidate, Wendell Wilkie. Following Roosevelt's reelection to a third term, Lewis resigned the CIO presidency and in 1942 withdrew the UMW from the organization he had helped found.

Following his resignation from the CIO, Lewis won significant concessions from mining interests in a series of mining strikes during World War II. In 1948, Lewis and the UMW were fined $2.1 million for civil and criminal contempt of court arising from UMW strikes in 1946 and 1948, but won royalties from the coal-mining companies on every ton of coal mined, which allowed for the financing of UMW welfare and retirement programs. An "open-end agreement" between the UMW and the Bituminous Coal Operators Association in 1951 halted strikes in the industry for several years, and in 1952 Lewis was instrumental in the passage of the first Federal Coal Mine Safety Act. After stepping down as president of the UMW in 1960, Lewis continued to serve until his death as president emeritus, chairman of the board of trustees, and chief executive officer of the Welfare and Retirement Fund. Lewis died in Washington, D.C., on June 11, 1969.

WILLIAM D. BAKER

See also: American Federation of Labor; automobile industry; Congress of Industrial Organizations; William Green; "little steel"; mining; Section 7 (National Industrial Recovery Act); strikes, general; strikes, sitdown; unions and union organizing; United Mine Workers.

Bibliography

Dubofsky, Melvyn, and Warren Van Tine. *John L. Lewis*. Urbana, IL: University of Illinois Press, 1986.

"Lewis, John L." In *Biographical Dictionary of American Labor Leaders*, ed. Gary M. Fink. Westport, CT: Greenwood Press, 1974.

"Lewis, John L." In *Current Biography 1942*, ed. Maxine Block. New York: H. W. Wilson, 1942.

Roberts, Ron E. *John L. Lewis: Hard Labor and Wild Justice*. Dubuque, IA: Kendall/Hunt, 1994.

Zieger, Robert H. *John L. Lewis: Labor Leader*. New York: Macmillan, 1988.

The most important and controversial labor leader of the 1930s, United Mine Workers chief John L. Lewis was instrumental in the creation of the Congress of Industrial Organizations. *(Brown Brothers)*

LEWIS, SINCLAIR

Nobel Prize for Literature winner in 1930 for his novels exploring and satirizing small-town American life in the 1910s and 1920s, Sinclair Lewis's most famous literary contribution to the Great Depression era was the 1935 novel *It Can't Happen Here*, about the rise of a fascist leader in the United States.

Born in Sauk Centre, Minnesota, in 1885, Lewis graduated from Yale University in 1907 and went to work as an editor at several publishing houses. Over the next two decades, Lewis wrote a number of journalistic pieces and novels, including *Babbitt* (1922), *Arrowsmith* (1925), and *Elmer Gantry* (1927).

It Can't Happen Here was Lewis's response to Adolf Hitler's takeover of Germany and, closer to home, the rise of Huey P. Long, the demagogic governor and senator of Louisiana, and his Share Our Wealth movement. The novel, depicting the takeover of the United States by a charismatic fascist leader, was turned into a theatrical production by the Federal Theater Project (FTP). With Lewis himself playing the lead role of Doremus Jessup, the production premiered in New York in 1935. Along with other productions, the play brought conservative press and political criticism that the FTP was under the control of leftists and Communists.

While Lewis continued to publish after World War II, his reputation had gone into decline. He died in 1951.

See also: literature; Share Our Wealth Society; Federal Theater Project; Nazism and Nazi Germany; Long, Huey P.

Bibliography

O'Connor, Richard. *Sinclair Lewis*. New York: McGraw-Hill, 1971.

Schorer, Mark. *Sinclair Lewis: An American Life*. New York: McGraw-Hill, 1961.

Winner of the Nobel Prize for Literature in 1930, Sinclair Lewis was author of the 1935 novel *It Can't Happen Here*, which depicted a fascist takeover of the United States. *(Library of Congress)*

LINDBERGH, CHARLES A.

The most famous aviator in American history after his pathbreaking solo flight across the Atlantic Ocean in 1927, Charles A. Lindbergh was a celebrity during the Great Depression for far more tragic and controversial reasons: in 1932, his infant son was kidnapped and killed which became a headline-making story; in 1938, Lindbergh was decorated by the Nazi government; and in 1940, he helped form the anti-interventionist America First Committee.

Lindbergh was born in Detroit in 1902; his father was a congressman from Minnesota, and the young Charles spent his early years between that state and Washington, D.C. He attended the University of Wisconsin for two years in the early 1920s before dropping out to go to aviation school in Nebraska. For the next few years, Lindbergh gave stunt-flying demonstrations and worked as an airmail pilot. After getting financial backing from some St. Louis businessmen, Lindbergh became the first to fly the Atlantic Ocean solo in 1927, becoming an immediate national hero.

In 1929, he married Anne Morrow, who gave birth to their first child, Charles Jr., in 1930. Two years later, the baby was kidnapped from the couple's New Jersey home and murdered. Because of Lindbergh's fame, the crime and the subsequent trial and execution of Bruno Richard Hauptmann brought the couple unwanted publicity. To flee the constant attention, they went to Europe, where Lindbergh toured the German air industry and was decorated by the Nazi government, an award that brought Lindbergh much criticism back in the United States.

Despite his warnings about Nazi air supremacy, Lindbergh remained adamantly opposed to U.S. aid to

Britain in its struggle against Nazi Germany from 1939 to 1941. In 1940, he joined with isolationist Senator Gerald Nye (R-ND) and General Robert Wood to form the anti-interventionist America First Committee. This activity, combined with his Nazi decoration, brought charges in the press that Lindbergh was a secret Nazi supporter. When President Franklin D. Roosevelt joined the chorus of criticism, Lindbergh resigned his commission in the Air Corps Reserve.

After the Japanese attack on Pearl Harbor in December 1941, the America First Committee was disbanded. Lindbergh, now a strong supporter of the war effort, became a consultant to aircraft companies producing warplanes and flew fifty combat missions as a civilian. After the war, Lindbergh worked as a consul-tant to Pan American Airways and the U.S. Defense Department. He died in 1974.

See also: Lindbergh kidnapping; America First Committee; World War II, early history of.

Bibliography

Cole, Wayne S. *Charles A. Lindbergh and the Battle Against American Intervention in World War II.* New York: Harcourt Brace Jovanovich, 1974.

Kennedy, Ludovic. *Crime of the Century: The Lindbergh Kidnapping and the Framing of Richard Hauptmann.* New York: Penguin, 1996.

Lindbergh, Charles Augustus. *Of Flight and Life.* New York: Charles Scribner's Sons, 1948.

LIPPMANN, WALTER

Essayist, newspaper columnist, and arguably the most influential political commentator of the 1930s, Walter Lippmann is remembered for, among other things, a 1932 column on Franklin D. Roosevelt that portrayed the Democratic presidential candidate as an "amiable" but ultimately lightweight political thinker.

Born in New York City in 1889, Lippmann graduated from Harvard University in 1909 and helped found *The New Republic* magazine in 1914. As a regular commentator for the liberal magazine, Lippmann influenced Woodrow Wilson's thinking on the formation of the League of Nations. After serving as editor of *The New Republic* from 1929 to 1931, Lippmann began writing his "Today and Tomorrow" column for the New York *Herald Tribune*, which was eventually syndicated in over 250 newspapers in the United States and twenty-five countries around the world.

As the Depression began, Lippmann was critical of President Herbert Hoover, saying he was too slow in his response to the economic difficulties and too supportive of the interests of big business. Yet, in the 1932 campaign, he dismissed Roosevelt as a "boy scout" who was "too eager to please."

As the Depression deepened, however, Lippmann advised president-elect Roosevelt in January 1933 to take on dictatorial powers to combat the Depression. But later in the 1930s, Lippmann warned of the growing bureaucratization of American society because of the plethora of New Deal programs and agencies. Always a liberal anti-Marxist, Lippmann grew increasingly suspicious of social democracy as well.

An ardent internationalist, Lippmann tried to drum up support for U.S. aid to Britain in the latter part of the 1930s. Continuing to write his column during and after the war, Lippmann coined the phrase the "Cold War" to define the growing tensions between America and the Soviet Union and advocated an interventionist American foreign policy. Lippmann died in 1974.

See also: *New Republic, The*; newspapers and magazines; World War II, early history of; Roosevelt, Franklin D.

Bibliography

Lippmann, Walter. *A New Social Order.* New York: The John Day Co., 1933.

Lippmann, Walter. *An Inquiry into the Principles of the Good Society.* Boston: Little, Brown, 1937.

Steel, Ronald. *Walter Lippmann and the American Century.* Boston: Little, Brown, 1980.

LOMBARD, CAROLE

One of the most popular comedic actresses in Hollywood films during the Great Depression era, Carole Lombard is best remembered for her roles in a series of fast-paced screwball comedies, including *Twentieth Century* (1934), *My Man Godfrey* (1936), and *Nothing Sacred* (1937).

Born Jane Alice Peters in Indiana in 1908, she was discovered by Hollywood director Alain Dwan when she was just twelve years old and became one of the bathing beauties featured in producer Max Sennett's silent short films of the 1920s. Her debut in feature films came with *High Voltage* in 1929.

Beautiful and talented—her costar in *Twentieth Century*, the legendary John Barrymore, said she was the best actress he had ever worked with—Lombard continued to make movies through the early 1940s. Perhaps her best-known role is as a spoiled rich girl who adopts a homeless person, played by William Powell, in *My Man Godfrey*.

Lombard was as famous for her personal life as for her film career, having married stars Powell and Clark Gable. Lombard's last film was Ernest Lubitsch's comedy about life in wartime Poland, *To Be or Not To Be*, with Jack Benny. Lombard died in 1942 in an airplane crash while on tour selling war bonds.

See also: films, feature; Gable, Clark; Powell, William.

Bibliography

Ott, Frederick W. *The Films of Carole Lombard.* Secaucus, NJ: Citadel Press, 1972.

Swindell, Larry. *Screwball: The Life of Carole Lombard.* New York: Morrow, 1975.

LOMBARDO, GUY

Bandleader and musician, Guy Lombardo hosted a New Year's eve radio show that may have been the most listened-to annual broadcast of the 1930s.

Born in London, Ontario, in 1902, Lombardo came from a musical family and was classically trained on the violin. He began his performing career in Cleveland in the 1920s and made his first national broadcast in 1927 from Chicago. Two years later, he moved to New York and began his annual winter show from the Roosevelt Room, including his New Year's eve broadcast that always concluded with the playing of "Auld Lang Syne."

As leader of his band The Royal Canadians, Lombardo was often dismissed as the "king of corn" for his old-fashioned, sentimental composing and conducting. But he was immensely popular from the 1930s to the 1960s. Lombardo died in 1977.

See also: music; radio.

Bibliography

Brown, Robert J. *Manipulating the Ether: The Power of Broadcast Radio in Thirties America.* Jefferson, NC: McFarland, 1998.

Dunning, John. *On the Air: The Encyclopedia of Old-Time Radio.* New York: Oxford University Press, 1998.

LONG, HUEY P.

Huey Pierce Long Jr. was born into a middle-class family in Winn Parish, Louisiana, on August 30, 1893. As a boy, he absorbed many of the ideas that came out of the strong populist and socialist traditions in the area. A gifted student, Long's imperiousness and persistent quarreling with school officials probably caused him to be expelled from high school in 1910. For the next four years, Long worked as a travelling salesman in the South and Midwest, selling canned goods and patent medicines. He met Rose McConnell in 1910 at a pie-baking contest in Shreveport, and the couple married two years later. They moved to New Orleans in 1914, where Long enrolled in law school at Tulane University. After less than a year of coursework, Long petitioned for a special bar examination, which he passed with ease. Long began practicing as a lawyer, winning a number of compensation suits for injured workers against large corporations.

For Long, though, the law served merely as a springboard for his political ambitions. In 1918, at age 25, he was elected to the Louisiana Railroad Commission. During the campaign, Long made use of techniques that would characterize his political activities throughout his career: heavy use of circulars and posters, withering attacks on opponents, and extensive travel through rural areas in an automobile to directly engage poor, rural voters. In addition, Long began to compile a mass mailing list, make contacts, cultivate allies, and thereby to establish a vibrant political machine that would form the basis of his power as Governor and Senator. It was also during this period that the outlines of Long's political vision began to publicly emerge. He immediately exploited the unrealized potential of his new office to attack the unregulated power of the companies that ran the railroad, telephone, telegraph, and pipeline companies. He worked incessantly to limit the powers of these utilities, reduce rates and improve services. While only modestly successful, Long gained significant public attention as an emerging political force and as a champion of "the little man" against the rich and privileged.

After beating back an attempted impeachment by his political foes in 1921, Long made his first run for governor as a Democrat in 1924. Sporting his trademark white linen suit, Long tirelessly stumped the state, handing out thousands of circulars, personally nailing posters to trees and signposts, sending literature to his ever expanding mailing list, and exploiting the power of radio to get his message out. Positioning himself as a political outsider, Long railed against the incumbent governor as a tool of corporate interests. He denounced Standard Oil, one of the state's largest businesses, as corrupt and predatory, and attacked the entrenched power of local political bosses. Although he lost the 1924 primary election, Long spent the next four years expanding his base of support. Large crowds gathered wherever he spoke, waving signs and banners proclaiming his new campaign slogan: "Every Man a King, But No One Wears a Crown." Long effectively tapped the anger and resentment of many poor Louisianans as well as their hopes and aspirations. Voters responded to Long's class-based politics by overwhelmingly electing him governor of Louisiana in 1928 at the age of thirty-five.

As governor, Long combined a compassion for the poor and downtrodden with a ruthless ambition for personal power. He quickly consolidated unprecedented power over all levels of the state government and forced through the legislature a program of progressive legislation that made good on his campaign promises. Among the numerous accomplishments of this early phase of Long's governorship was a measure to provide free textbooks to public and private school children, a bond issue that resulted in the paving of more than 5,000 miles of roads, and a bill authorizing the piping of cheap natural gas to New Orleans. Following a five-cent per barrel tax on refined oil in 1929, though, the Standard Oil Company and other wealthy Louisiana interests spearheaded another impeachment effort against Long. Narrowly escaping conviction in the state senate, Long quickly moved to further consolidate his power throughout the state and became increasingly ruthless in the pursuit of his goals. He mercilessly wielded his patronage power to reward allies and punish foes. When conservative foes attempted to block his plan to raze the old governor's mansion, he simply assembled a crew of convicts from the state prison, led them to the mansion, and personally oversaw its destruction. Similarly, to counter unfavorable press coverage in major Louisiana newspapers, Long

On March 8, 1935, Louisiana Senator Huey P. Long delivers a radio address in which he bitterly attacks the Roosevelt administration and outlines plans for his "Share Our Wealth" program. *(Brown Brothers)*

established his own newspaper and built an expensive sound truck to blitz the state. He also began to take on more visible trappings of power: chauffeured automobiles, a private police force, and expensive clothes. Long financed this personal power structure through the "deduct box," a system of automatic cash deductions from the salaries of all state employees. To his foes, the Long administration was a "virtual dictatorship"; to his allies, he was simply "the Kingfish."

Barred by state law from seeking a second term as governor in 1932, Long successfully ran for the U.S. Senate in 1930, and, with the aid of his private police force, installed his boyhood friend, Oscar "OK" Allen, in the governor's mansion. Long did not take his seat in Washington until 1932, opting instead to maintain his iron grip on state politics in Louisiana. While democratic institutions and processes undoubtedly continued to suffer and deteriorate under Long during this period, his list of accomplishments also grew: thousands of citizens were put to work on public projects, building roads and bridges, a medical school and a sports facility at Louisiana State University, an airport

in New Orleans, and a new capitol building; night schools for adults were established to combat illiteracy; the state's woefully inadequate public-health system was improved; and state supported school busses were supplied for public school students. As a result of this spate of activity, though, annual state spending increased from $29 million to 1928 to $83 million in 1931, and state debt rose from $11 million to $125 million over the same period.

Long supported Franklin Delano Roosevelt in the 1932 presidential election, but their relationship became increasingly adversarial as both men moved under the spotlight of national politics. Long's disappointment at the lack of patronage his state received once Roosevelt took office and the relatively moderate shape of most early New Deal programs, as well as his own national political ambitions, prompted him to increasingly oppose the president in the Senate. Long effectively used the filibuster to block or delay several key New Deal measures. On February 23, 1934, Long organized the "Share Our Wealth Society" with the goal of taxing the rich to give aid to the poor. The plan sought to eliminate poverty by guaranteeing every family a minimum annual income of $5,000, by providing old-age pensions to those over sixty years of age and free education through college, and by canceling all personal debt. These boldly redistributionary policies were to be paid for by steep taxes on all inherited fortunes over $1 million and by limiting annual individual incomes to a maximum of $1 million. By 1935, there were over 27,000 local "Share Our Wealth Society" clubs spread throughout every state (although most were in the South), and membership topped 7 million. Unlike other critics of the New Deal at the time, Long had a powerful popular base of support. As the 1936 presidential election approached, Long appeared to be the most serious political threat to Roosevelt's reelection bid. On September 10, 1935, though, Dr. Carl A. Weiss, the son-in-law of a political opponent in Louisiana, assassinated Long on the capitol steps of his home state, thereby ending the rapid ascent of one of the most colorful and controversial political figures of the Depression era.

PATRICK D. JONES

See also: Share Our Wealth Society; Document: Huey P. Long's "Every Man a King" Speech, 1934.

Bibliography

Williams, Thomas Harry. *Huey Long.* New York: Random House, 1981.

LOUIS, JOE

On June 22, 1937, boxer Joe Louis—popularly known as the "Brown Bomber"—knocked out James Braddock to take the heavyweight crown. Until he retired from boxing on March 1, 1949, Louis remained the heavyweight champion of the world, holding the title longer than any other boxer in the history of the sport.

Born Joseph Louis Barrow to sharecroppers in Lexington, Alabama in 1914, he moved with his family to Detroit in 1924, where he began his boxing career. After losing his first amateur bout, Louis went on to win the U.S. Amateur Athletic Union 175-pound-plus division championship in 1934. That same year, he turned professional. In 1935, he knocked out Primo Carnera and Max Baer, both former heavyweight champions.

In 1936, he met German heavyweight Max Schmeling—pride of Nazi Germany—but lost in a twelfth-round knockout. Hitler touted Schmeling's victory as proof of Aryan racial superiority. But Louis responded by winning seven fights and the right to take on Braddock in 1937. After that victory, he met Schmeling again a year later and knocked him out.

Louis would go on to beat a number of other previous and subsequent heavyweights, including Max Baer, Jack Sharkey, and Jersey Joe Walcott, over the next twelve years. These victories made Louis a hero in the African-American community. In 1942, Louis was inducted into the army and performed in 100 exhibition matches for the troops. While unwilling to speak out against racism in civilian society, Louis did criticize segregation in the military.

He continued to fight after the war until his retirement in 1948. But financial troubles forced him back into the ring until his knockout loss to Rocky Marciano in 1951. Louis then became a professional wrestler and a greeter at Las Vegas hotels. He died in 1981.

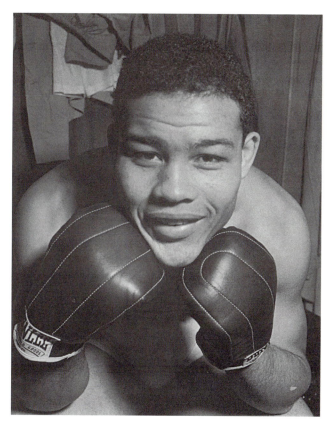

Known popularly as the "brown bomber," Joe Louis was the most accomplished heavy-weight boxer of his generation, winning the championship in 1937 and retaining it until his retirement twelve years later. *(Brown Brothers)*

See also: sports; Nazi Germany.

Bibliography

Barrow, Joe Louis, and Barbara Munder. *Joe Louis: 50 Years an American Hero.* New York: McGraw-Hill, 1988.

Mead, Chris. *Champion—Joe Louis: Black Hero in White America.* New York: Scribner, 1985.

LUCE, HENRY R.

Founder and owner of a vast publishing empire that, by the end of the 1930s, included *Time, Fortune*, and *Life* magazines, Henry R. Luce was an internationalist Republican who used his news outlets in the late 1930s to promote U.S. support for China in its struggle against Japanese invaders.

Born in China in 1898 to missionary parents, Luce spent the first dozen years of his life in the Asian country until he was sent to England and then the United States to attend preparatory schools. He then went to Yale University, where he edited the school paper.

He introduced the breezily written and stylishly designed newsweekly *Time* in 1922 and purchased the business magazine *Fortune* in 1930. The following year, he began the radio series *The March of Time*, following it up in 1935 with the newsreel series of the same name.

Still, Luce's greatest journalistic innovation is widely considered to be *Life* magazine. In 1937, he launched the photo-heavy magazine, featuring a picture by famed photographer Margaret Bourke-White on its premier issue cover. *Life* became the preeminent mass-distribution photo magazine of the late 1930s. While it did not invent the documentary photo-essay, it made it a popular news format and art genre.

Even as Luce was bringing fine photography to millions of magazine readers, he was also promoting his internationalist agenda, eagerly promoting the cause of the Chinese people struggling against Japanese invaders. Ultimately, Luce was a major figure behind the rising tensions between the United States and Japan in the late 1930s and early 1940s. At the same time, Luce's conservatism was shown in his bitter opposition to the Republican government in the Spanish Civil War, which he accused of being Communist-run. His 1941 book *The American Century* argued for an internationalist American foreign policy.

After the war, Luce's Time-Life empire introduced other magazines, including *Sports Illustrated*. Luce died in 1967.

See also: *Life*; newspapers and magazines; photography; *Time*; China; Spanish Civil War; World War II, early history of; Bourke-White, Margaret.

Bibliography

Baughman, James L. *Henry R. Luce and the Rise of the American News Media*. Boston: Twayne, 1987.

Jessup, John K., ed. *The Ideas of Henry Luce*. New York: Atheneum, 1969.

Luce, Henry R. *The American Century*. New York: Farrar & Rinehart, 1941.

MacARTHUR, DOUGLAS

Commander of American forces in the Pacific theater of World War II, Douglas MacArthur was the military commander charged with dispersing the Bonus Army, a group of veterans encamped in the nation's capital who—facing unemployment and poverty in the Great Depression—demanded an expedited payment of their World War I bonuses.

MacArthur, born in Little Rock, Arkansas, in 1880, came from a long line of military officers and graduated from West Point in 1903 at the top of his class. An aide to commanding officers and an officer in the engineering corps, MacArthur first served overseas during a brief U.S. occupation of Veracruz during the Mexican civil war.

During World War I, MacArthur reached the rank of brigadier general, commanding a full army division in France and in the occupation of the German Rhineland after the war. In the downsized military of the isolationist interwar period, MacArthur served as West Point superintendent, commander in the U.S. territory of the Philippines, and commander at stateside bases. He was made army chief of staff in 1930.

While MacArthur was one World War I veteran rising through the ranks, others were not so fortunate.

General Douglas MacArthur (*left*) supervised the forced removal of the Bonus Army from the nation's capital in the spring of 1932. He is shown in this 1932 photo with his subordinate, future World War II allied commander and U.S. President Dwight D. Eisenhower. (*Brown Brothers*)

In spring 1932, some 20,000 unemployed veterans came to Washington, D.C., demanding that their service bonus—promised to them for 1945—be paid immediately. While the House of Representatives passed a measure to do that, the Senate refused. Some veterans went home; thousands of others pitched camps in the Anacostia Flats section of the city.

By July, President Herbert Hoover and police authorities in Washington decided that the veterans should be moved. A dispute with police that resulted in the shooting of several veterans—and the death of one—led MacArthur to move against the veterans. The general gave them one hour to take their possessions and go, and when the time was up troops moved in with tear gas and bayonets. The sight of impoverished veterans under attack from U.S. troops tarnished Hoover's name.

In fact, Hoover never gave the order; MacArthur—in a pattern of insubordination to presidential commanders-in-chief that would continue through the Korean War—took the initiative on his own. Hoover did little to reprimand MacArthur. Many political observers at the time saw MacArthur's action as a move by the right wing to push Hoover to take tougher law-and-order measures against Depression-era protesters.

MacArthur also had strained relations with Franklin D. Roosevelt. When the new president ordered further cuts in the already diminished military in 1933, MacArthur spoke back in terms that the president considered highly insulting. Later, Roosevelt would describe MacArthur as one of the two most dangerous men in America, along with the populist Louisiana politician Huey P. Long.

MacArthur retired from the military in 1937, but he did not leave public life. In the later years of the decade, MacArthur—not surprisingly for an ex-military man—spoke out strongly against isolationists in Congress and insisted that the United States needed to beef up its military preparedness. In July 1941, he was recalled to active duty and dispatched to the Philippines, where he conducted a tough rear guard action against the advancing Japanese in the early days of America's involvement in World War II.

MacArthur would go on to command U.S. forces in the Pacific and would be the senior authority in the postwar occupation of Japan. The general was also in command in the Korean War, although his insistence on taking the war to China resulted in his firing by President Harry Truman. Returning to the United States as a military hero, MacArthur nevertheless faded from view as a public figure and died in 1964.

See also: Bonus Army; Bonus bills; World War II, early history of; Hoover, Herbert.

Bibliography

James, Dorris Clayton. *The Years of MacArthur: Volume One 1880–1941.* Boston: Houghton Mifflin, 1970.

MacArthur, Douglas. *Reminiscences.* New York: McGraw-Hill, 1978.

Manchester, William Raymond. *American Caesar: Douglas MacArthur, 1880–1964.* Boston: Little, Brown, 1978.

MacDONALD, RAMSAY

Labour Party prime minister of Great Britain at the outset of the Great Depression, Ramsay MacDonald was seen by many Labourites as a traitor to the party when—after offering his resignation in 1931—he changed his mind and formed a coalition with Liberals and Conservatives that ruled Britain until 1935.

Born James Ramsay MacDonald to an unwed domestic servant in Scotland in 1866, the future prime minister managed to graduate from the British equivalent of high school by tutoring fellow students. At nineteen, he became involved in leftist politics and worked for the socialist Fabian Society. In 1900, he was picked to be first secretary of the Labour Representation Committee (LRC), the predecessor of Britain's Labour Party.

In 1906, he joined twenty-eight other LRC members to win election to the House of Commons, when the LRC was renamed the Labour Party. Head of the party from 1911 to 1914, he was forced to resign after protesting Britain's declaration of war against Germany at the beginning of World War I and was defeated in the 1918 parliamentary election.

In 1922, he returned to Parliament and was chosen to lead the Labour opposition. Briefly prime minister in 1924, MacDonald returned to the office after his party won the general elections of 1929. MacDonald is best remembered for his efforts at international disarmament during his two years as prime minister from 1929 to 1931, but he was largely ineffective in combating the effects of the Depression.

Attempting to borrow gold to protect the pound, MacDonald was forced by the nation's creditors to cut government spending, including unemployment benefits. This unpopular move led to the resignation of his cabinet on August 23, 1935, which MacDonald joined. But next day, he announced that he had changed his mind and formed a coalition government with the Liberal and Conservative Parties.

Labour Party leaders denounced him as a turncoat, but MacDonald continued as prime minister in the coalition government through 1935. With Neville Chamberlain as his finance minister, he removed Britain from the gold standard, cut government expenditures, and raised tariffs, the latter a marked break from the country's traditional support of free trade. With the pound falling, exports grew. A drop in interest rates spurred the economy, and the country slowly revived from the depths of depression, even though unemployment remained high.

According to an agreement, MacDonald exchanged places with Stanley Baldwin, lord president of the council, ending his term as prime minister in June 1935. Resigning from the council post shortly thereafter, MacDonald went into retirement and died on a trip to South America in 1937.

See also: Great Britain; Baldwin, Stanley; Chamberlain, Neville.

Bibliography

Marquand, David. *Ramsay MacDonald*. London: Jonathan Cape, 1977.

Morgan, Austen. *J. Ramsay MacDonald*. Manchester, UK: Manchester University Press, 1987.

MacLEISH, ARCHIBALD

One of America's most respected poets and playwrights, librarian of Congress, and, during World War II, an assistant secretary of state, Archibald MacLeish was one of the earliest and most insistent voices warning against the threat of fascism both in the United States and around the world in the early 1930s.

Born in Glencoe, Illinois, in 1892, MacLeish went to Yale University and spent several years practicing law in Boston. In 1923, he left his job for France and a chance to devote himself full-time to poetry writing. After five years living and writing in Europe, MacLeish returned to the United States and published his impressions of the changing landscape of America in a collection of poems entitled *New Found Land* (1930).

By the early 1930s, MacLeish was infusing his poetry with paeans to liberal democracy and warnings against the threat of fascism. He called these his "public poems," and they included *Conquistador* (1932), *Rockefeller's City* (1933), *Public Speech* (1936), and *America Was Promises* (1939). At the same time, MacLeish wrote several radio dramas in verse on the same themes; *Fall of the City* (1937) and *Air Raid* (1938) are the best known.

MacLeish was appointed librarian of Congress in 1939 and then assistant secretary of state in 1944. MacLeish worked in several other government positions through 1949, when he took up a professorship at Harvard. He continued to write verse for books, the stage, and broadcast through much of the rest of his life. MacLeish died in 1982.

See also: fascism, domestic; literature; radio.

Bibliography

MacLeish, Archibald. *A Continuing Journey*. Boston: Houghton Mifflin, 1968.

Smith, Grover Cleveland. *Archibald MacLeish*. Minneapolis: University of Minnesota Press, 1971.

MAO ZEDONG

Chairman of the Chinese Communist Party, leader of the Chinese revolution, and chief of state of the People's Republic of China, Mao Zedong (the old-style transliteration was spelled Mao Tse-tung) spent the 1930s holding together communist forces besieged by the Kuomintang, or Nationalist Chinese, and Japanese invaders.

The son of a self-made, prosperous grain dealer, Mao was born in Hunan province in 1893 and ran away from home to study in the provincial capital of Ch'ang-sha with Nationalist reformers who were determined to overthrow the Manchu dynasty and establish a Chinese republic. When the revolution of 1911 broke out, Mao enlisted in the republican forces. Following the establishment of the republic, Mao drifted for a while and then returned to school, enrolling in Peking (now Beijing) University, the country's premier institution of higher learning. There, he became involved with the May Fourth Movement of 1919, which advocated Marxism-Leninism over western liberalism as the best future course for China.

In the early 1920s, Mao became active in the Chinese Communist Party, which was then in an alliance with the Kuomintang, organizing peasants in Hunan province into pro-revolutionary associations. After the death of Sun Yat-sen, who had led the Kuomintang since the revolution of 1911, a split had developed between the Communists and the Nationalists—now under the leadership of General Chiang Kai-shek—and Mao was forced to flee to Canton (now Guangzhou). Chiang then launched attacks on urban communist groups, forcing them to flee to mountains in southeastern China, where they set up the Kiangsi revolutionary government. During this period, Mao and the Communists developed their concept of rural, peasant-based revolution that would come to power by surrounding and choking off urban areas.

In 1934, Chiang led a new offensive against the

Communists, forcing Mao and 8,000 of his followers to make their "Long March" to the remote northwestern mountain enclave at Yenan. In 1936, however, a number of Nationalist generals forced Chiang to form an anti-Japanese alliance with the Communists, which the Nationalist leader reluctantly agreed to. (The Japanese had invaded the northern province of Manchuria in 1931 and were making threatening noises against the rest of China in the mid-1930s).

After the 1937 Japanese invasion of China, Mao divided his forces into small groups and spread them around the countryside, in order to both harass the Japanese forces and prepare the peasantry for communist revolution. In his mountain fortress of Yenan, he developed the theories of revolution that he would employ after the defeat of the Japanese in 1945, during the Chinese civil war from 1945 to 1949, and once in power as the leader of the new People's Republic of China after 1949.

From 1949 until 1958, Mao served as both chief of state of the newly proclaimed People's Republic of China and chairman of the Communist Party Central Committee. He resigned as chief of state in 1958 to concentrate on the Party's goals. Mao remained influential as a statesman, adviser, and Communist Party chairman until his death in 1976.

See also: China; Japan; Manchuria, invasion of; Chiang Kai-shek.

Bibliography

Short, Philip. *Mao: A Life*. New York: Henry Holt, 2000.

Snow, Edgar. *Red Star Over China*. New York: Random House, 1938.

Starr, John Bryan. *Continuing the Revolution: The Political Thought of Mao*. Princeton: Princeton University Press, 1979.

Terrill, Ross. *Mao: A Biography*. New York: Harper & Row, 1980.

MARCANTONIO, VITO

Elected from New York to the House of Representatives as a member of the leftist American Labor Party (ALP), Vito Marcantonio was perhaps the most radical member of Congress during his terms there from 1935 to 1951. He not only defended Communists but argued for civil rights legislation and increased funding for antipoverty programs.

Marcantonio was the son of an immigrant mother and a first-generation American-born father—both of Italian descent—and was born in Italian Harlem (now Spanish Harlem) in upper Manhattan in 1902. He was educated in New York City's public school system and became a political organizer for his future mentor and future mayor of New York, Fiorello La Guardia, who was running for Congress in 1922.

Radicalized in the heavily socialist districts of immigrant New York City in the 1920s and early 1930s, Marcantonio made close friends in the various communities of upper Manhattan, including African Americans, Puerto Ricans, Italians, Jews, and other immigrant groups. This formed the basis of a coalition that would put a man who was, for all intents and purposes, a socialist in the U.S. Congress for sixteen years.

Like La Guardia, however, Marcantonio started out as a progressive Republican, standing against the Democratic machine that ran New York. Unlike his mentor, Marcantonio left the Republicans to form the radical ALP in the mid-1930s. After winning his first two terms as a Republican, Marcantonio ran on the ALP ticket in 1939.

As an outsider, Marcantonio had a hard time in Congress, being excluded from all the important committees. Yet he was a master of parliamentary procedure and used those skills to advance his agenda of civil rights and more public funding for New York jobs programs. His efforts to prevent federal contracts from going to firms that practiced discrimination were repeatedly defeated.

Marcantonio continued to represent his Harlem district through the early Cold War and red scare of the late 1940s, until he was finally defeated in the 1950 election. When he died in 1954, the New York archbishop refused to give him a Catholic burial because he had broken with the church.

See also: African Americans; American Labor Party; Communist Party; Republican Party; La Guardia, Fiorello.

Bibliography

Jackson, Peter. "Vito Marcantonio and Ethnic Politics in New York." *Ethnic and Racial Studies*, vol. 6 (January 1983): 50–72.

Meyer, Gerald. *Vito Marcantonio: Radical Politician, 1902–1954*. Albany: State University of New York, 1989.

Rubinstein, Annette, ed. *I Vote My Conscience: Debates, Speeches, and Writings of Vito Marcantonio*. New York: Vito Marcantonio Memorial, 1956.

MARSHALL, GEORGE C.

After two decades of isolationist neglect in the 1920s and 1930s, United States Army chief of staff, General George C. Marshall was the man most responsible for organizing the rebuilding of America's military for World War II.

Born in the mining community of Uniontown, Pennsylvania in 1880, Marshall was the son of a well-off coal merchant. Although he did poorly at the Virginia Military Institute at first, he soon excelled and was head of his class by his senior year. After graduating in 1901, Marshall served in the Philippines and in France during World War I, becoming chief of operations of the First Army in 1918. Known for his quiet confidence and exceptional organizational abilities, Marshall continued to rise through the ranks even in the greatly shrunken military of the interwar years.

These abilities brought him to the attention of President Franklin D. Roosevelt, who appointed Marshall army chief of staff on September 1, 1939, the day Germany invaded Poland and two days before World War II began. But while Roosevelt greatly respected Marshall's abilities, the two disagreed about how the U.S. military buildup should proceed in the period between September 1939 and December 1941, when the United States officially entered the war. Marshall did not believe that the United States should expend its still limited military resources aiding the British, who he believed were on the verge of collapse. Instead, he felt that most of the resources should be focused on creating a potent U.S. military force. In the end, he was overruled by Roosevelt, who pushed a number of bills through Congress—most notably the Lend-Lease Act of early 1941—providing vast monetary and military aid to Britain and other countries fighting Nazi Germany and imperial Japan.

Marshall remained as chief of staff through the war and is largely credited with organizing America's military-industrial system for victory. After the war, he served as secretary of state from 1947 to 1949 and secretary of defense from 1950 to 1951. He is best known for the Marshall Plan, a massive aid program that helped rebuild Western Europe after the war, for which he won the Nobel Peace Prize in 1953. Marshall died in 1959.

See also: Lend-Lease Act; Great Britain; World War II, early history of; Roosevelt, Franklin D.; Document: Lend-Lease Act, March 11, 1941.

Bibliography

Mosley, Leonard. *Marshall: Hero for Our Times*. New York: Hearst Books, 1982.

Stoler, Mark A. *George C. Marshall: Soldier-Statesman of the American Century*. Boston: Twayne, 1989.

MARX BROTHERS

A group of zany comedic brothers who began their performance career on the stage and moved on to radio and screen, the Marx Brothers starred in a series of fast-moving, often slapstick comedy films in the 1930s that featured absurd dialogue, improbable situations, and offbeat characters.

There were five Marx Brothers originally: Chico (born 1886, originally Leonard); Harpo (born 1888, originally Adolph); Groucho (born 1890, originally Julius); Gummo (born 1893, originally Milton); and Zeppo (born 1901, originally Herbert). All were born in New York City.

In 1904, their mother put the brothers into a vaudeville act and they soon became a hit on the vaudeville circuit, though, by 1918, Gummo had left the troupe. By the early 1920s, they were starring on the Broadway stage, billed first as "The Four Nightingales" and then as the "Marx Brothers." Some of their Broadway hits, like *Cocoanuts* (1925) and *Animal Crackers* (1928), would later be turned into hit movies.

One of the most popular comedy teams in American film history, the Marx Brothers are shown here in a publicity still from the 1933 movie *Duck Soup*. Clockwise from top left are Zeppo, Groucho, Harpo, and Chico. *(Brown Brothers)*

After heading to Hollywood in the late 1920s, they turned out a string of box office hits in rapid succession, most of which have become classics of the American comedic movie tradition, including *Cocoanuts* (1929), *Animal Crackers* (1930), *Monkey Business* (1931), *Duck Soup* (1933), *A Night at the Opera* (1935), and *A Day at the Races* (1937).

Each of the Marx Brothers had his signature style. Groucho was usually the leader of the troupe, supplying strings of snappy one-liners that seemed like complete non sequiturs. Harpo, playing a mute, honked a large bicycle horn to make his points or grab attention. Chico, inexplicably, spoke with a heavy Italian accent, and Zeppo, the least comedic of the four, often played the straight man.

The group went their separate ways in the late 1930s, as Zeppo became an agent and Chico a band-leader. Of the four, Groucho had the longest lasting career after the Marx Brothers, appearing in several movies and hosting a popular television show, *You Bet Your Life*, in the 1950s.

Chico died in 1961; Harpo in 1964; Groucho in 1977; Gummo in 1977; and Zeppo in 1979.

See also: films, feature; radio.

Bibliography

Louvish, Simon. *Monkey Business: The Lives and Legends of the Marx Brothers: Groucho, Chico, Harpo, Zeppo, with added Gummo.* London: Faber and Faber, 1999.

Mitchell, Glenn. *The Marx Brothers Encyclopedia.* London: Batsford, 1996.

MAYER, LOUIS B.

Among the most powerful and influential Hollywood producers of the 1920s and 1930s, Louis B. Mayer was one of the cofounders of the Metro-Goldwyn-Mayer (MGM) studios and creator of the star system, whereby studios nurtured film stars and kept them under contract.

Born Eliezer Mayer in Minsk, Russia (now Belarus), in 1885, the future movie mogul emigrated to the United States as a child and worked for his father's scrap iron business. In 1907, he opened his first nickelodeon, or arcade movie theater, in Massachusetts. Within a decade or so, he owned the largest chain of movie theaters in New England.

To create a product to show on his screens, Mayer opened studios in Hollywood called Louis B. Mayer Pictures and Metro Pictures Corporation. In 1924, he merged his outfits with Samuel Goldwyn's Goldwyn Pictures Corporation to form MGM. During the 1920s and 1930s, and under Mayer's control, MGM focused on escapist entertainment that featured expensive sets and costumes and lots of pretty actresses, including *Grand Hotel* (1932) and *Dinner at Eight* (1933). Among the stars under contract at MGM were Clark Gable and Greta Garbo.

In 1934, Mayer helped organize business leaders to defeat the radical Upton Sinclair and his End Poverty in California campaign for governor on the Democratic ticket.

Mayer gave up control of the studio after the war and died in 1957.

See also: End Poverty in California; films, feature; Gable, Clark; Garbo, Greta; Goldwyn, Samuel; Sinclair, Upton.

Bibliography

Carey, Gary. *All the Stars in Heaven: Louis B. Mayer's MGM.* New York: Dutton, 1981.

Higham, Charles. *Merchant of Dreams: Louis B. Mayer, M.G.M., and the Secret Hollywood.* New York: D. I. Fine, 1993.

McCORMICK, ROBERT R.

Publisher of the conservative newspaper the *Chicago Tribune* during the 1930s, Robert R. McCormick was one of the most influential and outspoken critics of Franklin D. Roosevelt, lambasting both the administration's New Deal legislation in the early and middle part of the decade and its efforts to aid Britain in its fight against Nazi Germany in the late 1930s and early 1940s.

McCormick, born in Chicago in 1880, came from an illustrious heritage. His great-uncle, Cyrus McCormick, had invented the mechanical reaper in the nineteenth century and founded the McCormick Reaper Company (now International Harvester). His grandfather was Joseph Medill, who edited and published the *Chicago Tribune* from 1855 to 1899.

McCormick started out as a politician, serving in local city offices in the early 1900s. In 1911, he became president of the Chicago Tribune Company, coediting the paper with his cousin Joseph Medill Patterson. In World War I, he won a Distinguished Service Medal in France. In 1925, McCormick gained sole control of the newspaper.

With its 1-million-strong readership, McCormick's *Tribune* became the voice of Republican conservatism on domestic issues and midwestern isolationism on foreign ones. Not only did the archconservative McCormick label Franklin D. Roosevelt a "communist," he called Herbert Hoover "the greatest state socialist in history."

By the late 1930s, McCormick was speaking out forcefully against any American efforts to get involved in the conflicts in Europe and Asia, opposing every bill that promised aid to Britain and other countries fighting against Germany and Japan. He called the 1941 Lend-Lease Act, which provided military loans and aid to Britain, the "dictator bill," after Roosevelt. His paper also released a secret government military preparedness report on the eve of the Japanese attack on Pearl Harbor in early December 1941, which government officials and many members of the public considered an act bordering on treason. He was also an outspoken critic of post–World War II aid to Europe.

McCormick died in 1955.

See also: newspapers and magazines; Lend-Lease Act; World War II, early history of.

Bibliography

Edwards, Jerome E. *The Foreign Policy of Col. McCormick's Tribune, 1929–1941.* Reno: University of Nevada Press, 1971.

Smith, Richard Norton. *The Colonel: The Life and Legend of Robert R. McCormick, 1880–1955.* Boston: Houghton Mifflin, 1997.

MELLON, ANDREW W.

A wealthy financier and industrialist, Andrew W. Mellon was appointed secretary of the treasury by President Warren G. Harding in 1921 and served in that position nearly through the end of the Herbert Hoover administration in 1932. An archconservative, Mellon believed that the government should stay out of economic affairs and do as little as possible to counter the effects of the Great Depression. By the time of his resignation, Mellon was perhaps the second most detested public official in America, after the president himself.

Born into a wealthy banking family in Pittsburgh in 1855, Mellon attended Western University (now the University of Pittsburgh) and went into his father's business in 1874. By 1882, he was running the company, which, over the next thirty years, he expanded into various industries, including aluminum, steel, coal, and oil. He was also cofounder of Alcoa and Gulf Oil and, by the 1920s, among the richest men in America.

Appointed head of the treasury in 1921, Mellon was an early supply-side thinker. With the U.S. government facing a $24 billion World War I debt, he argued for lower taxes to encourage business and hence increase government revenue. Taxes, mostly for corporations and the rich, dropped significantly, just as the booming economy of the 1920s provided additional government revenue to pay down the debt, as Mellon had predicted.

Mellon's success made him a prime candidate for the Republican presidential nomination in 1928, especially for the party's most conservative, probusiness elements. When Hoover got the nod, Mellon's backers were able to make sure that Mellon stayed on at the Treasury, despite Hoover's dislike for his laissez-faire thinking.

When the market crashed in 1929 and the nation went into the Great Depression, Mellon argued that it was probably a good thing. "It will purge the rottenness out of the system," he said. "People will work harder, live a more moral life. Values will be adjusted, and enterprising people will pick up the wrecks from less competent people."

He offered little in the way of solutions and utterly opposed any efforts—either federally mandated or voluntary—to counter the negative effects of the economic collapse. He kept a tight rein on the money supply and fought anything that smacked of inflation.

He even turned down a request by Hoover to provide $1 million of his bank's money to a fund to rescue other financial institutions on the verge of bankruptcy, thereby helping to doom Hoover's voluntaristic approach to the bank crisis of the early 1930s. As the differences between Hoover and Mellon grew, the president tried to ease the treasury secretary out of office, finally appointing him to be ambassador to Britain, where he served for less than a year.

In 1937, the year he died, Mellon gave some $25 million in art from his vast collection to the national government.

See also: banking; budget, federal; Republican Party; stock market; Hoover, Herbert; Document: Hoover's Outline of Program to Secure Cooperation of Bankers to Relieve Financial Difficulties, October 6, 1931.

Bibliography

Koskoff, David E. *The Mellons: The Chronicle of America's Richest Family.* New York: Crowell, 1978.

O'Connor, Harvey. *Mellon's Millions: The Biography of a Fortune: The Life and Times of Andrew W. Mellon.* New York: John Day, 1933.

MITCHELL, CHARLES E.

Head of National City Bank (later Citibank, and now part of Citigroup) and its parent companies from 1916 until forced to resign in a stock scandal in 1933, Charles E. Mitchell was one of the biggest promoters of stock market speculation in the 1920s and became a symbol of the corruption and greed in the securities markets during the 1930s.

Born in small-town Massachusetts in 1877, Mitchell went to work for a utility company in Chicago and became president's assistant in 1903. Within a few years, he had left to become the assistant of a bank president in New York, where he worked until 1911, going on to form his own investment house C. E. Mitchell & Company. Five years after that, he helped to reorganize the National City Company, which was affiliated with the National City Bank. By 1929, he was president of both companies.

Known by the nickname "Sunshine Charlie," Mitchell was one of the most outspoken promoters of stock market speculation, by both commercial banks and the public at large. Even after the Federal Reserve Bank tried to dampen stock speculation by hiking in-

terest rates in early 1929, Mitchell flamboyantly responded by putting up $25 million of his bank's money to invest in securities. But Mitchell was also involved in some shady tax-evasion schemes at the same time, shifting assets to his wife and creating false losses to lower his tax burden in 1929.

When the stock market crash came, National City Bank's stock prices fell nearly 90 percent. To save the personal fortunes of the bank's top officials, Mitchell illegally made millions of dollars of the company's assets available to them in the form of interest-free loans.

In January 1933, as the nation's banking system went into near-total collapse, Mitchell was hauled in front of a Senate investigation committee, known as the Pecora committee, after its chief counsel, Ferdinand Pecora, and forced to explain his actions. Mitchell was bluntly honest, believing he had done nothing wrong. In the end, the investigation led to an indictment but not a conviction. But the scandals unearthed by Pecora contributed to the formation of the Securities and Exchange Commission.

After his trial, Mitchell returned to Wall Street

and opened a financial consulting firm and served on the board of another investment bank. He died in 1955.

See also: banking; stock market; Securities and Exchange Commission; Pecora, Ferdinand.

Bibliography

Klebaner, Benjamin Joseph. *American Commercial Banking: A History*. Boston: Twayne, 1990.

Wicker, Elmus. *The Banking Panics of the Great Depression*. New York: Cambridge University Press, 1996.

MOLEY, RAYMOND

A political scientist who helped put together the Brain Trust for Franklin D. Roosevelt in 1932, Raymond Moley was also the architect of Roosevelt's successful 1932 campaign for the presidency, which helped create the so-called New Deal Democratic Party coalition of workers and small farmers that would lead the country through the early 1950s.

Born in Berea, Ohio, in 1886, Moley graduated from Baldwin-Wallace College and became superintendent of schools in a nearby town. He then returned to school, earning a master's degree at Oberlin College in 1913 and a doctorate in political science from Columbia University in 1918. Focusing on criminal justice issues, he became a professor at Columbia in 1923.

At the university, Moley came to the attention of a Roosevelt business associate named Louis Howe, who convinced Moley to work on Roosevelt's 1928 run for the New York governor's office. But it was really in 1932, as Roosevelt geared up to run for the presidency, that the two men became close. Not only did Moley advise the presidential candidate, but he assembled for him a group of like-minded liberal advisers—known popularly as the Brain Trust—who worked on the campaign and helped shape much of the early New Deal legislation.

Moley, who was influenced by the populist tradition of William Jennings Bryan—with its emphasis on the little man versus the big financial interests—persuaded Roosevelt to take a similar approach to his campaign against incumbent Republican Herbert Hoover. Moley was responsible for Roosevelt's famous "Forgotten Man" speech and radio address at the beginning of the 1932 campaign, in which the candidate denounced what would later be called the "trickle-down" economics of helping big business in the hopes that it would create jobs and argued that the government would have to kill the "bacteria" that were poisoning the system.

Many listeners took this address to be a class-based attack on the rich, and many conservatives and even progressives in the party urged Roosevelt to back away from such inflammatory rhetoric. But Moley convinced Roosevelt to persist, saying that the Democratic Party must shift its orientation to the Left, becoming the defender of workers and farmers. This was not only the right thing to do, but it would make the Democrats invincible politically.

Moley, of course, was right, as proven by the 1932 Roosevelt landslide. Despite his advocacy of radical rhetoric during the campaign, however, Moley actually advocated close working relations between government and business to pull the country out of the Great Depression. Still, as leader of the Brain Trust, Moley also urged Roosevelt to take immediate and broad action to fight the Great Depression and was one of the architects of the Emergency Banking act of 1933, the Civilian Conservation Corps, the National Recovery Administration, and the Civil Works Administration.

Although Moley was a close personal adviser to Roosevelt through the first years of the administration, the two grew estranged politically as the administration turned to the Left in 1935, with its push for the so-called "soak the rich" tax plan, while Moley grew increasingly conservative. By 1936, he had left the Democratic Party and largely supported Republican candidates thereafter. Moley spent most of the rest of his life as a writer, publishing political books and memoirs, until his death in 1975.

See also: Brain Trust; Democratic Party; election of 1932; Civil Works Administration; Civilian Conservation Corps; Emergency Banking Act; National Recovery Administration; New Deal, first; Roosevelt, Franklin D; Documents: National Industrial Recovery Act, June 16, 1933; Fireside Chat on the National Recovery Administration, July 24, 1933.

Bibliography

Lash, Joseph P. *Dealers and Dreamers: A New Look at the New Deal*. New York: Doubleday, 1988.

Moley, Raymond. *After Seven Years*. New York: Harper and Brothers, 1939.

Moley, Raymond, and Eliot A. Rosen. *The First New Deal*. New York: Harcourt, Brace & World, 1966.

Moley, Raymond. *Realities and Illusions, 1886–1931: The Autobiography of Raymond Moley*. New York: Garland, 1980.

MORGENTHAU, HENRY, JR.

Secretary of the treasury through most of Franklin D. Roosevelt's presidency, Henry Morgenthau Jr. was also a close adviser to the president and played a critical role in the formation of the Social Security system.

Born in New York City in 1891, Morgenthau came from a well-off German Jewish family and became a social worker, volunteering at the Henry Street settlement house in New York. Despite his urban roots, Morgenthau was also an avid farmer and edited the *American Agriculturalist* from 1922 to 1933. His farm, near Roosevelt's Hyde Park estate in upstate New York, brought the two men together and made them close friends and confidants.

When Roosevelt was elected governor of New York State in 1928, he appointed Morgenthau state conservation commissioner and chairman of the agricultural advisory committee. Morgenthau was also active in Roosevelt's 1928 campaign and his 1932 candidacy for President.

Upon coming to the White House in 1933, Roosevelt appointed Morgenthau head of the Farm Credit Administration, which helped farmers refinance their mortgages. In 1934, Morgenthau was made secretary of the treasury. Efficient and hardworking, Morgenthau—between his 1934 appointment and his 1945 resignation—would end up supervising the spending of more money than all the treasury secretaries who had preceded him.

Even before being made secretary of the treasury, however, Morgenthau was advising the president on economic affairs. For a time after Roosevelt took the country off the gold standard in late 1933, he and Morgenthau would get together every morning to set the price at which the government would buy gold in order to lower the value of the dollar and spur inflation.

In 1934, Roosevelt appointed Morgenthau to serve on a committee of cabinet officers, under the leadership of labor secretary Frances Perkins, to work out the details of the Social Security Act. A fiscal conservative, Morgenthau insisted on making the system self-paying through increased payroll taxes and the exclusion of agricultural workers.

Morgenthau also pushed for a balanced budget and major cutbacks in government spending in late 1937. Adopted by Roosevelt, these two measures have often been blamed for the so-called Roosevelt recession of 1937–38.

On the international front, Morgenthau was an anti-isolationist who believed that the United States should support Britain in its struggle against Nazi Germany in the early days of World War II. But while a strong supporter of Lend-Lease, which provided military aid to Britain, he believed that the British should spend most of their hard currency before receiving the aid. Otherwise, Morgenthau argued, Americans would see it as a bailout.

At the same time, as the Nazi crisis worsened for German and European Jews in the late 1930s, Morgenthau became a liaison between Jewish leaders and the administration, trying to get more persecuted Jews visas to enter the United States.

During the war, Morgenthau—the only Jew in the cabinet—would be the most outspoken proponent of tough postwar punishment for Germany, but he resigned from the Treasury in April 1945, just before Roosevelt's death. During his retirement, Morgenthau wrote, farmed, and served in philanthropic organizations. He died in 1967.

See also: banking; budget, federal; gold standard; Social Security Act; Lend-Lease Act; refugees; Perkins, Frances; Roosevelt, Franklin D.

Bibliography

Blum, John Morton. *Roosevelt and Morgenthau*. Boston: Houghton Mifflin, 1970.

Blum, John Morton, ed. *From the Morgenthau Diaries* (3 vols). Boston: Houghton Mifflin, 1959–1967.

MUNI, PAUL

Among the most versatile and popular actors of the 1930s, Paul Muni starred in such Great Depression–era hits as Howard Hawk's *Scarface* (1932) and *I Am a Fugitive from a Chain Gang* (1932).

Born Muni Weisenfreund in Austria in 1895, the future star came from a family of Yiddish-speaking theater actors. In 1902, his family emigrated to the United States and immediately went to work in the Yiddish theater in America, with the young Muni participating. Although a star in this popular theater form by his late teens, Muni did not star in his first Broadway role until 1926.

Several hit roles on stage gave way to a movie career. In 1929, he starred in his first picture, *The Valiant* (1929), followed by a virtuoso performance playing seven different roles in *Seven Faces*, later that year.

Nevertheless, Muni is best remembered for his roles as the gangster with a fondness for his sister in *Scarface* and a prisoner in the politically controversial film about southern chain gangs, *I Am a Fugitive from a Chain Gang*. Muni also played in a number of other historical and literary pictures in the 1930s, including *The Good Earth* (1937), *The Life of Emile Zola* (1937), and *Juarez* (1939). He won an Academy Award for best actor for his title role in *The Story of Louis Pasteur* (1936).

After World War II, Muni continued to act in films, including *Inherit the Wind* (1955) and *The Last Angry Man* (1959). He died in 1967.

See also: films, feature; *Scarface*; Hawks, Howard.

Bibliography

Baxter, John. *Hollywood in the Thirties.* New York: Barnes, 1968.

Sklar, Robert. *Movie-Made America: A Cultural History of the American Movies.* New York: Random House, 1975.

MURPHY, FRANK

A Franklin D. Roosevelt appointee to the Supreme Court in 1940, Frank Murphy was also governor of Michigan in 1937 and 1938, presiding at the time of the great General Motors (GM) sit-down strike of late 1936 and early 1937. His decision not to send in troops to clear the factories has been viewed by historians as a major turning point in the history of government/union relations.

Born William Francis Murphy in Michigan in 1890, he received his law degree from the University of Michigan in 1914 and served in the military in World War I. After several minor government positions, Murphy was elected mayor of Detroit and became famous throughout the country for his aggressive measures on behalf of the city's mass numbers of unemployed auto and other workers.

From 1933 to 1936, Murphy was appointed to administer the territory of the Philippines, where he strongly supported the independence movement. Elected as governor of Michigan in 1936, Murphy took office on January 1, 1937, two days after GM's workers—under the leadership of the United Automobile Workers—had begun their strike at one of the company's key plants in Flint.

Although Murphy felt that the strikes were illegal, he refused to send in troops to force the strikers out, telling aides that he did not want to go down in history as "bloody Murphy." Instead, Murphy mobilized the Michigan National Guard to maintain order only, and he allowed the families of striking workers to collect state relief. Both measures endeared him to organized labor. Indeed, it was a momentous decision, marking one of the first times in American history that the government remained neutral in a major strike.

Ultimately, this position favored workers since GM, looking forward to better car sales, settled after several weeks. The sit-down strikes in Flint triggered hundreds of similar strikes across the country over the following weeks and months and contributed to the organizing of millions of workers in mass production industries in the late 1930s.

From 1939 to 1940, Murphy served as U.S. attorney general and established the Civil Rights Unit (now Division) of the Justice Department. Appointed to the Supreme Court in 1940, Murphy continued to fight for civil rights, dissenting from an opinion declaring the internment of Japanese constitutional. Murphy remained on the Court until his death in 1949.

See also: General Motors; strikes, sit-down; unions and union organizing; United Automobile Workers; Supreme Court.

Bibliography

Fine, Sidney. *Frank Murphy*. Ann Arbor: University of Michigan Press, 1975.

Lunt, Richard D. *The High Ministry of Government: The Political Career of Frank Murphy*. Detroit: Wayne State University Press, 1965.

MURRAY, PHILIP

Vice president of the United Mine Workers of America (UMWA) under John L. Lewis, Philip Murray was appointed head of the Steel Workers Organizing Committee (SWOC)in 1936, in which position he led one of the first successful mass production industry strikes in American history.

Although of Catholic Irish descent, Murray was born in Glasgow in 1886, after his family moved to Scotland to work in the coal mines. When he was sixteen, his family emigrated yet again, this time to the coal-mining region of western Pennsylvania. Murray worked in the mines and joined the United Mine Workers of America. By 1912, he had become a member of the national union's board of directors and, from 1920 to 1942, served as its vice president, under the leadership of the fiery and blunt-spoken Lewis.

In 1935, Murray joined Lewis in forming the Committee for Industrial Organization (precursor of the Congress of Industrial Organizations, CIO) with the American Federation of Labor. In 1936, Lewis appointed him head of SWOC (precursor of the United Steel Workers of America).

Murray, who set up SWOC's headquarters in the same Pittsburgh skyscraper where many steel company executives had their offices, successfully negotiated a contract with United States Steel in spring 1937 that recognized SWOC as the bargaining agent for the company's employees. This was at the time of the General Motors sit-down strikes, and U.S. Steel wanted to avoid a similar situation in its own plants.

But Murray was less successful organizing the several smaller steel companies known as "little steel." Indeed, Murray was reluctant at first to take them on, fearing that SWOC did not have the resources to support a strike. But the rank and file were eager and forced the issue. Ultimately, the "little steel" companies resorted to violent repression, including a Memorial Day attack in Chicago that left ten workers dead. The workers at the "little steel" companies would not be organized until 1941.

By that time, Murray had moved on to become president of the CIO. A strong supporter of the war effort, Murray worked to remove communist-led unions from the CIO in the late 1940s and early 1950s. He died in 1952.

See also: American Federation of Labor; Congress of Industrial Organizations; "little steel"; Memorial Day massacre; sit-down strikes; Steel Workers Organizing Committee; unions and union organizing; United Mine Workers; United States Steel; Lewis, John L.

Bibliography

Clark, Paul F., Peter Gottlieb, and Donald Kennedy, eds. *Forging a Union of Steel: Philip Murray, SWOC, and the United Steelworkers*. Ithaca, NY: International Labor Review Press, 1987.

Tate, Juanita. *Philip Murray as a Labor Leader*. Ann Arbor, MI: University Microfilms, 1970.

MURROW, EDWARD R.

One of the most respected broadcast journalists of all time, Edward R. Murrow worked for the Columbia Broadcasting System (CBS) radio network during the late 1930s and early 1940s. His broadcasts from London during the blitz of 1940, when Nazi Germany launched a massive aerial attack on Britain, helped rouse American sympathy for the British.

Murrow was born in Greensboro, North Carolina, in 1908 and studied political science and international relations at Washington State College. Upon graduation, he became assistant director of the Institute of International Education and in 1935 was hired as an executive at CBS, where he arranged for leading personalities to appear on the network.

In 1937, he was sent to London as CBS's European director. A year later, he was on his way to Poland when Adolf Hitler marched into Austria. Murrow quickly went to Vienna and covered the so-called *anschluss*, or union of Germany and Austria. Now a correspondent, Murrow covered the Munich conference, where British prime minister Neville Chamberlain agreed to let Hitler annex part of Czechoslovakia.

But it was during the Battle of Britain that Murrow, with his resonant voice, made himself a household name in America by broadcasting against the backdrop of explosions and sirens. Capturing the immediacy of war for the listening public back home, Murrow not only helped convince many of his fellow Americans that Nazi Germany had to be stopped, but also—almost single-handedly—created the tradition of on-the-scene, international broadcast reportage.

Murrow continued to broadcast from Europe during World War II and became an outspoken critic of anticommunist Senator Joseph McCarthy (R-WI) in the early 1950s. In the 1950s, he collaborated with Fred W. Friendly to produce *Christmas in Korea, See It Now,* and *Small World* for CBS television. In 1961, he was appointed by President John Kennedy to head the U.S. Information Agency, but was forced to resign in 1964 because of lung cancer. He died the following year.

See also: radio; Great Britain; Munich Conference; World War II, early history of.

Bibliography

Bliss, Edward, ed. *In Search of Light: The Broadcasts of Edward R. Murrow, 1938–1964.* New York: Knopf, 1967.

Persico, Joseph E. *Edward R. Murrow: An American Original.* New York: McGraw-Hill, 1988.

MUSSOLINI, BENITO

Officially prime minister of Italy from 1922 to 1943 but, in fact, the country's dictator during those years, Benito Mussolini—also known as Il Duce, Italian for "leader"—organized Europe's first fascist regime, launched his country into several wars of expansion in Europe and Africa, and allied himself with Nazi leader Adolf Hitler of Germany before and during World War II.

Born to a working-class but well-educated family in Predappio, Italy, in 1883, Mussolini was expelled from several boarding schools after attacking and even stabbing fellow students and teachers. Despite this record, Mussolini was able to pass his examinations and get his teaching diploma in 1902. Disliking teaching, he wandered from job to job, all the time reading deeply in philosophy and political science. Eventually, he turned to journalism and public speaking, working as a propagandist for a union and calling for violence against employers, for which he was jailed several times.

Once again returning to teaching and journalism, he joined the Socialist Party and became editor of its journal, doubling its circulation as he argued against nationalism and Italy's entry into World War I. He soon changed his mind and spoke out vociferously supporting the war, which got him thrown off the paper and out of the party. But a publisher who also favored entry into the war made him editor of a pro-war journal.

Benito Mussolini, Italian dictator from 1922 through 1943, is shown giving the fascist salute. (*Library of Congress*)

When Italy entered the war, Mussolini went off to fight as a sharpshooter and was wounded. Returning from the front, he denounced socialism and spoke out in favor of a dictatorship for the country. By 1919, he had created a paramilitary group to effect a takeover of the government. He called it the Fasci di Combattimento—"fasci" being a bundle of sticks, the symbol of ancient Roman power.

Surrounded by his supporters in black shirts, Mussolini was a highly theatrical speaker whose oratory caught the imagination of many Italians upset over the disruptions and chaos of the post–World War I era. By the summer of 1922, Mussolini had enough fascist supporters to make his move to take over the government in Rome, although he wanted the approval of King Victor Emmanuel III. But his followers went ahead and marched on Rome. The threat of a takeover prompted the king to issue a summons to Mussolini, who assumed the post of prime minister in October, becoming the youngest in Italian history. Fraudulent elections in 1924 created an illusion of legitimacy for Mussolini's government.

At first, Mussolini was popular, as he brutally quelled the strikes and rioting that had plagued the country. He launched a massive public works program that helped put many Italians to work, earning him much respect among conservative circles in other European countries and the United States. Mussolini also had extraterritorial ambitions. In 1935, he launched a successful attack on Ethiopia, the last remaining independent kingdom in Africa. When condemnations by the League of Nations failed to include an oil embargo, Mussolini felt emboldened.

Meanwhile, Mussolini's seizure of power provided a model for another would-be dictator, Adolf Hitler of Germany. After the latter's rise to power in 1933, Mussolini joined forces with him in the Rome-Berlin Axis, later to include militarist Japan as well. While Mussolini was wary of Hitler's ambitions, he also did not want to see Italy left behind in expanding into other countries. When Hitler launched his invasion of France, Italy, moving in soon after, seized southern parts of the country.

Later, Mussolini's Italy would prove itself less than competent in warfare. Its nearly-failed invasion of Albania was aided by the German army, and the Germans were forced to fortify Italy after Allied forces invaded the country in 1943. In July, the fascist Grand Council dismissed Mussolini from office and had him arrested. Imprisoned on Sardinia, he eventually made his way to the Abruzzi Mountains in northeast Italy, where he was rescued by the Germans.

But as German forces in Italy collapsed in the waning weeks of the war, Mussolini tried to escape from the country disguised as a German soldier. Recognized by an angry mob, he was shot to death on April 28, 1945, his body left to hang head down, in dishonor, in a Milan piazza.

See also: Ethiopian war; fascism, Italy; League of Nations; Nazi Germany; World War II, early history of; Hitler, Adolf.

Bibliography

Gregor, A. James. *Young Mussolini and the Intellectual Origins of Fascism.* Berkeley: University of California Press, 1979.

Kirkpatrick, Ivone, Sir. *Mussolini: A Study in Power.* New York: Avon Books, 1964.

Mack Smith, Denis. *Mussolini.* New York: Vintage Books, 1982.

Ridley, Jasper Godwin. *Mussolini.* New York: St. Martin's, 1998.

NELSON, GEORGE "BABY FACE"

One of the most notorious and vicious of the bank robbers who plagued the early Depression years, "Baby Face" Nelson was known for his teenage face and his casual disregard for life.

Born George Nelson in Chicago in 1908, Nelson became involved in petty crime at an early age, eventually becoming a labor racketeer. From 1929 to 1931, he worked for Al Capone and other gang leaders in Chicago, bootlegging liquor and enforcing gang rule. But Nelson proved too unpredictably violent even for Chicago gangsters of the Prohibition era, and he was soon blackballed from the various criminal organizations.

At that point, he went into robbing banks, holding up at least two with fellow gangster John Dillinger. Considered Public Enemy Number One by the Federal Bureau of Investigation, Nelson was shot down by its agents in a Chicago suburb on November 27, 1934.

See also: crime; Prohibition; Federal Bureau of Investigation; Capone, Al; Dillinger, John.

Bibliography

Ruth, David E. *Inventing the Public Enemy: The Gangster in American Culture, 1918–1934*. Chicago: University of Chicago Press, 1996.

NIEBUHR, REINHOLD

Perhaps the most influential American theologian of the Great Depression era, Reinhold Niebuhr emphasized the doctrine of "Christian realism" in his pathbreaking book *Moral Man and Immoral Society* (1932). Influenced by the prevailing thinking at the time that individualist greed of the 1920s had brought on the economic troubles of the 1930s, Niebuhr argued that a decent society must rid itself of pride, hypocrisy, and self-centered behavior if it is to survive on a morally sound basis.

Born the son of a German immigrant minister in Missouri in 1892, Niebuhr graduated from Elmhurst College in Illinois in 1910 and Eden Theological Seminary in St. Louis in 1913. He also received his divinity degree and master of arts from Yale. He was ordained a minister of the Evangelical and Reformed Church (now part of the United Church of Christ) in 1915. From that year until 1928, Niebuhr was pastor of the Bethel Evangelical Church in Detroit. He then went to teach at the Union Theological Seminary in New York, where he remained on the faculty until 1960.

Seeing the suffering among his working-class parishioners in Detroit led Niebuhr to join the Socialist Party, and he even ran for office several times as a Socialist. While influenced by Marxism in the 1930s, he disliked its ideological certitude. But his days with the Socialist Party came to an end in the middle 1930s because of its pacifist doctrine. Once a pacifist himself, Niebuhr eventually turned away from that doctrine and urged U.S. participation in the war against Nazi Germany.

After the war, Niebuhr became a liberal anticommunist and a founder of the like-minded Americans for Democratic Action. Niebuhr continued to write and teach for much of the rest of his life. He died in 1971.

See also: Socialist Party.

Bibliography

Fox, Richard Wrightman. *Reinhold Niebuhr: A Biography*. New York: Pantheon Books, 1985.

Merkley, Paul. *Reinhold Niebuhr: A Political Account*. Montreal: McGill-Queen's University Press, 1975.

Kegley, Charles W., ed. *Reinhold Niebuhr: His Religious, Social, and Political Thought*. 2nd ed. New York: Macmillan, 1984.

NORRIS, GEORGE W.

A progressive Republican senator from Nebraska, George W. Norris fought long and hard for public power projects throughout the 1920s, particularly along the Tennessee River in Muscle Shoals, Alabama, only to be thwarted by Republican presidents. But his plans helped form the foundation for the massive public power projects of the Tennessee Valley Authority, enacted by the Franklin D. Roosevelt administration in 1933.

Norris was born in Sandusky, Ohio, in 1861 and studied law at Northern Indiana Normal School (now Valparaiso University). Admitted to the Indiana bar in 1883, he moved to Nebraska two years later and started a practice. Active in politics, he was elected to the House of Representatives four times from 1902 to 1908. In 1912, he was elected to the Senate and served there almost to the end of his life.

Norris was both a progressive on domestic issues and an isolationist on foreign ones. He was one of a handful of senators voting against Woodrow Wilson's declaration of war against Germany in 1917, and he spoke out against U.S. entry into the League of Nations after the war. He broke with Herbert Hoover over the latter's moratorium on loan payments from World War I and fought against Roosevelt's efforts to get U.S. aid to Britain and others fighting Nazi Germany in the late 1930s. At the same time, he was a firm believer in the usefulness of cheap and abundant hydroelectric power, financed by the government. Throughout the 1920s, he tried to get a World War I hydroelectric project at Muscle Shoals, Alabama, out of mothballs, but the bills he got through Congress to do this were ve-toed, once by President Calvin Coolidge in 1925 and again by President Herbert Hoover in 1931. He was also the author—along with Democratic representative Fiorello La Guardia—of the Norris-La Guardia Anti-Injunction Act, which was reluctantly signed by Hoover. The act outlawed the so-called yellow-dog contract, whereby workers, in order to get a job, agreed never to join a union.

Not surprisingly, given his liberal politics, Norris abandoned the Republicans during the 1930s presidential elections and supported Roosevelt. And the Roosevelt administration borrowed from Norris's ideas and made them their own, including the Tennessee Valley Authority and the National Labor Relations Act of 1935.

Norris resigned from the Senate in 1943 and died the following year.

See also: utilities; National Labor Relations Act; Norris-La Guardia Anti-Injunction Act; Tennessee Valley Authority; Hoover, Herbert.

Bibliography

Norris, George. *Fighting Liberal: The Autobiography of George W. Norris.* New York: Macmillan, 1945.

Lowitt, Richard. *George Norris: The Making of a Progressive, 1861–1912.* Urbana: University of Illinois Press, 1963.

———. *George Norris: The Persistence of a Progressive, 1913–1933.* Urbana: University of Illinois Press, 1971.

———. *George Norris: The Triumph of a Progressive, 1933–1944.* Urbana: University of Illinois Press, 1978.

ODETS, CLIFFORD

Aplaywright and one of the founding members of the influential Group Theatre company, Clifford Odets is best known for his 1935 play about unions and union organizing, *Waiting for Lefty*.

Born in Philadelphia in 1906, Odets became involved in the theater at a young age and acted with several repertory companies in the 1920s before joining the newly formed Group Theatre in 1931. Like many other artists, Odets was strongly influenced by the human tragedy of the Great Depression and wrote about working people's plights.

In 1935, he achieved his first and greatest success with *Waiting for Lefty*, perhaps the finest example of 1930s agit-prop, or agitational propaganda, theater. It was said that New York audiences were so moved that they would jump out of their seats and shout "Strike!" Odets followed up *Lefty* with several other popular dramas, including *Awake and Sing* (1935), *Paradise Lost* (1935), and *Golden Boy* (1937), another big hit about an immigrant boy who becomes a prizefighter.

In the latter part of the decade, Odets moved to Hollywood and wrote screenplays. He continued to write for film and theater after World War II and died in 1963.

See also: films, feature; *Waiting for Lefty*.

Bibliography

Brenman-Gibson, Margaret. *Clifford Odets, American Playwright: The Years from 1906 to 1940*. New York: Atheneum, 1981.

Murray, Edward. *Clifford Odets: The Thirties and After*. New York: F. Ungar Publishing, 1968.

OLSON, FLOYD

Farmer-Labor Party governor of Minnesota from 1930 until his death in 1936, Floyd Olson was a self-professed "radical" who passed a number of key pieces of reform legislation and remained an outspoken critic of capitalism and an advocate of socialism throughout his life.

Born the son of an impoverished railroad worker in Minneapolis in 1891, he studied prelaw at the University of Minnesota, before dropping out in 1910 for lack of funds. For three years, he worked in various jobs out West, including a stint as a dockworker in Seattle, where he briefly joined the radical Industrial Workers of the World. In 1913, he returned to Minneapolis and earned his law degree from Northwestern Law College, taking classes at night. After graduating in 1915, he took a job with a local law firm and, in 1919, became assistant county attorney for Hennepin County, where Minneapolis is situated. The following year he became county attorney. Reelected twice, he served in that position until 1930.

An early member of the Farmer-Labor Party, which formed shortly after World War I, Olson ran on its ticket for governor in 1924, but lost. Declining to run in 1926 and 1928, he chose to make another run in 1930, since he believed that the Depression's impact on the economy made the reformist Farmer-Laborites a more viable party. And, indeed, he won with a large 200,000-vote edge, taking all but five counties in the state.

While Olson had to face a conservative legislature during his three terms in office, he nevertheless got bills passed expanding public works, establishing securities regulation, conserving natural resources, and encouraging farmer and worker cooperatives, a cause dear to the members of his party. He outraged state employers by agreeing to arbitrate a strike by truckers that shut Minneapolis down in 1934.

Though Olson was a leftist critic of the New Deal—believing that it was not socialist enough—he nevertheless supported Franklin D. Roosevelt in both the 1932 and 1936 elections. During the latter year, Olson decided to run for senator but died of cancer before the campaign began.

See also: Farmer-Labor Party; strikes, general.

Bibliography

Mayer, George H. *The Political Career of Floyd B. Olson*. Minneapolis: University of Minnesota Press, 1951.

McCurry, Dan C. *The Farmer-Labor Party: History, Platform, and Programs*. New York: Arno Press, 1975.

OWENS, JESSE

Arguably the best-known and most-accomplished track and field athlete of the 1930s, Jesse Owens won four gold medals at the 1936 Olympic Games in Berlin. Owens's feat was electrifying since, as an African American, he struck a blow against the notion of Aryan, or Germanic, racial superiority, which the Nazi-run games were supposed to highlight.

Born in Danville, Alabama, in 1913, Owens attended high school in Cleveland, where he competed on the track and field team. He won three events at the 1933 National Interscholastic Championships before going on to Ohio State University. On the track team there, he set records in the 100- and 220-yard dashes and the running broad jump (now the long jump).

In 1936, he was picked to run with the U.S. Olympic team in Berlin and tied the Olympic record in the 100-meter run. He broke the world record in the 220-meter run and the long jump and ran the final leg of the U.S. team's record-breaking 400-meter relay. Upon receiving his medals, however, Owens was shunned by the disheartened German dictator, Adolf Hitler, who refused to greet him or shake his hand. But, as Owens later remarked, he was not invited to shake President Franklin D. Roosevelt's hand either, when he came back to cheering parades.

After leaving track and field competition, Owens supported youth athletics, became a U.S. goodwill ambassador, and worked for a time on the Illinois State Athletic Commission. He died in 1980.

See also: sports; Nazi Germany; Olympic Games (Berlin 1936); Hitler, Adolf.

Jesse Owens, America's greatest male track athlete of the 1930s, won four gold medals at the Berlin Olympics of 1936. *(Brown Brothers)*

Bibliography

Baker, William J. *Jesse Owens: An American Life*. London: Collier Macmillan, 1986.

Owens, Jesse, and Paul G. Neimark. *Blackthink: My Life as Black Man and White Man*. New York: William Morrow, 1970.

PAIGE, LEROY ROBERT "SATCHEL"

Considered by baseball enthusiasts to be the greatest pitcher ever to play in the Negro League, and one of the best to play the game of baseball, period, Satchel Paige was nicknamed the "iron man" for his ability to pitch day after day.

Born Leroy Robert Paige in Mobile, Alabama, sometime between 1899 and 1906—Paige liked to keep people guessing about his age—the future right-hander grew up to stand over 6 feet, 3 inches, giving him a commanding presence on the mound. As a youth, he worked at train stations, handling bags and satchels— hence the nickname.

Paige began his career with the Mobile Tigers of the Negro Southern Association in 1924 and played for a number of teams before his belated entry into the newly integrated major leagues in 1948. Paige also worked as a pitcher on teams that barnstormed the Caribbean and Latin America.

In exhibition games against white U.S. teams in the 1930s, Paige excelled. He pitched a one-to-nothing victory over Dizzy Dean in 1934, the year Dean had a thirty-win season. But it is his record with the Negro League that stand out. According to Paige's own record-keeping, he pitched fifty-five no-hitters in the Negro League and won over 2,000 games. His endurance was extraordinary. At one point in the 1935 season, he pitched a game a day for twenty-nine days.

In 1948, Paige was finally welcomed into the majors and pitched for the Cleveland Indians from 1948 to 1949. He pitched on the American League All-Star team in 1952 and was the best relief pitcher on the St. Louis Browns from 1951 to 1953. In 1971, Paige became the first representative of the Negro League to be inducted into baseball's Hall of Fame. He died in 1982.

See also: African Americans; sports.

Leroy "Satchel" Paige of the Kansas City Monarchs, a Negro League team, was one of the greatest pitchers in the history of baseball. Paige threw fifty-five no-hitters in his twenty-nine-year career. *(Brown Brothers)*

Bibliography

Paige, Leroy, and David Lipman. *Maybe I'll Pitch Forever: A Great Baseball Player Tells the Hilarious Story Behind the Legend.* Lincoln: University of Nebraska Press, 1993.

Ribowsky, Mark. *Don't Look Back: Satchel Paige in the Shadows of Baseball.* New York: Simon & Schuster, 1994.

PARSONS, LOUELLA

Journalist and radio broadcaster Louella Parsons was one of the most influential and widely read gossip columnists in America during the 1930s, skewering Hollywood celebrities but also fiercely defending the film industry against critics from outside.

Born in Freeport, Illinois, in 1881, she attended Dixon College and worked as a drama critic for the Dixon *Morning Star*. In 1910, after an unsuccessful marriage and the birth of her only child in 1906, Parsons moved to Chicago, where she became a reporter for the *Tribune*. At the same time, she briefly worked at a local silent film studio, doing publicity and writing scripts.

In 1914, she moved to the *Record-Herald*, where she began writing one of the first movie columns in America. After William Randolph Hearst acquired the *Record-Herald* in 1918, Parsons moved to New York City's *Morning Telegraph*. After making some favorable remarks about Hearst's mistresses in one of her columns, Parsons was reassigned to Hearst's New York *American* and made motion picture editor. After a bout with tuberculosis and treatment in Palm Springs, Parsons was once again reassigned—this time to Hearst's Los Angeles *Examiner* in 1926. There, until 1965, she wrote her influential column on Hollywood, which eventually was syndicated in over 600 periodicals around the world. She also developed a bitter rivalry with columnist Hedda Hopper.

In 1931, Parsons also went into radio, briefly hosting a show for the Sunkist Orange Company. Three years later, she hosted the popular *Hollywood Hotel*, where she interviewed film celebrities for four years. Parsons was said to have enormous influence. When the secretive Orson Welles refused to let her on the set of *Citizen Kane*, a movie Parsons rightly believed was highly critical of Hearst, Parsons attacked Welles in print and, it is said, worked behind the scenes to make sure neither he nor his movie received an Academy Award.

Parsons resigned from her columnist position in 1965 due to ill health and died in 1972.

See also: films, feature; newspapers and magazines; radio; *Citizen Kane*; Hearst, William Randolph; Hopper, Hedda; Welles, Orson.

Bibliography

Eells, George. *Hedda and Louella*. New York: Putnam, 1972.

Parsons, Louella. *The Gay Illiterate*. Garden City, NY: Doubleday, Doran and Company, 1944.

PEEK, GEORGE

A businessman and agricultural expert, George Peek served as the first director of the Agricultural Adjustment Administration (AAA)—the New Deal's primary farm aid agency—in 1933, where he fought against efforts to limit farm production to bolster crop prices.

Born in rural Illinois in 1873, he briefly attended Northwestern University before joining the John Deere Plow Company, where he worked until 1917, rising through the ranks to become an executive. From 1917 to 1919, Peek worked at the War Industries Board, which converted America's economy to military production during World War I. From 1924 to 1928, he served as president and general manager of the Moline Plow Company, but quit after a dispute over business strategy with fellow executive Hugh Johnson, who would later become head of the National Recovery Administration. Peek also won a $280,000 lawsuit against the company for violation of his contract.

During those years, he and Johnson worked together on plans to aid the farm economy, which had been in a slump since the end of World War I. Together, they devised a program called "Equality for Agriculture," which involved the establishment of a government-run corporation that would buy up surpluses at parity, that is, at the prices paid for farm crops during the boom years immediately preceding World War I, and then dump them abroad at whatever price the market would bear.

When the Republicans refused to add the plan to their platform in 1928, Peek shifted his loyalty to the Democrats and endorsed Alfred Smith's candidacy for the presidency. Four years later, he backed Franklin D. Roosevelt and, after the AAA was created in May 1933, was appointed head. Peek immediately ran afoul of Agriculture Secretary Henry A. Wallace, a strong believer in production control, since Peek believed that the idea of overproduction was a myth. Instead, Peek advocated voluntary marketing agreements and an aggressive export policy.

With the conflict becoming increasingly intense, Roosevelt asked for Peek's resignation in December, then appointed him special adviser on foreign trade and president of the government-run Export-Import Bank. In 1935, Peek negotiated an 800,000-bale cotton barter deal with Nazi Germany, a move criticized by Roosevelt. Peek resigned from both his government posts and became an outspoken critic of the New Deal. In the elections of 1936 and 1940, Peek supported Republicans and, in 1940, joined the isolationist America First Committee. He died in 1943.

See also: agriculture; Agricultural Adjustment Administration; America First Committee; Johnson, Hugh; Roosevelt, Franklin D.; Wallace, Henry A.

Bibliography

Fite, Gilbert C. *George N. Peek and the Fight for Farm Parity*. Norman: University of Oklahoma Press, 1954.

Peek, George N. *Why Quit Our Own*. New York: Van Nostrand, 1936.

PEPPER, CLAUDE

A liberal supporter of the New Deal, Claude Pepper was a Democratic senator from Florida whose 1938 victory was aided by a strong effort from Franklin D. Roosevelt. Indeed, Roosevelt saw Pepper's victory as a vindication of the administration's liberal positions and his own continuing political popularity as president.

Pepper was born in small-town Alabama in 1900. After attending the University of Alabama, he received his law degree from Harvard in 1924. After several years in a private law practice in Florida, Pepper was elected to the state legislature, where he began his lifelong fight for the interests of senior citizens.

Appointed to the Senate in 1936 as a firm New Deal Democrat, Pepper faced an uphill primary battle in 1938 against a conservative. Roosevelt both spoke on Pepper's behalf and urged the candidate to take a conspicuous stand supporting the Fair Labor Standards Act (FLSA), then before Congress. The act, establishing a federal minimum wage and maximum hours for a workweek, was opposed by many southern business interests, who viewed it as a threat to their region's only industrial advantage—lower wages.

When Pepper won the primary and the general election, it proved the appeal of the FLSA, which was soon passed. Roosevelt also felt that his interference in the Florida election proved that he and his New Deal programs were still popular.

In the late 1930s, Pepper was an outspoken opponent of U.S. isolationism. He continued to serve in the Senate through 1950, but was ousted because of his position that the United States should cooperate with, rather than confront, the Soviet Union. Twelve years later, Pepper became a member of the House of Representatives, where he served until his death in 1989.

See also: election of 1938; Fair Labor Standards Act; Roosevelt, Franklin D.

Bibliography

Danese, Tracy E. *Claude Pepper and Ed Ball: Politics, Purpose, and Power*. Gainesville: University Press of Florida, 2000.

Pepper, Claude. *Pepper: Eyewitness to a Century*. San Diego: Harcourt Brace Jovanovich, 1987.

PERKINS, FRANCES

Secretary of labor through all four terms of Franklin D. Roosevelt's administration and the first woman ever to hold a cabinet post, Frances Perkins organized the committee that wrote the Social Security Act of 1935.

Born Fannie Coralie Perkins in Boston in 1882, the future cabinet member graduated from Mount Holyoke College in Massachusetts in 1902 and taught school for a time. A believer in the Social Gospel ideology of the Progressive Era—in which Protestants were supposed to realize their faith by helping the poor—Perkins went to work at Jane Addams' Hull House settlement house in Chicago. Returning to school, she received her master's degree in social economics from Columbia University in 1910.

From 1910 to 1912, Perkins served as executive secretary of the Consumers' League of New York, where she fought for women's and children's labor issues. For the next five years, she worked at the same position for the New York Committee on Safety, where she met Roosevelt. During the 1920s, she worked at the New York State Industrial Commission, becoming its chairperson from 1926 to 1929. In the latter year, newly elected Governor Roosevelt appointed her state industrial commissioner. When Roosevelt went to Washington in 1933, he made Perkins his secretary of labor.

The appointment disappointed many in the labor movement, and not just because she was a woman. As part of the Social Gospel tradition, Perkins believed that college-educated, middle-class reformers could do more for labor by enacting appropriate legislation than workers could do for themselves by organizing and striking. Still, she was a strong supporter of labor rights. As a consumer advocate and, like many of her generation, having been forever scarred by the Triangle Shirtwaist Company factory fire, in which more than a hundred women workers who had been locked in a factory died, Perkins did not trust employers to do the right thing either.

In office, Perkins was a strong supporter of the 1933 Civilian Conservation Corps and other public works programs. But it was her role in shaping the Social Security Act on which her legacy stands. In summer 1934, she was asked by the president to convene

Secretary of Labor Frances Perkins, the first woman cabinet member in American history, was instrumental in writing the Social Security Act of 1935. *(Brown Brothers)*

the Committee on Economic Security to draw up a federal plan for old-age pensions.

Fearing radical proposals being pushed by Francis Townsend and Huey P. Long, Roosevelt wanted to create a plan he considered more responsible by way of social insurance. Perkins and her group of experts had to balance what was politically feasible with what they felt could pass constitutional muster with a conservative Supreme Court.

Perkins enthusiastically supported the tax-offset feature of the act, which penalized states that did not go along with the program. But she only reluctantly accepted the idea of benefits being proportional to earnings and the exclusion of agricultural workers, the latter a concession to southern Democrats who wanted to keep black farm workers out of the program. The act passed Congress in 1935 and was ruled constitutional by the Court in 1937. The following year, Perkins helped draw up the Fair Labor Standards Act, establishing a federal minimum wage and a maximum workweek of forty-four hours.

Perkins continued to serve as labor secretary during the war, resigning two months after Roosevelt's death in April 1945, but stayed on as a Civil Service commissioner through 1953. Resigning from government, Perkins spent much of the rest of her life lecturing on industrial relations. She died in 1965.

See also: unions and union organizing; Civilian Conservation Corps; Fair Labor Standards Act; Social Security Act; Supreme Court.

Bibliography

Martin, George W. *Madame Secretary, Frances Perkins.* Boston: Houghton Mifflin, 1976.

Perkins, Frances. *The Roosevelt I Knew.* New York: Viking, 1946.

PORTER, COLE

One of most prolific and accomplished popular music composers in twentieth-century American history, Cole Porter is well known for sophisticated Depression-era musicals, including *The Gay Divorcee* (1932) and *Anything Goes* (1934).

Born the son of a millionaire banker in Peru, Indiana, in 1891, Porter was interested in music from a young age, publishing his first song at the age of eleven. He continued to write music while studying pre-law at Yale. As a law student at Harvard, Porter changed his studies to music, a move that upset his father, who wanted Cole to take over the family business.

Instead, Porter—a lifelong Francophile—went to study music in Paris. Upon his return to the United States, he wrote two Broadway musicals—*See America First* (1915) and *Hitchy-Koo* (1920). Both bombed. His first hit song was "Let's Do It" for the show *Paris* (1928). The tune included the catchy rhythms and sly, sexually charged lyrics that would become a hallmark of his musical writing style.

The songs Porter penned for his various hit shows of the 1930s have become American classics. They include, "Love for Sale" and "Night and Day" for *The Gay Divorcee*; "Anything Goes," "You're the Top," and "I Get a Kick Out of You" for *Anything Goes*; and "Just One of Those Things," "Begin the Beguine," and "It's De-Lovely" for *Red, Hot and Blue!*

Porter continued to write musicals from the 1930s to the 1950s, including *Kiss Me Kate* and *Can-Can*. Porter died in 1964.

See also: music.

Bibliography

McBrien, William. *Cole Porter: A Biography.* New York: Knopf, 1998.

Schwartz, Charles. *Cole Porter: A Biography.* New York: Dial Press, 1979.

POWELL, WILLIAM

The leading man in some of the Depression era's most memorable comedies, William Powell is best known for his starring role in *The Thin Man* series of films, about the detective couple Nick and Nora Charles.

Born in Pittsburgh in 1892, Powell was a devoted fan of the theater from a young age and dropped out of the University of Kansas in 1912 to pursue a stage-acting career in New York City. Over the next eight years, Powell acted in over 200 plays until a starring role in *Spanish Love* (1920) brought him to the attention of Hollywood. He worked in many silent films, but it as the coming of sound movies that established his career.

Beginning in 1929, Powell was cast in a series of movies as the sophisticated detective Philo Vance—a character that he would refine in the wildly popular *The Thin Man* (1934), playing opposite Myrna Loy and their precocious dog, Asta. Six more *Thin Man* movies would follow. In 1936, Powell was cast as a hobo adopted into a wealthy family by Carole Lombard (whom Powell had earlier married and divorced), in the huge screwball comedy hit *My Man Godfrey*.

In the years after World War II, as he became too old to play leading men, Powell became a consummate character actor playing in dozens of films. Over the years, he picked up three Academy Award nominations for best actor, though he never won. Powell died in 1984.

See also: films, feature; Lombard, Carole.

Bibliography

Baxt, George. *The William Powell and Myrna Loy Murder Case.* New York: St. Martin's, 1996.

Francisco, Charles. *Gentleman: The William Powell Story.* New York: St. Martin's, 1985.

RANDOLPH, A. PHILIP

President of the Brotherhood of Sleeping Car Porters (BSCP), the largest African-American union in American history, A. Philip Randolph was the architect behind the 1941 March on Washington Movement (MOWM). Although the march was never held, the threat of such a demonstration persuaded President Franklin D. Roosevelt to create the Fair Employment Practices Commission (FEPC), an agency charged with investigating and remedying racial discrimination in the nation's defense industries.

Born Asa Philip Randolph in Crescent City, Florida, in 1889, the future labor leader graduated from Cookman College, an all-black educational institution, in 1907. But racial discrimination kept Randolph in menial positions until he moved to New York City in 1911. There he attended City College, acted in amateur productions, and worked in a Harlem employment agency.

In 1917, he and National Urban League official Chandler Owen founded *The Messenger*, a socialist newspaper for an African-American readership. Eight years later, Randolph established the BSCP to organize the nation's 10,000 sleeping car porters. Only after changes in the Railway Labor Act were made in 1935 did the Pullman Sleeping Car Company recognize the union.

In the late 1930s, Randolph fought against racial injustice in hiring and promotions with the National Negro Congress, but dropped out after a while because of the many Communists in the organization. In 1940, he joined with Walter White, president of the National Association for the Advancement of Colored People (NAACP), to push for desegregation of the military. To achieve this, Randolph established the MOWM, with the aim of organizing a march of tens of thousands of demonstrators in Washington in summer 1941. Randolph refused Roosevelt's request to call off the march until the president, agreeing to end racial discrimination in the nation's burgeoning defense industries, issued Executive Order 8002, establishing the FEPC. Desegregation of the military, Randolph's initial demand, was not achieved until President Harry Truman's administration after World War II. As for the FEPC, it had a mixed record. Understaffed and underbudgeted, it could investigate only a fraction of the complaints filed.

Randolph continued to speak out for the desegregation of the military in the 1940s and for speedy implementation of the 1954 *Brown v. Board of Education* decision calling for integration of the nation's schools. He also spoke in front of 250,000 people at the 1963 March on Washington, a demonstration inspired in part by Randolph's efforts in 1941. Randolph died in 1979.

See also: African Americans; Brotherhood of Sleeping Car Porters; March on Washington Movement; railroads; Fair Employment Practices Committee.

Bibliography

Harris, William Hamilton. *Keeping the Faith: A. Philip Randolph, Milton P. Webster, and the Brotherhood of Sleeping Car Porters, 1925–37.* Urbana: University of Illinois Press, 1991.

Pfeffer, Paula F. *A. Philip Randolph: Pioneer of the Civil Rights Movement.* Baton Rouge: Louisiana State University Press, 1990.

RANKIN, JOHN

Democratic congressman from Mississippi from 1921 through 1953, John Rankin was both an opponent of civil rights legislation and a progressive supporter of the New Deal. He is best remembered for his advocacy of public power projects and as one of the legislative architects behind the creation of the Tennessee Valley Authority (TVA) Act of 1933.

Born in rural Mississippi in 1882, Rankin attended the University of Mississippi, graduating with a law degree in 1910. He worked at a private law firm for two years before becoming prosecuting attorney for Lee County, where he served until 1916. In 1915 and 1916, he ran unsuccessful campaigns for district attorney and for congressman from Lee County, respectively.

He served briefly as an enlisted man in World War I before returning to Tupelo, Mississippi, where he edited a weekly newspaper, the *New Era*. In 1920, Rankin ran successfully for Congress, and he would win reelection fifteen consecutive times. An ardent supporter of Franklin D. Roosevelt in 1932, Rankin—along with Republican Senator George Norris of Nebraska—was critical in getting the TVA passed. Rankin was also the key sponsor of legislation that created the Rural Electrification Administration in 1936. Yet despite this progressive record on public power, Rankin was an outspoken white supremacist who worked hard to prevent antilynching legislation from becoming law during the decade.

During World War II, he spoke out in support of Roosevelt's decision to imprison Japanese Americans. From 1945 to 1950, Rankin was a member of the House Un-American Activities Committee and was known to be one of the most vigorous anti-Communists in government. Rankin left Congress in 1953 and died in 1960.

See also: Rural Electrification Administration; Tennessee Valley Authority; Norris, George.

Bibliography

Vickers, Kenneth Wayne. "John Rankin: Democrat and Demagogue." Master's thesis, Mississippi State University, 1993.

RASKOB, JOHN J.

A very conservative industrialist and former Republican, John J. Raskob became the chairman of the national Democratic Party in 1928. Four years later, Raskob tried to block the nomination of Franklin Roosevelt but, failing that, tried to push the candidate in more conservative directions.

Born in upstate New York in 1879, Raskob served as a secretary to Pierre Samuel du Pont, a real estate and street railway executive in Ohio. When du Pont became treasurer of the E. I. du Pont de Nemours company in 1902, Raskob went to work there. Twelve years later, Raskob took over his former boss's position. By 1915, he and du Pont had bought enough stock in the new General Motors Corporation to join the board. Eventually appointed chairman of the company's finance committee, Raskob established credit and long-term financing to help sell cars.

In 1928, Raskob left General Motors to become chairman of the Democratic Party. That year, he backed the candidacy of Al Smith and tried to move him in more conservative directions. One of Raskob's pet issues was Prohibition, which he wanted to end. Raskob believed that a tax on alcohol would help eliminate income taxes for the rich and for corporations, which, he felt, were the productive elements of society and should not be taxed. After Smith's loss in the 1928 election, Raskob joined with the candidate in constructing the Empire State Building.

A great believer in the prosperity of the 1920s, Raskob is remembered for an article he wrote for the *Ladies' Home Journal* shortly before the stock market crash of 1929. Entitled "Everybody Ought to Be Rich,"
it urged average Americans to invest their savings on Wall Street.

In 1932, Raskob tried to block the candidacy of Roosevelt, thinking the New York governor was far too radical. When that failed, he backed Roosevelt reluctantly and, believing that the election was really a referendum on the presidency of Herbert Hoover, told the candidate to say as little as possible about what he would do when elected—a strategy largely adopted by Roosevelt. At the same time, Raskob supported a national sales tax to help balance the budget.

Once Roosevelt was in office, Raskob became alienated from the president. While he appreciated Roosevelt's rescue of the nation's banks in 1933, he disliked the public works programs and other New Deal legislation. In 1934, Raskob openly broke with Roosevelt and the Democrats to form the Liberty League, an organization of business executives strongly opposed to the New Deal. Raskob remained an outspoken critic of Roosevelt and the New Deal through the rest of the 1930s. He died in 1950.

See also: election of 1932; Empire State Building; General Motors; Liberty League; Prohibition; stock market; Roosevelt, Franklin D.; Smith, Al.

Bibliography

McElvaine, Robert S. *The Great Depression: America, 1929–1941.* New York: Times Books, 1993.

Mintz, Frank P. *The Liberty Lobby and the American Right: Race, Conspiracy, and Culture.* Westport, CT: Greenwood Press, 1985.

RAYBURN, SAM

As chairman of the House of Representatives Committee on Interstate and Foreign Commerce, Democratic Texas congressman Sam Rayburn was instrumental in the passage of key pieces of New Deal legislation, particularly in the area of business and securities legislation.

Born in rural Tennessee in 1882, Rayburn grew up on a farm and taught school as a young man. He entered politics as a state legislator in 1907, and passed the Texas bar in 1908. In 1913 he won election to the House of Representatives and served until his death in 1961, being elected twenty-five times in a row.

His longevity in office was typical of many southern Democrats, but Rayburn was more liberal than most. As committee chairman, he helped draw up the Federal Securities Act of 1933, the Securities Exchange Act of 1934, which established the Securities and Exchange Commission, the Federal Communications Act of 1934, the Rural Electrification Act of 1936, and the Public Utilities Holding Act of 1935, a controversial piece of legislation which Rayburn was instrumental in getting passed.

In 1937, the Texas congressman was made House Democratic leader and then Speaker of the House in 1940, serving in that position for the seventeen years between 1940 and 1961 that Democrats controlled the House. Rayburn died in 1961.

See also: Democratic Party; Federal Communications Commission; Public Utilities Holding Act; Rural Electrification Administration; Securities and Exchange Commission.

Bibliography

Mooney, Booth. *Roosevelt and Rayburn: A Political Partnership.* Philadelphia: Lippincott, 1971.

Steinberg, Alfred. *Sam Rayburn: A Biography.* New York: Hawthorn Books, 1975.

REED, STANLEY F.

Stanley F. Reed was the solicitor general between 1935 to 1938, responsible for defending New Deal legislation in a number of key Supreme Court cases, and a United States Supreme Court justice from 1938 to 1957.

Born in Minerva, Kentucky, in 1884, Reed studied law at the University of Virginia, Columbia University, and at the Sorbonne in Paris. After a four-year stint in the Kentucky state legislature, he served in army intelligence during World War I. Reed was appointed to the Federal Farm Board in 1929 and President Herbert Hoover made him counsel for the Reconstruction Finance Corporation in 1932.

Reed's most significant achievement of the Depression years was as the nation's solicitor general from 1935 to 1938, defending such programs as the National Recovery Administration (unsuccessfully) in the 1935 *Schechter v. United States* decision; the Agricultural Adjustment Act (unsuccessfully) in the 1936 *United States v. Butler et al.* decision; the National Labor Relations Act (successfully) in the 1937 *NLRB v. Jones & Laughlin* decision; and the Social Security Act (successfully) in the 1937 *Seward Machine v. Davis* and the *Helvering v. Davis* decisions.

In 1938, Reed became Roosevelt's second appointee to the Supreme Court. There, he issued several key civil liberties decisions in the 1940s and 1950s. Reed retired from the Court in 1957 and died in 1980.

See also: Agricultural Adjustment Act; *NLRB v. Jones & Laughlin;* National Labor Relations Act; Reconstruction Finance Corporation; *Schechter v. United States;* Social Security Act; Supreme Court; *United States v. Butler et al.*

Bibliography

Fassett, John D. *New Deal Justice: The Life of Stanley Reed of Kentucky.* New York: Vantage Press, 1994.

REUTHER, WALTER

President of the United Automobile Workers (UAW) and later of the Congress of Industrial Organizations (CIO), Walter Reuther was the lead organizer of the sit-down strikes against General Motors (GM) in 1936 and 1937 that ushered in a new age in the organization of workers in mass production industries.

Reuther was born in Wheeling, West Virginia, in 1907, the son of German immigrants and socialists. In 1927, he moved to Detroit, went to work at the Ford Motor Company, and took courses at a college that later became Wayne State University. Over the years, he became a skilled tool and die craftsman and a foreman. At the same time, he joined the leftist labor organization, the League for Industrial Democracy. In 1933, he was laid off from Ford. Pooling his money with his brother Victor, who would later join him in organizing auto workers, Reuther toured Nazi Germany and worked at a Ford-equipped auto factory in the Soviet Union. His experiences there permanently turned him against communism.

Upon his return to the United States, Reuther was elected to the new UAW's board in 1936 and became president of UAW Local 174. Late in that year, Reuther began his plans for organizing GM, the giant of the auto industry, through a sit-down strike at Fisher Body Plant Number One, a key plant in the corporation's archipelago of midwestern factories. Well organized and well disciplined, the workers held out at the plant for forty-four days between December 30, 1936, and February 11, 1937, forcing GM management to cave in and accept the UAW as the bargaining agent for the company's assembly-line workers.

This success, partly due to the state government's neutrality and the union-encouraging National Labor Relations Act, unleashed a wave of sit-down strikes across the country and—even in the absence of strikes—got U.S. Steel to accept unionization of its massive plants. Following the sit-down strikes, Reuther was made director of the GM department of the UAW in 1939 and president of the whole union from 1946 until his death.

After the war, Reuther became head of the CIO in 1952 and helped push through its merger with the American Federation of Labor in 1955. Reuther died in a plane crash in 1970.

See also: auto industry; Congress of Industrial Organizations; General Motors; strikes, sit-down; unions and union organizing; United Automobile Workers; National Labor Relations Act.

Bibliography

Cormier, Frank. *Reuther*. Englewood Cliffs, NJ: Prentice-Hall, 1970.

Gould, Jean. *Walter Reuther: Labor's Rugged Individualist*. New York: Dodd, Mead, 1972.

Lichtenstein, Nelson. *The Most Dangerous Man in Detroit: Walter Reuther and the Fate of American Labor*. New York: Basic Books, 1995.

RIVERA, DIEGO

Among Mexico's greatest artists of the twentieth century—and certainly the country's most influential—Diego Rivera is best known in the United States for his 1933 mural commissioned by Nelson Rockefeller for the RCA Building in New York City, a mural that was destroyed by Rockefeller for political reasons.

Rivera was born in Guanajuato, Mexico, in 1886 and began to study art at the age of ten. When his family insisted that he attend a military academy at thirteen, Rivera rebelled, enrolling instead in the Academy of San Carlos. His first exhibition took place at the academy in 1906.

For the next twenty years, Rivera traveled back and forth between Mexico and Europe, becoming involved in Communist Party politics and winning a reputation as a master visual chronicler of Mexican history and Mexican culture. He married fellow painter Frida Kahlo in 1929; the two had a tempestuous relationship, with many of their feuds carried out in public.

In 1930, Rivera traveled to San Francisco, where he painted two murals for the California School of Fine Arts. In 1932 and 1933, he painted twenty-seven murals covering the history of the auto industry at the Detroit Institute of Arts. In 1933, art collector Nelson Rockefeller, heir to an oil fortune, commissioned Rivera to paint a mural for the RCA Building. But Rivera's depiction of Soviet May Day celebrations offended his patron. When Rivera refused to paint over a prominent portrait of Lenin at the center of the mural, Rockefeller had the mural destroyed.

Rivera soon returned to Mexico, where he served as host to the exiled Soviet leader Leon Trotsky, although the two soon fell into a dispute. Rivera continued to paint and to participate in left-wing politics until the end of his life in 1957.

See also: arts, fine.

Mexican artist Diego Rivera works on an anti-Nazi mural for the offices of *The Workers Age*, a New York City newspaper, in 1933. Rivera's bold compositions influenced much of American public art of the Great Depression era. *(Brown Brothers)*

Bibliography

Herner de Larrea, Irene. *Diego Rivera's Mural at Rockefeller Center.* Mexico City: Edicupes, S. A. de C. V., 1990.

Kettenman, Andrea. *Diego Rivera (1886–1957): A Revolutionary Spirit in Modern Art.* New York: Taschen, 1997.

ROBESON, PAUL

A dramatic actor, a renowned bass singer, a civil rights activist, and a political radical, Paul Robeson is one of the great Renaissance men of the twentieth century, who performed in a number of racially and dramatically pathbreaking theatrical and cinematic productions in the 1930s, including the revival of the musical *Show Boat* in 1932 and the film *The Emperor Jones* (1933).

Robeson, born in Princeton, New Jersey, in 1898, came from a middle-class black family; his father was an escaped slave who attended college and became a minister, and his mother was a schoolteacher from one of Philadelphia's leading African-American families. Robeson won a scholarship to Rutgers University, where he became class valedictorian and an All-American in football. After graduating in 1919, Robeson studied law at Columbia University and joined an all-white law firm in 1923, soon leaving to become a performing artist.

At Columbia, Robeson had acted in amateur theatrical productions. His powerful bass voice and commanding presence made him a natural for the stage, and he played the title role in the revival of Eugene O'Neill's *The Emperor Jones* in 1923. He also starred in the premiere of the playwright's *All God's Chillun Got Wings* that same year. While performing on stage, Robeson was also pursuing a music career, signing a recording contract with the Victor Talking Machine Company to sing popular tunes and spirituals.

After starring in a famed 1930 production of *Othello* in London, Robeson went to Hollywood, where he starred in *The Emperor Jones, Showboat* (1936), *Song of Freedom* (1936), *The Proud Valley* (1940), and a number of other films. Later, Robeson would say that he was exploited in stereotypical roles in most of these films.

While in Britain in the 1930s, Robeson became interested in African culture and history, taking courses at the University of London and becoming active in the West African Students Union, where he met, among other future liberation leaders, Jomo Kenyatta of Kenya. Robeson also became involved in radical politics in these years, visiting the Soviet Union in 1934 and concluding that communism offered the best path for the liberation of people of African descent in the

Actor Paul Robeson poses for a publicity photo as the title character in the 1933 film *The Emperor Jones*, based on Eugene O'Neill's play of the same name. *(Brown Brothers)*

United States and around the world. In 1938, he traveled to Spain to sing for the troops fighting fascism in the civil war there. Returning to the United States in the following year, he became active in the union movement, recording a number of labor ballads and performing at union benefits.

Robeson's radicalism got him into trouble with U.S. authorities and much of white America after World War II. A radical audience at a Robeson concert in Peekskill, New York, was attacked by local toughs in 1949 and, in 1950, the State Department voided his passport. Unable to perform abroad and shunned in the United States, he made few public appearances in the 1950s. By 1958, he was performing again in the United States and had gotten his passport back, allowing him to hold concerts around the world. But the strain of the 1950s showed. In 1961, Robeson attempted suicide. Later in the 1960s and 1970s, he was heartened by the rise of black radicalism and experienced something of a revival. He died in 1976.

See also: African Americans; films, feature; music; Soviet Union; Spanish Civil War.

Bibliography

Duberman, Martin B. *Paul Robeson.* New York: Knopf, 1989.

Foner, Philip, ed. *Paul Robeson Speaks: Writings, Speeches, Interviews, 1918–1974.* New York: Brunner/Mazel, 1978.

Robeson, Paul. *Here I Stand.* Boston: Beacon Press, 1971.

Robeson, Susan. *The Whole World in His Hands: A Pictorial History of Paul Robeson.* Secaucus, NJ: Citadel Press, 1981.

ROBERTS, OWEN J.

Appointed by President Herbert Hoover to the Supreme Court in 1930, Owen J. Roberts was a moderate voice on the Court and considered a swing vote in a number of critical cases upholding the constitutionality of New Deal legislation.

Roberts was born in small-town Pennsylvania in 1875 and graduated from the University of Pennsylvania. Thereafter, he conducted a private law practice and taught law at the University of Pennsylvania. In 1924, he was appointed by President Calvin Coolidge to help prosecute the Teapot Dome scandal cases from the previous Warren G. Harding administration, leading to the conviction of former Interior Secretary Albert Fall in 1929. Hoover appointed him to the Supreme Court the following year.

While Roberts wrote decisions in key 1930s cases—including the 1934 *Nebbia v. New York*, which upheld the state's milk price-setting practices, thereby confirming the government's right to regulate business—he played a more crucial role as a swing vote on the Court.

In 1936, he joined the majority in ruling against a minimum-wage law but then reversed himself to confirm the legality of the minimum wage in the landmark *West Coast Hotel v. Parrish* decision of 1937. Many court observers believed that his switch was influenced by President Franklin D. Roosevelt's threats to pack the court with liberal justices. Roberts also provided a swing vote in the *NLRB v. Jones & Laughlin* case of 1937, upholding the National Labor Relations Act, and in various decisions ruling different aspects of the Social Security Act constitutional in 1937.

In late 1941, Roberts was appointed by the president to conduct an official investigation of the attack on Pearl Harbor. While largely blaming military unpreparedness, the report also concluded, without any documentation, that local Japanese-Americans were instrumental in the success of the surprise attack.

Roberts served on the Supreme Court until 1945 and died in 1955.

See also: court-packing plan; *NLRB v. Jones & Laughlin*; National Labor Relations Act; Social Security Act; Supreme Court; *West Coast Hotel v. Parrish*.

Bibliography

Leonard, Charles A. *A Search for a Judicial Philosophy: Mr. Justice Roberts and the Constitutional Revolution of 1937.* Port Washington, NY: Kennikat Press, 1971.

Roberts, Owen J. *The Court and the Constitution.* Cambridge: Harvard University Press, 1951.

ROBINSON, EDWARD G.

One of the most popular and accomplished film stars of the 1930s, Edward G. Robinson is perhaps best remembered for his starring role in *Little Caesar* (1930), where, say film enthusiasts, he literally invented the role of the Hollywood gangster.

Born Emmanuel Goldenberg in Bucharest, Romania, in 1893, Robinson emigrated to New York City with his family when he was ten years old. He attended City College, where he began to act in amateur productions. He made his professional debut on Broadway in 1915 and continued to act on the stage through 1930. At the same time, Robinson was breaking into film, with his first role being in the 1923 silent *The Bright Shawl*.

But his characteristic nasal, tough-guy voice was meant for the talking pictures that came out in the late 1920s, and Robinson became a star playing Caesar "Rico" Bandello in *Little Caesar*. Considered among the finest of the early talkies, it caught the anger of Depression-era audiences, depicting the gangster as ruthless and cutthroat.

In Howard Hawks's *Barbary Coast* (1935), Robinson played a nineteenth-century gang leader in San Francisco who equates business and crime in ways that also appealed to embittered audiences in the 1930s. Robinson also played roles on the other side of the criminal line, including a gang-fighting cop in the 1936 *Bullets or Ballots*.

Robinson continued to act in classic films like *Double Indemnity* (1944), *The Ten Commandments* (1956), and *The Cincinnati Kid* (1965) during and after World War II. Robinson received a lifetime achievement Academy Award after his death in 1973.

See also: films, feature; *Little Caesar;* Hawks, Howard.

With his distinctive voice and tough-guy demeanor, Edward G. Robinson was one of the most popular actors of the 1930s. *(Library of Congress)*

Bibliography

Hirsch, Foster. *Edward G. Robinson*. New York: Pyramid Publications, 1975.

Robinson, Edward G. *All My Yesterdays: An Autobiography*. New York: Hawthorn Books, 1973.

ROBINSON, JOSEPH T.

A conservative Democrat from Arkansas, Joseph T. Robinson was Senate majority leader from 1933 until 1937, playing a reluctant but generally effective steward of New Deal legislation through Congress.

Born in Lonoke, Arkansas, in 1872, Robinson was a lawyer in his hometown until elected to the House of Representatives in 1902. In 1912, he became governor of Arkansas. But he was in that post for just a few months when the legislature appointed him to replace the recently deceased Senator Jeff Davis.

In 1928, Robinson was picked as the party's vice presidential nominee on the losing Al Smith ticket. With the Franklin D. Roosevelt landslide and the Democratic takeover of Congress in 1933, Robinson was chosen Senate majority leader, where he spent the next four years getting New Deal legislation passed. The most famous piece of legislation that Robinson sponsored was the 1936 Robinson-Patman act, which banned chain stores from dumping products at below-profit to drive local competitors out of business. But as a southern conservative, he fought antilynching legislation and efforts to get blacks included in public works projects.

In 1937, Robinson took on the leading role in shepherding President Roosevelt's so-called court-packing plan through the Senate. The plan, designed to overcome the conservative majority on the Supreme Court, called for the appointment of one new justice for every sitting justice aged seventy or over. But the plan drew outraged criticism and charges of dictatorship against Roosevelt. Indeed, the fight was so stressful that it was said to have caused Robinson's fatal heart attack on July 14, 1937. Robinson's sudden death convinced Roosevelt that the plan was unlikely to pass Congress and he backed away from it.

See also: court-packing plan; Democratic Party; Roosevelt, Franklin D.; Smith, Al.

Bibliography

Weller, Cecil Edward. *Joe T. Robinson: Always a Loyal Democrat.* Fayetteville: University of Arkansas Press, 1998.

ROCKWELL, NORMAN

One of the most popular commercial artists of the Great Depression era, Norman Rockwell is best remembered for his sentimental but technically exacting portrayals of American life painted for the cover of the mass circulation magazine the *Saturday Evening Post.*

Born in New York City in 1894, Rockwell won a scholarship to the Art Students League and got his first freelance magazine assignment at the age of 17. In 1916, he produced his first cover for the *Saturday Evening Post.* For the next half-century, Rockwell would paint over 300 magazine covers.

Perhaps his most famous artwork was a series of four posters illustrating the "four freedoms" enunciated as the goals of U.S. participation in World War II by President Franklin D. Roosevelt. Thousands of these posters were distributed by the Office of War Information.

After the war, Rockwell weathered the various art movements of the era, continuing to produce his hyperrealistic paeans to traditional American life and values. Awarded the Presidential Medal of Freedom in 1977—America's highest peacetime honor—Rockwell died in 1978.

See also: arts, fine; newspapers and magazines; *Saturday Evening Post.*

Bibliography

Buechner, Thomas S. *Norman Rockwell: Artist and Illustrator.* New York: Abradale Press/Abrams, 1996.

Rockwell, Norman. *Norman Rockwell and the* Saturday Evening Post: *The Complete Cover Collection, 1916–1971.* New York: MJF Books, 1994.

Rockwell, Norman. *My Adventures As an Illustrator.* New York: Abrams, 1988.

RODGERS (RICHARD) AND HART (LORENZ)

The writing team of composer Richard Rodgers and lyricist Lorenz Hart produced some of the most memorable stage and film musicals of the twentieth century, including such Depression-era classics as *Love Me Tonight* (1932), *On Your Toes* (1936), *Babes in Arms* (1937), and *Pal Joey* (1940).

Both Rodgers and Hart were born in New York City, the former in 1902 and the latter in 1895. Rodgers studied music and theater at Columbia University and the Institute of Musical Art (now the Juilliard School of Music). Hart studied journalism at Columbia. Their first collaboration was on the 1919 musical show *Fly With Me.* They had their first big success in 1925 with the show *The Garrick Gaieties.* Another hit show, *A Connecticut Yankee,* was well-reviewed in 1927.

They produced fourteen shows for Broadway between 1926 and 1930, until the Depression dried up much of the funding for shows. They then turned to Hollywood and wrote musical scores for a number of movies. Among the memorable tunes penned by the team are "My Funny Valentine," "The Lady Is a Tramp," "Blue Moon," "With a Song in My Heart," and "Bewitched, Bothered and Bewildered."

After Hart's premature death in 1943, Rodgers teamed up with lyricist Oscar Hammerstein. Rodgers died in 1979.

See also: films, feature; music.

Bibliography

Marx, Samuel, and Jan Clayton. *Rodgers and Hart: Bewitched, Bothered, and Bedeviled.* New York: G. P. Putnam, 1976.

Rodgers, Richard. *Musical Stages: An Autobiography.* New York: Random House, 1975.

ROGERS, WILL

A popular newspaper columnist, author, and movie actor, Will Rogers is best remembered as America's premier humorist of the 1920s and 1930s, poking fun gently at American customs and politics.

Born William Penn Adair Rogers in the Oologah Indian Territory (later part of Oklahoma) in 1879, the future humorist was the son of a successful rancher and grew up learning the roping and cowboy tricks he would later exploit in Wild West shows and on the vaudeville stage.

He began performing on Broadway in the early 1900s and starred in showman Florenz Ziegfield's production of *Midnight Frolic* in 1915, in which he began commenting humorously on political affairs. He turned his routines into a good-natured newspaper column beginning in 1922 and authored a number of books of his oft-quoted sayings—known as "rogerisms." Even while writing and touring, Rogers was also launching a Hollywood acting career from 1918 on. Among his best-known films are *A Connecticut Yankee* (1931) and *State Fair* (1933).

While Rogers turned down a nomination to run for governor of Oklahoma on the Democratic ticket, he did serve as mayor of Beverly Hills and campaigned hard for Franklin D. Roosevelt in 1932. Rogers continued to write his columns and conduct humorous lecture tours until his death in an Alaskan airplane crash with famed pilot Wiley Post on August 15, 1935.

See also: films, feature; newspapers and magazines; radio.

Humorist, actor, and professional raconteur, Will Rogers was author of a popular syndicated newspaper column in the 1920s and 1930s. *(Brown Brothers)*

Bibliography

Carter, Joseph H. *Never Met a Man I Didn't Like: The Life and Writings of Will Rogers.* New York: Avon Books, 1991.

Rogers, Will, and Donald Day. *Autobiography.* Boston: Houghton Mifflin, 1949.

Sterling, Bryan B., and Frances N. Sterling. *A Will Rogers Treasury: Reflections and Observations.* New York: Crown Publishers, 1982.

ROOSEVELT, ELEANOR

Anna Eleanor Roosevelt, a niece of Theodore Roosevelt was born in 1884. In 1905, she married her distant cousin, Franklin Delano Roosevelt. As First Lady from 1933 to 1945, Eleanor Roosevelt was an experienced political leader, educator, and journalist.

THE 1920s

Throughout the 1920s, Eleanor Roosevelt helped lead the Women's City Club in New York, the National Consumer's League, the Women's Division of the Democratic State Committee, and the New York chapters of the League of Women Voters and the Women's Trade Union League. Repeatedly she goaded women's and other reform groups to set realistic goals, prioritize their tasks, and delegate assignments. As Democratic Women's Committee (DWC) vice president and finance chairman, Eleanor Roosevelt wrote articles discussing campaign strategies for the *Women's Democratic News*. As chair of the Civic League's City Planning Department, she coordinated its responses on housing and transportation issues, chaired its legislation committee, pushed through a reorganization plan, arbitrated disputes over child labor laws, promoted workmen's compensation, and, in a move that made banner headlines across New York state, strongly urged adoption of an amendment to the penal law legalizing the distribution of birth control information among married couples. In 1924, she chaired both the Bok Peace Prize Committee and the women's delegation to the platform committee of the Democratic National Convention and served as Al Smith's liaison to women voters. A staunch supporter of Robert Wagner's 1926 campaign for the U.S. Senate, she traveled New York as one of Wagner's leading speakers and debaters.

Eleanor Roosevelt then took to print to promote her candidates with the same level of energy she displayed in her speeches. She expanded her audience, broadened her themes, and carefully tailored her remarks to readers of the Civic League's *Weekly News*, *Women's Democratic News*, *Redbook*, *Current History*, and *North American Review*. Her persistent pragmatism attracted attention within the party and women's political organizations. Soon the media publicized her clout, treating her as a "woman [of influence] who speaks her political mind."

The 1928 election of Franklin D. Roosevelt as governor of New York presented a new challenge to both Roosevelts. Their relationship had begun to move away from a traditional marriage and more toward a professional collaboration between peers. Eleanor's discovery in 1918 of Franklin's affair with Lucy Mercer, Eleanor's secretary, destroyed marital intimacy and encouraged her to look elsewhere for closeness. Daughter Anna Roosevelt later recalled that her mother's discovery of the affair "spurred on" her activism and that her parents' "different priorities" became more apparent. As a result, by the time Franklin was elected governor in 1928, both he and Eleanor had developed their own personal and political support systems.

As the wife of the governor, Eleanor Roosevelt struggled to balance her commitment to political reform with her husband's political agenda. Her private loyalty was the DWC, whose newsletter she continued to edit covertly. Although she refrained from delivering "political speeches," she continued to travel the remote upstate regions with DWC organizer Molly Dewson. When postelection polls showed a 20 percent increase in the upstate Democratic vote, Franklin D. Roosevelt's campaign director, James Farley credited the victory to Eleanor Roosevelt's "real sense of politics." Aware of how difficult it was for a politician and his staff to face unpopular decisions, she urged the appointment of individuals who had the nerve to disagree openly with the governor. She lobbied successfully for Frances Perkins's appointment as New York state secretary of labor and for Nell Schwartz to fill the vacancy Perkins's appointment left on the state industrial commission. Eleanor strongly objected to Franklin's retaining any of previous Governor Al Smith's cabinet. In particular, she opposed Belle Moskowitz's reappointment as personal secretary to the governor and Robert Moses's reappointment as secretary of state.

Perhaps most important, Eleanor began to apply political finesse to resolve disagreements within Franklin's inner circle. She regularly settled conflicts between his intimates, personal adviser Louis Howe and campaign adviser James Farley and acted as a political stand-in when Franklin could not or chose not to participate in the discussion. Certainly there is no clearer indication of her prominence within this inner circle than its decision to send her to issue the admin-

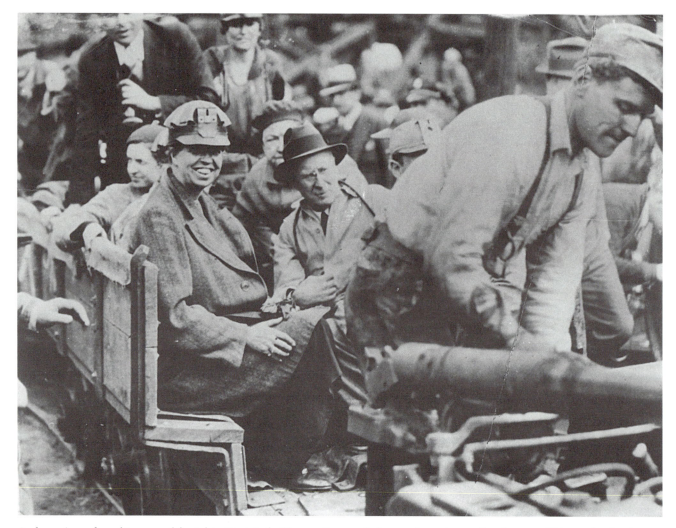

A champion of working people's rights, First Lady Eleanor Roosevelt is seen here descending into an Ohio coal mine in 1936. *(Brown Brothers)*

istration's rebuke of now Mayor Jimmy Walker's misconduct corruption.

ELEANOR ROOSEVELT AS FIRST LADY

Franklin D. Roosevelt was elected president in 1932, and the move to the White House presented Eleanor with a more complicated dilemma. Franklin insisted that she stop her political activities and he refused her offers to help with his mail, act as his unofficial ambassador, or serve as administrative assistant. Trapped by convention, she begrudgingly recognized that "the work [was his] work and the pattern his pattern" and that she "was one of those who served his purposes." She turned to Louis Howe and former journalist and now adviser Lorena Hickok for guidance. Hickok suggested that Eleanor capitalize on the good relations she

had developed with women journalists during the 1932 campaign by holding her own press conferences. Howe, respectful of her political acuity, urged her to continue to speak out and frequently advocated Eleanor's positions before Franklin and Howe urged her to reject the confines of the White House and reach out to Americans ravaged by the Depression. The favorable press she received for getting Roosevelt to reach out (as well as the popularity of her own press conferences) convinced the president that he had erred in curtailing her activity. By August, Eleanor Roosevelt had resumed writing, beginning a monthly column for *Pictorial Review*; by October, she had traveled 40,000 miles examining social and economic conditions; and by December, she had responded to the 300,000 letters she received from "forgotten Americans." Her observations and those of her correspondents only reinforced the impressions she had formed during the final days of the campaign. She returned to Washington convinced that relief programs alone could not counteract the Depression and that basic economic reforms were essential.

Her constituency expanded, and she began to promote her own version of the New Deal. Worried that Louisiana Senator Huey P. Long and popular radio preacher Charles Coughlin supporters felt neglected by the New Deal, she wanted to make herself available to them. Also concerned that the Federal Emergency Relief Administration (FERA) programs did not meet enough people's needs, she pressured FERA administrator Harry Hopkins to hire Hickok to tour the nation, observe FERA programs, and report to him on the programs' effectiveness. Hickok sent copies of these honest, harsh field reports to the White House, daily confirming the many obstacles that those seeking relief encountered.

Determined to make the New Deal as much an agenda of reform as of relief, Eleanor Roosevelt pressured Hopkins and Secretary of the Interior Harold Ickes to address those most marginalized by the administration's policies. She criticized the Economy Act for penalizing federally employed married women; urged the Civil Works Administration to hire unemployed women; carefully monitored the construction of the government's Arthurdale subsistence homestead at Morgantown, West Virginia; facilitated the creation of the National Youth Administration; and spurred the development of the Federal One Programs for writers, artists, and actors. Disappointed that Social Security did not cover the majority of Americans and include health coverage, she reinvigorated her call for a living wage, the right to organize, and safe working conditions.

Like Franklin, Eleanor thought fear the greatest threat to democracy. Unlike him, however, she paid close attention to democracy's most vocal critics, especially African Americans and student activists. She coordinated the famous 1934 meeting between Franklin and National Association for the Advancement of Colored People leader Walter White to discuss anti-lynching legislation; prodded Henry A. Wallace, National Youth Administration head Aubrey Williams, and emergency relief coordinator Harry Hopkins to resist jim crow relief practices; acted as black spokesperson Mary McLeod Bethune's White House ombudsman; and spoke out strongly against racial violence. Her 1938 defiance of Birmingham segregation laws at the Southern Conference for Human Welfare drew national attention. In 1939 she played a key role in enabling Marian Anderson to perform at the Lincoln Memorial after the singer had, for racial reasons, been denied permission by the Daughters of the American Revolution (DAR) to sing at Constitution Hall. The DAR's action prompted Roosevelt to resign from the organization. From 1936 to 1940, Eleanor lent the same vocal support to the left-wing American Youth Congress, despite the strong opposition of Franklin's aides, and worked with James Farley (DNC) and Molly Dewson, now head of the Women's Division of the DNC, to discuss the role of women in political elections.

Eleanor Roosevelt's skillful use of the media helped offset the criticism that her activism provoked. In December 1935, she began writing her daily syndicated column "My Day," which, by 1940, had a circulation equal to that of Walter Lippman and Dorothy Thompson. She continued to devote four weeks a year to a nationwide lecture tour. She expanded her audience by launching a monthly question-and-answer magazine column; appearing on radio; writing more than 100 articles for magazines, newsletters, and policy journals; and releasing the first installment of her autobiography (*This Is My Story*) and two small books on foreign policy (*This Troubled World*) and democratic values (*The Moral Basis of Democracy*). By the end of Franklin's second presidential term, Eleanor was recognized as a political force in her own right.

After World War II, Eleanor became a major supporter of the United Nations. She served as U.S. delegate to the U.N. General Assembly in 1945, from 1949 to 1952, and from 1961 to 1962. She also served as chair of the U.N.'s Commission on Human Rights. Her boundless energy and deep commitment to social, economic, and political issues led her to be the most active First Lady in American history. She died in 1962.

ALLIDA BLACK

See also: women; Anderson, Marion; Hickok, Lorena; Roosevelt, Franklin D.; Documents: Eleanor Roosevelt Press Conference Discussion on Married Women in the Labor Force, June 16, 1938; Eleanor Roosevelt Press Conference Discussion on Crossing Picket Lines, January 17, 1939; Eleanor Roosevelt Press Conference Discussion on Cuts in Works Progress Administration Jobs, January 31, 1939.

Bibliography

Black, Allida. *Casting Her Own Shadow: Eleanor Roosevelt and the Shaping of Postwar Liberalism.* New York: Columbia University Press, 1996.

———. *Courage in a Dangerous World: The Political Writings of Eleanor Roosevelt.* New York: Columbia University Press, 1999.

Cook, Blanche Wiesen. *Eleanor Roosevelt: A Life.* 2 Vols. New York: Viking, 1992.

Ware, Susan. *Beyond Suffrage: Women in the New Deal.* Cambridge: Harvard University Press, 1981.

ROOSEVELT, FRANKLIN DELANO

Franklin Delano Roosevelt, scion of a wealthy upstate New York family, became the thirty-second president of the United States on March 4, 1933. Assuming power during the depths of the Great Depression, he would lead the country through economic turmoil and World War II. Elected president an unprecedented four times, he died in office on April 12, 1945, less than a month before the surrender of Nazi Germany and the end of the conflict in Europe.

Formerly a state legislator, assistant secretary of the Navy, vice-presidential candidate, and two-term governor of New York, Roosevelt's inauguration as president brought a new optimism to the country. With his ebullient personality and his gift for conveying empathy, Roosevelt was also a master of the relatively new medium of radio, using it to establish a seemingly personal relationship with average citizens in their homes. He favored government activism in economic affairs and made it clear that he was willing to try almost any strategy to lift the country out of the Depression. Arguing that Americans wanted vigorous leadership from federal officials in Washington, D.C., he initiated a spate of new programs and agencies that vastly expanded the national government and made it a part of people's everyday lives.

Historians and economists argue about the efficacy of the New Deal, as the series of Roosevelt programs became known, in alleviating the economic crisis of the 1930s. Most argue that ultimately it was mobilization for World War II that finally brought the country out of the Great Depression. Nevertheless, Roosevelt accomplished much, not only expanding the federal government but staving off potentially more extremist politicians on both the Right and Left. Big business, which initially did little to oppose Roosevelt, turned on him during his first administration. But, say historians, it was Roosevelt who probably saved American capitalism at its greatest moment of crisis. For this, and for leading the country through the worst of World War II, most scholars place Roosevelt among the top tier of presidents and consider him the most influential American politician of the twentieth century.

YOUTH, MARRIAGE, AND LAW PRACTICE

Roosevelt was born on January 30, 1882, at Springwood, his family's estate in Hyde Park, New York, the only child of James and Sara Delano Roosevelt, members of a wealthy branch of an old New York family. Franklin was well tutored as a child, was an avid bird hunter and collector, and accompanied his parents on visits to European resorts. He entered Groton Preparatory School in Massachusetts in 1896, a school for the children of the Protestant American elite, which prepared him for his matriculation at Harvard College. His fifth cousin, Theodore Roosevelt, was elected vice president of the United States in 1900, the same year young Franklin entered college. Franklin was fairly popular if not overly studious, attributes accentuated with the elevation of his cousin to the presidency following William McKinley's assassination in 1901. Still, Franklin read considerably on his own and amassed a library on U.S. warships.

While in college, Franklin became engaged to marry another fifth cousin, Eleanor Roosevelt, Theodore's niece. Eleanor, then nineteen, independent, and committed to social relief, was already teaching in a woman's settlement house and serving as an investigator for the Consumers League. They were married after Franklin's graduation in 1905 and moved to New York City.

In New York, Franklin again followed Theodore's tracks and attended Columbia Law School, where he was a more marginal student than his cousin. Although he failed two courses and never completed his degree, he passed his bar exam. He entered the practice of a large Wall Street firm, Carter, Ledyard, and Milburn.

NEW YORK REFORMER

Roosevelt was recruited into politics by John E. Mack, the district attorney for Dutchess County and leader of the Democratic Party. In 1910, Mack asked Roosevelt to run for the New York assembly to replace Lewis Chanler, who was thought to be retiring from the seat that included Hyde Park in order to run for the state senate. Roosevelt accepted the idea only to learn that

Shown here with his signature cigarette holder and displaying his ebullient style of campaigning, Franklin D. Roosevelt was elected to an unprecedented four terms as president in 1932, 1936, 1940, and 1944. He died in office in 1945. *(Brown Brothers)*

Chanler had decided to run for reelection rather than risk running in the Republican-leaning senate district. Roosevelt chose to run for the senate seat as a party token, planning a high-profile, if likely unsuccessful, campaign. Roosevelt hired the only automobile in the district and campaigned ceaselessly for a month, running on a good-government ticket despite representing the party of the downstate Tammany Hall, the political machine that dominated New York City elections.

Franklin's side of the family had long voted Democratic, although Roosevelt did secure Theodore's Republican blessing to run on the other ticket, which turned out to be just as well. The year 1910 was good for Democrats, who won the New York governorship and both houses, as well as three-fifths of Congress. Roosevelt outdid the Democratic gubernatorial candidate in his own district, but still won his seat only by 15,708 to 14,568. Eleanor and Franklin moved to Albany with their first three children: Anna, born in 1906; James, born in 1907; and Elliott, born in 1910. They would later be joined by Franklin Jr., born in 1914, and John, born in 1916.

One of the first issues of the new session was the selection of the United States senator, then a task committed by the U.S. Constitution to the state legislatures. William F. Sheehan was being forced on the legislature by Boss Charles F. Murphy, the leader of Tammany Hall. Roosevelt and a few reformist Democrats joined the Republicans to defeat him, Roosevelt emerging as the leader of the insurgent Democrats and gaining national press for his stand and for his negotiations with the Tammany politicians. A protracted fight led to a compromise candidate, a more independent Tammany man, state justice James O'Gorman.

Roosevelt contracted typhoid in 1912, on the eve of his first reelection, and his campaign was run by his political operative, Louis McHenry Howe. Howe used direct mail and large media buys to promote farm issues, including attacks on the low prices New York City commissioners awarded upstate farmers to allow for higher profits by city merchants. Roosevelt won 15,590 votes to 13,889 for the Republican and 2,628 for the Bull Moose Party challengers, which was again a stronger margin than that of his party's candidate for governor. In Roosevelt's second term, he introduced not only a bill to remedy the farm price differential on which he had campaigned but also bills to promote agricultural cooperatives and farmers' credit, to develop state water programs, and to improve forestry.

WILSON AND WASHINGTON

In 1911, Roosevelt had supported New Jersey governor Woodrow Wilson's run for the Democratic presidential nomination. Wilson won the nomination and the election of 1912, rewarding Roosevelt with access that led to his first national office in March 1913, an appointment as assistant secretary of the navy, a position once held by his cousin Theodore. The Roosevelts moved to Washington, D.C.

Roosevelt, yachtsman and traveler, had long been fascinated by the sea and the navy, which was more preparation for his post than was had by his superior, Navy Secretary Josephus Daniels, a former newspaper editor from North Carolina. Roosevelt's snobbish mockery of Daniels's politics and southern manners was accepted by the secretary with benign tolerance, indeed even with support for his assistant's rash attempts to modernize navy yards, appease shipyard labor, and enlarge the fleet.

In 1914, Roosevelt made one of his few true blunders in politics, running for the U.S. Senate, whose members, according to the Seventeenth Amendment passed in 1913, were to be popularly elected for the first time. Roosevelt ran in the primary without the support of his president and against the candidate of the still-formidable Tammany machine, Ambassador James Gerard, in the primary. Gerard, who did not leave Germany to campaign, beat Roosevelt in the primary by 210,765 to 76,888 but was defeated in the general election. The Tammany machine was changing as it lost ground, and the 1914 fight was the last between it and Roosevelt, who would later support its reformers, particularly Al Smith.

The defeat saved Roosevelt for the navy, and he returned to his desk from the campaign trail just weeks after the assassination of Archduke Ferdinand triggered the onset of World War I. Roosevelt was a hawk and strongly for the Allies. Acting on advice from friendly admirals, including Alfred Thayer Mahan, Roosevelt argued for a dramatic increase in the Atlantic fleet, an argument strengthened when a German submarine torpedoed the passenger liner *Lusitania* in May 1915. Congress passed a huge increase to naval appropriations in 1916.

Germany's January 1917 announcement of unrestricted attacks on American shipping provoked the United States to war, and Roosevelt committed himself to full-scale mobilization. His most ingenious trick was to evade a restriction on munitions sales to citizens that threatened to leave merchant ships unprotected from

German attack, which he thwarted by a scheme to lease cannon to the private merchantmen.

In 1918, Roosevelt toured Europe, meeting Allied leaders, inspecting facilities, and—most important—stealing a taste of battle from the fringes. He returned on the eve of the armistice, in the grip of influenza and pneumonia but still seeking a commission in the fleet, which Wilson denied him. His return led to Eleanor's discovery of Franklin's affair with Lucy Mercer, who had been Eleanor's social secretary for several years. Franklin gave Mercer up, and the marriage was not dissolved, although it was never again to be intimate.

RETURN TO NEW YORK

In 1920, Roosevelt was nominated for vice president on the Democratic ticket with presidential nominee James Cox. The Republican ticket of Warren G. Harding and Calvin Coolidge won in a landslide, 16,152,220 to 9,147,553. Roosevelt laid plans for future elections but turned to private industry, spinning various investment schemes and becoming vice president in charge of the New York office of the Fidelity and Deposit Company of Maryland, a bonding company.

The following August, while boating and swimming near his family vacation retreat on Campobello Island in New Brunswick, Canada, Roosevelt contracted poliomyelitis. He suffered horribly and was for a time utterly paralyzed. He was hospitalized for seven weeks and despite years of exercise was never again able to walk unaided.

Despite this obstacle, Roosevelt pursued his political ambitions, and the fall of 1921 saw him writing letters to the victorious Democratic candidates in New York and corresponding with former governor Al Smith, whom Roosevelt recruited to a successful bid for reelection as governor in 1922. During this time, Franklin began to rely on Eleanor to act for him as both surrogate speaker and observer. Despite her initial shyness, her efforts to keep Franklin informed and his name on the front political burners were necessary to his success for the rest of his career.

Roosevelt's first public appearance after his illness was at the 1924 Democratic Party convention, when he nominated Al Smith to be president, coining Smith's tag as the "happy warrior of the political battlefield." Although Smith failed to get the nomination and the Democrats lost the election, Roosevelt reemerged as a national party leader.

Roosevelt turned down a nomination to the U.S. Senate in 1926, drifting from national view while he concentrated on restoring his health in Warm Springs, Georgia. But in 1928, he repeated his call for a Smith nomination, making one of the first political speeches broadcast nationally by radio. Smith, now more powerful than ever, won the Democratic nomination on the first ballot. During the state convention, Roosevelt, then in Georgia, was nominated by acclamation for governor of New York. In November, Smith lost the nation and the state, but Roosevelt won a slim victory, beating his Republican challenger Albert Ottinger 2,130,193 to 2,104,629.

Roosevelt's gubernatorial administration placed him squarely in the national eye. He hewed an independent course, turning from Smith and his appointees and relying on the advice of professors and experts such as Felix Frankfurter, Morris Cooke, and Henry Morgenthau Jr. He promoted a range of economic initiatives, notably tax relief for farmers and a water project to create cheaper utilities for consumers, programs that deepened his appeal in upstate New York. His bills, however, led to stalemate with the Republican-led legislature.

By 1930, the bank failures and farm foreclosures of the Depression had begun to be felt in both urban and rural areas. After an initially slow understanding of the depth of the crisis, Roosevelt created an emergency unemployment committee, which recommended direct relief to unemployed workers and an expansion of public works. He also turned to farm credit and consumer relief programs as a response, and he made these his platform for his reelection. He campaigned vigorously, using tours, radio, and a new press bureau he set up to transmit news from Albany to upstate newspapers. He spoke out on but did little about the difficult issues of Prohibition repeal and judicial corruption, denying the Republicans their two planned attack issues. He carried the whole state this time, defeating Republican Charles A. Tuttle by 1,770,342 to 1,045,341, the greatest popular-vote percentage of victory in his career.

The effects of the Depression were more keenly felt after the election, and Roosevelt used his electoral mandate to push relief and recovery measures through the state legislature. In 1931, over the opposition of the American Federation of Labor, he created the state Temporary Emergency Relief Administration, run by Harry Hopkins, which eventually would provide unemployment compensation to 10 percent of New York's families. He also won a limited workweek for women and children, more credit for crop production, and a large public works project for reforestation.

THE FIRST PRESIDENTIAL CAMPAIGN AND THE PROMISE OF THE NEW DEAL

Roosevelt's political advisers, Louis McHenry Howe and Thomas Farley, began preparing for Roosevelt's presidential nomination the day after his reelection as governor in 1930. Roosevelt, of course, was publicly coy about his ambitions, even while planning political alliances through the national Elks club and among state and national party officials. He announced his candidacy on January 23, 1932, a week before his fiftieth birthday.

Roosevelt's opponent for the nomination was Al Smith, whose hostility to his one-time ally had grown with Roosevelt's exile of Smith and his supporters from gubernatorial influence. Smith's strong ties to Tammany gave him a base in Roosevelt's back yard, and Smith remained popular in New York City and the northeastern coast.

Despite planning and care, Roosevelt could not secure the nomination before the Democratic convention. Early planning led to a disparate coalition of elites and populists and ran up strong primary victories in western and southern states. To win the party nomination through the primaries, however, a candidate needed two-thirds of the votes before the convention, and a series of state commitments to favorite sons—Oklahoma governor Alfalfa Bill Murray; Missouri senator James Reed; Maryland governor Albert Ritchie; Ohio governor George White (who had a potential commitment to a national candidacy for Ohioan Newton Baker); Illinois governor J. Hamilton Lewis; and Louisiana governor Huey P. Long—contributed to a stall in the Roosevelt machine. In April, Smith carried Massachusetts entirely and a share of Pennsylvania. Worse still, in May Roosevelt placed second behind the Speaker of the House, John Garner of Texas, although ahead of third-place Smith.

The Chicago convention opened with a blunder by the Roosevelt forces, who attempted to repeal the two-thirds rule in favor of nomination by a majority. This ploy antagonized many delegates, and Roosevelt dropped the plan. The first roll-call ballot gave Roosevelt 664½ ballots, Smith 203¾, Garner 90¼, and the remainder scattered among six other minor candidates. Roosevelt needed 104 more votes to get the nomination. Two more roll-call ballots that night led to slight Roosevelt gains, gotten by feverish work by Farley, chief of Roosevelt's floor lieutenants, while the candidate waited by the phone in Albany. The next day Farley played his last card and offered Garner a place

as Roosevelt's running mate. Garner's commitment to Roosevelt and release of his own delegates allowed Farley to bring Texas into the Roosevelt camp and then California, which started a Roosevelt roll and clinched the nomination.

Departing from tradition, Roosevelt flew to Chicago to accept the nomination in person. His speech, emphasizing his break with traditions—not just in politics but in tax reform, agriculture, tariffs, and the economy—closed with one of the most famous political promises in American history: "I pledge you, I pledge myself, to a new deal for the American people."

The phrase "new deal," innocuous in itself, was seized the next day by *New York World* cartoonist Rollin Kirby as a label for an airplane flying over a puzzled farmer with a hoe. The press grabbed up the phrase and applied it generally to Roosevelt's program as it evolved.

Winning the nomination was the hard part. In the general election, the ravaged economy and public perception of Republican fault made Democratic victory all but inevitable. Touring the country, Roosevelt promoted reform programs at each stop, thereby garnering continuing national press coverage for himself and his still vague plans. The campaign of unspecified reform paid off, and Roosevelt beat incumbent President Herbert Hoover 22,829,501 to 15,760,684 in the popular vote and 472 to 59 in winning the electoral votes. The Democrats gained thirteen Senate seats and ninety House seats, leaving them in control of the Senate 60 to 35 and the House 310 to 117.

THE FIRST ADMINISTRATION

Immediately after the election, Roosevelt began to plan for the country's recovery from the Depression. There were 13 million people unemployed, a quarter of the workforce; the winter was particularly harsh; industrial output had dropped 44 percent in three years; and the farm price system had collapsed. Hoover sought Roosevelt's alliance to support Hoover's strategy of careful development of a recovery or at least to make public statements to calm capital managers moving money out of the country. Roosevelt, however, kept his distance. He consulted with his Brain Trust, an array of lawyers, professors, and economists who had written speeches for the campaign and now argued over methods of recovery, based largely on new price stabilizing regulations and limited public works projects built on a balanced budget.

On February 13, 1933, Roosevelt was almost assassinated during a visit to Miami, Florida. A man named Joseph Zangara aimed a pistol at him but, thanks to a tug of his arm by a woman near him, shot instead Chicago mayor Anton Cermak, who was standing next to Roosevelt's car. Roosevelt himself took Cermak in his car to the hospital, where Cermak later died. Zangara, who believed that capitalists should have stopped his father from causing a chronic pain in his stomach and had earlier plotted to kill Herbert Hoover and King Victor Emmanuel III, was tried for Cermak's murder and executed.

Roosevelt's inauguration on March 4, 1933, broke with tradition, primarily when Roosevelt pronounced his entire oath of office, rather than uttering the traditional "I do" after the Chief Justice's recitation. His inaugural address called for calm, noting, "This great nation will endure as it has endured, will revive and prosper. . . . The only thing we have to fear is fear itself." It called also for action, either through Congress or through direct executive power, in order to achieve economic balance, lost through failures of the men who controlled the stock exchanges and commodity markets, and to raise the prices of goods and the ability of the consumer to purchase them.

The change of administration had panicked the markets, banks, and exchanges, whose leaders feared that a change from Hoover's fiscal caution would destroy them. A run on the banks three days before Roosevelt's inauguration was halted only by declarations of "banking holidays" in six states. Roosevelt convened a special session of Congress on Sunday, March 5, to impose a week-long bank closure, at the end of which the run had been averted.

Roosevelt and his Brain Trust worked feverishly, using the momentum of his new presidency to urge Congress to enact a raft of public works, private relief, and economic regulation to stimulate the economy and put people back to work. The result was a breathtaking procession of new laws presented and passed in the first hundred days of the new Congress. Between March 9 and June 16, it passed the Emergency Banking Act and the Economy Act; reduced the federal operating budget by $500 million; passed an Economy Act and the Beer-Wine Revenue Act; established the Civilian Conservation Corps (CCC); ended reliance on the gold standard; passed the Emergency Farm Mortgage Act and the Agricultral Adjustment Act (AAA); created the Tennessee Valley Authority (TVA); passed the Home Owners' Loan Act, the Federal Securities Act, and the Glass-Steagall Banking Reform Act, which prohibited commercial banks from making risky investments and established the Federal Deposit Insurance Corporation (FDIC); and passed the National Industrial Recovery Act (NIRA) and the Farm Credit Act. At the end of the hundred days, Roosevelt had signed fifteen new laws.

Quick relief for the unemployed was to be had through the TVA, enacted under Roosevelt's aegis after years of fruitless promotion by Nebraska senator George Norris. The TVA was to provide electricity to much of the poorest areas in America through a series of dams and hydroelectric projects, as well as improve shipping access for Midwest goods. Likewise, public works performed by the CCC would not only reduce unemployment but construct land management and building projects on public lands. The NIRA and the AAA were even more ambitious.

The NIRA reflected a two-pronged approach to industrial recovery. It provided a $3.3 billion appropriation for more public works, managed by the new Public Works Administration (PWA). The PWA, however, took several years to develop under Roosevelt's barriers against fraud and waste, and its effects were not seen until late in the administration. The NIRA also established the National Recovery Administration (NRA), which was to develop and administer industrial codes for each trade sector to bar unfair trade practices. The NIRA was also to set limits on price, quotas on production, and wage and hour standards; it also assured workers' rights to bargain collectively.

The Agricultural Adjustment Act showed even more promise. It established the Agricultural Adjustment Administration (AAA), which set production standards to raise the prices of farm goods and to grant subsidies to producers of wheat, corn, hogs, cotton, tobacco, rice, and milk. The trade of subsidies for quotas was meant to reduce the price-crippling surpluses without bankrupting more farmers. This law had some effect prior to its invalidation by the Supreme Court in 1936.

Roosevelt's mandate at the polls had made him temporarily invincible in Congress. The Emergency Banking Act, introduced on the first day of the session, was passed sight unseen, after just thirty-eight minutes of token debate. Roosevelt also gained popular support for his programs by appealing directly to the people through a combination of twice-weekly press conferences without written questions the first held on March 8, 1933—and so-called fireside chats, direct radio addresses, the first of which he made on March 13. In contrast to the regular press conferences, Roosevelt continued a pattern with the fireside chats that he had developed as governor, making them infrequent to heighten the public's interest.

The economic measures were largely extensions of Hoover's programs of short-term economic intervention, although they were extended by regulatory measures. Still, Roosevelt believed America could pull itself up by its bootstraps and that industrial and agricultural concerns could restore themselves to health, as long as they had sufficient markets, profit, credit, and room to maneuver without losing it all to the banks.

The National Recovery Administration (NRA) headed by former Brig. Gen. Hugh Johnson, put the economy at the forefront. Its efforts were to establish industrial codes, which were written by industry insiders. Despite some success in 1933, the codes grew overly complex, with over 13,000 pages of regulations interpreted by an additional 11,000 rulings in just two years. Johnson also set up a huge propaganda campaign promoting the "blue eagle" logo of the NRA, unveiled by the president in a July 1933 fireside chat. Merchants and employers under the blue eagle accepted a voluntary system of wage and hour limits. Congress grew leery of the blue eagle, though, concerned that Johnson's bureaucracy was creating monopolies, and Roosevelt appointed a National Recovery Review Board, chaired by Clarence Darrow, to investigate the concerns, which the board substantiated. Other criticism came from the left, as unions complained that the NIRA's collective bargaining provisions were unenforced.

The AAA likewise suffered from unpopularity as 1933 dragged on. Although the drought's destruction of much of the wheat crop shored up wheat prices, Agriculture Secretary Henry A. Wallace faced massive overproduction of cotton and pork. He ordered the destruction of 10 million acres of cotton and 6 million piglets, measures that increased resistance to the still-voluntary programs. The lost agricultural lands moved millions of tenant farmers and sharecroppers to the cities, where they became unskilled workers.

Meanwhile, economic conditions had reached their nadir. The dust bowl Midwest was in the tenth year of the drought and erosion of its farmland, and the slow response to the newly devalued dollar, continued overproduction in some regions and underproduction in others, and the lack of capital in the markets delayed the administration's progress. Strikes became more frequent throughout the country.

Roosevelt continued his reforms, pursuing further access of farmers to credit, the regulation of broadcasting with creation of the Federal Communications Commission, and a permanent securities regulation scheme with the creation of the Securities and Exchange Commission in 1934, appointing financier Joseph P. Kennedy as its first chair. Roosevelt created a federal housing loan program and the National Labor Relations Board. He also signaled to Congress his intent to create a retirement insurance fund along lines proposed by Francis Townsend, which would become the Social Security Administration the following year. As resistance to voluntary farm quotas grew, Roosevelt's advisers asked Congress to move toward involuntary quotas, which were passed for sugar and cotton.

Despite all the action, Roosevelt's bootstrap approach was faltering. Although new capital investment began again to grow in 1934, it was still half its 1931 levels. Payrolls had risen but only to two-thirds of their 1929 highs. Building construction, wholesale prices, and consumer spending had risen but barely.

Roosevelt's party support was crumbling. Opposition to the New Deal crystallized in August 1934 with the American Liberty League, backed by Democratic standard-bearers John W. Davis and Al Smith and Democratic Party chair John Raskob. Hoover published a book resonating Liberty League ideas, which were echoed in speeches and radio addresses by Huey P. Long in the South and Father Charles Coughlin in the North.

Even so, the public still trusted Roosevelt and the New Deal. The November 1934 elections surprised everyone by giving the Democrats nine more seats in both the Senate and the House, for majorities of 69 to 25 and 310 to 117, respectively.

THE "SECOND NEW DEAL" AND THE COURT

In his January 1935 State of the Union message, President Roosevelt set out an even more ambitious plan, moving from relief to job creation, as well as the fuller assurance of Social Security—an economic safety net for the old, the ill, and the unemployed. The results were dramatic new laws, appropriating $5 million for emergency relief and public works employment, embodied in the Resettlement Administration (RA) and the Works Progress Administration (WPA). The RA helped dislocated farmers to find new work in towns, particularly the new suburbs. The WPA created jobs for them, as well as for artisans, artists, writers, and other skilled workers. The WPA, run by Harry Hopkins, eventually employed over 8,500,000 people.

May 1935 saw a series of intense political fights that Roosevelt took personally. He vetoed a popular bill to allow World War I veterans early redemption of their bonuses, going personally to Congress to explain his concerns of inflation arising from the bill. In an intense fight, the House overrode the veto, but the Senate narrowly sustained it. Only a few days later, the Supreme Court handed down its opinion in *Schechter Poultry v. United States*, ruling unconstitutional large portions of the NIRA and most of the work of the NRA and opening a two-year battle between Roosevelt and the Court.

Perhaps the most enduring of Roosevelt's New Deal plans was enacted on August 14, when he signed into law the Social Security Act, establishing a national insurance program of worker payroll deductions that supported pension and disability payments. Still, that autumn was not wholly given to domestic law; as Roosevelt supported a neutrality act, forbidding Americans to sell arms to states declared by the president to be at war. Over the next year, as the German, Japanese, and Italian Axis was forged, Roosevelt privately contemplated a blockade, which did not materialize but did jumpstart naval expansion. Roosevelt personally observed massive naval maneuvers off San Diego in October 1935, the first president to watch naval war games.

He broke form again in January, giving his State of the Union address at night, the better to gain a radio audience. His warnings of war abroad were accompanied by plans for neutrality and increased defense. Throughout the winter, much of it spent by Roosevelt in his winter quarters, the Little White House in Warm Springs, Georgia, the Court set aside more of the New Deal statutes, after which Roosevelt operatives enacted replacement statutes that recast parts of the vacated acts.

The campaign of 1936 was the great referendum on the New Deal. In June, the Republicans nominated Kansas governor Alfred Landon for president, and a host of small parties on both the Left and Right attempted to mount national campaigns, all attacking the New Deal and Roosevelt. One third-party candidacy had ended the previous September with the assassination of Huey P. Long, but less well-known candidacies covered the spectrum.

At the Philadelphia convention, Roosevelt was renominated by his party by acclamation and given a party platform supporting the means and goals of the New Deal. The campaign was intense, made more so by the new device of national opinion polling by George Gallup and Elmo Roper, who had measured growing dissatisfaction with the administration in late 1935 and whose polls were followed with interest by the public itself.

The campaign was based on a series of noncampaigning inspections of PWA projects and drought-stricken areas, each stop providing Roosevelt with a platform for a speech on some grand theme. Even so,

Landon's forces were buoyed by massive press support—nearly 80 percent of editorials were for Landon—and a defection of campaign donations as well. The death that year of loyal electioneerer Louis Howe led to an expanded role for Eleanor Roosevelt, whom Franklin asked to investigate the operation of party headquarters and who toured and spoke for the campaign.

Despite the defection of the elites, Roosevelt won a staggering victory at the polls, winning every state but Maine and Vermont, by a margin of 27,757,333 to 16,684,231 popular votes and 528 to 8 electoral votes. Three percent of the popular vote went to the third-party candidates, the largest being William Lemke's Union Party, which polled over 5 percent in only four states.

Roosevelt gave his second inaugural address on January 20, 1937, two months earlier than any before, owing to the Twentieth Amendment to the Constitution. He called for remedies for "one-third of a nation ill-housed, ill-clad, ill-nourished."

The greatest opposition to his pursuit of relief continued to be the Supreme Court, and on February 5, he proposed to enlarge the Court to gain a majority of new appointees. The fight over the plan, which would add a new judge for each justice over seventy, was bitter and prolonged.

Meanwhile, the Court began to lean Roosevelt's way. On December 19, 1936, Justice Owen Roberts, a swing vote, had agreed with the liberals during a private conference to uphold a Washington State minimum-wage law. Chief Justice Charles Evans Hughes released the decision on March 27, 1937, making it appear that the Court had suddenly swung to support Roosevelt's plans in general. That support was actually ensured with the resignation of Justice Willis Van Devanter, allowing Roosevelt to appoint Alabama senator Hugo Black on August 12. The court-packing plan devolved into a generous retirement package for judges modifications of lower court rules, the rest dying in committee. The Court, however, would not muster another majority to oppose the New Deal.

RECOVERY, WAR, AND DEATH

By 1937, the recovery had begun to take noticeable hold. The number of commercial failures in 1936 and 1937 was a third of what it had been in 1931 and 1932. Investment was rising, stock prices had recovered, and prices were up. Roosevelt's budget for 1937–38 initially curtailed government spending in order to end deficit spending. The result was a sudden and definite recession, reversing growth back toward 1932 levels. A decline in stock value through the summer, an October dive in the stock markets, and increasing unemployment fueled the "Roosevelt recession." Finally, in April 1938, Roosevelt was persuaded by Harry Hopkins to embrace continued deficit spending to prime the pumps of industry and counter the Depression. By the middle of 1938 the crisis was over, and growth returned and continued to rise. Meanwhile, Roosevelt was more concerned with both labor relations and foreign affairs.

A massive sit-down strike at a General Motors plant in Flint, Michigan, in January 1937 was met with police assaults and blockades of food and heat. The strikers' successful hold-out led to a wave of strikes across the country. Ten strikers were killed in May at a steel strike in Chicago. Roosevelt refused to intervene directly on either side, but signed a new wage and hours law in June, and Congress passed a ban on child labor. Roosevelt, whose programs had directly benefited black workers as well as whites, also promoted an antilynching bill. Although the bill failed, it spurred preemptive state laws that dramatically reduced lynchings.

Europe and Asia were by then moving toward war, and Roosevelt was cautious of hasty action. He sent memoranda to the European powers seeking arbitration of German claims to Czechoslovakian Sudetenland, which reinforced British Prime Minister Neville Chamberlain's policy of appeasement. In December 1937, the Japanese sank the USS *Panay*, an American gunboat, on the Yangtze River in China. Rather than starting a war for which he knew American forces were unprepared, Roosevelt accepted Japan's apologies for the offense. At the same time, though, Roosevelt had begun overseeing a billion-dollar expansion of the fleet, and he consulted with his ambassador to Germany on Nazi activities against the European Jews.

In the midterm elections of November, Roosevelt turned on some of the conservatives of his own party who had not supported his legislation, opposing the reelection of some southerners. The Democrats lost ground but still retained control of the Senate by 69 to 23 and the House by 261 to 164. This Congress approved Roosevelt's half-billion dollar defense increase in January.

The year 1939 was consumed with diplomacy, but domestic administration continued as well. The New Deal programs were consolidated and enlarged, while some were phased out. The WPA and four other agencies were combined into the Federal Works Agency. Moreover, the need for continued defense buildup, made clear by the German invasion of Poland in September and British and French declarations of war

against Germany, was increasing industrial production and relieving unemployment throughout the nation. The Depression was over.

In fireside chats Roosevelt reassured the country of his policy of neutrality. He also closed the ports to powers at war and supported a new neutrality act. This act of 1939, however, which passed two months after thirty Americans died in the torpedoed S.S. *Athenia*, allowed for the sale of arms to belligerents. In the face of the German occupation of Norway, Denmark, Luxembourg, Belgium, Holland, and France, the Battle of Britain, and submarine blockades, Roosevelt followed with the provision of fifty World War I destroyers to Britain, in exchange for ninety-nine-year leases to the United States of British airbases in Newfoundland and the West Indies. In September 1940, Congress passed the first peacetime draft, the Selective Service Act, which provided initially for the induction of 900,000 men between the age of twenty and thirty-six, requiring service for one year.

Running with Henry A. Wallace, who had replaced Vice President Garner on the Democratic ticket, Roosevelt was elected to an unprecedented third term in November 1940, with the Democrats beating Republican Wendell Willkie by 27,313,041 to 22,348,480 popular votes, and 449 to 82 electoral votes. The results in Congress were mixed. The Republicans gained ground in the Senate, though they were still heavily in the minority of 28 to 66. In the House, the Democrats gained seven seats, enlarging their margin 268 to 162.

In January 1941, Roosevelt gave two of his greatest speeches. His State of the Union address, on January 6, sought "a world founded upon four essential human freedoms . . . freedom of speech and expression . . . freedom of every person to worship God in his own way . . . freedom from want . . . [and] freedom from fear." His inaugural address two weeks later set forth America's rationale for supporting Britain and its allies: "In the face of great perils never before encountered, our strong purpose is to protect and to perpetuate the integrity of democracy. For this we muster the spirit of America, and the faith of America."

Throughout 1941, war with Germany seemed increasingly certain. On March 11, after a bitter debate, Congress passed Roosevelt's Lend-Lease Act, allowing the United States to accept noncash loan promises for aid to Britain, Russia, and their allies. Lend-lease shipments were protected by the U.S. navy in the summer, which was ordered in the autumn to shoot on sight any German submarines. In August, Roosevelt met British prime minister Winston Churchill aboard the battleship HMS *Prince of Wales* to sign the Atlantic Charter, pledging to achieve "the final destruction of the Nazi tyranny."

War came first, however, with Japan. When Japan allied with the German-Italian Axis, Roosevelt restricted war-related exports to Japan, especially of oil. Throughout 1941, Japan negotiated to restore supplies but failed. This prompted Japan to attack the United States, and on December 7, 1941, the Japanese navy bombed Pearl Harbor, Hawaii. On December 8, Roosevelt asked Congress for a declaration of war, and on December 11, Germany and Italy declared war on the United States

Thus, the United States found itself allied with a surrounded Britain, an invaded Russia, and an occupied France against an Axis that had crushed the armies and navies of most of its opponents across the globe. Roosevelt, awakening American's vast military potential, took the lead in forging a common alliance against the Axis, although Russian policy under Joseph Stalin remained a mystery to him. Following Churchill's plan to relieve the continent by attacking German flanks, and against Stalin's demands for an early Western front, Roosevelt endorsed preliminary invasions of North Africa in November 1942, Sicily in July 1943, Italy in September 1943, and France in June 1944, while pursuing a predominantly naval strategy against Japan.

Roosevelt was reelected to a fourth term in 1944. Senator Harry Truman of Missouri had replaced Wallace on the Democratic ticket, and he and Roosevelt beat Republican Thomas E. Dewey by 25,602,504 to 22,006,285, and 432 electoral votes to 99. The Democrats kept control of the Senate by a margin of 56 to 38, but gained in the House, 242 to 190.

Roosevelt's last foreign trip was to the Yalta Conference in the Crimea, Soviet Union, in February 1945, to meet with Churchill and Stalin, from whom Roosevelt secured promises that Russia would enter the war against Japan after Germany's surrender and that Stalin would establish democratic governments in the nations of Eastern Europe occupied by his troops. Russia did enter the war, taking a few Pacific islands before Japan's surrender, but turned Eastern Europe into a communist empire.

By the time of his return from Yalta, Roosevelt was desperately weak from advanced arteriosclerosis, which he had had for more than a year. He addressed Congress sitting down, which was a rare public acknowledgment of the bodily weaknesses he had camouflaged so well so long. In April 1945, he went to his cottage in Warm Springs with his two cousins, Laura Delano and Margaret Suckley, and with the now-widowed Lucy Mercer Rutherford, with whom he had renewed rela-

tions. There, on April 12, he died of a massive cerebral hemorrhage.

STEVE SHEPPARD

Bibliography

Ackerman, Bruce. *We the People: Transformations.* Cambridge: Harvard University Press, 1998.

Burns, James McGregor. *Roosevelt, 1882–1940: The Lion and the Fox.* San Diego: Harcourt, Brace, 1956.

Cushman, Barry. *Rethinking the New Deal Court: The Structure of a Constitutional Revolution.* New York: Oxford University Press, 1998.

Friedel, Frank *Roosevelt: A Rendezvous with Destiny.* Boston: Little, Brown, 1990.

Goodwin, Doris Kearns. *No Ordinary Time: Franklin and Eleanor Roosevelt: The Home Front in World War II.* New York: Simon & Schuster, 1994.

Graham, Otis L. *An Encore for Reform: The Old Progressives and the New Deal.* New York: Oxford University Press, 1967.

Hughes, Charles Evans. *The Autobiographical Notes of Charles Evans Hughes.* Cambridge: Harvard University Press, 1973.

Kennedy, David M. *Freedom from Fear: The American People in Depression and War, 1929–1945.* New York: Oxford University Press, 1999.

Leuchtenberg, William E. *Franklin D. Roosevelt and the New Deal.* New York: Harper & Row, 1963.

———. *The Supreme Court Reborn: Constitutional Revolution in the Age of Roosevelt.* New York: Oxford University Press, 1995.

Louchheim, Katie. *The Making of the New Deal: The Insiders Speak.* Cambridge: Harvard University Press, 1983.

McElvaine, Robert S. *The Great Depression: America, 1929–1941.* New York: Times Books, 1993.

Mitchell, Broadus. *Depression Decade: From New Era Through New Deal, 1929–1941.* New York: Harper & Row, 1947.

Romasco, Albert U. *The Politics of Recovery: Roosevelt's New Deal.* New York: Oxford University Press, 1983.

Roosevelt, Eleanor. *Autobiography.* New York: Harper & Row, 1961.

Roosevelt, Franklin. *The Public Papers and Addresses of Franklin D. Roosevelt.* Compiled by Samuel I. Rosenman. 13 Vols. New York: Random House, 1950.

———. *FDR's Fireside Chats.* Ed. Russell D. Buhite and David W. Levy. Norman: University of Oklahoma Press, 1992.

Schlesinger, Arthur M. *Crisis of the Old Order, 1919–1933.* Cambridge, MA: Houghton Mifflin, 1957.

———. *The Coming of the New Deal.* Cambridge, MA: Houghton Mifflin, 1958.

———. *The Politics of Upheaval.* Cambridge, MA: Houghton Mifflin, 1960.

RUTH, GEORGE HERMAN "BABE"

Considered by most baseball fans as the greatest player in the game's history, Babe Ruth is best remembered in the Great Depression for calling the spot to which he would hit a home run during the 1932 World Series game against the Chicago Cubs.

Born George Herman Ruth in Baltimore in 1895, the future baseball star had a troubled youth and ended up in a reformatory school. Always a competitive athlete, Ruth won a try-out with the Orioles in Baltimore, when he earned his nickname from a local sportswriter. But before he could play there, his contract was sold to the Boston Red Sox.

At first a pitcher, Ruth was traded to the New York Yankees in 1920. His hitting prowess was quickly recognized and he soon changed the game by hitting the long balls and extra-base hits heretofore rare in baseball. Coming just after the "Black Sox" bribery scandal of 1919, in which Chicago White Sox players were found guilty of throwing the World Series, Ruth's hitting abilities electrified fans and returned the game to its status as the national sport.

During the 1920s, with Ruth as their premier home-run hitter, the Yankees stood unchallenged as the powerhouse of the American League. Ruth broke hitting record after hitting record, including sixty home runs in 1927, a season record that stood until 1961. So crucial was Ruth to the Yankees' success that their stadium is still nicknamed "The House That Ruth Built." Earning more than even President Herbert Hoover during the Depression, Ruth is reported to have remarked that he was having a better year than the president.

Ruth was also known as a great lover of children and often visited them in hospitals and orphanages. Weeks after his number 3 was retired by the Yankees in 1948, Ruth died.

See also: sports.

Bibliography

Smesler, Marshall. *The Life That Ruth Built: A Biography*. New York: Quadrangle, 1975.

Wagenheim, Kal. *Babe Ruth: His Life and Legend*. New York: Praeger, 1974.

SHAHN, BEN

A fine arts painter and graphic artist, Ben Shahn is perhaps best known for a 1931–32 series of paintings about the 1920s-era trial of anarchists Nicola Sacco and Bartolomeo Vanzetti. Shahn also worked on a number of important murals for public works projects during the Great Depression, painted in the social realism style of the day.

Born in Lithuania in 1898, Shahn emigrated to New York City in 1906 with his family. He worked as a lithographer's apprentice during his high school years from 1913 to 1917. He also attended New York University and the National Academy of Design. Between 1925 and 1929, he traveled and studied art in Europe.

His work on the Sacco and Vanzetti trial, with its emphasis on angular facial portraits and striking perspectives, won him critical acclaim. He followed up with a painting of the trial of labor leader Tom Mooney. Between 1933 and 1935, Shahn did a series of paintings about the Prohibition era for the New York City Public Works Art Project.

For the next three years, Shahn was hired to do paintings and photographs of rural America for the Farm Security Administration. In 1938 and 1939, Shahn collaborated with his wife Barnarda Brysen on a famous mural series for the Bronx post office. Also in 1939, Shahn painted three of his most famous works: *Seurat's Lunch*, *Handball*, and *Vacant Lot*.

During World War II, Shahn worked on posters for the government and the Congress of Industrial Organizations. After the war, he moved away from social realism and painted more personal pictures. Shahn died in 1969.

See also: arts, fine; Farm Security Administration.

Bibliography

Greenfeld, Howard. *Ben Shahn: An Artist's Life.* New York: Random House, 1998.

Prescott, Kenneth Wade. *The Complete Graphic Works of Ben Shahn.* New York: Quadrangle, 1973.

Shahn, Ben, and Margaret R. Weiss. *Ben Shahn, Photographer: An Album from the Thirties.* New York: Da Capo Press, 1973.

Shahn, Ben, and James Thrall Toby. *Paintings.* New York: G. Braziller, 1963.

SINCLAIR, UPTON

A muckraking journalist and novelist during the early twentieth century, Upton Sinclair ran for governor of California with his radical End Poverty in California campaign in 1934, polling over a million votes in the general election.

Born in Baltimore in 1878, Sinclair graduated from the City College of New York in 1897 and attended graduate school at Columbia University, working during the latter years of his schooling as a journalist. In 1906, he was sent by the socialist journal *Appeal to Reason* to expose the terrible working conditions in the meatpacking factories of Chicago. One of the results of this investigation was the best-selling novel *The Jungle* (1906), which, rather than awakening Americans to the harsh working conditions of the factories, exposed them to the unhealthy methods of meat production. The book helped spur the formation of the Food and Drug Administration.

Sinclair entered California politics in the 1920s, running for governor twice on the socialist ticket and getting few votes. In 1933, a group of influential left-wing Californians convinced him to run for governor on the Democratic ticket. To launch his campaign, Sinclair penned a tract entitled *I, Governor of California, and How I Ended Poverty: A True Story of the Future* (1933), which sold thousands of copies.

Sinclair called his 1934 campaign EPIC (an acronym for his program, End Poverty in California) and advocated "production for use," which called for the state to seize idle farms and factories and turn them into cooperatives run and owned by farmers and workers. To the surprise of the Democratic Party's leadership, the radical platform galvanized voters and gave Sinclair a victory in the primary.

Soon a number of left-wing writers, intellectuals, and a few Hollywood personalities rallied to his cause.

Upton Sinclair and his End Poverty in California campaign for governor in 1934 were defeated by a coalition of business leaders and officials from the Democratic and Republican parties. *(Brown Brothers)*

But mainstream Democrats and Republicans—along with the state's business community, spearheaded by MGM chairman Louis B. Mayer—banded together in a well-funded and-orchestrated media campaign to defeat him in the general election. After his defeat, Sinclair published *I, Candidate for Governor, And How I Got Licked* (1935).

Sinclair continued to write socially conscious essays, fiction, and his autobiography between the late 1930s and the end of his life in 1968.

See also: Democratic party; End Poverty in California; Mayer, Louis B.

Bibliography

Mitchell, Greg. *The Campaign of the Century: Upton Sinclair's Race for Governor of California and the Birth of Media Politics.* New York: Random House, 1992.

Sinclair, Upton. *The Autobiography of Upton Sinclair.* New York: Harcourt, Brace & World, 1962.

SLOAN, ALFRED P., JR.

More than any other individual, Alfred P. Sloan Jr. created the modern industrial giant General Motors (GM). As president and chief executive officer from 1923 to 1937, he helped the company overtake Ford as the world's leading producer of automobiles. But he was forced to resign in 1937 when he refused to negotiate with the United Automobile Workers (UAW).

Sloan was born in New Haven, Connecticut, in 1875, the son of a coffee and tea importer. He earned a degree in electrical engineering from the Massachusetts Institute of Technology in 1895. He then took over as president of the Hyatt Roller Bearing Company—a company in which his father had an interest—and helped it win numerous contracts with the rapidly growing automobile industry. Hyatt was acquired by GM in 1916; Sloan was made the larger company's vice president in 1918. After GM was taken over by financiers John J. Raskob and Pierre S. Du Pont in 1920, Sloan became operating vice president. Three years later, he was promoted to president and chief executive officer.

A brilliant administrator and business tactician, Sloan steered GM into unprecedented prosperity and power in the 1920s, but faced hard times with declining auto sales after the beginning of the Great Depression in 1929. By the mid-1930s, GM employees, restive under the pay cuts and speed-ups of the Depression years, were beginning to agitate for a union. The 1935 National Labor Relations Act—guaranteeing the right to organize—was yet another factor behind the union effort.

At the end of 1936, the UAW organized a sit-down strike at GM's critical Fisher Body Plant in Flint, Michigan. For forty-four days, the strikers refused to leave the factory while Sloan tried in vain to get Governor Frank Murphy to use the National Guard to oust them. Sloan was adamantly opposed to unionization and refused to speak with the UAW and its head, Walter Reuther. But the strike was hurting GM financially and earning it bad publicity. Rather than meet with union representatives, Sloan stepped down as president, though he stayed on as chief executive officer and became chairman of the board of directors. He resigned as chief executive officer and as chairman of the board in 1946 and 1956, respectively. Sloan was also a philanthropist and is best known for his contributions to the Sloan-Kettering Cancer Center in New York City. He died in 1966.

See also: General Motors; strikes, sit-down; United Automobile Workers; National Labor Relations Act; Murphy, Frank; Raskob, John; Reuther, Walter.

Bibliography

Fine, Sidney. *The Automobile Under the Blue Eagle.* Ann Arbor: University of Michigan Press, 1963.

Sloan, Alfred P., Jr. *My Years with General Motors.* Garden City, NY: Doubleday, 1963.

SMITH, ALFRED E.

Democratic nominee for president in the 1928 election, Alfred E. Smith—popularly known as the "happy warrior"—was a member of the conservative wing of his party that tried to prevent the nomination of Franklin D. Roosevelt in 1932 and opposed much of the New Deal legislation proposed by his administration.

Smith was born on New York City's immigrant Lower East Side in 1873 and dropped out of school to work at the Fulton fish market following his father's death. He began working for the Tammany Hall Democratic machine in 1895 and served in several appointed positions in the city government and city Democratic Party before winning a seat in the state assembly from 1903 to 1915.

Smith made a name for himself as a member of a commission investigating factory conditions after the disastrous Triangle Shirtwaist Company factory fire of 1911. In 1913, Smith became speaker of the assembly and in 1918 won an uphill battle for the gubernatorial office. While losing in the Republican landslide of 1920 (New York then had two-year gubernatorial terms), Smith was elected again from 1922 to 1928, when he ran for president as the first Catholic candidate of a major party.

Losing badly to Republican Herbert Hoover, Smith became involved in the construction of the Empire State Building in 1931 and—believing that the Democrats were a shoo-in to win the White House in the first presidential election of the Great Depression—sought the party's nomination in vain in 1932. Aligning himself with the conservative party chairman John Raskob, with whom he had worked on the Empire State Building project, Smith tried to block Roosevelt's nomination and became increasingly embittered toward the new president after he took office in 1933.

Once a liberal supporter of workers' rights and urban issues, Smith became increasingly conservative and even reactionary during the middle and late 1930s, joining up with Raskob and other big business leaders to form the anti–New Deal Liberty League. Smith even endorsed the Republican candidates for president in 1936 and 1940. Smith died in 1944.

The Democratic candidate for president in 1928, Al Smith (*right*) grew increasingly conservative in his political outlook in the 1930s and became an ardent opponent of President Franklin D. Roosevelt and the New Deal. (*Library of Congress*)

See also: Democratic party; election of 1932; Empire State Building; Liberty League; Raskob, John J.; Roosevelt, Franklin D.

Bibliography

O'Connor, Richard. *The First Hurrah: A Biography of Alfred E. Smith*. New York: Putnam, 1970.

Pringle, Henry Fowles. *Alfred E. Smith: A Critical Study*. New York: AMS Press, 1970.

Smith, Alfred Emanuel. *The Citizen and His Government*. New York: Harper & Brothers, 1935.

SMITH, ELLISON D.

Democratic senator from South Carolina from 1908 to 1944, Ellison D. Smith—often known as "Cotton Ed" for his advocacy of cotton farmers—was both a firm opponent of civil rights legislation and a progressive on economic matters, helping usher through Congress a number of key New Deal bills.

Born in small-town South Carolina in 1864, Smith graduated from Wofford College in 1889. He then returned home to run his family's cotton plantation. In 1896, he ran successfully for the South Carolina legislature as a moderately liberal candidate with populist leanings. After four years in the state capital, he lost a race for U.S. Congress. In 1905, he organized the short-lived Southern Cotton Association, a trade group for cotton producers, where he earned a reputation as both a friend of cotton farmers and a brilliant orator. In 1908, he won a seat in the U.S. Senate.

In the 1910s and 1920s, Smith fought against anti–poll tax legislation and antilynching laws. At the same time, he became a key member of the so-called agricultural bloc in Congress. He advocated federal price supports for cotton and other crops, as well as Washington money to fight the devastating boll weevil infestation of the South's primary crop. Smith was also a strong supporter of the Muscle Shoals public power project in Alabama, but was stymied by President Herbert Hoover.

Because of this, Smith became an ardent supporter of Franklin D. Roosevelt—a public power advocate—in 1932, helping Roosevelt win passage of the Tennessee Valley Authority, a public power project for the South that dwarfed Muscle Shoals. As head of the powerful Senate Committee on Agriculture and Forestry, however, Smith fought with the Agricultural Adjustment Administration over farm policy, favoring price supports rather than crop reduction.

An unredeemed white supremacist to the end, Smith voted against antilynching legislation in the 1930s and walked out of the Democratic convention in 1936 rather than listen to an invocation by an African-American minister. Smith's opposition to Roosevelt's defense preparedness programs of the early 1940s hurt him politically and he was denied the Democratic nomination for another Senate term in August 1944. He died three months later.

See also: agriculture; lynching; Agricultural Adjustment Administration; Tennessee Valley Authority.

Bibliography

Hollis, Daniel W. " 'Cotton Ed' Smith—Showman or Statesman?" In *South Carolina Historical Magazine* 71 (October 1970): 235–56.

SMITH, GERALD L. K.

Right-hand man to Huey P. Long and his Share Our Wealth movement (SOWM) in the early 1930s and head of the organization after Long's assassination, Gerald L. K. Smith helped form the populist Union Party in 1936, which ran a weak campaign against President Franklin D. Roosevelt's reelection.

Born in rural Wisconsin in 1898, Smith earned a degree in oratory from Valparaiso University of Indiana. Following in the footsteps of his father, grandfather, and great-grandfather, Smith became a minister in the Disciples of Christ Church and was appointed pastor in Shreveport, Louisiana, in 1929.

There, he became an ardent supporter of Governor Huey P. Long and resigned his church position to head the radical SOWM. After Long's death in 1935, Smith became associated with Dr. Francis Townsend, advocate of a national old-age pension plan, and Father Charles Coughlin, the popular radio priest who had organized the anti–New Deal, populist National Union for Social Justice. In 1936, Smith worked with Coughlin to form the Union Party, which ran populist North Dakota congressman William Lemke in an ineffectual bid for the presidency in 1936.

Smith's political influence peaked in 1936. But,

though he was a brilliant orator, his increasingly demagogic and anti-Semitic rhetoric was alienating voters and isolating him to the fringes of the American political scene. He became an ardent isolationist and supporter of fascist causes in the late 1930s and formed the racist and anti-Semitic Christian Nationalist Front after World War II.

Later in life, he helped found a religious theme park in the Arkansas Ozarks. Smith died in 1976.

See also: election of 1936; National Union for Social Justice; Share Our Wealth Society; Union Party; Coughlin, Father Charles; Long, Huey P.; Townsend, Francis.

Bibliography

Bennett, Davis H. *Demagogues in the Depression: American Radicals and the Union Party, 1932–1936.* New Brunswick, NJ: Rutgers University Press, 1969.

Jeansonne, Glen. *Gerald L. K. Smith, Minister of Hate.* New Haven: Yale University Press, 1988.

SMITH, KATE

With her long-running show on the Columbia Broadcasting System (CBS), Kate Smith was among the most popular radio singing personalities of the Great Depression era. She is best known for her 1938 rendition of Irving Berlin's patriotic song "God Bless America."

Born in Washington, D.C. in 1907, Smith showed her singing talents early as a chorister in her local church. As a child during World War I, she sang on tour, raising money for Liberty Loans and being introduced to President Woodrow Wilson for her efforts.

While her family preferred that she go into nursing, Smith was determined to continue her singing career, performing in amateur contests and, at sixteen, heading for the New York stage. Smith soon established herself as a dancer as well as a singer in several Broadway shows in the 1920s and early 1930s.

In 1930, she made her radio debut on popular crooner Rudy Vallee's show and was signed up the next year to host *The A & P Bandwagon*, a fifteen-minute musical show airing four nights a week on CBS. With her trademark opening tune—"When the Moon Comes Over the Mountain"—Smith was an immediate success, becoming known as the "first lady of radio" and earning $3,000 a week, more than any other woman in broadcasting. The show would continue until 1947.

During World War II, Smith traveled extensively, entertaining the troops and selling war bonds. In 1950, she moved to television and hosted a daytime variety show for housewives. In the 1960s, she made guest appearances on variety shows. Smith died in 1986.

See also: music; radio; Berlin, Irving; Vallee, Rudy.

Bibliography

Hayes, Richard K. *Kate Smith: A Biography.* Jefferson, NC: McFarland, 1995.

Pitts, Michael R. *Kate Smith: A Bio-bibliography.* Westport, CT: Greenwood Press, 1988.

STALIN, JOSEPH

Secretary of the Communist Party of the Soviet Union from 1922 to 1953 and dictator of the country from the late 1920s until his death in 1953, Joseph Stalin built the Soviet Union into a major industrial power in the 1930s, even as he conducted ruthless and bloody purges of thousands of government officials, party members, and others whom he deemed a threat to his rule.

Born Iosif Vissarionovich Dzhugashvili in Georgia, an imperial colony of czarist Russia, in 1879, Stalin attended religious schools and seminaries as a young man, even as he secretly read the writings of Karl Marx and other revolutionary theorists. In 1900, he became involved in the political underground, organizing labor demonstrations and strikes in the region's industrial centers in the Caucasus.

When the socialists of Russia divided into two wings—the Mensheviks (literally, "minor" wing but actually moderates) and the Bolsheviks (major wing, but signifying radicals)—Stalin joined up with the latter, calling for a violent revolution to overthrow the corrupt and decrepit czarist government. In 1912, Stalin was elected to the Bolshevik Party's Central Committee. Over the next decade, Stalin would engage in revolutionary activity and be arrested more than half a dozen times.

Slowly, he rose in the Bolshevik party's ranks and adopted the revolutionary name "Stalin," Russian for "steel." He was editor of the party's newspaper before going into internal exile in Siberia from 1913 to March 1917, when a democratic revolution overthrew the czarist government. Stalin played a key role in the takeover of the government by Bolsheviks during the October (1917) revolution and was a military leader during the Russian civil war from 1918 to 1920.

Also serving as commissar of the people for the nationalities of Russia from 1917 to 1923 and secretary general of the Central Committee of the Soviet Communist Party from 1922 on, Stalin consolidated his position within the powerful Politburo that actually ruled the country. He used these various positions to eliminate his rivals for power—including Bolshevik revolutionary leaders Leon Trotsky and Grigory Zinoviev—after Lenin's death in January 1924. By 1928, he was in total control of the party apparatus and the government, forcing Trotsky into exile in 1929 (and having him assassinated in Mexico in 1940).

Once in power, Stalin abandoned Lenin's New Economic Policy of mixed private enterprise and state control for a bureaucratic, state-run industrialization process organized through a series of five-year plans. Attempting to consolidate government control of the agricultural sector and establish state-run farming collectives, Stalin literally starved out or killed the landholding peasantry, a process that resulted in the deaths of an estimated 10 million people.

But, along with the bloodshed, Stalin's plans produced striking results, as the nation's industrial output soared, even if agriculture lagged. The indisputable accomplishments of the Soviet Union in the 1930s—especially when compared to the collapsed economies of the capitalist West—intrigued many liberal and left-wing thinkers and activists in Europe and the United States. Stalin encouraged this thinking by establishing tight controls over communist parties in Europe and the United States through the Comintern, or Communist International.

Between 1934 and 1938, Stalin launched a new campaign to consolidate his power, conducting mock trials that led to the executions of tens of thousands, including Zinoviev and Marshal Mikhail Tukhachevsky, head of the Soviet military. His ruthless elimination of anyone or any group that might challenge his power is widely seen to have weakened Soviet administration and the Soviet military at a time when it was being increasingly challenged by the rise of Nazi Germany. At the same time, beginning in the mid-1930s, Stalin ordered communist parties in the West to join other liberal forces in popular front governments to fight against fascism.

To head off the threat from Germany, Stalin signed a nonaggression treaty with Adolf Hitler in August 1939, which contained a secret clause for the division of Poland. A couple of weeks after Hitler invaded that eastern European country on September 1, Stalin moved his troops into the eastern half of Poland. (The nonaggression pact also ended the popular front phase of the Comintern.) In 1940, Stalin ordered the takeover of neighboring Finland as well, but faced tough partisan resistance.

In June 1941, Hitler launched the greatest invasion in history against the Soviet Union and nearly made it to Moscow before meeting fierce resistance.

While helping to industrialize the Soviet Union in the 1930s, dictator Joseph Stalin was responsible for the murder of millions of his fellow citizens whom he deemed enemies of communism. *(Library of Congress)*

For the next four years, Stalin presided over a brutal eastern front war with Nazi Germany that resulted in the latter's defeat and Soviet hegemony over Eastern Europe. Following Stalin's death in 1953, his successor, Nikita Khrushchev, exposed the crimes of Stalin at a 1956 Communist Party meeting and went about a de-Stalinization program within a liberalized Soviet Union.

See also: Nazi Germany; Nazi-Soviet nonaggression pact; Soviet Union; Hitler, Adolf.

Bibliography

Conquest, Robert. *The Great Terror: A Reassessment.* New York: Oxford University Press, 1990.

Lee, Stephen J. *Stalin and the Soviet Union.* New York: Routledge, 1999.

Rappoport, Helen. *Joseph Stalin: A Biographical Companion.* Santa Barbara: ABC-CLIO, 1999.

Tucker, Robert C. *Stalin in Power: The Revolution from Above, 1928–1941.* New York: W.W. Norton, 1990.

STEINBECK, JOHN

One of the most popular and prolific authors of the Great Depression era, John Steinbeck is best known for his 1939 naturalistic novel with mythic overtones, *The Grapes of Wrath,* which tells the story of a family of Oklahoma farmers driven from their land and forced to labor in the fields and orchards of California.

Born in Salinas, California, in 1902, Steinbeck attended Stanford University off and on during the 1920s, but never received a degree. Always determined to be a writer, Steinbeck performed manual labor to support himself and used his experiences in much of his later fiction.

Steinbeck's first novels—*Cup of Gold* (1929), *The Pastures of Heaven* (1932), and *To a God Unknown* (1933)—were released to an uninterested public. His first best-seller came with *Tortilla Flat* in 1935, a gentle portrayal of a Mexican-American community in California. His next novel, *In Dubious Battle* (1936), had a different tone altogether, offering a bitter story of a communist-organized agricultural strike. His novella *Of Mice and Men* (1937)—later turned into a play and a film—was the tragic tale of two unusual migrant farmworkers.

But it was *The Grapes of Wrath*—which won both the Pulitzer Prize and the National Book Award—that propelled Steinbeck to the top of the literary scene in America. Read by millions, it was made into a popular and critically acclaimed film by director John Ford in 1940.

Steinbeck continued to write fiction, essays, travelogues, and memoirs during and after World War II, even as his politics and world outlook grew increasingly conservative. His outspoken advocacy of U.S. participation in the Vietnam war undermined his popularity among college students in the 1960s. Among his most popular World War II and postwar books were *Cannery Row* (1945) and *East of Eden* (1952). He received the Nobel Prize for Literature in 1962 and died in 1968.

See also: films, feature; *Grapes of Wrath, The*; literature; Ford, John.

Bibliography

Fensch, Thomas, ed. *Conversations with John Steinbeck*. Jackson: University Press of Mississippi, 1988.

Parini, Jay. *John Steinbeck: A Biography*. New York: Henry Holt, 1995.

Steinbeck, Elaine, and Robert Wallsten, eds. *Steinbeck: A Life in Letters*. New York: Viking, 1975.

STIMSON, HENRY L.

Secretary of state under Republican President Herbert Hoover from 1929 to 1933 and secretary of war under Democratic Presidents Franklin D. Roosevelt and Harry Truman from 1940 to 1945, Henry L. Stimson was called the author of the policy known as the Stimson Doctrine that kept the United States from interfering in Asian conflicts in the 1930s. Later in the decade, however, he became an ardent internationalist, pushing even harder than Roosevelt for U.S. aid to Britain.

Born in New York City in 1867, Stimson practiced law between 1891 and 1906, when he became U.S. attorney for the southern district of New York for three years. Appointed secretary of war by President William Howard Taft from 1911 to 1913, Stimson fought in France during World War I as an artillery officer. After the war, he went back to his private law practice until appointed, in 1926, to mediate a dispute in Nicaragua by President Calvin Coolidge.

The following year he was appointed governor general of the U.S. territory of the Philippines, where he served until he was appointed secretary of state by Hoover in 1929. When Japan invaded Manchuria in 1931 and set up the puppet state of Manchukuo, Stimson issued his doctrine calling for nonrecognition of the new country. However, the Stimson Doctrine did not back up its "nonrecognition" economically and militarily. The lack of military and economic sanctions enabled Japan to build an empire during the 1930s. Ironically, Stimson himself was always in favor of stronger sanctions.

Out of public life following the end of Hoover's term in 1933, the Republican Stimson was picked by Roosevelt to be secretary of war again, as the president hoped to build bipartisan consensus for a more internationalist foreign policy. Stimson proved to be even a stronger proponent of aid to Britain than Roosevelt, delivering a radio address in 1940 calling for American escorts of British merchant convoys, a position Roosevelt himself was unwilling to take at that time.

In early 1941, Stimson testified before Congress in favor of the Lend-Lease Act, which offered billions in military aid to Britain and other countries fighting Nazi Germany and later Japan. Overall, Stimson was a strong supporter of Roosevelt's "short of war" strategy, calling on the United States to become an "arsenal of democracy" even as it refused to actually fight in World War II.

Stimson remained in office after Pearl Harbor, helping to organize the war effort, and he urged President Harry Truman to drop atomic bombs on Japan in August 1945. One month later he resigned. Stimson died in 1950.

See also: Great Britain; Japan; Lend-Lease Act; Manchuria, invasion of; World War II, early history of.

Bibliography

Hodgson, Godfrey. *The Colonel: The Life and Wars of Henry Stimson, 1867–1950*. New York: Knopf, 1990.

Morison, Elting Elmore. *Turmoil and Tradition: A Study of the Life and Times of Henry L. Stimson*. New York: Atheneum, 1964.

Stimson, Henry L. *On Active Service in Peace and War*. New York: Harper, 1948.

STONE, HARLAN FISKE

A liberal justice of the Supreme Court from 1925 to 1941, Harlan Fiske Stone was an outspoken critic of conservative judicial activism, whereby courts overturned reformist legislation on narrow constitutional principles. A supporter of the constitutionality of much New Deal legislation, he is perhaps best known for his dissenting opinion in *United States v. Butler et al.* (1936), which overturned the Agricultural Adjustment Act (AAA).

Born in small-town New Hampshire in 1872, Fiske graduated from Amherst College in 1894 and received a law degree four years later from Columbia University. In 1899, he began teaching there and became dean of the law school after 1910, even as he went into private practice.

In 1924, he was appointed attorney general by President Calvin Coolidge to help reorganize the Federal Bureau of Investigation, after its reputation was tarnished by the scandals of the Warren G. Harding administration. His success in this endeavor led to his appointment by Coolidge to the Supreme Court in the following year.

On the Court, Stone became a surprisingly liberal voice, frequently dissenting from the conservative decisions overturning the New Deal legislation of the Franklin D. Roosevelt administration in the mid-1930s. Stone dissented from the Court's decision that the AAA could not tax food processors in order to pay farmers not to grow crops, thereby encouraging higher agricultural prices. Such a tax was a violation of the Tenth Amendment, which reserved to the states all powers not explicitly given to the federal government under the Constitution. Stone called the decision "a tortured construction of the Constitution."

As the Court grew more liberal, Stone joined the majority in two 1937 decisions upholding the constitutionality of the National Labor Relations Act and the unemployment provisions of the Social Security Act. Stone, appointed chief justice in 1941, remained on the Court until his death in 1946.

See also: Agricultural Adjustment Act; Federal Bureau of Investigation; National Labor Relations Act; Social Security Act; *United States v. Butler et al.*

Bibliography

Konefsky, Samuel Joseph. *Chief Justice Stone and the Supreme Court.* New York: Macmillan, 1946.

Mason, Alpheus Thomas. *Harlan Fiske Stone: Pillar of the Law.* New York: Viking, 1956.

STRYKER, ROY E.

An economic adviser to Franklin D. Roosevelt and, from 1935 to 1943, an official at the Resettlement Administration (RA; known as the Farm Security Administration, FSA, after 1937), Roy E. Stryker is best remembered for the group of photographers he put together to chronicle rural conditions for the RA's Historical Section.

Born in rural Kansas in 1893, Stryker moved to Colorado with his family as a baby. He briefly studied at the Colorado School of Mines before serving in the infantry in France in World War I. After the war, he moved to New York and majored in economics at Columbia University, receiving his degree in 1924. In graduate school at Columbia, he met Professor Rexford Tugwell, who would serve as his mentor for many years. Tugwell was impressed with teaching assistant and amateur photographer Stryker's use of photographs to aid in explaining economic principles.

Indeed, when Tugwell was appointed to head up the Resettlement Administration in 1935, with the task of providing grants to poor farmers and moving them to better land, he put Stryker in charge of the Information Division's Historical Section. Since he had to convince Congress to supply funds to the agency, Tugwell needed to provide visual evidence of rural poverty.

Stryker put together a team of some of the best photographers in the country to work for the RA and its successor agency, the FSA. These included Dorothea

Lange, Walker Evans, Gordon Parks, Ben Shahn, Arthur Rothstein, and John Vachon.

In 1943, the FSA was shifted to the Office of War, which cut off Stryker's funding for photography that did not immediately aid the war effort. Before resigning, Stryker made sure that the more than 250,000 photographs put together by the FSA were safely stored in the Library of Congress.

After leaving government service, Stryker worked on photographic projects for private industry and as director of the Pittsburgh Photographic Library. He died in 1975.

See also: photography; Farm Security Administration; Resettlement Administration; Evans, Walker; Lange, Dorothea; Shahn, Ben; Tugwell, Rexford.

Bibliography

Hurley, Forrest Jack. *Portrait of a Decade: Roy Stryker and the Development of Documentary Photography in the Thirties.* Baton Rouge: Louisiana State University Press, 1972.

Stryker, Roy Emerson. *In This Proud Land: America 1935–1943 as Seen in the FSA Photographs.* Boston: New York Graphic Society, 1973.

SUTHERLAND, GEORGE

Among the more conservative of Supreme Court justices during the Great Depression era, George Sutherland was one of the so-called "four horsemen" who fundamentally opposed any extension of federal power and ruled several pieces of New Deal legislation unconstitutional.

Born Alexander George Sutherland in rural England in 1862, the future jurist immigrated with his Mormon family to Utah when he was an infant. Educated at Brigham Young Academy and the University of Michigan, Sutherland passed the bar in 1883 and began to practice law in Provo, Utah.

Elected to the Utah senate when the state entered the union in 1896, Sutherland was elected to the House of Representatives for one term in 1901 and then appointed to the Senate for two terms beginning in 1905. An adviser to President Warren G. Harding after 1920, he was appointed by him to the Supreme Court in 1922.

He ruled against minimum wage laws in the 1920s and joined the conservative majority in the 1935 *Schechter v. United States* decision, which ruled the National Recovery Administration unconstitutional, and the 1936 *United States v. Butler et al.* decision, which ruled the Agricultural Adjustment Act unconstitutional. As the Court turned more liberal after 1936 and President Franklin D. Roosevelt's threat to pack the court with pro–New Deal justices, Sutherland found himself in the minority, dissenting against the 1937 *NLRB v. Jones & Laughlin* decision declaring the National Labor Relations act constitutional.

Sutherland resigned from the Court in 1938 and died in 1942.

See also: Agricultural Adjustment Act; National Labor Relations Act; *NLRB v. Jones & Laughlin*; *Schechter Poultry Corporation v. United States*; Supreme Court; *United States v. Butler et al.*

Bibliography

Arkes, Hadley. *The Return of George Sutherland: Restoring a Jurisprudence of Natural Rights.* Princeton: Princeton University Press, 1994.

Paschal, Joel Francis. *Mr. Justice Sutherland: A Man Against the State.* Princeton: Princeton University Press, 1951.

TEMPLE, SHIRLEY

Among the best-known child movie stars in the history of American cinema, Shirley Temple acted, danced, and sang in a number of top box office hits during the 1930s, most notably alongside dancer Bill "Bojangles" Robinson in *The Little Colonel* and *The Littlest Rebel*, both made in 1935.

Born in Santa Monica, California, in 1928, Temple was sent to dance school and on studio auditions by her mother from the time she was three years old. She made her feature debut at age six in Fox Studio's *Stand Up and Cheer* (1934), where she stole the film with her "Baby Take a Bow" song-and-dance routine. Meanwhile, she had a simultaneous starring role in *Little Miss Marker* (1934). Together, the two films made Temple—with her blond curls and pouting charm—a star. Chipper and upbeat in the face of every on-screen problem, Temple appealed to Depression-era audiences.

In 1934 Temple also turned out *Now and Forever*, with Gary Cooper and Carole Lombard, and *Bright Eyes*, where she sang her signature song "On the Good Ship Lollipop." Always a professional even at such a young age, Temple continued to turn out films regularly during the late 1930s, including *Heidi* (1937), *Wee Willie Winkle* (1937), *Rebecca of Sunnybrook Farm* (1938), *The Little Princess* (1939), and *Susannah of the Mounties* (1939). By that time, she was making $300,000 a picture, an enormous sum for the time.

But as Temple grew older—she turned twelve in 1940—her success began to fade. After several unsuccessful films during and after World War II, Temple tried to make a go of it on television, but failed there too. In the 1960s, she became involved in Republican politics, which won her appointments as ambassador to Ghana in the 1970s and ambassador to Czechoslovakia in the 1980s. Temple remains involved in philanthropy and international affairs.

The most popular child actress of her generation, Shirley Temple is shown here chatting with cartoonist and studio executive Walt Disney. (*Brown Brothers*)

See also: films, feature; music; Cooper, Gary; Lombard, Carole.

Bibliography

Black, Shirley Temple. *Child Star, USA*. New York: Warner Books, 1989.

Windeler, Robert. *The Films of Shirley Temple*. New York: Citadel Press, 1995.

THOMAS, NORMAN

Socialist Party candidate for president six times between 1928 and 1948, Norman Thomas remained a critic of Franklin D. Roosevelt and the New Deal, claiming that the president's leadership and New Deal programs were insufficient to fight the economic ravages of the Depression or create a more equitable and just society.

Born in Marion, Ohio, in 1884, Thomas graduated from the Union Theological Seminary in New York in 1911 and became a Presbyterian minister at a church in Harlem. At the same time, he became chairman of the American Parish settlement house. A pacifist, civil libertarian, and opponent of America's entry into World War I, Thomas left his church position and joined the Socialist Party in 1918. When the party split over the Russian Revolution, Thomas rejected the wing that called for revolution—the future Communist Party of the United States—and remained with the more moderate wing that looked to electoral politics and unionism as the way toward socialism.

By the early 1920s, he had also become secretary of the new pacifist Fellowship of Reconciliation, a founder of the American Civil Liberties Union, associate editor of the left-wing magazine, *The Nation* and a codirector of the League for Industrial Democracy, a leftist union-support organization he helped found.

In 1924, Thomas ran for governor of New York on the Socialist ticket and, in 1928, made his first try for the presidency. With the onset of the Depression, the Socialists grew in strength and Thomas garnered nearly 1 million votes in the 1932 election.

While critical of much New Deal legislation, Thomas was particularly indignant at the effects of the 1933 Agricultural Adjustment Act and the Agricultural Adjustment Administration (AAA), which the act created. Under the act, farmers were paid by the government not to grow crops. But most of the payments went to the owners of large farms. In the South, this meant—in effect—that landlords were paid to throw sharecroppers off the land. When Thomas toured Arkansas in 1934 to highlight the problems of sharecroppers and support their Southern Tenant Farmers Union, he was literally chased out of the state by toughs hired by the landlords. He then went to President Roosevelt to say that the AAA must start including white and black

After being pelted with eggs at a Newark, New Jersey, rally in June 1938, Socialist Party leader Norman Thomas is led off a stage by detectives. *(Brown Brothers)*

sharecroppers. But the president, fearful of alienating key Democrats in Congress, said that Thomas did not understand the ways of the South and should not get involved. Incensed, Thomas argued that Roosevelt cared more about expediency than morality.

In 1935, a split occurred in the Socialist Party between the Marxist "Old Guard," who wanted to join with the Communist Party and its Popular Front-inspired alliance with Roosevelt, and the moderates under Thomas. The Communists argued that Roosevelt was the best chance to fight conservatism at home and to support the antifascist struggle abroad, which the Soviet Union was involved in. This split would lead Thomas to run against Roosevelt in 1936 and to increasingly oppose America's entry into the war against fascism.

Thomas and the Socialists' continued pacifism hurt their cause during World War II and their ranks were decimated by the anticommunist hysteria of the immediate postwar era. During the 1960s, Thomas became an outspoken critic of U.S. participation in Vietnam. He died in 1968.

See also: Communist Party; election of 1932; election of 1936; *Nation, The*; Popular Front; Socialist Party; Southern Tenant Farmers Union; Agricultural Adjustment Act; Roosevelt, Franklin D.

Bibliography

Johnpoll, Bernard K. *Pacifist's Progress: Norman Thomas and the Decline of American Socialism.* Chicago: Quadrangle Books, 1970.

Swanberg, W.A. *Norman Thomas: The Last Idealist.* New York: Scribner, 1976.

Thomas, Norman. *Socialism Re-examined.* New York: W. W. Norton, 1963.

THREE STOOGES, THE

A comedy trio whose slapstick antics have endured for years with audiences young and young-at-heart, the Three Stooges began as a vaudeville stage act and then moved to the movie screen in the early 1930s with a series of very popular shorts and a few feature films.

There were many Stooges over the years, but one remained in the act throughout—Moe Howard, the ringleader with the bowl-cut hairdo. Born Moses Horowitz in 1897, he formed a vaudeville routine in 1923 with his brother Shemp (born Samuel Horowitz in 1895); Shemp was the sad-sack character with the long bangs that fell over his face. The two essentially served as sidekicks to comedian Ted Healy, and the group was billed as "Ted Healy, and His Stooges" or, sometimes, "The Racketeers." After a string of other performers moved in and out of the act, the team added Larry Fine (born Louis Feinberg in 1902), the straight man with the curly hair, in 1925.

By the late 1920s, success on the vaudeville circuit had led Healy and his troupe to Broadway and, in 1930, to Hollywood in the modestly successful *Soup to Nuts* (1930). In 1932, Shemp left the trio and was replaced by Curly (born Jerome Lester Horowiz in 1903), the shaven-headed Stooge with the childlike demeanor. In 1933, the Stooges and Healy signed a contract with Metro-Goldwyn-Mayer (MGM) to make six feature films in one year.

But it was their short films that made the trio famous. In 1934, the group left MGM and Healy behind, signing on to Columbia Pictures, where they would remain for the next twenty-five years. It was during the early years at Columbia that the name and the characteristics of the Three Stooges emerged. Two of their most popular films came late in the Depression era and were send-ups of Adolf Hitler and the Nazis—*You Nazty Spy* (1940) and *I'll Never Say Heil Again* (1941).

The three continued to make feature-length and short films during World War II. In 1946, Curly suffered a stroke (he died in 1952) and was replaced by a returning Shemp. In 1955, Shemp died and was replaced by Joe Besser and, after 1959, by Joe "Curly Joe" De Rita. In these various groupings, the trio continued to make short and feature films through the 1960s. All three—Moe, Larry, and Joe De Rita—retired in the late 1960s. Moe and Larry died in 1975.

See also: films, feature.

Bibliography

Howard, Moe. *Moe Howard and the Three Stooges.* Secaucus, NJ: Citadel Press, 1977.

Kurson, Robert, and Martin Short. *The Official Three Stooges Encyclopedia: The Ultimate Knucklehead's Guide to Stoogedom.* Lincolnwood, IL: Contemporary Books, 1998.

TOWNSEND, FRANCIS

A California physician, Francis Townsend was the author of the so-called Townsend Plan to pay every American over the age of sixty a government stipend of $200 per month, on the condition that each recipient spend all of the money each month. Designed both to relieve the hardships of seniors and promote consumer spending, the idea was embraced by millions of Americans who formed Townsend Clubs across the country in the mid-1930s.

Born in a small-town in Illinois in 1867, Townsend graduated from Omaha Medical College in Nebraska and practiced medicine all of his life. In 1919, he moved to southern California, where he maintained a struggling practice. When the Great Depression hit in the early 1930s, Townsend, himself already in his sixties, was much troubled by the suffering he saw among his fellow older Americans.

Between September and December 1933, he published his plan in a series of letters to the editor of the *Telegraph*, a newspaper in Long Beach, California. He

Francis Townsend, shown here at the typewriter he used to compose his influential letters to the editor, devised a popular old-age pension plan that spurred the enactment of Social Security. *(Brown Brothers)*

explained his idea of paying seniors $200 a month, which would be financed by a small "transaction tax" at each stage in the production of goods.

While economists both inside and outside the Franklin D. Roosevelt administration pointed out the unworkability of the plan—it would cost far more than any "transaction tax" could raise—average Americans of all ages were intrigued. Working with a local real estate broker named Robert Clements, Townsend formed Old Age Revolving Pensions, Inc. (OARP) which created a network of clubs to support the plan. By January 1935, some 1,200 local clubs with a membership of nearly half a million had come into being. A year later, at the peak, there would be 7,000 branches of the OARP and over 2 million members.

Fearing that these people might join forces with radical politicians and parties, such as Huey P. Long's Share Our Wealth movement, and run against Roosevelt from the Left, the president began to formulate the Social Security Act, which Congress passed in 1935. Social Security undercut popular support for the Townsend Plan, as did Townsend's indictment for contempt of Congress when he refused to answer questions about the clubs' finances. Townsend was pardoned by Roosevelt in 1937.

Meanwhile, the OARP quickly faded from the political map, although Townsend himself reluctantly joined with the anti–New Deal Union Party of Father Charles Coughlin and Huey P. Long's successor, Gerald L. K. Smith, in their efforts to defeat Roosevelt in the 1936 presidential election.

From the late 1930s to the end of his life in 1960 at age 93, Townsend continued to practice medicine in southern California.

See also: election of 1936; Share Our Wealth Society; Townsend Plan; Union Party; Social Security Act; Coughlin, Father Charles; Long, Huey P.; Smith, Gerald L. K.

Bibliography

Gaydowski, J. D. "Eight Letters to the Editor: The Genesis of the Townsend National Recovery Plan." *Southern California Quarterly* 1970 52(4) 365–82.

Holtzman, Abraham. *The Townsend Movement: A Political Study.* New York: Bookman Associates, 1963.

Townsend, Francis. *New Horizons.* Chicago: J. L. Stewart, 1943.

TRACY, SPENCER

Considered by many cinema critics and moviegoers to be one of the finest actors in the history of Hollywood, Spencer Tracy somehow managed the difficult feat of becoming a top-billed leading man without looking particularly handsome.

Tracy was born in Milwaukee in 1900 and attended a Jesuit school, intending to go into the ministry. But he preferred the stage and, in 1922, enrolled at the American Academy of Dramatic Arts in New York City. After a number of small parts, he won his first starring role on Broadway in *The Last Mile* (1930), a prison drama. Director John Ford was so impressed by Tracy's performance that he starred the actor in his gangster film *Up the River* (1930).

While under contract to Fox between 1930 through 1935, Tracy was loaned out to other studios, where he made some of his most memorable pictures of the decade, notably *20,000 Years in Sing Sing* (1933). A series of scandals involving women and alcohol led Fox to release him to MGM in 1935. There he won three Best Actor Academy Award nominations in a row for *San Francisco* (1936), *Captains Courageous* (1937), and *Boys Town* (1938). He won the award for the last two, becoming the first actor ever to win two consecutive Academy Awards.

During World War II, Tracy partnered with Katharine Hepburn for the first time in *Woman of the Year* (1942), a collaboration that would prove one of the most enduring in Hollywood. Tracy continued to act through the 1960s, winning another Academy Award nomination for *Father of the Bride* (1950). Tracy died in 1967.

See also: films, feature; Metro-Goldwyn-Mayer; Ford, John; Hepburn, Katharine.

Bibliography

Davidson, Bill. *Spencer Tracy: Tragic Idol.* New York: Dutton, 1987.

Tozzi, Romano. *Spencer Tracy: 1900–1967.* New York: Galahad Books, 1973.

TUGWELL, REXFORD G.

One of President Franklin D. Roosevelt's Brain Trust, Rexford G. Tugwell was an economist who advocated a number of key New Deal agencies designed to lift the country out of the Great Depression and regulate the economy. As assistant secretary of agriculture, he was also instrumental in establishing the Agricultural Adjustment Administration (AAA).

Born in upstate New York in 1891, Tugwell attended the Wharton School of Finance at the University of Pennsylvania, earning several degrees there, including a doctorate in 1922. Even before finishing his dissertation, Tugwell was hired to teach at Columbia University in 1920.

In 1932, Tugwell was convinced by fellow Columbia professor and Roosevelt adviser Raymond Moley to join the so-called Brain Trust of advisers to the Democratic candidate for president and the likely winner of the 1932 election. A brilliant thinker and articulate advocate of his ideas, Tugwell argued that large-scale corporate enterprise was both inevitable and necessary for a modern economy. But, to ensure a functioning economy that distributed its output equitably, large-scale governmental regulation at the federal level was necessary.

Indeed, Tugwell believed that the cause of the Depression lay in corporate America's unwillingness to share fairly with workers the productivity of the 1920s. Now, with the economy having reached a level of maturity and unlikely to grow rapidly in the future, it was critical to make sure that it provided a decent living to all. Much of this theorizing was laid out in Tugwell's 1933 treatise, *Industrial Discipline and the Governmental Arts.*

After Roosevelt took office in 1933, Tugwell was appointed to the Agriculture Department, where he applied his economic ideas to the farm sector, which he believed was where the Depression had started and where it must first be combated. A major architect of the AAA, Tugwell felt that farmers had to be assured an adequate income in order to purchase the products of industrial America. To achieve this, he proposed a government agency that would pay farmers not to grow crops, in order to increase demand and lift prices.

In 1936, Tugwell left the Roosevelt administration and went into private business. Two years later, he was appointed to the New York City Planning Commission and, in 1941, to the chancellor's position at the University of Puerto Rico. He later became governor of the territory. From 1946 to 1957, he taught at the University of Chicago. His 1968 book—*The Brains Trust*, a revisionist history that argued that the anti–Depression programs of Herbert Hoover had inspired the early New Deal—won Tugwell the Bancroft Prize for history writing. He died in 1979.

See also: Brain Trust; election of 1932; Agricultural Adjustment Administration; taxation; Hoover, Herbert; Moley, Raymond; Roosevelt, Franklin D.

Bibliography

Namorato, Michael V. *Rexford G. Tugwell: A Biography.* New York: Praeger, 1988.

Tugwell, Rexford G. *The Brains Trust.* New York: Viking, 1968.

———. *The Diary of Rexford G. Tugwell: The New Deal, 1932–1935.* Westport, CT: Greenwood Press, 1992.

VALLÉE, RUDY

One of most popular crooners, or singers of popular songs, during the Great Depression era, Rudy Vallée also starred in a number of light movie comedies that featured his warbling singing style.

Born Hubert Prior Vallée in rural Vermont in 1901, the future radio star became a professional musician while attending Yale University in the 1920s. He was soon playing a number of instruments—including drums, clarinet, and saxophone—in Vincent Lopez's London Savoy Havana Band from 1924 to 1925. After earning his degree from Yale in 1927, he formed a dance band called the Yale Collegians, later the Connecticut Yankees, which featured Vallée singing through a hand-held megaphone.

He began his film career with *Vagabond Lover* (1929). During the 1930s, his broadcasts were among the most popular shows on radio. Vallée continued to sing and act through much of the rest of his life, dying in 1986.

See also: films, feature; music; radio.

Bibliography

Brown, Robert J. *Manipulating the Ether: The Power of Broadcast Radio in the Thirties.* Jefferson, NC: McFarland, 1998.

Vallée, Rudy. *Let the Chips Fall.* Harrisburg, PA: Stackpole Books, 1975.

VAN DEVANTER, WILLIS

A member of the so-called "four horsemen" of the 1930s Supreme Court, known for their conservatism and strict construction of the Constitution, Willis Van Devanter was a strong judicial opponent of any extension of federal power and voted frequently to rule pieces of New Deal legislation unconstitutional.

Van Devanter was born in Indiana in 1859 and graduated from the Cincinnati Law School in 1881. Three years later, he was hired as a railroad attorney and moved to Wyoming. Active in the territory's politics, he became city attorney of Cheyenne, a member of the territorial legislature, and, in 1888, chief justice of the territory's Supreme Court. When Wyoming entered the Union in 1890, he returned to his private practice.

In 1897, he was appointed assistant U.S. attorney general and, in 1903, a federal circuit judge. In 1910, President William Howard Taft appointed Van Devanter to the U.S. Supreme Court. On the Court until 1937, Van Devanter voted with the majority in *Schechter v. United States* and *United States v. Butler et al.*, which ruled unconstitutional the National Recovery Administration and the Agricultural Adjustment Administration, respectively.

In early 1937, President Franklin D. Roosevelt, frustrated at the Court's conservative opposition to the New Deal, offered his so-called court-packing plan, whereby one justice would be added to the bench for every justice over the age of seventy. As one of those justices over seventy, Van Devanter was outraged. But Roosevelt's plan, though stopped by congressional and public resistance, may have contributed to Van Devanter's decision to step down later in the year. He died in 1941.

See also: court-packing plan; Agricultural Adjustment Administration; National Recovery Administration; *Schechter v. United States*; Supreme Court; *United States v. Butler et al.*

Bibliography

Currie, David P. "Constitution in the Supreme Court: The New Deal, 1931–1940." *University of Chicago Law Review* 40 (1987): 504.

Cushman, Barry. *Rethinking the New Deal Court: The Structure of a Constitutional Revolution.* New York: Oxford University Press, 1998.

Leuchtenberg, William E. *The Supreme Court Reborn: Constitutional Revolution in the Age of Roosevelt.* New York: Oxford University Press, 1995.

VIDOR, KING

One of the most popular directors of the 1930s, King Vidor is known for the sensitivity of the subjects he portrayed in his movies, including issues of race, economic justice, and immigration.

Born King Wallis Vidor in Galveston, Texas, in 1894, the future director began his film career modestly enough as an assistant projectionist in a local nickelodeon. At twenty-one, he moved to Hollywood and worked in the film industry as prop man, scriptwriter, newsreel cameraman, and assistant director.

By 1918, Vidor was directing silent films, his first hit being *The Big Parade* (1925), a movie about World War I. Three years later, he directed *The Crowd*. Focused on the alienation of modern urban life, it is considered by film historians to be one of the finest movies of the silent era. A year later, he put out the musical *Hallelujah*!, the first major Hollywood movie with an all-black cast.

Among his films of the 1930s are *Street Scene* (1931), about working-class New Yorkers; *Our Daily Bread* (1934), focusing on the difficulties of farm life; a movie about Polish immigrants entitled *The Wedding Night* (1935); and *The Citadel* (1938), the story of a doctor in a Welsh mining town, which won Vidor a directorial Academy Award. Vidor also directed the Kansas scenes in *The Wizard of Oz* (1939).

Vidor continued to direct after World War II and is associated with such critical and popular successes as *Duel in the Sun* (1946), *The Fountainhead* (1949), and *War and Peace* (1956). He died in 1982.

See also: films, feature.

Bibliography

Durgnat, Raymond. *King Vidor, American.* Berkeley: University of California Press, 1988.

Vidor, King. *A Tree Is a Tree.* New York: Harcourt, Brace, 1953.

WAGNER, ROBERT F.

Democratic senator from New York and longtime advocate of the interests of organized labor, Robert F. Wagner is best known as the author of the National Labor Relations Act (NLRA) of 1935—sometimes referred to as the Wagner Act—the most important piece of labor legislation in American history.

Born in Germany in 1877, Wagner emigrated to the United States in 1886 and settled with his family in New York City's rough Hell's Kitchen neighborhood. A graduate of City College of New York, Wagner earned a law degree from New York University in 1900 and began to practice law in the city. Initiated into politics as a ward heeler, or local representative, of the Tammany Hall political machine, he was elected to the state senate in 1904.

He gained a reputation as a pro-labor representative through his work on the commission organized to investigate the state's factories after the Triangle Shirtwaist Company factory fire of 1911. In 1919, Wagner was appointed to serve on the New York State Supreme Court. In 1926, he won a U.S. Senate seat, to which he would be reelected three times.

During his first year in the Senate, Wagner began working on the labor issues that would preoccupy much of his term in office. He sponsored unsuccessful bills calling for more public works, better labor statistics, and a revamping of the U.S. Employment Service. Once the Depression began, Wagner worked hard to get a new public works bill passed, the so-called Wagner-Garner bill, which was vetoed by President Herbert Hoover in 1931.

Once Franklin D. Roosevelt became president, Wagner participated in drafting and passing a number of key pieces of New Deal legislation, including the National Industrial Recovery Act, the Federal Emergency Relief Administration, and the Civilian Conservation Corps. In 1934, he cosponsored the Wagner-Lewis unemployment bill, parts of which would be incorporated into the 1935 Social Security Act, which Wagner would also help draft.

But Wagner's most important contribution to the

New Deal was as author of the NLRA in 1935, which set liberal federal rules for union organizing and established the National Labor Relations Board to arbitrate labor disputes. Passage of the NLRA is considered by historians one of the key factors behind the sit-down strikes at General Motors in 1936–37 and the sudden explosion of union organizing in the nation's mass-production industries thereafter.

Also a believer in public housing, Wagner sponsored the Wagner-Steagall Housing Act. Although it established the United States Housing Authority, it was watered down by amendments that limited its budget.

As a senator from a state with a large Jewish population—and, perhaps, as a German immigrant himself, albeit non-Jewish—Wagner strongly advocated admitting refugees from Nazi Germany in the late 1930s. After the anti-Jewish attacks of *Kristallnacht* in 1938, Wagner sponsored an unsuccessful bill to bring 20,000 Jewish refugee children to the United States.

A strong supporter of U.S. intervention in the anti-Nazi struggle in the late 1930s and 1940s, Wagner sponsored a full-employment bill after the war, which was weakened by amendments. In ill health, Wagner resigned from the Senate in 1949 and died in 1953. His son, Robert Wagner, Jr., became mayor of New York in the 1950s and 1960s.

See also: Civilian Conservation Corps; Federal Emergency Relief Administration; National Industrial Recovery Act; National Labor Relations Act; Wagner-Steagall Housing Act; refugees.

Bibliography

Huthmacher, J. Joseph. *Senator Robert F. Wagner and the Rise of Urban Liberalism.* New York: Atheneum, 1968.

WALLACE, HENRY A.

Formerly a progressive Republican who changed his party affiliation to the Democrats in 1928, Henry A. Wallace was secretary of agriculture during President Franklin D. Roosevelt's first two terms in office and vice president during his third term.

Wallace was born in rural Iowa in 1888. His father was publisher of an influential farm journal, *Wallace's Farmer*, and secretary of agriculture in the administration of President Warren G. Harding in the early 1920s. The younger Wallace also became an agricultural expert, developing a high-yield corn hybrid that became widely adopted.

During the 1920s, Wallace grew increasingly concerned about the plight of farmers—the agricultural sector never seemed able to lift itself out of economic stagnation after World War I—and disenchanted with conservative Republican administrations that offered little in the way of farm relief.

Having switched to the Democratic Party, Wallace was introduced to Roosevelt when the latter was still governor of New York. Roosevelt—himself an amateur farmer—and Wallace established a close rapport, and Wallace worked on Roosevelt's 1932 presidential campaign.

In 1933, Roosevelt appointed Wallace secretary of agriculture. By his own admission, Wallace was more interested in big ideas and philosophy than the day-to-day administration of his agency. Still, Wallace did much to expand the government's role in regulating and aiding the agricultural sector. He helped draft and implement the landmark 1933 Agricultural Adjustment Act (AAA), which created the Agricultural Adjustment Administration (AAA). The AAA subsidized farmers not to grow crops so that farm prices and incomes would be raised.

But Wallace grew disenchanted with the AAA during a tour of the rural South in 1936. Seeing the plight of impoverished sharecroppers—many of whom were being thrown off the land by their landlords who took advantage of the AAA and stopped growing crops—Wallace began pushing for more liberal and egalitarian agricultural policies. At the same time, as a strong believer in scientific farming, Wallace promoted the Agriculture Department's Extension Service, to provide information and expertise to farmers.

By the late 1930s, the increasingly radical and antifascist Wallace pushed hard for an end to America's isolationist foreign policy, positions which paralleled Roosevelt's. Their mutual concern about the rise of Nazi Germany and militarist Japan led Roosevelt to pick Wallace to replace the conservative and anti-interventionist John Nance Garner as vice president.

During the war, Wallace spoke out against profiteering by big corporations, thereby earning the enmity of party conservatives, who got Roosevelt to remove him from the ballot in 1944 and pick the moderate

An agricultural expert, Henry A. Wallace served two terms as secretary of agriculture under President Franklin D. Roosevelt and served as Roosevelt's vice-president from 1941 to 1945. *(Corbis)*

Harry Truman instead. In 1948, Wallace ran for president against Truman on the Progressive Party ticket, winning more than 1 million votes. Wallace then retired to his farm, wrote extensively, and died in 1965.

See also: Democratic Party; election of 1932; election of 1940; Agricultural Adjustment Act; Roosevelt, Franklin D.

Bibliography

Blum, John Morton, ed. *The Price of Vision: The Diary of Henry A. Wallace, 1942–1946.* Boston: Houghton Mifflin, 1973.

Culver, John C., and John Hyde. *American Dreamer: The Life and Times of Henry A. Wallace.* New York: W.W. Norton, 2000.

Lord, Russell. *The Century of the Common Man, by Henry A. Wallace. Selected from Public Papers.* New York: Reynal & Hitchcock, 1943.

WARREN, ROBERT PENN

An important literary critic and writer of the Great Depression era, Robert Penn Warren was cofounder and editor of the *Southern Review*, perhaps the most influential literary journal of its day.

Born in Guthrie, Kentucky, in 1905, Warren studied at Tennessee's Vanderbilt University, the University of California at Berkeley, Yale, and, as a Rhodes scholar, at Oxford University. He published *I'll Take My Stand* in 1930, in which he defended traditional southern rural life against criticism emanating from the urban North.

In 1935, he joined with other southern writers and critics to found the *Southern Review*, in which he and other contributors examined a South in transition from traditional rural life to modern times. A proponent of the rigorous New Criticism, which closely examined the language of literary texts to find deep psychological meaning, Warren authored the influential *Understanding Poetry* in 1938, followed by *Understanding Fiction* in 1943.

He published his first novel, *Night Rider*, a historical fiction about tobacco wars at the turn of the twentieth century, in 1939. But his best-known novel was written after the war. *All the King's Men* (1946) offered a fictionalized account of the life and times of Huey P. Long. The book won the Pulitzer Prize in 1947 and was made into a popular and critically acclaimed film in 1949.

Warren continued to write novels, poetry, and literary criticism through much of the rest of his life. He died in 1989.

See also: literature; Long, Huey P.

One of the most influential literary critics of the 1930s, Robert Penn Warren is best known for the novel *All the King's Men*, a fictional recounting of the life and career of Louisiana politician Huey P. Long. *(Brown Brothers)*

Bibliography

Blotner, Joseph Leo. *Robert Penn Warren: A Biography.* New York: Random House, 1997.

Warren, Robert Penn. *A Robert Penn Warren Reader.* New York: Random House, 1987.

Watkins, Floyd C., John T. Hiers, and Mary Louise Weaks. *Talking with Robert Penn Warren* Athens: University of Georgia Press, 1990.

WEAVER, ROBERT C.

Special assistant to the administrator of the U.S. Housing Authority, Robert C. Weaver was the highest-ranking African-American official in the administration of President Franklin D. Roosevelt and an important member of the so-called "black cabinet," which advised the administration on issues of concern to the black community.

Born in Washington, D.C., in 1907, Weaver earned his doctorate in economics from Harvard University in 1934. Even before his dissertation was finished, Weaver was hired by Interior Secretary Harold Ickes to advise on race relations in housing issues. By 1937, he had risen to his post at the Housing Authority, where he served until 1940. During these years, he met with people like Mary McLeod Bethane to push for racial justice in the federal government and its programs.

During World War II, Weaver worked at various mobilization and defense agencies, advising and implementing antidiscrimination policies. He also published two studies on discrimination. An official in the administratioins of Presidents Harry Truman and, later, John F. Kennedy, he was appointed secretary of housing and urban development by President Lyndon Johnson in 1966, becoming the first black cabinet member in American history. He continued in public service until 1969 and then taught at Hunter College in New York City. He died in 1997.

See also: African Americans; "black cabinet"; Bethune, Mary McLeod; Ickes, Harold.

Special assistant to the administrator of the United States Housing Authority, Robert Weaver was the highest ranking African American in Franklin D. Roosevelt's administration. *(Library of Congress)*

Bibliography

Kirby, John B. *Black Americans in the Roosevelt Era: Liberalism and Race.* Knoxville: University of Tennessee Press, 1980.

Sitkoff, Harvard. *A New Deal for Blacks: The Emergence of Civil Rights as a National Issue.* Vol. 1, *The Depression Years.* New York: Oxford University Press, 1978.

Weaver, Robert C. *Negro Labor: A National Problem.* New York: Harcourt Brace 1946.

WEISMULLER, JOHNNY

A gold-medal-winning swimmer in the 1924 and 1928 Olympic Games, Johnny Weismuller became a film star in the 1930s, best known for his portrayal of Tarzan in a series of popular movies.

It is not certain where or when Weismuller was born—either in Romania or Pennsylvania, around 1904. If born in the former, he came to the United States as a baby. The discrepancy arose because his parents allegedly switched his identity with that of his younger brother so he could compete on the American Olympic team.

Attending school in Chicago through the junior high level, then dropping out, Weismuller emerged early in life as an exceptional athlete. In the early 1920s, he began competing in swimming and water polo, going on to win twenty-six national championships and five gold medals in swimming over the course of two Olympic Games, setting several world records along the way.

Featured in several short documentary films about his athletic abilities, Weismuller caught the attention of Metro-Goldwyn-Mayer studios, which was looking for someone to play Tarzan. The studio had gone through a number of actors, none of whom seemed to possess the athleticism that would win over audiences.

Weismuller was an immediate hit with his *Tarzan the Ape Man* (1932), with Maureen O'Sullivan as Jane. The two went on to star in four more Tarzan pictures during the Great Depression. After World War II, Weismuller moved to Columbia Pictures and starred in fifteen films set in Africa. He later ran the Swimming Pool Hall of Fame in Florida and worked as a host at Caesar's Palace in Las Vegas. Weismuller died in 1984.

See also: films, feature; Metro-Goldwyn-Mayer; sports.

Bibliography

Behlmer, Rudy. "Johnny Weismuller: Olympics to Tarzan." In *Films in Review*, July/August, 1996: 20–33.

Fury, David. *Kings of the Jungle: An Illustrated Reference to Tarzan on Screen and Television*. Jefferson, NC: McFarland and Company, 1994.

WELLES, ORSON

Writer, actor, director, and producer, Orson Welles was one of the most innovative, creative, and influential persons in the performing arts of the Great Depression era. Both a boy wonder and a Renaissance man, Welles is best known for innovative productions with the Federal Theater Project (FTP), his terrifying radio broadcast of H. G. Wells's *War of the Worlds* in 1938, and his landmark film *Citizen Kane* (1941).

Born George Orson Welles into a prominent family—Civil War Navy Secretary Gideon Welles was among his ancestors—in Kenosha, Wisconsin, in 1915, he met actors and artists through his wealthy father and traveled around the world with his family. With little formal education beyond high school—he studied briefly at the Art Institute of Chicago—he traveled to Ireland and began acting at the Gate Theatre in Dublin in 1931.

Returning to the United States in 1933, he acted with a Chicago company and then organized a drama festival in Woodstock, New York, at the age of nineteen. In 1936, he went to work for the FTP, directing a landmark all-black production of *Macbeth* in New York. The following year, he founded the influential and pathbreaking Mercury Theatre.

At the same time, he was becoming a radio actor and producer, even playing a role on the popular show *The Shadow*. On October 30, 1938, he offered a version of *The War of the Worlds*, about an invasion from Mars, told in a mock newscast style. The broadcast was so effective that it triggered mass panic along the eastern seaboard.

In 1940, Welles was hired by RKO pictures to write, direct, and produce films. His first was the controversial *Citizen Kane*, a fictionalized version of the life of William Randolph Hearst in which Welles co-wrote, produced, directed, and played the title role. Despite Hearst's efforts to kill the unflattering film by refusing to run reviews or ads for it in his chain of

Star of stage and film, Orson Welles was also an accomplished radio producer and actor, best known for his 1938 version of H. G. Wells's *War of the Worlds*, a broadcast whose realism struck fear in many listeners. (*Brown Brothers*)

newspapers, the movie was a critical and box office success; in fact, the visually innovative film is considered by many critics to be the greatest American movie of all time.

Welles continued to direct and star in critically acclaimed movies in the 1940s and 1950s and to work in the theater. But, always an outsider in Hollywood, his career began to wither by the 1960s. Welles died in 1985.

See also: *Citizen Kane*; films, feature; radio; *The War of the Worlds*; Federal Theater Project; Hearst, William Randolph.

Bibliography

Callow, Simon. *Orson Welles: The Road to Xanadu*. New York: Viking, 1996.

Thomson, David. *Rosebud: The Story of Orson Welles*. New York: Knopf, 1996.

Welles, Orson, and Peter Bogdanovich. *This Is Orson Welles*. New York: HarperCollins, 1992.

WELLES, SUMNER

An influential foreign policy adviser to President Franklin D. Roosevelt throughout much of his twelve-year administration and a top official in the State Department from 1933 to 1943, Sumner Welles is best known as the architect of the Good Neighbor policy, involving a major revamping of U.S. relations with Latin American countries.

Born Benjamin Sumner Welles in New York City in 1892, the future diplomat came from an influential American family that traced its roots in public service to the mid-nineteenth century and enjoyed a close friendship with the Roosevelt family. A graduate of Harvard in 1914, Welles entered the foreign service the following year and was assigned to the American embassy in Japan from 1915 to 1917.

Switching his specialty to Latin America, Welles was assigned to Buenos Aires and then became assistant chief of the Division of Latin American Affairs in 1920. Two years later, upset about Republican foreign policy initiatives, he resigned, but was quickly brought back in by Secretary of State Charles Evans Hughes to deal with a crisis in the Dominican Republic. Failing to get the United States to pull out of the country, Welles quit his State Department position in anger and wrote a critique of U.S. policy in the Caribbean country.

Impressed by the book, Roosevelt appointed Welles assistant secretary of state in 1933 and special presidential ambassador to Cuba, then undergoing one of its political crises. Applying the ideas that would lead to the Good Neighbor doctrine, Welles advised against direct U.S. intervention, but was nevertheless able to persuade the reigning dictator, Gerardo Machado, to resign. When this resulted in the rise of a revolutionary government, Welles returned to the United States in embarrassment.

Still convinced of the rightness of his ideas, Welles convinced Roosevelt to organize the Inter-American Peace Conference in 1936 to negotiate an end to a brutal war between Paraguay and Bolivia. In 1937, Welles was made undersecretary of state, which put him in charge of the department as Secretary Cordell Hull became increasingly sickly and absent from work.

After the breakout of war in Europe, Welles helped establish a neutrality zone for the Western Hemisphere. In 1940, Roosevelt sent Welles to Rome, Berlin, Paris, and London to try to negotiate a truce. In fact, both the president and Welles believed that U.S. entry into the war was inevitable and used the meetings to delay a Nazi attack in order to allow the Allies to become better prepared.

From 1942 to 1943, Welles chaired a committee within the State Department charged with creating a postwar international organization for cooperation, the future United Nations. Despite these accomplishments, Welles was growing increasingly erratic in his personal life. Heavy drinking and rumors of homosexual encounters led to the threat of a congressional investigation, forcing Welles to resign in September 1943.

In his later years, Welles wrote extensively about foreign policy. He died in 1961.

See also: Good Neighbor policy; World War II, early history of; Hull, Cordell; Roosevelt, Franklin D.

Bibliography

Gellman, Irwin. *Secret Affairs: Franklin Roosevelt, Cordell Hull, and Sumner Welles*. Baltimore: Johns Hopkins University Press, 1995.

Welles, Benjamin. *Sumner Welles: FDR's Global Strategist: A Biography*. New York: St. Martin's, 1997.

Welles, Sumner. *The Time for Decision*. New York: Harper & Brothers, 1944.

WEST, MAE

One of the most popular female stars of the 1930s, the quick-witted, wisecracking, buxom actress Mae West was famous for the overt sexuality and sexual innuendos that she displayed in such Depression-era films as *She Done Him Wrong* (1933) and *My Little Chickadee* (1940).

Born in Brooklyn, New York, either in 1892 or 1893, West began acting in the theater in 1901 and was a nationally touring vaudeville performer from about 1907 to the mid-1920s. At the same time, she began to sing and dance in Broadway productions, going on to write, produce, and star in them after 1926. She shocked audiences with her first production, *Sex*, in which she played a prostitute, a performance that got her jailed for "corrupting the morals of youth." But *Sex* was a hit, as were two other productions, *Diamond Lil* (1928) and *The Constant Sinner* (1931).

In 1932, West began starring in her signature sexually explicit (for the time) and comedic movies. Her first, *Night after Night* (1932), was followed by the highly successful *She Done Him Wrong* with Cary Grant, an adaptation of *Diamond Lil*, which featured one of the most memorable lines in cinematic history: "Come up and see me sometime." Indeed, West's films contributed to the rise of the Legion of Decency, a Catholic protest organization aimed at curbing what it saw to be the immoral excesses of Hollywood movies, and the Production Code Administration of 1934 founded in part to censor movie content.

Still, West toned down her sexuality only a bit in successive films, including *I'm No Angel* (1933), *Belle of the Nineties* (1934), *Klondike Annie* (1936), and *My Little Chickadee*, in which she played opposite W. C. Fields. A brilliant businesswoman, West produced her own films and made a great deal of money in Hollywood. She continued to act in film and on stage after the war, but became increasingly a caricature of her former self. She died in 1980.

See also: films, feature; Legion of Decency; Motion Picture Production Code/Production Code Administration; Fields, W. C.; Grant, Cary.

Bibliography

Hamilton, Marybeth. *"When I'm Bad, I'm Better": Mae West, Sex, and American Popular Entertainment*. New York: HarperCollins, 1993.

West, Mae. *Goodness Had Nothing to Do With It: The Autobiography of Mae West*. New York: Belvedere Publishers, 1981.

WHEELER, BURTON K.

A liberal Democratic senator from Montana, Burton K. Wheeler was the first member of the Senate to back Franklin D. Roosevelt for the 1932 presidential nomination and a firm and consistent supporter of New Deal legislation.

Born in Hudson, Massachusetts, in 1882, Wheeler earned a law degree from the University of Michigan in 1905, then moved to Montana to open a law practice. A member of the state assembly from 1910 to 1912, Wheeler was then appointed U.S. district attorney for Montana in 1913 and served in that position for five years. After a failed run for the governor's office in 1920, Wheeler was elected to the U.S. Senate in 1922, campaigning as an opponent of the state's big mining interests.

In 1924, Wheeler was Robert M. La Follette's vice presidential running mate on the 1924 Progressive Party ticket. Six years later, Wheeler came out early in favor of Roosevelt and became one of the president's key legislative whips, gathering votes for a host of New Deal legislation, most especially the controversial Public Utilities Holding Act of 1935. Two years later, however, Wheeler—like many other supporters—broke with Roosevelt over the president's plan to pack the Supreme Court with liberal justices.

In the late 1930s, Wheeler joined with other western progressives to oppose U.S. intervention in the increasingly tense European situation and became a leading spokesman for the isolationist America First Committee. However, once the Japanese attacked Pearl Harbor, the Montana senator supported the war effort wholeheartedly. Still, his outspoken opposition to the war was remembered by voters afterwards, who denied him the Democratic nomination in the senatorial primary election of 1946.

After leaving the Senate, Wheeler joined his son's Washington, D.C., law practice and died in 1975.

See also: court-packing plan; Public Utilities Holding Act; America First Committee.

Bibliography

Cole, Wayne S. *Roosevelt and the Isolationists, 1932–45*. Lincoln: University of Nebraska Press, 1983.

Wheeler, Burton K., and Paul F. Healy. *Yankee from the West: The Candid, Turbulent Life Story of the Yankee-born U.S. Senator from Montana*. Garden City, NY: Doubleday, 1962.

WHITE, WALTER FRANCIS

Executive secretary of the National Association for the Advancement of Colored People (NAACP) from 1931 to 1955, Walter Francis White was a major supporter of antilynching legislation in the 1930s and one of the key activists behind the establishment of the 1941 Fair Employment Practices Committee (FEPC), set up to ensure equal hiring practices in the nation's defense industries.

Born in Atlanta in 1893, White was so light-skinned that he frequently passed for Caucasian as a boy but claimed that the Atlanta antiblack race riot of 1906 reinforced his African-American consciousness. A graduate of black Atlanta University, White became involved in the local branch of the NAACP in 1916.

Two years later, he moved to New York, where he served as assistant to the organization's national executive secretary, James Weldon Johnson. White's investigation of lynchings led him to write two novels on the subject in the 1920s, as well as an important 1929 investigative report, *Rope and Faggot: A Biography of Judge Lynch*.

Upon assuming the leadership of the NAACP in 1931, White pressured Congress to enact antilynching legislation but, although various bills were introduced, none passed, due to the resistance of southern senators. A reluctant President Franklin D. Roosevelt refused to speak out in favor of such legislation for fear it would alienate congressional support for New Deal legislation. Though White and the NAACP did not take the initiative for the 1941 March on Washington Movement (MOWM)—calling for an end to segregation in the military—they soon joined up with the movement's organizer, A. Philip Randolph, head of the Brotherhood of Sleeping Car Porters. Although the march was called off and desegregation had to await an executive order by President Harry Truman in 1948, the threat of a march pushed Roosevelt to issue his own executive order, establishing the Fair Employment Practices Committee (FEPC).

White monitored the FEPC's limited progress during World War II and became a delegate to the 1945 meeting establishing the United Nations. White's last years at the helm of the NAACP saw the beginning of the organization's efforts to end segregation in public education, resulting in the historic 1954 *Brown v. Board of Education* decision. White died in 1955.

See also: Brotherhood of Sleeping Car Porters; lynching; March on Washington Movement; Fair Employment Practices Committee; Randolph, A. Philip.

Bibliography

White, Walter Francis. *A Man Called White: The Autobiography of Walter White*. New York: Viking, 1948.

Zangrando, Robert L. *The NAACP Crusade Against Lynching, 1909–1950*. Philadelphia: Temple University Press, 1980.

WHITNEY, RICHARD

President of the New York Stock Exchange (NYSE) at the time of the great crash of 1929, Richard Whitney would become a symbol to many Americans of the responsibility of the business community for the Great Depression, when he was tried and convicted on charges of fraud and larceny in 1938.

Born to a wealthy family in Beverly, Massachusetts in 1888, Whitney graduated from Harvard in 1923 and became principal broker for J. P. Morgan Company before taking over his father's investment firm and renaming it Richard Whitney and Company.

Amidst the stock market crash on October 24, 1929—so-called "black Thursday"—Whitney was asked by a group of major financiers to bolster the market by buying up huge lots of blue chip stocks. While the effort temporarily raised share values, it could not in the end halt the free-fall in stock prices.

In 1930, Whitney was elected by the members of the NYSE to serve as president, a position he was re-elected to five times in a row through 1935. In that position, Whitney maintained a confident exterior and repeated his contention that the stock market would soon revive.

In 1938, Whitney was investigated for misappropriation of some $30 million of his company's funds and sentenced to serve time. After spending more than three years in Sing Sing prison, Whitney returned to investment banking, but on a far more modest scale. He died in 1974.

See also: stock market.

Bibliography

Brooks, John. *Once in Golconda; a True Drama of Wall Street, 1920–1938*. New York: Harper & Row, 1969.

WILLIAMS, AUBREY

An official in the Reconstruction Finance Corporation (RFC) and an assistant to Harry Hopkins at the various New Deal relief and public works agencies he administered, Aubrey Williams is best known as the director of the National Youth Administration (NYA) within the Works Progress Administration.

Born in rural Alabama in 1890, Williams was an infant when his impoverished family moved to Birmingham. Dropping out of school at age nine to work, Williams took night classes and eventually earned a degree from the University of Cincinnati in 1920, after taking off a year to fight first with the French Foreign Legion and then with the American Fifth Field Artillery during World War I.

Although interested in becoming a clergyman, Williams turned instead to social work and served as executive secretary of the Wisconsin Conference of Social Work from 1922 to 1932. He then went to work for the RFC, helping southern and midwestern governors apply for unemployment funds for their states.

A year later, Williams was hired by Hopkins as the first field representative of the Federal Emergency Relief Administration, set up in early 1933 to disperse federal relief money. Hopkins and Williams convinced Roosevelt to set up the Civil Works Administration in late 1933, a public works program that Williams helped Hopkins run.

When Roosevelt established the more ambitious Works Progress Administration in 1935, Hopkins was again appointed to run it, and he picked Williams to assist him as head of the agency's National Youth Administration (NYA). Over the next eight years, the NYA provided money for vocational education for over 4 million high school and college students. Williams strongly advocated bringing blacks into the NYA, both as recipients of aid and jobs and in positions of authority. Mary McLeod Bethune was head of the NYA's Division of Negro Affairs.

Williams was always a controversial figure. With his outspoken criticism of capitalism and New Deal opponents, he became an increasing political liability for the president, who removed him from office in 1938 after Williams was charged with harboring Communists within the NYA. In 1945, those charges came back to haunt Williams when the Senate refused to confirm him as head of the Rural Electrification Administration. Williams was involved in the civil rights movement in his home state of Alabama in the 1950s and early 1960s. He died in 1965.

See also: public works; Civil Works Administration; Federal Emergency Relief Administration; National Youth Administration; Reconstruction Finance Corporation; Works Progress Administration; Bethune, Mary McLeod; Hopkins, Harry.

Bibliography

Reiman, Richard A. *The New Deal and American Youth: Ideas and Ideals in a Depression Decade.* Athens: University of Georgia Press, 1992.

Salmond, John A. *A Southern Rebel: The Life and Times of Aubrey Willis Williams, 1890–1965.* Chapel Hill: University of North Carolina Press, 1983.

WILLKIE, WENDELL L.

A corporate lawyer, businessman, and Democrat who switched to the Republican Party in opposition to New Deal regulation of private business, Wendell L. Willkie became the Republican candidate for the presidency in 1940, losing to Franklin D. Roosevelt by a substantial margin.

Born in Elwood, Indiana in 1892, Willkie graduated from Indiana University with a law degree in 1916 and joined the army during World War I. Following his service, he became a corporate lawyer and moved to New York City in 1929 to work for the Commonwealth and Southern Corporation, a utilities holding company, where he rapidly rose to become president in 1933.

During the early and middle 1930s, Willkie was largely a supporter of New Deal programs and refused to denounce all government regulation of the private sector, as many conservative business leaders did. But when that regulation affected him personally through the Public Utilities Holding Act of 1935, Willkie became an outspoken critic of Roosevelt and changed his political affiliation to Republican. By the late 1930s, he had become a prominent spokesman for the moderate business community and its opposition to increasing governmental regulation.

While there were other more prominent candidates for the Republican presidential nomination in 1940, none were odds-on favorites, opening up the process to a dark horse, or outside, candidate. Popular with small business owners and rank-and-file Republicans, Willkie exuded a bouncy confidence that spurred the spontaneous formation of hundreds of "Willkie for President" clubs across the country by the time of the Republican convention in summer 1940.

Nominated on the sixth ballot, Willkie campaigned as a New Dealer who could administer the agencies

A Wall Street lawyer and utility company executive, Wendell Willkie nevertheless managed to display the common touch in his unsuccessful run for the presidency on the Republican ticket in 1940. *(Library of Congress)*

more effectively and create a climate more conducive to business expansion and job growth. Just as he was moderate on domestic issues, he was not far away from Roosevelt on foreign ones, generally supporting the president's push to help Great Britain, which, after the fall of France in spring 1940, was fighting against Nazi Germany alone.

Willkie lost the election by a significant margin, winning only ten states, although this was an improvement over Alfred Landon's 1936 run, which had won only two for the Republicans. During the early 1940s, Willkie toured foreign capitals to bolster the anti-Axis alliance. In 1944, he sought the Republican presidential nomination again but failed to get it and died later in the year.

See also: election of 1940; Republican Party; utilities; Public Utilities Holding Act; Landon, Alfred; Roosevelt, Franklin D.

Bibliography

Johnson, Donald Bruce. *The Republican Party and Wendell Willkie.* Urbana: University of Illinois Press, 1960.

Willkie, Wendell. *This Is Wendell Willkie: A Collection of Speeches and Writings on Present-Day Issues.* New York: Dodd, Mead, 1940.

WILSON, EDMUND

Among the most influential American intellectuals of the twentieth century, Edmund Wilson is best known for two seminal and pathbreaking Depression-era books on literature and political thought, *Axel's Castle* (1931) and *To the Finland Station* (1940).

Born in Red Bank, New Jersey, in 1895, Wilson graduated from Princeton University and became a journalist, first as a newspaper reporter and then as managing editor of *Vanity Fair*, a popular arts magazine, in the early 1920s. He became associate editor of the liberal magazine *The New Republic* from 1926 to 1931, continuing to write essays on culture, politics, and ideas for it until 1940. Most of the essays were republished in a series of collections that came out between 1936 and 1941.

In 1931, Wilson published *Axel's Castle*, which ex-amined the work of the symbolist poets of the early twentieth century. *To the Finland Station* looked at the ideologues and thinkers behind the Russian Revolution of 1917.

From 1944 to 1948, Wilson reviewed books for the *New Yorker* and after World War II published poetry, fiction, nonfiction, and drama. He died in 1972.

See also: literature; newspapers and magazines.

Bibliography

Edel, Leon, ed. *The Thirties: From Notebooks and Diaries of the Period: Edmund Wilson.* New York: Farrar, Straus, and Giroux, 1980.

Meyers, Jeffrey. *Edmund Wilson: A Biography.* Boston: Houghton Mifflin, 1995.

WINCHELL, WALTER

A widely syndicated newspaper columnist in the 1920s, Walter Winchell shifted to radio in the early 1930s, becoming one of the most powerful and widely-listened-to personalities of the Great Depression era, influencing both public opinion and policy-makers on a number of critical issues.

Winchell was born Walter Winschel in Harlem, New York, in 1897. From a poor household, Winchell made money as a boy singing in a vaudeville theater. At age thirteen, he was "discovered" by a talent agent and went on tour until he was in his early twenties. Marrying a fellow performer, Winchell returned to New York to find other employment because his new wife wanted to get out of show business.

He took a job doing errands, writing copy, and editing at *The Vaudeville News* in 1920. Working night and day to make contacts, Winchell destroyed his marriage but earned a reputation as a man-about-town who had information on lots of important personages. In 1924, he was signed on to write a column on Broadway for the start-up *Evening Graphic*.

Winchell's column became one of the most popular in a city teeming with columnists. His unique writing style, with its puns and jokes, along with his willingness to explore taboo subjects like abortion and extramarital affairs, often through the use of unnamed sources, fascinated the public. By the end of the decade, Winchell was syndicated across the country.

Beginning in the early 1930s, Winchell did a weekly radio broadcast in the same style as his column—odd turns of phrase combined with exposés about forbidden topics. Winchell was also willing to air his opinions on the topics of the day. A strong supporter of President Franklin D. Roosevelt and the New Deal, Winchell lashed out at greedy businesses and unfeeling government bureaucrats. Indeed, he was often welcomed at the White House, where Roosevelt would offer Winchell exclusives while Winchell would promote Roosevelt's policies.

With the rise of Nazi Germany in the 1930s, Winchell became an outspoken internationalist, advocating a firm and decisive U.S. response to Adolf Hitler, including military aid to Great Britain. Increasingly vocal in his patriotism during World War II, Winchell began drifting farther to the right during the early years of the Cold War, when he became a stalwart supporter of the anticommunist crusades of Senator Joseph McCarthy. This conservatism put him out-of-touch with a liberalizing America in the 1950s and 1960s, and Winchell's influence declined. He died in 1972.

See also: newspapers and magazines; radio; World War II, early history of; Roosevelt, Franklin D.

Bibliography

Gabler, Neal. *Winchell: Gossip, Power, and the Culture of Celebrity.* New York: Knopf, 1994.

Klurfeld, Herman. *Winchell: His Life and Times.* New York: Praeger, 1976.

WOOD, GRANT

One of the most influential artists of the Great Depression era and a member of the so-called Midwestern Regionalist school of painting, Grant Wood is known for his depictions of rural American life, most notably the classic *American Gothic* of 1930.

Born near Anamosa, Iowa, in 1892, Wood studied crafts and design, as well as painting, as a young man. He studied at the Académie Julian in Paris in 1923. After a brief flirtation with impressionistic painting, Wood turned to the detailed, realist style that became his hallmark.

Wood's *American Gothic*, portraying a dour midwestern couple in front of their farm house, was an immediate sensation when exhibited at the Art Institute of Chicago. The painting—with its emphasis on regional culture and its simplified but highly realistic forms—is said by art critics to have influenced the social realism of the murals for public buildings commissioned by various public works programs of the New Deal later in the 1930s.

Wood continued to paint through the 1930s, though none of his other paintings remain as memorable as *American Gothic*. A professor of fine arts at the University of Iowa after 1934, Wood died in 1942.

See also: arts, fine; public works.

Bibliography

Dennis, James M. *Grant Wood: A Study in American Art and Culture.* Columbia: University of Missouri Press, 1986.

Garwood, Darrell. *Artist in Iowa: A Life of Grant Wood.* New York: W. W. Norton, 1944.

WRIGHT, RICHARD

Among the most widely read and critically acclaimed African-American novelists, Richard Wright is best known for his 1940 novel *Native Son*, about a young black man condemned to death for the accidental killing of a white woman.

Born in rural Mississippi in 1908, Wright was raised by a single mother forced to move around the South looking for work. Sent to high school in Memphis and then Chicago, Wright studied literature and attended meetings of the John Reed Club of leftist writers and intellectuals, eventually becoming active in the Communist Party. In 1935, he got a job writing travel guides for the Federal Writers' Project.

Hoping to fuse his radical politics and his literary ambition, Wright published *Uncle Tom's Children* in 1938, a critically acclaimed and popular collection of long stories about the effects of racism on American society. Two years later, he published *Native Son*, a book most critics consider Wright's greatest contribution to American literature. Although the original manuscript was toned down by editors who felt it was too inflammatory, the militancy of the book came through, appealing to Depression-era readers who made it a best seller. A Book-of-the-Month Club selection, it was later dramatized for Broadway by director Orson Welles.

Wright's memoir of his youth, *Black Boy*, was published in 1945. After the war, Wright settled in France, where he continued to write. He died in 1960.

See also: African Americans; Communist Party; literature; Federal Writers' Project; Welles, Orson.

Bibliography

Fabre, Michel. *The Unfinished Quest of Richard Wright*. Urbana: University of Illinois Press, 1993.

Gayle, Addison. *Richard Wright: Ordeal of a Native Son*. Garden City, NY: Anchor Press/Doubleday, 1980.

Novelist Richard Wright won critical acclaim and wide readership for his 1935 short story collection *Uncle Tom's Children* and his 1940 novel *Native Son*. (*Library of Congress*)

PART VI
DOCUMENTS

INTRODUCTION TO PART VI

Part VI of the *Encyclopedia of the Great Depression and the New Deal* is devoted to original historical documents. Some are reprinted in full; others, generally longer ones, are excerpted from their original sources. All relate to various entries in the encyclopedia; at the end of many entries, there are cross-references to appropriate documents. The documents included here are divided into four general sections: governmental, political, legal, and international.

The first category includes bills and legislation on domestic issues, veto statements, official letters, executive orders, and congressional committee reports. The second category—politics—includes major party platforms, key political speeches, and excerpts from press conferences. In the third category are excerpts from the majority rulings of key Supreme Court cases of the Great Depression era, while in the fourth category—international affairs—are official government statements and letters, State Department reports, speeches, legislation, and international agreements.

SECTION 1 Government

Domestic Bills, Acts, Veto Statements, Official Letters, Executive Orders, and Committee Reports

HOOVER'S APPEAL TO GOVERNORS FOR STIMULATION OF STATE PUBLIC WORKS, NOVEMBER 23, 1929

With collective local and state revenues and budgets several times greater than those of the federal government, President Herbert Hoover appealed to these jurisdictions to make moneys available for activities that would put unemployed Americans to work in the first days of the Great Depression

With view to giving strength to the present economic situation and providing for the absorption of any unemployment which might result from present disturbed conditions, I have asked for collective action of industry in the expansion of construction activities and in stabilization of wages. As I have publicly stated, one of the largest factors that can be brought to bear is that of the energetic yet prudent pursuit of public works by the Federal Government and state municipal and county authorities.

The Federal Government will exert itself to the utmost within its own province and I should like to feel that I have the cooperation of yourself and the municipal county and other local officials in the same direction. It would be helpful if road, street, public building and other construction of this type could be speeded up and adjusted in such fashion as to further employment.

I would also appreciate it if your officials would canvass the state, municipal and county programs and give me such information as you can as to the volume of expenditure that can be prudently arranged for the next twelve months and for the next six months and inform me thereof.

I am asking Secretary [Thomas] Lamont of the Department of Commerce to take in hand the detailed measures of cooperation with you which may arise in this matter.

From: William Starr Myers, ed. *The State Papers and Other Public Writings of Herbert Hoover.* Garden City, NY: Doubleday, Doran and Company, 1934.

VETO OF AMENDMENT TO WORLD WAR VETERANS' BONUS ACT, JUNE 26, 1930

In one of the costlier political blunders of his administration, President Herbert Hoover refused to provide additional benefits to the veterans of World War I and vetoed a congressional bill to that effect. Later, Hoover also refused to speed up bonuses due to veterans in 1945, desperate as many of these unemployed veterans were. When they marched on Washington in 1932, Hoover ordered the army to clear their squatter camps, earning him the enmity of millions of Americans.

To the House of Representatives:

I am returning herewith House bill 10381 without approval.

One of the most repugnant tasks which can fall to this office is to disapprove of measures intended to benefit our sick or disabled men who have served our country in war. Perhaps as much as any other person, I have full realization of the task, the hardships, and the dangers to which the Nation ordered its sons. In sentiment and in sympathy I should desire no greater satisfaction than to support just measures which are proposed for their benefit. But I want a square deal between veterans; not unjust discriminations between special groups, and I do not want wasteful or unnecessary expenditures.

The country already generously provides for the 280,000 men whose health or earning power is shown to have been impaired by their service in the war and for 91,000 dependents of the men who suffered or died. That is and should be a first charge upon the Nation.

This measure except for a small part adds nothing

to aid of veterans wounded or disabled in the war. It is a radical departure from our full commitment to provide compensation to men for war disability into the field of pension to men who have incurred disabilities as the incident of civil life since the war and having no valid relation to their military service. It provides that in respect to veterans who between the years 1923 and 1930 shall have become afflicted with any one of an extensive category of diseases and thus disabled, there is established a "presumption" that these diseases originated from their service, and that they should be "compensated" or pensioned upon the basis of men who suffered as the result of actual military service. This provision would give war disability benefits to from 75,000 to 100,000 men who were not disabled as the result of war. In other words, the bill purports to establish that men who have enjoyed good health for a minimum of 7 years (from 1918 to 1925) since the war, or a maximum of 12 years (to 1930) and who have then become afflicted, have received such affliction from their war service.

I am informed by the Director of the Veterans' Bureau that the medical council of the bureau, consisting of most eminent physicians and surgeons, supported by the whole experience of the bureau, agree conclusively that this legal "presumption" that affliction from diseases mentioned in the bill between 1925 and 1930, is not a physical possibility and that the presumption constitutes a wholly false and fictitious basis for legislation in veterans' aid. This is confirmed by a recent resolution of so eminent a body as the American Medical Association.

The spectacle of the Government practicing subterfuge in order to say that what did not happen in the war did happen in the war, impairs the integrity of government, reduces the respect for government, and undermines the morale of all the people.

The practical effects of this enactment of a fictitious "presumption" into law are widespread. It creates a long train of injustices and inequalities. The first is to place men of this class who have in fact been disabled in civil life since the war upon the same basis as the men who were wounded in battle and suffered the exposures of the trenches. But a second injustice immediately arises. The Veterans' Bureau estimates that there are somewhere in the neighborhood of 380,000 possible cases of disability incurred in civil life since the war amongst the 4,300,000 living veterans. By this legislation all except somewhere between 75,000 and 100,000 of these men are excluded from this aid by the Government except for benefits which they already receive by hospitalization, the bonus, and insurance. This

bill would, therefore, create a preferred group of one-third among the men who are suffering from disabilities incurred in civil life since the war.

The further injustice of this bill may become more apparent when it is realized that men who were enrolled in the Army who remained but comparatively a few days or weeks in service, without ever leaving their home states, will receive aid upon the same basis as those men who passed through the battle of the Argonne. They may come upon the Government pay roll for life in case of total disability at rates from $80 to $200 per month. Beyond this, again, under the provisions of this bill as it affects the existing law, many thousands of men who have in fact incurred their disabilities in civil life may receive larger allowances from the Government than the men actually wounded at the front.

It has been contended that the Government has the right to disprove the "presumption" that any of the long list of diseases enumerated in this bill are not of war origin. But the burden of such proof is placed upon the Government, and all the experience of the Veterans' Bureau shows that such rebuttal is ineffective as the evidence surrounding such questions as a rule can not be secured or made clear and conclusive.

Additional inequalities and injustices arise from certain other provisions. At the present time any veteran who may become ill or disabled as the incident of civil life is received in Government hospitals if there is a vacant bed, and given free treatment. This bill provides that such cases received in the hospitals shall in addition to free treatment also receive cash allowances, and that a dependency allowance under certain restrictions shall be made to their families. The number of men of this type who are taken into Federal hospitals depends upon the number of beds unoccupied by men actually disabled from illness or injury incurred during the war, that being the major purpose of the hospitals. It is, therefore, a matter of accident or luck as to whether a given veteran ill from sickness arising in civil life is able to secure these facilities. An ill and destitute veteran may not have the luck to find a bed, in which case he neither receives treatment nor does his family receive an allowance. Yet a veteran of independent means may be fortunate enough to secure both. This is neither equitable nor just.

This bill departs from the traditional basis upon which we have given support to the veterans of the Civil and Spanish Wars. We have always recognized the principle in that legislation that the veterans of less than 90 days' service, unless they have a disability incurred in line of duty, should be excluded from benefits, because such men have not been called to actual war service. Recently in the Spanish War Veterans' Bill, against my protest, this was reduced to 70 days, but in the bill we are here considering there is no requirement whatever of service, and a man with one day's service after enrollment is entitled to all of the benefits. Here we create at once an injustice between veterans of different wars and between men whose lives were endangered and those who incurred no risks.

There is no provision in this bill against men of independent means claiming benefits from the Government for these disabilities arising in civil life. Surely it is of vital importance to the taxpayers, who, directly or indirectly, include all veterans themselves, that they shall not be called upon to contribute to such men of independent means. Moreover, it is equally important that the amount the Nation can find for this burden should not be dissipated over those without need but should be devoted to those who are in actual need. A declaration of destitution and pauperism from veterans is not necessary. I have never advocated such a declaration. It can, however, easily be provided in any legislation that the Secretary of the Treasury should return to the Veterans' Bureau a statement of the men who are exempt from income taxes at some level to be determined by Congress.

I have already protested to Congress in other connections against the inclusion of compensation for disablement due to vicious habits. This bill contemplates compensation for some misconduct disabilities, the whole conception of which must be repugnant to decent family life.

No government can proceed with intelligence that does not take into account the fiscal effects of its actions. The bill in a wasteful and extravagant manner goes far beyond the financial necessities of the situation. General Hines, after renewed examination, reports that this bill as finally passed will cost $11,000,000 the first year; that this will increase to an annual burden of $235,000,000 and continue during the life of these veterans.

The provision in the bill for review after three years, in my view, will never relieve us from commitments once entered upon. And this is but a portion of the costs, because the bill as enacted contains indirect liabilities to the Government of uncertain but very large possibilities. The amendments to section 19 of the World War Veterans' Act will increase the liabilities of the Government by a total of over $40,000,000, and the amendments to section 206 or 209 of the act will increase liabilities to a substantial but uncertain amount.

These costs are beyond the capacity of the Government at the present time without increased taxation. They are larger than the veterans have themselves proposed.

Beyond this, and of vital importance, are the potential obligations which are created and must finally be met. For instance, if we attempt to set up a system of relief to veterans suffering from disabilities incurred in civil life by establishing the "presumptions" of this bill, then we can not with fairness stop with a preferred group of 75,000 to 100,000 men. We shall have to extend these "presumptions" step by step over the entire group of 380,000. The additional cost upon the basis of the first 100,000 could readily add another $150,000,000 or $200,000,000 a year.

If we are going to make cash allowances to men disabled from sickness or accident arising in civil life now in Government hospitals, together with cash allowances to their families, we must consider the fate of others in the same class who are so unfortunate as not to be able to find an empty bed. There are approximately 13,000 such cases of illness arising from civil life in the Federal hospitals at the present time. The medical council of the Veterans' Bureau states that there are at least 85,000 such cases that will eventually have a right to hospitalization if beds are available. In addition to hospitals now building, we should need to expend another $140,000,000 in construction to take care of such further cases, and then be faced with an annual maintenance cost of about $60,000,000 all in addition to what we are providing now. To this again must be added the cash allowance to the further number of men for whom we make additional beds available in hospitals, and the allowance to their families, which will in itself aggregate a further great annual sum.

It is disagreeable to point out these potentialities lest it be thought that the Government begrudges its veterans. I am not presenting these reasons in any such sense, but in order that Congress and the country may be apprised of the real magnitude of the burden imposed and of the injustices arising from this legislation.

Even if I were able to overlook these burdens, for monetary considerations are indeed secondary, I can not overlook the discriminations and injustices which this legislation creates, together with its failure to meet the real need that exists today among our veterans in a fundamental and sound manner.

From: William Starr Myers, ed. *The State Papers and Other Public Writings of Herbert Hoover.* Garden City, NY: Doubleday, Doran and Company, 1934.

HOOVER'S VETO OF MUSCLE SHOALS BILL, MARCH 3, 1931

A pet project of progressive Republicans, the federally financed construction of hydroelectric dams was seen by President Herbert Hoover as dangerously socialistic, in that they would compete with private enterprise. In this message, Hoover vetoed one of the most widely discussed projects, at Muscle Shoals, Alabama. Later, under the New Deal, Muscle Shoals would be one of the key elements in the Tennessee Valley Authority.

To the Senate:

I return herewith, without my approval, Senate Joint Resolution 49, "To provide for the national defense by the creation of a corporation for the operation of the Government properties at and near Muscle Shoals in the State of Alabama, to authorize the letting of the Muscle Shoals properties under certain conditions; and for other purposes."

This bill proposes the transformation of the war plant at Muscle Shoals, together with important expansions, into a permanently operated Government institution for the production and distribution of power and the manufacture of fertilizers. . . .

The plants at Muscle Shoals were originally built for a production of nitrates for use in war explosives. I am advised by the War Department that the very large development in the United States by private enterprise in the manufacture of synthetic nitrogen now affords an ample supply covering any possible requirements of war. It is therefore unnecessary to maintain this plant for any such purposes.

This bill provides that the President for a period of 12 months may negotiate a lease of the nitrate plants for fertilizer manufacture under detailed limitations, but in failure to make such a lease the bill makes it mandatory upon the Government to manufacture nitrogen fertilizers at Muscle Shoals by the employment of existing facilities or by modernizing existing plants or by any other process. . . .

I am firmly opposed to the Government entering into any business the major purpose of which is competition with our citizens. There are national emergencies which require that the Government should temporarily enter the field of business, but they must be emergency actions and in matters where the cost of the project is secondary to much higher considerations.

There are many localities where the Federal Government is justified in the construction of great dams and reservoirs, where navigation, flood control, reclamation or stream regulation are of dominant importance, and where they are beyond the capacity or purpose of private or local government capital to construct. In these cases power is often a by-product and should be disposed of by contract or lease. But for the Federal Government deliberately to go out to build up and expand an occasion to the major purpose of a power and manufacturing business is to break down the initiative and enterprise of the American people; it is destruction of equality of opportunity of our people; it is the negation of the ideals upon which our civilization has been based.

This bill raises one of the important issues confronting our people. That is squarely the issue of Federal Government ownership and operation of power and manufacturing business not as a minor by-product but as a major purpose. Involved in this question is the agitation against the conduct of the power industry. The power problem is not to be solved by the project in this bill. The remedy for abuses in the conduct of that industry lies in regulation and not by the Federal Government entering upon the business itself. I have recommended to the Congress on various occasions that action should be taken to establish Federal regulation of interstate power in cooperation with State authorities. This bill would launch the Federal Government upon a policy of ownership and operation of power utilities upon a basis of competition instead of by the proper Government function of regulation for the protection of all the people. I hesitate to contemplate the future of our institutions, of our country if the preoccupation of its officials is to be no longer the promotion of justice and equal opportunity but is to be devoted to barter in the markets. That is not liberalism, it is degeneration.

This proposal can be effectively opposed upon other and perhaps narrower grounds. The establishment of a Federal-operated power business and fertilizer factory in the Tennessee Valley means Federal control from Washington with all the vicissitudes of national politics and the tyrannies of remote bureaucracy imposed upon the people of that valley without voice by them in their own resources, the overriding of State and local government, the undermining of State and local responsibility. The very history of this project over the past 10 years should be a complete demonstration of the ineptness of the Federal Government to administer such enterprise and of the penalties which the local community suffers under it.

This bill distinctly proposes to enter the field of powers reserved to the States. It would deprive the adjacent States of the right to control rates for this power and would deprive them of taxes on property within their borders and would invade and weaken the authority of local government.

The real development of the resources and the industries of the Tennessee Valley can only be accomplished by the people in that valley themselves. Muscle Shoals can only be administered by the people upon the ground, responsible to their own communities, directing them solely for the benefit of their communities and not for purposes of pursuit of social theories or national politics. Any other course deprives them of liberty. . . .

From: *Message from the President of the United States to Senate, March 3, 1931*. Washington, DC: Government Printing Office, 1931.

HOOVER'S OUTLINE OF PROGRAM TO SECURE COOPERATION OF BANKERS TO RELIEVE FINANCIAL DIFFICULTIES, OCTOBER 6, 1931

The banking system was hard hit in the early years of the Great Depression, beset by depositor runs and liquidity crises. To combat this problem, President Herbert Hoover pleaded with major bankers to create a $500,000,000 fund that would be made available to failing banks. This voluntaristic approach was characteristic of Hoover. But his pleas went unheard as the major banks refused to cooperate.

The prolongation of the depression by the succession of events in Europe, affecting as they have both commodity and security prices, has produced in some localities in the United States an apprehension wholly unjustified in view of the thousand-fold resources we have for meeting any demand. Foolish alarm in these sections has been accompanied by wholly unjustifiable withdrawal of currency from the banks. Such action results in limiting the ability of the banks in these localities to extend credit to business men and farmers for the normal conduct of business but beyond this to be prepared to meet the possibility of unreasoning demands of depositors the banks are compelled to place their assets in liquid form by sales of securities and restriction of credits so as to enable them to meet unnecessary and unjustified drains. This affects the conduct of banking further afield. It is unnecessary to specify the unfortunate consequences of such a situation in the districts affected both in its further effect on national prices of agricultural products, upon se-

curities and upon the normal conduct of business and employment of labor. It is a deflationary factor and a definite impediment to agricultural and business recovery.

There is no justification for any such situation in view of the strength of our banking system, and the strong position of our Federal Reserve System. Our difficulty is a diffusion of resources and the primary need is to mobilize them in such a way as to restore in a number of localities the confidence of the banker in his ability to continue normal business and to dispel any conceivable doubt in the mind of those who do business with him.

In order to deal with this wholly abnormal situation and to bring about an early restoration of confidence, unity of action on the part of our bankers and cooperative action on the part of the Government is essential. Therefore, I propose the following definite program of action, to which I ask our citizens to give their full cooperation:

1. To mobilize the banking resources of the country to meet these conditions, I request the bankers of the Nation to form a national institution of at least $500,000,000. The purpose of this institution to be the rediscount of banking assets not now eligible for rediscount at the Federal Reserve Banks in order to assure our banks, being sound, that they may attain liquidity in case of necessity, and thereby enable them to continue their business without the restriction of

credits or the sacrifice of their assets. I have submitted my proposal to the leading bankers of New York. I have been advised by them that it will receive their support, and that at my request they will assume the leadership in the formation of such an organization. The members of the New York City Clearing House Association have unanimously agreed to contribute their share by pledging $150,000,000 which is two per cent of their net demand and time deposits. I have been assured from other large centers, as far as I have been able to reach, of their support also. I consider that it is in the national interest including the interest of all individual banks and depositors that all the banks of the country should support this movement to their full responsibility. It is a movement of national assurance and of unity of action in an American way to assist business, employment and agriculture.

2. On September 8th I requested the Governors of the Federal Reserve Banks to endeavor to secure the cooperation of the bankers of their territory to make some advances on the security of the assets of closed banks or to take over some of these assets in order that the receivers of those banks may pay some dividends to their depositors in advance of what would otherwise be the case pending liquidation. Such a measure will contribute to free many business activities and to relieve many families from hardship over the forthcoming winter, and in a measure reverse the process of deflation involved in the tying up of deposits. Several of the districts have already made considerable progress to this end, and I request that it should be taken up vigorously as a community responsibility.

3. In order that the above program of unification and solidarity of action may be carried out and that all parts of the country be enlisted, I request the Governors of the Federal Reserve Banks in each district to secure the appointment of working committees of bankers for each Reserve District to cooperate with the New York group and in carrying out the other activities which I have mentioned.

4. I shall propose to the Congress that the eligibility provisions of the Federal Reserve Act should be broadened in order to give greater liquidity to the assets of the banks, and thus a greater assurance to the bankers in the granting of credits by enabling them to obtain legitimate accommodation on sound security in times of stress. Such measures are already under con-

sideration by the Senate Committee upon Currency and Banking.

5. Furthermore, if necessity requires, I will recommend the creation of a Finance Corporation similar in character and purpose to the War Finance Corporation, with available funds sufficient for any legitimate call in support of credit.

6. I shall recommend to Congress the subscription of further capital stock by the Government to the Federal Land Banks (as was done at their founding) to strengthen their resources so that on the one hand the farmer may be assured of such accommodation as he may require and on the other hand their credit may be of such high character that they may obtain their funds at low rates of interest.

7. I have submitted the above mentioned proposals which require legislation to the members of Congress whose attendance I was able to secure on short notice at the evening's meeting—being largely the members of committees particularly concerned—and they approve of them in principle.

8. Premier [Pierre] Laval of France is visiting the United States. It is my purpose to discuss with him the question of such further arrangements as are imperative during the period of the depression with respect to intergovernmental debts. The policy of the American Government in this matter is well known and was set out by me in public statement on June 20th in announcing the American proposal for a year's postponement of debt payments. Our problem in this respect is one of such adjustment during the period of depression as will at the same time aid our own and world recovery. This being a subject first of negotiation with foreign governments was not submitted for determination at this evening's conference.

9. The times call for unity of action on the part of our people. We have met with great difficulties not of our own making. It requires determination to overcome these difficulties and above all to restore and maintain confidence. Our people owe it not only to themselves and in their own interest but they can by such an example of stability and purpose give hope and confidence in our own country and to the rest of the world.

From: William Starr Myers, ed. *The State Papers and Other Public Writings of Herbert Hoover.* Garden City, NY: Doubleday, Doran and Company, 1934.

NORRIS-LA GUARDIA ANTI-INJUNCTION BILL, MARCH 20, 1932

For much of U.S. history, companies and corporations have made effective use of the injunction to block activities by labor unions. Under such injunctions, labor unions could be prevented from picketing or organizing boycotts, under the threat of double and triple damages. This bill, introduced by Nebraska Senator George Norris and New York representative Fiorello La Guardia, would have blocked many of these injunctions. Vetoed by President Herbert Hoover, some of this legislation would be incorporated into the 1935 National Labor Relations Act.

AN ACT to amend the Judicial Code and to define and limit the jurisdiction of courts sitting in equity, and for other purposes.

Be it enacted, That no court of the United States, as herein defined, shall have jurisdiction to issue any restraining order or temporary or permanent injunction in a case involving or growing out of a labor dispute, except in a strict conformity with the provisions of this Act; nor shall any such restraining order or temporary or permanent injunction be issued contrary to the public policy declared in this Act....

SEC. 2. In the interpretation of this Act and in determining the jurisdiction and authority of the courts of the United States, as such jurisdiction and authority are herein defined and limited, the public policy of the United States is hereby declared as follows:

Whereas, under prevailing economic conditions, ... the individual unorganized worker is commonly helpless to exercise actual liberty of contract and to protect his freedom of labor, and thereby to obtain acceptable terms and conditions of employment, wherefore, though he should be free to decline to associate with his fellows, it is necessary that he should have full freedom of association, self-organization, and designation of representatives of his own choosing, to negotiate the terms and conditions of his employment, and that he shall be free from the interference, restraint, or coercion of employers of labor, or their agents, in the activities for the purpose of collective bargaining or other mutual aid or protection; therefore, the following definitions of, and limitations upon, the jurisdiction and authority of the courts of the United States are hereby enacted.

SEC. 3. Any undertaking or promise, such as is described in this section, or any other undertaking or promise in conflict with the public policy declared in section 2 of this Act, is hereby declared to be contrary to the public policy of the United States, shall not be enforceable in any court of the United States and shall not afford any basis for the granting of legal or equitable relief by any such court, including specifically the following:

Every undertaking or promise hereafter made, whether written or oral, express or implied constituting or contained in any contract or agreement of hiring or employment between any individual firm, company, association, or corporation, and any employee or prospective employee of the same, whereby,

a—Either party to such contract or agreement undertakes or promises not to join, become, or remain a member of any labor organization or of any employer organization; or

b—Either party to such contract or agreement undertakes or promises that he will withdraw from any employment relation in the event that he joins, becomes or remains a member of any labor organization or of any employer organization.

SEC. 4. No court of the United States shall have the jurisdiction to issue any restraining order or temporary or permanent injunction in any case involving or growing out of any labor dispute to prohibit any person or persons participating or interested in such dispute (as these terms are herein defined) from doing, whether singly or in concert, any of the following acts:

(a) Ceasing or refusing to perform any work or to remain in any relation of employment;

(b) Becoming or remaining a member of any labor organization or of any employer organization, regardless of any such undertaking or promise as is described in section 3 of this Act:

(c) Paying or giving to, or withholding from any person participating or interested in such labor dispute, any strike or employment benefits or insurance, or other moneys or things of value;

(d) By all lawful means aiding any person participating or interested in any labor dispute who is being proceeded against in, or is prosecuting, any action or suit in any court in the United States or of any state;

(e) Giving publicity to the extent of, or the facts involved in any labor dispute whether by advertising, speaking, patrolling, or by any other method not involving fraud or violence;

(f) Assembling peaceably to act or to organize to act in promotion of their interests in a labor dispute;

(g) Advising or notifying any persons of any intentions to do any of the acts heretofore specified;

(h) Agreeing with other persons to do or not to do any of the acts heretofore specified; and

(i) Advising, urging, or otherwise causing or inducing without fraud or violence the acts heretofore specified, regardless of any such undertaking or promise as is described in section 3 of this Act.

SEC. 5. No court of the United States shall have jurisdiction to issue a restraining order or temporary or permanent injunction upon the ground that any of the persons participating or interested in a labor dispute constitute or are engaged in an unlawful combination or conspiracy because of the doing in concert of the acts enumerated in section 4 of this Act.

SEC. 6. No officer or member of any organization or association, and no association or organization participating or interested in a labor dispute, shall be held responsible or liable in any court of the United States for the unlawful acts of individual officers, members, or agents, except upon clear proof of actual participation in, or actual authorization of, such acts, or of ratification of such acts after actual knowledge thereof.

SEC. 7. No court of the United States shall have jurisdiction to issue a temporary or permanent injunction in any case involving or growing out of a labor dispute as herein defined except after hearing the testimony of witnesses in open court (with opportunity for cross-examination) in support of the allegations of a complaint made under oath, and testimony in opposition thereto, if offered, and except after findings of fact by the court, to the effect—

(a) That unlawful acts have been threatened and will be committed unless restrained or have been committed and will be continued unless restrained, but no injunction or temporary restraining order shall be issued on account of any threat or unlawful act excepting against the person or persons, association, or organization making the threat or committing the unlawful act or actually authorizing or ratifying the same after actual knowledge thereof;

(b) That substantial and irreparable injury to complainant's property will follow;

(c) That as to each item of relief granted greater injury will be inflicted upon complainant by the denial of relief than will be inflicted upon defendants by the granting of relief;

(d) That complainant has no adequate remedy at law; and

(e) That the public officers charged with the duty to protect complainant's property are unable or unwilling to furnish adequate protection. . . .

SEC. 9. No restraining order or temporary or permanent injunctions shall be granted in a case involving or growing out of a labor dispute, except on the basis of findings of fact made and filed by the court in the record of the case prior to the issuance of such restraining order or injunction; and every restraining order or injunction granted in a case involving or growing out of a labor dispute shall include only a prohibition of such specific act or acts as may be expressly complained of in the bill of complaint or petition filed in such case and as shall be expressly included in said findings of fact made and filed by the court as provided herein. . . .

SEC. 11. In all cases arising under this Act in which a person shall be charged with contempt in a court of the United States (as herein defined), the accused shall enjoy the right to speedy and public trial by an impartial jury of the state and district wherein the contempt shall have been committed: Provided, That this right shall not apply to contempt committed in the presence of the court or so near thereto as to interfere directly with the administration of justice or to apply to the misbehavior, misconduct, or disobedience of any officer of the court in respect to the writs, orders, or process of the court. . . .

SEC. 13. . . .

(c) The term "labor dispute" includes any controversy concerning terms or conditions of employment, or concerning the association or representation of persons negotiating fixing, maintaining, changing, or seeking to arrange terms or conditions of employment regardless of whether or not the disputants stand in approximate relation of employer and employee. . . .

From: William Starr Myers, ed. *The State Papers and Other Public Writings of Herbert Hoover.* Garden City, NY: Doubleday, Doran and Company, 1934.

AGRICULTURAL ADJUSTMENT ACT, MAY 12, 1933

When urban and industrial America was plunged into the Great Depression following the stock market crash of 1929, agricultural America had been mired in an economic slump since the end of World War I. Bumper crops and deflation had reduced the value of most crops drastically, leading to massive numbers of farm failures. The Agricultural Adjustment Act was designed to boost crop prices by having the government pay farmers not to plant.

An Act to relieve the existing national economic emergency by increasing agricultural purchasing power. . . .

TITLE I—AGRICULTURAL ADJUSTMENT DECLARATION OF EMERGENCY

That the present acute economic emergency being in part the consequence of a severe and increasing disparity between the prices of agricultural and other commodities, which disparity has largely destroyed the purchasing power of farmers for industrial products, has broken down the orderly exchange of commodities, and has seriously impaired the agricultural assets supporting the national credit structure, it is hereby declared that these conditions in the basic industry of agriculture have affected transactions in agricultural commodities with a national public interest, have burdened and obstructed the normal currents of commerce in such commodities, and render imperative the immediate enactment of title I of this Act.

DECLARATION OF POLICY

SEC. 2. It is hereby declared to be the policy of Congress—

(1) To establish and maintain such balance between the production and consumption of agricultural commodities, and such marketing conditions therefor, as will reestablish prices to farmers at a level that will give agricultural commodities a purchasing power with respect to articles that farmers buy, equivalent to the purchasing power of agricultural commodities in the base period. The base period in the case of all agricultural commodities except tobacco shall be the prewar period, August 1909–July 1914. In the case of tobacco, the base period shall be the postwar period, August 1919–July 1929.

(2) To approach such equality of purchasing power by gradual correction of the present inequalities therein at as rapid a rate as is deemed feasible in view of the current consumptive demand in domestic and foreign markets.

(3) To protect the consumers' interest by readjusting farm production at such level as will not increase the percentage of the consumers' retail expenditures for agricultural commodities, or products derived therefrom, which is returned to the farmer, above the percentage which was returned to the farmer in the prewar period, August 1909–July 1914. . . .

SEC. 6. (a) The Secretary of Agriculture is hereby authorized to enter into option contracts with the producers of cotton to sell to any such producer an amount of cotton to be agreed upon not in excess of the amount of reduction in production of cotton by such producer below the amount produced by him in the preceding crop year, in all cases where such producer agrees in writing to reduce the amount of cotton produced by him in 1933 below his production in the previous year, by not less than 30 per centum, without increase in commercial fertilization per acre.

(b) To any such producer so agreeing to reduce production the Secretary of Agriculture shall deliver a nontransferable-option contract agreeing to sell to said producer an amount, equivalent to the amount of his agreed reduction, of the cotton in the possession and control of the Secretary.

(c) The producer is to have the option to buy said cotton at the average price paid by the Secretary for the cotton procured under section 3, and is to have the right at any time up to January 1, 1934, to exercise his option, upon proof that he has complied with his contract and with all the rules and regulations of the Secretary of Agriculture with respect thereto, by taking said cotton upon payment by him of his option price and all actual carrying charges on such cotton; or the Secretary may sell such cotton for the account of such producer, paying him the excess of the market price at the date of sale over the average price above referred to after deducting all actual and necessary carrying charges: Provided, That in no event shall the producer be held responsible or liable for financial loss incurred in the holding of such cotton or on account of the carrying charges therein: Provided further, That such agreement to curtail cotton production shall contain a further provision that such cotton producer shall not use the land taken out of cotton production for the production for sale, directly or indirectly, of any other nationally produced agricultural commodity or product. . . .

PART 2—COMMODITY BENEFITS

GENERAL POWERS

SEC. 8. In order to effectuate the declared policy, the Secretary of Agriculture shall have power—

(1) To provide for reduction in the acreage or reduction in the production for market, or both, of any basic agricultural commodity, through agreements with producers or by other voluntary methods, and to provide for rental or benefit payments in connection therewith or upon that part of the production of any basic agricultural commodity required for domestic consumption, in such amounts as the Secretary deems fair and reasonable, to be paid out of any moneys available for such payments. . . .

(2) To enter into marketing agreements with processors, associations of producers, and others engaged in the handling, in the current of interstate or foreign commerce of any agricultural commodity or project thereof, after due notice and opportunity for hearing to interested parties. The making of any such agreement shall not be held to be in violation of any of the antitrust laws of the United States, and any such agreement shall be deemed to be lawful. . . .

PROCESSING TAX

SEC. 9. (a) To obtain revenue for extraordinary expenses incurred by reason of the national economic emergency, there shall be levied processing taxes as hereinafter provided. When the Secretary of Agriculture determines that rental or benefit payments are to be made with respect to any basic agricultural commodity, he shall proclaim such determination, and a processing tax shall be in effect with respect to such commodity from the beginning of the marketing year therefor next following the date of such proclamation. The processing tax shall be levied, assessed, and collected upon the first domestic processing of the commodity whether of domestic production or imported and shall be paid by the processor. . . .

(b) The processing tax shall be at such rate as equals the difference between the current average farm price for the commodity and the fair exchange value of the commodity; except that if the Secretary has reason to believe that the tax at such rate will cause such reduction in the quantity of the commodity or products thereof domestically consumed as to result in the accumulation of surplus stocks of the commodity or products thereof or in the depression of the farm price of the commodity, then he shall cause an appropriate investigation to be made and afford due notice and opportunity for hearing to interested parties. If thereupon the Secretary finds that such result will occur, then the processing tax shall be at such rate as will prevent such accumulation of surplus stocks and depression of the farm price of the commodity. . . .

(c) For the purposes of part 2 of this title, the fair exchange value of a commodity shall be the price therefor that will give the commodity the same purchasing power, with respect to articles farmers buy, as such commodity had during the base period specified in section 2. . . .

(d) As used in part 2 of this title—

(1) In case of wheat, rice, and corn, the term "processing" means the milling or other processing (except cleaning and drying) of wheat, rice, or corn for market, including custom milling for toll as well as commercial milling, but shall not include the grinding or cracking thereof not in the form of flour for feed purposes only.

(2) In case of cotton, the term "processing" means the spinning, manufacturing, or other processing (except ginning) of cotton; and the term "cotton" shall not include cotton linters.

(3) In case of tobacco, the term "processing" means the manufacturing or other processing (except drying or converting into insecticides and fertilizers) of tobacco.

(4) In case of hogs, the term "processing" means the slaughter of hogs for market.

(5) In the case of any other commodity, the term "processing" means any manufacturing or other processing involving a change in the form of the commodity or its preparation for market, as defined by regulations of the Secretary of Agriculture; and in prescribing such regulations the Secretary shall give due weight to the customs of the industry.

(e) When any processing tax, or increase or decrease therein, takes effect in respect of a commodity the Secretary of Agriculture, in order to prevent pyramiding of the processing tax and profiteering in the sale of the products derived from the commodity, shall make public such information as he deems necessary regarding (1) the relationship between the processing tax and the price paid to producers of the commodity, (2) the effect of the processing tax upon prices to consumers of products of the commodity, (3) the relationship, in previous periods, between prices paid to the producers of the commodity and prices to consumers of the products thereof, and (4) the situation in foreign countries relating to prices paid to producers of the commodity and prices to consumers of the products thereof. . . .

From: *U.S. Statutes at Large.* 1933. Vol. 48, p. 31.

TENNESSEE VALLEY ACT, MAY 18, 1933

Long a pet project of progressives, such as Republican senator George Norris of Nebraska, federally financed hydroelectric systems got a major boost with the election of Franklin D. Roosevelt. Unlike Hoover, who vetoed the Muscle Shoals (Alabama) hydroelectric project, Roosevelt endorsed this project and was eager to expand it into a system of dams and other projects that would encompass the entire Tennessee River valley. The 1933 Tennessee Valley Act—creating the Tennessee Valley Authority—was the fulfillment of that dream.

AN ACT to improve the navigability and to provide for the flood control of the Tennessee River; to provide for reforestation and the proper use of marginal lands in the Tennessee Valley; to provide for the agricultural and industrial development of said valley; to provide for the national defense by the creation of a corporation for the operation of Government properties at and near Muscle Shoals in the State of Alabama, and for other purposes. . . .

Be it enacted, That for the purpose of maintaining and operating the properties now owned by the United States in the vicinity of Muscle Shoals, Alabama, . . . there is hereby created a body corporate by the name of the "Tennessee Valley Authority." . . .

SEC. 2. . . . (f) No director shall have financial interest in any public-utility corporation engaged in the business of distributing and selling power to the public nor in any corporation engaged in the manufacture, selling, or distribution of fixed nitrogen or fertilizer, or any ingredients thereof, nor shall any member have any interest in any business that may be adversely affected by the success of the Corporation as a producer of concentrated fertilizers or as a producer of electric power. . . .

(h) All members of the board shall be persons who profess a belief in the feasibility and wisdom of this Act. . . .

SEC. 3. . . . All contracts to which the Corporation is a party and which require the employment of laborers and mechanics in the construction, alteration, maintenance, or repair of buildings, dams, locks, or other projects shall contain a provision that not less than the prevailing rate of wages for work of a similar nature prevailing in the vicinity shall be paid to such laborers or mechanics. . . .

SEC. 4. Except as otherwise specifically provided in this Act, the Corporation. . . .

(f) May purchase or lease and hold such real and personal property as it deems necessary or convenient in the transaction of its business, and may dispose of any such personal property held by it. . . .

(h) Shall have power in the name of the United States of America to exercise the right of eminent domain, and in the purchase of any real estate or the acquisition of real estate by condemnation proceedings, the title to such real estate shall be taken in the name of the United States of America. . . .

(i) Shall have power to acquire real estate for the construction of dams, reservoirs, transmission lines, power houses, and other structures, and navigation projects at any point along the Tennessee River, or any of its tributaries. . . .

(j) Shall have power to construct dams, reservoirs, power houses, power structures, transmission lines, navigation projects, and incidental works in the Tennessee River and its tributaries, and to unite the various power installations into one or more systems by transmission lines.

SEC. 5. The board is hereby authorized....

(b) To arrange with farmers and farm organizations for large-scale practical use of the new forms of fertilizers under conditions permitting an accurate measure of the economic return they produce.

(c) To cooperate with National, State, district, or county experimental stations or demonstration farms, for the use of new forms of fertilizer or fertilizer practices during the initial or experimental period of their introduction.

(d) The board in order to improve and cheapen the production of fertilizer is authorized to manufacture and sell fixed nitrogen, fertilizer, and fertilizer ingredients at Muscle Shoals by the employment of existing facilities, by modernizing existing plants, or by any other process or processes that in its judgment shall appear wise and profitable for the fixation of atmospheric nitrogen or the cheapening of the production of fertilizer.

(e) Under the authority of this Act the board may make donations or sales of the product of the plant or plants operated by it to be fairly and equitably distributed through the agency of county demonstration agents, agricultural colleges, or otherwise as the board may direct, for experimentation, education, and introduction of the use of such products in cooperation with practical farmers so as to obtain information as to the value, effect, and best methods of their use.

(f) The board is authorized to make alterations, modifications, or improvements in existing plants and facilities, and to construct new plants.

(g) In the event it is not used for the fixation of nitrogen for agricultural purposes or leased, then the board shall maintain in standby condition nitrate plant numbered 2, or its equivalent, for the fixation of atmospheric nitrogen, for the production of explosives in the event of war or a national emergency, until the Congress shall by joint resolution release the board from this obligation, and if any part thereof be used by the board for the manufacture of phosphoric acid or potash the balance of nitrate plant numbered 2 shall be kept in stand-by condition.

(h) To establish, maintain, and operate laboratories and experimental plants, and to undertake experiments for the purpose of enabling the Corporation to furnish nitrogen products for military purposes, and nitrogen and other fertilizer products for agricultural purposes in the most economical manner and at the highest standard of efficiency....

(1) To produce, distribute, and sell electric power, as herein particularly specified.

(m) No products of the Corporation shall be sold for use outside of the United States, its Territories and possessions, except to the United States Government for the use of its Army and Navy, or to its allies in case of war.

SEC. 10. The board is hereby empowered and authorized to sell the surplus power not used in its operations, and for operation of locks and other works generated by it, to States, counties, municipalities, corporations, partnerships, or individuals, according to the policies hereinafter set forth; and to carry out said authority, the board is authorized to enter into contracts for such sale for a term not exceeding twenty years, and in the sale of such current by the board it shall give preference to States, counties, municipalities and cooperative organizations of citizens or farmers, not organized or doing business for profit, but primarily for the purpose of supplying electricity to its own citizens or members: ... In order to promote and encourage the fullest possible use of electric light and power on farms within reasonable distance of any of its transmission lines the board in its discretion shall have power to construct transmission lines to farms and small villages that are not otherwise supplied with electricity at reasonable rates, and to make such rules and regulations governing such sale and distribution of such electric power as in its judgment may be just and equitable: Provided further, That the board is hereby authorized and directed to make studies, experiments, and determinations to promote the wider and better use of electric power for agricultural and domestic use, or for small or local industries, and it may cooperate with State governments, or their subdivisions or agencies, with educational or research institutions, and with cooperatives or other organizations, in the application of electric power to the fuller and better balanced development of the resources of the region.

SEC. 11. It is hereby declared to be the policy of the Government so far as practical to distribute and sell the surplus power generated at Muscle Shoals equitably among the States, counties, and municipalities within transmission distance. This policy is further declared to be that the projects herein provided for shall be considered primarily as for the benefit of the people of the section as a whole and particularly the domestic and rural consumers to whom the power can economically be made available, and accordingly that sale to and use by industry shall be a secondary purpose, to be utilized principally to secure a sufficiently high load factor and revenue returns which will permit domestic and rural use at the lowest possible rates and in such manner as to encourage increased domestic and rural use of electricity. It is further hereby declared to be the policy of the Government to utilize the Muscle Shoals properties so far as may be necessary to improve, increase, and cheapen the production of fertilizer and fertilizer ingredients by carrying out the provision of this Act....

SEC. 22. To aid further the proper use, conservation, and development of the natural resources of the Tennessee River drainage basin and of such adjoining territory as may be related to or materially affected by the development consequent to this Act, and to provide for the general welfare of the citizens of said areas, the President is hereby authorized, by such means or methods as he may deem proper within the limits of appropriations made therefore by Congress, to make such surveys of and general plans for said Tennessee basin and adjoining territory as may be useful to the Congress and to the several States in guiding and controlling the extent, sequence, and nature of development that may be equitably and economically advanced through the expenditure of public funds, or through the guidance or control of public authority, all for the general purpose of fostering an orderly and proper physical, economic, and social development of said areas; and the President is further authorized in making said surveys and plans to cooperate with the States affected thereby, or subdivisions or agencies of such States, or with cooperative or other organizations, and to make such studies, experiments, or demonstrations as may be necessary and suitable to that end.

SEC. 23. The President shall, from time to time, as the work provided for in the preceding section progresses, recommend to Congress such legislation as he deems proper to carry out the general purposes stated in said section, and for the especial purpose of bringing about in said Tennessee drainage basin and adjoining territory in conformity with said general purposes (1) the maximum amount of flood control; (2) the maximum development of said Tennessee River for navigation purposes; (3) the maximum generation of electric power consistent with flood control and navigation; (4) the proper use of marginal lands; (5) the proper method of reforestation of all lands in said drainage basin suitable for reforestation; and (6) the economic and social well-being of the people living in said river basin....

From: *U.S. Statutes at Large.* 1933. Vol. 48, p. 58.

ABANDONMENT OF THE GOLD STANDARD, JUNE 5, 1933

Throughout the nineteenth and into the early twentieth centuries, the dollar was linked to gold. That is, any person holding American currency could have that money exchanged for a fixed amount of gold. The gold standard was considered the bulwark of a sound financial system. But it also kept the value of the dollar inordinately high, contributing to a deflation of prices. This deflation was seen by the Roosevelt administration as a major cause of the Depression. Thus three months after assuming office, President Franklin D. Roosevelt asked and got Congress to take the United States off the gold standard.

JOINT RESOLUTION to assure uniform value to the coins and currencies of the United States.

Whereas the holding of or dealing in gold affect the public interest, and are therefore subject to proper regulation and restriction; and

Whereas the existing emergency has disclosed that provisions of obligations which purport to give the obligee a right to require payment in gold or a particular kind of coin or currency of the United States, or in an amount of money of the United States measured thereby, obstruct the power of the Congress to regulate the value of the money of the United States, and are inconsistent with the declared policy of the Congress to maintain at all times the equal power of every dollar, coined or issued by the United States, in the markets and in the payment of debts. Now, therefore, be it

Resolved by the Senate and House of Representatives of the United States of America in Congress assembled, That (a) every provision contained in or made with respect to any obligation which purports to give the obligee a right to require payment in gold or a particular kind of coin or currency, or in an amount in money of the United States measured thereby, is declared to be against public policy; and no such provision shall be contained in or made with respect to any obligation hereafter incurred. Every obligation, heretofore or hereafter incurred, whether or not any such provision is contained therein or made with respect thereto, shall be discharged upon payment, dollar for dollar, in any coin or currency which at the time of payment is legal tender for public and private debts. Any such provision contained in any law authorizing obligations to be issued by or under authority of the United States, is hereby repealed, but the repeal of any such provision shall not invalidate any other provision or authority contained in such law.

(b) As used in this resolution, the term "obligation" means an obligation (including every obligation of and to the United States, excepting currency) payable in money of the United States; and the term "coin or currency" means coin or currency of the United States, including Federal Reserve notes and circulating notes of Federal Reserve banks and national banking associations.

SEC. 2. The last sentence of paragraph (1) of subsection (b) of section 43 of the act entitled "An act to relieve the existing national economic emergency by increasing agricultural purchasing power, to raise revenue for extraordinary expenses incurred by reason of such emergency, to provide emergency relief with respect to agricultural indebtedness, to provide for the orderly liquidation of joint-stock land banks, and for other purposes," approved May 12, 1933, is amended to read as follows:

"All coins and currencies of the United States (including Federal Reserve notes and circulating notes of Federal Reserve banks and national banking associations) heretofore or hereafter coined or issued shall be legal tender for all debts, public and private, public charges, taxes, duties, and dues, except that gold coins, when below the standard weight and limit of tolerance provided by law for the single piece, shall be legal tender only at valuation in proportion to their actual weight."

From: *U.S. Statutes at Large*. 1933. Vol. 48, p. 113.

NATIONAL INDUSTRIAL RECOVERY ACT, JUNE 16, 1933

The National Industrial Recovery Act was the linchpin legislation of the early New Deal. It set up the National Recovery Administration, a government agency created to regulate prices, wages, and other aspects of the industrial economy. It also included the first major public works project of the New Deal. While it did raise prices somewhat and helped stabilize the industrial sector of the economy, it was widely criticized for helping big business too much. Farmers also complained that it hurt them by raising prices on the things they bought. Workers also complained that Section 7(a) of the act, which supposedly guaranteed their right to organize, had little enforcement machinery behind it and was routinely evaded by business. In 1935, the act was declared unconstitutional by the Supreme Court in its Schechter Poultry Corporation v. United States *decision.*

An Act to encourage national industrial recovery, to foster fair competition, and to provide for the con-

struction of certain useful public works, and for other purposes.

TITLE I—INDUSTRIAL RECOVERY DECLARATION OF POLICY

SEC. 1. A national emergency productive of widespread unemployment and disorganization of industry, which burdens interstate and foreign commerce, affects the public welfare, and undermines the standards of living of the American people, is hereby declared to exist. It is hereby declared to be the policy of Congress to remove obstructions to the free flow of interstate and foreign commerce which tend to diminish the amount thereof; and to provide for the general welfare by promoting the organization of industry for the purpose of cooperative action among trade groups, to induce and maintain united action of labor and management under adequate governmental sanctions and supervision, to eliminate unfair competitive practices, to promote the fullest possible utilization of the present productive capacity of industries, to avoid undue restriction of production (except as may be temporarily required), to increase the consumption of industrial and agricultural products by increasing purchasing power, to reduce and relieve unemployment, to improve standards of labor, and otherwise to rehabilitate industry and to conserve natural resources.

ADMINISTRATIVE AGENCIES

SEC. 2. . . . (c) This title shall cease to be in effect and any agencies established here under shall cease to exist at the expiration of two years after the date of enactment of this Act, or sooner if the President shall by proclamation or the Congress shall by joint resolution declare that the emergency recognized by section 1 has ended.

CODES OF FAIR COMPETITION

SEC. 3. (a) Upon the application to the President by one or more trade or industrial associations or groups, the President may approve a code or codes of fair competition for the trade or industry or subdivision thereof, represented by the applicant or applicants, if the President finds (1) that such associations or groups impose no inequitable restrictions on admission to membership therein and are truly representative of such trades or industries or subdivisions thereof, and (2) that such code or codes are not designed to promote monopolies or to eliminate or oppress small enterprises and will not operate to discriminate against them, and will tend to effectuate the policy of this title: Provided, That such code or codes shall not permit monopolies or monopolistic practices: Provided further, That where such code or codes affect the services and welfare of persons engaged in other steps of the economic process, nothing in this section shall deprive such persons of the right to be heard prior to approval by the President of such code or codes. The President may, as a condition of his approval of any such code, impose such conditions (including requirements for the making of reports and the keeping of accounts) for the protection of consumers, competitors, employees, and others, and in furtherance of the public interest, and may provide such exceptions to and exemptions from the provisions of such code, as the President in

his discretion deems necessary to effectuate the policy herein declared.

(b) After the President shall have approved any such code, the provisions of such code shall be the standards of fair competition for such trade or industry or subdivision thereof. Any violation of such standards in any transaction in or affecting interstate or foreign commerce shall be deemed an unfair method of competition in commerce within the meaning of the Federal Trade Commission Act, as amended; but nothing in this title shall be construed to impair the powers of the Federal Trade Commission under such Act, as amended. . . .

(d) Upon his own motion, or if complaint is made to the President that abuses inimical to the public interest and contrary to the policy herein declared are prevalent in any trade or industry or subdivision thereof, and if no code of fair competition therefore has theretofore been approved by the President, the President, after such public notice and hearing as he shall specify, may prescribe and approve a code of fair competition for such trade or industry or subdivision thereof, which shall have the same effect as a code of fair competition approved by the President under subsection (a) of this section. . . .

AGREEMENTS AND LICENSES

SEC. 4. (a) The President is authorized to enter into agreements with, and to approve voluntary agreements between and among, persons engaged in a trade or industry, labor organizations, and trade or industrial organizations, associations, or groups, relating to any trade or industry, if in his judgment such agreements will aid in effectuating the policy of this title with respect to transactions in or affecting interstate or foreign commerce, and will be consistent with the requirements of clause (2) of subsection (a) of section 3 for a code of fair competition.

(b) Whenever the President shall find that destructive wage or price cutting or other activities contrary to the policy of this title are being practiced in any trade or industry or any subdivision thereof, and, after such public notice and hearing as he shall specify, shall find it essential to license business enterprises in order to make effective a code of fair competition or an agreement under this title or otherwise to effectuate the policy of this title, and shall publicly so announce, no person shall, after a date fixed in such announcement, engage in or carry on any business, in or affecting interstate or foreign commerce, specified in such announcement, unless he shall have first obtained a license issued pursuant to such regulations as the President shall prescribe. The President may suspend or revoke any such license, after due notice and opportunity for hearing, for violations of the terms or conditions thereof. Any order of the President suspending or revoking any such license shall be final if in accordance with law. . . .

SEC. 5. While this title is in effect . . . and for sixty days thereafter, any code, agreement, or license approved, prescribed, or issued and in effect under this title, and any action complying with the provisions thereof taken during such period, shall be exempt from the provisions of the antitrust laws of the United States.

Nothing in this Act, and no regulation thereunder, shall prevent an individual from pursuing the vocation of manual labor and selling or trading the products thereof; nor shall anything in this Act, or regulation thereunder, prevent anyone from marketing or trading the produce of his farm.

LIMITATIONS UPON APPLICATION OF TITLE

SEC. 6. (a) No trade or industrial association or group shall be eligible to receive the benefit of the provisions of this title until it files with the President a statement containing such information relating to the activities of the association or group as the President shall by regulation prescribe. . . .

SEC. 7. (a) Every code of fair competition, agreement, and license approved, prescribed, or issued under this title shall contain the following conditions: (1) That employees shall have the right to organize and bargain collectively through representatives of their own choosing, and shall be free from the interference, restraint, or coercion of employers of labor, or their agents, in the designation of such representatives or in selforganization or in other concerted activities for the purpose of collective bargaining or other mutual aid or protection; (2) that no employee and no one seeking employment shall be required as a condition of employment to join any company union or to refrain from joining, organizing, or assisting a labor organization of his own choosing; and (3) that employers shall comply with the maximum hours of labor, minimum rates of pay, and other conditions of employment, approved or prescribed by the President.

(b) The President shall, so far as practicable, afford every opportunity to employers and employees in any trade or industry or subdivision thereof with respect to which the conditions referred to in clauses (1) and (2) of subsection (a) prevail, to establish by mutual agreement, the standards as to the maximum hours of labor, minimum rates of pay, and such other conditions of employment as may be necessary in such trade or industry or subdivision thereof to effectuate the policy of this title; and the standards established in such agreements, when approved by the President, shall have the same effect as a code of fair competition. . . .

(c) Where no such mutual agreement has been approved by the President he may investigate the labor practices, policies, wages, hours of labor, and conditions of employment in such trade or industry or subdivision thereof, and upon the basis of such investigations, and after such hearings as the President finds advisable, he is authorized to prescribe a limited code of fair competition fixing such maximum hours of labor, minimum rates of pay, and other conditions of employment in the trade or industry or subdivision thereof investigated as he finds to be necessary to effectuate the policy of this title, which shall have the same effect as a code of fair competition approved by the President under subsection (a) of section 3. The President may differentiate according to experience and skill of the employees affected and according to the locality of employment; but no attempt shall be made to introduce any classification according to the nature of the work involved which might tend to set a maximum as well as a minimum wage.

(d) As used in this title, the term "person" includes any individual, partnership, association, trust, or corporation. . . .

OIL REGULATION

SEC. 9. (a) The President is further authorized to initiate before the Interstate Commerce Commission proceedings necessary to prescribe regulations to control the operations of oil pipe lines and to fix reasonable compensatory rates for the transportation of petroleum and its products by pipe lines, and the Interstate Commerce Commission shall grant preference to the hearings and determination of such cases.

(b) The President is authorized to institute proceedings to divorce from any holding company any pipe-line company controlled by such holding company which pipe-line company by unfair practices or by exorbitant rates in the transportation of petroleum or its products tends to create a monopoly.

(c) The President is authorized to prohibit the transportation in interstate and foreign commerce of petroleum and the products thereof produced or withdrawn from storage in excess of the amount permitted to be produced or withdrawn from storage by any State law or valid regulation or order prescribed thereunder, by any board, commission, officer, or other duly authorized agency of a State. . . .

TITLE II—PUBLIC WORKS AND CONSTRUCTION PROJECTS/FEDERAL EMERGENCY ADMINISTRATION OF PUBLIC WORKS

SEC. 201. (a) To effectuate the purposes of this title, the President is hereby authorized to create a Federal Emergency Administration of Public Works, all the powers of which shall be exercised by a Federal Emergency Administrator of Public Works, . . . and to establish such agencies, to accept and utilize such voluntary and uncompensated services, to appoint, without regard to the civil service laws, such officers and employees, and to utilize such Federal officers and employees, and, with the consent of the State, such State and local officers and employees as he may find necessary, to prescribe their authorities, duties, responsibilities, and tenure, and, without regard to the Classification Act of 1923, as amended, to fix the compensation of any officers and employees so appointed. The President may delegate any of his functions and powers under this title to such officers, agents, and employees as he may designate or appoint.

(b) The Administrator may, without regard to the civil service laws or the Classification Act of 1923, as amended, appoint and fix the compensation of such experts and such other officers and employees as are necessary to carry out the provisions of this title; and may make such expenditures (including expenditures for personal services and rent at the seat of government and elsewhere, for law books and books of reference, and for paper printing and binding) as are necessary to carry out the provisions of this title. . . .

(d) After the expiration of two years after the date of the enactment of this Act, or sooner if the President shall by proclamation or the Congress shall by joint resolution declare that the emergency recognized by section 1 has ended, the President shall not make any further loans or grants or enter upon any new construction under this title, and any agencies established hereunder shall cease to exist and any of their remaining functions shall be transferred to such departments of the Government as the President shall designate. . . .

SEC. 202. The Administrator, under the direction of the President, shall prepare a comprehensive program of public works, which shall include among other things the following: (a) Construction, repair, and improvement of public highways and park ways, public buildings, and any publicly owned instrumentalities and facilities; (b) conservation and development of natural resources, including control, utilization, and purification of waters, prevention of soil or coastal erosion, development of water power, transmission of electrical energy, and construction of river and harbor improvements and flood control and also the construction of any river or drainage improvement required to perform or satisfy any obligation incurred by the United States through a treaty with a foreign Government heretofore ratified and to restore or develop for the use of any State or its citizens water taken from or denied to them by performance on the part of the United States of treaty obligations heretofore assumed: Provided, That no river or harbor improvements shall be carried out unless they shall have heretofore or hereafter been adopted by the Congress or are recommended by the Chief of Engineers of the United States Army; (c) any projects of the character heretofore constructed or carried on either directly by public authority or with public aid to serve the interests of the general public; (d) construction, reconstruction, alteration, or repair under public regulation or control of low-cost housing and slumclearance projects; (e) any project (other than those included in the foregoing classes) of any character heretofore eligible for loans under subsection (a) of section 201 of the Emergency Relief and Construction Act of 1932, as amended, and paragraph (3) of such subsection (a) shall for such purposes be held to include loans for the construction or completion of hospitals the operation of which is partly financed from public funds, and of reservoirs and pumping plants and for the construction of dry docks, and if in the opinion of the President it seems desirable, the construction of naval vessels within the terms and/or limits established by the London Naval Treaty of

1930 and of aircraft required therefore and construction of heavier-than-air aircraft and technical construction for the Army Air Corps and such Army housing projects as the President may approve, and provision of original equipment for the mechanization or motorization of such Army tactical units as he may designate: Provided, however, That in the event of an international agreement for the further limitation of armament, to which the United States is signatory, the President is hereby authorized and empowered to suspend, in whole or in part, any such naval or military construction or mechanization and motorization of Army units. . . .

SEC. 203. (a) With a view to increasing employment quickly (while reasonably securing any loans made by the United States) the President is authorized and empowered, through the Administrator or through such other agencies as he may designate or create, (1) to construct, finance, or aid in the construction or financing of any public-works project included in the program prepared pursuant to section 202; (2) upon such terms as the President shall prescribe, to make grants to States, municipalities, or other public bodies for the construction, repair, or improvement of any such project, but no such grant shall be in excess of 30 per centum of the cost of the labor and materials employed upon such project; (3) to acquire by purchase, or by exercise of the power of eminent domain, any real or personal property in connection with the construction of any such project, and to sell any security acquired or any property so constructed or acquired or to lease any such property with or without the privilege of purchase: Provided, That all moneys received from any such sale or lease or the repayment of any loan shall be used to retire obligations issued pursuant to section 209 of this Act, in addition to any other moneys required to be used for such purpose. (4) to aid in the financing of such railroad maintenance and equipment as may be approved by the Interstate Commerce Commission as desirable for the improvement of transportation facilities; . . . Provided, That in deciding to extend any aid or grant hereunder to any State, county, or municipality the President may consider whether action is in process or in good faith assured therein reasonably designed to bring the ordinary current expenditures thereof within the prudently estimated revenues thereof. . . . (d) The President, in his discretion, and under such terms as he may prescribe, may extend any of the benefits of this title to any State, county, or municipality notwithstanding any constitutional or legal restriction or limitation on the right or

power of such State, county, or municipality to borrow money or incur indebtedness.

SEC. 204. (a) For the purpose of providing for emergency construction of public highways and related projects, the President is authorized to make grants to the highway departments of the several States in an amount not less than $400,000,000, to be expended by such departments in accordance with the provisions of the Federal Highway Act, approved November 9, 1921, as amended and supplemented.

SEC. 205. (a) Not less than $50,000,000 of the amount made available by this Act shall be allotted for (A) national forest highways, (B) national forest roads, trails, bridges, and related projects, (C) national park roads and trails in national parks owned or authorized, (D) roads on Indian reservations, and (E) roads through public lands, to be expended in the same manner as provided in paragraph (2) of section 301 of the Emergency Relief and Construction Act of 1932, in the case of appropriations allocated for such purposes, respectively, in such section 301, to remain available until expended. . . .

SEC. 206. All contracts let for construction projects and all loans and grants pursuant to this title shall contain such provisions as are necessary to insure (1) that no convict labor shall be employed on any such project; (2) that (except in executive, administrative, and supervisory positions), so far as practicable and feasible, no individual directly employed on any such project shall be permitted to work more than thirty hours in any one week; (3) that all employees shall be paid just and reasonable wages which shall be compensation sufficient to provide, for the hours of labor as limited, a standard of living in decency and comfort, (4) that in the employment of labor in connection with any such project, preference shall be given, where they are qualified, to ex-service men with dependents, and then in the following order: (A) To citizens of the United States and aliens who have declared their intention of becoming citizens, who are bona fide residents of the political subdivision and/or county in which the work is to be performed, and (B) to citizens of the United States and aliens who have declared their intention of becoming citizens, who are bona fide residents of the State, Territory, or district in which the work is to be performed: Provided, That these preferences shall apply only where such labor is available and qualified to perform the work to which the employment relates; and (5) that the maximum of human labor shall be used in lieu of machinery wherever practicable and consistent with sound economy and public advantage. . . .

SUBSISTENCE HOMESTEADS

SEC. 208. To provide for aiding the redistribution of the overbalance of population in industrial centers $25,000,000 is hereby made available to the President,

to be used by him through such agencies as he may establish and under such regulations as he may make, for making loans for and otherwise aiding in the purchase of subsistence homesteads. The moneys collected as repayment of said loans shall constitute a revolving fund to be administered as directed by the President for the purposes of this section.

From: *U.S. Statutes at Large.* 1933. Vol. 48, p. 195.

NATIONAL LABOR RELATIONS ACT, JULY 5, 1935

The National Labor Relations Act—or, as it was popularly known, the Wagner Act, after its chief sponsor, Democratic senator Robert Wagner of New York—represented a revolution in labor legislation. For the first time, the federal government guaranteed workers the right to organize independent unions, and it established the National Labor Relations Board to arbitrate disputes between employers and employees. The act unleashed a wave of union organizing, particularly in mass industries like steel and automobiles.

An Act to diminish the causes of labor disputes burdening or obstructing interstate and foreign commerce, to create a National Labor Relations Board, and for other purposes.

Be it enacted,

FINDINGS AND POLICY

SECTION 1. The denial by employers of the right of employees to organize and the refusal by employers to accept the procedure of collective bargaining lead to strikes and other forms of industrial strife or unrest, which have the intent or the necessary effect of burdening or obstructing commerce by (a) impairing the efficiency, safety, or operation of the instrumentalities of commerce; (b) occurring in the current of commerce, (c) materially affecting, restraining, or controlling the flow of raw materials or manufactured or processed goods from or into the channels of commerce, or the prices of such materials or goods in commerce; or (d) causing diminution of employment and wages in such volume as substantially to impair or disrupt the market for goods flowing from or into the channels of commerce.

The inequality of bargaining power between employees who do not possess full freedom of association or actual liberty of contract, and employers who are organized in the corporate or other forms of ownership association substantially burdens and affects the flow of commerce, and tends to aggravate recurrent business depressions, by depressing wage rates and the purchasing power of wage earners in industry and by preventing the stabilization of competitive wage rates and working conditions within and between industries.

Experience has proved that protection by law of the right of employees to organize and bargain collectively safeguards commerce from injury, impairment, or interruption, and promotes the flow of commerce by removing certain recognized sources of industrial strife and unrest, by encouraging practices fundamental to the friendly adjustment of industrial disputes arising out of differences as to wages, hours, or other working conditions, and by restoring equality of bargaining power between employers and employees.

It is hereby declared to be the policy of the United States to eliminate the causes of certain substantial obstructions to the free flow of commerce and to mitigate and eliminate these obstructions when they have occurred by encouraging the practice and procedure of collective bargaining and by protecting the exercise by workers of full freedom of association, self-organization, and designation of representatives of their own choosing, for the purpose of negotiating the terms and conditions of their employment or other mutual aid or protection.

SEC. 2. When used in this Act—

(1) The term "person" includes one or more individuals, partnerships, associations, corporations, legal representatives, trustees, trustees in bankruptcy, or receivers.

(2) The term "employer" includes any person acting in the interest of an employer, directly or indirectly but shall not include the United States or any State or political subdivision thereof or any person subject to the Railway Labor Act, as amended from time to time or any labor organization (other than when acting as an employer), or anyone acting in the capacity of officer or agent of such labor organization.

(3) The term "employee" shall include any employee, and shall not be limited to the employees of a particular employer, unless the Act explicitly states otherwise, and shall include any individual whose work has ceased as a consequence of or in connection with, any current labor dispute or because of any unfair labor practice, and who has not obtained any other regular and substantially equivalent employment, but shall not include any individual employed as an agricultural laborer, or in the domestic service of any family or person at his home, or any individual employed by his parent or spouse. . . .

(5) The term "labor organization" means any organization of any kind, or any agency or employee representation committee or plan, in which employees participate and which exists for the purpose, in whole or in part, of dealing with employers concerning grievances, labor disputes, wages, rates of pay, hours of employment, or conditions of work.

(6) The term "commerce" means trade, traffic commerce, transportation, or communication among the several States. . . .

(7) The term "affecting commerce" means in commerce or burdening or obstructing commerce or the free flow of commerce, or having led or tending to lead to a labor dispute burdening or obstructing commerce or the free flow of commerce. . . .

(9) The term "labor dispute" includes any controversy concerning terms, tenure or conditions of employment, or concerning the association or representation of persons in negotiating, fixing, maintaining, changing, or seeking to arrange terms or conditions of employment, regardless of whether the disputants stand in the proximate relation of employer and employee. . . .

NATIONAL LABOR RELATIONS BOARD

SEC. 3. (a) There is hereby created a board, to be known as the "National Labor Relations Board," which shall be composed of three members who shall be appointed by the President, by and with the advice and consent of the Senate. One of the original members shall be appointed for a term of one year, one for a term of three years, and one for a term of five years, but their successors shall be appointed for terms of five years each, except that any individual chosen to fill a vacancy shall be appointed only for the unexpired term of the member whom he shall succeed. The President shall designate one member to serve as chairman of the Board. Any member of the Board may be removed by the President, upon notice and hearing, for neglect of duty or malfeasance in office, but for no other cause. . . .

SEC. 6. (a) The Board shall have authority from time to time to make, amend and rescind such rules and regulations as may be necessary to carry out the provisions of this Act. Such rules and regulations shall be effective upon publication in the manner, which the Board shall prescribe.

RIGHTS OF EMPLOYEES

SEC. 7. Employees shall have the right of self-organization, to form, join, or assist labor organizations, to bargain collectively through representatives of their own choosing, and to engage in concerted activities, for the purpose of collective bargaining or other mutual aid or protection.

SEC. 8. It shall be an unfair labor practice for an employer—

(1) To interfere with, restrain, or coerce employees in the exercise of the rights guaranteed in section 7.

(2) To dominate or interfere with the formation or administration of any labor organization or contribute financial or other support to it: Provided, That subject to rules and regulations made and published by the Board pursuant to section 6 (a), an employer shall not be prohibited from permitting employees to confer with him during working hours without loss of time or pay.

(3) By discrimination in regard to hire or tenure of employment or any term or condition of employment to encourage or discourage membership in any labor organization: Provided, That nothing in this Act, or in the National Industrial Recovery Act (U. S. C., Supp. VII, title 15, secs. 701-712), as amended from time to time, or in any code or agreement approved or prescribed thereunder or in any other statute of the United States, shall preclude an employer from making an agreement with a labor organization (not established, maintained, or assisted by any action defined in this Act as an unfair labor practice) to require as a condition of employment membership therein, if such labor organization is the representative of the employ-

ees as provided in section 9 (a), in the appropriate collective bargaining unit covered by such agreement when made.

(4) To discharge or otherwise discriminate against an employee because he has filed charges or given testimony under this Act.

(5) To refuse to bargain collectively with the representatives of his employees, subject to the provisions of Section 9 (a).

REPRESENTATIVES AND ELECTIONS

SEC. 9. (a) Representatives designated or selected for the purposes of collective bargaining by the majority of the employees in a unit appropriate for such purposes, shall be the exclusive representatives of all the employees in such unit for the purposes of collective bargaining in respect to rates of pay, wages, hours of employment, or other conditions of employment: Provided, That any individual employee or a group of employees shall have the right at any time to present grievances to their employer.

(b) The Board shall decide in each case whether, in order to insure to employees the full benefit of their right to self-organization and to collective bargaining, and otherwise to effectuate the policies of this Act, the unit appropriate for the purposes of collective bargaining shall be the employer unit, craft unit, plant unit, or subdivision thereof.

(c) Whenever a question affecting commerce arises concerning the representation of employees, the Board may investigate such controversy and certify to the parties, in writing, the name or names of the representatives that have been designated or selected. In any such investigation, the Board shall provide for an appropriate hearing upon due notice, either in conjunction with a proceeding under section 10 or otherwise, and may take a secret ballot of employees, or utilize any other suitable method to ascertain such representatives.

(d) Whenever an order of the Board made pursuant to section 10 (c) is based in whole or in part upon facts certified following an investigation pursuant to subsection (c) of this section, and there is a petition for the enforcement or review of such order, such certification and the record of such investigation shall be included in the transcript of the entire record required to be filed under subsections 10 (e) or 10 (f), and thereupon the decree of the court enforcing, modifying, or setting aside in whole or in part the order of the Board shall

be made and entered upon the pleadings, testimony, and proceedings set forth in such transcript.

PREVENTION OF UNFAIR LABOR PRACTICES

SEC. 10. (a) The Board is empowered, as hereinafter provided, to prevent any person from engaging in any unfair labor practice (listed in section 8) affecting commerce. This power shall be exclusive, and shall not be affected by any other means of adjustment or prevention that has been or may be established by agreement, code, law, or otherwise.

(b) Whenever it is charged that any person has engaged in or is engaging in any such unfair labor practice, the Board, or any agent or agency designated by the Board for such purposes, shall have power to issue and cause to be served upon such person a complaint stating the charges in that respect, and containing a notice of hearing before the Board or a member thereof, or before a designated agent or agency, at a place therein fixed, not less than five days after the serving of said complaint. Any such complaint may be amended by the member, agent, or agency conducting the hearing or the Board in its discretion at any time prior to the issuance of an order based thereon. The person so complained of shall have the right to file an answer to the original or amended complaint and to appear in person or otherwise and give testimony at the place and time fixed in the complaint. In the discretion of the member, agent or agency conducting the hearing or the Board, any other person may be allowed to intervene in the said proceeding and to present testimony. In any such proceeding the rules of evidence prevailing in courts of law or equity shall not be controlling.

(c) The testimony taken by such member, agent or agency or the Board shall be reduced to writing and filed with the Board. Thereafter, in its discretion, the Board upon notice may take further testimony or hear argument. If upon all the testimony taken the Board shall be of the opinion that any person named in the complaint has engaged in or is engaging in any such unfair labor practice, then the Board shall state its findings of fact and shall issue and cause to be served on such person an order requiring such person to cease and desist from such unfair labor practice, and to take such affirmative action, including reinstatement of employees with or without back pay, as will effectuate the policies of this Act. Such order may further require such person to make reports from time to time showing the extent to which it [sic] has complied with the order. If upon all the testimony taken the Board shall be of the opinion that no person named in the complaint has engaged in or is engaging in any such unfair labor practice, then the Board shall state its findings of fact and shall issue an order dismissing the said complaint. . . .

(e) The Board shall have power to petition any circuit court of appeals of the United States, or if all the circuit courts of appeals to which application may be made are in vacation, any district court of the United States, within any circuit or district, respectively, wherein the unfair labor practice in question occurred or wherein such person resides or transacts business, for the enforcement of such order and for appropriate temporary relief or restraining order, and shall certify and file in the court a transcript of the entire record in the proceeding, including the pleadings and testimony upon which such order was entered and the findings and order of the Board. Upon such filing, the court shall cause notice thereof to be served upon such person, and thereupon shall have jurisdiction of the proceeding and of the question determined therein, and shall have power to grant such temporary relief or restraining order as it deems just and proper, and to make and enter upon the pleadings, testimony, and proceedings set forth in such transcript a decree enforcing, modifying, and enforcing as so modified, or setting aside in whole or in part the order of the Board. No objection that has not been urged before the Board, its member, agent or agency, shall be considered by the court, unless the failure or neglect to urge such objection shall be excused because of extraordinary circumstances. The findings of the Board as to the facts, if supported by evidence, shall be conclusive. . . . The Board may modify its findings as to the facts, or make new findings, by reason of additional evidence so taken and filed and it shall file such modified or new findings which, if supported by evidence, shall be conclusive, and shall file its recommendations, if any, for the modification or setting aside of its original order. The jurisdiction of the court shall be exclusive and its judgment and decree shall be final, except that the same shall be subject to review by the appropriate circuit court of appeals if application was made to the district court as hereinabove provided, and by the Supreme Court of the United States upon writ of certiorari or certification.

(f) Any person aggrieved by a final order of the Board granting or denying in whole or in part the relief sought may obtain a review of such order in any circuit court of appeals of the United States in the circuit wherein the unfair labor practice in question was alleged to have been engaged in or wherein such person resides or transacts business. . . .

(g) The commencement of proceedings under subsection (e) or (f) of this section shall not, unless specifically ordered by the court, operate as a stay of the Board's order. . . .

(i) Petitions filed under this Act shall be heard expeditiously, and if possible within ten days after they have been docketed.

INVESTIGATORY POWERS

SEC. 11. For the purpose of all hearings and investigations, . . .

(1) The Board, or its duly authorized agents or agencies, shall at all reasonable times have access to, for the purpose of examination, and the right to copy any evidence of any person being investigated or proceeded against that relates to any matter under investigation or in question. Any member of the Board shall have power to issue subpoenas requiring the attendance and testimony of witnesses and the production of any evidence that relates to any matter under investigation or in question, before the Board, its member, agent, or agency conducting the hearing or investigation. . . .

SEC. 12. Any person who shall willfully resist, prevent, impede, or interfere with any member of the Board or any of its agents or agencies in the performance of duties pursuant to this Act shall be punished by a fine of not more than $5,000 or by imprisonment for not more than one year, or both.

LIMITATIONS

SEC. 13. Nothing in this Act shall be construed so as to interfere with or impede or diminish in any way the right to strike. . . .

SEC. 15. If any provision of this Act, or the application of such provision to any person or circumstance, shall be held invalid, the remainder of this Act, or the application of such provision to persons or circumstances other than those as to which it is held invalid, shall not be affected thereby. . . .

From: *U.S. Statutes at Large.* 1935. Vol. 49 p. 449.

SOCIAL SECURITY ACTS, AUGUST 14, 1935

Arguably the most popular piece of legislation of the New Deal, the Social Security Act created America's first federal old-age pension fund. Virtually all nonagricultural employees were included in the program, which taxed both workers and employers in a continually revolving fund. While the immediate impetus for the act was the desperate circumstances of senior citizens in the Great Depression, there were also political considerations. With an old-age program of his own, radical reformer Francis Townsend of California—in an alliance with New Deal opponents Senator Huey P. Long of Louisiana and popular radio preacher Father Charles Coughlin—threatened to steal popular support from Franklin D. Roosevelt and the New Deal.

An Act to provide for the general welfare by establishing a system of Federal old-age benefits, and by enabling the several States to make more adequate provision for aged persons, blind persons, dependent and crippled children, maternal and child welfare, public health, and the administration of their unemployment compensation laws; to establish a Social Security Board; to raise revenue; and for other purposes. Be it enacted by the Senate and House of Representatives of the United States of America in Congress assembled,

TITLE I—GRANTS TO STATES FOR OLD-AGE ASSISTANCE APPROPRIATION

SECTION 1. For the purpose of enabling each State to furnish financial assistance, as far as practicable under the conditions in such State, to aged needy individuals, there is hereby authorized to be appropriated for the fiscal year ending June 30, 1936, the sum of $49,750,000, and there is hereby authorized to be appropriated for each fiscal year thereafter a sum sufficient to carry out the purposes of this title. The sums made available under this section shall be used for making payments to States which have submitted, and had approved by the Social Security Board established by Title VII, State plans for old-age assistance.

STATE OLD-AGE ASSISTANCE PLANS

SEC. 2. (a) A State plan for old-age assistance must (1) provide that it shall be in effect in all political subdivisions of the State, and, if administered by them, be mandatory upon them; (2) provide for financial participation by the State; (3) either provide for the establishment or designation of a single State agency to administer the plan, or provide for the establishment or designation of a single State agency to supervise the administration of the plan; (4) provide for granting to any individual, whose claim for old-age assistance is denied, an opportunity for a fair hearing before such State agency; (5) provide such methods of administration (other than those relating to selection, tenure of office, and compensation of personnel) as are found by the Board to be necessary for the efficient operation of the plan; (6) provide that the State agency will make such reports, in such form and containing such information, as the Board may from time to time require, and comply with such provisions as the Board may from time to time find necessary to assure the correctness and verification of such reports; and (7) provide that, if the State or any of its political subdivisions collects from the estate of any recipient of old-age assistance any amount with respect to old-age assistance furnished him under the plan, one-half of the net amount so collected shall be promptly paid to the United States. Any payment so made shall be deposited in the Treasury to the credit of the appropriation for the purposes of this title.

(b) The Board shall approve any plan which fulfills the conditions specified in subsection (a), except that it shall not approve any plan which imposes, as a condition of eligibility for old-age assistance under the plan—

(1) An age requirement of more than sixty-five years, except that the plan may impose, effective until January 1, 1940, an age requirement of as much as seventy years; or

(2) Any residence requirement which excludes any resident of the State who has resided therein five years during the nine years immediately preceding the application for old-age assistance and has resided therein

continuously for one year immediately preceding the application; or

(3) Any citizenship requirement which excludes any citizen of the United States.

PAYMENT TO STATES

SEC. 3. (a) From the sums appropriated therefore the Secretary of the Treasury shall pay to each State which has an approved plan for old-age assistance, for each quarter, beginning with the quarter commencing July 1, 1935, (1) an amount, which shall be used exclusively as old-age assistance, equal to one-half of the total of the sums expended during such quarter as old-age assistance under the State plan with respect to each individual who at the time of such expenditure is sixty-five years of age or older and is not an inmate of a public institution, not counting so much of such expenditure with respect to any individual for any month as exceeds $30, and (2) 5 per centum of such amount, which shall be used for paying the costs of administering the State plan or for old-age assistance, or both, and for no other purpose: Provided, That the State plan, in order to be approved by the Board, need not provide for financial participation before July 1, 1937 by the State, in the case of any State which the Board, upon application by the State and after reasonable notice and opportunity for hearing to the State, finds is prevented by its constitution from providing such financial participation.

(b) The method of computing and paying such amounts shall be as follows:

(1) The Board shall, prior to the beginning of each quarter, estimate the amount to be paid to the State for such quarter under the provisions of clause (1) of subsection (a), such estimate to be based on (A) a report filed by the State containing its estimate of the total sum to be expended in such quarter in accordance with the provisions of such clause, and stating the amount appropriated or made available by the State and its political subdivisions for such expenditures in such quarter, and if such amount is less than one-half of the total sum of such estimated expenditures, the source or sources from which the difference is expected to be derived, (B) records showing the number of aged individuals in the State, and (C) such other investigation as the Board may find necessary....

TITLE II—FEDERAL OLD-AGE BENEFITS/ OLD-AGE RESERVE ACCOUNT

SECTION 201. (a) There is hereby created an account in the Treasury of the United States to be known as the "Old-Age Reserve Account."...

OLD-AGE BENEFIT PAYMENTS

SEC. 202. (a) Every qualified individual shall be entitled to receive, with respect to the period beginning on the date he attains the age of sixty-five, or on January 1, 1942, whichever is the later, and ending on the date of his death, an old-age benefit (payable as nearly as practicable in equal monthly installments) as follows:

(1) If the total wages determined by the Board to have been paid to him, with respect to employment after December 31, 1936, and before he attained the age of sixty-five, were not more than $3,000, the old-age benefit shall be at a monthly rate of one-half of 1 per centum of such total wages;

(2) If such total wages were more than $3,000, the old-age benefit shall be at a monthly rate equal to the sum of the following:

(A) One-half of 1 per centum of $3,000; plus

(B) One-twelfth of 1 per centum of the amount by which such total wages exceeded $3,000 and did not exceed $45,000; plus

(C) One-twenty-fourth of 1 per centum of the amount by which such total wages exceeded $45,000.

(b) In no case shall the monthly rate computed under subsection (a) exceed $85....

PAYMENTS UPON DEATH

SEC. 203. (a) If any individual dies before attaining the age of sixty-five, there shall be paid to his estate an amount equal to 3 per centum of the total wages determined by the Board to have been paid to him, with respect to employment after December 31, 1936....

PAYMENTS TO AGED INDIVIDUALS NOT QUALIFIED FOR BENEFITS

SEC. 204. (a) There shall be paid in a lump sum to any individual who, upon attaining the age of sixty-five, is not a qualified individual, an amount equal to 3 one-half per centum of the total wages determined by the Board to have been paid to him, with respect to employment after December 31, 1936, and before he attained the age of sixty-five.

(b) After any individual becomes entitled to any payment under subsection (a), no other payment shall be made under this title in any manner measured by wages paid to him, except that any part of any payment under subsection (a) which is not paid to him before his death shall be paid to his estate. . . .

SEC. 210. . . .

(b) The term "employment" means any service, of whatever nature, performed within the United States by an employee for his employer, except—

(1) Agricultural labor;

(2) Domestic service in a private home;

(3) Casual labor not in the course of the employer's trade or business;

(4) Service performed as an officer or member of the crew of a vessel documented under the laws of the United States or of any foreign country;

(5) Service performed in the employ of the United States Government or of an instrumentality of the United States;

(6) Service performed in the employ of a State, a political subdivision thereof, or an instrumentality of one or more States or political subdivisions;

(7) Service performed in the employ of a corporation, community chest, fund, or foundation, organized and operated exclusively for religious, charitable, scientific, literary, or educational purposes, or for the prevention of cruelty to children or animals, no part of the net earnings of which inures to the benefit of any private shareholder or individual. . . .

TITLE III—GRANTS TO STATES FOR UNEMPLOYMENT COMPENSATION

ADMINISTRATION APPROPRIATION

SECTION 301. For the purpose of assisting the States in the administration of their unemployment compensation laws there is hereby authorized to be appropriated, for the fiscal year ending June 30, 1936, the sum of $4,000,000, and for each fiscal year thereafter the sum of $49,000,000, to be used as hereinafter provided.

PAYMENTS TO STATES

SEC. 302. (a) The Board shall from time to time certify to the Secretary of the Treasury for payment to each State which has an unemployment compensation law approved by the Board under Title IX, such amounts as the Board determines to be necessary for the proper administration of such law during the fiscal year in which such payment is to be made. The Board's determination shall be based on (1) the population of the State; (2) an estimate of the number of persons covered by the State law and of the cost of proper administration of such law, and (3) such other factors as the Board finds relevant. The Board shall not certify for payment under this section in any fiscal year a total amount in excess of the amount appropriated therefore for such fiscal year. . . .

PROVISIONS OF STATE LAWS

SEC. 303. (a) The Board shall make no certification for payment to any State unless it finds that the law of such State, approved by the Board under Title IX, includes provisions for—

(1) Such methods of administration (other than those relating to selection, tenure of office, and compensation of personnel) as are found by the Board to be reasonably calculated to insure full payment of unemployment compensation when due; and

(2) Payment of unemployment compensation solely through public employment offices in the State or such other agencies as the Board may approve; and

(3) Opportunity for a fair hearing, before an impartial tribunal, for all individuals whose claims for unemployment compensation are denied; and

(4) The payment of all money received in the unemployment fund of such State, immediately upon such receipt, to the Secretary of the Treasury to the credit of the Unemployment Trust Fund established by section 904; and

(5) Expenditure of all money requisitioned by the State agency from the Unemployment Trust Fund, in the payment of unemployment compensation, exclusive of expenses of administration; and

(6) The making of such reports, in such form and containing such information, as the Board may from time to time require, and compliance with such provisions as the Board may from time to time find nec-

essary to assure the correctness and verification of such reports; and

(7) Making available upon request to any agency of the United States charged with the administration of public works or assistance through public employment, the name, address, ordinary occupation and employment status of each recipient of unemployment compensation, and a statement of such recipient's rights to further compensation under such law.

(b) Whenever the Board, after reasonable notice and opportunity for hearing to the State agency charged with the administration of the State law, finds that in the administration of the law there is—

(1) a denial, in a substantial number of cases, of unemployment compensation to individuals entitled thereto under such law; or

(2) a failure to comply substantially with any provision specified in subsection (a);

the Board shall notify such State agency that further payments will not be made to the State until the Board is satisfied that there is no longer any such denial or failure to comply. Until it is so satisfied it shall make no further certification to the Secretary of the Treasury with respect to such State. . . .

TITLE IV—GRANTS TO STATES FOR AID TO DEPENDENT CHILDREN

APPROPRIATION

SECTION 401. For the purpose of enabling each State to furnish financial assistance, as far as practicable under the conditions in such State, to needy dependent children, there is hereby authorized to be appropriated for the fiscal year ending June 30, 1936, the sum of $24,750,000, and there is hereby authorized to be appropriated for each fiscal year thereafter a sum sufficient to carry out the purposes of this title. The sums made available under this section shall be used for making payments to States which have submitted, and had approved by the Board, State plans for aid to dependent children. . . .

PAYMENT TO STATES

SEC. 403. (a) From the sums appropriated therefore, the Secretary of the Treasury shall pay to each State which has an approved plan for aid to dependent chil-

dren, for each quarter, beginning with the quarter commencing July 1, 1935, an amount, which shall be used exclusively for carrying out the State plan, equal to one-third of the total of the sums expended during such quarter under such plan, not counting so much of such expenditure with respect to any dependent child for any month as exceeds $18, or if there is more than one dependent child in the same home, as exceeds $18 for any month with respect to one such dependent child and $12 for such month with respect to each of the other dependent children. . . .

DEFINITIONS

SEC. 406. When used in this title—

(a) The term "dependent child" means a child under the age of sixteen who has been deprived of parental support or care by reason of the death, continued absence from the home, or physical or mental incapacity of a parent, and who is living with his father, mother, grandfather, grandmother, brother, sister, stepfather, stepmother, stepbrother, stepsister, uncle, or aunt, in a place of residence maintained by one or more of such relatives as his or their own home. . . .

TITLE V—GRANTS TO STATES FOR MATERNAL AND CHILD WELFARE

PART 1—MATERNAL AND CHILD HEALTH SERVICES APPROPRIATION

SECTION 501. For the purpose of enabling each State to extend and improve, as far as practicable under the conditions in such State, services for promoting the health of mothers and children, especially in rural areas and in areas suffering from severe economic distress, there is hereby authorized to be appropriated for each fiscal year, beginning with the fiscal year ending June 30, 1936, the sum of $3,800,000. The sums made available under this section shall be used for making payments to States which have submitted, and had approved by the Chief of the Children's Bureau, State plans for such services.

ALLOTMENTS TO STATES

SEC. 502. (a) Out of the sums appropriated pursuant to section 501 for each fiscal year the Secretary of Labor shall allot to each State $20,000, and such part of $1,800,000 as he finds that the number of live births in such State bore to the total number of live births in the United States, in the latest calendar year for which the Bureau of the Census has available statistics.

(b) Out of the sums appropriated pursuant to section 501 for each fiscal year the Secretary of Labor shall allot to the States $980,000 (in addition to the allotments made under subsection (a)), according to the financial need for each State for assistance in carrying out its State plan, as determined by him after taking into consideration the number of live births in such State. . . .

APPROVAL OF STATE PLANS

SEC. 503. (a) A State plan for maternal and child-health services must (1) provide for financial participation by the State; (2) provide for the administration of the plan by the State health agency or the supervision of the administration of the plan by the State health agency; (3) provide such methods of administration (other than those relating to selection, tenure of office, and compensation of personnel) as are necessary for the efficient operation of the plan; (4) provide that the State health agency will make such reports, in such form and containing such information, as the Secretary of Labor may from time to time require, and comply with such provisions as he may from time to time find necessary to assure the correctness and verification of such reports; (5) provide for the extension and improvement of local maternal and child-health services administered by local child-health units; (6) provide for cooperation with medical, nursing, and welfare groups and organizations; and (7) provide for the development of demonstration services in needy areas and among groups in special need. . . .

PART 2—SERVICES FOR CRIPPLED CHILDREN APPROPRIATION

SEC. 511. For the purpose of enabling each State to extend and improve (especially in rural areas and in areas suffering from severe economic distress), as far as practicable under the conditions in such State, services for locating crippled children, and for providing medical, surgical, corrective, and other services and care, and facilities for diagnosis, hospitalization, and aftercare, for children who are crippled or who are suf-fering from conditions which lead to crippling, there is hereby authorized to be appropriated for each fiscal year, beginning with the fiscal year ending June 30, 1936, the sum of $2,850,000. The sums made available under this section shall be used for making payments to States which have submitted, and had approved by the Chief of the Children's Bureau, State plans for such services.

ALLOTMENTS TO STATES

SEC. 512. (a) Out of the sums appropriated pursuant to section 511 for each fiscal year the Secretary of Labor shall allot to each State $20,000, and the remainder to the States according to the need of each State as determined by him after taking into consideration the number of crippled children in such State in need of the services referred to in section 511 and the cost of furnishing such services to them.

PART 3—CHILD WELFARE SERVICES

SEC. 521 (a) For the purpose of enabling the United States, through the Children's Bureau, to cooperate with State public-welfare agencies in establishing, extending, and strengthening, especially in predominantly rural areas, public-welfare services (hereinafter in this section referred to as "child-welfare services") for the protection and care of homeless, dependent, and neglected children, and children in danger of becoming delinquent, there is hereby authorized to be appropriated for each fiscal year, beginning with the fiscal year ending June 30, 1936, the sum of $1,500,000. Such amount shall be allotted by the Secretary of Labor for use by cooperating State public-welfare agencies on the basis of plans developed jointly by the State agency and the Children's Bureau, to each State, $10,000, and the remainder to each State on the basis of such plans, not to exceed such part of the remainder as the rural population of such State bears to the total rural population of the United States. The amount so allotted shall be expended for payment of part of the cost of district county or other local child-welfare services in areas predominantly rural, and for developing State services for the encouragement and assistance of adequate methods of community child-welfare organization in areas predominantly rural and other areas of special need. . . .

PART 4—VOCATIONAL REHABILITATION

SEC. 531. (a) In order to enable the United States to cooperate with the States and Hawaii in extending and strengthening their programs of vocational rehabilitation of the physically disabled, and to continue to carry out the provisions and purposes of the Act entitled "An Act to provide for the promotion of vocational rehabilitation of persons disabled in industry or otherwise and their return to civil employment," approved June 2, 1920, . . . there is hereby authorized to be appropriated for the fiscal years ending June 30, 1936, and June 30, 1937, the sum of $841,000 for each such fiscal year in addition to the amount of the existing authorization, and for each fiscal year thereafter the sum of $1,938,000.

TITLE VI—PUBLIC HEALTH WORK APPROPRIATION

SECTION 601. For the purpose of assisting States, counties, health districts, and other political subdivisions of the States in establishing and maintaining adequate public health services, including the training of personnel for State and local health work, there is hereby authorized to be appropriated for each fiscal year, beginning with the fiscal year ending June 30, 1936, the sum of $8,000,000 to be used as hereinafter provided.

STATE AND LOCAL PUBLIC HEALTH SERVICES

SEC. 602. (a) The Surgeon General of the Public Health Service, with the approval of the Secretary of the Treasury, shall, at the beginning of each fiscal year, allot to the States the total of (1) the amount appropriated for such year pursuant to section 601; and (2) the amounts of the allotments under this section for the preceding fiscal year remaining unpaid to the States at the end of such fiscal year. The amounts of such allotments shall be determined on the basis of (1) the population; (2) the special health problems; and (3) the financial needs; of the respective States. Upon making such allotments the Surgeon General of the Public Health Service shall certify the amounts thereof to the Secretary of the Treasury.

(b) The amount of an allotment to any State under subsection (a) for any fiscal year, remaining unpaid at the end of such fiscal year, shall be available for allotment to States under subsection (a) for the succeeding fiscal year, in addition to the amount appropriated for such year.

(c) Prior to the beginning of each quarter of the fiscal year, the Surgeon General of the Public Health Service shall, with the approval of the Secretary of the Treasury, determine in accordance with rules and regulations previously prescribed by such Surgeon General after consultation with a conference of the State and Territorial health authorities, the amount to be paid to each State for such quarter from the allotment to such State, and shall certify the amount so determined to the Secretary of the Treasury. Upon receipt of such certification, the Secretary of the Treasury shall, through the Division of Disbursement of the Treasury Department and prior to audit or settlement by the General Accounting Office, pay in accordance with such certification.

(d) The moneys so paid to any State shall be expended solely in carrying out the purposes specified in section 601, and in accordance with plans presented by the health authority of such State and approved by the Surgeon General of the Public Health Service.

INVESTIGATIONS

SEC. 603. (a) There is hereby authorized to be appropriated for each fiscal year, beginning with the fiscal year ending June 30, 1936, the sum of $2,000,000 for expenditure by the Public Health Service for investigation of disease and problems of sanitation. . . .

TITLE VII—SOCIAL SECURITY BOARD ESTABLISHMENT

SECTION 701. There is hereby established a Social Security Board to be composed of three members to be appointed by the President, by and with the advice and consent of the Senate. During his term of membership on the Board, no member shall engage in any other business, vocation, or employment. Not more than two of the members of the Board shall be members of the same political party. Each member shall receive a salary at the rate of $10,000 a year and shall hold office for a term of six years. . . .

DUTIES OF SOCIAL SECURITY BOARD

SEC. 702. The Board shall perform the duties imposed upon it by this Act and shall also have the duty of studying and making recommendations as to the most effective methods of providing economic security through social insurance, and as to legislation and matters of administrative policy concerning old-age pensions, unemployment compensation, accident compensation, and related subjects. . . .

TITLE VIII—TAXES WITH RESPECT TO EMPLOYMENT INCOME TAX ON EMPLOYEES

SECTION 801. In addition to other taxes, there shall be levied, collected, and paid upon the income of every individual a tax equal to the following percentages of the wages (as defined in section 811) received by him after December 31, 1936, with respect to employment (as defined in section 811) after such date:

(1) With respect to employment during the calendar years 1937, 1938, and 1939, the rate shall be 1 per centum.

(2) With respect to employment during the calendar years 1940, 1941, and 1942, the rate shall be 1.36 per centum.

(3) With respect to employment during the calendar years 1943, 1944, and 1945, the rate shall be 2 per centum.

(4) With respect to employment during the calendar years 1946, 1947, and 1948, the rate shall be 2 per centum.

(5) With respect to employment after December 31, 1948, the rate shall be 3 per centum.

DEDUCTION OF TAX FROM WAGES

SEC. 802. (a) The tax imposed by section 801 shall be collected by the employer of the taxpayer, by deducting the amount of the tax from the wages as and when paid. . . .

EXCISE TAX ON EMPLOYERS

SEC. 804. In addition to other taxes, every employer shall pay an excise tax, with respect to having individuals in his employ, equal to the following percentages of the wages (as defined in section 811) paid by him after December 31, 1936, with respect to employment (as defined in section 811) after such date:

(1) With respect to employment during the calendar years 1937, 1938, and 1939, the rate shall be 1 per centum.

(2) With respect to employment during the calendar years 1940, 1941, and 1942, the rate shall be 1½ per centum.

(3) With respect to employment during the calendar years 1943, 1944, and 1945, the rate shall be 2 per centum.

(4) With respect to employment during the calendar years 1946, 1947, and 1948, the rate shall be 2½ per centum.

(5) With respect to employment after December 31, 1948, the rate shall be 3 per centum. . . .

DEFINITIONS

SEC. 811. When used in this title— . . .

(b) The term "employment" means any service, of whatever nature, performed within the United States by an employee for his employer, except—
    (1) Agricultural labor;
    (2) Domestic service in a private home;
    (3) Casual labor not in the course of the employer's trade or business;
    (4) Service performed by an individual who has attained the age of sixty-five;
    (5) Service performed as an officer or member of the crew of a vessel documented under the laws of the United States or of any foreign country;
    (6) Service performed in the employ of the United States Government or of an instrumentality of the United States;

(7) Service performed in the employ of a State, a political subdivision thereof, or an instrumentality of one or more States or political subdivisions;

(8) Service performed in the employ of a corporation, community chest, fund, or foundation, organized and operated exclusively for religious, charitable, scientific, literary, or educational purposes, or for the prevention of cruelty to children or animals, no part of the net earnings of which inures to the benefit of any private shareholder or individual.

TITLE IX—TAX ON EMPLOYERS OF EIGHT OR MORE/IMPOSITION OF TAX

SECTION 901. On and after January 1, 1936, every employer shall pay for each calendar year an excise tax, with respect to having individuals in his employ, equal to the following percentages of the total wages payable by him with respect to employment during such calendar year:

(1) With respect to employment during the calendar year 1936 the rate shall be 1 per centum;

(2) With respect to employment during the calendar year 1937 the rate shall be 2 per centum;

(3) With respect to employment after December 31, 1937, the rate shall be 3 per centum. . . .

CERTIFICATION OF STATE LAWS

SEC. 903. (a) The Social Security Board shall approve any State law submitted to it, within thirty days of such submission, which it finds provides that—

(1) All compensation is to be paid through public employment offices in the State or such other agencies as the Board may approve;

(2) No compensation shall be payable with respect to any day of unemployment occurring within two years after the first day of the first period with respect to which contributions are required;

(3) All money received in the unemployment fund shall immediately upon such receipt be paid over to the Secretary of the Treasury to the credit of the Unemployment Trust Fund. . . .

(5) Compensation shall not be denied in such State to any otherwise eligible individual for refusing to accept new work under any of the following conditions: (A) If the position offered is vacant due directly to a strike, lockout, or other labor dispute; (B) if the wages, hours, or other conditions of the work offered are substantially less favorable to the individual than those prevailing for similar work in the locality; (C) if as a condition of being employed the individual would be required to join a company union or to resign from or refrain from joining any bona fide labor organization.

UNEMPLOYMENT TRUST FUND

SEC. 904. (a) There is hereby established in the Treasury of the United States a trust fund to be known as the "Unemployment Trust Fund. . . ."

(b) It shall be the duty of the Secretary of the Treasury to invest such portion of the Fund as is not, in his judgment, required to meet current withdrawals. Such investment may be made only in interest bearing obligations of the United States or in obligations guaranteed as to both principal and interest by the United States. . . .

INTERSTATE COMMERCE

SEC. 906. No person required under a State law to make payments to an unemployment fund shall be relieved from compliance therewith on the ground that he is engaged in interstate commerce, or that the State law does not distinguish between employees engaged in interstate commerce and those engaged in intrastate commerce.

DEFINITIONS

SEC. 907. When used in this title—

(a) The term "employer" does not include any person unless on each of some twenty days during the taxable year, each day being in a different calendar week, the total number of individuals who were in his employ for some portion of the day (whether or not at the same moment of time) was eight or more. . . .

TITLE X—GRANTS TO STATES FOR AID TO THE BLIND APPROPRIATION

SECTION 1001. For the purpose of enabling each State to furnish financial assistance, as far as practicable under the conditions in such State, to needy individuals who are blind there is hereby authorized to be appropriated for the fiscal year ending June 30, 1936, the sum of $3,000,000, and there is hereby authorized to be appropriated for each fiscal year thereafter a sum sufficient to carry out the purposes of this title. The sums made available under this section shall be used for making payments to States which have submitted, and had approved by the Social Security Board, State plans for aid to the blind....

From: *U.S. Statutes at Large.* 1935. Vol. 49, p. 620.

REFORM OF THE FEDERAL JUDICIARY, 1937

Frustrated by a conservative Supreme Court that ruled many of the New Deal programs unconstitutional, President Franklin D. Roosevelt attempted to create a liberal majority by adding one justice to the court for every sitting justice over the age of seventy. While Roosevelt claimed this was to ease the judicial burden on elderly justices, opponents saw it as an attempt to pack the court with liberal New Deal supporters. While the Constitution does not indicate how many judges should sit on the court, by the 1930s, precedent had dictated nine. Adding more, Roosevelt's opponents said, was a dictatorial attempt to upset the constitutional balance of power. Ultimately, Roosevelt lost the fight—in that he did not get the legislation passed—but won the war. Several conservative judges soon resigned, while those that remained became more amenable to ruling New Deal programs constitutional. Included here are the piece of legislation Roosevelt introduced; his radio address to the nation explaining the legislation; and a report by the Senate Judiciary Committee condemning the Roosevelt court-packing plan.

1. PROPOSED BILL

Be it enacted, That—(a) When any judge of a court of the United States, appointed to hold his office during good behavior, has heretofore or hereafter attained the age of seventy years and has held a commission or commissions as judge of any such court or courts at least ten years, continuously or otherwise, and within six months thereafter has neither resigned nor retired, the President, for each such judge who has not so resigned or retired, shall nominate, and by and with the advice and consent of the Senate, shall appoint one additional judge to the court to which the former is commissioned: Provided, That no additional judge shall be appointed hereunder if the judge who is of retirement age dies, resigns, or retires prior to the nomination of such additional judge.

(b) The number of judges of any court shall be permanently increased by the number appointed thereto under the provisions of subsection (a) of this section. No more than fifty judges shall be appointed thereunder, nor shall any judge be so appointed if such appointment would result in (1) more than fifteen members of the Supreme Court of the United States, (2) more than two additional members so appointed to a circuit court of appeals, the Court of Claims, the United States Court of Customs and Patent Appeals, or the Customs Court, or (3) more than twice the number of judges now authorized to be appointed for any district or in the case of judges appointed for more than one district, for any such group of districts....

(d) An additional judge shall not be appointed under the provisions of this section when the judge who is of retirement age is commissioned to an office as to which Congress has provided that a vacancy shall not be filled.

SEC. 2. (a) Any circuit judge hereafter appointed may be designated and assigned from time to time by the Chief Justice of the United States for service in the circuit court of appeals for any circuit. Any district judge hereafter appointed may be designated and assigned from time to time by the Chief Justice of the United States for service in any district court or, subject to the authority of the Chief Justice, by the senior circuit judge of his circuit for service in any district court within the circuit. A district judge designated and assigned to another district hereunder may hold court separately and at the same time as the district judge in such district. . . . The designation and assignment of any judge may be terminated at any time by order of the Chief Justice or the senior circuit judge, as the case may be. . . .

SEC. 3 (a) The Supreme Court shall have power to appoint a proctor. It shall be his duty (1) to obtain and, if deemed by the Court to be desirable, to publish information as to the volume, character, and status of litigation in the district courts and circuit courts of appeals, and such other information as the Supreme Court may from time to time require by order, and it shall be the duty of any judge, clerk, or marshal of any court of the United States promptly to furnish such information as may be required by the proctor; (2) to investigate the need of assigning district and circuit judges to other courts and to make recommendations thereon to the Chief Justice; (3) to recommend, with the approval of the Chief Justice, to any court of the United States methods for expediting cases pending on its dockets; and (4) to perform such other duties consistent with his office as the Court shall direct. . . .

SEC. 5. When used in this Act—

(a) The term "judge of retirement age" means a judge of a court of the United States appointed to hold his office during good behavior who has attained the age of seventy years and has held a commission or commissions as judge of any such court or courts at least ten years continuous or otherwise, and within six months thereafter, whether or not he is eligible for retirement, has neither resigned nor retired. . . .

2. ADDRESS BY THE PRESIDENT OF THE UNITED STATES, MARCH 9, 1937

. . . Tonight, sitting at my desk in the White House I make my first radio report to the people in my second term of office. . . .

The American people have learned from the depression. For in the last three national elections an overwhelming majority of them voted a mandate that the Congress and the President begin the task of providing that protection—not after long years of debate, but now.

The courts, however, have cast doubts on the ability of the elected Congress to protect us against catastrophe by meeting squarely our modern social and economic conditions.

We are at a crisis in our ability to proceed with that protection. It is a quiet crisis. There are no lines of depositors outside closed banks. But to the far-sighted it is far-reaching in its possibilities of injury to America.

I want to talk with you very simply about the need for present action in this crisis—the need to meet the unanswered challenge of one-third of a nation ill-nourished, ill-clad, ill-housed.

Last Thursday I described the American form of government as a three-horse team provided by the Constitution to the American people so that their field might be plowed. The three horses are, of course, the three branches of government—the Congress, the executive, and the courts. Two of the horses are pulling in unison today; the third is not. Those who have intimated that the President of the United States is trying to drive that team overlook the simple fact that the President, as Chief Executive, is himself one of the three horses.

It is the American people themselves who are in the driver's seat.

It is the American people themselves who want the furrow plowed.

It is the American people themselves who expect the third horse to pull in unison with the other two.

I hope that you have reread the Constitution of the United States. Like the Bible, it ought to be read again and again.

It is an easy document to understand when you remember that it was called into being because the Articles of Confederation under which the Original Thirteen States tried to operate after the Revolution showed the need of a National Government with power enough to handle national problems. In its preamble the Constitution states that it was intended to form a more perfect Union and promote the general welfare; and the powers given to the Congress to carry out those purposes can be best described by saying that they were all the powers needed to meet each and every problem which then had a national character and which could not be met by merely local action.

But the framers went further. Having in mind that in succeeding generations many other problems then undreamed of would become national problems, they gave to the Congress the ample broad powers "to levy taxes and provide for the common defense and general welfare of the United States."

That, my friends, is what I honestly believe to have been the clear and underlying purpose of the patriots who wrote a Federal Constitution to create a National

Government with national power, intended as they said, "to form a more perfect union . . . for ourselves and our posterity."

For nearly 20 years there was no conflict between the Congress and the Court. Then, in 1803, . . . The Court claimed the power to declare it [a statute] unconstitutional and did so declare it. But a little later the Court itself admitted that it was an extraordinary power to exercise and through Mr. Justice Washington laid down this limitation upon it: "It is but a decent respect due to the wisdom, the integrity, and the patriotism of the legislative body, by which any law is passed, to presume in favor of its validity until its violation of the Constitution is proved beyond all reasonable doubt."

But since the rise of the modern movement for social and economic progress through legislation, the Court has more and more often and more and more boldly asserted a power to veto laws passed by the Congress and State legislatures in complete disregard of this original limitation.

In the last four years the sound rule of giving statutes the benefit of all reasonable doubt has been cast aside. The Court has been acting not as a judicial body, but as a policy-making body.

When the Congress has sought to stabilize national agriculture, to improve the conditions of labor, to safeguard business against unfair competition, to protect our national resources, and in many other ways to serve our clearly national needs, the majority of the Court has been assuming the power to pass on the wisdom of these acts of the Congress—and to approve or disapprove the public policy written into these laws.

That is not only my accusation. It is the accusation of most distinguished Justices of the present Supreme Court. I have not the time to quote to you all the language used by dissenting Justices in many of these cases. But in the case holding the Railroad Retirement Act unconstitutional, for instance, Chief Justice Hughes said in a dissenting opinion that the majority opinion was "a departure from sound principles," and placed "an unwarranted limitation upon the commerce clause." And three other Justices agreed with him.

In the case holding the A.A.A. unconstitutional, Justice Stone said of the majority opinion that it was a "tortured construction of the Constitution." And two other Justices agreed with him.

In the case holding the New York Minimum Wage Law unconstitutional, Justice Stone said that the majority were actually reading into the Constitution their own "personal economic predilections," and that if the legislative power is not left free to choose the methods of solving the problems of poverty, subsistence, and health of large numbers in the community, then "government is to be rendered impotent." And two other Justices agreed with him.

In the face of these dissenting opinions, there is no basis for the claim made by some members of the Court that something in the Constitution has compelled them regretfully to thwart the will of the people.

In the face of such dissenting opinions, it is perfectly clear that as Chief Justice Hughes has said, "We are under a Constitution, but the Constitution is what the judges say it is."

The Court in addition to the proper use of its judicial functions has improperly set itself up as a third House of the Congress—a superlegislature, as one of the Justices has called it—reading into the Constitution words and implications which are not there, and which were never intended to be there.

We have, therefore, reached the point as a Nation where we must take action to save the Constitution from the Court and the Court from itself. We must find a way to take an appeal from the Supreme Court to the Constitution itself. We want a Supreme Court which will do justice under the Constitution—not over it. In our courts we want a government of laws and not of men.

I want—as all Americans want—an independent Judiciary as proposed by the framers of the Constitution. That means a Supreme Court that will enforce the Constitution as written—that will refuse to amend the Constitution by the arbitrary exercise of judicial power—amendment by judicial say-so. It does not mean a judiciary so independent that it can deny the existence of facts universally recognized.

How, then, could we proceed to perform the mandate given us? It was said in last year's Democratic platform, "If these problems cannot be effectively solved within the Constitution, we shall seek such clarifying amendment as will assure the power to enact those laws, adequately to regulate commerce, protect public health and safety, and safeguard economic security." In other words, we said we would seek an amendment only if every other possible means by legislation were to fail.

When I commenced to review the situation with the problem squarely before me, I came by a process of elimination to the conclusion that short of amendments the only method which was clearly constitutional, and would at the same time carry out other much-needed reforms, was to infuse new blood into all our courts. We must have men worthy and equipped to carry out impartial justice. But at the same time we must have judges who will bring to the courts a present-day sense of the Constitution—judges who will retain in the courts the judicial functions of a court and reject the legislative powers which the courts have today assumed.

In 45 out of 48 States of the Union, judges are chosen not for life but for a period of years. In many States judges must retire at the age of 70. Congress has provided financial security by offering life pensions at full pay for Federal judges on all courts who are willing to retire at 70. In the case of Supreme Court Justices, that pension is $20,000 a year. But all Federal judges, once appointed, can, if they choose, hold office for life no matter how old they may get to be.

What is my proposal? It is simply this: Whenever a judge or justice of any Federal court has reached the age of 70 and does not avail himself of the opportunity to retire on a pension, a new member shall be appointed by the President then in office, with the approval, as required by the Constitution, of the Senate of the United States.

That plan has two chief purposes: By bringing into the judicial system a steady and continuing stream of new and younger blood, I hope, first, to make the administration of all Federal justice speedier and therefore less costly; secondly, to bring to the decision of social and economic problems younger men who have had personal experience and contact with modern facts and circumstances under which average men have to live and work. This plan will save our National Constitution from hardening of the judicial arteries.

The number of judges to be appointed would depend wholly on the decision of present judges now over 70 or those who would subsequently reach the age of 70.

If, for instance, any one of the six Justices of the Supreme Court now over the age of 70 should retire as provided under the plan, no additional place would be created. Consequently, although there never can be more than 15, there may be only 14, or 13, or 12, and there may be only 9.

There is nothing novel or radical about this idea. It seeks to maintain the Federal bench in full vigor. It has been discussed and approved by many persons of high authority even since a similar proposal passed the House of Representatives in 1869.

Why was the age fixed at 70? Because the laws of many States, the practice of the civil service, the regulations of the Army and Navy, and the rules of many of our universities and of almost every great private business enterprise commonly fix the retirement age at 70 years or less.

The statute would apply to all the courts in the Federal system. There is general approval so far as the lower Federal courts are concerned. The plan has met opposition only so far as the Supreme Court of the United States itself is concerned. If such a plan is good for the lower courts it certainly ought to be equally good for the highest court, from which there is no appeal.

Those opposing this plan have sought to arouse prejudice and fear by crying that I am seeking to "pack" the Supreme Court and that a baneful precedent will be established.

What do they mean by the words "packing the Court"?

Let me answer this question with a bluntness that will end all honest misunderstanding of my purposes.

If by that phrase "packing the Court" it is charged that I wish to place on the bench spineless puppets who would disregard the law and would decide specific cases as I wished them to be decided, I make this answer: That no President fit for his office would appoint, and no Senate of honorable men fit for their office would confirm, that kind of appointees to the Supreme Court.

But if by that phrase the charge is made that I would appoint and the Senate would confirm Justices worthy to sit beside present members of the Court who understand those modern conditions; that I will appoint Justices who will not undertake to override the judgment of the Congress on legislative policy; that I will appoint Justices who will act as Justices and not as legislators—if the appointment of such Justices can be called "packing the Courts"—then I say that I, and with me the vast majority of the American people, favor doing just that thing—now.

Is it a dangerous precedent for the Congress to change the number of the Justices? The Congress has always had, and will have, that power. The number of Justices has been changed several times before—in the administrations of John Adams and Thomas Jefferson, both signers of the Declaration of Independence, Andrew Jackson, Abraham Lincoln, and Ulysses S. Grant.

I suggest only the addition of Justices to the bench in accordance with a clearly defined principle relating to a clearly defined age limit. Fundamentally, if in the future America cannot trust the Congress it elects to refrain from abuse of our constitutional usages, democracy will have failed far beyond the importance to it of any kind of precedent concerning the judiciary.

We think it so much in the public interest to maintain a vigorous judiciary that we encourage the retirement of elderly judges by offering them a life pension at full salary. Why then should we leave the fulfillment of this public policy to chance or make it dependent upon the desire or prejudice of any individual Justice?

It is the clear intention of our public policy to provide for a constant flow of new and younger blood into the judiciary. Normally, every President appoints a large number of district and circuit judges and a few members of the Supreme Court. Until my first term practically every President of the United States had appointed at least one member of the Supreme Court. President Taft appointed five members and named a Chief Justice; President Wilson three, President Harding four including a Chief Justice; President Coolidge one; President Hoover three, including a Chief Justice.

Such a succession of appointments should have provided a court well balanced as to age. But chance and the disinclination of individuals to leave the Supreme Bench have now given us a Court in which five Justices will be over 75 years of age before next June and one over 70. Thus a sound public policy has been defeated.

I now propose that we establish by law an assurance against any such ill-balanced Court in the future. I propose that hereafter, when a judge reaches the age of 70, a new and younger judge shall be added to the Court automatically. In this way I propose to enforce a sound public policy by law instead of leaving the composition of our Federal courts, including the highest, to be determined by chance or the personal decision of individuals.

If such a law as I propose is regarded as establishing a new precedent, is it not a most desirable precedent?

Like all lawyers, like all Americans, I regret the necessity of this controversy. But the welfare of the United States, and indeed of the Constitution itself, is what we all must think about first. Our difficulty with the Court today rises not from the Court as an institution but from human beings within it. But we cannot yield our constitutional destiny to the personal judgment of a few men who, being fearful of the future, would deny us the necessary means of dealing with the present.

This plan of mine is no attack on the Court; it seeks to restore the Court to its rightful and historic place in our system of constitutional government and to have it resume its high task of building anew on the Constitution "a system of living law."

I have thus explained to you the reasons that lie behind our efforts to secure results by legislation within the Constitution. I hope that thereby the difficult process of constitutional amendment may be rendered unnecessary.

I am in favor of action through legislation—

First, because I believe that it can be passed at this session of the Congress.

Second, because it will provide a reinvigorated, liberal-minded judiciary necessary to furnish quicker and cheaper justice from bottom to top.

Third, because it will provide a series of Federal courts willing to enforce the Constitution as written, and unwilling to assert legislative powers by writing into it their own political and economic policies.

During the past half century the balance of power between the three great branches of the Federal Government has been tipped out of balance by the courts in direct contradiction of the high purposes of the framers of the Constitution. It is my purpose to restore that balance. You who know me will accept my solemn assurance that in a world in which democracy is under attack I seek to make American democracy succeed.

3. ADVERSE REPORT FROM THE COMMITTEE ON THE JUDICIARY

The Committee on the Judiciary, to whom was referred the bill to reorganize the judicial branch of the Government, after full consideration, having unanimously amended the measure, hereby report the bill adversely with the recommendation that it do not pass....

THE ARGUMENT

The committee recommends that the measure be rejected for the following primary reasons:

I. The bill does not accomplish any one of the objectives for which it was originally offered.

II. It applies force to the judiciary and in its initial and ultimate effect would undermine the independence of the courts.

III. It violates all precedents in the history of our Government and would in itself be a dangerous precedent for the future.

IV. The theory of the bill is in direct violation of the spirit of the American Constitution and its employment would permit alteration of the Constitution without the people's consent or approval; it undermines the protection our constitutional system gives to minorities and is subversive of the rights of individuals.

V. It tends to centralize the Federal district judiciary by the power of assigning judges from one district to another at will.

VI. It tends to expand political control over the judicial department by adding to the powers of the legislative and executive departments respecting the judiciary. . . .

OBJECTIVES AS ORIGINALLY STATED

As offered to the Congress, this bill was designed to effectuate only three objectives, described as follows in the President's message:

1. To increase the personnel of the Federal courts "so that cases may be promptly decided in the first instance, and may be given adequate and prompt hearing on all appeals";

2. To "invigorate all the courts by the permanent infusion of new blood";

3. To "grant to the Supreme Court further power and responsibility in maintaining the efficiency of the entire Federal judiciary."

The third of these purposes was to be accomplished by the provisions creating the office of the Proctor and dealing with the assignment of judges to courts other than those to which commissioned.

The first two objectives were to be attained by the provisions authorizing the appointment of not to exceed 50 additional judges when sitting judges of retirement age, as defined in the bill, failed to retire or resign. How totally inadequate the measure is to achieve either of the named objectives, the most cursory examination of the facts reveals. . . .

QUESTION OF AGE NOT SOLVED

The next question is to determine to what extent "the persistent infusion of new blood" may be expected from this bill.

It will be observed that the bill before us does not and cannot compel the retirement of any judge, whether on the Supreme Court or any other court, when he becomes 70 years of age. It will be remembered that the mere attainment of three score and ten by a particular judge does not, under this bill, require the appointment of another. The man on the bench may be 80 years of age, but this bill will not authorize the President to appoint a new judge to sit beside him unless he has served as a judge for 10 years. In other words, age itself is not penalized; the penalty falls only when age is attended with experience.

No one should overlook the fact that under this bill the President, whoever he may be and whether or not he believes in the constant infusion of young blood in the courts, may nominate a man 69 years and 11 months of age to the Supreme Court, or to any court, and if confirmed, such nominee, if he never had served as a judge, would continue to sit upon the bench unmolested by this law until he had attained the ripe age of 79 years and 11 months.

We are told that "modern complexities call also for a constant infusion of new blood in the courts, just as it is needed in executive functions of the Government and in private business." Does this bill provide for such? The answer is obviously no. As has been just demonstrated, the introduction of old and inexperienced blood into the courts is not prevented by this bill.

More than that, the measure, by its own terms, makes impossible the "constant" or "persistent" infusion of new blood. It is to be observed that the word is "new," not "young."

The Supreme Court may not be expanded to more than 15 members. No more than two additional members may be appointed to any circuit court of appeals, to the Court of Claims, to the Court of Customs and Patent Appeals, or to the Customs Court, and the number of judges now serving in any district or group of districts may not be more than doubled. There is, therefore, a specific limitation of appointment regardless of age. That is to say, this bill, ostensibly designed to provide for the infusion of new blood, sets up insuperable obstacles to the "constant" or "persistent" operation of that principle. . . .

It thus appears that the bill before us does not with certainty provide for increasing the personnel of the Federal judiciary, does not remedy the law's delay, does not serve the interest of the "poorer litigant" and does not provide for the "constant" or "persistent infusion of new blood" into the judiciary. What, then, does it do?

THE BILL APPLIES FORCE TO THE JUDICIARY

The answer is clear. It applies force to the judiciary. It is an attempt to impose upon the courts a course of action, a line of decision which, without that force, without that imposition, the judiciary might not adopt. . . .

Those of us who hold office in this Government, however humble or exalted it may be, are creatures of the Constitution. To it we owe all the power and authority we possess. Outside of it we have none. We are bound by it in every official act.

We know that this instrument, without which we would not be able to call ourselves presidents, judges, or legislators, was carefully planned and deliberately framed to establish three coordinate branches of government, every one of them to be independent of the others. For the protection of the people, for the preservation of the rights of the individual, for the maintenance of the liberties of minorities, for maintaining the checks and balances of our dual system, the three branches of the Government were so constituted that the independent expression of honest difference of opinion could never be restrained in the people's servants and no one branch could overawe or subjugate the others. That is the American system. It is immeasurably more important, immeasurably more sacred to the people of America, indeed, to the people of all the world than the immediate adoption of any legislation however beneficial.

That judges should hold office during good behavior is the prescription. It is founded upon historic experience of the utmost significance. Compensation at stated times, which compensation was not to be diminished during their tenure, was also ordained. Those comprehensible terms were the outgrowths of experience which was deep-seated. . . . This judicial system is the priceless heritage of every American.

By this bill another and wholly different cause is proposed for the intervention of executive influence, namely, age. Age and behavior have no connection; they are unrelated subjects. By this bill, judges who have reached 70 years of age may remain on the bench and have their judgment augmented if they agree with the new appointee, or vetoed if they disagree. This is far from the independence intended for the courts by the framers of the Constitution. This is an unwarranted influence accorded the appointing agency, contrary to the spirit of the Constitution. The bill sets up a plan which has as its stability the changing will or inclination of an agency not a part of the judicial system. Constitutionally, the bill can have no sanction. The effect of the bill, as stated by the Attorney General to the committee, and indeed by the President in both his message and speech, is in violation of the organic law.

OBJECT OF PLAN ACKNOWLEDGED

No amount of sophistry can cover up this fact. The effect of this bill is not to provide for an increase in the number of Justices composing the Supreme Court. The effect is to provide a forced retirement or, failing in this, to take from the Justices affected a free exercise of their independent judgment. . . .

Let us, for the purpose of the argument, grant that the Court has been wrong, wrong not only in that it has rendered mistaken opinions but wrong in the far more serious sense that it has substituted its will for the congressional will in the matter of legislation. May we nevertheless safely punish the Court?

Today it may be the Court which is charged with forgetting its constitutional duties. Tomorrow it may be the Congress. The next day it may be the Executive. If we yield to temptation now to lay the lash upon the Court, we are only teaching others how to apply it to ourselves and to the people when the occasion seems to warrant. Manifestly, if we may force the hand of the Court to secure our interpretation of the Constitution, then some succeeding Congress may repeat the process to secure another and a different interpretation and one which may not sound so pleasant in our ears as that for which we now contend.

There is a remedy for usurpation or other judicial wrongdoing. If this bill be supported by the toilers of this country upon the ground that they want a Court which will sustain legislation limiting hours and providing minimum wages, they must remember that the procedure employed in the bill could be used in another administration to lengthen hours and to decrease wages. If farmers want agricultural relief and favor this bill upon the ground that it gives them a Court which will sustain legislation in their favor, they must remember that the procedure employed might some day be used to deprive them of every vestige of a farm relief.

When members of the Court usurp legislative powers or attempt to exercise political power, they lay themselves open to the charge of having lapsed from that "good behavior" which determines the period of their official life. But, if you say, the process of impeachment is difficult and uncertain, the answer is, the people made it so when they framed the Constitution. It is not for us, the servants of the people, the instruments of the Constitution, to find a more easy way to do that which our masters made difficult.

But, if the fault of the judges is not so grievous as to warrant impeachment, if their offense is merely that they have grown old, and we feel, therefore, that there should be a "constant infusion of new blood," then obviously the way to achieve that result is by constitutional amendment fixing definite terms for the members of the judiciary or making mandatory their retirement at a given age. Such a provision would indeed provide for the constant infusion of new blood, not only now but at all times in the future. The plan before us is but a temporary expedient which operates once and then never again, leaving the Court as permanently expanded to become once more a court of old men, gradually year by year falling behind the times....

A MEASURE WITHOUT PRECEDENT

This bill is an invasion of judicial power such as has never before been attempted in this country. It is true that in the closing days of the administration of John Adams, a bill was passed creating 16 new circuit judges while reducing by one the number of places on the Supreme Court. It was charged that this was a bill to use the judiciary for a political purpose by providing official positions for members of a defeated party. The repeal of that law was the first task of the Jefferson administration.

Neither the original act nor the repealer was an attempt to change the course of judicial decision. And never in the history of the country has there been such an act. The present bill comes to us, therefore, wholly without precedent.

It is true that the size of the Supreme Court has been changed from time to time, but in every instance after the Adams administration, save one, the changes were made for purely administrative purposes in aid of the Court, not to control it....

A PRECEDENT OF LOYALTY TO THE CONSTITUTION

Shall we now, after 150 years of loyalty to the constitutional ideal of an untrammeled judiciary, duty bound to protect the constitutional rights of the humblest citizen even against the Government itself, create the vicious precedent which must necessarily undermine our system? The only argument for the increase which survives analysis is that Congress should enlarge the Court so as to make the policies of this administration effective.

We are told that a reactionary oligarchy defies the will of the majority, that this is a bill to "unpack" the Court and give effect to the desires of the majority; that is to say, a bill to increase the number of Justices for the express purpose of neutralizing the views of some of the present members. In justification we are told, but without authority, by those who would ra-

tionalize this program, that Congress was given the power to determine the size of the Court so that the legislative branch would be able to impose its will upon the judiciary. This amounts to nothing more than the declaration that when the Court stands in the way of a legislative enactment, the Congress may reverse the ruling by enlarging the Court. When such a principle is adopted, our constitutional system is overthrown!

This, then, is the dangerous precedent we are asked to establish. When proponents of the bill assert, as they have done, that Congress in the past has altered the number of Justices upon the Supreme Court and that this is reason enough for our doing it now, they show how important precedents are and prove that we should now refrain from any action that would seem to establish one which could be followed hereafter whenever a Congress and an executive should become dissatisfied with the decisions of the Supreme Court.

This is the first time in the history of our country that a proposal to alter the decisions of the court by enlarging its personnel has been so boldly made. Let us meet it. Let us now set a salutary precedent that will never be violated. Let us, of the Seventy-fifth Congress, in words that will never be disregarded by any succeeding Congress, declare that we would rather have an independent Court, a fearless Court, a Court that will dare to announce its honest opinions in what it believes to be the defense of the liberties of the people, than a Court that, out of fear or sense of obligation to the appointing power, or factional passion, approves any measure we may enact. We are not the judges of the judges. We are not above the Constitution.

Even if every charge brought against the so-called "reactionary" members of this Court be true, it is far better that we await orderly but inevitable change of personnel than that we impatiently overwhelm them with new members. Exhibiting this restraint, thus demonstrating our faith in the American system, we shall set an example that will protect the independent American judiciary from attack as long as this Government stands....

True it is, that courts like Congresses, should take account of the advancing strides of civilization. True it is that the law, being a progressive science, must be pronounced progressively and liberally; but the milestones of liberal progress are made to be noted and counted with caution rather than merely to be encountered and passed. Progress is not a mad mob march; rather, it is a steady, invincible stride....

If, under the "hydraulic pressure" of our present need for economic justice, we destroy the system under which our people have progressed to a higher degree of justice and prosperity than that ever enjoyed by any other people in all the history of the human race, then we shall destroy not only all opportunity for further advance but everything we have thus far achieved. . . .

Even if the case were far worse than it is alleged to be, it would still be no argument in favor of this bill to say that the courts and some judges have abused their power. The courts are not perfect, nor are the judges. The Congress is not perfect, nor are Senators and Representatives. The Executive is not perfect. These branches of government and the office under them are filled by human beings who for the most part strive to live up to the dignity and idealism of a system that was designed to achieve the greatest possible measure of justice and freedom for all the people. We shall destroy the system when we reduce it to the imperfect standards of the men who operate it. We shall strengthen it and ourselves, we shall make justice and liberty for all men more certain when, by patience and self-restraint, we maintain it on the high plane on which it was conceived.

Inconvenience and even delay in the enactment of legislation is not a heavy price to pay for our system. Constitutional democracy moves forward with certainty rather than with speed. The safety and the permanence of the progressive march of our civilization are far more important to us and to those who are to come after us than the enactment now of any particular law. The Constitution of the United States provides ample opportunity for the expression of popular will to bring about such reforms and changes as the people may deem essential to their present and future welfare. It is the people's charter of the powers granted those who govern them. . . .

SUMMARY

We recommend the rejection of this bill as a needless, futile, and utterly dangerous abandonment of constitutional principle.

It was presented to the Congress in a most intricate form and for reasons that obscured its real purpose.

It would not banish age from the bench nor abolish divided decisions.

It would not affect the power of any court to hold laws unconstitutional nor withdraw from any judge the authority to issue injunctions.

It would not reduce the expense of litigation nor speed the decision of cases.

It is a proposal without precedent and without justification.

It would subjugate the courts to the will of Congress and the President and thereby destroy the independence of the judiciary, the only certain shield of individual rights.

It contains the germ of a system of centralized administration of law that would enable an executive so minded to send his judges into every judicial district in the land to sit in judgment on controversies between the Government and the citizen.

It points the way to the evasion of the Constitution and establishes the method whereby the people may be deprived of their right to pass upon all amendments of the fundamental law.

It stands now before the country, acknowledged by its proponents as a plan to force judicial interpretation of the Constitution, a proposal that violates every sacred tradition of American democracy.

Under the form of the Constitution it seeks to do that which is unconstitutional.

Its ultimate operation would be to make this Government one of men rather than one of law, and its practical operation would be to make the Constitution what the executive or legislative branches of the Government choose to say it is—an interpretation to be changed with each change of administration.

It is a measure which should be so emphatically rejected that its parallel will never again be presented to the free representatives of the free people of America.

WILLIAM H. KING.
FREDERICK VAN NUYS.
PATRICK McCARRAN.
CARL A. HATCH.
EDWARD R. BURKE.
TOM CONNALLY.
JOSEPH C. O'MAHONEY.
WILLIAM E. BORAH.
WARREN R. AUSTIN.
FREDERICK STEIWER.

From: U.S. Senate. 1937. Committee on the Judiciary. 75th Cong., 1st Sess. S. Rep. 711.

WAGNER–STEAGALL NATIONAL HOUSING ACT, SEPTEMBER 1, 1937

Throughout the Great Depression, homelessness grew as a problem. Added to the homeless problem was the mass of substandard housing in America's cities and rural areas. While the National Recovery Act earmarked sums for public housing, the amount was insignificant. The Housing Act of 1937—sponsored by Democratic New York Senator Robert Wagner—put relatively large sums of federal money in the service of public housing for the first time in American history.

An Act to provide financial assistance to the States and political subdivisions thereof for the elimination of unsafe and insanitary housing conditions, for the eradication of slums, for the provision of decent, safe, and sanitary dwellings for families of low income, and for the reduction of unemployment and the stimulation of business activity, to create a United States Housing Authority, and for other purposes.

DECLARATION OF POLICY

SECTION 1. It is hereby declared to be the policy of the United States to promote the general welfare of the Nation by employing its funds and credit, as provided in this Act, to assist the several States and their political subdivisions to alleviate present and recurring unemployment and to remedy the unsafe and insanitary housing conditions and the acute shortage of decent, safe, and sanitary dwellings for families of low income in rural or urban communities that are injurious to the health, safety, and morals of the citizens of the Nation.

DEFINITIONS

SEC. 2. When used in this Act—

(1) The term "low-rent housing" means decent, safe, and sanitary dwellings within the financial reach of families of low income and developed and administered to promote serviceability, efficiency, economy, and stability, and embraces all necessary appurtenances thereto. The dwellings in low-rent housing as defined in this Act shall be available solely for families whose net income at the time of admission does not exceed five times the rental (including the value or cost to them of heat, light, water, and cooking fuel) of the dwellings to be furnished such families, except that in the case of families with three or more minor dependents, such ratio shall not exceed six to one.

(2) The term "families of low income" means families who are in the lowest income group and who cannot afford to pay enough to cause private enterprise in their locality or metropolitan area to build an adequate supply of decent, safe, and sanitary dwellings for their use.

(3) The term "slum" means any area where dwellings predominate which, by reason of dilapidation, overcrowding, faulty arrangement or design, lack of ventilation, light or sanitation facilities, or any combination of these factors, are detrimental to safety, health, or morals....

UNITED STATES HOUSING AUTHORITY

SEC. 3. (a) There is hereby created in the Department of the Interior and under the general supervision of the Secretary thereof a body corporate of perpetual duration to be known as the United States Housing Authority, which shall be an agency and instrumentality of the United States.

(b) The powers of the Authority shall be vested in and exercised by an Administrator, who shall be appointed by the President, by and with the advice and consent of the Senate. The Administrator shall serve for a term of five years and shall be removable by the President upon notice and hearing for neglect of duty or malfeasance but for no other cause.

SEC. 4....

(e) The Authority, including but not limited to its franchise, capital, reserves, surplus, loans, income, assets, and property of any kind, shall be exempt from all taxation now or hereafter imposed by the United States or by any State, county, municipality, or local taxing authority. Obligations, including interest thereon, issued by public housing agencies in connection with low-rent-housing or slum-clearance projects, and the income derived by such agencies from such projects, shall be exempt from all taxation now or hereafter imposed by the United States....

LOANS FOR LOW-RENT-HOUSING AND SLUM-CLEARANCE PROJECTS

SEC. 9. The Authority may make loans to public-housing agencies to assist the development, acquisition, or administration of low-rent-housing or slum-clearance projects by such agencies. Where capital grants are made pursuant to section 11 the total amount of such loans outstanding on any one project and in which the Authority participates shall not exceed the development or acquisition cost of such project less all such capital grants, but in no event shall said loans exceed 90 per centum of such cost. In the case of annual contributions in assistance of low rentals as provided in section 10 the total of such loans outstanding on any one project and in which the Authority participates shall not exceed 90 per centum of the development or acquisition cost of such project. Such loans shall bear interest at such rate not less than the going Federal rate at the time the loan is made, plus one-half of one per centum, shall be secured in such manner, and shall be repaid within such period not exceeding sixty years, as may be deemed advisable by the Authority.

ANNUAL CONTRIBUTIONS IN ASSISTANCE OF LOW RENTALS

SEC. 10. (a) The Authority may make annual contributions to public housing agencies to assist in achieving and maintaining the low-rent character of their housing projects. The annual contributions for any such project shall be fixed in uniform amounts, and shall be paid in such amounts over a fixed period of years. No part of such annual contributions by the Authority shall be made available for any project unless and until the State, city, county, or other political subdivision in which such project is situated shall contribute, in the form of cash or tax remissions, general or special, or tax exemptions, at least 20 per centum of the annual contributions herein provided. The Authority shall embody the provisions for such annual contributions in a contract guaranteeing their payment over such fixed period: Provided, That no annual contributions shall be made, and the Authority shall enter into no contract guaranteeing any annual contribution in connection with the development of any low-rent-housing or slum-clearance project involving the construction of new dwellings, unless the project includes the elimination by demolition, condemnation, and effective closing, or the compulsory repair or improvement of unsafe or insanitary dwellings situated in the locality or metropolitan area, substantially equal in number to the number of newly constructed dwellings provided by the project; except that such elimination may, in the discretion of the Authority, be deferred in any locality or metropolitan area where the shortage of decent, safe, or sanitary housing available to families of low income is so acute as to force dangerous overcrowding of such families.

(b) Annual contributions shall be strictly limited to the amounts and periods necessary, in the determination of the Authority, to assure the low-rent character of the housing projects involved. Toward this end the Authority may prescribe regulations fixing the maximum contributions available under different circumstances, giving consideration to cost, location, size, rent-paying ability of prospective tenants, or other factors bearing upon the amounts and periods of assistance needed to achieve and maintain low rentals. Such regulations may provide for rates of contribution based upon development, acquisition or administration cost, number of dwelling units, number of persons housed, or other appropriate factors....

(e) The Authority is authorized, on and after the date of the enactment of this Act, to enter into contracts which provide for annual contributions aggregating not more than $5,000,000 per annum, on or after July 1, 1938, to enter into additional such contracts which provide for annual contributions aggregating not more than $7,500,000 per annum, and on or after July 1, 1939, to enter into additional such contracts which provide for annual contributions aggregating not more than $7,500,000 per annum. Without further authorization from Congress, no new contracts for annual contributions beyond those herein authorized shall be entered into by the Authority. The faith of the United States is solemnly pledged to the payment of all annual contributions contracted for pursuant to this section, and there is hereby authorized to be appropriated in each fiscal year, out of any money in the Treasury not otherwise appropriated, the amounts necessary to provide for such payments.

CAPITAL GRANTS IN ASSISTANCE OF LOW RENTALS

SEC. 11. (a) As an alternative method of assistance to that provided in section 10, when any public housing agency so requests and demonstrates to the satisfaction of the Authority that such alternative method is better suited to the purpose of achieving and maintaining low rentals and to the other purposes of this Act, capital grants may be made to such agency for such purposes. . . .

(b) Pursuant to subsection (a) of this section, the Authority may make a capital grant for any low-rent-housing or slum-clearance project, which shall in no case exceed 25 per centum of its development or acquisition cost.

(d) The Authority is authorized, on or after the date of the enactment of this Act to make capital grants (pursuant to subsection (b) of this section) aggregating not more than $10,000,000, on or after July 1, 1938, to make additional capital grants aggregating not more than $10,000,000, and on or after July 1, 1939, to make additional capital grants aggregating not more than $10,000,000. Without further authorization from Congress, no capital grants beyond those herein authorized shall be made by the Authority.

(e) To supplement any capital grant made by the Authority in connection with the development of any low-rent-housing or slum-clearance project, the President may allocate to the Authority, from any funds available for the relief of unemployment, an additional capital grant to be expended for payment of labor used in such development: Provided, That such additional capital grant shall not exceed 15 per centum of the development cost of the low-rent-housing or slum-clearance project involved.

(f) No capital grant pursuant to this section shall be made for any low-rent housing or slum-clearance project unless the public housing agency receiving such capital grant shall also receive, from the State, political subdivision thereof, or otherwise, a contribution for such project (in the form of cash, land, or the value, capitalized at the going Federal rate of interest, of community facilities or services for which a charge is usually made, or tax remissions or tax exemptions) in an amount not less than 20 per centum of its development or acquisition cost.

DISPOSAL OF FEDERAL PROJECTS

SEC. 12. . . .

(b) As soon as practicable the Authority shall sell its Federal projects or divest itself of their management through leases.

GENERAL POWERS OF THE AUTHORITY

SEC. 13. . . .

(5) No contract for any loan, annual contribution, or capital grant made pursuant to this Act shall be entered into by the Authority with respect to any project hereafter initiated costing more than $4,000 per family-dwelling-unit or more than $1,000 per room (excluding land, demolition, and non-dwelling facilities); except that in any city the population of which exceeds 500,000 any such contract may be entered into with respect to a project hereafter initiated costing not to exceed $5,000 per family-dwelling-unit or not to exceed $1,250 per room (excluding land, demolition, and non-dwelling facilities), if in the opinion of the Authority such higher family-dwelling-unit cost or cost per room is justified by reason of higher costs of labor and materials and other construction costs. With respect to housing projects on which construction is hereafter initiated, the Authority shall make loans, grants, and annual contributions only for such low-rent-housing projects as it finds are to be undertaken in such a manner (a) that such projects will not be of elaborate or expensive design or materials, and economy will be promoted both in construction and administration, and (b) that the average construction cost of the dwelling units (excluding land, demolition, and non-dwelling facilities) in any such project is not greater than the average construction cost of dwelling units currently produced by private enterprise, in the locality or metropolitan area concerned, under the legal building requirements applicable to the proposed site, and under labor standards not lower than those prescribed in this Act.

FINANCIAL PROVISIONS

SEC. 17. The Authority shall have a capital stock of $1,000,000, which shall be subscribed by the United States and paid by the Secretary of the Treasury out of any available funds. . . .

SEC. 20. (a) The Authority is authorized to issue obligations, in the form of notes, bonds, or otherwise, which it may sell to obtain funds for the purposes of this Act. The Authority may issue such obligations in an amount not to exceed $100,000,000 on or after the date of enactment of this Act, an additional amount not to exceed $200,000,000 on or after July 1, 1938, and an additional amount not to exceed $200,000,000 on or after July 1, 1939. Such obligations shall . . . bear such rates of interest not exceeding 4 per centum per annum.

(b) Such obligations shall be exempt, both as to principal and interest, from all taxation (except surtaxes, estate, inheritance, and gift taxes) now or hereafter imposed by the United States or by any State, county, municipality, or local taxing authority.

(c) Such obligations shall be fully and unconditionally guaranteed upon their face by the United States as to the payment of both interest and principal, and, in the event that the Authority shall be unable to make any such payment upon demand when due, payments shall be made to the holder by the Secretary of the Treasury with money hereby authorized to be appropriated for such purpose out of any money in the Treasury not otherwise appropriated.

SEC. 21. . . .
(d) Not more than 10 per centum of the funds provided for in this Act, either in the form of a loan, grant, or annual contribution, shall be expended within any one State.

From: *U.S. Statutes at Large.* 1937. Vol. 50, p. 888.

HATCH ACT, AUGUST 2, 1939

The 1939 Hatch Act was ostensibly written to keep politics out of public works and the civil service, by banning political activity by federal officeholders. In fact, the act was the product of anti–New Deal forces in Congress that feared that public works projects were being used to build Democratic Party constituencies.

An Act to prevent pernicious political activities.

Be it enacted, That it shall be unlawful for any person to intimidate, threaten, or coerce, or to attempt to intimidate, threaten, or coerce, any other person for the purpose of interfering with the right of such other person to vote or to vote as he may choose, or of causing such other person to vote for, or not to vote for, any candidate for the office of President, Vice President, Presidential elector, Member of the Senate, or Member of the House of Representatives at any election. . . .

SEC. 2. It shall be unlawful for any person employed in any administrative position by the United States, or by any department, independent agency, or other agency of the United States (including any corporation controlled by the United States or any agency thereof, and any corporation all of the capital stock of which is owned by the United States or any agency thereof), to use his official authority for the purpose of interfering with, or affecting the election or the nomination of any candidate for the office of President, Vice President, Presidential elector, Member of the Senate, or Member of the House of Representatives, Delegates or Commissioners from the Territories and insular possessions.

SEC. 3. It shall be unlawful for any person, directly or indirectly, to promise any employment, position, work, compensation, or other benefit, provided for or made possible in whole or in part by any Act of Congress, to any person as consideration, favor, or reward for any political activity or for the support of or opposition to any candidate or any political party in any election.

SEC. 4. Except as may be required by the provisions of subsection (b), section 9 of this Act, it shall be unlawful for any person to deprive, attempt to deprive, or threaten to deprive, by any means, any person of any employment, position, work, compensation, or other benefit provided for or made possible by any Act of Congress appropriating funds for work relief or relief purposes, on account of race, creed, color, or any political activity, support of, or opposition to any candidate or any political party in any election.

SEC. 5. It shall be unlawful for any person to solicit or receive or be in any manner concerned in soliciting or receiving any assessment, subscription, or contribution for any political purpose whatever from any person known by him to be entitled to or receiving compensation, employment, or other benefit provided for or made possible by any Act of Congress appropriating funds for work relief or relief purposes.

SEC. 6. It shall be unlawful for any person for political purposes to furnish or to disclose, or to aid or assist in furnishing or disclosing, any list or names of persons receiving compensation, employment, or benefits provided for or made possible by any Act of Congress appropriating, or authorizing the appropriation of, funds for work relief or relief purposes, to a political candidate, committee, campaign manager, or to any person for delivery to a political candidate, committee, or campaign manager, and it shall be unlawful for any person to receive any such list or names for political purposes.

SEC. 7. No part of any appropriation made by any Act, heretofore or hereafter enacted, making appropriations for work relief, relief, or otherwise to increase employment by providing loans and grants for public-works projects, shall be used for the purpose of, and no authority conferred by any such Act upon any person shall be exercised or administered for the purpose of, interfering with, restraining, or coercing any individual in the exercise of his right to vote at any election.

SEC. 8. Any person who violates any of the foregoing provisions of this Act upon conviction thereof shall be fined not more than $1,000 or imprisoned for not more than one year, or both.

SEC. 9. (a) It shall be unlawful for any person employed in the executive branch of the Federal Government, or any agency or department thereof, to use his official authority or influence for the purpose of interfering with an election or affecting the result thereof. No officer or employee in the executive branch of the Federal Government, or any agency or department thereof, shall take any active part in political management or in political campaigns. All such persons shall retain the right to vote as they may choose and to express their opinions on all political subjects. For the purposes of this section the term "officer" or "employee" shall not be construed to include (1) the President and Vice President of the United States, (2) persons whose compensation is paid from the appropriation for the office of the President; (3) heads and assistant heads of executive departments; (4) officers who are appointed by the President by and with the advice and consent of the Senate, and who determine policies to be pursued by the United States in its relations with foreign powers or in the Nation-wide administration of Federal laws.

(b) Any person violating the provisions of this section shall be immediately removed from the position or office held by him, and thereafter no part of the funds appropriated by any Act of Congress for such position or office shall be used to pay the compensation of such person.

SEC. 9A. (1) It shall be unlawful for any person employed in any capacity by any agency of the Federal Government, whose compensation, or any part thereof, is paid from funds authorized or appropriated by any Act of Congress, to have membership in any political party or organization which advocates the overthrow of our constitutional form of government in the United States.
(2) Any person violating the provisions of this section shall be immediately removed from the position or office held by him, and thereafter no part of the funds appropriated by any Act of Congress for such position or office shall be used to pay the compensation of such person.

SEC. 10. All provisions of this Act shall be in addition to, not in substitution for, of existing law.

SEC. 11. If any provision of this Act, or the application of such provision to any person or circumstance, is held invalid, the remainder of the Act, and the application of such provision to other persons or circumstances, shall not be affected thereby.

From: *U.S. Statutes at Large.* 1939. Vol. 53, p. 1147.

SECTION 2 Domestic Politics

Platforms, Speeches, and Press Conferences

HOOVER'S "RUGGED INDIVIDUALISM" SPEECH, OCTOBER 22, 1928

Herbert Hoover—Republican candidate for president in 1928—delivered this address in New York City shortly before the election. Much of Hoover and the Republican Party's philosophy was captured in the speech, including the fear that an overreliance on federal government programs would enervate the American people and the private sector. After three years of the Depression, when many Americans were crying out for Washington to do something about the economic slump, these words would come back to haunt Hoover when he ran for reelection against Franklin D. Roosevelt in 1932.

This campaign now draws near a close. The platforms of the two parties defining principles and offering solutions of various national problems have been presented and are being earnestly considered by our people. . . .

In my acceptance speech I endeavored to outline the spirit and ideals by which I would be guided in carrying that platform into administration. Tonight I will not deal with the multitude of issues which have been already well canvassed. I intend rather to discuss some of those more fundamental principles and ideals upon which I believe the government of the United States should be conducted. . . .

After the war, when the Republican party assumed administration of the country, we were faced with the problem of determination of the very nature of our national life. During one hundred and fifty years we have builded [sic] up a form of self-government and a social system which is peculiarly our own. It differs essentially from all others in the world. It is the American system. It is just as definite and positive a political and social system as has ever been developed on earth. It is founded upon a particular conception of self-government in which decentralized local responsibility is the very base. Further than this, it is founded upon the conception that only through ordered liberty, freedom, and equal opportunity to the individual will his initiative and enterprise spur on the march of progress. And in our insistence upon equality of opportunity has our system advanced beyond all the world.

During the war we necessarily turned to the government to solve every difficult economic problem. The government having absorbed every energy of our people for war, there was no other solution. For the preservation of the state the Federal Government became a centralized despotism which undertook unprecedented responsibilities, assumed autocratic powers, and took over the business of citizens. To a large degree we regimented our whole people temporarily into a socialistic state. However justified in time of war if continued in peace-time it would destroy not only our American system but with it our progress and freedom as well.

When the war closed, the most vital of all issues both in our own country and throughout the world was whether governments should continue their wartime ownership and operation of many instrumentalities of production and distribution. We were challenged with a peace-time choice between the American system of rugged individualism and a European philosophy of diametrically opposed doctrines—doctrines of paternalism and state socialism. The acceptance of these ideas would have meant the destruction of self-government through centralization of government. It would have meant the undermining of the individual initiative and enterprise through which our people have grown to unparalleled greatness.

The Republican Party from the beginning resolutely turned its face away from these ideas and these war practices. . . . When the Republican Party came into full power it went at once resolutely back to our fundamental conception of the state and the rights and responsibilities of the individual. Thereby it restored confidence and hope in the American people, it freed and stimulated enterprise, it restored the government to its position as an umpire instead of a player in the economic game. For these reasons the American people have gone forward in progress while the rest of the world has halted, and some countries have even gone backwards. If anyone will study the causes of retarded recuperation in Europe, he will find much of it due to stifling of private initiative on one hand, and overloading of the government with business on the other.

There has been revived in this campaign, however, a series of proposals which, if adopted, would be a long step toward the abandonment of our American system and a surrender to the destructive operation of governmental conduct of commercial business. Because the country is faced with difficulty and doubt over certain national problems—that is[,] prohibition, farm relief, and electrical power—our opponents propose that we must thrust government a long way into the businesses which give rise to these problems. In effect, they abandon the tenets of their own party and turn to state socialism as a solution for the difficulties presented by all three. It is proposed that we shall change from prohibition to the state purchase and sale of liquor. If their agricultural relief program means anything, it means that the government shall directly or indirectly buy and sell and fix prices of agricultural products. And we are to go into the hydroelectric power business. In other words, we are confronted with a huge program of government in business.

There is, therefore, submitted to the American people a question of fundamental principle. That is: shall we depart from the principles of our American political and economic system, upon which we have advanced beyond all the rest of the world, in order to adopt methods based on principles destructive of its very foundations? And I wish to emphasize the seriousness of these proposals. I wish to make my position clear; for this goes to the very roots of American life and progress.

I should like to state to you the effect that this projection of government in business would have upon our system of self-government and our economic system. That effect would reach to the daily life of every man and woman. It would impair the very basis of liberty and freedom not only for those left outside the fold of expanded bureaucracy but for those embraced within it.

Let us first see the effect upon self-government. When the Federal Government undertakes to go into commercial business it must at once set up the organization and administration of that business, and it immediately finds itself in a labyrinth, every alley of which leads to the destruction of self-government.

Commercial business requires a concentration of responsibility. Self-government requires decentralization and many checks and balances to safeguard liberty. Our Government to succeed in business would need to become in effect a despotism. There at once begins the destruction of self-government.

It is a false liberalism that interprets itself into the government operation of commercial business. Every step of bureaucratizing of the business of our country poisons the very roots of liberalism—that is, political

equality, free speech, free assembly, free press, and equality of opportunity. It is the road not to more liberty, but to less liberty. Liberalism should be found not striving to spread bureaucracy but striving to set bounds to it. True liberalism seeks all legitimate freedom first in the confident belief that without such freedom the pursuit of all other blessings and benefits is vain. That belief is the foundation of all American progress, political as well as economic.

Liberalism is a force truly of the spirit, a force proceeding from the deep realization that economic freedom cannot be sacrificed if political freedom is to be preserved. Even if Governmental conduct of business could give us more efficiency instead of less efficiency, the fundamental objection to it would remain unaltered and unabated. It would destroy political equality. It would increase rather than decrease abuse and corruption. It would stifle initiative and invention. It would undermine the development of leadership. It would cramp and cripple the mental and spiritual energies of our people. It would extinguish equality and opportunity. It would dry up the spirit of liberty and progress. For these reasons primarily it must be resisted. For a hundred and fifty years liberalism has found its true spirit in the American system, not in the European systems.

I do not wish to be misunderstood in this statement. I am defining a general policy. It does not mean that our government is to part with one iota of its national resources without complete protection to the public interest. I have already stated that where the government is engaged in public works for purposes of flood control, of navigation, of irrigation, of scientific research or national defense, or in pioneering a new art, it will at times necessarily produce power or commodities as a by-product. But they must be a by-product of the major purpose, not the major purpose itself.

Nor do I wish to be misinterpreted as believing that the United States is free-for-all and devil-take-the-hindmost. The very essence of equality of opportunity and of American individualism is that there shall be no domination by any group or combination in this republic, whether it be business or political. On the contrary, it demands economic justice as well as political and social justice. It is no system of laissez faire.

I feel deeply on this subject because during the war I had some practical experience with governmental operation and control. I have witnessed not only at home but abroad the many failures of government in business. I have seen its tyrannies, its injustices, its destructions of self-government, its undermining of the very instincts which carry our people forward to progress. I have witnessed the lack of advance, the lowered standards of living, the depressed spirits of people working under such a system. My objection is based not upon theory or upon a failure to recognize wrong or abuse, but I know the adoption of such methods would strike at the very roots of American life and would destroy the very basis of American progress.

Our people have the right to know whether we can continue to solve our great problems without abandonment of our American system. I know we can. . . .

And what have been the results of the American system? Our country has become the land of opportunity to those born without inheritance, not merely because of the wealth of its resources and industry but because of this freedom of initiative and enterprise. Russia has natural resources equal to ours. Her people are equally industrious, but she has not had the blessings of one hundred and fifty years of our form of government and our social system.

By adherence to the principles of decentralized self-government, ordered liberty, equal opportunity, and freedom to the individual, our American experi-

ment in human welfare has yielded a degree of well-being unparalleled in all the world. It has come nearer to the abolition of poverty, to the abolition of fear of want, than humanity has ever reached before. Progress of the past seven years is the proof of it. This alone furnishes the answer to our opponents, who ask us to introduce destructive elements into the system by which this has been accomplished. . . .

I have endeavored to present to you that the greatness of America has grown out of a political and social system and a method of control of economic forces distinctly its own—our American system—which has carried this great experiment in human welfare farther than ever before in all history. We are nearer today to the ideal of the abolition of poverty and fear from the lives of men and women than ever before in any land. And I again repeat that the departure from our American system by injecting principles destructive to it which our opponents propose, will jeopardize the very liberty and freedom of our people, and will destroy equality of opportunity not alone to ourselves but to our children. . . .

From: *Hoover, Herbert: The New Day Campaign Speeches of Herbert Hoover*, p. 149. Stanford CA: University Press, 1928.

HOOVER'S PRESS CONFERENCE WARNING AGAINST DEFICIT SPENDING, FEBRUARY 25, 1930

Like many other politicians and economists of his generation, President Herbert Hoover feared that deficit spending by the government would only exacerbate the economic depression. Unlike John Maynard Keynes and later economic thinkers, who argued that pump-priming was essential to counter the effects of deflation and unemployment, Hoover worried that—by borrowing through deficit spending—the government would compete with the private sector for scarce capital. Below is a press conference statement—with a press handout—Hoover offered on February 25, 1930.

The President said:

It should be understood that the unprecedented drive now in progress for new legislation and for expansion of established services which increase expenditures beyond the Budget, only in a small percent originates

with members of Congress or heads of Government Departments. It originates from different sections of the country itself and from various groups and organizations each vigorously supporting their own projects. Many of these projects are worthy and no doubt can and should be undertaken some time over future years, especially when funds are free by completion of legislation already adopted.

I hope that the people at home will realize that the Government cannot undertake every worthy social, economic, military and naval expansion, increases in pay to Government employees, expanded pension systems, or public improvement project—and will support the Members of Congress in their cooperation with the Administration to hold down these new proposals for additional expenditures. We have enough resources to take care of the Budget, and such necessities as marginal cases of disability among veterans, and the speeding up of public works that we have undertaken to assist employment, and some proposals of lesser importance, but this is not the time for general expansion of public expenditure.

[Accompanying statement of the Director of the Budget giving list of excessive projects]

The Director of the Budget, under instruction of the President, has prepared a survey of the various projects which have been presented to Congress and the Administration, which will involve additional expenditure beyond the present authorizations and beyond the present Budget.

These demands are being made upon Congress and the Administration from different sections of the country and from different interested groups. The amounts below are a summary of these projects and are given in the amount of additional expenditure that would be imposed upon the Federal Budget during the first year of their operation. These are not the totals projected which are very much larger, but simply the annual addition to the Budget. Many of the items would be permanent and increasing annually:

Public Roads	$350,000,000
Rivers and Harbors	35,000,000
Compensation to property owners for rights of way in flood control	100,000,000

Loans to Levee Districts	100,000,000
Protection to Forests	10,000,000
Eradication of Pests	20,000,000
Expansion of Agricultural Services	20,000,000
Scientific Research	5,000,000
Development of Columbia River	45,000,000
Reclamation Service	100,000,000
National Parks and Memorials	50,000,000
Indian Service	5,000,000
Naval Construction	50,000,000
Military Aviation	25,000,000
Increased Army and Navy Pay	80,000,000
Army-Navy Hospital Barracks and Posts	15,000,000
Employment Services	5,000,000
Disaster Relief	15,000,000
Increase in Spanish War Veterans Service	45,000,000
Increase in Civil War Veterans Service	40,000,000
Increase in World War Veterans Service	400,000,000
Increase Civil Service Pensions	20,000,000
Increase Civil Service Pay	100,000,000
Education	100,000,000
	$1,735,000,000

The present Federal income is approximately $4,000,000,000 per annum and such a program would imply an increase in taxes of 40%.

In addition to the above list, other projects are being urged but are not regarded as imminent, which would impose a further expenditure of fully $1,500,000,000 per annum.

From: William Starr Myers, ed. *The State Papers and Other Public Writings of Herbert Hoover.* Garden City, NY: Doubleday, Doran and Company, 1934.

HOOVER'S LINCOLN BIRTHDAY ADDRESS, FEBRUARY 12, 1931

Like his successor Franklin D. Roosevelt, President Herbert Hoover used the radio to convey messages to the American people, though most historians believe that he was not nearly as effective in manipulating the new medium. In this address from February 1931, Hoover explains his philosophy of relief, arguing that the federal government role should be minimal. Too much reliance on the federal government would, he said, weaken the morale and enterprise of the American people.

By the magic of the radio I am able to address several hundred public gatherings called this evening through-

out our country in celebration of the birth of Abraham Lincoln.

It is appropriate that I should speak from this room in the White House where Lincoln strived and accomplished his great service to our country.

His invisible presence dominates these halls, ever recalling that infinite patience and that indomitable will which fought and won the fight for those firmer foundations and greater strength to government by the people. From these windows he looked out upon that great granite shaft which was then in construction to mark the country's eternal tribute to the courage and uncompromising strength of the founder of this Union of states.

Here are the very chairs in which he meditated upon his problems. Above the mantelpiece hangs his portrait with his Cabinet, and upon this fireplace is written:

"In this room Abraham Lincoln signed the Emancipation Proclamation of January 1, 1863, whereby 4,000,000 slaves were given their freedom and slavery forever prohibited in these United States."

It was here that he toiled by day and by night that the Union created by the fathers might be preserved and that slavery might be ended.

Most of the business of this room in Lincoln's time was concerned with the conduct of war against destructive forces. From here he could oft hear the sound of approaching cannon, and yet the thought that he should desert his place, this city and this house, never entered into his considerations. Lincoln was a builder in an epoch of destruction. It was his assignment by Providence to restore the national edifice, so badly shattered in its social and economic structure that it had well-nigh failed. His undying idealism and inflexible resolve builded [sic] a new temple of the national soul in which our succeeding generations have since dwelt secure and free and of a richer life.

And if Lincoln could today resurvey the scene of his country he would find a union more solidly knit and more resolute in its common purpose than ever in its history. He would find the states of the South recovered from the wounds of war, inspired by the splendid leadership of a new generation to a brilliant renaissance of industry and culture.

He would indeed find the consummation of that great moving appeal of his inaugural in which he said: "The mystic chords of memory stretching from every battlefield and patriot grave to every living heart and hearthstone all over this broad land will yet swell the chorus of the Union when again touched, as surely they will be, by the better angels of our nature." It was indeed a great prophecy.

If Lincoln were living, he would find that this race of liberated slaves, starting a new life without a shred but the clothes in which they stood, without education, without organization, has today by its own endeavors progressed to an amazingly high level of self-reliance and well-being. To Lincoln it would have been incredible that within a lifetime the millions of children of these slaves would be graduating from the public schools and colleges, that the race could have built [sic] itself homes and accumulated itself a wealth in lands and savings; that it should have carried on with success every calling and profession in our country.

While the dramatic period of Lincoln's life was engrossed with these tremendous problems, yet he was a man of many interests. He was a believer in party government. He realized, as we also must realize, that fundamentally our whole selfgovernment is conceived and born of majority rule, and to enable the majority to express itself we must have party organization. Lincoln led in founding the Republican Party and he gloried in his party. His tradition has dominated it to this day. It was and is a party of responsibility; it was and is a party of the Constitution.

While many of the issues of that time are dead and gone, some of our present problems were equally vivid in his day. You will find Lincoln addressing the country in strong and urgent support of the protective tariff with vivid declamation against the party opposing that policy. You will find him advocating Federal Government aid in internal development of waterways, rivers and harbors, and transportation. You will find him pounding at the public mind against nullification and for adherence to constitutional processes of government. No stronger statement has ever been made than that of Lincoln upon obedience to law as the very foundation of our Republic.

In Lincoln's day the dominant problem in our form of government turned upon the issue of states rights. Though less pregnant with disaster, the dominant problem today in our form of government turns in large degree upon the issue of the relationship of Federal, state, and local government responsibilities. We are faced with unceasing agitation that the Federal Government shall assume new financial burdens, that it shall undertake increased burdens in regulation of abuses and in the prosecution of crime.

It is true that since Lincoln's time many forces have swept across state borders and have become more potent than the state or local community can deal with alone either financially or by jurisdiction. Our concept of Federal, state, and local responsibilities is possible of no unchangeable definitions and it must shift with the moving forces in the Nation, but the time has come when we must have more national consideration and decision of the part which each shall assume in these responsibilities.

The Federal Government has assumed many new responsibilities since Lincoln's time, and will probably assume more in the future when the states and local communities can not alone cure abuse or bear the entire cost of national programs, but there is an essential principle that should be maintained in these matters. I am convinced that where Federal action is essential then in most cases it should limit its responsibilities to supplement the states and local communities, and that it should not assume the major role or the entire responsibility, in replacement of the states or local government. To do otherwise threatens the whole foundation of local government, which is the very basis of self-government.

The moment responsibilities of any community, particularly in economic and social questions, are shifted from any part of the Nation to Washington, then that community has subjected itself to a remote bureaucracy with its minimum of understanding and of sympathy. It has lost a large part of its voice and its control of its own destiny. Under Federal control the varied conditions of life in our country are forced into standard molds, with all their limitations upon life, either of the individual or the community. Where people divest themselves of local government responsibilities they at once lay the foundation for the destruction of their liberties.

And buried in this problem lies something even deeper. The whole of our governmental machinery was devised for the purpose that through ordered liberty we give incentive and equality of opportunity to every individual to rise to that highest achievement of which he is capable. At once when government is centralized there arises a limitation upon the liberty of the individual and a restriction of individual opportunity. The true growth of the Nation is the growth of character in its citizens. The spread of government destroys initiative and thus destroys character. Character is made in the community as well as in the individual by assuming responsibilities, not by escape from them. Carried to its logical extreme, all this shouldering of individual and community responsibility upon the Government can lead but to the superstate where every man becomes the servant of the State and real liberty is lost. Such was not the government that Lincoln sought to build.

There is an entirely different avenue by which we may both resist this drift to centralized government and at the same time meet a multitude of problems. That is to strengthen in the Nation a sense and an organization of self-help and cooperation to solve as many problems as possible outside of government. We are today passing through a critical test in such a problem arising from the economic depression.

Due to lack of caution in business and to the impact of forces from an outside world, one-half of which is involved in social and political revolution, the march of our prosperity has been retarded. We are projected into temporary unemployment, losses, and hardships. In a Nation rich in resources, many people were faced with hunger and cold through no fault of their own. Our national resources are not only material supplies and material wealth but a spiritual and moral wealth in kindliness, in compassion, in a sense of obligation of neighbor to neighbor and a realization of responsibility by industry, by business, and the community for its social security and its social welfare.

The evidence of our ability to solve great problems outside of Government action and the degree of moral strength with which we emerge from this period will be determined by whether the individuals and the local communities continue to meet their responsibilities.

Throughout this depression I have insisted upon organization of these forces through industry, through local government and through charity, that they should meet this crisis by their own initiative, by the assumption of their own responsibilities. The Federal Government has sought to do its part by example in the expansion of employment, by affording credit to drought sufferers for rehabilitation, and by cooperation with the community, and thus to avoid the opiates of Government charity and the stifling of our national spirit of mutual self-help.

We can take courage and pride in the effective work of thousands of voluntary organizations for provision of employment, for relief of distress, that have sprung up over the entire Nation. Industry and business have recognized a social obligation to their employees as never before. The State and local governments are being helpful. The people are themselves succeeding in this task. Never before in a great depression has there been so systematic a protection against distress; never before has there been so little social disorder; never before has there been such an outpouring of the spirit of self-sacrifice and of service.

The ever-growing complexity of modern life, with its train of evermore perplexing and difficult problems, is a challenge to our individual characters and to our devotion to our ideals. The resourcefulness of America when challenged has never failed. Success is not gained by leaning upon government to solve all the problems before us. That way leads to enervation of will and destruction of character. Victory over this depression and over our other difficulties will be won by the resolution of our people to fight their own battles in their own communities, by stimulating their ingenuity to solve their own problems, by taking new courage to be masters of their own destiny in the struggle of life. This is not the easy way, but it is the American way. And it was Lincoln's way.

The ultimate goal of the American social ideal is equality of opportunity and individual initiative. These are not born of bureaucracy. This ideal is the expression of the spirit of our people. This ideal obtained at the birth of the Republic. It was the ideal of Lincoln. It is the ideal upon which the Nation has risen to unparalleled greatness.

We are going through a period when character and courage are on trial, and where the very faith that is within us is under test. Our people are meeting this test. And they are doing more than the immediate task of the day. They are maintaining the ideals of our American system. By their devotion to these ideals we shall come out of these times stronger in character, in courage, and in faith.

From: William Starr Myers, ed. *The State Papers and Other Public Writings of Herbert Hoover.* Garden City, NY: Doubleday, Doran and Company, 1934.

DEMOCRATIC PARTY PLATFORM, 1932

The Democratic Party platform for the election year 1932 was essentially a vague and conservative document, reflecting the predilections of the party leaders and the party's presidential nominee Franklin D. Roosevelt. The vagueness reflected the Roosevelt campaign of 1932 which essentially promised action to deal with the economic problems facing the country, but little in the way of specific programs. At the same time, the platform argues for a sound currency and an insistence that all international debt obligations to the United States be paid—positions that Republicans supported as well. More liberal economic thinkers believed that both positions were likely to prolong the Depression. Still, there were some differences with the Republicans, most notably, a call for more government regulation of the economy and the repeal of the anti-alcohol Volstead act.

In this time of unprecedented economic and social distress the Democratic Party declares its conviction that the chief causes of this condition were the disastrous policies pursued by our government since the World War, of economic isolation, fostering the merger of competitive businesses into monopolies and encouraging the indefensible expansion and contraction of credit for private profit at the expense of the public.

Those who were responsible for these policies have abandoned the ideals on which the war was won and thrown away the fruits of victory, thus rejecting the greatest opportunity in history to bring peace, prosperity, and happiness to our people and to the world.

They have ruined our foreign trade, destroyed the values of our commodities and products, crippled our banking system, robbed millions of our people of their life savings, and thrown millions more out of work, produced wide-spread poverty and brought the government to a state of financial distress unprecedented in time of peace.

The only hope for improving present conditions, restoring employment, affording permanent relief to the people, and bringing the nation back to the proud position of domestic happiness and of financial, industrial, agricultural and commercial leadership in the world lies in a drastic change in economic governmental policies.

We believe that a party platform is a covenant with the people to be faithfully kept by the party when entrusted with power, and that the people are entitled to know in plain words the terms of the contract to which they are asked to subscribe. We hereby declare this to be the platform of the Democratic Party:

The Democratic Party solemnly promises by appropriate action to put into effect the principles, policies, and reforms herein advocated, and to eradicate the policies, methods, and practices condemned. We advocate an immediate and drastic reduction of governmental expenditures by abolishing useless commissions and offices, consolidating departments and bureaus, and eliminating extravagance to accomplish a saving of not less than twenty-five per cent in the cost of the Federal Government. And we call upon the Democratic Party in the states to make a zealous effort to achieve a proportionate result.

We favor maintenance of the national credit by a federal budget annually balanced on the basis of accurate executive estimates within revenues, raised by a system of taxation levied on the principle of ability to pay.

We advocate a sound currency to be preserved at all hazards and an international monetary conference called on the invitation of our government to consider the rehabilitation of silver and related questions.

We advocate a competitive tariff for revenue with a fact-finding tariff commission free from executive interference, reciprocal tariff agreements with other nations, and an international economic conference designed to restore international trade and facilitate exchange.

We advocate the extension of federal credit to the states to provide unemployment relief wherever the diminishing resources of the states makes it impossible for them to provide for the needy; expansion of the federal program of necessary and useful construction effected with a public interest, such as adequate flood control and waterways.

We advocate the spread of employment by a substantial reduction in the hours of labor, the encouragement of the shorter week by applying that principle in government service; we advocate advance planning of public works.

We advocate unemployment and old-age insurance under state laws.

We favor the restoration of agriculture, the nation's basic industry; better financing of farm mortgages through recognized farm bank agencies at low rates of interest on an amortization plan, giving preference to credits for the redemption of farms and homes sold under foreclosure.

Extension and development of the Farm Cooperative movement and effective control of crop surpluses so that our farmers may have the full benefit of the domestic market.

The enactment of every constitutional measure that will aid the farmers to receive for their basic farm commodities prices in excess of cost.

We advocate a Navy and an Army adequate for national defense, based on a survey of all facts affecting the existing establishments, that the people in time of peace may not be burdened by an expenditure fast approaching a billion dollars annually.

We advocate strengthening and impartial enforcement of the anti-trust laws, to prevent monopoly and unfair trade practices, and revision thereof for the better protection of labor and the small producer and distributor.

The conservation, development, and use of the nation's water power in the public interest.

The removal of government from all fields of private enterprise except where necessary to develop public works and natural resources in the common interest.

We advocate protection of the investing public by requiring to be filed with the government and carried in advertisements of all offerings of foreign and domestic stocks and bonds true information as to bonuses, commissions, principal invested, and interests of the sellers.

Regulation to the full extent of federal power, of:

(a) Holding companies which sell securities in interstate commerce;

(b) Rates of utilities companies operating across state lines;

(c) Exchanges in securities and commodities.

We advocate quicker methods of realizing on assets for the relief of depositors of suspended banks, and a more rigid supervision of national banks for the protection of depositors and the prevention of the use of their moneys in speculation to the detriment of local credits.

The severance of affiliated security companies from, and the divorce of the investment banking business from, commercial banks, and further restriction of federal reserve banks in permitting the use of federal reserve facilities for speculative purposes.

We advocate the full measure of justice and generosity for all war veterans who have suffered disability or disease caused by or resulting from actual service in time of war and for their dependents.

We advocate a firm foreign policy, including peace with all the world and the settlement of international disputes by arbitration; no interference in the internal affairs of other nations; and sanctity of treaties and the maintenance of good faith and of good will in financial obligations; adherence to the World Court with appending reservations; the Pact of Paris abolishing war as an instrument of national policy, to be made effective by provisions for consultation and conference in case of threatened violations of treaties.

International agreements for reduction of armaments and cooperation with nations of the Western Hemisphere to maintain the spirit of the Monroe Doctrine.

We oppose cancellation of the debts owing to the United States by foreign nations.

Independence for the Philippines; ultimate statehood for Puerto Rico.

The employment of American citizens in the operation of the Panama Canal.

Simplification of legal procedure and reorganization of the judicial system to make the attainment of justice speedy, certain, and at less cost.

Continuous publicity of political contributions and expenditures; strengthening of the Corrupt Practices Act and severe penalties for misappropriation of campaign funds.

We advocate the repeal of the Eighteenth Amendment. To effect such repeal we demand that the Congress immediately propose a Constitutional Amendment to truly represent the conventions in the states called to act solely on that proposal; we urge the enactment of such measures by the several states as will actually promote temperance, effectively prevent the return of the saloon, and bring the liquor traffic into the open under complete supervision and control by the states.

We demand that the Federal Government effectively exercise its power to enable the states to protect themselves against importation of intoxicating liquors in violation of their laws.

Pending repeal, we favor immediate modification of the Volstead Act; to legalize the manufacture and sale of beer and other beverages of such alcoholic content as is permissible under the Constitution and to provide therefrom a proper and needed revenue.

We condemn the improper and excessive use of money in political activities.

We condemn paid lobbies of special interests to influence members of Congress and other public servants by personal contact.

We condemn action and utterances of high public officials designed to influence stock exchange prices.

We condemn the open and covert resistance of administrative officials to every effort made by Congressional Committees to curtail the extravagant expenditures of the government and to revoke improvident subsidies granted to favorite interests.

We condemn the extravagance of the Farm Board, its disastrous action which made the government a speculator in farm products, and the unsound policy of restricting agricultural products to the demands of domestic markets.

We condemn the usurpation of power by the State Department in assuming to pass upon foreign securities offered by international bankers as a result of which billions of dollars in questionable bonds have been sold to the public upon the implied approval of the Federal Government.

And in conclusion, to accomplish these purposes and to recover economic liberty, we pledge the nominees of this convention the best efforts of a great party whose founder announced the doctrine which guides us now in the hour of our country's need: equal rights to all; special privilege to none.

From: George Thomas Kurian, ed. *The Encyclopedia of the Democratic Party.* Armonk, NY: M. E. Sharpe, 1997.

ROOSEVELT'S NEW DEAL SPEECH TO DEMOCRATIC CONVENTION, JULY 2, 1932

When the Democrats convened in Chicago for their 1932 convention, they were optimistic about their electoral chances. Out of power—both in the White House and Congress—for twelve years, they believed that both the tough economic times and their candidate, New York governor Franklin D. Roosevelt, promised them victory. Roosevelt's acceptance speech—full of his characteristic optimism—buoyed Democratic spirits even more.

I appreciate your willingness after these six arduous days to remain here, for I know well the sleepless hours which you and I have had. I regret that I am late, but I have no control over the winds of Heaven and could only be thankful for my Navy training.

The appearance before a National Convention of its nominee for President, to be formally notified of his selection, is unprecedented and unusual, but these are unprecedented and unusual times. I have started out on the tasks that lie ahead by breaking the absurd traditions that the candidate should remain in professed ignorance of what has happened for weeks until he is formally notified of that event many weeks later.

My friends, may this be the symbol of my intention to be honest and to avoid all hypocrisy or sham, to avoid all silly shutting of the eyes to the truth in this campaign. You have nominated me and I know it, and I am here to thank you for the honor.

Let it also be symbolic that in so doing I broke traditions. Let it be from now on the task of our Party to break foolish traditions. We will break foolish traditions and leave it to the Republican leadership, far more skilled in that art, to break promises.

Let us now and here highly resolve to resume the country's interrupted march along the path of real progress, of real justice, of real equality for all of our citizens, great and small. Our indomitable leader in that interrupted march is no longer with us, but there still survives today his spirit. Many of his captains, thank

God, are still with us, to give us wise counsel. Let us feel that in everything we do there still lives with us, if not the body, the great indomitable, unquenchable, progressive soul of our Commander-in-Chief, Woodrow Wilson.

I have many things on which I want to make my position clear at the earliest possible moment in this campaign. That admirable document, the platform which you have adopted, is clear. I accept it one hundred per cent.

And you can accept my pledge that I will leave no doubt or ambiguity on where I stand on any question of moment in this campaign.

As we enter this new battle, let us keep always present with us some of the ideals of the Party: The fact that the Democratic Party by tradition and by the continuing logic of history, past and present, is the bearer of liberalism and of progress and at the same time of safety to our institutions. And if this appeal fails, remember well, my friends, that a resentment against the failure of Republican leadership—and note well that in this campaign I shall not use the words "Republican Party," but I shall use, day in and day out, the words, "Republican leadership"—the failure of Republican leaders to solve our troubles may degenerate into unreasoning radicalism.

The great social phenomenon of this depression, unlike others before it, is that it has produced but a few of the disorderly manifestations that too often attend upon such times.

Wild radicalism has made few converts, and the greatest tribute that I can pay to my countrymen is that in these days of crushing want there persists an orderly and hopeful spirit on the part of the millions of our people who have suffered so much. To fail to offer them a new chance is not only to betray their hopes but to misunderstand their patience.

To meet by reaction that danger of radicalism is to invite disaster. Reaction is no barrier to the radical. It is a challenge, a provocation. The way to meet that danger is to offer a workable program of reconstruction, and the party to offer it is the party with clean hands. This, and this only, is a proper protection against blind reaction on the one hand and an improvised, hit-or-miss, irresponsible opportunism on the other.

There are two ways of viewing the Government's duty in matters affecting economic and social life. The first sees to it that a favored few are helped and hopes that some of their prosperity will leak through, sift through, to labor, to the farmer, to the small business man. That theory belongs to the party of Toryism and

I had hoped that most of the Tories left this country in 1776.

But it is not and never will be the theory of the Democratic Party. This is no time for fear, for reaction or for timidity. Here and now I invite those nominal Republicans who find that their conscience cannot be squared with the groping and the failure of their party leaders to join hands with us; here and now, in equal measure, I warn those nominal Democrats who squint at the future with their faces turned toward the past, and who feel no responsibility to the demands of the new time, that they are out of step with their Party.

Yes, the people of this country want a genuine choice this year, not a choice between two names for the same reactionary doctrine. Ours must be a party of liberal thought, of planned action, of enlightened international outlook, and of the greatest good to the greatest number of our citizens.

Now it is inevitable—and the choice is that of the times—it is inevitable that the main issue of this campaign should revolve about the clear fact of our economic condition, a depression so deep that it is without precedent in modern history. It will not do merely to state, as do Republican leaders to explain their broken promises of continued inaction, that the depression is worldwide. That was not their explanation of the apparent prosperity of 1918. The people will not forget the claim made by them then that prosperity was only a domestic product manufactured by a Republican President and a Republican Congress. If they claim paternity for the one they cannot deny paternity for the other.

I cannot take up all the problems today. I want to touch on a few that are vital. Let us look a little at the recent history and the simple economics, the kind of economics that you and I and the average man and woman talk.

In the years before 1929 we know that this country had completed a vast cycle of building and inflation; for ten years we expanded on the theory of repairing the wastes of the War, but actually expanding far beyond that, and also beyond our natural and normal growth. Now it is worth remembering, and the cold figures of finance prove it, that during that time there was little or no drop in the prices that the consumer had to pay, although those same figures proved that the cost of production fell very greatly; corporate profit resulting from this period was enormous, at the same time little of that profit was devoted to the reduction of prices. The consumer was forgotten. Very little of it went into increased wages; the worker was forgotten, and by no means an adequate proportion was even paid out in dividends, the stockholder was forgotten. And, incidentally, very little of it was taken by taxation to the beneficent Government of those years.

What was the result? Enormous corporate surpluses piled up—the most stupendous in history. Where, under the spell of delirious speculation, did those surpluses go? Let us talk economics that the figures prove and that we can understand. Why, they went chiefly in two directions: first, into new and unnecessary plants which now stand stark and idle; and second, into the callmoney [speculative money] market of Wall Street, either directly by the corporations, or indirectly through the banks. Those are the facts. Why blink at them?

Then came the crash. You know the story. Surpluses invested in unnecessary plants became idle. Men lost their jobs; purchasing power dried up; banks became frightened and started calling loans. Those who had money were afraid to part with it. Credit contracted. Industry stopped. Commerce declined, and unemployment mounted.

And there we are today.

Translate that into human terms. See how the events of the past three years have come home to specific groups of people: first, the group dependent on industry; second, the group dependent on agriculture; third, and made up in large part of members of the first two groups, the people who are called "small investors and depositors." In fact, the strongest possible tie between the first two groups, agriculture and industry, is the fact that the savings and to a degree the security of both are tied together in that third group—the credit structure of the Nation.

Never in history have the interests of all the people been so united in a single economic problem. Picture to yourself, for instance, the great groups of property owned by millions of our citizens, represented by credits issued in the form of bonds and mortgages—Government bonds of all kinds, Federal, State, county, municipal; bonds of industrial companies, of utility companies; mortgages on real estate in farms and cities, and finally the vast investments of the Nation in the railroads. What is the measure of the security of each of those groups? We know well that in our complicated, interrelated credit structure if any one of these credit groups collapses they may all collapse. Danger to one is danger to all.

How, I ask, has the present Administration in Washington treated the interrelationship of these credit groups? The answer is clear: It has not recognized that interrelationship existed at all. Why, the Nation asks, has Washington failed to understand that all of these groups, each and every one, the top of the pyramid and the bottom of the pyramid, must be considered together, that each and every one of them is dependent on every other; each and every one of them affecting the whole financial fabric?

Statesmanship and vision, my friends, require relief to all at the same time.

Just one word or two on taxes, the taxes that all of us pay toward the cost of Government of all kinds.

I know something of taxes. For three long years I have been going up and down this country preaching that Government—Federal and State and local—costs too much. I shall not stop that preaching. As an immediate program of action we must abolish useless offices. We must eliminate unnecessary functions of Government—functions, in fact, that are not definitely essential to the continuance of Government. We must merge, we must consolidate subdivisions of Government, and, like the private citizen, give up luxuries which we can no longer afford.

By our example at Washington itself, we shall have the opportunity of pointing the way of economy to local government, for let us remember well that out of every tax dollar in the average State in this Nation, forty cents enter the treasury in Washington, D.C., ten or twelve cents only go to the State capitals, and forty-eight cents are consumed by the costs of local government in counties and cities and towns.

I propose to you, my friends, and through you, that Government of all kinds, big and little, be made solvent and that the example be set by the President of the United States and his Cabinet.

And talking about setting a definite example, I congratulate this convention for having had the courage fearlessly to write into its declaration of principles what an overwhelming majority here assembled really thinks about the Eighteenth Amendment. This convention wants repeal. Your candidate wants repeal. And I am confident that the United States of America wants repeal.

Two years ago the platform on which I ran for Governor the second time contained substantially the same provision. The overwhelming sentiment of the people of my State, as shown by the vote of that year, extends, I know, to the people of many of the other States. I say to you now that from this date on the Eighteenth Amendment is doomed. When that happens, we as Democrats must and will, rightly and morally, enable the States to protect themselves against the importation of intoxicating liquor where such importation may violate their State laws. We must rightly and morally prevent the return of the saloon.

To go back to this dry subject of finance, because it all ties in together—the Eighteenth Amendment has something to do with finance, too—in a comprehensive planning for the reconstruction of the great credit groups, including Government credit, I list an important place for that prize statement of principle in the platform here adopted calling for the letting in of the light of day on issues of securities, foreign and domestic, which are offered for sale to the investing public.

My friends, you and I as common-sense citizens know that it would help to protect the savings of the Country from the dishonesty of crooks and from the lack of honor of some men in high financial places. Publicity is the enemy of crookedness.

And now one word about unemployment, and incidentally about agriculture. I have favored the use of certain types of public works as a further emergency means of stimulating employment and the issuance of bonds to pay for such public works, but I have pointed out that no economic end is served if we merely build without building for a necessary purpose. Such works, of course, should insofar as possible be self-sustaining if they are to be financed by the issuing of bonds. So as to spread the [work] of all kinds as widely as possible, we must take definite steps to shorten the working day and the working week.

Let us use common sense and business sense. Just as one example, we know that a very hopeful and immediate means of relief, both for the unemployed and for agriculture, will come from a wide plan of the converting of many millions of acres of marginal and unused land into timberland through reforestation. There are tens of millions of acres east of the Mississippi River alone in abandoned farms, in cut-over land, now growing up in worthless brush. Why, every European Nation has a definite land policy, and has had one for generations. We have none. Having none, we face a future of soil erosion and timber famine. It is clear that economic foresight and immediate employment march hand in hand in the call for the reforestation of these vast areas. In so doing, employment can be given to a million men. That is the kind of public work that is self-sustaining, and therefore capable of being financed by the issuance of bonds which are made secure by the fact that the growth of tremendous crops will provide adequate security for the investment.

Yes, I have a very definite program for providing employment by that means. I have done it, and I am doing it today in the State of New York. I know that the Democratic Party can do it successfully in the Nation. That will put men to work, and that is an example of the action that we are going to have.

Now as a further aid to agriculture, we know perfectly well—but have we come out and said so clearly and distinctly?—we should repeal immediately those provisions of law that compel the Federal Government to go into the market to purchase, to sell, to speculate in farm products in a futile attempt to reduce farm surpluses. And [the Republicans] are the people who are talking of keeping Government out of business. The practical way to help the farmer is by an arrangement that will, in addition to lightening some of the impoverishing burdens from his back, do something toward the reduction of the surpluses of staple commodities that hang on the market. It should be our aim to add to the world prices of staple products the amount of a reasonable tariff protection, to give agriculture the same protection that industry has today.

And in exchange for this immediately increased return I am sure that the farmers of this Nation would agree ultimately to such planning of their production as would reduce the surpluses and make it unnecessary in later years to depend on dumping those surpluses abroad in order to support domestic prices. That result has been accomplished in other Nations; why not in America, too?

Farm leaders and farm economists, generally, agree that a plan based on that principle is a desirable first step in the reconstruction of agriculture. It does not in itself furnish a complete program, but it will serve in great measure in the long run to remove the pall of a surplus without the continued perpetual threat of world dumping. Final voluntary reduction of surplus is a part of our objective, but the long continuance and the present burden of existing surpluses make it necessary to repair great damage of the present by immediate emergency measures.

Such a plan as that, my friends, does not cost the Government any money, nor does it keep the Government in business or in speculation.

As to the actual wording of a bill, I believe that the Democratic Party stands ready to be guided by whatever the responsible farm groups themselves agree on. That is a principle that is sound; and again I ask for action.

One more word about the farmer, and I know that every delegate in this hall who lives in the city knows why I lay emphasis on the farmer. It is because one-half of our population, over fifty million people, are dependent on agriculture; and, my friends, if those fifty million people have no money, no cash, to buy what is produced in the city, the city suffers to an equal or greater extent.

That is why we are going to make the voters understand this year that this Nation is not merely a Nation of independence, but it is, if we are to survive, bound to be a Nation of interdependence—town and city, and North and South, East and West. That is our goal, and that goal will be understood by the people of this country no matter where they live.

Yes, the purchasing power of that half of our population dependent on agriculture is gone. Farm mortgages reach nearly ten billions of dollars today and interest charges on that alone are five hundred sixty million dollars a year. But that is not all. The tax burden caused by extravagant and inefficient local government is an additional factor. Our most immediate concern should be to reduce the interest burden on these mortgages.

Rediscounting of farm mortgages under salutary restrictions must be expanded and should, in the future, be conditioned on the reduction of interest rates. Amortization payments, maturities should likewise in this crisis be extended before rediscount is permitted where the mortgagor is sorely pressed. That, my friends, is another example of practical, immediate relief: Action.

I aim to do the same thing, and it can be done, for the small home-owner in our cities and villages. We can lighten his burden and develop his purchasing power. Take away, my friends, that spectre of too high an interest rate. Take away that spectre of the due date just a short time away. Save homes; save homes for thousands of self-respecting families, and drive out that spectre of insecurity from our midst.

Out of all the tons of printed paper, out of all the hours of oratory, the recriminations, the defenses, the happy-thought plans in Washington and in every State, there emerges one great, simple, crystal-pure fact that during the past ten years a Nation of one hundred twenty million people has been led by the Republican leaders to erect an impregnable barbed wire entanglement around its borders through the instrumentality of tariffs which have isolated us from all the other human beings in all the rest of the round world. I accept that admirable tariff statement in the platform of this convention. It would protect American business and American labor. By our acts of the past we have invited and received the retaliation of other nations. I propose an invitation to them to forget the past, to sit at the table with us, as friends, and to plan with us for the restoration of the trade of the world.

Go into the home of the business man. He knows what the tariff has done for him. Go into the home of the factory worker. He knows why goods do not move.

Go into the home of the farmer. He knows how the tariff has helped to ruin him.

At last our eyes are open. At last the American people are ready to acknowledge that Republican leadership was wrong and that the Democracy is right.

My program, of which I can only touch on these points, is based upon this simple moral principle: the welfare and the soundness of a nation depend first upon what the great mass of the people wish and need; and second, whether or not they are getting it.

What do the people of America want more than anything else? To my mind, they want two things: work, with all the moral and spiritual values that go with it; and with work, a reasonable measure of security—security for themselves and for their wives and children. Work and security—these are more than words. They are more than facts. They are the spiritual values, the true goal toward which our efforts of reconstruction should lead. These are the values that this program is intended to gain; these are the values we have failed to achieve by the leadership we now have.

Our Republican leaders tell us economic laws—sacred, inviolable, unchangeable—cause panics which no one could prevent. But while they prate of economic laws, men and women are starving. We must lay hold of the fact that economic laws are not made by nature. They are made by human beings.

Yes, when—not if—when we get the chance, the Federal Government will assume bold leadership in distress relief. For years Washington has alternated between putting its head in the sand and saying there is no large number of destitute people in our midst who need food and clothing, and then saying the States should take care of them, if there are. Instead of planning two and a half years ago to do what they are now trying to do, they kept putting it off from day to day, week to week, and month to month, until the conscience of America demanded action.

I say that while primary responsibility for relief rests with localities now, as ever, yet the Federal Government has always had and still has a continuing responsibility for the broader public welfare. It will soon fulfill that responsibility.

And now, just a few words about our plans for the next four months. By coming here instead of waiting for a formal notification, I have made it clear that I believe we should eliminate expensive ceremonies and that we should set in motion at once, tonight, my friends, the necessary machinery for an adequate presentation of the issues to the electorate of the Nation.

I myself have important duties as Governor of a great State, duties which in these times are more arduous and more grave than at any previous period. Yet I feel confident that I shall be able to make a number of short visits to several parts of the Nation. My trips will have as their first objective the study at first hand, from the lips of men and women of all parties and all occupations, of the actual conditions and needs of every part of an interdependent country.

One word more: Out of every crisis, every tribulation, every disaster, mankind rises with some share of greater knowledge, of higher decency, of purer purpose. Today we shall have come through a period of loose thinking, descending morals, an era of selfishness, among individual men and women and among nations. Blame not Governments alone for this. Blame ourselves in equal share. Let us be frank in acknowledgment of the truth that many amongst us have made obeisance to Mammon, that the profits of speculation, the easy road without toil, have lured us from the old barricades. To return to higher standards we must abandon the false prophets and seek new leaders of our own choosing.

Never before in modern history have the essential differences between the two major American parties stood out in such striking contrast as they do today. Republican leaders not only have failed in material things, they have failed in national vision, because in disaster they have held out no hope, they have pointed out no path for the people below to climb back to places of security and of safety in our American life.

Throughout the Nation, men and women, forgotten in the political philosophy of the Government of the last years look to us here for guidance and for more equitable opportunity to share in the distribution of national wealth.

On the farms, in the large metropolitan areas, in the smaller cities and in the villages, millions of our citizens cherish the hope that their old standards of living and of thought have not gone forever. Those millions cannot and shall not hope in vain.

I pledge you, I pledge myself, to a new deal for the American people. Let us all here assembled constitute ourselves prophets of a new order of competence and of courage. This is more than a political campaign; it is a call to arms. Give me your help, not to win votes alone, but to win in this crusade to restore America to its own people.

From: B. D. Zevin, ed. *Nothing to Fear: The Selected Addresses of Franklin Delano Roosevelt, 1932–1945*. Boston: Houghton Mifflin, 1946.

REPUBLICAN PARTY PLATFORM, 1932

Although much longer and far more detailed than the Democratic platform of the same year, the Republican Party platform of 1932 did not differ much from it in overall philosophy. On the critical issue of dealing with the Great Depression, both called for more economic discipline on the part of the federal government, that is, a conservative deflationary fiscal policy that, as later economists argued, merely prolonged the crisis. There were a few notable differences, however. The most important, perhaps, concerned Prohibition. Democrats wanted to end it; Republicans were committed to continuing it.

We, the representatives of the Republican Party, in convention assembled, renew our pledge to the principles and traditions of our party and dedicate it anew to the service of the nation.

We meet in a period of widespread distress and of an economic depression that has swept the world. The emergency is second only to that of a great war. The human suffering occasioned may well exceed that of a period of actual conflict.

The supremely important problem that challenges our citizens and government alike is to break the back of the depression, to restore the economic life of the nation and to bring encouragement and relief to the thousands of American families that are sorely afflicted.

The people themselves, by their own courage, their own patient and resolute effort in the readjustments of their own affairs, can and will work out the cure. It is our task as a party, by leadership and a wise determination of policy, to assist that recovery.

To that task we pledge all that our party possesses in capacity, leadership, resourcefulness and ability. Republicans, collectively and individually, in nation and State, hereby enlist in a war which will not end until the promise of American life is once more fulfilled.

LEADERSHIP

For nearly three years the world has endured an economic depression of unparalleled extent and severity.

The patience and courage of our people have been severely tested, but their faith in themselves, in their institutions and in their future remains unshaken. When victory comes, as it will, this generation will hand on to the next a great heritage unimpaired.

This will be due in large measure to the quality of the leadership that this country has had during this crisis. We have had in the White House a leader wise, courageous, patient, understanding, resourceful, ever present at his post of duty, tireless in his efforts and unswervingly faithful to American principles and ideals.

At the outset of the depression, when no man could foresee its depth and extent, the President succeeded in averting much distress by securing agreement between industry and labor to maintain wages and by stimulating programs of private and governmental construction. Throughout the depression unemployment has been limited by the systematic use of part-time employment as a substitute for the general discharge of employees. Wage scales have not been reduced except under compelling necessity. As a result there have been fewer strikes and less social disturbance than during any similar period of hard times.

The suffering and want occasioned by the great drought of 1930 were mitigated by the prompt mobilization of the resources of the Red Cross and of the government. During the trying winters of 1930–31 and 1931–32 a nation-wide organization to relieve distress was brought into being under the leadership of the President. By the spring of 1931 the possibility of a business upturn in the United States was clearly discernible when, suddenly, a train of events was set in motion in Central Europe which moved forward with extraordinary rapidity and violence, threatening the credit structure of the world and eventually dealing a serious blow to this country.

The President foresaw the danger. He sought to avert it by proposing a suspension of intergovernmental debt payments for one year, with the purpose of relieving the pressure at the point of greatest intensity. But the credit machinery of the nations of Central Europe could not withstand the strain, and the forces of disintegration continued to gain momentum until in September Great Britain was forced to depart from the gold standard. This momentous event, followed by a tremendous raid on the dollar, resulted in a series of bank suspensions in this country, and the hoarding of currency on a large scale.

Again the President acted. Under his leadership the National Credit Association came into being. It mobilized our banking resources, saved scores of banks from failure, helped restore confidence and proved of inestimable value in strengthening the credit structure.

By the time the Congress met, the character of our problems was clearer than ever. In his message to Congress the President outlined a constructive and definite program which in the main has been carried out; other portions may yet be carried out.

The Railroad Credit Corporation was created. The capital of the Federal Land Banks was increased. The Reconstruction Finance Corporation came into being and brought protection to millions of depositors, policy-holders and others.

Legislation was enacted enlarging the discount facilities of the Federal Reserve System, and, without reducing the legal reserves of the Federal Reserve Banks, releasing a billion dollars of gold, a formidable protection against raids on the dollar and a greatly enlarged basis for an expansion of credit.

An earlier distribution to depositors in closed banks has been brought about through the action of the Reconstruction Finance Corporation. Above all, the national credit has been placed in an impregnable position by provision for adequate revenue and a program of drastic curtailment of expenditures. All of these measures were designed to lay a foundation for the resumption of business and increased employment.

But delay and the constant introduction and consideration of new and unsound measures has kept the country in a state of uncertainty and fear, and offset much of the good otherwise accomplished.

The President has recently supplemented his original program to provide for distress, to stimulate the revival of business and employment, and to improve the agricultural situation; he recommended extending the authority of the Reconstruction Finance Corporation to enable it:

(a) To make loans to political subdivisions of public bodies or private corporations for the purpose of starting construction of income-producing or self-liquidating projects which will at once increase employment;

(b) To make loans upon security of agricultural commodities so as to insure the carrying of normal stocks of those commodities, and thus stabilize their loan value and price levels;

(c) To make loans to the Federal Farm Board to enable extension of loans to farm cooperatives and loans for export of agricultural commodities to quarters unable to purchase them;

(d) To loan up to $300,000,000 to such States as are unable to meet the calls made on them by their citizens for distress relief.

The President's program contemplates an attack on

a broad front, with far-reaching objectives, but entailing no danger to the budget. The Democratic program, on the other hand, contemplates a heavy expenditure of public funds, a budget unbalanced on a large scale, with a doubtful attainment of at best a strictly limited objective.

We strongly endorse the President's program.

UNEMPLOYMENT AND RELIEF

True to American traditions and principles of government, the administration has regarded the relief problem as one of State and local responsibility. The work of local agencies, public and private, has been coordinated and enlarged on a nation-wide scale under the leadership of the President.

Sudden and unforeseen emergencies such as the drought have been met by the Red Cross and the Government. The United States Public Health Service has been of inestimable benefit to stricken areas.

There has been magnificent response and action to relieve distress by citizens, organizations and agencies, public and private throughout the country.

PUBLIC ECONOMY

Constructive plans for financial stabilization cannot be completely organized until our national, State and municipal governments not only balance their budgets but curtail their current expenses as well to a level which can be steadily and economically maintained for some years to come.

We urge prompt and drastic reduction of public expenditure and resistance to every appropriation not demonstrably necessary to the performance of government, national or local.

The Republican Party established and will continue to uphold the gold standard and will oppose any measure which will undermine the government's credit or impair the integrity of our national currency. Relief by currency inflation is unsound in principle and dishonest in results. The dollar is impregnable in the marts of the world today and must remain so. An ailing body cannot be cured by quack remedies. This is no time to experiment upon the body politic.

BANKS AND THE BANKING SYSTEM

The efficient functioning of our economic machinery depends in no small measure on the aid rendered to trade and industry by our banking system. There is need of revising the banking laws so as to place our banking structure on a sounder basis generally for all concerned, and for the better protection of the depositing public there should be more stringent supervision and broader powers vested in the supervising authorities. We advocate such a revision.

One of the serious problems affecting our banking system has arisen from the practice of organizing separate corporations by the same interests as banks, but participating in operations which the banks themselves are not permitted legally to undertake. We favor requiring reports of and subjecting to thorough and periodic examination all such affiliates of member banks until adequate information has been acquired on the basis of which this problem may definitely be solved in a permanent manner.

INTERNATIONAL CONFERENCE

We favor the participation by the United States in an international conference to consider matters relating to monetary questions, including the position of silver, exchange problems, and commodity prices, and possible cooperative action concerning them.

HOME LOAN DISCOUNT BANK SYSTEM

The present Republican administration has initiated legislation for the creation of a system of Federally supervised home loan discount banks, designed to serve the home owners of all parts of the country and to encourage home ownership by making possible long term credits for homes on more stable and more favorable terms.

There has arisen in the last few years a disturbing trend away from home ownership. We believe that everything should be done by Governmental agencies, national, State and local, to reverse this tendency; to aid home owners by encouraging better methods of home financing; and to relieve the present inequitable tax burden on the home. In the field of national legislation we pledge that the measures creating a home loan discount system will be pressed in Congress until adopted.

AGRICULTURE

Farm distress in America has its root in the enormous expansion of agricultural production during the war, the deflation of 1919–1920 and the dislocation of markets after the war. There followed, under Republican administrations, a long record of legislation in aid of the cooperative organization of farmers and in providing farm credit. The position of agriculture was gradually improved. In 1928 the Republican Party pledged further measures in aid of agriculture, principally tariff protection for agricultural products and the creation of a Federal Farm Board "clothed with the necessary power to promote the establishment of a farm marketing system of farmer-owned and controlled stabilization corporations."

Almost the first official act of President Hoover was the calling of a special session of Congress to redeem these party pledges. They have been redeemed.

The 1930 tariff act increased the rates on agricultural products by 30 per cent, upon industrial products only 12 per cent. That act equalized, so far as legislation can do so, the protection afforded the farmer with the protection afforded industry, and prevented a vast flood of cheap wool, grain, livestock, dairy and other products from entering the American market.

By the agricultural marketing act, the Federal Farm Board was created and armed with broad powers and ample funds. The object of that act, as stated in its preamble, was:

"To promote the effective merchandising of agricultural commodities in interstate and foreign commerce so that . . . agriculture will be placed on the basis of economic equality with other industries . . . by encouraging the organization of producers into effective association for their own control . . . and by promoting the establishment of a farm marketing system of producer owned and producer-controlled cooperative associations."

The Federal Farm Board, created by the agricultural marketing act, has been compelled to conduct its operations during a period in which all commodity prices, industrial as well as agricultural, have fallen to disastrous levels. A period of decreasing demand and of national calamities such as drought and flood has intensified the problem of agriculture.

Nevertheless, after only a little more than two years' efforts, the Federal Farm Board has many achievements of merit to its credit. It has increased the membership of the cooperative farms marketing associations to coordinate efforts of the local associations. By cooperation with other Federal agencies, it has made available to farm marketing associations a large value of credit, which, in the emergency, would not have otherwise been available. Larger quantities of farm products have been handled cooperatively than ever before in the history of the cooperative movement. Grain

crops have been sold by the farmer through his association directly upon the world market.

Due to the 1930 tariff act and the agricultural marketing act, it can truthfully be stated that the prices received by the American farmer for his wheat, corn, rye, barley, oats, flaxseed, cattle, butter and many other products, cruelly low though they are, are higher than the prices received by the farmers of any competing nation for the same products.

The Republican Party has also aided the American farmer by relief of the sufferers in the drought-stricken areas, through loans for rehabilitation and through road building to provide employment, by the development of the inland waterway system, by the perishable product act, by the strengthening of the extension system, and by the appropriation of $125,000,000 to recapitalize the Federal land banks and enable them to extend time to worthy borrowers.

The Republican Party pledges itself to the principle of assistance to cooperative marketing associations, owned and controlled by the farmers themselves, through the provisions of the agricultural marketing act, which will be promptly amended or modified as experience shows to be necessary to accomplish the objects set forth in the preamble of that act.

TARIFF AND THE MARKETING ACT

The party pledges itself to make such revision of tariff schedules as economic changes require to maintain the parity of protection to agriculture with other industry.

The American farmer is entitled not only to tariff schedules on his products but to protection from substitutes therefor.

We will support any plan which will help to balance production against demand, and thereby raise agricultural prices, provided it is economically sound and administratively workable without burdensome bureaucracy.

The burden of taxation borne by the owners of farm land constitutes one of the major problems of agriculture.

President Hoover has aptly and truly said, "Taxes upon real property are easiest to enforce and are the least flexible of all taxes. The tendency under pressure of need is to continue these taxes unchanged in times of depression, despite the decrease in the owner's income. Decreasing price and decreasing income results in an increasing burden upon property owners . . . which is now becoming almost unbearable. The tax burden upon real estate is wholly out of proportion to that upon other forms of property and income. There is no farm relief more needed today than tax relief."

The time has come for a reconsideration of our tax systems, Federal, State and local, with a view to developing a better coordination, reducing duplication and relieving unjust burdens. The Republican Party pledges itself to this end.

More than all else, we point to the fact that, in the administration of executive departments, and in every plan of the President for the coordination of national effort and for strengthening our financial structure, for expanding credit, for rebuilding the rural credit system and laying the foundations for better prices, the President has insisted upon the interest of the American farmer.

The fundamental problem of American agriculture is the control of production to such volume as will balance supply with demand. In the solution of this problem the cooperative organization of farmers to plan production, and the tariff, to hold the home market for American farmers, are vital elements. A third element equally as vital is the control of the acreage of land under cultivation, as an aid to the efforts of the farmer to balance production.

We favor a national policy of land utilization which looks to national needs, such as the administration has already begun to formulate. Such a policy must foster reorganization of taxing units in areas beset by tax delinquency and divert lands that are submarginal for crop production to other uses. The national welfare plainly can be served by the acquisition of submarginal lands for watershed protection, grazing, forestry, public parks and game preserves. We favor such acquisition.

THE TARIFF

The Republican Party has always been the staunch supporter of the American system of a protective tariff. It believes that the home market, built up under that policy, the greatest and richest market in the world, belongs first to American agriculture, industry and labor. No pretext can justify the surrender of that market to such competition as would destroy our farms, mines and factories, and lower the standard of living which we have established for our workers.

Because many foreign countries have recently abandoned the gold standard, as a result of which the costs of many commodities produced in such countries have, at least for the time being, fallen materially in terms of American currency, adequate tariff protection is today particularly essential to the welfare of the American people.

The Tariff Commission should promptly investigate individual commodities so affected by currency depreciation and report to the President any increase in duties found necessary to equalize domestic with foreign costs of production.

To fix the duties on some thousands of commodities, subject to highly complex conditions, is necessarily a difficult technical task. It is unavoidable that some of the rates established by legislation should, even at the time of their enactment, be too low or too high. Moreover, a subsequent change in costs or other conditions may render obsolete a rate that was before appropriate. The Republican Party has, therefore, long supported the policy of a flexible tariff, giving power to the President, after investigation by an impartial commission and in accordance with prescribed principles, to modify the rates named by the Congress.

We commend the President's veto of the measure, sponsored by Democratic Congressmen, which would have transferred from the President to Congress the authority to put into effect the findings of the Tariff Commission. Approval of the measure would have returned tariff making to politics and destroyed the progress made during ten years of effort to lift it out of log-rolling methods. We pledge the Republican Party to a policy which will retain the gains made and enlarge the present scope of greater progress.

We favor the extension of the general Republican principle of tariff protection to our natural resource industries, including the products of our farms, forests, mines and oil wells, with compensatory duties on the manufactured and refined products thereof.

VETERANS

Our country is honored whenever it bestows relief on those who have faithfully served its flag. The Republican Party, appreciative of this solemn obligation and honor, has made its sentiments evident in Congress.

Increased hospital facilities have been provided, payments in compensation have more than doubled and in the matter of rehabilitations, pensions and insurance, generous provision has been made.

The administration of laws dealing with the relief of the veterans and their dependents has been a difficult task, but every effort has been made to carry service to the veterans and bring about not only a better and generous interpretation of the law but a sympathetic consideration of the many problems of the veteran.

We believe that every veteran incapacitated in any degree by reason of illness should be cared for and compensated, so far as compensation is possible, by a grateful nation, and that the dependents of those who lost their lives in war or whose death since the war in which service was rendered is traceable to service causes, should be provided for adequately. Legislation should be in accord with this principle.

Disability from causes subsequent and not attributable to war and the support of dependents of deceased veterans whose death is unconnected with war have been to some measure accepted obligations of the nation as a part of the debt due.

A careful study should be made of existing veterans' legislation with a view to elimination of inequalities and injustices and effecting all possible economies, but without departing from our purpose to provide on a sound basis full and adequate relief for our service disabled men, their widows and orphans.

FOREIGN AFFAIRS

Our relations with foreign nations have been carried on by President Hoover with consistency and firmness, but with mutual understanding and peace with all nations. The world has been overwhelmed with economic strain which has provoked extreme nationalism in every quarter, has overturned many governments, stirred the springs of suspicion and distrust and tried the spirit of international cooperation, but we have held to our own course steadily and successfully.

The party will continue to maintain its attitude of protecting our national interests and policies wherever threatened but at the same time promoting common understanding of the varying needs and aspirations of other nations and going forward in harmony with other peoples without alliances or foreign partnerships.

The facilitation of world intercourse, the freeing of commerce from unnecessary impediments, the settlement of international difficulties by conciliation and the methods of law and the elimination of war as a resort of national policy have been and will be our party program.

FRIENDSHIP AND COMMERCE

We believe in and look forward to the steady enlargement of the principles of equality of treatment between nations great and small, the concessions of sovereignty and self-administration to every nation which is capable of carrying on stable government and conducting sound orderly relationships with other peoples, and the cultivation of trade and intercourse on the basis of uniformity of opportunity of all nations.

In pursuance of these principles, which have steadily gained favor in the world, the administration has asked no special favors in commerce, has protested discriminations whenever they arose, and has steadily cemented this procedure by reciprocal treaties guaranteeing equality for trade and residence.

The historic American plan known as the most favored-nation principle has been our guiding program, and we believe that policy to be the only one consistent with a full development of international trade, the only one suitable for a country having as wide and diverse a commerce as America, and the one most appropriate for us in view of the great variety of our industrial, agricultural and mineral products and the traditions of our people.

Any other plan involves bargains and partnerships with foreign nations, and as a permanent policy is unsuited to America's position.

Conditions in the Pacific

Events in the Far East, involving the employment of arms on a large scale in a controversy between Japan and China, have caused worldwide concern in the past year and sorely tried the bulwarks erected to insure peace and pacific means for the settlement of international disputes.

The controversy has not only threatened the security of the nations bordering the Pacific but has challenged the maintenance of the policy of the open door in China and the administrative and political integrity of that people, programs which upon American initiation were adopted more than a generation ago and secured by international treaty.

The President and his Secretary of State have maintained throughout the controversy a just balance between Japan and China, taking always a firm position to avoid entanglements in the dispute, but consistently upholding the established international policies and the treaty rights and interests of the United States, and never condoning developments that endangered the obligation of treaties or the peace of the world.

Throughout the controversy our government has acted in harmony with the governments represented in the League of Nations, always making it clear that American policy would be determined at home, but always lending a hand in the common interest of peace and order.

In the application of the principles of the Kellogg pact the American Government has taken the lead, following the principle that a breach of the pact or a threat of infringement thereof was a matter of international concern wherever and however brought about.

As a further step the Secretary of State, upon the instruction of the President, adopted the principle later enlarged upon in his letter to the chairman of the Committee on Foreign Relations of the Senate that this government would not recognize any situation, treaty or agreement brought about between Japan and China by force and in defiance of the covenants of the Kellogg pact.

This principle, associated as it is with the name of President Hoover, was later adopted by the Assembly of the League of Nations at Geneva as a rule for the conduct of all those governments. The principle remains today as an important contribution to international law and a significant moral and material barrier to prevent a nation obtaining the fruits of aggressive warfare. It thus opens a new pathway to peace and order.

We favor enactment by Congress of a measure that will authorize our government to call or participate in an international conference in case of any threat of non-fulfillment of Article 2 of the Treaty of Paris (Kellogg-Briand pact).

Latin-America

The policy of the administration has proved to our neighbors of Latin-America that we have no imperialistic ambitions, but that we wish only to promote the welfare and common interest of the independent nations in the western hemisphere.

We have aided Nicaragua in the solution of its troubles by sending a team of observers, at the request of the Nicaraguan Government, to supervise the coming election. After that they will all be returned to the United States.

In Haiti, in accord with the recommendations of the Forbes commission, appointed by the President, the various services of supervision are being rapidly withdrawn, and only those will be retained which are mandatory under the treaties.

Throughout Latin-America the policy of the government of the United States has been and will, under Republican leadership, continue to be one of frank and friendly understanding.

World Court

The acceptance by America of membership in the World Court has been approved by three successive Republican Presidents and we commend this attitude of supporting in this form the settlement of international disputes by the rule of law. America should join its influence and gain a voice in this institution, which would offer us a safer, more judicial and expeditious instrument for the constantly recurring questions between us and other nations than is now available by arbitration.

Reduction of Armament

Conscious that the limitation of armament will contribute to security against war, and that the financial burdens of military preparation have been shamefully increased throughout the world, the Administration under President Hoover has made steady efforts and marked progress in the direction of proportional reduction of arms by agreement with other nations.

Upon his initiative a treaty between the chief naval powers at London in 1930, following the path marked by the Washington Conference of 1922, established a limitation of all types of fighting ships on a proportionate basis as between the three great naval powers. For the first time, a general limitation of a most costly branch of armament was successfully accomplished.

In the Geneva disarmament conference, now in progress, America is an active participant and a representative delegation of our citizens is laboring for progress in a cause to which this country has been an earnest contributor. This policy will be pursued.

Meanwhile maintenance of our navy on the basis of parity with any nation is a fundamental policy to which the Republican Party is committed. While in the interest of necessary government retrenchment, humanity and relief of the taxpayer we shall continue to exert our full influence upon the nations of the world in the cause of reduction of arms, we do not propose to reduce our navy defenses below that of any other nation.

NATIONAL DEFENSE

Armaments are relative and, therefore, flexible and subject to changes as necessity demands. We believe that in time of war every material resource in the nation should bear its proportionate share of the burdens occasioned by the public need and that it is a duty of government to perfect plans in time of peace whereby this objective may be attained in war.

We support the essential principles of the National Defense Act as amended in 1920 and by the Air Corps Act of 1926, and believe that the army of the United States has, through successive reductions accomplished in the last twelve years, reached an irreducible minimum consistent with the self-reliance, self-respect and security of this country.

WAGES AND WORK

We believe in the principle of high wages.

We favor the principle of the shorter working week and shorter work day—with its application to government as well as to private employment, as rapidly and as constructively as conditions will warrant.

We favor legislation designed to stimulate, encourage and assist in home building.

IMMIGRATION

The restriction of immigration is a Republican policy. Our party formulated and enacted into law the quota system, which for the first time has made possible an adequate control of foreign immigration.

Rigid examination of applicants in foreign countries prevented the coming of criminals and other undesirable classes, while other provisions of the law have enabled the President to suspend immigration of foreign wage-earners who otherwise, directly or indirectly, would have increased unemployment among native-born and legally resident foreign-born wage-earners in this country. As a result, immigration is now less than at any time during the past one hundred years.

We favor the continuance and strict enforcement of our present laws upon this subject.

DEPARTMENT OF LABOR

We commend the constructive work of the United States Department of Labor.

LABOR

Collective bargaining by responsible representatives of employers and employees of their own choice, without the interference of anyone, is recognized and approved.

Legislation, such as laws, prohibiting alien contract labor, peonage labor and the shanghaiing of sailors; the eight-hour law on government contracts and in government employment; provision for railroad safety devices, of methods of conciliation, mediation and arbitration in industrial labor disputes, including the adjustment of railroad disputes; the providing of compensation for injury to government employees (the forerunner of Federal workers' compensation acts), and other laws to aid and protect labor are of Republican origin, and have had and will continue to have the unswerving support of the party.

EMPLOYMENT

We commend the constructive work of the United States Employment Service in the Department of Labor. This service was enlarged and its activities extended through an appropriation made possible by the President with the cooperation of the Congress. It has done high service for the unemployed in the ranks of civil life and in the ranks of the former soldiers of the World War.

FREEDOM OF SPEECH

Freedom of speech, press and assemblages are fundamental principles upon which our form of government rests. These vital principles should be preserved and protected.

PUBLIC UTILITIES

Supervision, regulation and control of interstate public utilities in the interest of the public is an established policy of the Republican Party, to the credit of which stands the creation of the Interstate Commerce Commission, with its authority to assure reasonable transportation rates, sound railway finance and adequate service.

As proof of the progress made by the Republican Party in government control of public utilities, we cite the reorganization under this administration of the Federal Power Commission, with authority to administer the Federal water power act. We urge legislation to authorize this commission to regulate the charges for electric current when transmitted across State lines.

TRANSPORTATION

The promotion of agriculture, commerce and industry requires coordination of transportation by rail, highway, air and water. All should be subjected to appropriate and constructive regulation.

The public will, of course, select the form of transportation best fitted to its particular service, but the terms of competition fixed by public authority should operate without discrimination, so that all common carriers by rail, highway, air and water shall operate under conditions of equality.

Inland Waterways

The Republican Party recognizes that low-cost transportation for bulk commodities will enable industry to develop in the midst of agriculture in the Mississippi Valley, thereby creating a home market for farm products in that section. With a view to aiding agriculture in the middle west the present administration has pushed forward as rapidly as possible the improvement of the Mississippi waterway system, and we favor the continued vigorous prosecution of these works to the end that agriculture and industry in that great area may enjoy the benefits of these improvements at the earliest possible date.

Railroads

The railroads constitute the backbone of our transportation system and perform an essential service for the country. The railroad industry is our largest employer of labor and the greatest consumer of goods. The restoration of their credit and the maintenance of their ability to render adequate service are of paramount importance to the public, to their many thousands of employees and to savings banks, insurance companies and other similar institutions, to which the savings of the people have been entrusted.

Merchant Marine

We should continue to encourage the further development of the merchant marine under American registry and ownership.

Under the present administration the American merchant fleet has been enlarged and strengthened until it now occupies second place among the merchant marines of the world.

By the gradual retirement of the government from the field of ship operations and marked economies in costs, the United States Shipping Board will require no appropriation for the fiscal year 1933 for ship operations.

St. Lawrence Seaway

The Republican Party stands committed to the development of the Great Lakes–St. Lawrence seaway. Under the direction of President Hoover negotiation of a treaty with Canada for this development is now at a favorable point. Recognizing the inestimable benefits which will accrue to the nation from placing the ports of the Great Lakes on an ocean base, the party reaffirms allegiance to this great project and pledges its best efforts to secure its early completion.

Highways

The Federal policy to cooperate with the States in the building of roads was thoroughly established when the Federal highway act of 1921 was adopted under a Republican Congress. Each year since that time appropriations have been made which have greatly increased the economic value of highway transportation and helped to raise the standards and opportunities of rural life.

We pledge our support to the continuation of this policy in accordance with our needs and resources.

CRIME

We favor the enactment of rigid penal laws that will aid the States in stamping out the activities of gangsters, racketeers and kidnappers. We commend the intensive and effective drive made upon these public enemies by President Hoover and pledge our party to further efforts to the same purpose.

NARCOTICS

The Republican Party pledges itself to continue the present relentless warfare against the illicit narcotic traffic and the spread of the curse of drug addiction among our people. This administration has by treaty greatly strengthened our power to deal with this traffic.

CIVIL SERVICE

The merit system has been amply justified since the organization of the Civil Service by the Republican Party. As a part of our governmental system it is now unassailable. We believe it should remain so.

THE EIGHTEENTH AMENDMENT

The Republican Party has always stood and stands to-day for obedience to and enforcement of the law as the very foundation of orderly government and civilization. There can be no national security otherwise. The duty of the President of the United States and the officers of the law is clear. The law must be enforced as they find it enacted by the people. To these courses of action we pledge our nominees.

The Republican Party is and always has been the party of the Constitution. Nullification by non-observance by individuals or State action threatens the stability of government.

While the Constitution makers sought a high degree of permanence, they foresaw the need of changes and provided for them. Article V limits the proposals of amendments to two methods: (1) Two-thirds of both houses of Congress may propose amendments or (2) on application of the Legislatures of two-thirds of the States a national convention shall be called by Congress to propose amendments. Thereafter ratification must be had in one of two ways: (1) By the Legislatures of three-fourths of the several States or (2) by conventions held in three-fourths of the several States. Congress is given power to determine the mode of ratification.

Referendums without constitutional sanction cannot furnish a decisive answer. Those who propose them innocently are deluded by false hopes; those who propose them knowingly are deceiving the people.

A nation-wide controversy over the Eighteenth Amendment now distracts attention from the constructive solution of many pressing national problems. The principle of national prohibition as embodied in the amendment was supported and opposed by members of both great political parties. It was submitted to the States by members of Congress of different political faith and ratified by State Legislatures of different political majorities. It was not then and is not now a partisan political question.

Members of the Republican Party hold different opinions with respect to it and no public official or member of the party should be pledged or forced to choose between his party affiliations and his honest convictions upon this question.

We do not favor a submission limited to the issue of retention or repeal, for the American nation never in its history has gone backward, and in this case the progress which has been thus far made must be preserved, while the evils must be eliminated.

We therefore believe that the people should have an opportunity to pass upon a proposed amendment the provision of which, while retaining in the Federal Government power to preserve the gains already made in dealing with the evils inherent in the liquor traffic, shall allow the States to deal with the problem as their citizens may determine, but subject always to the power of the Federal Government to protect those States where prohibition may exist and safeguard our citizens everywhere from the return of the saloon and attendant abuses.

Such an amendment should be promptly submitted to the States by Congress, to be acted upon by State conventions called for that sole purpose in accordance with the provisions of Article V of the Constitution and adequately safeguarded so as to be truly representative.

CONSERVATION

The wise use of all natural resources freed from monopolistic control is a Republican policy, initiated by Theodore Roosevelt. The Roosevelt, Coolidge and Hoover reclamation projects bear witness to the continuation of that policy. Forestry and all other conservation activities have been supported and enlarged.

The conservation of oil is a major problem to the industry and the nation. The administration has sought to bring coordination of effort through the States, the producers and the Federal Government. Progress has been made and the effort will continue.

THE NEGRO

For seventy years the Republican Party has been the friend of the American Negro. Vindication of the rights of the Negro citizen to enjoy the full benefits of life, liberty and the pursuit of happiness is traditional in the Republican Party, and our party stands pledged to maintain equal opportunity and rights for Negro citizens. We do not propose to depart from that tradition nor to alter the spirit or letter of that pledge.

HAWAII

We believe that the existing status of self-government which for many years has been enjoyed by the citizens of the Territory of Hawaii should be maintained, and that officials appointed to administer the government should be bona-fide residents of the Territory.

PUERTO RICO

Puerto Rico being a part of the United States and its inhabitants American citizens, we believe that they are entitled to a good-faith recognition of the spirit and purposes of their organic act.

We, therefore, favor the inclusion of the island in all legislative and administrative measures enacted or adopted by Congress or otherwise for the economic benefit of their fellow-citizens of the mainland.

We also believe that, in so far as possible, all officials appointed to administer the affairs of the island government should be qualified by at least five years of bona-fide residence therein.

ALASKA

We favor the policy of giving to the people of Alaska the widest possible territorial self-government and the selection so far as possible of bona-fide residents for positions in that Territory and the placing of its citizens on an equality with those in the several States.

WELFARE WORK AND CHILDREN

The children of our nation, our future citizens, have had the most solicitous thought of our President. Child welfare and protection has been a major effort of this administration. The organization of the White House Conference on Child Health and Protection is regarded as one of the outstanding accomplishments of this administration.

Welfare work in all its phases has had the support of the President and aid of the administration. The work of organized agencies—local, State and Federal—has been advanced and an increased impetus given by

that recognition and help. We approve and pledge a continuation of that policy.

INDIANS

We favor the fullest protection of the property rights of the American Indians and the provision for them of adequate educational facilities.

REORGANIZATION OF GOVERNMENT BUREAUS

Efficiency and economy demand reorganization of government bureaus. The problem is nonpartisan and must be so treated if it is to be solved. As a result of years of study and personal contact with conflicting activities and wasteful duplication of effort, the President is particularly fitted to direct measures to correct the situation. We favor legislation by Congress which will give him the required authority.

DEMOCRATIC FAILURE

The vagaries of the present Democratic House of Representatives offer characteristic and appalling proof of the existing incapacity of that party for leadership in a national crisis. Individualism running amuck has displaced party discipline and has trampled under foot party leadership. A bewildered electorate has viewed the spectacle with profound dismay and deep misgivings.

Goaded to desperation by their confessed failure, the party leaders have resorted to "pork barrel" legislation to obtain a unity of action which could not otherwise be achieved. A Republican President stands resolutely between the helpless citizen and the disaster threatened by such measures; and the people, regardless of party, will demand his continued service.

Many times during his useful life has Herbert Hoover responded to such a call, and his response has never disappointed. He will not disappoint us now.

PARTY GOVERNMENT

The delays and differences which recently hampered efforts to obtain legislation imperatively demanded by prevailing critical conditions strikingly illustrate the menace to self-government brought about by the weakening of party ties and party fealty.

Experience has demonstrated that coherent political parties are indispensable agencies for the prompt and effective operation of the functions of our government under the Constitution.

Only by united party action can consistent, well-planned and wholesome legislative programs be enacted. We believe that the majority of the Congressmen elected in the name of a party have the right and duty to determine the general policies of that party requiring Congressional action, and that Congressmen belonging to that party are, in general, bound to adhere to such policies. Any other course inevitably makes of Congress a body of detached delegates which, instead of representing the collective wisdom of our people, become the confused voices of a heterogeneous group of unrelated local prejudices.

We believe that the time has come when Senators and Representatives of the United States should be impressed with the inflexible truth that their first concern should be the welfare of the United States and the well-being of all of its people, and that stubborn pride of individual opinions is not a virtue, but an obstacle to the orderly and successful achievement of the objects of representative government.

Only by cooperation can self-government succeed. Without it election under a party aegis becomes a false pretense.

We earnestly request that Republicans throughout the Union demand that their representatives in the Congress pledge themselves to these principles, to the end that the insidious influences of party disintegration may not undermine the very foundations of the Republic.

CONCLUSION

In contrast with the Republican policies and record, we contrast those of the Democratic as evidenced by the action of the House of Representatives under Democratic leadership and control, which includes:

1. The issuance of fiat currency.

2. Instructions to the Federal Reserve Board and the Secretary of the Treasury to attempt to manipulate commodity prices.

3. The guarantee of bank deposits.

4. The squandering of the public resources and the unbalancing of the budget through pork-barrel appropriations which bear little relation to distress and would tend through delayed business revival to decrease rather than increase employment.

Generally on economic matters we pledge the Republican Party:

1. To maintain unimpaired the national credit.

2. To defend and preserve a sound currency and an honest dollar.

3. To stand steadfastly by the principle of a balanced budget.

4. To devote ourselves fearlessly and unremittingly to the task of eliminating abuses and extravagance and of drastically cutting the cost of government so as to reduce the heavy burden of taxation.

5. To use all available means consistent with sound financial and economic principles to promote an expansion of credit to stimulate business and relieve unemployment.

6. To make a thorough study of the conditions which permitted the credit and the credit machinery of the country to be made available, without adequate check, for wholesale speculation in securities, resulting in ruinous consequences to millions of our citizens and to the national economy, and to correct those conditions so that they shall not recur.

Recognizing that real relief to unemployment must come through a revival of industrial activity and agriculture, to the promotion of which our every effort must be directed, our party in State and nation undertakes to do all in its power that is humanly possible to see that distress is fully relieved in accordance with American principles and traditions.

No successful solution of the problems before the country today can be expected from a Congress and a President separated by partisan lines or opposed in purposes and principles. Responsibility cannot be placed unless a clear mandate is given by returning to Washington a Congress and a Chief Executive united in principles and program.

The return to power of the Republican Party with that mandate is the duty of every voter who believes in the doctrines of the party and its program as herein stated. Nothing else, we believe, will insure the orderly recovery of the country and that return to prosperous days which every American so ardently desires.

The Republican Party faces the future unafraid!

With courage and confidence in ultimate success, we will strive against the forces that strike at our social and economic ideals, our political institutions.

From: George Thomas Kurian, ed. *The Encyclopedia of the Republican Party*. Armonk, NY: M. E. Sharpe, 1997.

HOOVER CAMPAIGN SPEECH, OCTOBER 31, 1932

In this—one of the last campaign speeches President Herbert Hoover delivered in the 1932 presidential race—the candidate lays out his philosophical opposition to the programs outlined by his Democratic rival for the presidency, Franklin D. Roosevelt. Hoover argued that Roosevelt's call for more federal government involvement in the economy would destroy the American way of entrepreneurialism and voluntarism.

This campaign is more than a contest between two men. It is more than a contest between two parties. It is a contest between two philosophies of government.

We are told by the opposition that we must have a change, that we must have a new deal. It is not the change that comes from normal development of national life to which I object, but the proposal to alter the whole foundations of our national life which have been builded [sic] through generations of testing and struggle, and of the principles upon which we have builded [sic] the Nation. The expressions our opponents use must refer to important changes in our economic and social system and our system of Government, otherwise they are nothing but vacuous words. And I realize that in this time of distress many of our people are asking whether our social and economic system is incapable of that great primary function of providing security and comfort of life to all of the firesides of our 25,000,000 homes in America, whether our social system provides for the fundamental development and progress of our people, whether our form of government is capable of originating and sustaining that security and progress.

This question is the basis upon which our opponents are appealing to the people in their fears and distress. They are proposing changes and so-called new deals which would destroy the very foundations of our American system.

Our people should consider the primary facts before they come to the judgment—not merely through political agitation, the glitter of promise, and the discouragement of temporary hardships—whether they will support changes which radically affect the whole system which has been builded [sic] up by 150 years of the toil of our fathers. They should not approach the question in the despair with which our opponents would clothe it.

Our economic system has received abnormal shocks during the past three years, which temporarily dislocated its normal functioning. These shocks have in a large sense come from without our borders, but I say to you that our system of government has enabled us to take such strong action as to prevent the disaster which would otherwise have come to our Nation. It has enabled us further to develop measures and programs which are now demonstrating their ability to bring about restoration and progress.

We must go deeper than platitudes and emotional appeals of the public platform in the campaign, if we will penetrate to the full significance of the changes which our opponents are attempting to float upon the wave of distress and discontent from the difficulties we are passing through. We can find what our opponents would do after searching the record of their appeals to discontent, group and sectional interest. We must search for them in the legislative acts which they sponsored and passed in the Democratic-controlled House of Representatives in the last session of Congress. We must look into measures for which they voted and which were defeated. We must inquire whether or not the presidential and vice presidential candidates have disavowed these acts. If they have not, we must conclude that they form a portion and are a substantial indication of the profound changes proposed.

And we must look still further than this as to what revolutionary changes have been proposed by the candidates themselves.

We must look into the type of leaders who are campaigning for the Democratic ticket, whose philosophies have been well known all their lives, whose demands for a change in the American system are frank and forceful. I can respect the sincerity of these men in their desire to change our form of government and our social and economic system, though I shall do my best tonight to prove they are wrong. I refer particularly to Senator [George] Norris, Senator [Robert] La Follette, Senator [Bronson] Cutting, Senator Huey Long, Senator [Burton] Wheeler, William R. Hearst, and other exponents of a social philosophy different from the traditional American one. Unless these men feel assurance of support to their ideas they certainly would not be supporting these candidates and the Democratic Party. The seal of these men indicates that they have sure confidence that they will have voice in the administration of our government.

I may say at once that the changes proposed from all these Democratic principals and allies are of the most profound and penetrating character. If they are brought about this will not be the America which we have known in the past.

Let us pause for a moment and examine the American system of government, of social and economic life, which it is now proposed that we should alter. Our system is the product of our race and of our experience in building a nation to heights unparalleled in the whole history of the world. It is a system peculiar to the American people. It differs essentially from all others in the world. It is an American system.

It is founded on the conception that only through ordered liberty, through freedom to the individual, and equal opportunity to the individual will his initiative and enterprise be summoned to spur the march of progress.

It is by the maintenance of equality of opportunity and therefore of a society absolutely fluid in freedom of the movement of its human particles that our individualism departs from the individualism of Europe. We resent class distinction because there can be no rise for the individual through the frozen strata of classes, and no stratification of classes can take place in a mass livened by the free rise of its particles. Thus in our ideals the able and ambitious are able to rise constantly from the bottom to leadership in the community.

This freedom of the individual creates of itself the necessity and the cheerful willingness of men to act cooperatively in a thousand ways and for every purpose as occasion arises; and it permits such voluntary cooperations to be dissolved as soon as they have served their purpose, to be replaced by new voluntary associations for new purposes.

There has thus grown within us, to gigantic importance, a new conception. That is, this voluntary cooperation within the community. Cooperation to perfect the social organization; cooperation for the care of those in distress; cooperation for the advancement of knowledge, of scientific research, of education; for cooperative action in the advancement of many phases of economic life. This is self-government by the people outside of Government; it is the most powerful development of individual freedom and equal opportunity that has taken place in the century and a half since our fundamental institutions were founded.

It is in the further development of this cooperation and a sense of its responsibility that we should find solution for many of our complex problems, and not by the extension of government into our economic and social life. The greatest function of government is to build up that cooperation, and its most resolute action should be to deny the extension of bureaucracy. We have developed great agencies of cooperation by the assistance of the Government which promote and protect the interests of individuals and the smaller units of business. The Federal Reserve System, in its strengthening and support of the smaller banks; the Farm Board, in its strengthening and support of the farm cooperatives; the Home Loan Banks, in the mobilizing of building and loan associations and savings banks; the Federal Land Banks, in giving independence and strength to land mortgage associations; the great mobilization of relief to distress, the mobilization of business and industry in measures of recovery, and a score of other activities are not socialism—they are the essence of protection to the development of free men.

The primary conception of this whole American system is not the regimentation of men but the cooperation of free men. It is founded upon the conception of responsibility of the individual to the community, of the responsibility of local government to the state, of the state to the National Government.

It is founded on a peculiar conception of self-government designed to maintain this equal opportunity to the individual, and through decentralization it brings about and maintains these responsibilities. The centralization of government will undermine responsibilities and will destroy the system.

Our government differs from all previous conceptions, not only in this decentralization but also in the separation of functions between the legislative, executive and judicial arms of government, in which the independence of the judicial arm is the keystone of the whole structure.

It is founded on a conception that in times of emergency, when forces are running beyond control of individuals or other cooperative action, beyond the control of local communities and of states, then the great reserve powers of the Federal Government shall be brought into action to protect the community. But when these forces have ceased there must be a return of state, local, and individual responsibility.

The implacable march of scientific discovery with its train of new inventions presents every year new problems to government and new problems to the social order. Questions often arise whether, in the face of the growth of these new and gigantic tools, democracy can remain master in its own house, can preserve the fundamentals of our American system. I contend that it can; and I contend that this American system of ours has demonstrated its validity and superiority over any other system yet invented by [the] human mind.

It has demonstrated it in the face of the greatest test of our history—that is the emergency which we have faced in the past three years.

When the political and economic weakness of many nations of Europe, the result of the World War and its aftermath, finally culminated in collapse of their institutions, the delicate adjustment of our economic and social life received a shock unparalleled in our history. No one knows that better than you of New York. No one knows its causes better than you. That the crisis was so great that many of the leading banks sought directly or indirectly to convert their assets into gold or its equivalent with the result that they practically ceased to function as credit institutions; that many of our citizens sought flight for their capital to other countries; that many of them attempted to hoard gold in large amounts. These were but indications of the flight of confidence and of the belief that our government could not overcome these forces.

Yet these forces were overcome—perhaps by narrow margins—and this action demonstrates what the courage of a nation can accomplish under the resolute leadership in the Republican Party. And I say the Republican Party, because our opponents, before and during the crisis, proposed no constructive program; though some of their members patriotically supported ours. Later on the Democratic House of Representatives did develop the real thought and ideas of the Democratic Party, but it was so destructive that it had to be defeated, for it would have destroyed, not healed.

In spite of all these obstructions we did succeed. Our form of government did prove itself equal to the task. We saved this Nation from a quarter of a century of chaos and degeneration, and we preserved the savings, the insurance policies, gave a fighting chance to men to hold their homes. We saved the integrity of our government and the honesty of the American dollar. And we installed measures which today are bringing back recovery. Employment, agriculture, business—all of these show the steady, if slow, healing of our enormous wound.

I therefore contend that the problem of today is to continue these measures and policies to restore this American system to its normal functioning, to repair the wounds it has received, to correct the weaknesses and evils which would defeat that system. To enter upon a series of deep changes to embark upon this inchoate new deal which has been propounded in this campaign would be to undermine and destroy our American system.

Before we enter upon such courses, I would like for you to consider what the results of this American system have been during the last thirty years—that is, one single generation. For if it can be demonstrated that by means of this, our unequaled political, social, and economic system, we have secured a lift in the standards of living and a diffusion of comfort and hope to men and women, the growth of equal opportunity, the widening of all opportunity, such as had never been seen in the history of the world, then we should not tamper with it or destroy it; but on the contrary we should restore it and, by its gradual improvement and perfection, foster it into new performance for our country and for our children.

Now, if we look back over the last generation we find that the number of our families and, therefore, our homes, have increased from sixteen to twenty-five million, or 62 per cent. In that time we have builded [sic] for them 15,000,000 new and better homes. We have equipped 20,000,000 homes with electricity; thereby we have lifted infinite drudgery from women and men. The barriers of time and space have been swept away. Life has been made freer, the intellectual vision of every individual has been expanded by the installation of 20,000,000 telephones, 12,000,000 radios, and the service of 20,000,000 automobiles. Our cities have been made magnificent with beautiful buildings, parks and playgrounds. Our countryside has been knit together with splendid roads. We have increased by twelve times the use of electrical power and thereby taken sweat from the backs of men. In this broad sweep real wages and purchasing power of men and women have steadily increased. New comforts have steadily come to them. The hours of labor have decreased, the 12-hour day has disappeared, even the 9-hour day has almost gone. We are now advancing the 5-day week. The portals of opportunity to our children have ever widened. While our population grew by but 62 per cent, we have increased the number of children in high schools by 700 per cent, those in institutions of higher learning by 300 per cent. With all our spending we multiplied by six times the savings in our banks and in our building and loan associations. We multiplied by 1,200 per cent the amount of our life insurance. With the enlargement of our leisure we have come to a fuller life; we gained new visions of hope, we more nearly realize our national aspirations and give increasing scope to the creative power of every individual and expansion of every man's mind.

Our people in those 30 years grew in the sense of social responsibility. There is profound progress in the relation of the employer and employed. We have more nearly met with a full hand the most sacred obligation of man, that is, the responsibility of a man to his neighbor. Support to our schools, hospitals, and institutions for the care of the afflicted surpassed in totals of billions the proportionate service in any period of history in any nation in the world.

Three years ago there came a break in this progress. A break of the same type we have met fifteen times in a century and yet we have overcome them. But 18 months later came a further blow by shocks transmitted to us by the earthquakes of the collapse in nations throughout the world as the aftermath of the World War. The workings of our system were dislocated. Millions of men and women are out of jobs. Business men and farmers suffer. Their distress is bitter. I do not seek to minimize the depth of it. We may thank God that in view of this storm 30,000,000 still have their jobs; yet this must not distract our thoughts from the suffering of the other 10,000,000.

But I ask you what has happened. This 30 years of incomparable improvement in the scale of living, the advance of comfort and intellectual life, inspiration, and ideals did not arise without right principles animating the American system which produced them. Shall that system be discarded because vote-seeking men appeal to distress and say that the machinery is all wrong and that it must be abandoned or tampered with? Is it not more sensible to realize the simple fact that some extraordinary force has been thrown into the mechanism, temporarily deranging its operation? Is it not wiser to believe that the difficulty is not with the principles upon which our American system is founded and designed through all these generations of inheritance? Should not our purpose be to restore the normal working of that system which has brought to us such immeasurable benefits, and not destroy it?

And in order to indicate to you that the proposals of our opponents will endanger or destroy our system, I propose to analyze a few of the proposals of our opponents in their relation to these fundamentals.

First. A proposal of our opponents which would break down the American system is the expansion of Government expenditure by yielding to sectional and group raids on the Public Treasury. The extension of Government expenditures beyond the minimum limit necessary to conduct the proper functions of the Government enslaves men to work for the Government. If we combine the whole governmental expenditures— National, state, and municipal—we will find that before the World War each citizen worked, theoretically, 25 days out of each year for the Government. In 1924 he worked 46 days a year for the Government. Today he works for the support of all forms of government 61 days out of the year.

No nation can conscript its citizens for this proportion of men's time without national impoverishment and destruction of their liberties. Our Nation cannot do it without destruction to our whole conception of the American system. The Federal Government has been forced in this emergency to unusual expenditures but in partial alleviation of these extraordinary and unusual expenditures, the Republican Administration has made a successful effort to reduce the ordinary running expenses of the Government. Our opponents have persistently interfered with such policies. I only need recall to you that the Democratic House of Representatives passed bills in the last session that would have increased our expenditures by $3,500,000,000, or 87 per cent. Expressed in day [s of] labor, this would have meant the conscription of 16 days' additional work from every citizen for the Government. This I stopped. Furthermore, they refused to accept recommendations from the Administration in respect to $150,000,000 to $200,000,000 of reductions in ordinary expenditures, and finally they forced upon us increasing expenditure of $322,000,000. In spite of this, the ordinary expenses of the Government have been reduced upwards of $200,000,000 during this present administration. They will be decidedly further reduced. But the major point I wish to make—the disheartening part of these proposals of our opponents—is that they represent successful pressures of minorities. They would appeal to sectional and group political support, and thereby impose terrific burdens upon every home in the country. These things can and must be resisted. But they can only be resisted if there shall be live and virile public support to the Administration, in opposition to political log rolling and the sectional and group raids on the Treasury for distribution of public money, which is cardinal in the congeries of elements which make up the Democratic party.

These expenditures proposed by the Democratic House of Representatives for the benefit of special groups and special sections of our country directly undermine the American system. Those who pay are, in the last analysis, the man who works at the bench, the desk, and on the farm. They take away his comfort, stifle his leisure, and destroy his equal opportunity.

Second. Another proposal of our opponents which would destroy the American system is that of inflation of the currency. The bill which passed the last session of the Democratic House called upon the Treasury of the United States to issue $2,300,000,000 in paper currency that would be unconvertible into solid values. Call it what you will, greenbacks or fiat money. It was that nightmare which overhung our own country for years after the Civil War.

In our special situation today the issuance of greenbacks means the immediate departure of this country from the gold standard, as there could be no provision for the redemption of such currency in gold. The new currency must obviously go to immediate and constantly fluctuating discount when associated with currency convertible in gold.

The oldest law of currency is that bad money drives out the good, for a population—every individual—will hoard good currency and endeavor to get rid of the bad. The invariable effect is the withdrawal of a vast sum of good currency from circulation, and at once the Government is forced to print more and more bad paper currency. No candidate and no speaker in this campaign has disavowed this action of the Democratic House. In spite of this visible experience within recollection of this generation, with all its pitiable results, fiat money is proposed by the Democratic Party as a potent measure for relief from this depression.

The use of this expedient by nations in difficulty since the war in Europe has been one of the most tragic disasters to equality of opportunity, the independence of man.

I quote from a revealing speech by Mr. Owen D. Young upon the return of the Dawes Commission:

> . . . he stated, "the currency of Germany was depreciating so rapidly that the industries paid their wages daily, and sometimes indeed twice a day. Standing with the lines of employees was another line of wives and mothers waiting for the marks. The wife grabbed the paper from her husband's hand and rushed to the nearest provision store to spend it quickly before the rapid depreciation had cut its purchasing power in two.
>
> When the chairman of the syndicate of the German Trade Unions, Herr Grasseman, appeared before the Dawes Committee, I put to him this question: 'What can this committee do for German labor?'
>
> I expected the answer to be some one of the slogans of labor: An 8-hour day, old age or disability pensions, insurance against unemployment—something of that kind. Much to my surprise the answer came promptly.
>
> 'What your committee must do for German labor is

to give us a stable currency. Do you know,' Herr Grasseman said, 'that for many months it has been impossible for a wage earner in Germany to perform any of his moral obligations?

> 'Knowing that a child was coming to the family at a certain time, there was no way by which the husband, through effort or sacrifice or savings, could guarantee his wife a doctor and a nurse when that event arrived. One knowing that his mother was stricken with a fatal disease could not by any extra effort or sacrifice or saving be in a position to insure her a decent burial on her death.
>
> 'Your committee must,' Herr Grasseman added, 'just as a basic human thing, give us a stable currency and thereby insure to the worker that his wages will have the same purchasing power when he wants to spend them as they had when he earned them.' "

And I ask: Is that the preservation of opportunity and the protection of men by government?

Third. In the last session the Congress, under the personal leadership of the Democratic Vice Presidential candidate, and their allies in the Senate, enacted a law to extend the Government into personal banking business. This I was compelled to veto, out of fidelity to the whole American system of life and government. I may repeat a part of that veto message—and it remains unchallenged by any Democratic leader. I said:

> It would mean loans against security for any conceivable purpose on any conceivable security to anybody who wants money. It would place the Government in private business in such fashion as to violate the very principle of public relations upon which we have builded [sic] our Nation, and renders insecure its very foundations. Such action would make the Reconstruction Corporation the greatest banking and money-lending institution of all history. It would constitute a gigantic centralization of banking and finance to which the American people have been properly opposed over a hundred years. The purpose of the expansion is no longer in the spirit of solving a great major emergency but to establish a privilege whether it serves a great national end or not.

I further stated:

> It would require the setting up of a huge bureaucracy, to establish branches in every county and town in the United States. Every political pressure would be assembled for particular persons. It would be within the power of these agencies to dictate the welfare of millions of people, to discriminate between competitive business at will, and to deal favor and disaster amongst them. The

organization would be constantly subjected to conspiracies and raids of predatory interests, individuals, and private corporations. Huge losses and great scandals must inevitably result. It would mean the squandering of public credit to be ultimately borne by the taxpayer.

I stated further that—

This proposal violates every sound principle of public finance and of our government. Never before has so dangerous a suggestion been made to our country. Never before has so much power for evil been placed at the unlimited discretion of seven individuals.

They failed to pass this bill over my veto. But you must not be deceived. This is still in their purposes as a part of the new deal.

Fourth. Another proposal of our opponents which would wholly alter our American system of life is to reduce the protective tariff to a competitive tariff for revenue. The protective tariff and its results upon our economic structure has become gradually embedded into our economic life since the first protective tariff act passed by the American Congress under the administration of George Washington. There have been gaps at times of Democratic control when this protection has been taken away. But it has been so embedded that its removal has never failed to bring disaster. Whole towns, communities, and forms of agriculture with their homes, schools and churches have been built up under this system of protection. The grass will grow in streets of a hundred cities, a thousand towns; the weeds will overrun the fields of millions of farms if that protection be taken away. Their churches and school houses will decay.

Incidentally another one of the proposals of our opponents which is to destroy equal opportunity both between individuals and communities is their promise to repeal the independent action of the bipartisan Tariff Commission and thereby return the determination of import duties to the old logrolling greed of group or sectional interest of congressional action in review of the tariff.

Fifth. Another proposal is that the Government go into the power business. Three years ago, in view of the extension of the use of transmission of power over state borders and the difficulties of state regulatory bodies in the face of this interstate action, I recommended to the Congress that such interstate power should be placed under regulation by the Federal Government in cooperation with the state authorities.

That recommendation was in accord with the principles of the Republican Party over the past 50 years, to provide regulation where public interest had developed in tools of industry which was beyond control and regulation of the states.

I succeeded in creating an independent Power Commission to handle such matters, but the Democratic House declined to approve the further powers to this commission necessary for such regulation.

I have stated unceasingly that I am opposed to the Federal Government going into the power business. I have insisted upon rigid regulation. The Democratic candidate has declared that under the same conditions which may make local action of this character desirable, he is prepared to put the Federal Government into the power business. He is being actively supported by a score of Senators in this campaign, many of whose expenses are being paid by the Democratic National Committee, who are pledged to Federal Government development and operation of electrical power.

I find in the instructions to campaign speakers issued by the Democratic National Committee that they are instructed to criticize my action in the veto of the bill which would have put the Government permanently into the operation of power at Muscle Shoals with a capital from the Federal Treasury of over $100,000,000. In fact 31 Democratic Senators, being all except 3, voted to override that veto. In that bill was the flat issue of the Federal Government permanently in competitive business. I vetoed it because of principle and not because it was especially the power business. In that veto I stated that I was firmly opposed to the Federal Government entering into any business, the major purpose of which is competition with our citizens. I said:

There are national emergencies which require that the Government should temporarily enter the field of business but that they must be emergency actions and in matters where the cost of the project is secondary to much higher consideration. There are many localities where the Federal Government is justified in the construction of great dams and reservoirs, where navigation, flood control, reclamation or stream regulation are of dominant importance, and where they are beyond the capacity or purpose of private or local government capital to construct. In these cases, power is often a by-product and should be disposed of by contract or lease. But for the Federal Government to deliberately go out to build up and expand such an occasion to the major purpose of a power and manufacturing business is to break down the initiative and enterprise of the American people; it is destruction of equality of opportunity amongst our people; it is the negation of the ideals upon which our civilization has been based.

This bill raises one of the important issues confronting our people. That is squarely the issue of Federal Government ownership and operation of power and manufacturing business not as a minor by-product but as a major purpose. Involved in this question is the agitation against the conduct of the power industry. The power problem is not to be solved by the Federal Government going into the power business, nor is it to be solved by the project in this bill. The remedy for abuses in the conduct of that industry lies in regulation and not by the Federal Government entering upon the business itself. I have recommended to the Congress on various occasions that action should be taken to establish Federal regulation of interstate power in cooperation with state authorities. This bill would launch the Federal Government upon a policy of ownership of power utilities upon a basis of competition instead of by the proper Government function of regulation for the protection of all the people. I hesitate to contemplate the future of our institutions, of our government, and of our country if the preoccupation of its officials is to be no longer the promotion of justice and equal opportunity but is to be devoted to barter in the markets. That is not liberalism; it is degeneration.

From their utterances in this campaign and elsewhere we are justified in the conclusion that our opponents propose to put the Federal Government in the power business with all its additions to Federal bureaucracy, its tyranny over state and local governments, its undermining of state and local responsibilities and initiative.

Sixth. I may cite another instance of absolutely destructive proposals to our American system by our opponents.

Recently there was circulated through the unemployed in this country a letter from the Democratic candidate in which he stated that he

> would support measures for the inauguration of self-liquidating public works such as the utilization of water resources, flood control, land reclamation, to provide employment for all surplus labor at all times.

I especially emphasize that promise to promote "employment for all surplus labor at all times." At first I could not believe that anyone would be so cruel as to hold out a hope so absolutely impossible of realization to these 10,000,000 who are unemployed. But the authenticity of this promise has been verified. And I protest against such frivolous promises being held out to a suffering people. It is easily demonstrable that no such employment can be found. But the point I wish to make here and now is the mental attitude and spirit of the Democratic Party to attempt it. It is another mark of the character of the new deal and the destructive changes which mean the total abandonment of every principle upon which this government and the American system is founded. If it were possible to give this employment to 10,000,000 people by the Government, it would cost upwards of $9,000,000,000 a year.

The stages of this destruction would be first the destruction of Government credit, the value of Government securities, the destruction of every fiduciary trust in our country, insurance policies and all. It would pull down the employment of those who are still at work by the high taxes and the demoralization of credit upon which their employment is dependent. It would mean the pulling and hauling of politics for projects and measures, the favoring of localities, sections, and groups. It would mean the growth of a fearful bureaucracy which, once established, could never be dislodged. If it were possible, it would mean one-third of the electorate with Government jobs earnest to maintain this bureaucracy and to control the political destinies of the country.

Incidentally, the Democratic candidate has said on several occasions that we must reduce surplus production of agricultural products and yet he proposes to extend this production on a gigantic scale through expansion of reclamation and new agricultural areas to the ruin of the farmer.

I have said before, and I want to repeat on this occasion that the only method by which we can stop the suffering and unemployment is by returning our people to their normal jobs in their normal homes, carrying on their normal functions of living. This can be done only by sound processes of protecting and stimulating recovery of the existing economic system upon which we have builded [sic] our progress thus far—preventing distress and giving such sound employment as we can find in the meantime.

Seventh. Recently, at Indianapolis, I called attention to the statement made by Governor Roosevelt in his address on October 5 with respect to the Supreme Court of the United States. He said:

> After March 4, 1929, the Republican Party was in complete control of all branches of the Government—Executive, Senate and House, and, I may add for good measure, in order to make it complete, the Supreme Court as well.

I am not called upon to defend the Supreme Court of the United States from this slurring reflection. Fortunately that court has jealously maintained over the years its high standard of integrity, impartiality, and freedom from influence of either the Executive or Congress, so that the confidence of the people is sound and unshaken.

But is the Democratic candidate really proposing his conception of the relation of the Executive and the Supreme Court? If that is his idea, he is proposing the most revolutionary new deal, the most stupendous breaking of precedent, the most destructive undermining of the very safeguard of our form of government yet proposed by a presidential candidate.

Eighth. In order that we may get at the philosophical background of the mind which pronounces the necessity for profound change in our American system and a new deal, I would call your attention to an address delivered by the Democratic candidate in San Francisco, early in October.

He said:

> Our industrial plant is built. The problem just now is whether under existing conditions it is not overbuilt. Our last frontier has long since been reached. There is practically no more free land. There is no safety valve in the western prairies where we can go for a new start. . . .
>
> The mere building of more industrial plants, the organization of more corporations is as likely to be as much a danger as a help. . . . Our task now is not the discovery of natural resources or necessarily the production of more goods, it is the sober, less dramatic business of administering the resources and plants already in hand . . . establishing markets for surplus production, of meeting the problem of under-consumption, distributing the wealth and products more equitably and adopting the economic organization to the service of the people. . . .

There are many of these expressions with which no one would quarrel. But I do challenge the whole idea that we have ended the advance of America, that this country has reached the zenith of its power, the height of its development. That is the counsel of despair for the future of America. That is not the spirit by which we shall emerge from this depression. That is not the spirit that made this country. If it is true, every American must abandon the road of countless progress and unlimited opportunity. I deny that the promise of American life has been fulfilled, for that means we have begun the decline and fall. No nation can cease to move forward without degeneration of spirit.

I could quote from gentlemen who have emitted this same note of pessimism in economic depressions going back for 100 years. What Governor Roosevelt has overlooked is the fact that we are yet but on the frontiers of development of science, and of invention. I have only to remind you that discoveries in electricity, the internal-combustion engine, the radio—all of which have sprung into being since our land was settled—have in themselves represented the greatest advances in America. This philosophy upon which the Governor of New York proposes to conduct the Presidency of the United States is the philosophy of stagnation, of despair. It is the end of hope. The destinies of this country should not be dominated by that spirit in action. It would be the end of the American system.

I have recited to you the progress of this last generation. Progress in that generation was not due to the opening up of new agricultural land; it was due to the scientific research, the opening of new invention, new flashes of light from the intelligence of our people. These brought the improvements in agriculture and in industry. There are a thousand inventions for comfort in the lockers of science and invention which have not yet come to light; all are but on their frontiers. As for myself I am confident that if we do not destroy this American system, if we continue to stimulate scientific research, if we continue to give it the impulse of initiative and enterprise, if we continue to build voluntary cooperative action instead of financial concentration, if we continue to build it into a system of free men, my children will enjoy the same opportunity that have [sic] come to me and to the whole 120,000,000 of my countrymen. I wish to see American Government conducted in this faith and in this hope.

If these measures, these promises, which I have discussed, or these failures to disavow these projects, this attitude of mind, mean anything, they mean the enormous expansion of the Federal Government; they mean the growth of bureaucracy such as we have never seen in our history. No man who has not occupied my position in Washington can fully realize the constant battle which must be carried on against incompetence, corruption, tyranny of government expanded into business activities. If we first examine the effect on our form of government of such a program, we come at once to the effect of the most gigantic increase in expenditure ever known in history. That alone would break down the savings, the wages, the equality of opportunity among our people. These measures would transfer vast responsibilities to the Federal Government from the states, the local governments, and the individuals. But that is not all; they would break down our form of government. Our legislative bodies can not delegate their authority to any dictator, but without such delegation every member of these bodies is impelled in representation of the interest of his constituents constantly to seek privilege and demand service in the use of such agencies. Every time the Federal Government extends its arm, 531 Senators and Congressmen become actual boards of directors of that business.

Capable men can not be chosen by politics for all the various talents required. Even if they were supermen, if there were no politics in the selection of the Congress, if there were no constant pressure for this and for that, so large a number would be incapable as a board of directors of any institution. At once when these extensions take place by the Federal Government, the authority and responsibility of state governments and institutions are undermined. Every enterprise of private business is at once halted to know what Federal action is going to be. It destroys initiative and courage. We can do no better than quote that great statesman of labor, the late Samuel Gompers, in speaking of a similar situation:

> It is a question of whether it shall be government ownership or private ownership under control. If I were a minority of one in this convention, I would want to cast my vote so that the men of labor shall not willingly enslave themselves to government in their industrial effort.

We have heard a great deal in this campaign about reactionaries, conservatives, progressives, liberals, and radicals. I have not yet heard an attempt by any one of the orators who mouth these phrases to define the principles upon which they base these classifications. There is one thing I can say without any question of doubt—that is, that the spirit of liberalism is to create free men; it is not the regimentation of men. It is not the extension of bureaucracy. I have said in this city before now that you can not extend the mastery of government over the daily life of a people without somewhere making it master of people's souls and thoughts. Expansion of government in business means that the Government in order to protect itself from the political consequences of its errors is driven irresistibly without peace to greater and greater control of the Nation's press and platform. Free speech does not live many hours after free industry and free commerce die. It is a false liberalism that interprets itself into Government operation of business. Every step in that direction poisons the very roots of liberalism. It poisons political equality, free speech, free press, and equality of oppor-

tunity. It is the road not to liberty but to less liberty. True liberalism is found not in striving to spread bureaucracy, but in striving to set bounds to it. True liberalism seeks all legitimate freedom first in the confident belief that without such freedom the pursuit of other blessings is in vain. Liberalism is a force truly of the spirit proceeding from the deep realization that economic freedom can not be sacrificed if political freedom is to be preserved.

Even if the Government conduct of business could give us the maximum of efficiency instead of least efficiency, it would be purchased at the cost of freedom. It would increase rather than decrease abuse and corruption, stifle initiative and invention, undermine development of leadership, cripple mental and spiritual energies of our people, extinguish equality of opportunity, and dry up the spirit of liberty and progress. Men who are going about this country announcing that they are liberals because of their promises to extend the Government in business are not liberals, they are reactionaries of the United States.

And I do not wish to be misquoted or misunderstood. I do not mean that our government is to part with one iota of its national resources without complete protection to the public interest. I have already stated that democracy must remain master in its own house. I have stated that abuse and wrongdoing must be punished and controlled. Nor do I wish to be misinterpreted as stating that the United States is a free-for-all and devil-take-the-hindermost society.

The very essence of equality of opportunity of our American system is that there shall be no monopoly or domination by any group or section in this country, whether it be business, sectional or a group interest. On the contrary, our American system demands economic justice as well as political and social justice; it is not a system of laissez faire.

I am not setting up the contention that our American system is perfect. No human ideal has ever been perfectly attained, since humanity itself is not perfect. But the wisdom of our forefathers and the wisdom of the 30 men who have preceded me in this office hold to the conception that progress can only be attained as the sum of accomplishments of free individuals, and they have held unalterably to these principles.

In the ebb and flow of economic life our people in times of prosperity and ease naturally tend to neglect the vigilance over their rights. Moreover, wrongdoing is obscured by apparent success in enterprise. Then insidious diseases and wrongdoings grow apace. But we have in the past seen in times of distress and difficulty that wrongdoing and weakness come to the surface and our people, in their endeavors to correct these wrongs, are tempted to extremes which may destroy rather than build.

It is men who do wrong, not our institutions. It is men, who violate the laws and public rights. It is men, not institutions, which must be punished.

In my acceptance speech four years ago at Palo Alto I stated that—

> One of the oldest aspirations of the human race was the abolition of poverty. By poverty I mean the grinding by under-nourishment, cold, ignorance, fear of old age of those who have the will to work.

I stated that—

> In America today we are nearer a final triumph over poverty than in any land. The poorhouse has vanished from amongst us; we have not reached that goal, but given a chance to go forward, we shall, with the help of God, be in sight of the day when poverty will be banished from this Nation.

Our Democratic friends have quoted this passage many times in this campaign. I do not withdraw a word of it. When I look about the world even in these times of trouble and distress I find it more true in this land than anywhere else under the traveling sun. I am not ashamed of it, because I am not ashamed of holding ideals and purposes for the progress of the American people. Are my Democratic opponents prepared to state that they do not stand for this ideal or this hope? For my part, I propose to continue to strive for it, and I hope to live to see it accomplished.

One of the most encouraging and inspiring phases of this whole campaign has been the unprecedented interest of our younger men and women. It is in this group that we find our new homes being founded, our new families in which the children are being taught those basic principles of love and faith and patriotism. It is in this group that we find the starting of business and professional careers with courageous and hopeful faces turned to the future and its promise. It is this group who must undertake the guardianship of our American system and carry it forward to its greater achievements.

Inevitably in the progress of time, our country and its institutions will be entirely in their hands. The burdens of the depression have fallen on the younger generation with equal and perhaps greater severity than upon the elders. It has affected not only their economic well-being, but has tended also to shatter many illusions. But their faith in our country and its institutions has not been shaken. I am confident that they will resist any destruction to our American system of political, economic and social life.

It is a tribute to America and its past and present leaders and even more a tribute to this younger generation that, contrary to the experience of other countries, we can say tonight that the youth of America is more staunch than many of their elders. I can ask no higher tribute from my party for the maintenance of the American system and the program of my administration than the support being given by the younger men and women of our country. It has just been communicated to me that tonight at this time, in every county and almost every precinct of our country, 3,000,000 members of the Young Republican League are meeting for the support of a Republican victory November 8th—a victory for the American system.

My countrymen, the proposals of our opponents represent a profound change in American life—less in concrete proposal, bad as that may be, than by implication and by evasion. Dominantly in their spirit they represent a radical departure from the foundations of 150 years which have made this the greatest nation in the world. This election is not a mere shift from the ins to the outs. It means deciding the direction our Nation will take over a century to come.

My conception of America is a land where men and women may walk in ordered liberty, where they may enjoy the advantages of wealth not concentrated in the hands of a few but diffused through the lives of all, where they build and safeguard their homes, give to their children full opportunities of American life, where every man shall be respected in the faith that his conscience and his heart direct him to follow, where people secure in their liberty shall have leisure and impulse to seek a fuller life. That leads to the release of the energies of men and women, to the wider vision and higher hope; it leads to opportunity for greater and greater service not alone of man to man in our country but from our country to the world. It leads to health in body and a spirit unfettered, youthful, eager with a vision stretching beyond the farthest horizons with an open mind, sympathetic and generous. But that must be builded [sic] upon our experience with the past, upon the foundations which have made our country great. It must be the product of our truly American system.

From: William Starr Myers, ed. *The State Papers and Other Public Writings of Herbert Hoover*, Garden City, NY: Doubleday, Doran and Company, 1934.

ROOSEVELT'S FIRST INAUGURAL ADDRESS, MARCH 4, 1933

Perhaps the most famous of Franklin D. Roosevelt's addresses, his first inaugural attempted to reassure the nation that a new and vigorous leadership had taken charge. With candor unusual in such an address, Roosevelt let the American people know that he was quite aware of the dire economic situation facing the country. But his words of hope—that "the only thing we have to fear is fear itself"—were intended to infuse courage into his listeners. And by the accounts of the day in the press and elsewhere, his reassurance appeared to work.

I am certain that my fellow Americans expect that on my induction into the Presidency I will address them with a candor and a decision which the present situation of our Nation impels. This is preeminently the time to speak the truth, the whole truth, frankly and boldly. Nor need we shrink from honestly facing conditions in our country today. This great Nation will endure as it has endured, will revive and will prosper. So, first of all, let me assert my firm belief that the only thing we have to fear is fear itself—nameless, unreasoning, unjustified terror which paralyzes needed efforts to convert retreat into advance. In every dark hour of our national life a leadership of frankness and vigor has met with that understanding and support of the people themselves which is essential to victory. I am convinced that you will again give that support to leadership in these critical days.

In such a spirit on my part and on yours we face our common difficulties. They concern, thank God, only material things. Values have shrunken to fantastic levels; taxes have risen; our ability to pay has fallen; government of all kinds is faced by serious curtailment of income; the means of exchange are frozen in the currents of trade; the withered leaves of industrial enterprise lie on every side; farmers find no markets for their produce; the savings of many years in thousands of families are gone.

More important, a host of unemployed citizens face the grim problem of existence, and an equally great number toil with little return. Only a foolish optimist can deny the dark realities of the moment.

Yet our distress comes from no failure of substance. We are stricken by no plague of locusts. Compared with the perils which our forefathers conquered because they believed and were not afraid, we have still much to be thankful for. Nature still offers her bounty and human efforts have multiplied it. Plenty is at our doorstep, but a generous use of it languishes in the very sight of the supply. Primarily this is because rulers of the exchange of mankind's goods have failed through their own stubbornness and their own incompetence, have admitted their failure, and have abdicated. Practices of the unscrupulous money changers stand indicted in the court of public opinion, rejected by the hearts and minds of men.

True they have tried, but their efforts have been cast in the pattern of an outworn tradition. Faced by failure of credit they have proposed only the lending of more money. Stripped of the lure of profit by which to induce our people to follow their false leadership, they have resorted to exhortations, pleading tearfully for restored confidence. They know only the rules of a generation of self-seekers. They have no vision, and when there is no vision the people perish.

The money changers have fled from their high seats in the temple of our civilization. We may now restore that temple to the ancient truths. The measure of the restoration lies in the extent to which we apply social values more noble than mere monetary profit.

Happiness lies not in the mere possession of money; it lies in the joy of achievement, in the thrill of creative effort. The joy and moral stimulation of work no longer must be forgotten in the mad chase of evanescent profits. These dark days will be worth all they cost us if they teach us that our true destiny is not to be ministered unto but to minister to ourselves and to our fellow men.

Recognition of the falsity of material wealth as the standard of success goes hand in hand with the abandonment of the false belief that public office and high political position are to be valued only by the standards of pride of place and personal profit; and there must be an end to a conduct in banking and in business which too often has given to a sacred trust the likeness of callous and selfish wrongdoing. Small wonder that confidence languishes, for it thrives only on honesty, on honor, on the sacredness of obligations, on faithful protection, on unselfish performance; without them it cannot live.

Restoration calls, however, not for changes in

ethics alone. This Nation asks for action, and action now.

Our greatest primary task is to put people to work. This is no unsolvable problem if we face it wisely and courageously. It can be accomplished in part by direct recruiting by the Government itself, treating the task as we would treat the emergency of a war, but at the same time, through this employment, accomplishing greatly needed projects to stimulate and reorganize the use of our natural resources.

Hand in hand with this we must frankly recognize the overbalance of population in our industrial centers and, by engaging on a national scale in a redistribution, endeavor to provide a better use of the land for those best fitted for the land. The task can be helped by definite efforts to raise the values of agricultural products and with this the power to purchase the output of our cities. It can be helped by preventing realistically the tragedy of the growing loss through foreclosure of our small homes and our farms. It can be helped by insistence that the Federal, State, and local Governments act forthwith on the demand that their cost be drastically reduced. It can be helped by the unifying of relief activities which today are often scattered, uneconomical, and unequal. It can be helped by national planning for and supervision of all forms of transportation and of communications and other utilities which have a definitely public character. There are many ways in which it can be helped, but it can never be helped merely by talking about it. We must act and act quickly.

Finally, in our progress toward a resumption of work we require two safeguards against a return of the evils of the old order: there must be a strict supervision of all banking and credits and investments, so that there will be an end to speculation with other people's money; and there must be provision for an adequate but sound currency.

These are the lines of attack. I shall presently urge upon a new Congress, in special session, detailed measures for their fulfillment, and I shall seek the immediate assistance of the several States.

Through this program of action we address ourselves to putting our own national house in order and making income balance outgo. Our international trade relations, though vastly important, are in point of time and necessity secondary to the establishment of a sound national economy. I favor as a practical policy the putting of first things first. I shall spare no effort to restore world trade by international economic readjustment, but the emergency at home cannot wait on that accomplishment.

The basic thought that guides these specific means

of national recovery is not narrowly nationalistic. It is the insistence, as a first consideration, upon the interdependence of the various elements in and parts of the United States—a recognition of the old and permanently important manifestation of the American spirit of the pioneer. It is the way to recovery. It is the immediate way. It is the strongest assurance that the recovery will endure.

In the field of world policy I would dedicate this Nation to the policy of the good neighbor—the neighbor who resolutely respects himself and, because he does so, respects the rights of others—the neighbor who respects his obligations and respects the sanctity of his agreements in and with a world of neighbors.

If I read the temper of our people correctly, we now realize as we have never realized before our interdependence on each other; that we cannot merely take but we must give as well; that if we are to go forward, we must move as a trained and loyal army willing to sacrifice for the good of a common discipline, because without such discipline no progress is made, no leadership becomes effective. We are, I know, ready and willing to submit our lives and property to such discipline, because it makes possible a leadership which aims at a larger good. This I propose to offer, pledging that the larger purposes will bind upon us all as a sacred obligation with a unity of duty hitherto evolved only in time of armed strife.

With this pledge taken, I assume unhesitatingly the leadership of this great army of our people dedicated to a disciplined attack upon our common problems.

Action in this image and to this end is feasible under the form of government which we have inherited from our ancestors. Our Constitution is so simple and practical that it is possible always to meet extraordinary needs by changes in emphasis and arrangement without loss of essential form. That is why our constitutional system has proved itself the most superbly enduring political mechanism the modern world has produced. It has met every stress of vast expansion of territory, of foreign wars, of bitter internal strife, of world relations.

It is to be hoped that the normal balance of Executive and legislative authority may be wholly adequate to meet the unprecedented task before us. But it may be that an unprecedented demand and need for undelayed action may call for temporary departure from that normal balance of public procedure.

I am prepared under my constitutional duty to recommend the measures that a stricken Nation in the midst of a stricken world may require. These measures, or such other measures as the Congress may build out of its experience and wisdom, I shall seek, within my constitutional authority, to bring to speedy adoption.

But in the event that the Congress shall fail to take one of these two courses, and in the event that the national emergency is still critical, I shall not evade the clear course of duty that will then confront me. I shall ask the Congress for the one remaining instrument to meet the crisis—broad Executive power to wage a war against the emergency, as great as the power that would be given to me if we were in fact invaded by a foreign foe.

For the trust reposed in me I will return the courage and the devotion that befit the time. I can do no less.

We face the arduous days that lie before us in the warm courage of national unity; with the clear consciousness of seeking old and precious moral values;

with the clean satisfaction that comes from the stern performance of duty by old and young alike. We aim at the assurance of a rounded and permanent national life.

We do not distrust the future of essential democracy. The people of the United States have not failed. In their need they have registered a mandate that they want direct, vigorous action. They have asked for discipline and direction under leadership. They have made me the present instrument of their wishes. In the spirit of the gift I take it.

In this dedication of a Nation we humbly ask the blessing of God. May He protect each and every one of us. May He guide me in the days to come.

From: B. D. Zevin, ed. *Nothing to Fear: The Selected Addresses of Franklin Delano Roosevelt, 1932–1945*. Boston: Houghton Mifflin, 1946.

FIRESIDE CHAT ON THE BANKING CRISIS, MARCH 12, 1933

President Franklin D. Roosevelt inaugurated his famous series of radio chats to the American people with a discussion of the banking crisis he faced upon coming to office in March 1933. As the transcript below indicates, Roosevelt—a master of the new medium—understood the power of radio to create a sense of intimacy with the audience. In this address, he spoke in plain, commonsense terms about the cause of the crisis and what his new administration was doing to fix it. Perhaps as much as any legislation or executive action, this fireside chat helped alleviate the panic gripping the nation's banks in early 1933.

I want to talk for a few minutes with the people of the United States about banking—with the comparatively few who understand the mechanics of banking but more particularly with the overwhelming majority who use banks for the making of deposits and the drawing of checks. I want to tell you what has been done in the last few days, why it was done, and what the next steps are going to be. I recognize that the many proclamations from State capitols and from Washington, the legislation, the Treasury regulations, etc., couched for the most part in banking and legal terms, should be explained for the benefit of the average citizen. I owe this in particular because of the fortitude and good temper with which everybody has accepted the inconvenience

and hardships of the banking holiday. I know that when you understand what we in Washington have been about I shall continue to have your cooperation as fully as I have had your sympathy and help during the past week.

First of all, let me state the simple fact that when you deposit money in a bank the bank does not put the money into a safe deposit vault. It invests your money in many different forms of credit—bonds, commercial paper, mortgages and many other kinds of loans. In other words, the bank puts your money to work to keep the wheels of industry and of agriculture turning around. A comparatively small part of the money you put into the bank is kept in currency—an amount which in normal times is wholly sufficient to cover the cash needs of the average citizen. In other words, the total amount of all the currency in the country is only a small fraction of the total deposits in all of the banks.

What, then, happened during the last few days of February and the first few days of March? Because of undermined confidence on the part of the public, there was a general rush by a large portion of our population to turn bank deposits into currency or gold—a rush so great that the soundest banks could not get enough currency to meet the demand. The reason for this was that on the spur of the moment it was, of course, impossible to sell perfectly sound assets of a bank and convert them into cash except at panic prices far below their real value.

By the afternoon of March third scarcely a bank in the country was open to do business. Proclamations temporarily closing them in whole or in part had been issued by the Governors in almost all the States.

It was then that I issued the proclamation providing for the nationwide bank holiday, and this was the first step in the Government's reconstruction of our financial and economic fabric.

The second step was the legislation promptly and patriotically passed by the Congress confirming my proclamation and broadening my powers so that it became possible in view of the requirement of time to extend the holiday and lift the ban of that holiday gradually. This law also gave authority to develop a program of rehabilitation of our banking facilities. I want to tell our citizens in every part of the Nation that the national Congress—Republicans and Democrats alike—showed by this action a devotion to public welfare and a realization of the emergency and the necessity for speed that is difficult to match in our history.

The third stage has been the series of regulations permitting the banks to continue their functions to take care of the distribution of food and household necessities and the payment of payrolls.

This bank holiday, while resulting in many cases in great inconvenience, is affording us the opportunity to supply the currency necessary to meet the situation. No sound bank is a dollar worse off than it was when it closed its doors last Monday. Neither is any bank which may turn out not to be in a position for immediate opening. The new law allows the twelve Federal Reserve Banks to issue additional currency on good assets and thus the banks which reopen will be able to meet every legitimate call. The new currency is being sent out by the Bureau of Engraving and Printing in large volume to every part of the country. It is sound currency because it is backed by actual, good assets.

A question you will ask is this: why are all the banks not to be reopened at the same time? The answer is simple. Your Government does not intend that the history of the past few years shall be repeated. We do not want and will not have another epidemic of bank failures.

As a result, we start tomorrow, Monday, with the opening of banks in the twelve Federal Reserve Bank cities—those banks which on first examination by the Treasury have already been found to be all right. This will be followed on Tuesday by the resumption of all their functions by banks already found to be sound in cities where there are recognized clearing houses. That means about two hundred fifty cities of the United States.

On Wednesday and succeeding days banks in smaller places all through the country will resume business, subject, of course, to the Government's physical ability to complete its survey. It is necessary that the reopening of banks be extended over a period in order to permit the banks to make applications for necessary loans, to obtain currency needed to meet their requirements and to enable the Government to make common sense checkups.

Let me make it clear to you that if your bank does not open the first day you are by no means justified in believing that it will not open. A bank that opens on one of the subsequent days is in exactly the same status as the bank that opens tomorrow.

I know that many people are worrying about State banks not members of the Federal Reserve System. These banks can and will receive assistance from member banks and from the Reconstruction Finance Corporation. These State banks are following the same course as the National banks except that they get their licenses to resume business from the State authorities, and these authorities have been asked by the Secretary of the Treasury to permit their good banks to open up on the same schedule as the national banks. I am confident that the State Banking Departments will be as careful as the national Government in the policy relating to the opening of banks and will follow the same broad policy.

It is possible that when the banks resume a very few people who have not recovered from their fear may again begin withdrawals. Let me make it clear that the banks will take care of all needs—and it is my belief that hoarding during the past week has become an exceedingly unfashionable pastime. It needs no prophet to tell you that when the people find that they can get their money—that they can get it when they want it for all legitimate purposes—the phantom of fear will soon be laid. People will again be glad to have their money where it will be safely taken care of and where they can use it conveniently at any time. I can assure you that it is safer to keep your money in a reopened bank than under the mattress.

The success of our whole great national program depends, of course, upon the cooperation of the public—on its intelligent support and use of a reliable system.

Remember that the essential accomplishment of

the new legislation is that it makes it possible for banks more readily to convert their assets into cash than was the case before. More liberal provision has been made for banks to borrow on these assets at the Reserve Banks and more liberal provision has also been made for issuing currency on the security of these good assets. This currency is not fiat currency. It is issued only on adequate security, and every good bank has an abundance of such security.

One more point before I close. There will be, of course, some banks unable to reopen without being reorganized. The new law allows the Government to assist in making these reorganizations quickly and effectively and even allows the Government to subscribe to at least a part of new capital which may be required.

I hope you can see from this elemental recital of what your Government is doing that there is nothing complex, or radical, in the process.

We had a bad banking situation. Some of our bankers had shown themselves either incompetent or dishonest in their handling of the people's funds. They had used the money entrusted to them in speculations and unwise loans. This was, of course, not true in the vast majority of our banks, but it was true in enough of them to shock the people for a time into a sense of insecurity and to put them into a frame of mind where they did not differentiate, but seemed to assume that the acts of a comparative few had tainted them all. It was the Government's job to straighten out this situation and do it as quickly as possible. And the job is being performed.

I do not promise you that every bank will be reopened or that individual losses will not be suffered, but there will be no losses that possibly could be avoided; and there would have been more and greater losses had we continued to drift. I can even promise you salvation for some at least of the sorely pressed banks. We shall be engaged not merely in reopening sound banks but in the creation of sound banks through reorganization.

It has been wonderful to me to catch the note of confidence from all over the country. I can never be sufficiently grateful to the people for the loyal support they have given me in their acceptance of the judgment that has dictated our course, even though all our processes may not have seemed clear to them.

After all, there is an element in the readjustment of our financial system more important than currency, more important than gold, and that is the confidence of the people. Confidence and courage are the essentials of success in carrying out our plan. You people must have faith; you must not be stampeded by rumors or guesses. Let us unite in banishing fear. We have provided the machinery to restore our financial system; it is up to you to support and make it work.

It is your problem no less than it is mine. Together we cannot fail.

From: B. D. Zevin, ed. *Nothing to Fear: The Selected Addresses of Franklin Delano Roosevelt, 1932–1945*. Boston: Houghton Mifflin, 1946.

SPEECH ON THE NATIONAL RECOVERY ADMINISTRATION, JULY 24, 1933

Not one of his fireside chats but a radio appeal to the American people, the following address by President Franklin D. Roosevelt was intended to rally support for the National Industry Recovery Act and the Agricultural Adjustment Act. The first of these two pieces of legislation—introduced in 1933—were intended to regulate American business and industry in such a way as to raise prices and wages. The National Recovery Adminstration also created the Public Works Administration, which offered public works jobs to millions of Americans. Meanwhile, the Agricultural Adjustment Act was designed to lift farm prices through limits on production and subsidies

to farmers who plowed crops under. Since businesses, workers, and farmers would participate on a voluntary basis, the Roosevelt administration created an outreach program to draw them in. This radio appeal was part of the effort to recruit the American people to participate in these programs.

After the adjournment of the historical special session of the Congress five weeks ago I purposely refrained from addressing you for two very good reasons.

First, I think that we all wanted the opportunity of a little quiet thought to examine and assimilate in a mental picture the crowding events of the hundred days which had been devoted to the starting of the wheels of the New Deal.

Secondly, I wanted a few weeks in which to set up the new administrative organization and to see the first fruits of our careful planning.

I think it will interest you if I set forth the fundamentals of this planning for national recovery; and this I am very certain will make it abundantly clear to you that all of the proposals and all of the legislation since the fourth day of March have not been just a collection of haphazard schemes, but rather the orderly component parts of a connected and logical whole.

Long before Inauguration Day I became convinced that individual effort and local effort and even disjointed Federal effort had failed and of necessity would fail and, therefore, that a rounded leadership by the Federal Government had become a necessity both of theory and of fact. Such leadership, however, had its beginning in preserving and strengthening the credit of the United States Government, because without that no leadership was a possibility. For years the Government had not lived within its income. The immediate task was to bring our regular expenses within our revenues. That has been done.

It may seem inconsistent for a government to cut down its regular expenses and at the same time to borrow and to spend billions for an emergency. But it is not inconsistent because a large portion of the emergency money has been paid out in the form of sound loans which will be repaid to the Treasury over a period of years; and to cover the rest of the emergency money we have imposed taxes to pay the interest and the installments on that part of the debt.

So you will see that we have kept our credit good. We have built a granite foundation in a period of confusion. That foundation of the Federal credit stands there broad and sure. It is the base of the whole recovery plan.

Then came the part of the problem that concerned the credit of the individual citizens themselves. You and I know of the banking crisis and of the great danger to the savings of our people. On March sixth every national bank was closed. One month later ninety per cent of the deposits in the national banks had been made available to the depositors. Today only about five per cent of the deposits in national banks are still tied up. The condition relating to State banks, while not quite so good on a percentage basis, is showing a steady reduction in the total of frozen deposits—a result much better than we had expected three months ago.

The problem of the credit of the individual was made more difficult because of another fact. The dollar was a different dollar from the one with which the average debt had been incurred. For this reason large numbers of people were actually losing possession of and title to their farms and homes. All of you know the financial steps which have been taken to correct this inequality. In addition the Home Loan Act, the Farm Loan Act and the Bankruptcy Act were passed.

It was a vital necessity to restore purchasing power by reducing the debt and interest charges upon our people, but while we were helping people to save their credit it was at the same time absolutely essential to do something about the physical needs of hundreds of thousands who were in dire straits at that very moment. Municipal and State aid were being stretched to the limit. We appropriated half a billion dollars to supplement their efforts and in addition, as you know, we have put three hundred thousand young men into practical and useful work in our forests and to prevent flood and soil erosion. The wages they earn are going in greater part to the support of the nearly one million people who constitute their families.

In this same classification we can properly place the great public works program running to a total of over three billion dollars—to be used for highways and ships and flood prevention and inland navigation and thousands of self-sustaining State and municipal improvements. Two points should be made clear in the allotting and administration of these projects: first, we are using the utmost care to choose labor-creating, quick-acting, useful projects, avoiding the smell of the pork barrel; and second, we are hoping that at least half of the money will come back to the Government from projects which will pay for themselves over a period of years.

Thus far I have spoken primarily of the foundation stones—the measures that were necessary to reestablish credit and to head people in the opposite direction by preventing distress and providing as much work as possible through governmental agencies. Now I come to the links which will build us a more lasting prosperity. I have said that we cannot attain that in a Nation half boom and half broke. If all of our people have work and fair wages and fair profits, they can buy the products of their neighbors, and business is good. But if you take away the wages and the profits of half of them, business is only half as good. It does not help much if the fortunate half is very prosperous; the best way is for everybody to be reasonably prosperous.

For many years the two great barriers to a normal

prosperity have been low farm prices and the creeping paralysis of unemployment. These factors have cut the purchasing power of the country in half. I promised action. Congress did its part when it passed the Farm and the Industrial Recovery Acts. Today we are putting these two Acts to work and they will work if people understand their plain objectives.

First, the Farm Act: It is based on the fact that the purchasing power of nearly half our population depends on adequate prices for farm products. We have been producing more of some crops than we consume or can sell in a depressed world market. The cure is not to produce so much. Without our help the farmers cannot get together and cut production, and the Farm Bill gives them a method of bringing their production down to a reasonable level and of obtaining reasonable prices for their crops. I have clearly stated that this method is in a sense experimental, but so far as we have gone we have reason to believe that it will produce good results.

It is obvious that if we can greatly increase the purchasing power of the tens of millions of our people who make a living from farming and the distribution of farm crops, we shall greatly increase the consumption of those goods which are turned out by industry.

That brings me to the final step—bringing back industry along sound lines.

Last autumn, on several occasions, I expressed my faith that we can make possible by democratic self-discipline in industry general increases in wages and shortening of hours sufficient to enable industry to pay its own workers enough to let those workers buy and use the things that their labor produces. This can be done only if we permit and encourage cooperative action in industry, because it is obvious that without united action a few selfish men in each competitive group will pay starvation wages and insist on long hours of work. Others in that group must either follow suit or close up shop. We have seen the result of action of that kind in the continuing descent into the economic hell of the past four years.

There is a clear way to reverse that process: If all employers in each competitive group agree to pay their workers the same wages—reasonable wages—and require the same hours—reasonable hours—then higher wages and shorter hours will hurt no employer. Moreover, such action is better for the employer than unemployment and low wages, because it makes more buyers for his product. That is the simple idea which is the very heart of the Industrial Recovery Act.

On the basis of this simple principle of everybody doing things together, we are starting out on this na-

tionwide attack on unemployment. It will succeed if our people understand it—in the big industries, in the little shops, in the great cities and in the small villages. There is nothing complicated about it and there is nothing particularly new in the principle. It goes back to the basic idea of society and of the Nation itself that people acting in a group can accomplish things which no individual acting alone could even hope to bring about.

Here is an example. In the Cotton Textile Code and in other agreements already signed, child labor has been abolished. That makes me personally happier than any other one thing with which I have been connected since I came to Washington. In the textile industry—an industry which came to me spontaneously and with a splendid cooperation as soon as the Recovery Act was signed—child labor was an old evil. But no employer acting alone was able to wipe it out. If one employer tried it, or if one State tried it, the costs of operation rose so high that it was impossible to compete with the employers or States which had failed to act. The moment the Recovery Act was passed, this monstrous thing which neither opinion nor law could reach through years of effort went out in a flash. As a British editorial put it, we did more under a Code in one day than they in England had been able to do under the common law in eighty-five years of effort. I use this incident, my friends, not to boast of what has already been done but to point the way to you for even greater cooperative efforts this summer and autumn.

We are not going through another winter like the last. I doubt if ever any people so bravely and cheerfully endured a season half so bitter. We cannot ask America to continue to face such needless hardships. It is time for courageous action, and the Recovery Bill gives us the means to conquer unemployment with exactly the same weapon that we have used to strike down child labor.

The proposition is simply this:

If all employers will act together to shorten hours and raise wages we can put people back to work. No employer will suffer, because the relative level of competitive cost will advance by the same amount for all. But if any considerable group should lag or shirk, this great opportunity will pass us by and we shall go into another desperate winter. This must not happen.

We have sent out to all employers an agreement which is the result of weeks of consultation. This agreement checks against the voluntary codes of nearly all the large industries which have already been submitted. This blanket agreement carries the unanimous approval of the three boards which I have appointed to advise in this, boards representing the great leaders in labor, in industry, and in social service. The agreement has already brought a flood of approval from every State, and from so wide a cross-section of the common calling of industry that I know it is fair for all. It is a plan—deliberate, reasonable and just—intended to put into effect at once the most important of the broad principles which are being established, industry by industry, through codes. Naturally, it takes a good deal of organizing and a great many hearings and many months, to get these codes perfected and signed, and we cannot wait for all of them to go through. The blanket agreements, however, which I am sending to every employer will start the wheels turning now, and not six months from now.

There are, of course, men, a few men, who might thwart this great common purpose by seeking selfish advantage. There are adequate penalties in the law, but I am now asking the cooperation that comes from opinion and from conscience. These are the only instruments we shall use in this great summer offensive against unemployment. But we shall use them to the limit to protect the willing from the laggard and to make the plan succeed.

In war, in the gloom of night attack, soldiers wear a bright badge on their shoulders to be sure that comrades do not fire on comrades. On that principle, those who cooperate in this program must know each other at a glance. That is why we have provided a badge of honor for this purpose, a simple design with a legend, "We do our part," and I ask that all those who join with me shall display that badge prominently. It is essential to our purpose.

Already all the great, basic industries have come forward willingly with proposed codes, and in these codes they accept the principles leading to mass reemployment. But, important as is this heartening demonstration, the richest field for results is among the small employers, those whose contribution will be to give new work for from one to ten people. These smaller employers are indeed a vital part of the backbone of the country, and the success of our plan lies largely in their hands.

Already the telegrams and letters are pouring into the White House—messages from employers who ask that their names be placed on this special Roll of Honor. They represent great corporations and companies, and partnerships and individuals. I ask that even before the dates set in the agreements which we have sent out, the employers of the country who have not already done so—the big fellows and the little fellows—shall at once write or telegraph to me personally at the White House, expressing their intentions of going through with the plan. And it is my purpose to keep posted in the post office of every town, a Roll of Honor of all those who join with me.

I want to take this occasion to say to the twenty-four Governors who are now in conference in San Francisco, that nothing thus far has helped in strengthening this great movement more than their resolutions adopted at the very outset of their meeting, giving this plan their instant and unanimous approval, and pledging to support it in their States.

To the men and women whose lives have been darkened by the fact or the fear of unemployment, I am justified in saying a word of encouragement because the codes and the agreements already approved, or about to be passed upon, prove that the plan does raise wages, and that it does put people back to work. You can look on every employer who adopts the plan as one who is doing his part, and those employers deserve well of everyone who works for a living. It will be clear to you, as it is to me, that while the shirking employer may undersell his competitor, the saving he thus makes is made at the expense of his country's welfare.

While we are making this great common effort there should be no discord and dispute. This is no time to cavil or to question the standard set by this universal agreement. It is time for patience and understanding and cooperation. The workers of this country have rights under this law which cannot be taken from them, and nobody will be permitted to whittle them away but, on the other hand, no aggression is now necessary to attain those rights. The whole country will be united to get them for you. The principle that applies to the employers applies to the workers as well, and I ask you workers to cooperate in the same spirit.

When Andrew Jackson, "Old Hickory," died, someone asked, "Will he go to Heaven?" and the answer was, "He will if he wants to." If I am asked whether the American people will pull themselves out of this depression, I answer, "They will if they want to." The essence of the plan is a universal limitation of hours of work per week for any individual by common consent, and a universal payment of wages above a minimum, also by common consent. I cannot guarantee the success of this nationwide plan, but the people of this country can guarantee its success. I have no faith in "cure-alls" but I believe that we can greatly influence economic forces. I have no sympathy with the professional economists who insist that things must run their course and that human agencies can have no influence on economic ills. One reason is that I happen to know that professional economists have changed their definition of economic laws every five or ten years for a very long time, but I do have faith, and retain faith, in the strength of the common purpose, and in the strength of unified action taken by the American people.

That is why I am describing to you the simple purposes and the solid foundations upon which our program of recovery is built. That is why I am asking the employers of the Nation to sign this common covenant with me—to sign it in the name of patriotism and humanity. That is why I am asking the workers to go along with us in a spirit of understanding and of helpfulness.

From: B. D. Zevin, ed. *Nothing to Fear: The Selected Addresses of Franklin Delano Roosevelt, 1932–1945.* Boston: Houghton Mifflin, 1946.

HUEY P. LONG'S "EVERY MAN A KING" SPEECH, FEBRUARY 23, 1934

By 1934, many of Franklin D. Roosevelt's early supporters were turning against him and his New Deal programs, as inadequately radical to solve the economic crisis gripping the country. Most potent among these critics was Senator Huey P. Long of Louisiana. A populist demagogue, Long had created the Share Our Wealth Society as both a vehicle for his own political ambitions and as a campaign to redistribute the country's wealth from the rich to the poor. Long's plans would not be realized since he died by an assassin's bullet in 1935.

I contend, my friends, that we have no difficult problem to solve in America, and that is the view of nearly everyone with whom I have discussed the matter here in Washington and elsewhere throughout the United States—that we have no very difficult problem to solve.

It is not the difficulty of the problem which we have; it is the fact that the rich people of this country—and by rich people I mean the superrich—will not allow us to solve the problems, or rather the one little problem that is afflicting this country, because in order to cure all of our woes it is necessary to scale down the big fortunes, that we may scatter the wealth to be shared by all of the people. . . .

How many of you remember the first thing that the Declaration of Independence said? It said, "We hold these truths to be self-evident, that there are certain inalienable rights for the people, and among them are life, liberty, and the pursuit of happiness"; and it said, further, "We hold the view that all men are created equal."

Now, what did they mean by that? Did they mean, my friends, to say that all men were created equal and that that meant that any one man was born to inherit $10 billion and that another child was to be born to inherit nothing?

Did that mean, my friends, that someone would come into this world without having had an opportunity, of course, to have hit one lick of work, should be born with more than it and all of its children and children's children could ever dispose of, but that another one would have to be born into a life of starvation?

That was not the meaning of the Declaration of Independence when it said that all men are created equal or "That we hold that all men are created equal."

Nor was it the meaning of the Declaration of Independence when it said that they held that there were certain rights that were inalienable—the right of life, liberty, and the pursuit of happiness.

Is that right of life, my friends, when the young children of this country are being reared into a sphere which is more owned by 12 men than it is by 120 million people?

Is that, my friends, giving them a fair shake of the dice or anything like the inalienable right of life, liberty, and the pursuit of happiness, or anything resembling the fact that all people are created equal; when we have today in America thousands and hundreds of thousands and millions of children on the verge of starvation in a land that is overflowing with too much to eat and too much to wear?

I do not think you will contend that, and I do not think for a moment that they will contend it. . . .

We have in America today more wealth, more goods, more food, more clothing, more houses than we have ever had. We have everything in abundance here.

We have the farm problem, my friends, because we have too much cotton, because we have too much wheat, and have too much corn, and too much potatoes.

We have a home-loan problem because we have too many houses, and yet nobody can buy them and live in them.

We have trouble, my friends, in the country, because we have too much money owing, the greatest indebtedness that has ever been given to civilization, where it has been shown that we are incapable of distributing the actual things that are here, because the people have not money enough to supply themselves with them, and because the greed of a few men is such that they think it is necessary that they own everything, and their pleasure consists in the starvation of the masses, and in their possessing things they cannot use, and their children cannot use, but who bask in the splendor of sunlight and wealth, casting darkness and despair and impressing it on everyone else. . . .

Now, my friends, if you were off on an island where there were 100 lunches, you could not let one man eat up the hundred lunches, or take the hundred lunches and not let anybody else eat any of them. If you did, there would not be anything else for the balance of the people to consume.

So, we have in America today, my friends, a condition by which about 10 men dominate the means of activity in at least 85 percent of the activities that you own. They either own directly everything or they have got some kind of mortgage on it, with a very small percentage to be excepted. They own the banks, they own the steel mills, they own the railroads, they own the bonds, they own the mortgages, they own the stores, and they have chained the country from one end to the other until there is not any kind of business that a small, independent man could go into today and make a living, and there is not any kind of business that a small independent man can go into and make any money to buy an automobile with; and they have finally and gradually and steadily eliminated everybody from the fields in which there is a living to be made, and still they have got little enough sense to think they ought to be able to get more business out of it anyway.

If you reduce a man to the point where he is starving to death and bleeding and dying, how do you expect that man to get hold of any money to spend with you? It is not possible.

Then, ladies and gentlemen, how do you expect people to live, when the wherewith cannot be had by the people? . . .

Both of these men, Mr. [Herbert] Hoover and Mr. [Franklin] Roosevelt, came out and said there had to be a decentralization of wealth, but neither one of them did anything about it. But, nevertheless, they recognized the principle. The fact that neither one of them ever did anything about it is their own problem that I am not undertaking to criticize; but had Mr. Hoover carried out what he says ought to be done, he would be retiring from the President's office, very probably, three years from now, instead of one year ago, and had Mr. Roosevelt proceeded along the lines that he stated were necessary for the decentralization of wealth, he would have gone, my friends, a long way already, and within a few months he would have probably reached a solution of all of the problems that afflict this country today.

But I wish to warn you now that nothing that has been done up to this date has taken one dime away from these big-fortune holders; they own just as much as they did, and probably a little bit more; they hold just as many of the debts of the common people as they ever held, and probably a little bit more; and unless we, my friends, are going to give the people of this country a fair shake of the dice, by which they will all get something out of the funds of this land, there is not a chance on the topside of this God's eternal earth by which we can rescue this country and rescue the people of this country.

It is necessary to save the Government of the country, but it is much more necessary to save the people of America. We love this country. We love this Government. It is a religion, I say. It is a kind of religion people have read of, when women, in the name of religion, would take their infant babes and throw them into the burning flame, where they would be instantly devoured by the all-consuming fire, in days gone by; and there probably are some people of the world even today, who, in the name of religion, throw their own babes to destruction; but in the name of our good Government people today are seeing their own children hungry, tired, half-naked, lifting their tear-dimmed eyes into the sad faces of their fathers and mothers, who cannot give them food and clothing they both needed, and which is necessary to sustain them, and that goes on day by day, and night after night, when day gets into darkness and blackness, knowing those children would arise in the morning without being fed, and probably go to bed at night without being fed.

Yet in the name of our Government, and all alone, those people undertake and strive as hard as they can to keep a good government alive, and how long they can stand that no one knows. If I were in their place tonight, the place where millions are, I hope that I would have what I might say—I cannot give you the word to express the kind of fortitude they have; that is the word—I hope that I might have the fortitude to praise and honor my Government that had allowed me here in this land, where there is too much to eat and too much to wear, to starve in order that a handful of men can have so much more than they can ever eat or they can ever wear.

Now, we have organized a society, and we call it share-our-wealth society, a society with the motto "Every man a king."

Every man a king, so there would be no such thing as a man or woman who did not have the necessities of life, who would not be dependent upon the whims and caprices and ipsi [sic] dixit of the financial martyrs for a living. What do we propose by this society? We propose to limit the wealth of big men in the country. There is an average of $15,000 in wealth to every family in America. That is right here today.

We do not propose to divide it up equally. We do not propose a division of wealth, but we propose to limit poverty that we will allow to be inflicted upon any man's family. We will not say we are going to try to guarantee any equality, or $15,000 to families. No; but we do say that one third of the average is low enough for any one family to hold, that there should be a guaranty of a family wealth of around $5,000; enough for a home, an automobile, a radio, and the ordinary conveniences, and the opportunity to educate their children; a fair share of the income of this land thereafter to that family so there will be no such thing as merely the select to have those things, and so there will be no such thing as a family living in poverty and distress.

We have to limit fortunes. Our present plan is that we will allow no one man to own more than $50 million. We think that with that limit we will be able to carry out the balance of the program. It may be necessary that we limit it to less than $50 million. It may be necessary, in working out of the plans, that no man's fortune would be more than $10 million or $15 million. But be that as it may, it will still be more than any one man, or any one man and his children and their children, will be able to spend in their lifetimes; and it it is not necessary or reasonable to have wealth piled up beyond that point where we cannot prevent poverty among the masses.

Another thing we propose is [an] old-age pension of $30 a month for everyone that is 60 years old. Now, we do not give this pension to a man making $1,000 a year, and we do not give it to him if he has $10,000 in property, but outside of that we do.

We will limit hours of work. There is not any necessity of having over-production. . . .

We will not have any trouble taking care of the agricultural situation. All you have to do is balance your production with your consumption. You simply have to abandon a particular crop that you have too much of, and all you have to do is store the surplus for the next year, and the Government will take it over. . . .

Those are the things we propose to do. "Every man a king." Every man to eat when there is something to eat; all to wear something when there is something to wear. That makes us all a sovereign. . . .

Get together in your community tonight or tomorrow and organize one of our share-our-wealth societies. If you do not understand it, write me and let me send you the platform; let me give you the proof of it.

This is Huey P. Long talking, United States Senator, Washington, D.C. Write me and let me send you the data on this proposition. Enroll with us. Let us make known to the people what we are going to do. I will send you a button, if I have got enough of them left. We have got a little button that some of our friends designed, with our message around the rim of the button, and in the center "Every man a king." Many thousands of them are meeting through the United States, and every day we are getting hundreds and hundreds of letters. Share-our-wealth societies are now being organized, and people have it within their power to relieve themselves from this terrible situation.

Look at what the Mayo brothers announced this week, these greatest scientists of all the world today, who are entitled to have more money than all the Morgans and the Rockefellers, or anyone else, and yet the Mayos turn back their big fortunes to be used for treating the sick, and said they did not want to lay up fortunes in this earth, but wanted to turn them back where they would do some good; but the other big capitalists are not willing to do that, are not willing to do what these men, 10 times more worthy, have already done, and it is going to take a law to require them to do it.

From: *Congressional Record.* 73rd Cong., 2nd Sess., 1934, p. 3450.

ROOSEVELT'S FIRESIDE ADDRESS ON SOCIAL SECURITY ACTS, JANUARY 17, 1935

Facing challenges to the New Deal from Francis Townsend and his plan to provide the elderly with $200 a month in government payments, Franklin D. Roosevelt proposed the much more modest—and economically sound—Social Security program. Utilizing a combination of worker and employer taxes, Social Security was self-funding, and it has remained the most popular and long-lasting of all the New Deal programs introduced in the 1930s.

In addressing you on June eighth, 1934, I summarized the main objectives of our American program. Among these was, and is, the security of the men, women, and children of the Nation against certain hazards and vicissitudes of life. This purpose is an essential part of our task. In my annual message to you I promised to submit a definite program of action. This I do in the form of a report to me by a Committee on Economic Security, appointed by me for the purpose of surveying the field and of recommending the basis of legislation.

I am gratified with the work of this Committee and of those who have helped it: The Technical Board on Economic Security drawn from various departments of the Government, the Advisory Council on Economic Security, consisting of informed and public-spirited private citizens and a number of other advisory groups, including a committee on actuarial consultants, a medical advisory board, a dental advisory committee, a hospital advisory committee, a public-health advisory committee, a child-committee and an advisory committee on employment relief. All of those who participated in this notable task of planning this major legislative proposal are ready and willing, at any time, to consult with and assist in any way the appropriate Congressional committees and members, with respect to detailed aspects.

It is my best judgment that this legislation should be brought forward with a minimum of delay. Federal action is necessary to, and conditioned upon, the action of States. Forty-four legislatures are meeting or will meet soon. In order that the necessary State action may be taken promptly it is important that the Federal Government proceed speedily.

The detailed report of the Committee sets forth a series of proposals that will appeal to the sound sense of the American people. It has not attempted the impossible, nor has it failed to exercise sound caution and consideration of all of the factors concerned: the national credit, the rights and responsibilities of States, the capacity of industry to assume financial responsibilities and the fundamental necessity of proceeding in a manner that will merit the enthusiastic support of citizens of all sorts.

It is overwhelmingly important to avoid any danger of permanently discrediting the sound and necessary policy of Federal legislation for economic security by attempting to apply it on too ambitious a scale before actual experience has provided guidance for the permanently safe direction of such efforts. The place of such a fundamental in our future civilization is too precious to be jeopardized now by extravagant action. It is a sound idea—a sound ideal. Most of the other advanced countries of the world have already adopted it and their experience affords the knowledge that social insurance can be made a sound and workable project.

Three principles should be observed in legislation on this subject. First, the system adopted, except for the money necessary to initiate it, should be self-sustaining in the sense that funds for the payment of insurance benefits should not come from the proceeds of general taxation. Second, excepting in old-age insurance, actual management should be left to the States subject to standards established by the Federal Government. Third, sound financial management of the funds and the reserves, and protection of the credit structure of the Nation should be assured by retaining Federal control over all funds through trustees in the Treasury of the United States.

At this time, I recommend the following types of legislation looking to economic security:

1. Unemployment compensation.

2. Old-age benefits, including compulsory and voluntary annuities.

3. Federal aid to dependent children through grants to States for the support of existing mothers' pension systems and for services for the protection and

care of homeless, neglected, dependent, and crippled children.

4. Additional Federal aid to State and local public-health agencies and the strengthening of the Federal Public Health Service. I am not at this time recommending the adoption of so-called "health insurance," although groups representing the medical profession are cooperating with the Federal Government in the further study of the subject and definite progress is being made.

With respect to unemployment compensation, I have concluded that the most practical proposal is the levy of a uniform Federal payroll tax, ninety per cent of which should be allowed as an offset to employers contributing under a compulsory State unemployment compensation act. The purpose of this is to afford a requirement of a reasonably uniform character for all States cooperating with the Federal Government and to promote and encourage the passage of unemployment compensation laws in the States. The ten per cent not thus offset should be used to cover the costs of Federal and State administration of this broad system. Thus, States will largely administer unemployment compensation, assisted and guided by the Federal Government. An unemployment compensation system should be constructed in such a way as to afford every practicable aid and incentive toward the larger purpose of employment stabilization. This can be helped by the intelligent planning of both public and private employment. It also can be helped by correlating the system with public employment so that a person who has exhausted his benefits may be eligible for some form of public work as is recommended in this report. Moreover, in order to encourage the stabilization of private employment, Federal legislation should not foreclose the States from establishing means for inducing industries to afford an even greater stabilization of employment.

In the important field of security for our old people, it seems necessary to adopt three principles: First, noncontributory old-age pensions for those who are now too old to build up their own insurance. It is, of course, clear that for perhaps thirty years to come funds will have to be provided by the States and the Federal Government to meet these pensions. Second, compulsory contributory annuities which in time will establish a self-supporting system for those now young and for future generations. Third, voluntary contributory annuities by which individual initiative can increase the annual amounts received in old age. It is proposed that the Federal Government assume one-half of the cost of the old-age pension plan, which ought ultimately to be supplanted by self-supporting annuity plans.

The amount necessary at this time for the initiation of unemployment compensation, old-age security, children's aid, and the promotion of public health, as outlined in the report of the Committee on Economic Security, is approximately one hundred million dollars.

The establishment of sound means toward a greater future economic security of the American people is dictated by a prudent consideration of the hazards involved in our national life. No one can guarantee this country against the dangers of future depressions but we can reduce these dangers. We can eliminate many of the factors that cause economic depressions, and we can provide the means of mitigating their results. This plan for economic security is at once a measure of prevention and a method of alleviation.

We pay now for the dreadful consequence of economic insecurity—and dearly. This plan presents a more equitable and infinitely less expensive means of meeting these costs. We cannot afford to neglect the plain duty before us. I strongly recommend action to attain the objectives sought in this report.

From: B. D. Zevin, ed. *Nothing to Fear: The Selected Addresses of Franklin Delano Roosevelt, 1932–1945.* Boston: Houghton Mifflin, 1946.

ROOSEVELT'S FIRESIDE CHAT ON WORK RELIEF PROGRAMS, APRIL 28, 1935

With unemployment remaining at painfully high levels through the first two years of the New Deal, President Franklin D. Roosevelt introduced a new public works program known as the Works Progress Administration (WPA). Lasting until 1943, the WPA hired millions of unemployed persons and put them to work building public projects of all kinds. Part of the program was the famous Federal One, which put thousands of artists, musicians, writers, and actors to work creating art projects for the people. In the following address, Roosevelt introduces the plan for the WPA to the American people in one of his radio fireside chats.

Since my annual message to the Congress on January fourth, last, I have not addressed the general public over the air. In the many weeks since that time the Congress has devoted itself to the arduous task of formulating legislation necessary to the country's welfare. It has made and is making distinct progress.

Before I come to any of the specific measures, however, I want to leave in your minds one clear fact. The Administration and the Congress are not proceeding in any haphazard fashion in this task of government. Each of our steps has a definite relationship to every other step. The job of creating a program for the Nation's welfare is, in some respects, like the building of a ship. At different points on the coast where I often visit they build great seagoing ships. When one of these ships is under construction and the steel frames have been set in the keel, it is difficult for a person who does not know ships to tell how it will finally look when it is sailing the high seas.

It may seem confused to some, but out of the multitude of detailed parts that go into the making of the structure, the creation of a useful instrument for man ultimately comes. It is that way with the making of a national policy. The objective of the Nation has greatly changed in three years. Before that time individual self-interest and group selfishness were paramount in public thinking. The general good was at a discount.

Three years of hard thinking have changed the picture. More and more people, because of clearer thinking and a better understanding, are considering the whole rather than a mere part relating to one section, or to one crop, or to one industry, or to an individual private occupation. That is a tremendous gain for the principles of democracy. The overwhelming majority of people in this country know how to sift the wheat from the chaff in what they hear and what they read. They know that the process of the constructive rebuilding of America cannot be done in a day or a year, but that it is being done in spite of the few who seek to confuse them and to profit by their confusion. Americans as a whole are feeling a lot better—a lot more cheerful than for many, many years.

The most difficult place in the world to get a clear and open perspective of the country as a whole is Washington. I am reminded sometimes of what President Wilson once said: "So many people come to Washington who know things that are not so, and so few people who know what the people of the United States are thinking about." That is why I occasionally leave this scene of action for a few days to go fishing or back home to Hyde Park so that I can have a chance to think quietly about the country as a whole. "To get away from the trees," as they say, "and to look at the whole forest." This duty of seeing the country in a long-range perspective is one which, in a very special manner, attaches to this office to which you have chosen me. Did you ever stop to think that there are, after all, only two positions in the Nation that are filled by the vote of all of the voters—the President and the Vice-President? That makes it particularly necessary for the Vice-President and for me to conceive of our duty toward the entire country. Tonight, therefore, I speak to and of the American people as a whole.

My most immediate concern is in carrying out the purposes of the great work program just enacted by the Congress. Its first objective is to put men and women now on the relief rolls to work and, incidentally, to assist materially in our already unmistakable march toward recovery. I shall not confuse my discussion by a multitude of figures. So many figures are quoted to prove so many things. Sometimes it depends upon what paper you read and what broadcast you hear. Therefore, let us keep our minds on two or three simple essential facts in connection with this problem of unemployment. It is true that while business and industry are definitely better our relief rolls are still too large. However, for the first time in five years the relief rolls have declined instead of increased during the winter months. They are still declining. The simple fact is that many millions more people have private work today than two years ago today or one year ago today and every day that passes offers more chances to work for those who want to work. In spite of the fact that unemployment remains a serious problem here as in every other nation, we have come to recognize the possibility and the necessity of certain helpful remedial measures. These measures are of two kinds. The first is to make provisions intended to relieve, to minimize, and to prevent future unemployment; the second is to establish the practical means to help those who are unemployed in this present emergency. Our social security legislation is an attempt to answer the first of these questions; our Works Relief program, the second.

The program for social security now pending before the Congress is a necessary part of the future unemployment policy of the Government. While our present and projected expenditures for work relief are wholly within the reasonable limits of our national credit resources, it is obvious that we cannot continue to create governmental deficits for that purpose year after year. We must begin now to make provision for the future. That is why our social security program is an important part of the complete picture. It proposes, by means of old-age pensions, to help those who have reached the age of retirement to give up their jobs and thus give to the younger generation greater opportunities for work and to give to all a feeling of security as they look toward old age.

The unemployment insurance part of the legislation will not only help to guard the individual in future periods of lay-off against dependence upon relief, but it will, by sustaining purchasing power, cushion the shock of economic distress. Another helpful feature of unemployment insurance is the incentive it will give to employers to plan more carefully in order that unemployment may be prevented by the stabilizing of employment itself.

Provisions for social security, however, are protections for the future. Our responsibility for the immediate necessities of the unemployed has been met by the Congress through the most comprehensive work plan in the history of the Nation. Our problem is to put to work three and one-half million employable persons now on the relief rolls. It is a problem quite as much for private industry as for the Government.

We are losing no time getting the Government's vast work relief program under way and we have every reason to believe that it should be in full swing by autumn. In directing it, I shall recognize six fundamental principles:

(1) The projects should be useful.

(2) Projects shall be of a nature that a considerable proportion of the money spent will go into wages for labor.

(3) Projects will be sought which promise ultimate return to the Federal Treasury of a considerable proportion of the costs.

(4) Funds allotted for each project should be actually and promptly spent and not held over until later years.

(5) In all cases projects must be of a character to give employment to those on the relief rolls.

(6) Projects will be allocated to localities or relief areas in relation to the number of workers on relief rolls in those areas.

I next want to make it clear exactly how we shall direct the work.

(1) I have set up a Division of Applications and Information to which all proposals for the expenditure of money must go for preliminary study and consideration.

(2) After the Division of Applications and Information has sifted these projects, they will be sent to an Allotment Division composed of representatives of the more important governmental agencies charged with carrying on work relief projects. The group will also include representatives of cities, and of labor, farming, banking and industry. This Allotment Division will consider all of the recommendations submitted to it and such projects as they approve will be next submitted to the President who under the Act is required to make final allocations.

(3) The next step will be to notify the proper Government agency in whose field the project falls, and also to notify another agency which I am creating—a Progress Division. This Division will have the duty of coordinating the purchase of materials and supplies and of making certain that people who are employed will be taken from the relief rolls. It will also have the responsibility of determining work payments in various localities, of making full use of existing employment services and of assisting people engaged in relief work to move as rapidly as possible back into private employment when such employment is available. Moreover, this Division will be charged with keeping projects moving on schedule.

(4) I have felt it to be essentially wise and prudent to avoid, so far as possible, the creation of new governmental machinery for supervising this work. The

National Government now has at least sixty different agencies with the staff and the experience and the competence necessary to carry on the two hundred and fifty or three hundred kinds of work that will be undertaken. These agencies, therefore, will simply be doing on a somewhat enlarged scale, the same sort of things that they have been doing. This will make certain that the largest possible portion of the funds allotted will be spent for actually creating new work and not for building up expensive overhead organizations here in Washington.

For many months preparations have been under way. The allotment of funds for desirable projects has already begun. The key men for the major responsibilities of this great task already have been selected. I well realize that the country is expecting before this year is out to see the "dirt fly," as they say, in carrying on the work, and I assure my fellow citizens that no energy will be spared in using these funds effectively to make a major attack upon the problem of unemployment.

Our responsibility is to all of the people in this country. This is a great national crusade to destroy enforced idleness which is an enemy of the human spirit generated by this depression. Our attack upon these enemies must be without stint and without discrimination. No sectional, no political distinctions can be permitted.

It must, however, be recognized that when an enterprise of this character is extended over more than three thousand counties throughout the Nation, there may be occasional instances of inefficiency, bad management, or misuse of funds. When cases of this kind occur, there will be those, of course, who will try to tell you that the exceptional failure is characteristic of the entire endeavor. It should be remembered that in every big job there are some imperfections. There are chiselers in every walk of life, there are those in every industry who are guilty of unfair practices; every profession has its black sheep, but long experience in Government has taught me that the exceptional instances of wrongdoing in Government are probably less numerous than in almost every other line of endeavor. The most effective means of preventing such evils in this Works Relief program will be the eternal vigilance of the American people themselves. I call upon my fellow citizens everywhere to cooperate with me in making this the most efficient and the cleanest example of public enterprise the world has ever seen.

It is time to provide a smashing answer for those cynical men who say that a Democracy cannot be honest and efficient. If you will help, this can be done. I,

therefore, hope you will watch the work in every corner of this Nation. Feel free to criticize. Tell me of instances where work can be done better, or where improper practices prevail. Neither you nor I want criticism conceived in a purely fault-finding or partisan spirit, but I am jealous of the right of every citizen to call to the attention of his or her Government examples of how the public money can be more effectively spent for the benefit of the American people.

I now come, my friends, to a part of the remaining business before the Congress. It has under consideration many measures which provide for the rounding out of the program of economic and social reconstruction with which we have been concerned for two years. I can mention only a few of them tonight, but I do not want my mention of specific measures to be interpreted as lack of interest in or disapproval of many other important proposals that are pending.

The National Industrial Recovery Act expires on the sixteenth of June. After careful consideration, I have asked the Congress to extend the life of this useful agency of Government. As we have proceeded with the administration of this Act, we have found from time to time more and more useful ways of promoting its purposes. No reasonable person wants to abandon our present gains—we must continue to protect children, to enforce minimum wages, to prevent excessive hours, to safeguard, define and enforce collective bargaining, and, while retaining fair competition, to eliminate, so far as humanly possible, the kinds of unfair practices by selfish minorities which unfortunately did more than anything else to bring about the recent collapse of industries.

There is likewise pending before the Congress legislation to provide for the elimination of unnecessary holding companies in the public utility field.

I consider this legislation a positive recovery measure. Power production in this country is virtually back to the 1929 peak. The operating companies in the gas and electric utility field are by and large in good condition. But under holding company domination the utility industry has long been hopelessly at war within itself and with public sentiment. By far the greater part of the general decline in utility securities had occurred before I was inaugurated. The absentee management of unnecessary holding company control has lost touch with, and has lost the sympathy of, the communities it pretends to serve. Even more significantly it has given the country as a whole an uneasy apprehension of over-concentrated economic power.

A business that loses the confidence of its customers and the good-will of the public cannot long continue to be a good risk for the investor. This legislation will serve the investor by ending the conditions which have caused that lack of confidence and goodwill. It will put the public utility operating industry on a sound basis for the future, both in its public relations and in its internal relations.

This legislation will not only in the long run result in providing lower electric and gas rates to the consumer but it will protect the actual value and earning power of properties now owned by thousands of investors who have little protection under the old laws against what used to be called frenzied finance. It will not destroy values.

Not only business recovery, but the general economic recovery of the Nation will be greatly stimulated by the enactment of legislation designed to improve the status of our transportation agencies. There is need for legislation for the regulation of interstate transportation by buses and trucks, for the regulation of transportation by water, for the strengthening of our Merchant Marine and Air Transport, for the strengthening of the Interstate Commerce Commission to enable it to carry out a rounded conception of the national transportation system in which the benefits of private ownership are retained while the public stake in these important services is protected by the public's Government.

Finally, the reestablishment of public confidence in the banks of the Nation is one of the most hopeful results of our efforts as a Nation to reestablish public confidence in private banking. We all know that private banking actually exists by virtue of the permission of and regulation by the people as a whole, speaking through their Government. Wise public policy, however, requires not only that banking be safe but that its resources be most fully utilized in the economic life of the country. To this end it was decided more than twenty years ago that the Government should assume the responsibility of providing a means by which the credit of the Nation might be controlled, not by a few private banking institutions, but by a body with public prestige and authority. The answer to this demand was the Federal Reserve System. Twenty years of experience with this system have justified the efforts made to create it, but these twenty years have shown by experience definite possibilities for improvement. Certain proposals made to amend the Federal Reserve Act deserve prompt and favorable action by the Congress. They are a minimum of wise readjustments of our Federal Reserve System in the light of past experience and present needs.

These measures I have mentioned are, in large part, the program which under my constitutional duty I have recommended to the Congress. They are essential factors in a rounded program for national recovery. They contemplate the enrichment of our national life by a sound and rational ordering of its various elements and wise provisions for the protection of the weak against the strong.

Never since my Inauguration in March, 1933, have I felt so unmistakably the atmosphere of recovery. But it is more than the recovery of the material basis of our individual lives. It is the recovery of confidence in our democratic processes and institutions. We have survived all of the arduous burdens and the threatening dangers of a great economic calamity. We have in the darkest moments of our national trials retained our faith in our own ability to master our destiny. Fear is vanishing and confidence is growing on every side, faith is being renewed in the vast possibilities of human beings to improve their material and spiritual status through the instrumentality of the democratic form of government. That faith is receiving its just reward. For that we can be thankful to the God who watches over America.

From: B. D. Zevin, ed. *Nothing to Fear: The Selected Addresses of Franklin Delano Roosevelt, 1932–1945.* Boston: Houghton Mifflin, 1946.

DEMOCRATIC PARTY PLATFORM, 1936

The 1936 Democratic platform—part of the campaign to get President Franklin D. Roosevelt reelected—was composed largely of two messages: the extraordinary accomplishments of the New Deal and of Roosevelt's first term in office, and a commitment to keep up the pace of reform. In fact, the second Roosevelt administration was largely devoid of major new programs. Notably underplayed in the platform were foreign affairs, despite growing tensions in Europe and Asia. To the degree that a platform is important in a campaign, this one was particularly successful, as Roosevelt won reelection with the largest mandate in over a century.

We hold this truth to be self-evident—that the test of a representative government is its ability to promote the safety and happiness of the people.

We hold this truth to be self-evident—that 12 years of Republican leadership left our Nation sorely stricken in body, mind, and spirit; and that three years of Democratic leadership have put it back on the road to restored health and prosperity.

We hold this truth to be self-evident—that 12 years of Republican surrender to the dictatorship of a privileged few have been supplanted by a Democratic leadership which has returned the people themselves to the places of authority, and has revived in them new faith and restored the hope which they had almost lost.

We hold this truth to be self-evident—that this three-year recovery in all the basic values of life and the reestablishment of the American way of living has been brought about by humanizing the policies of the Federal Government as they affect the personal, financial, industrial, and agricultural well-being of the American people.

We hold this truth to be self-evident—that government in a modern civilization has certain inescapable obligations to its citizens, among which are:

(1) Protection of the family and the home.

(2) Establishment of a democracy of opportunity for all the people.

(3) Aid to those overtaken by disaster.

These obligations, neglected through 12 years of the old leadership, have once more been recognized by American Government. Under the new leadership they will never be neglected.

FOR THE PROTECTION OF THE FAMILY AND THE HOME

(1) We have begun and shall continue the successful drive to rid our land of kidnappers and bandits. We shall continue to use the powers of government to end the activities of the malefactors of great wealth who defraud and exploit the people.

Savings and Investment

(2) We have safeguarded the thrift of our citizens by restraining those who would gamble with other people's savings, by requiring truth in the sale of securities; by putting the brakes upon the use of credit for speculation; by outlawing the manipulation of prices in stock and commodity markets; by curbing the overweening power and unholy practices of utility holding companies; by insuring fifty million bank accounts.

Old Age and Social Security

(3) We have built foundations for the security of those who are faced with the hazards of unemployment and old age; for the orphaned, the crippled, and the blind. On the foundation of the Social Security Act we are determined to erect a structure of economic security for all our people, making sure that this benefit shall keep step with the ever-increasing capacity of America to provide a high standard of living for all its citizens.

Consumer

(4) We will act to secure to the consumer fair value, honest sales and a decreased spread between the price he pays and the price the producer receives.

Rural Electrification

(5) This administration has fostered power rate yardsticks in the Tennessee Valley and in several other parts of the Nation. As a result, electricity has been made

available to the people at a lower rate. We will continue to promote plans for rural electrification and for cheap power by means of the yardstick method.

Housing

(6) We maintain that our people are entitled to decent, adequate housing at a price which they can afford. In the last three years, the Federal Government, having saved more than two million homes from foreclosure, has taken the first steps in our history to provide decent housing for people of meager incomes. We believe every encouragement should be given to the building of new homes by private enterprise; and that the Government should steadily extend its housing program toward the goal of adequate housing for those forced through economic necessities to live in unhealthy and slum conditions.

Veterans

(7) We shall continue just treatment of our war veterans and their dependents.

FOR THE ESTABLISHMENT OF A DEMOCRACY OF OPPORTUNITY

Agriculture

We have taken the farmers off the road to ruin.

We have kept our pledge to agriculture to use all available means to raise farm income toward its prewar purchasing power. The farmer is no longer suffering from 15-cent corn, 3-cent hogs, 22-cent beef at the farm, 5-cent wool, 30-cent wheat, 5-cent cotton, and 3-cent sugar.

By Federal legislation, we have reduced the farmer's indebtedness and doubled his net income. In cooperation with the States and through the farmer's own committees, we are restoring the fertility of his land and checking the erosion of his soil. We are bringing electricity and good roads to his home.

We will continue to improve the soil conservation and domestic allotment program with payments to farmers.

We will continue a fair-minded administration of agricultural laws, quick to recognize and meet new problems and conditions. We recognize the gravity of the evils of farm tenancy, and we pledge the full cooperation of the Government in the refinancing of farm indebtedness at the lowest possible rates of interest and over a long term of years.

We favor the production of all the market will absorb, both at home and abroad, plus a reserve supply sufficient to insure fair prices to consumers; we favor judicious commodity loans on seasonal surpluses; and we favor assistance within Federal authority to enable farmers to adjust and balance production with demand, at a fair profit to the farmers.

We favor encouragement of sound, practical farm cooperatives.

By the purchase and retirement of ten million acres of sub-marginal land, and assistance to those attempting to eke out an existence upon it, we have made a good beginning toward proper land use and rural rehabilitation.

The farmer has been returned to the road to freedom and prosperity. We will keep him on that road.

Labor

We have given the army of America's industrial workers something more substantial than the Republican's dinner pail full of promises. We have increased the worker's pay and shortened his hours; we have undertaken to put an end to the sweated labor of his wife and children; we have written into the law of the land his right to collective bargaining and self-organization free from the interference of employers; we have provided Federal machinery for the peaceful settlement of labor disputes.

We will continue to protect the worker and we will guard his rights, both as wage-earner and consumer, in the production and consumption of all commodities, including coal and water power and other natural resource products.

The worker has been returned to the road to freedom and prosperity. We will keep him on that road.

Business

We have taken the American business man out of the red. We have saved his bank and given it a sounder foundation; we have extended credit; we have lowered interest rates; we have undertaken to free him from the ravages of cutthroat competition.

The American business man has been returned to the road to freedom and prosperity. We will keep him on that road.

Youth

We have aided youth to stay in school; given them constructive occupation; opened the door to opportunity which 12 years of Republican neglect had closed.

Our youth have been returned to the road to freedom and prosperity. We will keep them on that road.

MONOPOLY AND CONCENTRATION OF ECONOMIC POWER

Monopolies and the concentration of economic power, the creation of Republican rule and privilege, continue to be the master of the producer, the exploiter of the consumer, and the enemy of the independent operator. This is a problem challenging the unceasing effort of untrammeled public officials in every branch of the Government. We pledge vigorously and fearlessly to enforce the criminal and civil provisions of the existing anti-trust laws, and to the extent that their effectiveness has been weakened by new corporate devices or judicial construction, we propose by law to restore their efficacy in stamping out monopolistic practices and the concentration of economic power.

AID TO THOSE OVERTAKEN BY DISASTER

We have aided and will continue to aid those who have been visited by widespread drought and floods, and have adopted a Nation-wide flood-control policy.

Unemployment

We believe that unemployment is a national problem, and that it is an inescapable obligation of our Government to meet it in a national way. Due to our stimulation of private business, more than five million people have been re-employed; and we shall continue to maintain that the first objective of a program of economic security is maximum employment in private industry at adequate wages. Where business fails to supply such employment, we believe that work at prevailing wages should be provided in cooperation with State and local governments on useful public projects, to the end that the national wealth may be increased, the skill and energy of the worker may be utilized, his morale maintained, and the unemployed assured the opportunity to earn the necessities of life.

The Constitution

The Republican platform proposes to meet many pressing national problems solely by action of the separate States. We know that drought, dust storms, floods, minimum wages, maximum hours, child labor, working conditions in industry and monopolistic and unfair business practices cannot be adequately handled exclusively by 48 separate State legislatures, 48 separate State administrations, and 48 separate State courts. Transactions and activities which inevitably overflow State boundaries call for both State and Federal treatment.

We have sought and will continue to seek to meet these problems through legislation within the Constitution.

If these problems cannot be effectively solved by legislation within the Constitution, we shall seek such clarifying amendment as will assure to the legislatures of the several States and to the Congress of the United States, each within its proper jurisdiction, the power to enact those laws which the State and Federal legislatures, within their respective spheres, shall find necessary, in order adequately to regulate commerce, protect public health and safety and safeguard economic security. Thus we propose to maintain the letter and spirit of the Constitution.

THE MERIT SYSTEM IN GOVERNMENT

For the protection of government itself and promotion of its efficiency, we pledge the immediate extension of the merit system through the classified civil service—which was first established and fostered under Democratic auspices—to all non-policy-making positions in the Federal service.

We shall subject to the civil service law all continuing positions which, because of the emergency, have been exempt from its operation.

CIVIL LIBERTIES

We shall continue to guard the freedom of speech, press, radio, religion and assembly which our Constitution guarantees; with equal rights to all and special privileges to none.

GOVERNMENT FINANCE

The administration has stopped deflation, restored values and enabled business to go ahead with confidence.

When national income shrinks, government income is imperiled. In reviving national income, we have fortified government finance. We have raised the public credit to a position of unsurpassed security. The interest rate on Government bonds has been reduced to the lowest point in twenty-eight years. The same Government bonds which in 1932 sold under 83 are now selling over 104.

We approve the objective of a permanently sound currency so stabilized as to prevent the former wide fluctuations in value which injured in turn producers, debtors, and property owners on the one hand, and wage-earners and creditors on the other, a currency which will permit full utilization of the country's resources. We assert that today we have the soundest currency in the world.

We are determined to reduce the expenses of government. We are being aided therein by the recession in unemployment. As the requirements of relief decline and national income advances, an increasing percentage of Federal expenditures can and will be met from current revenues, secured from taxes levied in accordance with ability to pay. Our retrenchment, tax and recovery programs thus reflect our firm determination to achieve a balanced budget and the reduction of the national debt at the earliest possible moment.

FOREIGN POLICY

In our relationship with other nations, this Government will continue to extend the policy of Good Neighbor. We reaffirm our opposition to war as an instrument of national policy, and declare that disputes between nations should be settled by peaceful means. We shall continue to observe a true neutrality in the disputes of others; to be prepared resolutely to resist aggression against ourselves; to work for peace and to take the profits out of war; to guard against being drawn, by political commitments, international banking or private trading, into any war which may develop anywhere.

We shall continue to foster the increase in our for-eign trade which has been achieved by this administration; to seek by mutual agreement the lowering of those tariff barriers, quotas and embargoes which have been raised against our exports of agricultural and industrial products; but continue as in the past to give adequate protection to our farmers and manufacturers against unfair competition or the dumping on our shores of commodities and goods produced abroad by cheap labor or subsidized by foreign governments.

THE ISSUE

The issue in this election is plain. The American people are called upon to choose between a Republican administration that has and would again regiment them in the service of privileged groups and a Democratic administration dedicated to the establishment of equal economic opportunity for all our people.

We have faith in the destiny of our Nation. We are sufficiently endowed with natural resources and with productive capacity to provide for all a quality of life that meets the standards of real Americanism.

Dedicated to a government of liberal American principles, we are determined to oppose equally, the despotism of Communism and the menace of concealed Fascism.

We hold this final truth to be self-evident—that the interests, the security and the happiness of the people of the United States of America can be perpetuated only under democratic government as conceived by the founders of our Nation.

From: George Thomas Kurian, ed. *The Encyclopedia of the Democratic Party.* Armonk, NY: M. E. Sharpe, 1997.

REPUBLICAN PARTY PLATFORM, 1936

The Republican Party platform—supporting the candidacy of Governor Alfred Landon of Kansas—begins with a lengthy diatribe against the New Deal and its vast extension of federal powers. In its place, the Republicans proposed an enhancement of state and local authority to combat the continuing depression, as well as a return to the more voluntaristic economic recovery programs of the Herbert Hoover administration. The lack of appeal of these planks can be attested to by the drubbing Landon and congressional Republicans received by the electorate in 1936.

America is in peril. The welfare of American men and women and the future of our youth are at stake. We dedicate ourselves to the preservation of their political liberty, their individual opportunity and their character as free citizens, which today for the first time are threatened by government itself.

For three long years the New Deal Administration has dishonored American traditions and flagrantly betrayed the pledges upon which the Democratic Party sought and received public support.

The powers of Congress have been usurped by the President.

The integrity and authority of the Supreme Court have been flouted.

The rights and liberties of American citizens have been violated.

Regulated monopoly has displaced free enterprise.

The New Deal Administration constantly seeks to usurp the rights reserved to the States and to the people.

It has insisted on the passage of laws contrary to the Constitution.

It has intimidated witnesses and interfered with the right of petition.

It has dishonored our country by repudiating its most sacred obligations.

It has been guilty of frightful waste and extravagance, using public funds for partisan political purposes.

It has promoted investigations to harass and intimidate American citizens, at the same time denying investigations into its own improper expenditures.

It has created a vast multitude of new offices, filled them with its favorites, set up a centralized bureaucracy, and sent out swarms of inspectors to harass our people.

It has bred fear and hesitation in commerce and industry, thus discouraging new enterprises, preventing employment and prolonging the depression.

It secretly has made tariff agreements with our foreign competitors, flooding our markets with foreign commodities.

It has coerced and intimidated voters by withholding relief to those opposing its tyrannical policies.

It has destroyed the morale of our people and made them dependent upon government.

Appeals to passion and class prejudice have replaced reason and tolerance.

To a free people, these actions are insufferable. This campaign cannot be waged on the traditional differences between the Republican and Democratic parties. The responsibility of this election transcends all previous political divisions. We invite all Americans, irrespective of party, to join it in defense of American institutions.

CONSTITUTIONAL GOVERNMENT AND FREE ENTERPRISE

We pledge ourselves:

1. To maintain the American system of Constitutional and local self-government, and to resist all attempts to impair the authority of the Supreme Court of the United States, the final protector of the rights of our citizens against the arbitrary encroachments of the legislative and executive branches of government. There can be no individual liberty without an independent judiciary.

2. To preserve the American system of free enterprise, private competition, and equality of opportunity, and to seek its constant betterment in the interests of all.

REEMPLOYMENT

The only permanent solution of the unemployment problem is the absorption of the unemployed by industry and agriculture. To that end, we advocate:

Removal of restrictions on production.

Abandonment of all New Deal policies that raise production costs, increase the cost of living, and thereby restrict buying, reduce volume and prevent reemployment.

Encouragement instead of hindrance to legitimate business.

Withdrawal of government from competition with private payrolls.

Elimination of unnecessary and hampering regulations. Adoption of such other policies as will furnish a chance for individual enterprise, industrial expansion, and the restoration of jobs.

RELIEF

The necessities of life must be provided for the needy, and hope must be restored pending recovery. The administration of relief is a major failing of the New Deal. It has been faithless to those who must deserve our sympathy. To end confusion, partisanship, waste and incompetence, we pledge:

1. The return of responsibility for relief administration to non-political local agencies familiar with community problems.

2. Federal grants-in-aid to the States and territories while the need exists, upon compliance with these conditions: (a) a fair proportion of the total relief burden to be provided from the revenues of States and local governments; (b) all engaged in relief administration to be selected on the basis of merit and fitness; (c) adequate provision to be made for the encouragement of

those persons who are trying to become self-supporting.

3. Undertaking of Federal public works only on their merits and separate from the administration of relief.

4. A prompt determination of the facts concerning relief and unemployment.

SECURITY

Real security will be possible only when our productive capacity is sufficient to furnish a decent standard of living for all American families and to provide a surplus for future needs and contingencies. For the attainment of that ultimate objective, we look to the energy, self-reliance and character of our people, and to our system of free enterprise.

Society has an obligation to promote the security of the people, by affording some measure of protection against involuntary unemployment and dependency in old age. The New Deal policies, while purporting to provide social security, have, in fact, endangered it.

We propose a system of old age security, based upon the following principles:

1. We approve a pay-as-you-go policy, which requires of each generation the support of the aged and the determination of what is just and adequate.

2. Every American citizen over sixty-five should receive the supplementary payment necessary to provide a minimum income sufficient to protect him or her from want.

3. Each state and territory, upon complying with simple and general minimum standards, should receive from the federal government a graduated contribution in proportion to its own, up to a fixed maximum.

4. To make this program consistent with sound fiscal policy the Federal revenues for this purpose must be provided from the proceeds of a direct tax widely distributed. All will be benefited and all should contribute.

We propose to encourage adoption by the states and territories of honest and practical measures for meeting the problems of unemployment insurance.

The unemployment insurance and old age annuity sections of the present Social Security Act are unworkable and deny benefits to about two-thirds of our adult population, including professional men and women and all those engaged in agriculture and domestic service, and the self-employed while imposing heavy tax burdens upon all. The so-called reserve fund estimated at forty-seven billion dollars for old age insurance is

no reserve at all, because the fund will contain nothing but the Government's promise to pay, while the taxes collected in the guise of premiums will be wasted by the Government in reckless and extravagant political schemes.

LABOR

The welfare of labor rests upon increased production and the prevention of exploitation. We pledge ourselves to:

Protect the right of labor to organize and to bargain collectively through representatives of its own choosing without interference from any source.

Prevent governmental job holders from exercising autocratic powers over labor.

Support the adoption of state laws and interstate compacts to abolish sweatshops and child labor, and to protect women and children with respect to maximum hours, minimum wages and working conditions. We believe that this can be done within the Constitution as it now stands.

AGRICULTURE

The farm problem is an economic and social, not a partisan problem, and we propose to treat it accordingly. Following the wreck of the restrictive and coercive A.A.A. [Agricultural Adjustment Administration], the New Deal Administration has taken to itself the principles of the Republican policy of soil conservation and land retirement. This action opens the way for a non-political and permanent solution. Such a solution cannot be had under a New Deal Administration which misuses the program to serve partisan ends, to promote scarcity and to limit by coercive methods the farmer's control over his own farm.

Our paramount object is to protect and foster the family type of farm, traditional in American life, and to promote policies which will bring about an adjustment of agriculture to meet the needs of domestic and foreign markets. As an emergency measure, during the agricultural depression, federal benefits payments or grants-in-aid when administered within the means of the Federal government are consistent with a balanced budget.

We propose:

1. To facilitate economical production and increased consumption on a basis of abundance instead of scarcity.

2. A national land-use program, including the acquisition of abandoned and non-productive farm lands by voluntary sale or lease, subject to approval of the legislative and executive branches of the States concerned, and the devotion of such land to appropriate public use, such as watershed protection and flood prevention, reforestation, recreation, and conservation of wild life.

3. That an agricultural policy be pursued for the protection and restoration of the land resources, designed to bring about such a balance between soil-building and soil-depleting crops as will permanently insure productivity, with reasonable benefits to cooperating farmers on family type farms, but so regulated as to eliminate the New Deal's destructive policy towards the dairy and live-stock industries.

4. To extend experimental aid to farmers developing new crops suited to our soil and climate.

5. To promote the industrial use of farm products by applied science.

6. To protect the American farmer against the importation of all live-stock, dairy, and agricultural products, substitutes thereof, and derivatives therefrom, which will depress American farm prices.

7. To provide effective quarantine against imported live-stock, dairy and other farm products from countries which do not impose health and sanitary regulations fully equal to those required of our own producers.

8. To provide for ample farm credit at rates as low as those enjoyed by other industries, including commodity and live-stock loans, and preference in land loans to the farmer acquiring or refinancing a farm as a home.

9. To provide for decentralized, non-partisan control of the Farm Credit Administration and the election by National Farm Loan Associations of at least one-half of each Board of Directors of the Federal Land Banks, and thereby remove these institutions from politics.

10. To provide in the case of agricultural products of which there are exportable surpluses, the payment of reasonable benefits upon the domestically consumed portion of such crops in order to make the tariff effective. These payments are to be limited to the production level of the family type farm.

11. To encourage and further develop cooperative marketing.

12. To furnish Government assistance in disposing of surpluses in foreign trade by bargaining for foreign markets selectively by countries both as to exports and imports. We strenuously oppose so-called reciprocal treaties which trade off the American farmer.

13. To give every reasonable assistance to producers in areas suffering from temporary disaster, so that they may regain and maintain a self-supporting status.

TARIFF

Nearly sixty percent of all imports into the United States are now free of duty. The other forty percent of imports compete directly with the product of our industry. We would keep on the free list all products not grown or produced in the United States in commercial quantities. As to all commodities that commercially compete with our farms, our forests, our mines, our fisheries, our oil wells, our labor and our industries, sufficient protection should be maintained at all times to defend the American farmer and the American wage earner from the destructive competition emanating from the subsidies of foreign governments and the imports from low-wage and depreciated-currency countries.

We will repeal the present Reciprocal Trade Agreement Law. It is futile and dangerous. Its effect on agriculture and industry has been destructive. Its continuation would work to the detriment of the wage earner and the farmer.

We will restore the principle of the flexible tariff in order to meet changing economic conditions here and abroad and broaden by careful definition the powers of the Tariff Commission in order to extend this policy along non-partisan lines.

We will adjust tariffs with a view to promoting international trade, the stabilization of currencies, and the attainment of a proper balance between agriculture and industry.

We condemn the secret negotiations of reciprocal trade treaties without public hearing or legislative approval.

MONOPOLIES

A private monopoly is indefensible and intolerable. It menaces and, if continued, will utterly destroy constitutional government and the liberty of the citizen.

We favor the vigorous enforcement of the criminal laws, as well as the civil laws, against monopolies and trusts and their officials, and we demand the enactment of such additional legislation as is necessary to make it impossible for private monopoly to exist in the United States.

We will employ the full powers of the government to the end that monopoly shall be eliminated and that free enterprise shall be fully restored and maintained.

REGULATION OF BUSINESS

We recognize the existence of a field within which governmental regulation is desirable and salutary. The authority to regulate should be vested in an independent tribunal acting under clear and specific laws establishing definite standards. Their determinations on law and facts should be subject to review by the Courts. We favor Federal regulation, within the Constitution, of the marketing of securities to protect investors. We favor also Federal regulation of the interstate activities of public utilities.

CIVIL SERVICE

Under the New Deal, official authority has been given to inexperienced and incompetent persons. The Civil Service has been sacrificed to create a national political machine. As a result the Federal Government has never presented such a picture of confusion and inefficiency.

We pledge ourselves to the merit system, virtually destroyed by New Deal spoilsmen. It should be restored, improved and extended.

We will provide such conditions as offer an attractive permanent career in government service to young men and women of ability, irrespective of party affiliations.

GOVERNMENT FINANCE

The New Deal Administration has been characterized by shameful waste, and general financial irresponsibility. It has piled deficit upon deficit. It threatens national bankruptcy and the destruction through inflation of insurance policies and savings bank deposits.

We pledge ourselves to:

Stop the folly of uncontrolled spending.

Balance the budget—not by increasing taxes but by cutting expenditures, drastically and immediately.

Revise the Federal tax system and coordinate it with State and local tax systems.

Use the taxing power for raising revenue and not for punitive or political purposes.

MONEY AND BANKING

We advocate a sound currency to be preserved at all hazards.

The first requisite to a sound and stable currency is a balanced budget.

We oppose further devaluation of the dollar.

We will restore to the Congress the authority lodged with it by the Constitution to coin money and regulate the value thereof by repealing all the laws delegating this authority to the Executive.

We will cooperate with other countries toward stabilization of currencies as soon as we can do so with due regard for our National interests and as soon as other nations have sufficient stability to justify such action.

FOREIGN AFFAIRS

We pledge ourselves to promote and maintain peace by all honorable means not leading to foreign alliances or political commitments.

Obedient to the traditional foreign policy of America and to the repeatedly expressed will of the American people, we pledge that America shall not become a member of the League of Nations nor of the World Court nor shall America take on any entangling alliances in foreign affairs.

We shall promote, as the best means of securing and maintaining peace by the pacific settlement of disputes, the great cause of international arbitration through the establishment of free, independent tribunals, which shall determine such disputes in accordance with law, equity and justice.

NATIONAL DEFENSE

We favor an army and navy, including air forces, adequate for our National Defense.

We will cooperate with other nations in the limitation of armaments and control of traffic in arms.

BILL OF RIGHTS

We pledge ourselves to preserve, protect and defend, against all intimidation and threat, freedom of religion, speech, press and radio; and the right of assembly and petition and immunity from unreasonable searches and seizures.

We offer the abiding security of a government of laws as against the autocratic perils of a government of men.

FURTHERMORE

1. We favor the construction by the Federal Government of head-water storage basins to prevent floods, subject to the approval of the legislative and executive branches of the government of the States whose lands are concerned.

2. We favor equal opportunity for our colored citizens. We pledge our protection of their economic status and personal safety. We will do our best to further their employment in the gainfully occupied life of America, particularly in private industry, agriculture, emergency agencies and the Civil Service.

We condemn the present New Deal policies which would regiment and ultimately eliminate the colored citizen from the country's productive life, and make him solely a ward of the Federal Government.

3. To our Indian population we pledge every effort on the part of the national government to ameliorate living conditions for them.

4. We pledge continuation of the Republican policy of adequate compensation and care for veterans disabled in the service of our country and for their widows, orphans and dependents.

5. We shall use every effort to collect the war debt due us from foreign countries, amounting to $12,000,000—one-third of our national debt. No effort has been made by the present administration even to reopen negotiations.

6. We are opposed to legislation which discriminates against women in Federal and State employment.

CONCLUSION

We assume the obligations and duties imposed upon government by modern conditions. We affirm our unalterable conviction that, in the future as in the past, the fate of the nation will depend, not so much on the wisdom and power of government, as on the character and virtue, self-reliance, industry and thrift of the people and on their willingness to meet the responsibilities essential to the preservation of a free society.

Finally, as our party affirmed in its first Platform in 1856: "Believing that the spirit of our institutions as well as the Constitution of our country guarantees liberty of conscience and equality of rights among our citizens we oppose all legislation tending to impair them," and "we invite the affiliation and cooperation of the men of all parties, however differing from us in other respects, in support of the principles herein declared."

The acceptance of the nomination tendered by the Convention carries with it, as a matter of private honor and public faith, an undertaking by each candidate to be true to the principles and program herein set forth.

From: George Thomas Kurian, ed. *The Encyclopedia of the Republican Party.* Armonk, NY: M. E. Sharpe, 1997.

ROOSEVELT CAMPAIGN SPEECH, OCTOBER 14, 1936

President Franklin D. Roosevelt's 1936 pursuit of reelection contained a strong populist current, as this Chicago speech from late in the campaign indicates. Having been criticized by industry and the Republicans for being socialistic and antibusiness, Roosevelt returned the attacks. He argued that the individualistic pursuit of profit had led the country into its current economic difficulties and that restraints on it were necessary to get the nation back on the road to economic recovery. He also pointed out how business—rescued by the New Deal programs of the first administration—was turning against reform now that business was back on its financial feet.

I seem to have been here before. Four years ago I dropped into this city from the airways—an old friend come in a new way—to accept in this hall the nomination for the Presidency of the United States. I came to a Chicago fighting with its back to the wall—factories closed, markets silent, banks shaky, ships and trains empty. Today those factories sing the song of industry; markets hum with bustling movement; banks are secure; ships and trains are running full. Once again it is Chicago as Carl Sandburg saw it—"The City of the Big Shoulders"—the city that smiles. And with Chicago a whole Nation that had not been cheerful for years is full of cheer once more.

On this trip through the Nation I have talked to farmers, I have talked to miners, I have talked to industrial workers; and in all that I have seen and heard one fact has been clear as crystal—that they are part and parcel of a rounded whole, and that none of them can succeed in his chosen occupation if those in the other occupations fail in their prosperity. I have driven home that point.

Tonight, in this center of business, I give the same message to the business men of America—to those who make and sell the processed goods the Nation uses and to the men and women who work for them.

To them I say:

Do you have a deposit in the bank? It is safer today than it has ever been in our history. It is guaranteed. Last October first marked the end of the first full year in fifty-five years without a single failure of a national bank in the United States. Is that not on the credit side of the Government's account with you?

Are you an investor? Your stocks and bonds are up to five- and six-year high levels.

Are you a merchant? Your markets have the precious life-blood of purchasing power. Your customers on the farms have better incomes and smaller debts. Your customers in the cities have more jobs, surer jobs, better jobs. Did not your Government have something to do with that?

Are you in industry? Industrial earnings, industrial profits are the highest in four, six, or even seven years! Bankruptcies are at a new low. Your Government takes some credit for that.

Are you in railroads? Freight loadings are steadily going up. Passenger receipts are steadily going up—have in some cases doubled—because your Government made the railroads cut rates and make money.

Are you a middleman in the great stream of farm products? The meat and grain that move through your yards and elevators have a steadier supply, a steadier demand and steadier prices than you have known for years. And your Government is trying to keep it that way.

Some people say that all this recovery has just happened. But in a complicated modern world recoveries from depressions do not just happen. The years from 1919 to 1933, when we waited for recovery just to happen, prove the point.

But in 1933 we did not wait. We acted. Behind the growing recovery of today is a story of deliberate Government acceptance of responsibility to save business, to save the American system of private enterprise and economic democracy—a record unequaled by any modern Government in history.

What had the previous Administration in Washington done for four years? Nothing. Why? For a very fundamental reason. That Administration was not industrially-minded or agriculturally-minded or business-minded. It was high-finance-minded—manned and controlled by a handful of men who in turn controlled and by one financial device or another took their toll from the greater part of all other business and industry.

Let me make one simple statement. When I refer to high finance I am not talking about all great bankers, or all great corporation executives, or all multimillionaires—any more than Theodore Roosevelt, in using the term "malefactors of great wealth," implied that all men of great wealth were "malefactors." I do not even imply that the majority of them are bad citizens. The opposite is true.

Just in the same way, the overwhelming majority of business men in this country are good citizens and the proportion of those who are not is probably about the same proportion as in the other occupations and professions of life.

When I speak of high finance as a harmful factor in recent years, I am speaking about a minority which includes the type of individual who speculates with other people's money—and you in Chicago know the kind I refer to—and also the type of individual who says that popular government cannot be trusted and, therefore, that the control of business of all kinds and, indeed, of Government itself should be vested in the hands of one hundred or two hundred all-wise individuals controlling the purse-strings of the Nation.

High finance of this type refused to permit Government credit to go directly to the industrialist, to the business man, to the homeowner, to the farmer. They wanted it to trickle down from the top, through the intricate arrangements which they controlled and by which they were able to levy tribute on every business in the land.

They did not want interest rates to be reduced by the use of Government funds, for that would affect the rate of interest which they themselves wanted to charge. They did not want Government supervision over financial markets through which they manipulated their monopolies with other people's money.

And in the face of their demands that Government do nothing that they called "unsound," the Government, hypnotized by its indebtedness to them, stood by and let the depression drive industry and business toward bankruptcy.

America is an economic unit. New means and methods of transportation and communications have made us economically as well as politically a single Nation.

Because kidnappers and bank robbers could in high-powered cars speed across state lines it became necessary, in order to protect our people, to invoke the power of the Federal Government.

In the same way speculators and manipulators from across State lines, and regardless of State laws, have lured the unsuspecting and the unwary to financial destruction.

In the same way across state lines, there have been built up intricate corporate structures, piling bond upon stock and stock upon bond—huge monopolies which were stifling independent business and private enterprise.

There was no power under Heaven that could protect the people against that sort of thing except a people's Government at Washington. All that this Administration has done, all that it proposes to do—and this it does propose to do—is to use every power and authority of the Federal Government to protect the commerce of America from the selfish forces which ruined it.

Always, month in and month out, during these three and a half years, your Government has had but one sign on its desk—"Seek only the greater good of the greater number of Americans." And in appraising the record, remember two things. First, this Administration was called upon to act after a previous Administration and all the combined forces of private enterprise had failed. Secondly, in spite of all the demand for speed, the complexity of the problem and all the vast sums of money involved, we have had no Teapot Dome.

We found when we came to Washington in 1933, that the business and industry of the Nation were like a train which had gone off the rails into a ditch. Our first job was to get it out of the ditch and start it up the track again as far as the repair shops. Our next job was to make repairs—on the broken axles which had gotten it off the road, on the engine which had been worn down by gross misuse.

What was it that the average business man wanted Government to do for him—to do immediately in 1933?

1. Stop deflation and falling prices—and we did it.
2. Increase the purchasing power of his customers who were industrial workers in the cities—and we did it.
3. Increase the purchasing power of his customers on the farms—and we did it.
4. Decrease interest rates, power rates and transportation rates—and we did it.
5. Protect him from the losses due to crime, bank robbers, kidnappers, blackmailers—and we did it.

How did we do it? By a sound monetary policy which raised prices. By reorganizing the banks of the Nation and insuring their deposits. By bringing the business men of the Nation together and encouraging them to pay higher wages, to shorten working hours, and to discourage that minority among their own members who were engaging in unfair competition and unethical business practices.

Through the AAA [Agricultural Adjustment Administration], through our cattle-buying program, through our program of drought relief and flood relief, through the Farm Credit Administration, we raised the income of the customers of business who lived on the farms. By our program to provide work for the unemployed, by our CCC [Civilian Conservation Corps] camps, and other measures, greater purchasing power was given to those who lived in our cities.

Money began going round again. The dollars paid out by Government were spent in the stores and shops of the Nation; and spent again to the wholesaler; and spent again to the factory; and spent again to the wage earner; and then spent again in another store and shop. The wheels of business began to turn again; the train was back on the rails.

Mind you, it did not get out of the ditch itself, it was hauled out by your Government.

And we hauled it along the road. PWA [Public Works Administration], WPA [Works Progress Administration], both provided normal and useful employment for hundreds of thousands of workers. Hundreds of millions of dollars got into circulation when we liquidated the assets of closed banks through the Reconstruction Finance Corporation; millions more when we loaned money for home building and home financing through the Federal Housing program; hundreds of millions more in loans and grants to enable municipalities to build needed improvements; hundreds of millions more through the CCC camps.

I am not going to talk tonight about how much our program to provide work for the unemployed meant to the Nation as a whole. That cannot be measured in dollars and cents. It can be measured only in terms of the preservation of the families of America.

But so far as business goes, it can be measured in terms of sales made and goods moving.

The train of American business is moving ahead.

But you people know what I mean when I say it is clear that if the train is to run smoothly again the cars will have to be loaded more evenly. We have made a definite start in getting the train loaded more evenly, in order that axles may not break again.

For example, we have provided a sounder and cheaper money market and a sound banking and securities system. You business men know how much legitimate business you lost in the old days because your customers were robbed by fake securities or impoverished by shaky banks.

By our monetary policy we have kept prices up and lightened the burden of debt. It is easier to get credit. It is easier to repay.

We have encouraged cheaper power for the small factory owner to lower his cost of production.

We have given the business man cheaper transportation rates.

But above all, we have fought to break the deadly grip which monopoly has in the past been able to fasten on the business of the Nation.

Because we cherished our system of private property and free enterprise and were determined to preserve it as the foundation of our traditional American system, we recalled the warning of Thomas Jefferson that "widespread poverty and concentrated wealth cannot long endure side by side in a democracy."

Our job was to preserve the American ideal of economic as well as political democracy, against the abuse of concentration of economic power that had been insidiously growing up among us in the past fifty years, particularly during the twelve years of preceding Administrations. Free economic enterprise was being weeded out at an alarming pace.

During those years of false prosperity and during the more recent years of exhausting depression, one business after another, one small corporation after another, their resources depleted, had failed or had fallen into the lap of a bigger competitor.

A dangerous thing was happening. Half of the industrial corporate wealth of the country had come under the control of less than two hundred huge corporations. That is not all. These huge corporations in some cases did not even try to compete with each other. They themselves were tied together by interlocking directors, interlocking bankers, interlocking lawyers.

This concentration of wealth and power has been built upon other people's money, other people's business, other people's labor. Under this concentration independent business was allowed to exist only by sufferance. It has been a menace to the social system as well as to the economic system which we call American democracy.

There is no excuse for it in the cold terms of industrial efficiency.

There is no excuse for it from the point of view of the average investor.

There is no excuse for it from the point of view of the independent businessman.

I believe, I have always believed, and I will always believe in private enterprise as the backbone of economic well-being in the United States.

But I know, and you know, and every independent business man who has had to struggle against the competition of monopolies knows, that this concentration of economic power in all-embracing corporations does not represent private enterprise as we Americans cherish it and propose to foster it. On the contrary, it represents private enterprise which has become a kind of private government, a power unto itself—a regimentation of other people's money and other people's lives.

Back in Kansas I spoke about bogey men and fairy tales which the real Republican leaders, many of whom are part of this concentrated power, are using to spread fear among the American people.

You good people have heard about these fairy tales and bogeymen too. You have heard about how antagonistic to business this Administration is supposed to be. You have heard all about the dangers which the business of America is supposed to be facing if this Administration continues.

The answer to that is the record of what we have done. It was this Administration which saved the system of private profit and free enterprise after it had been dragged to the brink of ruin by these same leaders who now try to scare you.

Look at the advance in private business in the last three and a half years; and read there what we think about private business.

Today for the first time in seven years the banker, the storekeeper, the small factory owner, the industrialist, can all sit back and enjoy the company of their own ledgers. They are in the black. That is where we want them to be; that is where our policies aim them to be; that is where we intend them to be in the future.

Some of these people really forget how sick they were. But I know how sick they were. I have their fever charts. I know how the knees of all of our rugged individualists were trembling four years ago and how their hearts fluttered. They came to Washington in great numbers. Washington did not look like a dangerous bureaucracy to them then. Oh, no! It looked like an emergency hospital. All of the distinguished patients wanted two things—a quick hypodermic to end the pain and a course of treatment to cure the disease. They wanted them in a hurry; we gave them both. And now most of the patients seem to be doing very nicely. Some of them are even well enough to throw their crutches at the doctor.

The struggle against private monopoly is a struggle for, and not against, American business. It is a struggle to preserve individual enterprise and economic freedom.

I believe in individualism. I believe in it in the arts, the sciences and professions. I believe in it in business. I believe in individualism in all of these things—up to the point where the individualist starts to operate at the expense of society. The overwhelming majority of American business men do not believe in it beyond that point. We have all suffered in the past from individualism run wild. Society has suffered and business has suffered.

Believing in the solvency of business, the solvency of farmers and the solvency of workers, I believe also in the solvency of Government. Your Government is solvent.

The net Federal debt today is lower in proportion to the income of the Nation and in proportion to the wealth of the Nation than it was on March fourth, 1933.

In the future it will become lower still because with the rising tide of national income and national wealth, the very causes of our emergency spending are starting to disappear. Government expenditures are coming down and Government income is going up. The opportunities for private enterprise will continue to expand.

The people of America have no quarrel with business. They insist only that the power of concentrated wealth shall not be abused.

We have come through a hard struggle to preserve democracy in America. Where other Nations in other parts of the world have lost that fight, we have won.

The business men of America and all other citizens have joined in a firm resolve to hold the fruits of that victory, to cling to the old ideals and old fundamentals upon which America has grown great.

From: B. D. Zevin, ed. *Nothing to Fear: The Selected Addresses of Franklin Delano Roosevelt, 1932–1945.* Boston: Houghton Mifflin, 1946.

ROOSEVELT'S SECOND INAUGURAL ADDRESS, JANUARY 20, 1937

In his second inaugural address, President Franklin D. Roosevelt chose to emphasize two themes. One concerned the great strides the nation had made during the first administration and through the programs of the New Deal. At the same time, Roosevelt pointed out that the country had a long way to go. In perhaps the most famous line from the address, the reelected president said: "I see one-third of a nation ill-housed, ill-clad, ill-nourished." Ironically, the second administration would be known more for its lack of new programs than for its commitment to continue the New Deal reforms.

When four years ago we met to inaugurate a President, the Republic, single-minded in anxiety, stood in spirit here. We dedicated ourselves to the fulfillment of a vision—to speed the time when there would be for all the people that security and peace essential to the pursuit of happiness. We of the Republic pledged ourselves to drive from the temple of our ancient faith those who had profaned it; to end by action, tireless and unafraid, the stagnation and despair of that day. We did those first things first.

Our covenant with ourselves did not stop there. Instinctively we recognized a deeper need—the need to find through government the instrument of our united purpose to solve for the individual the ever-rising problems of a complex civilization. Repeated attempts at their solution without the aid of government had left us baffled and bewildered. For, without that aid, we had been unable to create those moral controls over the services of science which are necessary to make science a useful servant instead of a ruthless master of mankind. To do this we knew that we must find practical controls over blind economic forces and blindly selfish men.

We of the Republic sensed the truth that democratic government has innate capacity to protect its people against disasters once considered inevitable, to solve problems once considered unsolvable. We would not admit that we could not find a way to master economic epidemics just as, after centuries of fatalistic suffering, we had found a way to master epidemics of disease. We refused to leave the problems of our common welfare to be solved by the winds of chance and the hurricanes of disaster.

In this we Americans were discovering no wholly new truth; we were writing a new chapter in our book of self-government.

This year marks the one hundred and fiftieth anniversary of the Constitutional Convention which made us a nation. At that Convention our forefathers found the way out of the chaos which followed the Revolutionary War; they created a strong government with powers of united action sufficient then and now to solve problems utterly beyond individual or local solution. A century and a half ago they established the Federal Government in order to promote the general welfare and secure the blessings of liberty to the American people.

Today we invoke those same powers of government to achieve the same objectives.

Four years of new experience have not belied our historic instinct. They hold out the clear hope that government within communities, government within the separate States, and government of the United States can do the things the times require without yielding its democracy. Our tasks in the last four years did not force democracy to take a holiday.

Nearly all of us recognize that as intricacies of human relationships increase, so power to govern them also must increase—power to stop evil; power to do good. The essential democracy of our Nation and the safety of our people depend not upon the absence of power, but upon lodging it with those whom the people can change or continue at stated intervals through an honest and free system of elections. The Constitution of 1787 did not make our democracy impotent.

In fact, in these last four years, we have made the exercise of all power more democratic; for we have begun to bring private autocratic powers into their proper subordination to the public's government. The legend that they were invincible—above and beyond the processes of a democracy—has been shattered. They have been challenged and beaten.

Our progress out of the depression is obvious. But that is not all that you and I mean by the new order of things. Our pledge was not merely to do a patchwork job with second-hand materials. By using the new materials of social justice we have undertaken to erect on the old foundations a more enduring structure for the better use of future generations.

In that purpose we have been helped by achievements of mind and spirit. Old truths have been relearned; untruths have been unlearned. We have always known that heedless self-interest was bad morals; we know now that it is bad economics. Out of the collapse of a prosperity whose builders boasted their practicality has come the conviction that in the long run economic morality pays. We are beginning to wipe out the line that divides the practical from the ideal; and in so doing we are fashioning an instrument of unimagined power for the establishment of a morally better world.

This new understanding undermines the old admiration of worldly success as such. We are beginning to abandon our tolerance of the abuse of power by those who betray for profit the elementary decencies of life.

In this process evil things formerly accepted will not be so easily condoned. Hard-headedness will not so easily excuse hard-heartedness. We are moving toward an era of good feeling. But we realize that there can be no era of good feeling save among men of good will.

For these reasons I am justified in believing that the greatest change we have witnessed has been the change in the moral climate of America.

Among men of good will, science and democracy together offer an ever-richer life and ever-larger satisfaction to the individual. With this change in our moral climate and our rediscovered ability to improve our economic order, we have set our feet upon the road of enduring progress.

Shall we pause now and turn our back upon the road that lies ahead? Shall we call this the promised land? Or, shall we continue on our way? For "each age is a dream that is dying, or one that is coming to birth."

Many voices are heard as we face a great decision. Comfort says, "Tarry a while." Opportunism says, "This is a good spot." Timidity asks, "How difficult is the road ahead?"

True, we have come far from the days of stagnation and despair. Vitality has been preserved. Courage and confidence have been restored. Mental and moral horizons have been extended.

But our present gains were won under the pressure of more than ordinary circumstance. Advance became imperative under the goad of fear and suffering. The times were on the side of progress.

To hold to progress today, however, is more difficult. Dulled conscience, irresponsibility, and ruthless self-interest already reappear. Such symptoms of prosperity may become portents of disaster! Prosperity already tests the persistence of our progressive purpose.

Let us ask again: Have we reached the goal of our vision of that fourth day of March, 1933? Have we found our happy valley?

I see a great nation, upon a great continent, blessed with a great wealth of natural resources. Its hundred and thirty million people are at peace among themselves; they are making their country a good neighbor among the nations. I see a United States which can demonstrate that, under democratic methods of government, national wealth can be translated into a spreading volume of human comforts hitherto unknown, and the lowest standard of living can be raised far above the level of mere subsistence.

But here is the challenge to our democracy: In this nation I see tens of millions of its citizens—a substantial part of its whole population—who at this very moment are denied the greater part of what the very lowest standards of today call the necessities of life.

I see millions of families trying to live on incomes so meager that the pall of family disaster hangs over them day by day.

I see millions whose daily lives in city and on farm continue under conditions labeled indecent by a so-called polite society half a century ago.

I see millions denied education, recreation, and the opportunity to better their lot and the lot of their children.

I see millions lacking the means to buy the products of farm and factory and by their poverty denying work and productiveness to many other millions.

I see one-third of a nation ill-housed, ill-clad, ill-nourished.

It is not in despair that I paint you that picture. I paint it for you in hope—because the Nation, seeing and understanding the injustice in it, proposes to paint it out. We are determined to make every American citizen the subject of his country's interest and concern; and we will never regard any faithful, law-abiding group within our borders as superfluous. The test of our progress is not whether we add more to the abundance of those who have much; it is whether we provide enough for those who have too little.

If I know aught of the spirit and purpose of our Nation, we will not listen to Comfort, Opportunism, and Timidity. We will carry on.

Overwhelmingly, we of the Republic are men and women of good will; men and women who have more than warm hearts of dedication; men and women who have cool heads and willing hands of practical purpose as well. They will insist that every agency of popular government use effective instruments to carry out their will.

Government is competent when all who compose it work as trustees for the whole people. It can make constant progress when it keeps abreast of all the facts. It can obtain justified support and legitimate criticism when the people receive true information of all that government does.

If I know aught of the will of our people, they will demand that these conditions of effective government shall be created and maintained. They will demand a Nation uncorrupted by cancers of injustice and, therefore, strong among the nations in its example of the will to peace.

Today we reconsecrate our country to long-cherished ideals in a suddenly changed civilization. In every land there are always at work forces that drive men apart and forces that draw men together. In our personal ambitions we are individualists. But in our seeking for economic and political progress as a nation, we all go up, or else we all go down, as one people.

To maintain a democracy of effort requires a vast amount of patience in dealing with differing methods, a vast amount of humility. But out of the confusion of many voices rises an understanding of dominant public need. Then political leadership can voice common ideals, and aid in their realization.

In taking again the oath of office as President of the United States, I assume the solemn obligation of leading the American people forward along the road over which they have chosen to advance.

While this duty rests upon me I shall do my utmost to speak their purpose and to do their will, seeking Divine guidance to help us each and every one to give light to them that sit in darkness and to guide our feet into the way of peace.

From: B. D. Zevin, ed. *Nothing to Fear: The Selected Addresses of Franklin Delano Roosevelt, 1932–1945.* Boston: Houghton Mifflin, 1946.

ELEANOR ROOSEVELT'S PRESS CONFERENCE DISCUSSION ON MARRIED WOMEN IN THE LABOR FORCE, JUNE 16, 1938

During the Great Depression, an attitude arose that employed married women should either quit or be laid off, so that their jobs could be given to men, single women, and others who were heads of households. This attitude was put into practice by many employers. In this June 1938 press conference, First Lady Eleanor Roosevelt was asked her opinion of married women in the workforce. She gave a nuanced response, saying that blanket opinions about married women in the workforce needed to be thought through and decisions made on a case-by-case basis.

For some people work is almost a necessity to development. It may be that it's not always the keeping of a home which is the type of which they are supposed to do and that you can't deny permanently to any human being the right. You might say temporarily, because in this situation perhaps you couldn't take a salary for a length of time if there is a stress of some kind, but you certainly can't deny that human being the right of development permanently.

I have always cited the fact that work was necessary to the development of the country and dignified the individual and was of value to the community, and that any young man who could live on his income without working and who did not work has always had the feeling that he was a slacker.

Why we should feel that in an age when someone's work is not needed in the home, she should, out of necessity, be made a slacker, is something I have never been able to understand in the value of citizens to every community.

I think the theory on which we have built does not go with the theory we are trying to push on women today. It was all right when your home required every bit of work that you could get out of every woman in the house; because then the full capacity was being used and there were all kinds of ways of using it, and today it doesn't require that anymore. Therefore, we are really forcing upon women a position which we have held from the beginning in this country was not good for the country.

I think she, [the woman] herself, decides that. Actually, the families there [in an old-fashioned home] are very, large. A mother could hardly leave home a minute. Being large families, there are a good many girls who have wanted to work, but it's left entirely to them. I mean, nobody decides for them. They decide for themselves.

It happens that in the factory, girls and women are employed, not men. I think there may be one or two men, but it's almost entirely women and girls. That was understandable, because there were quite a number of young women and girls who really needed work, because they would have just been an added burden on their families if there had not been some outlet for their work. But, of course, they married very young and have very large families. So how long any one of them will continue is up to them.

If you had looked into family after family, you would have found that a number of the girls marry the minute they leave high school. They may work a short time, but a family begins to arrive very quickly, and for a short time they can't work.

There are one or two women who have been able to work because their children were old enough not to need them so much at home or helped at home or something of that sort. That's not a question that's decided by the individual. It's decided by the families.

A short time ago, I got a number of letters [questioning employment of women], and it wasn't merely drawing my attention, because one of the heads of a department here got a letter which he sent to me—I think because he had a sense of bewilderment as to what it was all about—and I got the answer for him and decided that perhaps the answer would be valuable in the country as a whole, because I had had several letters.

I am always getting letters from people who have theories of the way you can do away with unemployment. That had been one of the ways.

Not for women to give up their work. I think you have to realize that there are always individual situations.

I, for instance, I know of a family where the woman was working, and working to give a very much better education to her children. There was no real reason why she couldn't do it, because the children were grown and almost of college age. But there developed in their community a very serious employment situation. It was a temporary situation, but it was almost a necessity to cut down in the kind of work in which her husband was employed.

They did cut a number of employees, and she voluntarily took the cut, and the children did manage to pull themselves through. She did go back, but it was an exceptional situation that had to be met over a temporary period. It happened to be a situation which the employees understood as well as the employer.

I can't think that you could lay down hard and fast rules, that individual situations do arise, and people should be allowed to use their own intelligence about that. You can't ever, I don't think, say that any one thing will ever fit every situation. It doesn't. It's like saying such and such a thing is always right. You and I know such and such a thing is never always right. It may be right for one person and wrong for another person in almost the same situation. So that laying down hard and fast rules is very difficult, and I think you should leave a certain flexibility to allow for judgment.

I think if the single woman has to support herself, the question does not arise if she is under more moral obligation than a man.

So I think it boils down to a married woman, and then comes the question whether the man or woman should be the main support in a family. My own instinct is a feeling that most women, if it comes to a decision, have more ability to find employment for themselves than most men have. But that doesn't always hold true.

I happen to know of a couple where the woman earns money and the man runs a farm. It's the kind of work which doesn't bring in a large amount of income but which makes living a very pleasant, happy thing, and he is happy and does the kind of thing he enjoys. It's a happy family. My instinct is to say that, as a rule, a woman is more adjustable.

Who is going to be the person to decide whether it is a woman's duty to stay at home and take care of her family?

Second, who should say that where the skills of the woman were such that she could do that particular job better than anybody else, better than she could do any other, probably it would be economically sound as well as spiritually a good thing? On the other hand, there may be a great many people for whom it would neither be spiritually or economically the best thing for their children or for that individual.

From: Maurine Beasley, ed., *The White House Press Conferences of Eleanor Roosevelt.* New York: Garland, 1983.

ELEANOR ROOSEVELT'S PRESS CONFERENCE DISCUSSION ON CROSSING PICKET LINES, JANUARY 17, 1939

In January 1939, the waitresses at the George Mason Hotel in Alexandria, Virginia, were on strike, protesting that prospective tips were being considered in establishing the waitresses' minimum wage. With President Franklin D. Roosevelt's birthday celebration scheduled for the hotel on January 30, First Lady Eleanor Roosevelt was asked if she would cross the picket line. She said that she would not and that the practice of including tips in setting the minimum wage was wrong, both for the workers and the public. Eleanor Roosevelt's response reflected her deep sympathies for working women.

Well, I certainly won't go if the strike is still on. I won't go through the picket line.

I have been once or twice where it had been discussed and the strikers had been willing that I should attend something. I think that came up once about some engagement which had been made. But that was an arrangement made with the strikers, that they should call off their picket line at that particular time.

But I wouldn't be willing to go to anything till some decision had been arrived at, unless it was arranged in that way. Something of that kind had been done.

This is an old question; this is nothing new. There has been for many years this question of basic pay where tips are unavailable. It has been argued over and over again.

It seems to me that now it ought to be very quickly resolved, because there should be discussion. It should be easy to establish the facts, and one should be able to arrive at a conclusion as to whether it is a fair thing to ask any people to accept that type of work on the basis of tips.

It never has seemed to me quite fair to the public, any more than toward a worker. For that type of work, it means that it does put a burden on the public not only to pay for what they are supposed to pay for, which is the food they consume, but to remember that part of the service is a direct charge on them. But a great many people don't realize that fact, and that works a hardship on the worker and may result in the public not always being fairly treated because they don't realize the obligation.

Minimum wage standards should not include an allowance for tips.

From: Maurine Beasley, ed. *The White House Press Conferences of Eleanor Roosevelt.* New York: Garland, 1983.

ELEANOR ROOSEVELT'S PRESS CONFERENCE DISCUSSION ON CUTS IN WORKS PROGRESS ADMINISTRATION JOBS, JANUARY 31, 1939

Although holding no official capacity in the administration of her husband, First Lady Eleanor Roosevelt was often called upon to explain its policies and politics. In a January 1939 press conference, a reporter asked her to explain recent cuts in the Works Progress Administration (WPA), the major public works program of the late New Deal era. In her answer, she both minimized the importance of these cuts and placed blame on Congress. She also explained the role that the WPA should play in the American economy.

It seems to me that this [bill cutting back Works Progress Administration funding] was billed as an economic gesture. It's only a gesture, because it's not sufficient to be a real economy.

As the bill went through the Senate, it doesn't seem to me to mean a great deal, because the cuts won't be made until April 1; and the President is told that if he thinks there is the need, he may make application for money at that time. He could make application now, because he knows exactly what the need will be. It's not likely to change between now and the middle of March, when he will have to make his next application.

I think that once we actually made the cuts that amount represented, it would mean in human lives quite a serious difficulty. I'm only judging that from letters I have had on the cuts which went into effect in New York City in February as a perfectly normal decrease, the kind of thing they have done right along. Immediately, you had certain specific circumstances which showed that there would be, of course, a number of people who would not immediately get on Social Security, if that was the reason they were taken off, and who would have a very hard time.

The trouble with all these things is that the things don't always synchronize that you expect to synchronize, and the human element in general has rather a bad time. But when you talk of it in money, it is a very different thing from when you talk of it in people. That is the thing that bothers me, so long as the responsible people think of it entirely from the point of view of the money and not from the point of view of the people.

I wish very much that the letters, instead of coming to me, who can do nothing, would go directly to the responsible people who have the real power; because, after all, the people who are doing the work, who really have the responsibility, should be the people who get the true picture. I think that probably the letters sent to me should go to them. The letters should go to their own representatives or to their local people, and it would reflect the conditions to their representatives.

Relief was based on the fact that you had no other method of support, and any people who take relief and they [don't] state what they have are doing something which is not contemplated in relief. I personally feel that anything which is below subsistence amount should be included in giving the subsistence grant and should not bar you from relief, because the fact that you have ten dollars or five dollars does not give you enough to live on. But you should not hide that.

I think there is one criticism that can be made, because it does give a loophole to people who are critical of the whole program. Say, we come across some who had private resources and they don't say how much the private resources were or anything else. I don't know, but I don't feel that it [statement of insufficient resources] does actually bar you as badly. If you have a house, you have to turn it in or you can't have relief. But I don't think a thing which was below the subsistence amount would bar you.

What is criticized? For example, I have a letter of criticism of the WPA in a certain place, and it's from someone who wants to be on WPA and was refused. She states, in a general way, that WPA is not honestly run, because she knows people on WPA who are running automobiles and never had them before.

I wrote back to say, 'Would you mind giving me the names of the people? If you can give me one or two, I will have them investigated.' I question very much if I shall have any names.

That's the type of criticism that you get, and that is why, to avoid all appearance of evil, you should be very careful to have stated anything at all; because it won't be said so and so had ten dollars a month and was thereafter granted fifteen. It will be said so and so was found to have private means; and unless it is stated in the report that so and so has ten dollars a month, you have no way of checking it.

I wish very much that where people have a small home in which they can live more cheaply by keeping it, they could be allowed to keep it. I think each case should be considered as an individual case, because I have had cases where the keeping of the home would make it impossible to live on the sum of money which you could live on if you live in a different way in a different place.

I think it should be allowed when it really increases well-being. But it should not be allowed when it means raising the amount they get or else living on a lower standard because they haven't got enough after keeping the home and eating properly. It is almost impossible to make a hard and fast rule. You have to consider every case. But, of course, that rule was made with the idea in mind that it would often cost more to live in what they have had than was fair to give to them.

I had a letter the other day: 'My husband is working on a WPA job. On that he works so many days a week. If we live on that, I can't give my children certain advantages which they ought to have.' One of them had a talent for music. She was evidently a very intelligent woman. She wanted her children to have every possible advantage. She said, however, 'My husband has a chance to get work on other days, part time work, and if he takes that, I can give my children the advantages they should have. But if he takes it and it is found out, he will be off WPA. It is straight business. [I d]on't feel it is wrong to oblige people to live at a lower standard than they [can] achieve?'

The answer is simply that WPA is set up so that nobody, as far as possible, lives below a subsistence level. But it is not set up, and can't be, to give the greatest amount of advantage possible to every family. And if you can get work of any kind, you should take it and not take WPA, because it's taking it away from someone, perhaps, who needs it more than you do.

I wrote back and said that, sad though it is, the advantages had to be given through their own effort or through the effort of the children themselves and could not be given, under the present circumstances, by an agency which was not set up to give people advantages but had been set up to keep them alive through an emergency period. It seems to trouble her, but you hate to dampen the desire to give advantages, because that is a normal desire for advancement which is very understandable in this country. It always has been the backbone of all our effort.

I should think if there were openings and people on relief were qualified, they should be advanced [to supervisory positions]. If on relief there are people who have the ability, take them. I think they should be taken, but other people are taken. The reason there are those rules is sometimes to prevent jealousy. The next thing is that someone has had a person that they have had to advance. If they happen to be Democrats, the Republicans will say this is run for the benefit of the Democrats, and vice-versa.

From: Maurine Beasley, ed. *The White House Press Conferences of Eleanor Roosevelt.* New York: Garland, 1983.

DEMOCRATIC PARTY PLATFORM, 1940

The Democratic Convention of 1940 was held at a time of great crisis in world affairs. Germany had recently defeated much of Western Europe, leaving Great Britain to struggle on alone against the Nazi juggernaut. The Democratic Party platform reflected this situation, placing defense against foreign aggression at the top of the agenda. Still, Franklin D. Roosevelt—running for an unprecedented third term—had a difficult year ahead of him convincing an isolationist Congress and public that it was in America's interest to defend Britain, and later Russia, against Nazi aggression.

The world is undergoing violent change. Humanity, uneasy in this machine age, is demanding a sense of security and dignity based on human values.

No democratic government which fails to recognize this trend—and take appropriate action can survive.

That is why the Government of this nation has moved to keep ahead of this trend; has moved with speed incomprehensible to those who do not see this trend.

Outside the Americas, established institutions are being overthrown and democratic philosophies are being repudiated by those whose creed recognizes no power higher than military force, no values other than a false efficiency.

What the founding fathers realized upon this continent was a daring dream, that men could have not only physical security, not only efficiency, but something else in addition that men had never had before—the security of the heart that comes with freedom, the peace of mind that comes from a sense of justice.

To this generation of Americans it is given to defend this democratic faith as it is challenged by social maladjustment within and totalitarian greed without. The world revolution against which we prepare our defense is so threatening that not until it has burned itself out in the last corner of the earth will our democracy be able to relax its guard.

In this world crisis, the purpose of the Democratic Party is to defend against external attack and justify by internal progress the system of government and way of life from which the Democratic Party takes its name.

FULFILLING THE AMERICAN IDEAL

Toward the modern fulfillment of the American ideal, the Democratic Party, during the last seven years, has labored successfully:

1. To strengthen democracy by defensive preparedness against aggression, whether by open attack or secret infiltration;

2. To strengthen democracy by increasing our economic efficiency; and

3. To strengthen democracy by improving the welfare of the people.

These three objectives are one and inseparable. No nation can be strong by armaments alone. It must possess and use all the necessary resources for producing goods plentifully and distributing them effectively. It must add to these factors of material strength the unconquerable spirit and energy of a contented people, convinced that there are no boundaries to human progress and happiness in a land of liberty.

Our faith that these objectives can be attained is made unshakeable by what has already been done by the present Administration, in stopping the waste and exploitation of our human and natural resources, in restoring to the average man and woman a stake in the preservation of our democracy, in enlarging our national armaments, and in achieving national unity.

We shall hold fast to these gains. We are proud of our record. Therefore the Party in convention assembled endorses wholeheartedly the brilliant and courageous leadership of President Franklin D. Roosevelt and his statesmanship and that of the Congress for the past seven trying years. And to our President and great leader we send our cordial greetings.

WE MUST STRENGTHEN DEMOCRACY AGAINST AGGRESSION

The American people are determined that war, raging in Europe, Asia and Africa, shall not come to America.

We will not participate in foreign wars, and we will

not send our army, naval or air forces to fight in foreign lands outside of the Americas, except in case of attack. We favor and shall rigorously enforce and defend the Monroe Doctrine.

The direction and aim of our foreign policy has been, and will continue to be, the security and defense of our own land and the maintenance of its peace.

For years our President has warned the nation that organized assaults against religion, democracy and international good faith threatened our own peace and security. Men blinded by partisanship brushed aside these warnings as war-mongering and officious intermeddling. The fall of twelve nations was necessary to bring their belated approval of legislative and executive action that the President had urged and undertaken with the full support of the people. It is a tribute to the President's foresight and action that our defense forces are today at the peak of their peacetime effectiveness.

Weakness and unpreparedness invite aggression. We must be so strong that no possible combination of powers would dare to attack us. We propose to provide America with an invincible air force, a navy strong enough to protect all our seacoasts and our national interests, and a fully equipped and mechanized army. We shall continue to coordinate these implements of defense with the necessary expansion of industrial productive capacity and with the training of appropriate personnel. Outstanding leaders of industry and labor have already been enlisted by the Government to harness our mighty economic forces for national defense.

Experience of other nations gives warning that total defense is necessary to repel attack, and that partial defense is no defense.

We have seen the downfall of nations accomplished through internal dissension provoked from without. We denounce and will do all in our power to destroy the treasonable activities of disguised anti-democratic and un-American agencies which would sap our strength, paralyze our will to defend ourselves, and destroy our unity by inciting race against race, class against class, religion against religion and the people against their free institutions.

To make America strong, and to keep America free, every American must give of his talents and treasure in accordance with his ability and his country's needs. We must have democracy of sacrifice as well as democracy of opportunity.

To insure that our armaments shall be implements of peace rather than war, we shall continue our traditional policies of the good neighbor; observe and advocate international respect for the rights of others and

for treaty obligations; cultivate foreign trade through desirable trade agreements; and foster economic collaboration with the Republics of the Western Hemisphere.

In self-defense and in good conscience, the world's greatest democracy cannot afford heartlessly or in a spirit of appeasement to ignore the peace-loving and liberty-loving peoples wantonly attacked by ruthless aggressors. We pledge to extend to these peoples all the material aid at our command, consistent with law and not inconsistent with the interests of our own national self-defense—all to the end that peace and international good faith may yet emerge triumphant.

We do not regard the need for preparedness as a warrant for infringement upon our civil liberties, but on the contrary we shall continue to protect them, in the keen realization that the vivid contrast between the freedom we enjoy and the dark repression which prevails in the lands where liberty is dead, affords warning and example to our people to confirm their faith in democracy.

WE MUST STRENGTHEN DEMOCRACY BY INCREASING OUR ECONOMIC EFFICIENCY

The well-being of the land and those who work upon it is basic to the real defense and security of America.

The Republican Party gives its promises to the farmer and its allegiance to those who exploit him.

Since 1932 farm income has been doubled; six million farmers, representing more than 80 percent of all farm families, have participated in an effective soil conservation program; the farm debt and the interest rate on farm debt have been reduced, and farm foreclosures have been drastically curtailed; rural highways and farm-to-market roads have been vastly improved and extended; the surpluses on the farms have been used to feed the needy; low-cost electricity has been brought to five million farm people as a result of the rural electrification program; thousands of impoverished farm families have been rehabilitated; and steps have been taken to stop the alarming growth of farm tenancy, to increase land ownership, and to mitigate the hardships of migratory farm labor.

The Land and the Farmer

We pledge ourselves

To make parity as well as soil conservation payments until such time as the goal of parity income for agriculture is realized.

To extend and enlarge the tenant-purchase program until every deserving tenant farmer has a real opportunity to have a farm of his own.

To refinance existing farm debts at lower interest rates and on longer and more flexible terms.

To continue to provide for adjustment of production through democratic processes to the extent that excess surpluses are capable of control.

To continue the program of rehabilitation of farmers who need and merit aid.

To preserve and strengthen the ever-normal granary on behalf of the national defense, the consumer at home and abroad, and the American farmer.

To continue to make commodity loans to maintain the ever-normal granary and to prevent destructively low prices.

To expand the domestic consumption of our surpluses by the food and cotton stamp plan, the free school lunch, low-cost milk and other plans for bringing surplus farm commodities to needy consumers.

To continue our substantially increased appropriations for research and extension work through the land-grant colleges, and for research laboratories established to develop new outlets for farm products.

To conserve the soil and water resources for the benefit of farmers and the nation. In such conservation programs we shall, so far as practicable, bring about that development in forests and other permanent crops as will not unduly expand livestock and dairy production.

To safeguard the farmer's foreign markets and expand his domestic market for all domestic crops.

To enlarge the rural electrification [sic].

To encourage farmer-owned and controlled cooperatives.

To continue the broad program launched by this Administration for the coordinated development of our river basins through reclamation and irrigation, flood control, reforestation and soil conservation, stream purification, recreation, fish and game protection, low-cost power, and rural industry.

To encourage marketing agreements in aid of producers of dairy products, vegetables, fruits and specialty crops for the purpose of orderly marketing and the avoidance of unfair and wasteful practices.

To extend crop insurance from wheat to other crops as rapidly as experience justifies such extension.

To safeguard the family-sized farm in all our programs.

To finance these programs adequately in order that they may be effective.

In settling new lands reclaimed from desert by projects like Grand Coulee, we shall give priority to homeless families who have lost their farms. As these new lands are brought into use, we shall continue by Federal purchase to retire from the plow sub-marginal lands so that an increased percentage of our farmers may be able to live and work on good land.

These programs will continue to be in the hands of locally elected farmer committees to the largest extent possible. In this truly democratic way, we will continue to bring economic security to the farmer and his family, while recognizing the dignity and freedom of American farm life.

Industry and the Worker

Under Democratic auspices, more has been done in the last seven years to foster the essential freedom, dignity and opportunity of the American worker than in any other administration in the nation's history. In consequence, labor is today taking its rightful place as a partner of management in the common cause of higher earnings, industrial efficiency, national unity and national defense.

A far-flung system of employment exchanges has brought together millions of idle workers and available jobs. The workers' right to organize and bargain collectively through representatives of their own choosing is being enforced. We have enlarged the Federal machinery for the mediation of labor disputes. We have enacted an effective wage and hour law. Child labor in factories has been outlawed. Prevailing wages to workers employed on Government contracts have been assured.

We pledge to continue to enforce fair labor standards; to maintain the principles of the National Labor Relations Act; to expand employment training and opportunity for our youth, older workers, and workers displaced by technological changes; to strengthen the orderly processes of collective bargaining and peaceful settlement of labor disputes; and to work always for a just distribution of our national income among those who labor.

We will continue our efforts to achieve equality of opportunity for men and women without impairing the social legislation which promotes true equality by safeguarding the health, safety and economic welfare of women workers. The right to work for compensation in both public and private employment is an inalienable privilege of women as well as men, without distinction as to marital status.

The production of coal is one of our most important basic industries. Stability of production, employment, distribution and price are indispensable to the public welfare. We pledge continuation of the Federal Bituminous Coal Stabilization Act, and sympathetic consideration of the application of similar legislation to the anthracite coal industry, in order to provide additional protection for the owners, miners and consumers of hard coal.

We shall continue to emphasize the human element in industry and strive toward increasingly wholehearted cooperation between labor and industrial management.

Capital and the Business Man

To make democracy strong, our system of business enterprise and individual initiative must be free to gear its tremendous productive capacity to serve the greatest good of the greatest number.

We have defended and will continue to defend all legitimate business.

We have attacked and will continue to attack unbridled concentration of economic power and the exploitation of the consumer and the investor.

We have attacked the kind of banking which treated America as a colonial empire to exploit; the kind of securities business which regarded the Stock Exchange as a private gambling club for wagering other people's money; the kind of public utility holding companies which used consumers' and investors' money to suborn a free press, bludgeon legislatures and political conventions, and control elections against the interest of their customers and their security holders.

We have attacked the kind of business which levied tribute on all the rest of American business by the extortionate methods of monopoly.

We did not stop with attack—we followed through with the remedy. The American people found in themselves, through the democratic process, ability to meet the economic problems of the average American business where concentrated power had failed.

We found a broken and prostrate banking and financial system. We restored it to health by strengthening banks, insurance companies and other financial institutions. We have insured 62 million bank accounts, and protected millions of small investors in the security and commodity markets. We have thus revived confidence, safeguarded thrift, and opened the road to all honorable business.

We have made credit at low interest rates available to small-business men, thus unfastening the oppressive yoke of a money monopoly, and giving the ordinary citizen a chance to go into business and stay in business.

We recognize the importance of small business concerns and new enterprises in our national economy, and favor the enactment of constructive legislation to safeguard the welfare of small business. Independent small-scale enterprise, no less than big business, should be adequately represented on appropriate governmental boards and commissions, and its interests should be examined and fostered by a continuous research program.

We have provided an important outlet for private capital by stimulating home building and low-rent housing projects. More new homes were built throughout the nation last year than in any year since 1929.

We have fostered a well-balanced American merchant marine and the world's finest system of civil aeronautics, to promote our commerce and our national defense.

We have steered a steady course between a bankruptcy-producing deflation and a thrift-destroying inflation, so that today the dollar is the most stable and sought-after currency in the world—a factor of immeasurable benefit in our foreign and domestic commerce.

We shall continue to oppose barriers which impede trade among the several states. We pledge our best efforts in strengthening our home markets, and to this end we favor the adjustment of freight rates so that no section or state will have undue advantage over any other.

To encourage investment in productive enterprise, the tax-exempt privileges of future Federal, state and local bonds should be removed.

We have enforced the anti-trust laws more vigorously than at any time in our history, thus affording the maximum protection to the competitive system.

We favor strict supervision of all forms of the insurance business by the several states for the protection of policyholders and the public.

The full force of our policies, by raising the national income by thirty billion dollars from the low of 1932, by encouraging vast reemployment, and by elevating the level of consumer demand, has quickened the flow of buying and selling through every artery of industry and trade.

With mass purchasing power restored and many abuses eliminated, American business stands at the threshold of a great new era, richer in promise than any we have witnessed—an era of pioneering and progress beyond the present frontiers of economic activity—in transportation, in housing, in industrial expansion, and in the new utilization of the products of the farm and the factory.

We shall aid business in redeeming America's promise.

Electric Power

During the past seven years the Democratic Party has won the first major victories for the people of the nation in their generation-old contest with the power monopoly.

These victories have resulted in the recognition of certain self-evident principles and the realization of vast benefits by the people. These principles, long opposed by the Republican Party, are:

That the power of falling water is a gift from God, and consequently belongs not to a privileged few, but to all the people, who are entitled to enjoy its benefits;

That the people have the right through their government to develop their own power sites and bring low-cost electricity to their homes, farms and factories;

That public utility holding companies must not be permitted to serve as the means by which a few men can pyramid stocks upon stocks for the sole purpose of controlling vast power empires.

We condemn the Republican policies which permitted the victimizing of investors in the securities of private power corporations, and the exploitation of the people by unnecessarily high utility costs.

We condemn the opposition of utility power interests which delayed for years the development of national defense projects in the Tennessee Valley, and which obstructed river basin improvements and other public projects bringing low-cost electric power to the people. The successful power developments in the Tennessee and Columbia River basins show the wisdom of the Democratic Party in establishing government-owned and operated hydroelectric plants in the interests of power and light consumers.

Through these Democratic victories, whole regions have been revived and restored to prosperous habitation. Production costs have been reduced. Industries have been established which employ men and capital. Cheaper electricity has brought vast economic benefits to thousands of homes and communities.

These victories of the people must be safeguarded. They will be turned to defeat if the Republican Party should be returned to power. We pledge our Party militantly to oppose every effort to encroach upon the inherent right of our people to be provided with this primary essential of life at the lowest possible cost.

The nomination of a utility executive [Wendell

Willkie] by the Republican Party as its presidential candidate raises squarely the issue, whether the nation's water power shall be used for all the people or for the selfish interests of a few. We accept that issue.

Development of Western Resources

We take satisfaction in pointing out the incomparable development of the public land states under the wise and constructive legislation of this Administration. Mining has been revived, agriculture fostered, reclamation extended and natural resources developed as never before in a similar period. We pledge the continuance of such policies, based primarily on the expansion of opportunity for the people, as will encourage the full development, free from financial exploitation, of the great resources—mineral, agricultural, livestock, fishing and lumber—which the West affords.

Radio

Radio has become an integral part of the democratically accepted doctrine of freedom of speech, press, assembly and religion. We urge such legislative steps as may be required to afford the same protection from censorship that is now afforded the press under the Constitution of the United States.

WE MUST STRENGTHEN DEMOCRACY BY IMPROVING THE WELFARE OF THE PEOPLE

We place human resources first among the assets of a democratic society.

Unemployment

The Democratic Party wages war on unemployment, one of the gravest problems of our times, inherited at its worst from the last Republican administration. Since we assumed office, nine million additional persons have gained regular employment in normal private enterprise. All our policies—financial, industrial and agricultural—will continue to accelerate the rate of this progress.

By public action, where necessary to supplement private reemployment, we have rescued millions from idleness that breeds weakness, and given them a real stake in their country's well being. We shall continue to recognize the obligation of Government to provide work for deserving workers who cannot be absorbed by private industry.

We are opposed to vesting in the states and local authorities the control of Federally financed work relief. We believe that this Republican proposal is a thinly disguised plan to put the unemployed back on the dole.

We will continue energetically to direct our efforts toward the employment in private industry of all those willing to work, as well as the fullest employment of money and machines. This we pledge as our primary objective. To further implement this objective, we favor calling, under the direction of the President, a national unemployment conference of leaders of government, industry, labor and farm groups.

There is work in our factories, mines, fields, forests and river basins, on our coasts, highways, railroads and inland waterways. There are houses to be built to shelter our people. Building a better America means work and a higher standard of living for every family, and a richer and more secure heritage for every American.

Social Security

The Democratic Party, which established social security for the nation, is dedicated to its extension. We pledge to make the Social Security Act increasingly effective, by covering millions of persons not now protected under its terms; by strengthening our unemployment insurance system and establishing more adequate and uniform benefits, through the Federal equalization fund principle; by progressively extending and increasing the benefits of the old-age and survivors insurance system, including protection of the permanently disabled; and by the early realization of a minimum pension for all who have reached the age of retirement and are not gainfully employed.

Health

Good health for all the people is a prime requisite of national preparedness in its broadest sense. We have advanced public health, industrial hygiene, and maternal and child care. We are coordinating the health functions of the Federal Government. We pledge to expand these efforts, and to provide more hospitals and health centers and better health protection wherever the need exists, in rural and urban areas, all through the cooperative efforts of the Federal, state and local governments, the medical, dental, nursing and other scientific professions, and the voluntary agencies.

Youth and Education

Today, when the youth of other lands is being sacrificed in war, this nation recognizes the full value of the sound youth program established by the Administration. The National Youth Administration and Civilian Conservation Corps have enabled our youth to complete their education, have maintained their health, trained them for useful citizenship, and aided them to secure employment.

Our public works have modernized and greatly expanded the nation's schools. We have increased Federal aid for vocational education and rehabilitation, and undertaken a comprehensive program of defense-industry training. We shall continue to bring to millions of children, youths and adults, the educational and economic opportunities otherwise beyond their reach.

Slum-Clearance and Low-Rent Housing

We have launched a soundly conceived plan of loans and contributions to rid America of overcrowded slum dwellings that breed disease and crime, and to replace them by low-cost housing projects within the means of low-income families. We will extend and accelerate this plan not only in the congested city districts, but also in the small towns and farm areas, and we will make it a powerful arm of national defense by supplying housing for the families of enlisted personnel and for workers in areas where industry is expanding to meet defense needs.

Consumers

We are taking effective steps to insure that, in this period of stress, the cost of living shall not be increased by speculation and unjustified price rises.

Negroes

Our Negro citizens have participated actively in the economic and social advances launched by this Administration, including fair labor standards, social security benefits, health protection, work relief projects, decent housing, aid to education, and the rehabilitation of low-income farm families. We have aided more than half a million Negro youths in vocational training, education and employment. We shall continue to strive for complete legislative safeguards against discrimination in government service and benefits, and in the national defense forces. We pledge to uphold due process and the equal protection of the laws for every citizen regardless of race, creed or color.

Veterans

We pledge to continue our policy of fair treatment of America's war veterans and their dependents, in just tribute to their sacrifices and their devotion to the cause of liberty.

Indians

We favor and pledge the enactment of legislation creating an Indian Claims Commission for the special purpose of entertaining and investigating claims presented by Indian groups, bands and tribes, in order that our Indian citizens may have their claims against the Government considered, adjusted, and finally settled at the earliest possible date.

Civil Service

We pledge the immediate extension of a genuine system of merit to all positions in the executive branch of the Federal Government except actual bona fide policy-making positions. The competitive method of selecting employees shall be improved until experience and qualification shall be the sole test in determining fitness for employment in the Federal service. Promotion and tenure in Federal service shall likewise depend upon fitness, experience and qualification. Arbitrary and unreasonable rules as to academic training shall be abolished, all to the end that a genuine system of efficiency and merit shall prevail throughout the entire Federal service.

Territories and District of Columbia

We favor a larger measure of self-government leading to statehood for Alaska, Hawaii and Puerto Rico. We favor the appointment of residents to office, and equal treatment of the citizens of each of these three territories. We favor the prompt determination and payment of any just claims by Indian and Eskimo citizens of Alaska against the United States.

We also favor the extension of the right of suffrage to the people of the District of Columbia.

TRUE FIRST LINE OF DEFENSE

We pledge to continue to stand guard on our true first line of defense—the security and welfare of the men, women and children of America.

OUR DEMOCRATIC FAITH

Democracy is more than a political system for the government of a people. It is the expression of a people's faith in themselves as human beings. If this faith is permitted to die, human progress will die with it. We believe that a mechanized existence, lacking the spiritual quality of democracy, is intolerable to the free people of this country.

We therefore pledge ourselves to fight, as our fathers fought, for the right of every American to enjoy freedom of religion, speech, press, assembly, petition, and security in his home.

It is America's destiny, in these days of rampant despotism, to be the guardian of the world heritage of liberty and to hold aloft and aflame, the torch of Western civilization.

The Democratic Party rededicates itself to this faith in democracy, to the defense of the American system of government, the only system under which men are masters of their own souls, the only system under which the American people, composed of many races and creeds, can live and work, play and worship in peace, security and freedom.

Firmly relying upon a continuation of the blessings of Divine Providence upon all our righteous endeavors to preserve forever the priceless heritage of American liberty and peace, we appeal to all the liberal-minded men and women of the nation to approve this platform and to go forward with us by wholeheartedly supporting the candidates who subscribe to the principles which it proclaims.

From: George Thomas Kurian, ed. *The Encyclopedia of the Democratic Party.* Armonk, NY: M. E. Sharpe, 1997.

REPUBLICAN PARTY PLATFORM, 1940

The Republican Party of 1940 was very different from the Republican Party of 1932 and 1936. Its nominee, Wendell Willkie, was a former Democrat who actually supported most New Deal programs. In addition, like his opponent, President Franklin D. Roosevelt, Willkie was a staunch internationalist who believed that America's national security was closely linked to that of Britain and the anti-Nazi struggle. Ironically, many of the candidate's positions were not included in the platform, reflecting the persisting divisions within the party.

The Republican party, in representative Convention assembled, submits to the people of the United States the following declaration of its principles and purposes:

We state our general objectives in the simple and comprehensive words of the Preamble to the Constitution of the United States.

Those objectives as there stated are these:

To form a more perfect Union; establish justice; insure domestic tranquility; provide for the common defense, promote the general welfare and secure the blessings of liberty to ourselves and our posterity.

Meeting within the shadow of Independence Hall where those words were written we solemnly reaffirm them as a perfect statement of the ends for which we as a party propose to plan and to labor.

The record of the Roosevelt Administration is a record of failure to attain any one of those essential objectives.

Instead of leading us into More Perfect Union the Administration has deliberately fanned the flames of class hatred.

Instead of the Establishment of Justice the Administration has sought the subjection of the Judiciary to Executive discipline and domination.

Instead of insuring Domestic Tranquility the Administration has made impossible the normal friendly relation between employers and employees and has even succeeded in alienating both the great divisions of Organized Labor.

Instead of Providing for the Common Defense the Administration, notwithstanding the expenditure of billions of our dollars, has left the Nation unprepared to resist foreign attack.

Instead of promoting the General Welfare the Administration has Domesticated the Deficit, Doubled the Debt, Imposed Taxes where they do the greatest economic harm, and used public money for partisan political advantage.

Instead of the Blessings of Liberty the Administration has imposed upon us a Regime of Regimentation which has deprived the individual of his freedom and has made of America a shackled giant.

Wholly ignoring these great objectives, as solemnly declared by the people of the United States, the New Deal Administration has for seven long years whirled in a turmoil of shifting, contradictory and overlapping administrations and policies. Confusion has reigned supreme. The only steady undeviating characteristic has been the relentless expansion of the power of the Federal government over the everyday life of the farmer, the industrial worker and the business man. The emergency demands organization—not confusion. It demands free and intelligent cooperation—not incompetent domination. It demands a change.

The New Deal Administration has failed America.

It has failed by seducing our people to become continuously dependent upon government, thus weakening their morale and quenching the traditional American spirit.

It has failed by viciously attacking our industrial system and sapping its strength and vigor.

It has failed by attempting to send our Congress home during the world's most tragic hour, so that we might be eased into the war by word of deed during the absence of our elected representatives from Washington.

It has failed by disclosing military details of our equipment to foreign powers over protests by the heads of our armed defense.

It has failed by ignoring the lessons of fact concerning modern, mechanized, armed defense.

In these and countless other ways the New Deal Administration has either deliberately deceived the American people or proved itself incompetent to handle the affairs of our government.

The zero hour is here. America must prepare at once to defend our shores, our homes, our lives and our most cherished ideals.

To establish a first line of defense we must place

in official positions men of faith who put America first and who are determined that her governmental and economic system be kept unimpaired.

Our national defense must be so strong that no unfriendly power shall ever set foot on American soil. To assure this strength our national economy, the true basis of America's defense, must be free of unwarranted government interference.

Only a strong and sufficiently prepared America can speak words of reassurance and hope to the liberty-loving peoples of the world.

NATIONAL DEFENSE

The Republican Party is firmly opposed to involving this Nation in foreign war.

We are still suffering from the ill effects of the last World War: a war which cost us a twenty-four billion dollar increase in our national debt, billions of uncollectible foreign debts, and the complete upset of our economic system, in addition to the loss of human life and irreparable damage to the health of thousands of our boys.

The present National Administration has already spent for all purposes more than fifty-four billion dollars; has boosted the national debt and current federal taxes to an all-time high; and yet by the President's own admission we are still wholly unprepared to defend our country, its institutions and our individual liberties in a war that threatens to engulf the whole world; and this in spite of the fact that foreign wars have been in progress for two years or more and that military information concerning these wars and the rearmament programs of the warring nations has been at all times available to the National Administration through its diplomatic and other channels.

The Republican party stands for Americanism, preparedness and peace. We accordingly fasten upon the New Deal full responsibility for our unpreparedness and for the consequent danger of involvement in war.

We declare for the prompt, orderly and realistic building of our national defense to the point at which we shall be able not only to defend the United States, its possessions, and essential outposts from foreign attack, but also efficiently to uphold in war the Monroe Doctrine. To this task the Republican party pledges itself when entrusted with national authority. In the meantime we shall support all necessary and proper defense measures proposed by the Administration in its belated effort to make up for lost time; but we deplore explosive utterances by the President directed at other governments which serve to imperil our peace; and we condemn all executive acts and proceedings which might lead to war without the authorization of the Congress of the United States.

Our sympathies have been profoundly stirred by invasion of unoffending countries and by disaster to nations whose ideals most closely resemble our own. We favor the extension to all peoples fighting for liberty, or whose liberty is threatened, of such aid as shall not be in violation of international law or inconsistent with the requirements of our own national defense.

We believe that the spirit which should animate our entire defensive policy is determination to preserve not our material interests merely, but those liberties which are the priceless heritage of America.

RE-EMPLOYMENT

The New Deal's failure to solve the problem of unemployment and revive opportunity for our youth presents a major challenge to representative government and free enterprise. We propose to recreate opportunity for the youth of America and put our idle millions back to work in private industry, business, and agriculture. We propose to eliminate needless administrative restrictions, thus restoring lost motion to the wheels of individual enterprise.

RELIEF

We shall remove waste, discrimination, and politics from relief—through administration by the States with Federal grants-in-aid on a fair and nonpolitical basis, thus giving the man and woman on relief a larger share of the funds appropriated.

SOCIAL SECURITY

We favor the extension of necessary old age benefits on an ear-marked pay-as-you-go basis to the extent that the revenues raised for this purpose will permit. We favor the extension of the unemployment compensation provisions of the Social Security Act, wherever practicable, to those groups and classes not now included. For such groups as may thus be covered we favor a system of unemployment compensation with experience rating provisions, aimed at protecting the worker in the regularity of his employment and providing adequate compensation for reasonable periods when that regularity of employment is interrupted. The administration should be left with the States with a minimum of Federal control.

LABOR RELATIONS

The Republican party has always protected the American worker.

We shall maintain labor's right of free organization and collective bargaining.

We believe that peace and prosperity at home require harmony, teamwork, and understanding in all relations between worker and employer. When differences arise, they should be settled directly and voluntarily across the table.

Recent disclosures respecting the administration of the National Labor Relations Act require that this Act be amended in fairness to employers and all groups of employees so as to provide true freedom for, and orderliness in self-organization and collective bargaining.

AGRICULTURE

A prosperous and stable agriculture is the foundation of our economic structure. Its preservation is a national and nonpolitical social problem not yet solved, despite many attempts. The farmer is entitled to a profit-price for his products. The Republican party will put into effect such governmental policies, temporary and permanent, as will establish and maintain an equitable balance between labor, industry, and agriculture by expanding industrial and business activity, eliminating unemployment, lowering production costs, thereby creating increased consumer buying power for agricultural products.

Until this balance has been attained, we propose to provide benefit payments, based upon a widely applied, constructive soil conservation program free from government-dominated production control, but administered, as far as practicable, by farmers themselves; to restrict the major benefits of these payments to operators of family-type farms; to continue all present benefit payments until our program becomes operative; and to eliminate the present extensive and costly bureaucratic interference.

We shall provide incentive payments, when necessary, to encourage increased production of agricultural commodities, adaptable to our soil and climate, not now produced in sufficient quantities for our home markets, and will stimulate the use and processing of all farm products in industry as raw materials.

We shall promote a cooperative system of adequate farm credit, at lowest interest rates commensurate with the cost of money, supervised by an independent governmental agency, with ultimate farmer ownership and control; farm commodity loans to facilitate orderly marketing and stabilize farm income; the expansion of sound, farmer-owned and farmer-controlled cooperative associations; and the support of educational and extension programs to achieve more efficient production and marketing.

We shall foster Government refinancing, where necessary, of the heavy Federal farm debt load through an agency segregated from cooperative credit.

We shall promote a national land use program for Federal acquisition, without dislocation of local tax returns, of non-productive farm lands by voluntary sale or lease subject to approval of the States concerned; and the disposition of such lands to appropriate public uses including watershed protection and flood prevention, reforestation, recreation, erosion control, and the conservation of wild life.

We advocate a foreign trade policy which will end one-man tariff making, afford effective protection to farm products, regain our export markets, and assure an American price level for the domestically consumed portion of our export crops.

We favor effective quarantine against imported livestock, dairy, and other farm products from countries which do not impose health and sanitary standards equal to our own domestic standards.

We approve the orderly development of reclamation and irrigation, project by project and as conditions justify.

We promise adequate assistance to rural communities suffering disasters from flood, drought, and other natural causes.

We shall promote stabilization of agricultural income through intelligent management of accumulated surpluses, and through the development of outlets by supplying those in need at home and abroad.

TARIFF AND RECIPROCAL TRADE

We are threatened by unfair competition in world markets and by the invasion of our home markets, especially by the products of state-controlled foreign economies.

We believe in tariff protection for Agriculture, Labor, and Industry, as essential to our American standard of living. The measure of the protection shall be determined by scientific methods with due regard to the interest of the consumer.

We shall explore every possibility of reopening the channels of international trade through negotiations so conducted as to produce genuine reciprocity and expand our exports.

We condemn the manner in which the so-called reciprocal trade agreements of the New Deal have been put into effect without adequate hearings, with undue haste, without proper consideration of our domestic producers, and without Congressional approval. These defects we shall correct.

MONEY

The Congress should reclaim its constitutional powers over money, and withdraw the President's arbitrary authority to manipulate the currency, establish bi-metallism, issue irredeemable paper money, and debase the gold and silver coinage. We shall repeal the Thomas Inflation Amendment of 1933 and the (foreign) Silver Purchase Act of 1934, and take all possible steps to preserve the value of the Government's huge holdings of gold and re-introduce gold into circulation.

JOBS AND IDLE MONEY

Believing it possible to keep the securities market clean without paralyzing it, we endorse the principle of truth in securities in the Securities Act. To get billions of idle dollars and a multitude of idle men back to work and to promote national defense, these acts should be revised and the policies of the Commission changed to encourage the flow of private capital into industry.

TAXATION

Public spending has trebled under the New Deal, while tax burdens have doubled. Huge taxes are necessary to pay for New Deal waste and for neglected national defense. We shall revise the tax system and remove those practices which impede recovery and shall apply policies which stimulate enterprise. We shall not use the taxing power as an instrument of punishment or to secure objectives not otherwise obtainable under existing law.

PUBLIC CREDIT

With urgent need for adequate defense, the people are burdened by a direct and contingent debt exceeding fifty billion dollars. Twenty-nine billion of this debt has been created by New Deal borrowings during the past seven years. We pledge ourselves to conserve the public credit for all essential purposes by levying taxation sufficient to cover necessary civil expenditure, a substantial part of the defense cost, and the interest and retirement of the national debt.

PUBLIC SPENDING

Millions of men and women still out of work after seven years of excessive spending refute the New Deal theory that "deficit spending" is the way to prosperity and jobs. Our American system of private enterprise, if permitted to go to work, can rapidly increase the wealth, income, and standard of living of all the people. We solemnly pledge that public expenditures, other than those required for full national defense and relief, shall be cut to levels necessary for the essential services of government.

EQUAL RIGHTS

We favor submission by Congress to the States of an amendment to the Constitution providing for equal rights for men and women.

NEGRO

We pledge that our American citizens of Negro descent shall be given a square deal in the economic and political life of this nation. Discrimination in the civil service, the army, navy, and all other branches of the Government must cease. To enjoy the full benefits of life, liberty and pursuit of happiness universal suffrage must be made effective for the Negro citizen. Mob violence shocks the conscience of the nation and legislation to curb this evil should be enacted.

UN-AMERICAN ACTIVITIES

We vigorously condemn the New Deal encouragement of various groups that seek to change the American form of government by means outside the Constitution. We condemn the appointment of members of such un-American groups to high positions of trust in the national Government. The development of the treacherous so called Fifth Column, as it has operated in war-stricken countries, should be a solemn warning to America. We pledge the Republican Party to get rid of such borers from within.

IMMIGRATION

We favor the strict enforcement of all laws controlling the entry of aliens. The activities of undesirable aliens should be investigated and those who seek to change by force and violence the American form of government should be deported.

VETERANS

We pledge adequate compensation and care for veterans disabled in the service of our country, and for their widows, orphans, and dependents.

INDIANS

We pledge an immediate and final settlement of all Indian claims between the Government and the Indian citizenship of the nation.

HAWAII

Hawaii, sharing the nation's obligations equally with the several States, is entitled to the fullest measure of home rule; and to equality with the several States in the rights of her citizens and in the application of our national laws.

PUERTO RICO

Statehood is a logical aspiration of the people of Puerto Rico who were made citizens of the United States by Congress in 1917; legislation affecting Puerto Rico, in so far as feasible, should be in harmony with the realization of that aspiration.

GOVERNMENT AND BUSINESS

We shall encourage a healthy, confident, and growing private enterprise, confine Government activity to essential public services, and regulate business only so as to protect consumer, employee, and investor and without restricting the production of more and better goods at lower prices.

MONOPOLY

Since the passage of the Sherman Anti-trust Act by the Republican party we have consistently fought to preserve free competition with regulation to prevent abuse. New Deal policy fosters Government monopoly, restricts production, and fixes prices. We shall enforce anti-trust legislation without prejudice or discrimination. We condemn the use or threatened use of criminal indictments to obtain through consent decrees objectives not contemplated by law.

GOVERNMENT COMPETITION

We promise to reduce to the minimum Federal competition with business. We pledge ourselves to establish honest accounting and reporting by every agency of the Federal Government and to continue only those enterprises whose maintenance is clearly in the public interest.

FREE SPEECH

The principles of a free press and free speech, as established by the Constitution, should apply to the radio. Federal regulation of radio is necessary in view of the natural limitations of wave lengths, but this gives no excuse for censorship. We oppose the use of licensing to establish arbitrary controls. Licenses should be revocable only when, after public hearings, due cause for cancellation is shown.

SMALL BUSINESS

The New Deal policy of interference and arbitrary regulation has injured all business, but especially small business. We promise to encourage the small business man by removing unnecessary bureaucratic regulation and interference.

STOCK AND COMMODITY EXCHANGES

We favor regulation of stock and commodity exchanges. They should be accorded the fullest measure of self-control consistent with the discharge of their public trust and the prevention of abuse.

INSURANCE

We condemn the New Deal attempts to destroy the confidence of our people in private insurance institutions. We favor continuance of regulation of insurance by the several States.

GOVERNMENT REORGANIZATION

We shall reestablish in the Federal Civil Service a real merit system on a truly competitive basis and extend it to all non-policy-forming positions.

We pledge ourselves to enact legislation standardizing and simplifying quasi-judicial and administrative agencies to insure adequate notice and hearing, impartiality, adherence to the rules of evidence and full judicial review of all questions of law and fact.

Our greatest protection against totalitarian government is the American system of checks and balances. The constitutional distribution of legislative, executive, and judicial functions is essential to the preservation of this system. We pledge ourselves to make it the basis of all our policies affecting the organization and operation of our Republican form of government.

THIRD TERM

To insure against the overthrow of our American system of government we favor an amendment to the Constitution providing that no person shall be President of the United States for more than two terms.

A PLEDGE OF GOOD FAITH

The acceptance of the nominations made by this Convention carries with it, as a matter of private honor and public faith, an undertaking by each candidate to be true to the principles and program herein set forth.

We earnestly urge all patriotic men and women, regardless of former affiliations, to unite with us in the support of our declaration of principles to the end that "government of the people, by the people and for the people shall not perish from this earth."

From: George Thomas Kurian, ed. *The Encyclopedia of the Republican Party*. Armonk, NY: M. E. Sharpe, 1997.

ROOSEVELT'S THIRD INAUGURAL ADDRESS, JANUARY 20, 1941

While President Franklin D. Roosevelt's first two inaugural addresses were largely dedicated to domestic issues—notably, efforts to overcome the ravaging economic effects of the Great Depression—the third inaugural address, delivered on January 20, 1941, focused on international affairs. As Roosevelt delivered the speech, he was in the midst of a major campaign to convince the Congress and the American people to provide military aid to Great Britain in the form of lend-lease and other measures.

On each national day of Inauguration since 1789, the people have renewed their sense of dedication to the United States.

In Washington's day the task of the people was to create and weld together a Nation.

In Lincoln's day, the task of the people was to preserve that Nation from disruption within.

In this day, the task of the people is to save that Nation and its institutions from disruption from without.

To us there has come a time, in the midst of swift happenings, to pause for a moment and take stock—to recall what our place in history has been, and to rediscover what we are and what we may be. If we do not, we risk the real peril of isolation.

Lives of nations are determined not by the count

of years, but by the lifetime of the human spirit. The life of a man is threescore years and ten: a little more, a little less. The life of a nation is the fullness of the measure of its will to live.

There are men who doubt this. There are men who believe that democracy, as a form of government and a frame of life, is limited or measured by a kind of mystical and artificial fate—that, for some unexplained reason, tyranny and slavery have become the surging wave of the future—and that freedom is an ebbing tide.

But we Americans know that this is not true.

Eight years ago, when the life of this Republic seemed frozen by a fatalistic terror, we proved that this is not true. We were in the midst of shock—but we acted. We acted quickly, boldly, decisively.

These later years have been living years—fruitful years for the people of this democracy. For they have brought to us greater security and, I hope, a better understanding that life's ideals are to be measured in other than material things.

Most vital to our present and our future is this experience of a democracy which successfully survived crisis at home; put away many evil things; built new structures on enduring lines; and, through it all, maintained the fact of its democracy.

For action has been taken within the three-way framework of the Constitution of the United States. The coordinate branches of the Government continue freely to function. The Bill of Rights remains inviolate. The freedom of elections is wholly maintained. Prophets of the downfall of American democracy have seen their dire predictions come to naught.

Democracy is not dying.

We know it because we have seen it revive—and grow.

We know it cannot die—because it is built on the unhampered initiative of individual men and women joined together in a common enterprise—an enterprise undertaken and carried through by the free expression of a free majority.

We know it because democracy alone, of all forms of government, enlists the full force of men's enlightened will.

We know it because democracy alone has constructed an unlimited civilization capable of infinite progress in the improvement of human life.

We know it because, if we look below the surface, we sense it still spreading on every continent—for it is the most humane, the most advanced, and in the end the most unconquerable of all forms of human society.

A nation, like a person, has a body—a body that must be fed and clothed and housed, invigorated and rested, in a manner that measures up to the objectives of our time.

A nation, like a person, has a mind—a mind that must be kept informed and alert, that must know itself, that understands the hopes and the needs of its neighbors—all the other nations that live within the narrowing circle of the world.

And a nation, like a person, has something deeper, something more permanent, something larger than the sum of all its parts. It is that something which matters most to its future—which calls forth the most sacred guarding of its present.

It is a thing for which we find it difficult—even impossible—to hit upon a single, simple word.

And yet we all understand what it is—the spirit—the faith of America. It is the product of centuries. It was born in the multitudes of those who came from many lands—some of high degree, but mostly plain people—who sought here, early and late, to find freedom more freely.

The democratic aspiration is no mere recent phase in human history. It is human history. It permeated the ancient life of early peoples. It blazed anew in the middle ages. It was written in Magna Carta.

In the Americas its impact has been irresistible. America has been the New World in all tongues, to all peoples, not because this continent was a new-found land, but because all those who came here believed they could create upon this continent a new life—a life that should be new in freedom.

Its vitality was written into our own Mayflower Compact, into the Declaration of Independence, into the Constitution of the United States, into the Gettysburg Address.

Those who first came here to carry out the longings of their spirit, and the millions who followed, and the stock that sprang from them—all have moved forward constantly and consistently toward an ideal which in itself has gained stature and clarity with each generation.

The hopes of the Republic cannot forever tolerate either undeserved poverty or self-serving wealth.

We know that we still have far to go; that we must more greatly build the security and the opportunity and the knowledge of every citizen, in the measure justified by the resources and the capacity of the land.

But it is not enough to achieve these purposes alone. It is not enough to clothe and feed the body of this Nation, and instruct and inform its mind. For there is also the spirit. And of the three, the greatest is the spirit.

Without the body and the mind, as all men know, the Nation could not live.

But if the spirit of America were killed, even though the Nation's body and mind, constricted in an alien world, lived on, the America we know would have perished.

That spirit—that faith—speaks to us in our daily lives in ways often unnoticed, because they seem so obvious. It speaks to us here in the capital of the Nation. It speaks to us through the processes of governing in the sovereignties of forty-eight States. It speaks to us in our counties, in our cities, in our towns and in our villages.

It speaks to us from the other nations of the hemisphere, and from those across the seas—the enslaved, as well as the free. Sometimes we fail to hear or heed these voices of freedom because to us the privilege of our freedom is such an old, old story.

The destiny of America was proclaimed in words of prophecy spoken by our first President in his first Inaugural in 1789—words almost directed, it would seem, to this year of 1941: "The preservation of the sacred fire of liberty and the destiny of the republican model of government are justly considered . . . deeply, . . . finally, staked on the experiment intrusted to the hands of the American people."

If we lose that sacred fire—if we let it be smothered with doubt and fear—then we shall reject the destiny which Washington strove so valiantly and so triumphantly to establish. The preservation of the spirit and faith of the Nation does, and will, furnish the highest justification of every sacrifice that we may make in the cause of national defense.

In the face of great perils never before encountered, our strong purpose is to protect and to perpetuate the integrity of democracy.

For this we muster the spirit of America, and the faith of America.

We do not retreat. We are not content to stand still. As Americans, we go forward, in the service of our country, by the will of God.

From: B. D. Zevin, ed. *Nothing to Fear: The Selected Addresses of Franklin Delano Roosevelt, 1932–1945.* Boston: Houghton Mifflin, 1946.

SECTION 3 Court Cases

UNITED STATES V. ONE BOOK CALLED "ULYSSES," 1933

In this landmark decision of 1933, a federal court permitted the importation of James Joyce's classic work of Irish fiction, Ulysses. In doing so, the court redefined the meaning of the Tariff Act of 1890, which gave the Customs Bureau the right to seize anything it deemed "obscene." The judge in the case said the government must distinguish between "obscene" materials and those with literary merit.

The motion for a decree dismissing the libel herein is granted, and, consequently, of course, the Government's motion for a decree of forfeiture and destruction is denied. . . .

II. I have read "Ulysses" once in its entirety and I have read those passages of which the Government particularly complains several times. In fact, for many weeks, my spare time has been devoted to the consideration of the decision which my duty would require me to make in this matter.

III. The reputation of "Ulysses" in the literary world, however, warranted me taking such time as was necessary to enable me to satisfy myself as to the intent with which the book was written, for, of course, in any case where a book is claimed to be obscene it must first be determined, whether the intent with which it was written was what is called, according to the usual phrase, pornographic,—that is, written for the purpose of exploiting obscenity.

If the conclusion is that the book is pornographic that is the end of the inquiry and forfeiture must follow.

But in "Ulysses," in spite of its unusual frankness, I do not detect anywhere the leer of the sensualist. I hold, therefore, that it is not pornographic.

IV. In writing "Ulysses," Joyce sought to make a serious experiment in a new, if not wholly novel, literary genre. He takes persons of the lower middle class living in Dublin in 1904 and seeks not only to describe what they did on a certain day early in June of that year as they went about the City bent on their usual occupation, but also to tell what many of them thought about the while.

Joyce has attempted—it seems to me, with astonishing success—to show how the screen of consciousness with its ever-shifting kaleidoscopic impressions carries as it were on a plastic palimpsest, not only what is in the focus of each man's observation of the actual things about him, but also in a penumbral zone residua of past impressions, some recent and some drawn up by association from the domain of the subconscious. He shows how each of these impressions affects the life and behavior of the character which he is describing.

What he seeks to get is not unlike the result of a double or, if that is possible, a multiple exposure on a cinema film which would give a clear foreground with a background visible but somewhat blurred and out of focus in varying degrees.

To convey by words an effect which obviously lends itself more appropriately to a graphic technique, accounts, it seems to me, for much of the obscurity which meets a reader of "Ulysses." And it also explains another aspect of the book, which I have further to consider, namely, Joyce's sincerity and his honest effort to show exactly how the minds of his characters operate.

If Joyce did not attempt to be honest in developing the technique which he has adopted in "Ulysses" the result would be psychologically misleading and thus unfaithful to his chosen technique. Such an attitude would be artistically inexcusable.

It is because Joyce has been loyal to his technique and has not funked its necessary implications, but has honestly attempted to tell fully what his characters think about, that he has been the subject of so many attacks and that his purpose has been so often misunderstood and misrepresented. For his attempt sincerely and honestly to realize his objective has required him incidentally to use certain words which are generally considered dirty words and has led at times to what many think is a too poignant preoccupation with sex in the thoughts of his characters.

The words which are criticized as dirty are old Saxon words known to almost all men and, I venture, to many women and are such words as would be naturally and habitually used, I believe, by the types of folk whose life, physical and mental, Joyce is seeking to describe. In respect of the recurrent emergence of the theme of sex in the minds of his characters, it must always be remembered that his locale was Celtic and his season Spring.

Whether or not one enjoys such a technique as Joyce uses is a matter of taste on which disagreement or argument is futile, but to subject that technique to the standards of some other technique seems to me to be little short of absurd.

Accordingly, I hold that "Ulysses" is a sincere and honest book and I think that the criticisms of it are entirely disposed of by its rationale.

V. Furthermore, "Ulysses" is an amazing tour de force when one considers the success which has been in the main achieved with such a difficult objective as Joyce set for himself. As I have stated, "Ulysses" is not an easy book to read. It is brilliant and dull, intelligible and obscure by turns. In many places it seems to me to be disgusting, but although it contains, as I have mentioned above, many words usually considered dirty, I have not found anything that I consider to be dirt for dirt's sake. Each word of the book contributes like a bit of mosaic to the detail of the picture which Joyce is seeking to construct for his readers.

If one does not wish to associate with such folk as Joyce describes, that is one's own choice. In order to avoid indirect contact with them one may not wish to read "Ulysses"; that is quite understandable. But when such a real artist in words, as Joyce undoubtedly is, seeks to draw a true picture of the lower middle class in a European city, ought it to be impossible for the American public legally to see that picture?

To answer this question it is not sufficient merely to find, as I have found above, that Joyce did not write "Ulysses" with what is a commonly called pornographic intent, I must endeavor to apply a more objective standard to his book in order to determine its effect in the result, irrespective of the intent with which it was written.

VI. The statute under which the libel is filed only denounces, in so far as we are here concerned the importation into the United States from any foreign country of "any obscene book." Section 305 of the Tariff Act of 1930, Title 19 United States Code, Section 1305. It does not marshal against books the spectrum of condemnatory adjectives found, commonly, in laws dealing with matters of this kind. I am therefore, only required to determine whether "Ulysses" is obscene within the legal definition of that word.

The meaning of the word "obscene" as legally defined by the Courts is: tending to stir the sex impulses or to lead to sexually impure and lustful thoughts. . . .

Whether a particular book would tend to excite such impulses and thoughts must be tested by the Court's opinion as to its effect on a person with average sex instincts—what the French would call *l'homme moyen sensual*—who plays, in this branch of legal inquiry, the same role of hypothetical reagent as does the "reasonable man" in the law of torts and "the man learned in the art" on questions of invention in patent law.

The risk involved in the use of such a reagent arises from the inherent tendency of the trier of facts, however fair he may intend to be, to make his reagent too much subservient to his own idiosyncrasies. Here, I have attempted to avoid this, if possible, and to make my reagent herein more objective than he might otherwise be, by adopting the following course.

After I had made my decision in regard to the aspect of "Ulysses," now under consideration, I checked my impressions with two friends of mine who in my opinion answered to the above stated requirements for my reagent.

These literary assessors—as I might properly describe them—were called on separately, and neither knew that I was consulting the other. They are men whose opinion on literature and on life I value most highly. They had both read "Ulysses," and, of course, were wholly unconnected with this cause.

Without letting either of my assessors know what my decision was, I gave to each of them the legal definition of obscene and asked each whether in his opinion "Ulysses" was obscene within that definition.

I was interested to find that they both agreed with my opinion: that reading "Ulysses" in its entirety, as a book must be read on such a test as this, did not tend to excite sexual impulses or lustful thoughts but that its net effect on them was only that of somewhat tragic and very powerful commentary on the inner lives of men and women.

It is only with the normal person that the law is concerned. Such a test as I have described, therefore, is the only proper test of obscenity in the case of a book like "Ulysses" which is a sincere and serious attempt to devise a new literary method for the observation and description of mankind.

I am quite aware that owing to some of its scenes "Ulysses" is a rather strong draught to ask some sensitive, though normal, persons to take. But my considered opinion, after long reflection, is that whilst in many places the effect of "Ulysses" on the reader undoubtedly is somewhat emetic, nowhere does it tend to be an aphrodisiac.

"Ulysses" may, therefore, be admitted into the United States.

From: 5 Federal Supplement 182 (1933).

SCHECHTER POULTRY CORPORATION V. UNITED STATES, 1935

In one of the key Supreme Court decisions of the New Deal era, the majority of justices—with Chief Justice Charles Evans Hughes writing the decision—ruled elements of the 1933 National Industrial Recovery Act (NIRA), the legislation that created the National Recovery Administration, unconstitutional. The justices concurred with the plaintiff, the Schechter Poultry Corporation of Brooklyn, that Congress could not establish an executive department agency with such sweeping economic authority. At the same time, the decision left untouched other provisions of the NIRA, including the public works component.

Hughes, C. J. Petitioners were convicted in the District Court of the United States for the Eastern District of New York on eighteen counts of an indictment charging violations of what is known as the "Live Poultry Code," and on an additional count for conspiracy to commit such violations. By demurrer to the indictment and appropriate motions on the trial, the defendants contended (1) that the Code had been adopted pursuant to an unconstitutional delegation by Congress of legislative power; (2) that it attempted to regulate intrastate transactions which lay outside the authority of Congress; and (3) that in certain provisions it was repugnant to the due process clause of the Fifth Amendment.

The defendants are slaughterhouse operators. . . . A. L. A. Schechter Poultry Corporation and Schechter Live Poultry Market are corporations conducting wholesale poultry slaughterhouse markets in Brooklyn, New York City. Defendants ordinarily purchase their live poultry from commission men at the West Washington Market in New York City or at the railroad terminals serving the City, but occasionally they purchase from commission men in Philadelphia. They buy the poultry for slaughter and resale. After the poultry is trucked to their slaughterhouse markets in Brooklyn, it is there sold, usually within twenty-four hours, to retail poultry dealers and butchers who sell directly to consumers. The poultry purchased from defendants is immediately slaughtered, prior to delivery, by shochtim [religiously-sanctioned butchers] in defendants' employ. Defendants do not sell poultry in interstate commerce.

The "Live Poultry Code" was promulgated under section 3 of the National Industrial Recovery Act. That section authorizes the President to approve "codes of fair competition." Such a code may be approved for a trade or industry, upon application by one or more trade or industrial associations or groups, if the President finds (1) that such associations or groups "impose no inequitable restrictions on admission to membership therein and are truly representative," and (2) that such codes are not designed "to promote monopolies or to eliminate or oppress small enterprises and will not operate to discriminate against them, and will tend to effectuate the policy" of Title I of the act. Such codes "shall not permit monopolies or monopolistic practices." As a condition of his approval, the President may "impose such conditions (including requirements for the making of reports and the keeping of accounts) for the protection of consumers, competitors, employees, and others, and in furtherance of the public interest, and may provide such exceptions to and exemptions from the provisions of such code as the President in his discretion deems necessary to effectuate the policy herein declared." Where such a code has not been approved, the President may prescribe one, either on his own motion or on complaint. Violation of any provision of a code (so approved or prescribed) "in any transaction in or affecting interstate or foreign commerce" is made a misdemeanor punishable by a fine of not more than $500 for each offense, and each day the violation continues is to be deemed a separate offense.

The "Live Poultry Code" was approved by the President on April 13, 1934. Its divisions indicate its nature and scope. The Code has eight articles entitled (1) purposes, (2) definitions, (3) hours, (4) wages, (5) general labor provisions, (6) administration, (7) trade practice provisions, and (8) general.

The declared purpose is "To effect the policies of title I of the National Industrial Recovery Act." The Code is established as "a code for fair competition for the live poultry industry of the metropolitan area in and about the City of New York." That area is described as embracing the five boroughs of New York City, the counties of Rockland, Westchester, Nassau and Suffolk in the State of New York, the counties of Hudson and Bergen in the State of New Jersey, and the county of Fairfield in the State of Connecticut.

The "industry" is defined as including "every person engaged in the business of selling, purchasing for resale, transporting, or handling and/or slaughtering live poultry, from the time such poultry comes into the New York metropolitan area to the time it is first sold in slaughtered form," and such "related branches" as may from time to time be included by amendment. Employers are styled "members of the industry," and the term employee is defined to embrace "any and all persons engaged in the industry, however compensated," except "members."

The Code fixes the number of hours for work-days. It provides that no employee, with certain exceptions, shall be permitted to work in excess of forty (40) hours in any one week, and that no employee, save as stated "shall be paid in any pay period less than at the rate of fifty (50) cents per hour." The article containing "general labor provisions" prohibits the employment of any person under sixteen years of age, and declares that employees shall have the right of "collective bargaining," and freedom of choice with respect to labor organizations, in the terms of section 7 (a) of the Act. The minimum number of employees, who shall be employed by slaughterhouse operators, is fixed, the number being graduated according to the average volume of weekly sales.

The seventh article, containing "trade practice provisions," prohibits various practices which are said to constitute "unfair methods of competition."

Of the eighteen counts of the indictment upon which the defendants were convicted, aside from the count for conspiracy, two counts charged violation of the minimum wage and maximum hour provisions of the Code, and ten counts were for violation of the requirement (found in the "trade practice provisions") of "straight killing." The charges in the ten counts respectively, were that the defendants in selling to retail dealers and butchers had permitted "selections of individual chickens taken from particular coops and half coops."

Of the other six counts, one charged the sale to a butcher of an unfit chicken; two counts charged the making of sales without having the poultry inspected or approved in accordance with regulations or ordinances of the City of New York; two counts charged the making of false reports or the failure to make reports relating to the range of daily prices and volume of sales for certain periods; and the remaining count was for sales to slaughterers or dealers who were without licenses required by the ordinances and regulations of the City of New York.

First. Two preliminary points are stressed by the Government with respect to the appropriate approach to the important questions presented. We are told that the provision of the statute authorizing the adoption of codes must be viewed in the light of the grave national crisis with which Congress was confronted. Undoubtedly, the conditions to which power is addressed are always to be considered when the exercise of power is challenged. Extraordinary conditions may call for extraordinary remedies. But the argument necessarily stops short of an attempt to justify action which lies outside the sphere of constitutional authority. Extraordinary conditions do not create or enlarge constitutional power. The Constitution established a national government with powers deemed to be adequate, as they have proved to be both in war and peace, but these powers of the national government are limited by the constitutional grants. Those who act under these grants are not at liberty to transcend the imposed limits because they believe that more or different power is necessary. Such assertions of extra-constitutional authority were anticipated and precluded by the explicit terms of the Tenth Amendment.—"The powers not delegated to the United States by the Constitution, nor prohibited by it to the States, are reserved to the States respectively, or to the people."

The further point is urged that the national crisis demanded a broad and intensive cooperative effort by those engaged in trade and industry, and that this necessary cooperation was sought to be fostered by permitting them to initiate the adoption of codes. But the statutory plan is not simply one for voluntary effort. It does not seek merely to endow voluntary trade or industrial associations or groups with privileges or immunities. It involves the coercive exercise of the lawmaking power. The codes of fair competition, which the statute attempts to authorize, are codes of laws. If valid they place all persons within their reach under the obligation of positive law, binding equally those who assent and those who do not assent. Violations of the provisions of the codes are punishable as crimes.

Second. The question of the delegation of legislative power. For a statement of the authorized objectives and content of the "codes of fair competition" we are referred repeatedly to the "Declaration of Policy" in section one of Title I of the Recovery Act. Thus, the approval of a code by the President is conditioned on his finding that it "will tend to effectuate the policy of this title." Sec. 3 (a). The President is authorized to impose such conditions "for the protection of consumers, competitors, employees, and others, and in furtherance of the public interest, and may provide such exceptions to and exemptions from the provisions of such code as the President in his discretion deems necessary to effectuate the policy herein declared." Id. The "policy herein declared" is manifestly that set forth in section one. That declaration embraces a broad range of objectives. Among them we find the elimination of "unfair competitive practices." . . .

We think the conclusion is inescapable that the authority sought to be conferred by section 3 was not merely to deal with "unfair competitive practices" which offend against existing law, and could be the subject of judicial condemnation without further legislation, or to create administrative machinery for the application of established principles of law to particular instances of violation. Rather, the purpose is clearly disclosed to authorize new and controlling prohibitions through codes of laws which would embrace what the formulators would propose, and what the President would approve, or prescribe, as wise and beneficent measures for the government of trades and industries in order to bring about their rehabilitation, correction and development, according to the general declaration of policy in section one. Codes of laws of this sort are styled "codes of fair competition."

We find no real controversy upon this point and we must determine the validity of the Code in question in this aspect.

The question, then, turns upon the authority which section 3 of the Recovery Act vests in the President to approve or prescribe. If the codes have standing as penal statutes, this must be due to the effect of the executive action. But Congress cannot delegate legislative power to the President to exercise an unfettered discretion to make whatever laws he thinks may be needed or advisable for the rehabilitation and expansion of trade or industry.

Accordingly we turn to the Recovery Act to ascertain what limits have been set to the exercise of the President's discretion. First, the President, as a condition of approval, is required to find that the trade or industrial associations or groups which propose a code, "impose no inequitable restrictions on admission to membership" and are "truly representative." That condition, however, relates only to the status of the initiators of the new laws and not to the permissible scope of such laws. Second, the President is required to find that the code is not "designed to promote monopolies

or to eliminate or oppress small enterprises and will not operate to discriminate against them." And, to this is added a proviso that the code "shall not permit monopolies or monopolistic practices." But these restrictions leave virtually untouched the field of policy envisaged by section one and, in that wide field of legislative possibilities, the proponents of a code, refraining from monopolistic designs, may roam at will and the President may approve or disapprove their proposals as he may see fit.

Nor is the breadth of the President's discretion left to the necessary implications of this limited requirement as to his findings. As already noted, the President in approving a code may impose his own conditions, adding to or taking from what is proposed, as "in his discretion" he thinks necessary "to effectuate the policy" declared by the Act. Of course, he has no less liberty when he prescribes a code of his own motion or on complaint, and he is free to prescribe one if a code has not been approved. The Act provides for the creation by the President of administrative agencies to assist him, but the action or reports of such agencies, or of his other assistants,—their recommendations and findings in relation to the making of codes—have no sanction beyond the will of the President, who may accept, modify or reject them as he pleases. Such recommendations or findings in no way limit the authority which section 3 undertakes to vest in the President with no other conditions than those there specified. And this authority relates to a host of different trades and industries, thus extending the President's discretion to all the varieties of laws which he may deem to be beneficial in dealing with the vast array of commercial and industrial activities throughout the country.

Such a sweeping delegation of legislative power finds no support in the decisions upon which the Government especially relies.

To summarize and conclude upon this point: Section 3 of the Recovery Act is without precedent. It supplies no standards for any trade, industry or activity. It does not undertake to prescribe rules of conduct to be applied to particular states of fact determined by appropriate administrative procedure. Instead of prescribing rules of conduct, it authorizes the making of codes to prescribe them. For that legislative undertaking, section 3 sets up no standards, aside from the statement of the general aims of rehabilitation, correction and expansion described in section one. In view of the scope of that broad declaration, and of the nature of the few restrictions that are imposed, the discretion of the President in approving or prescribing codes, and thus enacting laws for the government of trade and industry throughout the country, is virtually unfettered. We think that the code-making authority thus conferred is an unconstitutional delegation of legislative power.

Second. The question of the application of the provisions of the Live Poultry Code to intrastate transactions. This aspect of the case presents the question whether the particular provisions of the Live Poultry Code, which the defendants were convicted for violating and for having conspired to violate, were within the regulating power of Congress.

These provisions relate to the hours and wages of those employed by defendants in their slaughterhouses in Brooklyn and to the sales there made to retail dealers and butchers.

(1) Were these transactions "in" interstate commerce? Much is made of the fact that almost all the poultry coming to New York is sent there from other States. But the code provisions, as here applied, do not concern the transportation of the poultry from other States to New York, or the transactions of the commission men or others to whom it is consigned, or the sales made by such consignees to defendants. When defendants had made their purchases, whether at the West Washington Market in New York City or at the railroad terminals serving the City, or elsewhere, the poultry was trucked to their slaughterhouses in Brooklyn for local disposition. The interstate transactions in relation to that poultry then ended. Defendants held the poultry at their slaughterhouse markets for slaughter and local sale to retail dealers and butchers who in turn sold directly to consumers. Neither the slaughtering nor the sales by defendants were transactions in interstate commerce.

The undisputed facts thus afford no warrant for the argument that the poultry handled by defendants at their slaughterhouse markets was in a "current" or "flow" of interstate commerce and was thus subject to congressional regulation. The mere fact that there may be a constant flow of commodities into a State does not mean that the flow continues after the property has arrived and has become commingled with the mass of property within the State and is there held solely for local disposition and use. So far as the poultry here in question is concerned, the flow in interstate commerce had ceased. The poultry had come to a permanent rest within the State. It was not held, used, or sold by defendants in relation to any further transactions in interstate commerce and was not destined for transportation to other states. Hence, decisions which deal with a stream of interstate commerce—where

goods come to rest within a State temporarily and are later to go forward in interstate commerce—and with the regulations of transactions involved in that practical continuity of movement, are not applicable here.

(2) Did the defendants' transactions directly "affect" interstate commerce so as to be subject to federal regulation? The power of Congress extends not only to the regulation of transactions which are part of interstate commerce, but to the protection of that commerce from injury.

In determining how far the federal government may go in controlling intrastate transactions upon the ground that they "affect" interstate commerce, there is a necessary and well-established distinction between direct and indirect effects. The precise line can be drawn only as individual cases arise, but the distinction is clear in principle. Direct effects are illustrated by the railroad cases we have cited, as e.g., the effect of failure to use prescribed safety appliances on railroads which are the highways of both interstate and intrastate commerce, injury to an employee engaged in interstate transportation by the negligence of an employee engaged in an intrastate movement, the fixing of rates for intrastate transportation which unjustly discriminate against interstate commerce. But where the effect of intrastate transactions upon interstate commerce is merely indirect, such transactions remain within the domain of state power. If the commerce clause were construed to reach all enterprises and transactions which could be said to have an indirect effect upon interstate commerce, the federal authority would embrace practically all the activities of the people and the authority of the State over its domestic concerns would exist only by sufferance of the federal government. Indeed, on such a theory, even the development of the State's commercial facilities would be subject to federal control.

The distinction between direct and indirect effects has been clearly recognized in the application of the Anti-Trust Act. Where a combination or conspiracy is formed, with the intent to restrain interstate commerce or to monopolize any part of it, the violation of the statute is clear. But where that intent is absent, and the objectives are limited to intrastate activities, the fact that there may be an indirect effect upon interstate commerce does not subject the parties to the federal statute, notwithstanding its broad provisions.

While these decisions related to the application of the federal statute, and not to its constitutional validity, the distinction between direct and indirect effects of intrastate transactions upon interstate commerce must be recognized as a fundamental one, essential to the maintenance of our constitutional system. Otherwise as we have said, there would be virtually no limit to the federal power and for all practical purposes we should have a completely centralized government. We must consider the provisions here in question in the light of this distinction.

The question of chief importance relates to the provisions of the Code as to the hours and wages of those employed in defendants' slaughterhouse markets. It is plain that these requirements are imposed in order to govern the details of defendants' management of their local business. The persons employed in slaughtering and selling in local trade are not employed in interstate commerce. Their hours and wages have no direct relation to interstate commerce. The question of how many hours these employees should work and what they should be paid differs in no essential respect from similar questions in other local businesses which handle commodities brought into a State and there dealt in as a part of its internal commerce. This appears from an examination of the considerations urged by the Government with respect to conditions in the poultry trade. Thus, the Government argues that hours and wages affect prices; that slaughterhouse men sell at a small margin above operating costs; that labor represents 50 to 60 percent of these costs; that a slaughterhouse operator paying lower wages or reducing his cost by exacting long hours of work, translates his saving into lower prices; that this results in demands for a cheaper grade of goods; and that the cutting of prices brings about demoralization of the price structure. Similar conditions may be adduced in relation to other businesses. The argument of the Government proves too much. If the federal government may determine the wages and hours of employees in the internal commerce of a State, because of their relation to cost and prices and their indirect effect upon interstate commerce, it would seem that a similar control might be exerted over other elements of cost, also affecting prices, such as the number of employees, rents, advertising, methods of doing business, etc. All the processes of production and distribution that enter into cost could likewise be controlled. If the cost of doing an intrastate business is in itself the permitted object of federal control, the extent of the regulation of cost would be a question of discretion and not of power.

The Government also makes the point that efforts to enact state legislation establishing high labor standards have been impeded by the belief that unless similar action is taken generally, commerce will be diverted from the States adopting such standards, and that this fear of diversion has led to demands for federal legislation on the subject of wages and hours. The apparent implication is that the federal authority under the commerce clause should be deemed to extend to the establishment of rules to govern wages and hours in intrastate trade and industry generally throughout the country, thus overriding the authority of the States to deal with domestic problems arising from labor conditions in their internal commerce.

It is not the province of the Court to consider the economic advantages or disadvantages of such a centralized system. It is sufficient to say that the Federal Constitution does not provide for it. Our growth and development have called for wide use of the commerce power of the federal government in its control over the expanded activities of interstate commerce, and in protecting that commerce from burdens, interferences, and conspiracies to restrain and monopolize it. But the authority of the federal government may not be pushed to such an extreme as to destroy the distinction, which the commerce clause itself establishes, between commerce "among the several States" and the internal concerns of a State. The same answer must be made to the contention that is based upon the serious economic situation which led to the passage of the Recovery Act,—the fall in prices, the decline in wages and employment, and the curtailment of the market for commodities. Stress is laid upon the great importance of maintaining wage distributions which would provide the necessary stimulus in starting "the cumulative forces making for expanding commercial activity." Without in any way disparaging this motive, it is enough to say that the recuperative efforts of the federal government must be made in a manner consistent with the authority granted by the Constitution.

We are of the opinion that the attempt through the provisions of the Code to fix the hours and wages of employees of defendants in their intrastate business was not a valid exercise of federal power.

On both the grounds we have discussed, the attempted delegation of legislative power, and the attempted regulation of intrastate transactions which affect interstate commerce only indirectly, we hold the code provisions here in question to be invalid and that the judgment of conviction must be reversed.

Justice [Benjamin] Cardozo delivered a concurring opinion with which Justice [Harlan] Stone concurred.

From: 295 U.S. 495 (1935).

UNITED STATES V. BUTLER ET AL., 1936

Among the critical Supreme Court decisions of the New Deal era, the 1936 United States *v.* Butler et al. *ruling declared the Agricultural Adjustment Act of 1933 unconstitutional. The conservative majority of the nine justices decided that tax placed on companies that processed food—used that tax to pay farmers for not growing crops—was a violation of the Tenth Amendment, which reserved to the states all powers that were not explicitly granted to the federal government by the Constitution. This narrow interpretation angered President Franklin D. Roosevelt and contributed to his unpopular and unsuccessful efforts to add new and more liberal justices to the Court.*

Roberts, Owen J.: In this case we must determine whether certain provisions of the Agricultural Adjustment Act, 1933, conflict with the federal Constitution.

Title I of the statute is captioned "Agricultural Adjustment." Section 1 recites that an economic emergency has arisen, due to disparity between the prices of agricultural and other commodities, with consequent destruction of farmers' purchasing power and breakdown in orderly exchange, which, in turn, have affected transactions in agricultural commodities with a national public interest and burdened and obstructed the normal currents of commerce, calling for the enactment of legislation.

Section 2 declares it to be the policy of Congress:

"To establish and maintain such balance between the production and consumption of agricultural commodities, and such marketing conditions therefor, as will reestablish prices to farmers at a level that will give agricultural commodities a purchasing power with respect to articles that farmers buy, equivalent to the purchasing power of agricultural commodities in the base period."

The base period, in the case of cotton, and all other commodities except tobacco, is designated as that between August, 1909, and July, 1914.

The further policies announced are an approach to the desired equality by gradual correction of present inequalities "at as rapid a rate as is deemed feasible in view of the current consumptive demand in domestic and foreign markets," and the protection of consumers' interest by readjusting farm production at such level as will not increase the percentage of the consumers' retail expenditures for agricultural commodities or products derived therefrom, which is returned to the farmer, above the percentage returned to him in the base period.

Section 8 provides, amongst other things, that "In order to effectuate the declared policy," the Secretary of Agriculture shall have power

"(1) To provide for reduction in the acreage or reduction in the production for market, or both, of any basic agricultural commodity, through agreements with producers or by other voluntary methods, and to provide for rental or benefit payments in connection therewith or upon that part of the production of any basic agricultural commodity required for domestic consumption, in such amounts as the Secretary deems fair and reasonable, to be paid out of any moneys available for such payments." . . .

"(2) To enter into marketing agreements with processors, associations of producers, and others engaged in the handling, in the current of interstate or foreign commerce, of any agricultural commodity or product thereof, after due notice and opportunity for hearing to interested parties."

"(3) To issue licenses permitting processors, associations of producers, and others to engage in the handling, in the current of interstate or foreign commerce, of any agricultural commodity or product thereof, or any competing commodity or product thereof."

It will be observed that the Secretary is not required, but is permitted, if, in his un-controlled judgment, the policy of the act will so be promoted, to make agreements with individual farmers for a reduction of acreage or production upon such terms as he may think fair and reasonable.

Section 9 (a) enacts:

"To obtain revenue for extraordinary expenses incurred by reason of the national economic emergency, there shall be levied processing taxes as hereinafter provided. When the Secretary of Agriculture determines that rental or benefit payments are to be made with respect to any basic agricultural commodity, he shall proclaim such determination, and a processing tax shall be in effect with respect to such commodity from the beginning of the marketing year therefor next following the date of such proclamation. The processing tax shall be levied, assessed, and collected upon the first domestic processing of the commodity, whether of domestic production or imported, and shall be paid by the processor." . . .

Section 9 (b) fixes the tax "at such rate as equals the difference between the current average farm price for the commodity and the fair exchange value," with power in the Secretary, after investigation, notice, and hearing, to readjust the tax so as to prevent the accumulation of surplus stocks and depression of farm prices.

Section 9 (c) directs that the fair exchange value of a commodity shall be such a price as will give that commodity the same purchasing power with respect to articles farmers buy as it had during the base period and that the fair exchange value and the current average farm price of a commodity shall be ascertained by the Secretary from available statistics in his department.

Section 12 (a) appropriates $100,000,000 "to be available to the Secretary of Agriculture for administrative expenses under this title and for rental and benefit payments . . ."; and Section 12 (b) appropriates the proceeds derived from all taxes imposed under the act "to be available to the Secretary of Agriculture for expansion of markets and removal of surplus agricultural products . . . Administrative expenses, rental and benefit payments, and refunds on taxes."

Section 15 (d) permits the Secretary, upon certain conditions to impose compensating taxes on commodities in competition with those subject to the processing tax. . . .

On July 14, 1933, the Secretary of Agriculture, with the approval of the President, proclaimed that he had determined rental and benefit payments should be made with respect to cotton; that the marketing year for that commodity was to begin August 1, 1933; and calculated and fixed the rates of processing and floor taxes on cotton in accordance with the terms of the act.

The United States presented a claim to the respondents as receivers of the Hoosac Mills Corporation for processing and floor taxes on cotton levied under sections 9 and 16 of the act. The receivers recommended that the claim be disallowed. The District Court found the taxes valid and ordered them paid. Upon appeal the Circuit Court of Appeals reversed the order. The judgment under review was entered prior to the adop-

tion of the amending act of August 24, 1935, and we are therefore concerned only with the original act.

First. At the outset the United States contends that the respondents have no standing to question the validity of the tax. The position is that the act is merely a revenue measure levying an excise upon the activity of processing cotton,—a proper subject for the imposition of such a tax,—the proceeds of which go into the federal treasury and thus become available for appropriation for any purpose. It is said that what the respondents are endeavoring to do is to challenge the intended use of the money pursuant to Congressional appropriation when, by confession, that money will have become the property of the Government and the taxpayer will no longer have any interest in it. . . .

The tax can only be sustained by ignoring the avowed purpose and operation of the act, and holding it a measure merely laying on excise upon processors to raise revenue for the support of government. Beyond cavil the sole object of the legislation is to restore the purchasing power of agricultural products to a parity with that prevailing in an earlier day; to take money from the processor and bestow it upon farmers who will reduce their acreage for the accomplishment of the proposed end, and, meanwhile, to aid these farmers during the period required to bring the prices of their crops to the desired level.

The tax plays an indispensable part in the plan of regulation. As stated by the Agricultural Adjustment Administrator, it is "the heart of the law"; a means of "accomplishing one or both of two things intended to help farmers attain parity prices and purchasing power." . . .

The statute not only avows an aim foreign to the procurement of revenue for the support of government, but by its operation shows the exaction laid upon processors to be the necessary means for the intended control of agricultural production. . . .

It is inaccurate and misleading to speak of the exaction from processors prescribed by the challenged act as a tax, or to say that as a tax it is subject to no infirmity. A tax, in the general understanding of the term, and as used in the Constitution, signifies an exaction for the support of the Government. The word has never been thought to connote the expropriation of money from one group for the benefit of another. We may concede that the latter sort of imposition is constitutional when imposed to effectuate regulation of a matter in which both groups are interested and in respect of which there is a power of legislative regulation. But manifestly no justification for it can be found unless as an integral part of such regulation. The exaction cannot be [w]rested out of its setting, denominated an excise for raising revenue and legalized by ignoring its purpose as a mere instrumentality for bringing about a desired end. To do this would be to shut our eyes to what all others than we can see and understand. *Child Labor Tax Case, 259 U. S. 20, 37.*

We conclude that the act is one regulating agricultural production, that the tax is a mere incident of such regulation and that the respondents have standing to challenge the legality of the exaction.

It does not follow that as the act is not an exertion of the taxing power and the exaction not a true tax, the statute is void or the exaction uncollectible. For, to paraphrase what was said in the Head Money Cases (supra), p. 596, if this is an expedient regulation by Congress, of a subject within one of its granted powers, "and the end to be attained is one falling within that power, the act is not void, because, within a loose and more extended sense than was used in the Constitution," the exaction is called a tax.

Second. The Government asserts that even if the respondents may question the propriety of the appropriation embodied in the statute their attack must fail because Article I, Section 3 of the Constitution authorizes the contemplated expenditure of the funds raised by the tax. This contention presents the great and the controlling question in the case. We approach its decision with a sense of our grave responsibility to render judgment in accordance with the principles established for the governance of all three branches of the Government.

There should be no misunderstanding as to the function of this court in such a case. It is sometimes said that the court assumes a power to overrule or control the action of the people's representatives. This is a misconception. The Constitution is the supreme law of the land ordained and established by the people. All legislation must conform to the principles it lays down. When an act of Congress is appropriately challenged in the courts as not conforming to the constitutional mandate the judicial branch of the Government has only one duty,—to lay the article of the Constitution which is invoked beside the statute which is challenged and to decide whether the latter squares with the former. All the court does, or can do, is to announce its considered judgment upon the question. The only power it has, if such it may be called, is the power of judgment. This court neither approves nor condemns any legislative policy. Its delicate and difficult office is to ascertain and declare whether the legislation is in accordance with, or in contravention of, the provisions of the Constitution; and, having done that, its duty ends.

The question is not what power the federal Government ought to have but what powers in fact have been given by the people. It hardly seems necessary to reiterate that ours is a dual form of government; that in every state there are two governments,—the state and the United States. Each State has all governmental powers save such as the people, by their Constitution, have conferred upon the United States, denied to the States, or reserved to themselves. The federal union is a government of delegated powers. It has only such as are expressly conferred upon it and such as are reasonably to be implied from those granted. In this respect we differ radically from nations where all legislative power without restriction or limitation, is vested in a parliament or other legislative body subject to no restrictions except the discretion of its members.

Article I, Section 8, of the Constitution vests sundry powers in the Congress. But two of its clauses have any bearing upon the validity of the statute under review.

The third clause endows the Congress with power "to regulate Commerce . . . among the several States." Despite a reference in its first section to a burden upon, and an obstruction of the normal currents of commerce, the act under review does not purport to regulate transactions in interstate or foreign commerce. Its stated purpose is the control of agricultural production, a purely local activity in an effort to raise the prices paid the farmer. Indeed, the Government does not attempt to uphold the validity of the act on the basis of the commerce clause, which, for the purpose of the present case, may be put aside as irrelevant.

The clause thought to authorize the legislation,— the first,—confers upon the Congress power "to lay and collect Taxes, Duties, Imposts and Excises, to pay the Debts and provide for the common Defence and general Welfare of the United States. . . ." It is not contended that this provision grants power to regulate agricultural production upon the theory that such legislation would promote the general welfare. The Government concedes that the phrase "to provide for the general welfare" qualifies the power "to lay and collect taxes." The view that the clause grants power to provide for the general welfare, independently of the taxing power, has never been authoritatively accepted. . . . The true construction undoubtedly is that the only thing granted is the power to tax for the purpose of providing funds for payment of the nation's debts and making provision for the general welfare.

Nevertheless the Government asserts that warrant is found in this clause for the adoption of the Agricultural Adjustment Act. The argument is that Congress may appropriate and authorize the spending of moneys for the "general welfare"; that the phrase should be liberally construed to cover anything conducive to national welfare; that decision as to what will promote such welfare rests with Congress alone, and the courts may not review its determination; and finally that the appropriation under attack was in fact for the general welfare of the United States. . . . Since the foundation of the nation sharp differences of opinion have persisted as to the true interpretation of the phrase. Madison asserted it amounted to no more than a reference to the other powers enumerated in the subsequent clauses of the same section; that, as the United States is a government of limited and enumerated powers, the grant of power to tax and spend for the general national welfare must be confined to the enumerated legislative fields committed to the Congress. In this view the phrase is mere tautology, for taxation and appropriation are or may be necessary incidents of the exercise of any of the enumerated legislative powers. Hamilton, on the other hand, maintained the clause confers a power separate and distinct from those later enumerated, is not restricted in meaning by the grant of them, and Congress consequently has a substantive power to tax and to appropriate, limited only by the requirement that it shall be exercised to provide for the general welfare of the United States. Each contention has had the support of those whose views are entitled to weight. This court has noticed the question, but has never found it necessary to decide which is the true construction. Mr. Justice Story, in his Commentaries, espouses the Hamiltonian position. We shall not review the writings of public men and commentators or discuss the legislative practice. Study of all these leads us to conclude that the reading advocated by Mr. Justice Story is the correct one. While, therefore, the power to tax is not unlimited, its confines are set in the clause which confers it, and not in those of section 8 which bestow and define the legislative powers of the Congress. It results that the power of Congress to authorize expenditure of public moneys for public purposes is not limited by the direct grants of legislative power found in the Constitution.

But the adoption of the broader construction leaves the power to spend subject to limitations. . . .

That the qualifying phrase must be given effect all advocates of broad construction admit. Hamilton, in his well known Report on Manufactures, states that the purpose must be "general, and not local." . . .

We are not now required to ascertain the scope of the phrase "general welfare of the United States" or to determine whether an appropriation in aid of agriculture falls within it. Wholly apart from that question, another principle embedded in our Constitution pro-

hibits the enforcement of the Agricultural Adjustment Act. The act invades the reserved rights of the states. It is a statutory plan to regulate and control agricultural production, a matter beyond the powers delegated to the federal government. The tax, the appropriation of the funds raised, and the direction for their disbursement, are but parts of the plan. They are but means to an unconstitutional end.

From the accepted doctrine that the United States is a government of delegated powers, it follows that those not expressly granted, or reasonably to be implied from such as are conferred, are reserved to the states or to the people. To forestall any suggestion to the contrary, the Tenth Amendment was adopted. The same proposition, otherwise stated, is that powers not granted are prohibited. None to regulate agricultural production is given, and therefore legislation by Congress for that purpose is forbidden.

It is an established principle that the attainment of a prohibited end may not be accomplished under the pretext of the exertion of powers which are granted. . . .

These principles are as applicable to the power to lay taxes as to any other federal power . . .

The power of taxation, which is expressly granted, may, of course, be adopted as a means to carry into operation another power also expressly granted. But resort to the taxing power to effectuate an end which is not legitimate, not within the scope of the Constitution, is obviously inadmissible. . . .

Third. If the taxing power may not be used as the instrument to enforce a regulation of matters of state concern with respect to which the Congress has no authority to interfere, may it, as in the present case, be employed to raise the money necessary to purchase a compliance which the Congress is powerless to command? The Government asserts that whatever might be said against the validity of the plan, if compulsory, it is constitutionally sound because the end is accomplished by voluntary cooperation. There are two sufficient answers to the contention. The regulation is not in fact voluntary. The farmer, of course, may refuse to comply, but the price of such refusal is the loss of benefits. The amount offered is intended to be sufficient to exert pressure on him to agree to the proposed regulation. The power to confer or withhold unlimited benefits is the power to coerce or destroy. If the cotton grower elects not to accept the benefits, he will receive less for his crops; those who receive payments will be able to undersell him. The result may well be financial ruin. The coercive purpose and intent of the statute is not obscured by the fact that it has not been perfectly successful. It is pointed out that, because there still remained a minority whom the rental and benefit payments were insufficient to induce to surrender their independence of action, the Congress has gone further and, in the Bankhead Cotton Act, used the taxing power in a more directly minatory fashion to compel submission. This progression only serves more fully to expose the coercive purpose of the so-called tax imposed by the present act. It is clear that the Department of Agriculture has properly described the plan as one to keep a non-cooperating minority in line. This is coercion by economic pressure. The asserted power of choice is illusory. . . .

But if the plan were one for purely voluntary cooperation it would stand no better so far as federal power is concerned. At best it is a scheme for purchasing with federal funds submission to federal regulation of a subject reserved to the states.

It is said that Congress has the undoubted right to appropriate money to executive officers for expenditure under contracts between the government and individuals; that much of the total expenditures is so made. But appropriations and expenditures under contracts for proper governmental purposes cannot justify contracts which are not within federal power. And contracts for the reduction of acreage and the control of production are outside the range of that power. An appropriation to be expended by the United States under contracts calling for violation of a state law clearly would offend the Constitution. Is a statute less objectionable which authorizes expenditure of federal moneys to induce action in a field in which the United States has no power to intermeddle? The Congress cannot invade state jurisdiction to compel individual action; no more can it purchase such action.

We are referred to numerous types of federal appropriation which have been made in the past, and it is asserted no question has been raised as to their validity. We need not stop to examine or consider them. . . .

Congress has no power to enforce its commands on the farmer to the ends sought by the Agricultural Adjustment Act. It must follow that it may not indirectly accomplish those ends by taxing and spending to purchase compliance. The Constitution and the entire plan of our government negative any such use of the power to tax and to spend as the act undertakes to authorize. It does not help to declare that local conditions throughout the nation have created a situation of national concern; for this is but to say that whenever there is a widespread similarity of local conditions, Congress may ignore constitutional limitations upon its own powers and usurp those reserved to the states. If, in lieu of compulsory regulation of subjects within the

states' reserved jurisdiction, which is prohibited, the Congress could invoke the taxing and spending power as a means to accomplish the same end, clause 1 of Section 8 of Article I would become the instrument for total subversion of the governmental powers reserved to the individual states.

If the act before us is a proper exercise of the federal taxing power, evidently the regulation of all industry throughout the United States may be accomplished by similar exercises of the same power. It would be possible to exact money from one branch of an industry and pay it to another branch in every field of activity which lies within the province of the states. The mere threat of such a procedure might well induce the surrender of rights and the compliance with federal regulation as the price of continuance in business. A few instances will illustrate the thought. . . .

A possible result of sustaining the claimed federal power would be that every business group which thought itself under-privileged might demand that a tax be laid on its vendors or vendees the proceeds to be appropriated to the redress of its deficiency of income. . . .

Until recently no suggestion of the existence of any such power in the federal government has been advanced. The expressions of the framers of the Constitution, the decisions of this court interpreting that instrument and the writings of great commentators will be searched in vain for any suggestion that there exists in the clause under discussion or elsewhere in the Constitution, the authority whereby every provision and every fair implication from that instrument may be subverted, the independence of the individual states obliterated, and the United States converted into a central government exercising uncontrolled police power in every state of the Union, superseding all local control or regulation of the affairs or concerns of the states.

Hamilton himself, the leading advocate of broad interpretation of the power to tax and to appropriate for the general welfare, never suggested that any power granted by the Constitution could be used for the destruction of local self-government in the states. Story countenances no such doctrine. It seems never to have occurred to them, or to those who have agreed with them, that the general welfare of the United States, (which has aptly been termed "an indestructible Union, composed of indestructible States,") might be served by obliterating the constituent members of the Union. But to this fatal conclusion the doctrine contended for would inevitably lead. And its sole premise is that, though the makers of the Constitution, in erecting the federal government, intended sedulously to limit and define its powers, so as to reserve to the states and the people sovereign power, to be wielded by the states and their citizens and not to be invaded by the United States, they nevertheless by a single clause gave power to the Congress to tear down the barriers, to invade the states' jurisdiction, and to become a parliament of the whole people, subject to no restrictions save such as are self-imposed. The argument when seen in its true character and in the light of its inevitable results must be rejected. The judgment is affirmed.

From: 297 U.S. 1 (1936).

ASHWANDER V. TENNESSEE VALLEY AUTHORITY, 1936

The Tennessee Valley Authority (TVA) was one of the most ambitious programs of the New Deal. It created a vast network of hydroelectric dams that would provide publicly generated power to a region encompassing no less than six southern states. The TVA was also meant to be a model for similar projects in other parts of the country. Conservatives feared that the TVA was the first step on the road to the nationalization of the country's utilities. But in the Ashwander v. Tennessee Valley Authority decision of 1936, the Supreme Court ruled that the TVA was constitutional. The decision represented one of the first major Court victories for the Roosevelt administration and the New Deal.

Hughes, Charles Evans: On January 4, 1934, the Tennessee Valley Authority, an agency of the Federal Government, entered into a contract with the Alabama Power Company, providing (1) for the purchase by the Authority from the Power Company of certain transmission lines, sub-stations, and auxiliary properties for $1,000,000, (2) for the purchase by the Authority from the Power Company of certain real property for $150,000, (3) for an interchange of hydroelectric energy, and in addition for the sale by the Authority to the Power Company of its "surplus power" on stated terms, and (4) for mutual restrictions as to the areas to be served in the sale of power. The contract was amended and supplemented in minor particulars on February 13 and May 24, 1934.

The Alabama Power Company is a corporation organized under the laws of Alabama and is engaged in the generation of electric energy and its distribution generally throughout that State, its lines reaching 66 counties. The transmission lines to be purchased by the Authority extend from Wilson Dam, at the Muscle Shoals plant owned by the United States on the Tennessee River in northern Alabama, into seven counties in that State, within a radius of about 50 miles. These lines serve a population of approximately 190,000, including about 10,000 individual customers, or about one-tenth of the total number served directly by the Power Company. The real property to be acquired by the Authority (apart from the transmission lines above mentioned and related properties) is adjacent to the area known as the "Joe Wheeler dam site," upon which the Authority is constructing the Wheeler Dam. . . .

Plaintiffs are holders of preferred stock of the Alabama Power Company. Conceiving the contract with the Tennessee Valley Authority to be injurious to the corporate interests and also invalid, because beyond the constitutional power of the Federal Government, they submitted their protest to the board of directors of the Power Company and demanded that steps should be taken to have the contract annulled. . . . Going beyond that particular challenge, and setting forth the pronouncements, policies and programs of the Authority, plaintiffs sought a decree restraining these activities as repugnant to the Constitution, and also asked a general declaratory decree with respect to the rights of the Authority in various relations.

The defendants, including the Authority and its directors, the Power Company and its mortgage trustee, and the municipalities within the described area, filed answers and the case was heard upon evidence. The District Court made elaborate findings and entered a final decree annulling the contract of January 4, 1934, and enjoining the transfer of the transmission lines and auxiliary properties. The court also enjoined the defendant municipalities from making or performing any contracts with the Authority for the purchase of power, and from accepting or expending any funds received from the Authority or the Public Works Administration for the purpose of constructing a public distribution system to distribute power which the Authority supplied. The court gave no consideration to plaintiff's request for a general declaratory decree.

The Authority, its directors, and the city of Florence appealed from the decree and the case was severed as to the other defendants. Plaintiffs took a cross appeal.

The Circuit Court of Appeals limited its discussion to the precise issue with respect to the effect and validity of the contract of January 4, 1934. The District Court had found that the electric energy required for the territory served by the transmission lines to be purchased under that contract is available at Wilson Dam without the necessity for any interconnection with any other dam or power plant. The Circuit Court of Appeals accordingly considered the constitutional authority for the construction of Wilson Dam and for the disposition of the electric energy there created. In the view that the Wilson Dam had been constructed in the exercise of the war and commerce powers of the Congress and that the electric energy there available was the property of the United States and subject to its disposition, the Circuit Court of Appeals decided that the decree of the District Court was erroneous and should be reversed. The court also held that plaintiffs should take nothing by their cross appeal. 78 F. (2d) 578. On plaintiffs' application we granted writs of certiorari, 296 United States.

First. The right of plaintiffs to bring this suit. . . .

We think that plaintiffs have made a sufficient showing to entitle them to bring suit and that a constitutional question is properly presented and should be decided.

Second. The scope of the issue. We agree with the Circuit Court of Appeals that the question to be determined is limited to the validity of the contract of January 4, 1934. The pronouncements, policies and program of the Tennessee Valley Authority and its directors, their motives and desires, did not give rise to a justiciable controversy save as they had fruition in action of a definite and concrete character constituting an actual or threatened interference with the rights of the persons complaining. The judicial power does not extend to the determination of abstract questions. . . .

As it appears that the transmission lines in question run from the Wilson Dam and that the electric energy generated at that dam is more than sufficient to supply all the requirements of the contract, the questions that are properly before us relate to the constitutional authority for the construction of the Wilson Dam and for the disposition, as provided in the contract, of the electric energy there generated.

Third. The constitutional authority for the construction of the Wilson Dam. The Congress may not, "under the pretext of executing its powers, pass laws for the accomplishment of objects not entrusted to the government." Chief Justice Marshall, in *McCulloch v. Maryland; Linder v. United States*, 268 U.S. 15, 17. The Government's argument recognizes this essential limi-

tation. The Government's contention is that the Wilson Dam was constructed, and the power plant connected with it was installed, in the exercise by the Congress of its war and commerce powers, that is, for the purposes of national defense and the improvement of navigation. . . .

We may take judicial notice of the international situation at the time the Act of 1916 was passed, and it cannot be successfully disputed that the Wilson Dam and its auxiliary plants, including the hydro-electric power plant, are, and were intended to be, adapted to the purposes of national defense. While the District Court found that there is no intention to use the nitrate plants or the hydro-electric units installed at Wilson Dam for the production of war materials in time of peace, "the maintenance of said properties in operating condition and the assurance of an abundant supply of electric energy in the event of war, constitute national defense assets." This finding has ample support.

The Act of 1916 also had in view "improvements to navigation." Commerce includes navigation. "All America understands, and has uniformly understood," said Chief Justice Marshall in *Gibbons v. Ogden*, "the word 'commerce,' to comprehend navigation." The power to regulate interstate commerce embraces the power to keep the navigable rivers of the United States free from obstructions to navigation and to remove such obstructions when they exist. "For these purposes," said the Court in *Gilman v. Philadelphia*, 3 Wall. 713, 725, "Congress possesses all the powers which existed in the States before the adoption of the national Constitution, and which have always existed in the Parliament in England." . . .

The Tennessee River is a navigable stream, although there are obstructions at various points because of shoals, reefs and rapids. The improvement of navigation on this river has been a matter of national concern for over a century. . . .

While, in its present condition, the Tennessee River is not adequately improved for commercial navigation, and traffic is small, we are not at liberty to conclude either that the river is not susceptible of development as an important waterway, or that Congress has not undertaken that development, or that the construction of the Wilson Dam was not an appropriate means to accomplish a legitimate end.

The Wilson Dam and its power plant must be taken to have been constructed in the exercise of the constitutional functions of the Federal Government.

Fourth. The constitutional authority to dispose of electric energy generated at the Wilson Dam. The Government acquired full title to the dam site, with all riparian rights. The power of falling water was an inevitable incident of the construction of the dam. That water power came into the exclusive control of the Federal Government. The mechanical energy was convertible into electric energy, and the water power, the right to convert it into electric energy, and the electric energy thus produced, constitute property belonging to the United States.

Authority to dispose of property constitutionally acquired by the United States is expressly granted to the Congress by section 3 of Article IV of the Constitution. This section provides:

> The Congress shall have Power to dispose of and make all needful Rules and Regulations respecting the Territory or other Property belonging to the United States; and nothing in this Constitution shall be so construed as to Prejudice any Claims of the United States, or of any particular State.

To the extent that the power of disposition is thus expressly conferred, it is manifest that the Tenth Amendment is not applicable. And the Ninth Amendment (which petitioners also invoke) in insuring the maintenance of the rights retained by the people does not withdraw the rights which are expressly granted to the Federal Government. The question is as to the scope of the grant and whether there are inherent limitations which render invalid the disposition of property with which we are now concerned.

The occasion for the grant was the obvious necessity of making provision for the government of the vast territory acquired by the United States. The power to govern and to dispose of that territory was deemed to be indispensable to the purposes of the cessions made by the States. . . . The grant was made in broad terms, and the power of regulation and disposition was not confined to territory, but extended to "other property belonging to the United States," so that the power may be applied, as Story says, "to the due regulation of all other personal and real property rightfully belonging to the United States." And so, he adds, "it has been constantly understood and acted upon."

This power of disposal was early construed to embrace leases, thus enabling the Government to derive profit through royalties. . . . The policy, early adopted and steadily pursued, of segregating mineral lands from other public lands and providing for leases, pointed to the recognition both of the full power of disposal and of the necessity of suitably adapting the methods of disposal to different sorts of property. . . .

But when Congress thus reserved mineral lands for special disposal, can it be doubted that Congress could have provided for mining directly by its own agents, instead of giving that right to lessees on the payment of royalties? Upon what ground could it be said that the Government could not mine its own gold, silver, coal, lead, or phosphates in the public domain, and dispose of them as property belonging to the United States? That it could dispose of its land but not of what the land contained? It would seem to be clear that under the same power of disposition which enabled the Government to lease and obtain profit from sales by its lessees, it could mine and obtain profit from its own sales.

The question is whether a more limited power of disposal should be applied to the water power, convertible into electric energy, and to the electric energy thus produced at the Wilson Dam constructed by the Government in the exercise of its constitutional functions. If so, it must be by reason either of (1) the nature of the particular property, or (2) the character of the "surplus" disposed of, or (3) the manner of disposition.

(1) That the water power and the electric energy generated at the dam are susceptible of disposition as property belonging to the United States is well established. . . .

(2) The argument is stressed that, assuming that electric energy generated at the dam belongs to the United States, the Congress has authority to dispose of this energy only to the extent that it is a surplus necessarily created in the course of making munitions of war or operating the works for navigation purposes; that is, that the remainder of the available energy must be lost or go to waste. We find nothing in the Constitution which imposes such a limitation. It is not to be deduced from the mere fact that the electric energy is only potentially available until the generators are operated. The Government has no less right to the energy thus available by letting the water course over its turbines than it has to use the appropriate processes to reduce to possession other property within its control, as, for example, oil which it may recover from a pool beneath its lands, and which is reduced to possession by boring oil wells and otherwise might escape its grasp. And it would hardly be contended that, when the Government reserves coal on its lands, it can mine the coal and dispose of it only for the purpose of heating public buildings or for other governmental operations. Or, if the Government owns a silver mine that it can obtain the silver only for the purpose of storage or coinage. Or that when the Government extracts the oil it has reserved, it has no constitutional power to sell it. Our decisions recognize no such restriction. The

United States owns the coal, or the silver, or the lead, or the oil, it obtains from its lands, and it lies in the discretion of the Congress, acting in the public interest, to determine of how much of the property it shall dispose.

We think that the same principle is applicable to electric energy. The argument pressed upon us leads to absurd consequences in the denial, despite the broad terms of the constitutional provision, of a power of disposal which the public interest may imperatively require. Suppose, for example, that in the erection of a dam for the improvement of navigation, it became necessary to destroy a dam and power plant which had previously been erected by a private corporation engaged in the generation and distribution of energy which supplied the needs of neighboring communities and business enterprises. Would anyone say that, because the United States had built its own dam and plant in the exercise of its constitutional functions, and had complete ownership and dominion over both, no power could be supplied to the communities and enterprises dependent on it, not because of any unwillingness of the Congress to supply it, or of any overriding governmental need, but because there was no constitutional authority to furnish the supply? Or that, with abundant power available, which must otherwise be wasted, the supply to the communities and enterprises whose very life may be at stake must be limited to the slender amount of surplus unavoidably involved in the operation of the navigation works, because the Constitution does not permit any more energy to be generated and distributed? In the case of *The Green Bay Canal Company*, where the government works supplanted those of the Canal Company, the Court found no difficulty in sustaining the Government's authority to grant to the Canal Company the water powers which it had previously enjoyed, subject, of course, to the dominant control of the Government. And in the case of *United States v. Chandler Dunbar Company . . .* the statutory provision to which the Court referred, was "that any excess of water in the St. Marys River at Sault Sainte Marie over and above the amount now or hereafter required for the uses of navigation shall be leased for power purposes by the Secretary of War upon such terms and conditions as shall be best calculated in his judgment to insure the development thereof." It was to the leasing, under this provision, "of any excess of power over the needs of the Government" that the Court saw no valid objection. . . .

(3) We come then to the question as to the validity of the method which had been adopted in disposing of the surplus energy generated at the Wilson Dam. The constitutional provision is silent as to the method of disposing of property belonging to the United States. That method, of course, must be an appropriate means of disposition according to the nature of the property, it must be one adopted in the public interest as distinguished from private or personal ends, and we may assume that it must be consistent with the foundation principles of our dual system of government and must not be contrived to govern the concerns reserved to the States. In this instance, the method of disposal embraces the sale of surplus energy by the Tennessee Valley Authority to the Alabama Power Company, the interchange of energy between the Authority and the Power Company, and the purchase by the Authority from the Power Company of certain transmission lines.

As to the mere sale of surplus energy, nothing need be added to what we have said as to the constitutional authority to dispose. The Government could lease or sell and fix the terms. Sales of surplus energy to the Power Company by the Authority continued a practice begun by the Government several years before. The contemplated interchange of energy is a form of disposition and presents no questions which are essentially different from those that are pertinent to sales.

The transmission lines which the Authority undertakes to purchase from the Power Company lead from the Wilson Dam to a large area within about fifty miles of the dam. These lines provide the means of distributing the electric energy, generated at the dam, to a large population. They furnish a method of reaching a market. The alternative method is to sell the surplus energy at the dam, and the market there appears to be limited to one purchaser, the Alabama Power Company, and its affiliated interests. We know of no constitutional ground upon which the Federal Government can be denied the right to seek a wider market. We suppose that in the early days of mining in the West, if the Government had undertaken to operate a silver mine on its domain, it could have acquired the mules or horses and equipment to carry its silver to market. And the transmission lines for electric energy are but a facility for conveying to market that particular sort of property, and the acquisition of these lines raises no different constitutional question, unless in some way there is an invasion of the rights reserved to the State or to the people. We had no basis for concluding that the limited undertaking with the Alabama Power Company amounts to such an invasion. Certainly the Alabama Power Company has no constitutional right to insist that it shall be the sole purchaser of the energy generated at the Wilson Dam; that the energy shall be sold to it or go to waste.

We limit our decision to the case before us, as we have defined it. The argument is earnestly presented that the Government by virtue of its ownership of the dam and power plant could not establish a steel mill and make and sell steel products, or a factory to manufacture clothing or shoes for the public, and thus attempt to make its ownership of energy, generated at its dam, a means of carrying on competitive commercial enterprises and thus drawing to the Federal Government the conduct and management of business having no relation to the purposes for which the Federal Government was established. The picture is eloquently drawn but we deem it to be irrelevant to the issue here. The Government is not using the water power at the Wilson Dam to establish any industry or business. It is not using the energy generated at the dam to manufacture commodities of any sort for the public. The Government is disposing of the energy itself which simply is the mechanical energy, incidental to falling water at the dam, converted into the electric energy which is susceptible of transmission. The question here is simply as to the acquisition of the transmission lines as a facility for the disposal of that energy. And the Government rightly conceded at the bar, in substance, that it was without constitutional authority to acquire or dis-

pose of such energy except as it comes into being in the operation of works constructed in the exercise of some power delegated to the United States. As we have said, these transmission lines lead directly from the dam, which has been lawfully constructed, and the question of the constitutional right of the Government to acquire or operate local or urban distribution systems is not involved. We express no opinion as to the validity of such an effort, as to the status of any other dam or power development in the Tennessee Valley, whether connected with or apart from the Wilson Dam, or as to the validity of the Tennessee Valley Authority Act or of the claims made in the pronouncements and program of the Authority apart from the questions we have discussed in relation to the particular provisions of the contract of January 4, 1934, affecting the Alabama Power Company.

The decree of the Circuit Court of Appeals is affirmed.

Affirmed.

Brandeis, Justice delivered a separate opinion in which Justices Stone, Roberts and Cardozo concurred. Justice McReynolds dissented.

From: 297 U.S. 288 (1936).

NATIONAL LABOR RELATIONS BOARD V. JONES & LAUGHLIN STEEL CORPORATION, 1937

A critical decision of the New Deal era, the National Labor Relations Board v. Jones & Laughlin Steel Corporation *ruling declared that the National Labor Relations Act (Wagner Act) was constitutional. The act—which was interpreted by unions to mean that the federal government supported labor organizing—unleashed a mass wave of such organizing and a series of major sit-down strikes. Corporate America opposed the bill vehemently and challenged it numerous times in the courts. But this first key decision made it clear that an increasingly liberal court was willing to back New Deal legislation like the National Labor Relations Act.*

Hughes, Charles Evans: In a proceeding under the National Labor Relations Act of 1935, the National Labor Relations Board found that the petitioner, Jones & Laughlin Steel Corporation had violated the Act by en-

gaging in unfair labor practices affecting commerce. The proceeding was instituted by the Beaver Valley Lodge No. 200, affiliated with the Amalgamated Association of Iron, Steel and Tin Workers of America, a labor organization. The unfair labor practices charged were that the corporation was discriminating against members of the union with regard to hire and tenure of employment, and was coercing and intimidating its employees in order to interfere with their self-organization. The discriminatory and coercive action alleged was the discharge of certain employees.

The National Labor Relations Board, sustaining the charge ordered the corporation to cease and desist from such discrimination and coercion, to offer reinstatement to ten of the employees named, to make good their losses in pay, and to post for thirty days notices that the corporation would not discharge or discriminate against members, or those desiring to become members, of the labor union. As the corporation failed to comply, the Board petitioned the Circuit Court of Appeals to enforce the order. The court denied the petition, holding that the order lay beyond the range of federal power. 83 F. (2d) 998. We granted certiorari.

The scheme of the National Labor Relations Act may be briefly stated. Respondent, appearing specially for the purpose of objecting to the jurisdiction of the Board, filed its answer. Respondent admitted the discharges, but alleged that they were made because of inefficiency or violation of rules or for other good reasons and were not ascribable to union membership or activities. As an affirmative defense respondent challenged the constitutional validity of the statute and its applicability in the instant case.

Contesting the ruling of the Board, the respondent argues (1) that the Act is in reality a regulation of labor relations and not of interstate commerce; (2) that the Act can have no application to the respondent's relations with its production employees because they are not subject to regulation by the federal government: and (3) that the provisions of the Act violate Section 2 of Article III and the Fifth and Seventh Amendments of the Constitution of the United States.

The facts as to the nature and scope of the business of the Jones & Laughlin Steel Corporation have been found by the Labor Board and, so far as they are essential to the determination of this controversy, they are not in dispute. The Labor Board has found: The corporation is organized under the laws of Pennsylvania and has its principal office at Pittsburgh. It is engaged in the business of manufacturing iron and steel in plants situated in Pittsburgh and nearby Aliquippa, Pennsylvania. It manufactures and distributes a widely diversified line of steel and pig iron, being the fourth largest producer of steel in the United States. With its subsidiaries—nineteen in number—it is a completely integrated enterprise, owning and operating ore, coal and limestone properties, lake and river transportation facilities and terminal railroads located at its manufacturing plants. It owns or controls mines in Michigan and Minnesota. It operates four ore steamships on the Great Lakes, used in the transportation of ore to its factories. It owns coal mines in Pennsylvania. It operates towboats and steam barges used in carrying coal to its factories. It owns limestone properties in various places in Pennsylvania and West Virginia. It owns the Monongahela connecting railroad which connects the plants of the Pittsburgh works and forms an interconnection with the Pennsylvania New York Central and

Baltimore and Ohio Railroad systems. It owns the Aliquippa and Southern Railroad Company which connects the Aliquippa works with the Pittsburgh and Lake Erie, part of the New York Central system. Much of its product is shipped to its warehouses in Chicago, Detroit, Cincinnati and Memphis,—to the last two places by means of its own barges and transportation equipment in Long Island City, New York, and in New Orleans it operates structural steel fabricating shops in connection with the warehousing of semi-finished materials sent from its works. Through one of its wholly-owned subsidiaries it owns leases and operates stores, warehouses and yards for the distribution of equipment and supplies for drilling and operating oil and gas mills and for pipe lines, refineries and pumping stations. It has sales offices in twenty cities in the United States and a wholly-owned subsidiary which is devoted exclusively to distributing its product in Canada. Approximately 75 per cent of its product is shipped out of Pennsylvania.

Summarizing these operations, the Labor Board concluded that the works in Pittsburgh and Aliquippa "might be likened to the heart of a self-contained, highly-integrated body. They draw in the raw materials from Michigan, Minnesota, West Virginia, Pennsylvania in part through arteries and by means controlled by the respondent; they transform the materials and then pump them out to all parts of the nation through the vast mechanism which the respondent has elaborated."

To carry on the activities of the entire steel industry, 33,000 men mine ore, 44,000 men mine coal, 4,000 men quarry limestone, 16,000 men manufacture coke, 343,000 men manufacture steel, and 83,000 men transport its product. Respondent has about 10,000 employees in its Aliquippa plant, which is located in a community of about 30,000 persons.

Practically all the factual evidence in the case, except that which dealt with the nature of respondent's business, concerned its relations with the employees in the Aliquippa plant whose discharge was the subject of the complaint. These employees were active leaders in the labor union.

While respondent criticises the evidence and the attitude of the Board, which is described as being hostile toward employers and particularly toward those who insisted upon their constitutional rights, respondent did not take advantage of its opportunity to present evidence to refute that which was offered to show discrimination and coercion. In this situation, the record presents no ground for setting aside the order of the Board so far as the facts pertaining to the circumstances and purpose of the discharge of the employees are concerned. Upon that point it is sufficient to say that the evidence supports the findings of the Board that respondent discharged these men "because of their union activity and for the purpose of discouraging membership in the union." We turn to the questions of law which respondent urges in contesting the validity and application of the Act.

First. The scope of the Act.—The Act is challenged in its entirety as an attempt to regulate all industry, thus invading the reserved powers of the States over their local concerns. It is asserted that the references in the Act to interstate and foreign commerce are colorable at best; that the Act is not a true regulation of such commerce or of matters which directly affect it but on the contrary has the fundamental object of placing under the compulsory supervision of the federal government all industrial labor relations within the nation. The argument seeks support in the broad words of the preamble and in the sweep of the provisions of the Act, and it is further insisted that its legislative history shows an essential universal purpose in the light of which its scope cannot be limited by either construction or by the application of the separability clause.

If this conception of terms, intent and consequent inseparability were sound, the Act would necessarily fall by reason of the limitation upon the federal power which inheres in the constitutional grant, as well as because of the explicit reservation of the Tenth Amendment. *Schechter Corporation v. United States*, 295 United States 495, 549, 550, 554. The authority of the federal government may not be pushed to such an extreme as to destroy the distinction, which the commerce clause itself establishes, between commerce "among the several States" and the internal concerns of a State. That distinction between what is national and what is local in the activities of commerce is vital to the maintenance of our federal system.

But we are not at liberty to deny effect to specific provisions, which Congress has constitutional power to enact, by superimposing upon them inferences from general legislative declarations of an ambiguous character, even if found in the same statute. The cardinal principle of statutory construction is to save and not to destroy. We have repeatedly held that as between two possible interpretations of a statute, by one of which it would be unconstitutional and by the other valid, our plain duty is to adopt that which will save the act. Even to avoid a serious doubt the rule is the same.

We think it clear that the National Labor Relations Act may be construed so as to operate within the sphere of constitutional authority. The jurisdiction conferred upon the Board, and invoked in this instance, is found in Section 10 (a), which provides:

> SEC. 10 (a). The Board is empowered, as hereinafter provided, to prevent any person from engaging in any unfair labor practice (listed in section 8) affecting commerce.

The critical words of this provision, prescribing the limits of the Board's authority in dealing with the labor practices, are "affecting commerce." The Act specifically defines the "commerce" to which it refers (sec. 2 (6)):

There can be no question that the commerce thus contemplated by the Act (aside from that within a Territory or the District of Columbia) is interstate and foreign commerce in the constitutional sense. The Act also defines the term "affecting commerce" (sec. 2 (7)):

This definition is one of exclusion as well as inclusion. The grant of authority to the Board does not purport to extend to the relationship between all industrial employees and employers. Its terms do not impose collective bargaining upon all industry regardless of effects upon interstate or foreign commerce. It purports to reach only what may be deemed to burden or obstruct that commerce and, thus qualified, it must be construed as contemplating the exercise of control within constitutional bounds. It is a familiar principle that acts which directly burden or obstruct interstate or foreign commerce, or its free flow, are within the reach of the congressional power. Acts having that effect are not rendered immune because they grow out of labor disputes. It is the effect upon commerce, not the source of the injury, which is the criterion. Whether or not particular action does affect commerce in such a close and intimate fashion as to be subject to federal control, and hence to lie within the authority conferred upon the Board, is left by the statute to be determined as individual cases arise. We are thus to inquire whether in the instant case the constitutional boundary has been passed.

Second. The unfair labor practices in question.—The unfair labor practices found by the Board are those defined in Section 8, subdivisions (1) and (3). These provide:

> SEC. 8. It shall be an unfair labor practice for an employer—
> (1) To interfere with, restrain, or coerce employees in the exercise of the rights guaranteed in section 7.
> (3) By discrimination in regard to hire or tenure of em-

ployment or any term or condition of employment to encourage or discourage membership in any labor organization. . . .

Section 8, subdivision (1), refers to Section 7, which is as follows:

SEC. 7. Employees shall have the right to self-organization, to form, join, or assist labor organizations, to bargain collectively through representatives of their own choosing, and to engage in concerted activities, for the purpose of collective bargaining or other mutual aid or protection.

Thus, in its present application, the statute goes no further than to safeguard the right of employees to self-organization and to select representatives of their own choosing for collective bargaining or other mutual protection without restraint or coercion by their employer.

That is a fundamental right. Employees have as clear a right to organize and select their representatives for lawful purposes as the respondent has to organize its business and select its own officers and agents. Discrimination and coercion to prevent the free exercise of the right of employees to self-organization and representation is a proper subject for condemnation by competent legislative authority. Long ago we stated the reason for labor organizations. We said that they were organized out of the necessities of the situation; that a single employee was helpless in dealing with an employer; that he was dependent ordinarily on his daily wage for the maintenance of himself and family; that if the employer refused to pay him the wages that he thought fair, he was nevertheless unable to leave the employ and resist arbitrary and unfair treatment; that union was essential to give laborers opportunity to deal on an equality with their employer. *American Steel Foundries v. Tri-City Central Trades Council*, 257 United States 184, 209. We reiterated these views when we had under consideration the Railway Labor Act of 1926. Fully recognizing the legality of collective action on the part of employees in order to safeguard their proper interests, we said that Congress was not required to ignore this right but could safeguard it. Congress could seek to make appropriate collective action of employees an instrument of peace rather than of strife. We said that such collective action would be a mockery if representation were made futile by interference with freedom of choice. Hence the prohibition by Congress of interference with the selection of representatives for the purpose of negotiation and conference between employers and employees, "instead of

being an invasion of the constitutional right of either, was based on the recognition of the rights of both." We have reasserted the same principle in sustaining the application of the Railway Labor Act as amended in 1934.

Third. The application of the Act to employees engaged in production.—The principle involved.—Respondent says that whatever may be said of employees engaged in interstate commerce, the industrial relations and activities in the manufacturing department of respondent's enterprise are not subject to federal regulation. The argument rests upon the proposition that manufacturing in itself is not commerce.

The Government distinguishes these cases. The various parts of respondent's enterprise are described as interdependent and as thus involving "a great movement of iron ore, coal and limestone along well-defined paths to the steel mills, thence through them, and thence in the form of steel products into the consuming centers of the country—a definite and well-understood course of business." It is urged that these activities constitute a "stream" or "flow" of commerce, of which the Aliquippa manufacturing plant is the focal point, and that industrial strife at that point would cripple the entire movement. Reference is made to our decision sustaining the Packers and Stockyards Act. The Court found that the stockyards were but a "throat" through which the current of commerce flowed and the transactions which there occurred could not be separated from that movement.

Respondent contends that the instant case presents material distinctions.

We do not find it necessary to determine whether these features of defendant's business dispose of the asserted analogy to the "stream of commerce" cases. The congressional authority to protect interstate commerce from burdens and obstructions is not limited to transactions which can be deemed to be an essential part of a "flow" of interstate or foreign commerce. Burdens and obstructions may be due to injurious action springing from other sources. The fundamental principle is that the power to regulate commerce is the power to enact "all appropriate legislation" for "its protection and advancement"; to adopt measures "to promote its growth and insure its safety"; "to foster, protect, control and restrain." That power is plenary and may be exerted to protect interstate commerce "no matter what the source of the dangers which threaten it." Although activities may be intrastate in character when separately considered, if they have such a close and substantial relation to interstate commerce that their control is essential or appropriate to protect that commerce from burdens and obstructions, Congress cannot be denied the power to exercise that control. Undoubtedly the scope of this power must be considered in the light of our dual system of government and may not be extended so as to embrace effects upon interstate commerce so indirect and remote that to embrace them, in view of our complex society, would effectually obliterate the distinction between what is national and what is local and create a completely centralized government. The question is necessarily one of degree.

That intrastate activities, by reason of close and intimate relation to interstate commerce, may fall within federal control is demonstrated in the case of carriers who are engaged in both interstate and intrastate transportation. There federal control has been found essential to secure the freedom of interstate traffic from interference or unjust discrimination and to promote the efficiency of the interstate service. It is manifest that intrastate rates deal primarily with a local activity. But in rate-making they bear such a close relation to interstate rates that effective control of the one must embrace some control over the other. Under the Transportation Act, 1920, Congress went so far as to authorize the Interstate Commerce Commission to establish a state-wide level of intrastate rates in order to prevent an unjust discrimination against interstate commerce. Other illustrations are found in the broad requirements of the Safety Appliance Act and the Hours of Service Act. It is said that this exercise of federal power has relation to the maintenance of adequate instrumentalities of interstate commerce. But the agency is not superior to the commerce which uses it. The protective power extends to the former because it exists as to the latter.

The close and intimate effect which brings the subject within the reach of federal power may be due to activities in relation to productive industry although the industry when separately viewed is local. This has been abundantly illustrated in the application of the federal Anti-Trust Act.

Upon the same principle, the Anti-Trust Act has been applied to the conduct of employees engaged in production.

It is thus apparent that the fact that the employees here concerned were engaged in production is not determinative. The question remains as to the effect upon interstate commerce of the labor practice involved.

Fourth. Effects of the unfair labor practice in respondent's enterprise.—Giving full weight to respondent's contention with respect to a break in the complete continuity of the "stream of commerce" by reason of re-

spondent's manufacturing operations, the fact remains that the stoppage of those operations by industrial strife would have a most serious effect upon interstate commerce. In view of respondent's far-flung activities, it is idle to say that the effect would be indirect or remote. It is obvious that it would be immediate and might be catastrophic. We are asked to shut our eyes to the plainest facts of our national life and to deal with the question of direct and indirect effects in an intellectual vacuum. Because there may be but indirect and remote effects upon interstate commerce in connection with a host of local enterprises throughout the country, it does not follow that other industrial activities do not have such a close and intimate relation to interstate commerce as to make the presence of industrial strife a matter of the most urgent national concern. When industries organize themselves on a national scale, making their relation to interstate commerce the dominant factor in their activities, how can it be maintained that their industrial labor relations constitute a forbidden field into which Congress may not enter when it is necessary to protect interstate commerce from the paralyzing consequences of industrial war? We have often said that interstate commerce itself is a practical conception. It is equally true that interferences with that commerce must be appraised by a judgment that does not ignore actual experience.

Experience has abundantly demonstrated that the recognition of the right of employees to self-organization and to have representatives of their own choosing for the purpose of collective bargaining is often an essential condition of industrial peace. Refusal to confer and negotiate has been one of the most prolific causes of strife. This is such an outstanding fact in the history of labor disturbances that it is a proper subject of judicial notice and requires no citation of instances. But with respect to the appropriateness of the recognition of self-organization and representation in the promotion of peace, the question is not essentially different in the case of employees in industries of such a character that interstate commerce is put in jeopardy from the case of employees of transportation companies. And of what avail is it to protect the facility of transportation, if interstate commerce is throttled with respect to the commodities to be transported!

These questions have frequently engaged the attention of Congress and have been the subject of many inquiries. The steel industry is one of the great basic industries of the United States, with ramifying activities affecting interstate commerce at every point. The Government aptly refers to the steel strike of 1919–1920 with its far-reaching consequences. The fact that there appears to have been no major disturbance in that industry in the more recent period did not dispose of the possibilities of future and like dangers to interstate commerce which Congress was entitled to foresee and to exercise its protective power to forestall. It is not necessary again to detail the facts as to respondent's enterprise. Instead of being beyond the pale, we think that it presents in a most striking way the close and intimate relation which a manufacturing industry may have to interstate commerce and we have no doubt that Congress had constitutional authority to safeguard the right of respondent's employees to self-organization and freedom in the choice of representatives for collective bargaining.

Fifth. The means which the Act employs.—Questions under the due process clause and other constitutional restrictions.—Respondent asserts its right to conduct its business in an orderly manner without being subjected to arbitrary restraints. What we have said points to the fallacy in the argument. Employees have their correlative right to organize for the purpose of securing the redress of grievances and to promote agreements with employers relating to rates of pay and conditions of work. Restraint for the purpose of preventing an unjust interference with that right cannot be considered arbitrary or capricious.

The Act does not compel agreements between employers and employees. It does not compel any agreement whatever. It does not prevent the employer "from refusing to make a collective contract and hiring individuals on whatever terms the employer may by unilateral action determine." The Act expressly provides in Section 9 (a) that any individual employee or a group of employees shall have the right at any time to present grievances to their employer. The theory of the Act is that free opportunity for negotiation with accredited representatives of employees is likely to promote industrial peace and may bring about the adjustments and agreements which the Act in itself does not attempt to compel. As we said in *Texas & N.O.R. Co. v. Railway Clerks, supra,* and repeated in *Virginian Railway Co. v. System Federation, No. 40,* the

cases of *Adair v. United States,* 208 United States 161, and *Coppage v. Kansas,* 236 United States 1, are inapplicable to legislation of this character. The Act does not interfere with the normal exercise of the right of the employer to select its employees or to discharge them. The employer may not, under cover of that right, intimidate or coerce its employees with respect to their self-organization and representation, and, on the other hand, the Board is not entitled to make its authority a pretext for interference with the right of discharge when that right is exercised for other reasons than such intimidation and coercion. The true purpose is the subject of investigation with full opportunity to show the facts. It would seem that when employers freely recognize the right of their employees to their own organizations and their unrestricted right of representation there will be much less occasion for controversy in respect to the free and appropriate exercise of the right of selection and discharge.

The Act has been criticised as one-sided in its application; that it fails to provide a more comprehensive plan. But we are dealing with the power of Congress, not with a particular policy or with the extent to which policy should go. We have frequently said that the legislative authority, exerted within its proper field, need not embrace all the evils within its reach. The Constitution does not forbid "cautious advance, step by step," in dealing with the evils which are exhibited in activities within the range of legislative power. The question in such cases is whether the legislature, in what it does prescribe, has gone beyond constitutional limits.

Our conclusion is that the order of the Board was within its competency and that the Act is valid as here applied. The judgment of the Circuit Court of Appeals is reversed and the cause is remanded for further proceedings in conformity with this opinion.

McReynolds, Justice, Van DeVanter, Justice, Sutherland, Justice, and Butler, Justice dissented.

From: 301 U.S. 1 (1937).

WEST COAST HOTEL COMPANY V. PARRISH, 1937

Through the late nineteenth and early twentieth centuries, state and federal legislative efforts to establish minimum wages and regulate the conditions of employment, including for women and children, were declared unconstitutional by federal courts. In the 1937 West Coast Hotel Company v. Parrish *decision, the Supreme Court reversed direction, overthrowing* Adkins v. Children's Hospital, *(1923) and allowing a Washington state law fixing the minimum wage for women and minors to stand. The decision reflected the increasingly liberal thinking of the court, following President Franklin D. Roosevelt's threats to add new liberal justices.*

Hughes, Charles Evans: This case presents the question of the constitutional validity of the minimum wage law of the State of Washington.

The Act, entitled "Minimum Wages for Women," authorizes the fixing of minimum wages for women and minors. . . . It provides:

SEC. 1. The welfare of the State of Washington demands that women and minors be protected from conditions of labor which have a pernicious effect on their health and morals. The State of Washington, therefore, exercising herein its police and sovereign power declares that inadequate wages and unsanitary conditions of labor exert such pernicious effect.

SEC. 2. It shall be unlawful to employ women or minors in any industry or occupation within the State of Washington under conditions of labor detrimental to their health or morals, and it shall be unlawful to employ women workers in any industry within the State of Washington at wages which are not adequate for their maintenance.

SEC. 3. There is hereby created a commission to be known as the "Industrial Welfare Commission" for the State of Washington, to establish such standards of wages and conditions of labor for women and minors employed within the State of Washington, as shall be held hereunder to be reasonable and not detrimental to health and morals, and which shall be sufficient for the decent maintenance of women.

Further provisions required the Commission to ascertain the wages and conditions of labor of women and minors within the State. Public hearings were to be held. If after investigation the Commission found that in any occupation, trade or industry the wages paid to women were "inadequate to supply them necessary cost of living and to maintain the workers in health," the Commission was empowered to call a conference of representatives of employers and employees together with disinterested persons representing the public. The conference was to recommend to the Commission, on its request, an estimate of a minimum wage adequate for the purpose above stated, and on the approval of such a recommendation it became the duty of the Commission to issue an obligatory order fixing minimum wages. Any such order might be reopened and the question reconsidered with the aid of the former conference or a new one. Special licenses were authorized for the employment of women who were "physically defective or crippled by age or otherwise," and also for apprentices, at less than the prescribed minimum wage.

By a later Act the Industrial Welfare Commission was abolished and its duties were assigned to the Industrial Welfare Committee consisting of the Director of Labor and Industries, the Supervisor of Industrial Insurance, the Supervisor of Industrial Relations, the Industrial Statistician and the Supervisor of Women in Industry. Laws of 1921 (Washington) chap. 7.

The appellant conducts a hotel. The appellee Elsie Parrish was employed as a chambermaid and (with her husband) brought this suit to recover the difference between the wages paid her and the minimum wage fixed pursuant to the state law. The minimum wage was $14.50 per week of 48 hours. The appellant challenged the act as repugnant to the due process clause of the Fourteenth Amendment of the Constitution of the United States. The Supreme Court of the State, reversing the trial court, sustained the statute and directed judgment for the plaintiffs. *Parrish v. West Coast Hotel Co.*, 185 Wash. 581. The case is here on appeal.

The appellant relies upon the decision of this Court in *Adkins v. Children's Hospital*, which held invalid the District of Columbia Minimum Wage Act which was attacked under the due process clause of the Fifth Amendment.

The recent case of *Morehead v. New York ex rel. Tipaldo*, 298 United States 587, came here on certiorari to the New York court which had held the New York minimum wage act for women to be invalid. A minority of this Court thought that the New York statute was distinguishable in a material feature from that involved in the Adkins case and that for that and other reasons the New York statute should be sustained. But the Court of Appeals of New York had said that it found no material difference between the two statutes and this Court held that the "meaning of the statute" as fixed by the decision of the state court "must be accepted here as if the meaning had been specifically expressed in the enactment." Id., p. 609. That view led to the affirmance by this Court of the judgment in the *Morehead* case, as the Court considered that the only question before it was whether the *Adkins* case was distinguishable and that reconsideration of that decision had not been sought. . . .

We think that the question which was not deemed to be open in the *Morehead* case is open and is necessarily presented here. The Supreme Court of Washington has upheld the minimum wage statute of that State. It has decided that the statute is a reasonable exercise of the police power of the State. In reaching that conclusion the state court has invoked principles long established by this Court in the application of the Fourteenth Amendment. The state court has refused to regard the decision in the *Adkins* case as determinative and has pointed to our decisions both before and since that case as justifying its position. We are of the opinion that this ruling of the state court demands on our part a reexamination of the *Adkins* case. The importance of the question, in which many States having similar laws are concerned, the close division by which the decision in the *Adkins* case was reached, and the economic conditions which have supervened, and in the light of which the reasonableness of the exercise of the protective power of the State must be considered, make it not only appropriate, but we think imperative, that in deciding the present case the subject should receive fresh consideration.

The history of the litigation of this question may be briefly stated. The minimum wage statute of Washington was enacted over twenty-three years ago. Prior to the decision in the instant case it had twice been held valid by the Supreme Court of the State. *Larsen v. Rice*, 100 Wash. 642; *Spokane Hotel Co. v. Younger*, 113 Wash. 359. The Washington statute is essentially the same as that enacted in Oregon in the same year. Laws of 1913 (Oregon) chap. 62. The validity of the latter act was sustained by the Supreme Court of Oregon in *Stettler v. O'Hara*, 69 Ore. 519 and *Simpson v. O'Hara*, 70 Ore. 261. These cases, after reargument, were affirmed here by an equally divided court, in 1917. 243 United States 629. The law of Oregon thus continued

in effect. The District of Columbia Minimum Wage Law (40 Stat. 960) was enacted in 1918. The statute was sustained by the Supreme Court of the District in the *Adkins* case. Upon appeal the Court of Appeals of the District first affirmed that ruling but on rehearing reversed it and the case came before this Court in 1923. The judgment of the Court of Appeals holding the Act invalid was affirmed, but with Chief Justice Taft, Mr. Justice Holmes and Mr. Justice Sanford dissenting, and Mr. Justice Brandeis taking no part. The dissenting opinions took the ground that the decision was at variance with the principles which this Court had frequently announced and applied. In 1925 and 1927, the similar minimum wage statutes of Arizona and Arkansas were held invalid upon the authority of the *Adkins* case. The Justices who had dissented in that case bowed to the ruling and Mr. Justice Brandeis dissented. *Murphy v. Sardell*, 269 United States 530; *Donham v. West-Nelson Co.*, 273 United States 657. The question did not come before us again until the last term in the *Morehead* case, as already noted. In that case, briefs supporting the New York statute were submitted by the States of Ohio, Connecticut, Illinois, Massachusetts, New Hampshire, New Jersey and Rhode Island. 298 U. S., p. 604, *note*. Throughout this entire period the Washington statute now under consideration has been in force.

The principle which must control our decision is not in doubt. The constitutional provision invoked is the due process clause of the Fourteenth Amendment governing the States, as the due process clause invoked in the *Adkins* case governed Congress. In each case the violation alleged by those attacking minimum wage regulation for women is deprivation of freedom of contract. What is this freedom? The Constitution does not speak of freedom of contract. It speaks of liberty and prohibits the deprivation of liberty without due process of law. In prohibiting that deprivation the Constitution does not recognize an absolute and uncontrollable liberty. Liberty in each of its phases has its history and connotation. But the liberty safeguarded is liberty in a social organization which requires the protection of law against the evils which menace the health, safety, morals and welfare of the people. Liberty under the Constitution is thus necessarily subject to the restraints of due process, and regulation which is reasonable in relation to its subject and is adopted in the interests of the community is due process.

This essential limitation of liberty in general governs freedom of contract in particular. More than twenty-five years ago we set forth the applicable principle in these words, after referring to the cases where the liberty guaranteed by the Fourteenth Amendment had been broadly described:

> But it was recognized in the cases cited, as in many others, that freedom of contract is a qualified and not an absolute right. There is no absolute freedom to do as one wills or to contract as one chooses. The guaranty of liberty does not withdraw from legislative supervision that wide department of activity which consists of the making of contracts, or deny to government the power to provide restrictive safeguards. Liberty implies the absence of arbitrary restraint, not immunity from reasonable regulations and prohibitions imposed in the interests of the community. *Chicago, Burlington & Quincy R. R. Co. v. McGuire*, 219 U.S s49, 56s.

This power under the Constitution to restrict freedom of contract has had many illustrations. That it may be exercised in the public interest with respect to contracts between employer and employee is undeniable. Thus statutes have been sustained limiting employment in underground mines and smelters to eight hours a day (*Holden v. Hardy*); in requiring redemption in cash of store orders or other evidences of indebtedness issued in the payment of wages (*Knoxville Iron Co. v. Harbison*, 183 U.S. 13); in forbidding the payment of seamen's wages in advance (*Patterson v. Bark Eudora*, 190 United States 169); in making it unlawful to contract to pay miners employed at quantity rates upon the basis of screened coal instead of the weight of the coal as originally produced in the mine (*McLean v. Arkansas*, 211 United States 539); in prohibiting contracts limiting liability for injuries to employees (*Chicago, Burlington & Quincy R. R. Co. v. McGuire*); in limiting hours of work of employees in manufacturing establishments (*Bunting v. Oregon*); and in maintaining workmen's compensation laws (*New York Central R. R. Co. v. White*, 243 United States 188; *Mountain Timber Co. v. Washington*, 243 United States 219). In dealing with the relation of employer and employed, the legislature has necessarily a wide field of discretion in order that there may be suitable protection of health and safety, and that peace and good order may be promoted through regulations designed to insure wholesome conditions of work and freedom from oppression. *Chicago, Burlington & Quincy R. R. Co. v. McGuire*, supra, p. 570.

The point that has been strongly stressed that adult employees should be deemed competent to make their own contracts was decisively met nearly forty years ago in *Holden v. Hardy*, supra, where we pointed out the inequality in the footing of the parties. . . .

It is manifest that this established principle is peculiarly applicable in relation to the employment of women in whose protection the State has a special interest. That phase of the subject received elaborate consideration in *Muller v. Oregon*, where the constitutional authority of the State to limit the working hours of women was sustained. . . . Again, in *Quong Wing v. Kirkendall*, 223 United States 59, 63, in referring to a differentiation with respect to the employment of women, we said that the Fourteenth Amendment did not interfere with state power by creating a "fictitious equality." We referred to recognized classifications on the basis of sex with regard to hours of work and in other matters, and we observed that the particular points at which that difference shall be enforced by legislation were largely in the power of the State. In later rulings this Court sustained the regulation of hours of work of women employees in *Riley v. Massachusetts*, 232 United States 671 (factories), *Miller v. Wilson*, 236 United States 373 (hotels), and *Bosley v. McLaughlin*, 236 United States 385 (hospitals).

This array of precedents and the principles they applied were thought by the dissenting Justices in the *Adkins* case to demand that the minimum wage statute be sustained. The validity of the distinction made by the Court between a minimum wage and a maximum of hours in limiting liberty of contract was especially challenged. That challenge persists and is without any satisfactory answer. . . .

One of the points which was pressed by the Court in supporting its ruling in the *Adkins* case was that the standard set up by the District of Columbia Act did not take appropriate account of the value of the services rendered. . . .

The minimum wage to be paid under the Washington statute is fixed after full consideration by representatives of employers, employees and the public. It may be assumed that the minimum wage is fixed in consideration of the services that are performed in the particular occupations under normal conditions. Provision is made for special licenses at less wages in the case of women who are incapable of full service. The statement of Mr. Justice Holmes in the *Adkins* case is pertinent:

> This statute does not compel anybody to pay anything. It simply forbids employment at rates below those fixed as the minimum requirement of health and right living. It is safe to assume that women will not be employed at even the lowest wages allowed unless they earn them, or unless the employer's business can sustain the burden. In short the law in its character and operation is like

hundreds of so-called police laws that have been upheld. 261 United States, p. 570.

And Chief Justice Taft forcibly pointed out the consideration which is basic in a statute of this character:

> Legislatures which adopt a requirement of maximum hours or minimum wages may be presumed to believe that when sweating employers are prevented from paying unduly low wages by positive law they will continue their business, abating that part of their profits, which were wrung from the necessities of their employees, and will concede the better terms required by the law; and that while in individual cases hardship may result, the restriction will enure to the benefit of the general class of employees in whose interest the law is passed and so to that of the community at large. Id., p. 563.

We think that the views thus expressed are sound and that the decision in the *Adkins* case was a departure from the true application of the principles governing the regulation by the State of the relation of employer and employed. Those principles have been reenforced by our subsequent decisions. Thus in *Radice v. New York*, 264 United States 292, we sustained the New York statute which restricted the employment of women in restaurants at night. In *O'Gorman v. Hartford Fire Insurance Company*, 282 United States 251, which upheld an act regulating the commissions of insurance agents, we pointed to the presumption of the constitutionality of a statute dealing with a subject within the scope of the police power and to the absence of any factual foundation of record for deciding that the limits of power had been transcended. In *Nebbia v. New York*, dealing with the New York statute providing for minimum prices for milk, the general subject of the regulation of the use of private property and of the making of private contracts received an exhaustive examination and we again declared that if such laws "have a reasonable relation to a proper legislative purpose, and are neither arbitrary nor discriminatory, the requirements of due process are satisfied"; that "with the wisdom of the policy adopted, with the adequacy or practicability of the law enacted to forward it, the courts are both incompetent and unauthorized to deal"; that "times without number we have said that the legislature is primarily the judge of the necessity of such an enactment, that every possible presumption is in favor of its validity, and that though the court may hold views inconsistent with the wisdom of the law, it may not be annulled unless palpably in excess of legislative power."

With full recognition of the earnestness and vigor which characterize the prevailing opinion in the *Adkins* case, we find it impossible to reconcile that ruling with these well-considered declarations. What can be closer to the public interest than the health of women and their protection from unscrupulous and overreaching employers? And if the protection of women is a legitimate end of the exercise of state power, how can it be said that the requirement of the payment of a minimum wage fairly fixed in order to meet the very necessities of existence is not an admissible means to that end? The legislature of the State was clearly entitled to consider the situation of women in employment, the fact that they are in the class receiving the least pay, that their bargaining power is relatively weak, and that they are the ready victims of those who would take advantage of their necessitous circumstances. The legislature was entitled to adopt measures to reduce the evils of the "sweating system," the exploiting of workers at wages so low as to be insufficient to meet the bare cost of living thus making their very helplessness the occasion of a most injurious competition. The legislature had the right to consider that its minimum wage requirements would be an important aid in carrying out its policy of protection. The adoption of similar requirements by many States evidences a deep seated conviction both as to the presence of the evil and as to the means adapted to check it. Legislative response to that conviction cannot be regarded as arbitrary or capricious and that is all we have to decide. Even if the wisdom of the policy be regarded as debatable and its effects uncertain, still the legislature is entitled to its judgment.

There is an additional and compelling consideration which recent economic experience has brought into a strong light. The exploitation of a class of workers who are in an unequal position with respect to bargaining power and are thus relatively defenceless against the denial of a living wage is not only detrimental to their health and well being but casts a direct burden for their support upon the community. What these workers lose in wages the taxpayers are called upon to pay. The bare cost of living must be met. We may take judicial notice of the unparalleled demands for relief which arose during the recent period of depression and still continue to an alarming extent despite the degree of economic recovery which has been achieved. It is unnecessary to cite official statistics to establish what is of common knowledge through the length and breadth of the land. While in the instant case no factual brief has been presented, there is no reason to doubt that the State of Washington has encountered the same social problem that is present elsewhere. The community is not bound to provide what is in effect a subsidy for unconscionable employers. The community may direct its law-making power to correct the abuse which springs from their selfish disregard of the public interest. The argument that the legislation in question constitutes an arbitrary discrimination, because it does not extend to men, is unavailing. This Court has frequently held that the legislative authority, acting within its proper field, is not bound to extend its regulation to all cases which it might possibly reach. The legislature "is free to recognize degrees of harm and it may confine its restrictions to those classes of cases where the need is deemed to be clearest." If "the law presumably hits the evil where it is most felt, it is not to be overthrown because there are other instances to which it might have been applied." There is no "doctrinaire requirement" that the legislation should be couched in all embracing terms. This familiar principle has repeatedly been applied to legislation which singles out women, and particular classes of women, in the exercise of the State's protective power. Their relative need in the presence of the evil, no less than the existence of the evil itself, is a matter for the legislative judgment.

Our conclusion is that the case of *Adkins v. Children's Hospital,* supra, should be, and it is, overruled. The judgment of the Supreme Court of the State of Washington is affirmed.

Sutherland, Justice, Van Devanter, Justice, McReynolds, Justice, Butler, Justice dissented.

From: 300 U.S. 379 (1937).

CHIEF JUSTICE CHARLES EVANS HUGHES'S OPINION ON ADMISSION OF A NEGRO STUDENT TO THE UNIVERSITY OF MISSOURI LAW SCHOOL, 1938

Predating by some sixteen years the Brown v. Board of Education *decision of 1954—which ordered the racial integration of the nation's public schools—this 1938 decision ruled that the segregation of the University of Missouri law school was an unconstitutional violation of the civil rights of African-American students. Gradually, the Court would move from postgraduate schools to universities and, finally, with* Brown, *to public schools as well.*

Hughes, Charles Evans, Justice: . . . The state court stresses the advantages that are afforded by the law schools of the adjacent states—Kansas, Nebraska, Iowa, and Illinois—which admit nonresident Negroes. The court considered that these were schools of high standing where one desiring to practice law in Missouri can get "as sound, comprehensive, valuable legal education" as in the University of Missouri; that the system of education in the former is the same as that in the latter and is designed to give the students a basis for the practice of law in any state where the Anglo-American system of law obtains; that the law school of the University of Missouri does not specialize in Missouri law and that the course of study and the casebooks used in the five schools are substantially identical.

Petitioner insists that for one intending to practice in Missouri, there are special advantages in attending a law school there, both in relation to the opportunities for the particular study of Missouri law and for the observation of the local courts, and also in view of the prestige of the Missouri law school among the citizens of the state, his prospective clients. Proceeding with its examination of relative advantages, the state court found that the difference in distances to be traveled afforded no substantial ground of complaint and that there was an adequate appropriation to meet the full tuition fees which petitioner would have to pay.

We think that these matters are beside the point. The basic consideration is not as to what sort of opportunities other states provide, or whether they are as good as those in Missouri, but as to what opportunities Missouri itself furnishes to white students and denies to Negroes solely upon the ground of color. The admissibility of laws separating the races in the enjoyment of privileges afforded by the state rests wholly upon the equality of the privileges which the laws give to the separated groups within the state. The question here is not of a duty of the state to supply legal training, or of the quality of the training which it does supply, but of its duty when it provides such training to furnish it to the residents of the state upon the basis of an equality of right.

By the operation of the laws of Missouri a privilege has been created for white law students which is denied to Negroes by reason of their race. The white resident is afforded legal education within the state; the Negro resident having the same qualifications is refused it there and must go outside the state to obtain it. That is a denial of the equality of legal right to the enjoyment of the privilege which the state has set up, and the provision for the payment of tuition fees in another state does not remove the discrimination.

The equal protection of the laws is "a pledge of the protection of equal laws." *Yick Wo v. Hopkins*, 118 United States 356, 369. Manifestly, the obligation of the state to give the protection of equal laws can be performed only where its laws operate, that is, within its own jurisdiction. It is there that the equality of legal right must be maintained. That obligation is imposed by the Constitution upon the states severally as governmental entities—each responsible for its own laws establishing the rights and duties of persons within its borders. It is an obligation the burden of which cannot be cast by one state upon another, and no state can be excused from performance by what another state may do or fail to do. That separate responsibility of each state within its own sphere is of the essence of statehood maintained under our dual system.

It seems to be implicit in respondents' argument that if other states did not provide courses for legal education, it would nevertheless be the constitutional duty of Missouri when it supplied such courses for white students to make equivalent provision for Negroes. But that plain duty would exist because it rested upon the state independently of the action of other states. We find it impossible to conclude that what otherwise would be an unconstitutional discrimination, with respect to the legal right to the enjoyment of opportunities within the state, can be justified by requiring resort to opportunities elsewhere. That resort may mitigate the inconvenience of the discrimination but cannot serve to validate it.

Nor can we regard the fact that there is but a limited demand in Missouri for the legal education of Negroes as excusing the discrimination in favor of whites. We had occasion to consider a cognate question in the case of *McCabe v. Atchison, T. & S. F. Ry. Co.* There the argument was advanced, in relation to the provision by a carrier of sleeping cars, dining and chair cars, that the limited demand by Negroes justified the state in permitting the furnishing of such accommodations exclusively for white persons.

We found that argument to be without merit. It made, we said, the constitutional right "depend upon the number of persons who may be discriminated against, whereas the essence of the constitutional right is that it is a personal one. Whether or not particular facilities shall be provided may doubtless be conditioned upon there being a reasonable demand therefor, but, if facilities are provided, substantial equality of treatment of persons traveling under like conditions cannot be refused. It is the individual who is entitled to the equal protection of the laws, and if he is denied by a common carrier, acting in the matter under the authority of a state law, a facility or convenience in the course of his journey which under substantially the same circumstances is furnished to another traveler, he may properly complain that his constitutional privilege has been invaded." *Id.*, pp. 161, 162.

Here, petitioner's right was a personal one. It was as an individual that he was entitled to the equal protection of the laws, and the state was bound to furnish him within its borders facilities for legal education substantially equal to those which the state there afforded for persons of the white race, whether or not other Negroes sought the same opportunity.

It is urged, however, that the provision for tuition outside the state is a temporary one—that it is intended to operate merely pending the establishment of a law department for Negroes at Lincoln University. While in that sense the discrimination may be termed temporary, it may nevertheless continue for an indefinite period by reason of the discretion given to the curators of Lincoln University and the alternative of arranging for tuition in other states, as permitted by the state law as construed by the state court, so long as the curators find it unnecessary and impracticable to provide facilities for the legal instruction of Negroes within the state. In that view, we cannot regard the discrimination as excused by what is called its temporary character.

We do not find that the decision of the state court turns on any procedural question. The action was for mandamus, but it does not appear that the remedy would have been deemed inappropriate if the asserted federal right had been sustained. In that situation the remedy by mandamus was found to be a proper one in *University of Maryland v. Murray*, supra.

In the instant case, the state court did note that petitioner had not applied to the management of Lincoln University for legal training. But, as we have said, the state court did not rule that it would have been the duty of the curators to grant such an application, but on the contrary took the view, as we understand it, that the curators were entitled under the state law to refuse such an application and in its stead to provide for petitioner's tuition in an adjacent state.

That conclusion presented the federal question as to the constitutional adequacy of such a provision while equal opportunity for legal training within the state was not furnished, and this federal question the state court entertained and passed upon. We must conclude that in so doing the court denied the federal right which petitioner set up and the question as to the cor-rectness of that decision is before us. We are of the opinion that the ruling was error, and that petitioner was entitled to be admitted to the law school of the state university in the absence of other and proper provision for his legal training within the state.

The judgment of the Supreme Court of Missouri is reversed and the cause is remanded for further proceedings not inconsistent with this opinion.

From: U.S. (1938)

SECTION 4 International Affairs

HOOVER'S PROPOSAL FOR ONE-YEAR MORATORIUM ON INTERGOVERNMENTAL DEBTS, JUNE 20, 1931

During World War I, the United States loaned billions of dollars to its allies in Europe, especially England and France. In addition, Germany was saddled with reparations payments to the Allies. During the course of the 1920s, many of these European countries fell behind in their payments, a situation that grew worse with the onset of the Great Depression in 1929. With the passage of the Smoot-Hawley tariff, which raised rates on imports to unprecedented levels, Europeans found it difficult to trade with the United States and gain the dollars they needed to pay back the loans, creating an international payments crisis. To alleviate this crisis, President Herbert Hoover ordered a moratorium on payments, though he refused to cancel the debts altogether, as some economists suggested.

President [Herbert Hoover] made the following statement:

The American Government proposes the postponement during one year of all payments on intergovernmental debts, reparations and relief debts, both principal and interest, of course, not including obligations of governments held by private parties. Subject to confirmation by Congress, the American Government will postpone all payments upon the debts of foreign governments to the American Government payable during the fiscal year beginning July 1 next, conditional on a like postponement for one year of all payments on intergovernmental debts owing the important creditor powers.

The purpose of this action is to give the forthcoming year to the economic recovery of the world and to help free the recuperative forces already in motion in the United States from retarding influences from abroad.

The world wide depression has affected the countries of Europe more severely than our own. Some of these countries are feeling to a serious extent the drain of this depression on national economy. The fabric of intergovernmental debts, supportable in normal times, weighs heavily in the midst of this depression.

From a variety of causes arising out of the depression such as the fall in the price of foreign commodities and the lack of confidence in economic and political stability abroad there is an abnormal movement of gold into the United States which is lowering the credit stability of many foreign countries. These and the other difficulties abroad diminish buying power for our exports and in a measure are the cause of our continued unemployment and continued lower prices to our farmers.

Wise and timely action should contribute to relieve the pressure of these adverse forces in foreign countries and should assist in the reestablishment of confidence, thus forwarding political peace and economic stability in the world.

Authority of the President to deal with this problem is limited as this action must be supported by the Congress. It has been assured the cordial support of leading members of both parties in the Senate and the House. The essence of this proposition is to give time to permit debtor governments to recover their national prosperity. I am suggesting to the American people that they be wise creditors in their own interest and be good neighbors.

I wish to take this occasion also to frankly state my views upon our relations to German reparations and the debts owed to us by the allied Governments of Europe. Our government has not been a party to, or exerted any voice in determination of reparation obligations. We purposely did not participate in either general reparations or the division of colonies or property. The repayments of debts due to us from the Allies for the advances for war and reconstruction were settled upon a basis not contingent upon German reparations or related thereto. Therefore, reparations are necessarily wholly a European problem with which we have no relation.

I do not approve in any remote sense of the cancellation of the debts to us. World confidence would not be enhanced by such action. None of our debtor nations have ever suggested it. But as the basis of the settlement of these debts was the capacity under normal conditions of the debtor to pay, we should be consistent with our own policies and principles if we take into account the abnormal situation now existing in the world. I am sure the American people have no desire to attempt to extract any sum beyond the capacity of any debtor to pay and it is our view that broad vision requires that our government should recognize the situation as it exists.

This course of action is entirely consistent with the policy which we have hitherto pursued. We are not involved in the discussion of strictly European problems, of which the payment of German reparations is one. It represents our willingness to make a contribution to the early restoration of world prosperity in which our own people have so deep an interest.

I wish further to add that while this action has no bearing on the conference for limitation of land armaments to be held next February, inasmuch as the burden of competitive armaments has contributed to bring about this depression, we trust that by this evidence of our desire to assist we shall have contributed to the good will which is so necessary in the solution of this major question.

From: William Starr Myers, ed. *The State Papers and Other Public Writings of Herbert Hoover*. Garden City, NY: Doubleday, Doran and Company, 1934.

ROOSEVELT'S LETTER TO SOVIET DIPLOMAT MAKSIM LITVINOV ON U.S. RECOGNITION OF THE SOVIET UNION, NOVEMBER 16, 1933

In 1917, Communists—known as Bolsheviks—seized power during a revolution in Russia. The new state, eventually calling itself the Soviet Union, was not recognized by the United States at the time. Indeed, the United States participated in a multination invasion force to isolate the new revolutionary government. Upon coming to office in March 1933, President Franklin D. Roosevelt made recognition of the Soviet Union one of his first foreign policy initiatives. The following two letters from Roosevelt to Russian Foreign Minister Maksim Litvinov announce Washington's intention to recognize the government in Moscow.

The White House, Washington
November 16, 1933

My dear Mr. Litvinov:

I am very happy to inform you that as a result of our conversations the Government of the United States has decided to establish normal diplomatic relations with the Government of the Union of Soviet Socialist Republics and to exchange ambassadors.

I trust that the relations now established between our peoples may forever remain normal and friendly, and that our Nations henceforth may cooperate for their mutual benefit and for the preservation of the peace of the world.

I am, my dear Mr. Litvinov,

Very sincerely yours,
Franklin D. Roosevelt

The White House, Washington
November 16, 1933

My dear Mr. Litvinov:

I am glad to have received the assurance expressed in your note to me of this date that it will be the fixed policy of the Government of the Union of Soviet Socialist Republics:

1. To respect scrupulously the indisputable right of the United States to order its own life within its own jurisdiction in its own way and to refrain from interfering in any manner in the internal affairs of the United States, its territories or possessions.

2. To refrain, and to restrain all persons in Government service and all organizations of the Government or under its direct or indirect control, including organizations in receipt of any financial assistance from it, from any act overt or covert liable in any way whatsoever to injure the tranquillity, prosperity, order, or security of the whole or any part of the United States, its territories or possessions, and, in particular, from any act tending to incite or encourage armed intervention, or any agitation or propaganda having as an aim, the violation of the territorial integrity of the United States, its territories or possessions, or the bringing

about by force of a change in the political or social order of the whole or any part of the United States, its territories or possessions.

3. Not to permit the formation or residence on its territory of any organization or group—and to prevent the activity on its territory of any organization or group, or of representatives or officials of any organization or group—which makes claim to be the Government of, or makes attempt upon the territorial integrity of, the United States, its territories or possessions; not to form, subsidize, support or permit on its territory military organizations or groups having the aim of armed struggle against the United States, its territories or possessions and to prevent any recruiting on behalf of such organizations and groups.

4. Not to permit the formation or residence on its territory of any organization or group—and to prevent the activity on its territory of any organization or

group, or of representatives or officials of any organization or group—which has as an aim the overthrow or the preparation for the overthrow of, or the bringing about by force of a change in the political or social order of the whole or any part of the United States, its territories or possessions.

It will be the fixed policy of the Executive of the United States within the limits of the powers conferred by the Constitution and the laws of the United States to adhere reciprocally to the engagements above expressed.

I am, my dear Mr. Litvinov,

Very sincerely yours,
Franklin D. Roosevelt

From: Samuel Rosenman, ed. *Public Papers and Addresses of Franklin D. Roosevelt*, Vol. 2, p. 471. New York: Random House, 1938–1950.

STATE DEPARTMENT REPORT ON NAZI GERMANY, APRIL 17, 1934

While the United States remained staunchly isolationist in the early and middle 1930s, its foreign diplomats kept on eye on developments in Europe, most especially the rise to power of the Nazi regime in Germany. This report, filed by Douglas Miller, the acting commercial attaché in Berlin, makes it quite clear that American policy-makers were aware of the racist and expansionist policies of the new regime under Adolf Hitler.

The fundamental purpose [of German government policy] is to secure a greater share of the world's future for the Germans, the expansion of German territory and growth of the German race until it constitutes the largest and most powerful nation in the world, and ultimately, according to some Nazi leaders, until it dominates the entire globe.

The German people suffering from a traditional inferiority complex, smarting from their defeat in the war and the indignities of the post-war period, disillusioned in their hopes of a speedy return to prosperity along traditional lines, inflamed by irresponsible demagogic slogans and flattered by the statement that their German racial inheritance gives them inherent superior rights over other peoples, have to a large mea-

sure adopted the National Socialist point of view for the time being.

ECONOMIC AIMS

There are two other purposes subsidiary to the main purpose. Germany is to be made the economic center of a self-sustaining territorial block whose dependent nations in Central and Eastern Europe will look to Berlin for leadership. This block is to be so constituted that it can defy war time blockade and be large enough to give the peoples in it the benefits of free trade now enjoyed by the 48 American States. In accordance with this purpose, an agricultural self-sufficiency program has been adopted, foreign foodstuffs are being rigorously excluded or the imported supply secured in increasing quantities from Central and Southeastern Europe. A hereditary peasantry has been set up, firmly attached to the soil through the prohibition of the sale or mortgaging of the peasants' land or crops. An increasing number of commodities have been placed under Government monopolies with fixed prices to consumers and producers; the principle of the *numerus clausus* or fixed number of persons engaged in any occupation has been increasingly adopted. The National Socialist conception of the correct or Government-fixed price instead of the price fixed by supply and demand has been introduced.

SOCIAL AIMS

The second subsidiary purpose is the welding of all individuals in the present and future Greater Germany into a homogeneous racial family, gladly obedient to the will of its leader, with class and cultural differences inside the country eliminated, but a sharp line drawn between Germans and the foreign world outside. In carrying out this purpose, the Jews are to be entirely eliminated, the Slavic or eastern elements in the population to be minimized and eventually bred out of the race. A national religion is in process of organization; trade unions, political parties and all social, political, cultural, trade or other organizations not affiliated with the National Socialist party, have been abolished, the individual's rights have been largely taken away. In the future the nation is to count for everything, the individual for nothing. Germany is to engage in a gigantic struggle with the rest of the world to grow at the expense of its neighbors. The German population owes the nation the patriotic duty of supporting it and bringing forward all necessary sacrifices to reach the common goal.

RETENTION OF POWER

To these long-distance objectives must be added the fourth and most important purpose of all, namely to retain control at all costs. The National Socialist party may compromise on distant objectives, if necessary, but cannot compromise on a question of retaining its absolute hold on the German people. This control had been gained by making most irresponsible and extravagant promises; by the studied use of the press, the radio, public meetings, parades, flags, uniforms, and all methods of working on popular psychology and finally by the use of force. This control once lost, could never be regained. It is absolutely necessary for the party to continue to make a show of success and to keep popular enthusiasm and fanaticism alive. There must be no open criticism or grumbling, even discussion of the future form of the State, the form in which industry is to be organized, or the laws regarding the hereditary peasantry is prohibited. Since the German public is politically inept and unusually docile, the Nazi movement

has been able to dominate the situation for the past year, but the hard facts of the economic situation are beginning to be felt by the more intelligent Germans, particularly bankers, business men, professional men and persons who have touch with the outside world.

DANGER OF WAR

The Nazis are not satisfied with the existing map of Europe. They are at heart belligerent and aggressive. True, they desire nothing more than a period of peace for several years in which they can gradually re-arm and discipline their people. This period may be 5 years, 10 years, or longer, but the more completely their experiments succeed the more certain is a large-scale war in Europe some day.

NAZIS WANT TO WIPE OUT 1918

In estimating the aims and purposes of the National Socialist movement, we must not make the mistake of putting too much reliance on public statements designed for consumption abroad which breathe the spirit of [peace and good will] and assert the intention of the Government to promote the welfare of the German people and good relations with their neighbors. Nor should we imagine that the present Government leaders will feel and act as we would in their circumstances, namely think only of Germany's welfare. The real emotional drive behind the Nazi program is not so much love of their own country as dislike of other countries. The Nazis will never be content in merely promoting the welfare of the German people. They desire to be feared and envied by foreigners and to wipe out the memory of 1918 by inflicting humiliations in particular upon the French, the Poles, the Czechs and anybody else they can get their hands on.

A careful examination of Hitler's book and his public speeches reveals the fact that he cannot be considered as absolutely sane and normal on this subject. The same is true of many other Nazi leaders. They have capitalized on the wounded inferiority complex of the German people, and magnified their own bitter feelings into a cult of dislike against the foreign world which is past the bounds of ordinary good sense and reason. Let us repeat this fact and let it sink in, the National Socialist movement is building a tremendous military machine, physically very poorly armed, but morally aggressive and belligerent. The control of this machine lies in the hands of narrow, ignorant and unscrupulous adventurers who have been slightly touched with madness from brooding over Germany's real or imagined wrongs, as well as the slights and indignities thrown in their own individual way as they attempted to organize the movement. Power of this kind concentrated in hands like these is dangerous. The Nazis are determined to secure more power and more territory in Europe. If this is voluntarily given to them by peaceful means, well and good, but if not, they will certainly use force. That is the only meaning behind the manifold activities of the movement in Germany today.

From: *Peace and War: United States Foreign Policy, 1931.* Washington, DC: Government Printing Office, 1943, pp. 211–214.

STATE DEPARTMENT REPORT ON IMPERIAL JAPAN, DECEMBER 27, 1934

While the vast majority of Americans were preoccupied with the country's own internal economic difficulties in the early and middle 1930s, U.S. personnel stationed at embassies abroad—particularly in Japan, Germany, and Italy—were taking note of the ominous developments in these countries. In this report American ambassador in Tokyo Joseph Grew argues that the United States should not concede hegemony over the Far East to Japan, for fear it will only strengthen militarists in that country.

. . . The thought which is uppermost in my mind is that the United States is faced, and will be faced in future, with two main alternatives. One is to be prepared to withdraw from the Far East, gracefully and gradually perhaps, but not the less effectively in the long run, permitting our treaty rights to be nullified, the Open Door to be closed, our vested economic interests to be dissolved and our commerce to operate unprotected. There are those who advocate this course, and who have advocated it to me personally on the ground that any other policy will entail the risk of eventual war with Japan. . . . In their opinion, "the game is not worth the candle" because the United States can continue to subsist comfortably even after relinquishing its varied interests in the Far East, thereby eliminating the risk of future war.

The other main alternative is to insist, and to continue to insist, not aggressively yet not the less firmly on the maintenance of our legitimate rights and interests in this part of the world and, so far as practicable, to support the normal development of those interests constructively and progressively.

There has already been abundant indication that the present Administration in Washington proposes to follow the second of these alternatives. For purposes of discussion we may therefore, I assume, discard the hypothesis of withdrawal and examine the future outlook with the assurance that our Government has not the slightest intention of relinquishing the legitimate rights, vested interests, non-discriminatory privileges for equal opportunity and healthful commercial development of the United States in the Far East. . . .

The administration of that policy from day to day becomes a matter of diplomacy, sometimes delicate, always important, for much depends on the method and manner of approach to the various problems with which we have been, are, and will continue to be faced. With the ultra-sensitiveness of the Japanese, arising out of a marked inferiority complex which manifests itself in the garb of an equally marked superiority complex, with all its attendant bluster, chauvinism, xenophobia and organized national propaganda, the method and manner of dealing with current controversies assume a significance and importance often out of all proportion to the nature of the controversy.

It is difficult for those who do not live in Japan to appraise the present temper of the country. An American Senator, according to reports, has recently recommended that we should accord parity to Japan in order to avoid future war. Whatever the Senator's views may be concerning the general policy that we should follow in the Far East, he probably does not realize what harm that sort of public statement does in strengthening the Japanese stand and in reinforcing the aggressive ambitions of the expansionists. The Japanese press of course picks out such statements by prominent Americans and publishes them far and wide, thus confirming the general belief in Japan that the pacifist element in the United States is preponderantly strong and in the last analysis will control the policy and action of our Government. Under such circumstances there is a general tendency to characterize our diplomatic representations as bluff and to believe that they can safely be disregarded without fear of implementation. It would be helpful if those who share the Senator's views could hear and read some of the things that are constantly being said and written in Japan, to the effect that Japan's destiny is to subjugate and rule the world [sic], and could realize the expansionist ambitions which lie not far from the surface in the minds of certain elements in the Army and Navy, the patriotic societies and the intense nationalists throughout the country. Their aim is to obtain trade control and eventually predominant political influence in China, the Philippines, the Straits Settlements, Siam and the Dutch East Indies, the Maritime Provinces [of the Soviet Union] and Vladivostok, one step at a time, as in Korea and Manchuria, pausing intermittently to consolidate and then continuing as soon as the intervening obstacles can be overcome by diplomacy or force. With such dreams of empire cherished by many, and with an army and navy capable of taking the bit in their own teeth and running away with it regardless of the restraining influence of the saner heads of the Government in Tokyo (a risk which unquestionably exists and of which we have already had ample evidence in the Manchurian affair), we would be reprehensibly somnolent if we were to trust to the security of treaty restraints or international comity to safeguard our own interests or, indeed, our own property.

I may refer here to my dispatch No. 608 of December 12, 1933, a re-reading of which is respectfully invited because it applies directly to the present situation. That dispatch reported a confidential conversation with the Netherlands Minister, General Pabst, a shrewd and rational colleague with long experience in Japan, in which the Minister said that in his opinion the Japanese Navy, imbued as it is with patriotic and chauvinistic fervor and with a desire to emulate the deeds of the Army in order not to lose caste with the public, would be perfectly capable of descending upon and occupying Guam at a moment of crisis or, indeed, at any other moment, regardless of the ulterior consequences. I do not think that such an insane step is likely, yet the action of the Army in Manchuria, judged from the point of view of treaty rights and international comity, might also have been judged as insensate. The important fact is that under present circumstances, and indeed under circumstances which may continue in future (although the pendulum of chauvinism throughout Japanese history has swung to and fro in periodic cycles of intensity and temporary relaxation) the armed forces of the country are perfectly capable of overriding the restraining control of the Government and of committing what might well amount to national "hara-kiri" in a mistaken conception of patriotism.

When Japanese speak of Japan's being the "stabilizing factor" and the "guardian of peace" of East Asia, what they have in mind is a *Pax Japonica* with eventual complete commercial control, and, in the minds of some, eventual complete political control of East Asia. While Ambassador Saito may have been misquoted in a recent issue of the Philadelphia Bulletin as saying that Japan will be prepared to fight to maintain that conception of peace, nevertheless that is precisely what is in the minds of many Japanese today. There is a swashbuckling temper in the country, largely developed by military propaganda, which can lead Japan during the next few years, or in the next few generations, to any extremes unless the saner minds in the Government prove able to cope with it and to restrain the country from national suicide.

The efficacy of such restraint is always problematical. Plots against the Government are constantly being hatched. We hear, for instance, that a number of young officers of the 3rd Infantry Regiment and students from the Military Academy in Tokyo were found on November 22 to have planned to assassinate various high members of the Government, including [prime minister] Count Makino, and that students of the Military Academy were confined to the school area for a few days after the discovery of that plot, which had for its object the placing in effect at once of the provisions of the now celebrated "Army pamphlet" (see dispatch No. 1031 of November 1, 1934). A similar alleged plot to attack the politicians at the opening of the extraordinary session of the Diet—-another May 1st incident—is also said to have been discovered and nipped in the bud. Such plots aim to form a military dictatorship. It is of course impossible to substantiate these rumors, but they are much talked about and it is unlikely that so much smoke would materialize without some fire. I wish that more Americans could come out here and live here and gradually come to sense the real potential risks and dangers of the situation instead of speaking and writing academically on a subject which they know nothing whatever about, thereby contributing ammunition to the Japanese military and extremists who are stronger than they have been for many a day. The idea that a great body of liberal thought lying just beneath the surface since 1931 would be sufficiently strong to emerge and assume control with a little foreign encouragement is thoroughly mistaken. The liberal thought is there, but it is inarticulate and largely impotent, and in all probability will remain so for some time to come.

At this point I should like to make the following observation. From reading this dispatch, and perhaps from other reports periodically submitted by the Embassy, one might readily get the impression that we are developing something of an "anti-Japanese" complex. This is not the case. One can dislike and disagree with certain members of a family without necessarily feeling hostility to the family itself. For me there are no finer people in the world than the type of Japanese exemplified by such men as . . . and a host of others. I am rather inclined to place . . . in the same general category; if he could have his way unhampered by the military I believe that he would steer the country into safer and saner channels. One of these friends once sadly remarked to us: "We Japanese are always putting our worst foot foremost, and we are too proud to explain ourselves." This is profoundly true. Theirs has been and is a "bungling diplomacy." They habitually play their cards badly. The declaration of the oil monopoly in Manchuria at this particular juncture, thereby tending to drive Great Britain into the other camp at a moment when closer Anglo-Japanese cooperation was very much in view, was [a case in point]. While it is true that the military and the extremists are primarily responsible for the "bungling diplomacy" of Japan, the Japanese as a race tend to be inarticulate, more at home in action than with words. . . .

Theodore Roosevelt enunciated the policy "Speak softly but carry a big stick." If our diplomacy in the Far East is to achieve favorable results, and if we are to reduce the risk of an eventual war with Japan to a minimum, that is the only way to proceed. Such a war may be unthinkable, and so it is, but the spectre of it is always present and will be present for some time to come. It would be criminally short-sighted to discard it from our calculations, and the best possible way to avoid it is to be adequately prepared, for preparedness is a cold fact which even the chauvinists, the military, the patriots and the ultra-nationalists in Japan, for all their bluster concerning "provocative measures" in the United States, can grasp and understand. The Soviet Ambassador recently told me that a prominent Japanese had said to him that the most important factor in avoiding a Japanese attack on the Maritime Provinces was the intensive Soviet military preparations in Siberia and Vladivostok. I believe this to be true, and again, and yet again, I urge that our own country be adequately prepared to meet all eventualities in the Far East.

The Counselor, the Naval Attaché and the Military Attaché of this Embassy, having separately read this dispatch, have expressed to me their full concurrence with its contents both in essence and detail.

From: *Peace and War: United States Foreign Policy, 1931.* Washington, DC: Government Printing Office, 1943, pp. 237–244, *passim.*

ROOSEVELT ON THE GOOD NEIGHBOR POLICY, DECEMBER 1, 1936

Among the most important foreign policy initiatives of the early Franklin D. Roosevelt administration was the so-called Good Neighbor policy, a shift in the relations maintained between the United States and its Latin American neighbors. Partly initiated in response to overtures made to various Latin American countries by Nazi Germany, the Good Neighbor policy outlined the end to decades of unilateral U.S. interference in the internal affairs of Latin American countries. In this speech to the Inter-American Conference for the Maintenance of Peace, given at Buenos Aires in December 1936, Roosevelt outlines the Good Neighbor policy to the delegates.

On the happy occasion of the convening of this Conference I address you thus, because members of a family need no introduction or formalities when, in pursuance of excellent custom, they meet together for their common good.

As a family we appreciate the hospitality of our host, President Justo, and the Government and people of Argentina; and all of us are happy that to our friend Dr. Saavedra Lamas has come the well-deserved award of the Nobel Prize for great service in the cause of world peace.

Three years ago the American family met in nearby Montevideo, the great capital of the Republic of Uruguay. They were dark days. A shattering depression, unparalleled in its intensity, held us, with the rest of the world, in its grip. And in our own Hemisphere a tragic war was raging between two of our sister Republics [Bolivia and Paraguay].

Yet, at that conference there was born not only

hope for our common future but a greater measure of mutual trust between the American democracies than had ever existed before. In this Western Hemisphere the night of fear has been dispelled. Many of the intolerable burdens of economic depression have been lightened and, due in no small part to our common efforts, every Nation of this Hemisphere is today at peace with its neighbors.

This is no conference to form alliances, to divide the spoils of war, to partition countries, to deal with human beings as though they were pawns in a game of chance. Our purpose, under happy auspices, is to assure the continuance of the blessings of peace.

Three years ago, recognizing that a crisis was being thrust upon the New World, with splendid unanimity our twenty-one Republics set an example to the whole world by proclaiming a new spirit, a new day, in the affairs of this Hemisphere.

While the succeeding period has justified in full measure all that was said and done at Montevideo, it has unfortunately emphasized the seriousness of threats to peace among other Nations. Events elsewhere have served only to strengthen our horror of war and all that war means. The men, women, and children of the Americas know that warfare in this day and age means more than the mere clash of armies: they see the destruction of cities and of farms; they foresee that children and grandchildren, if they survive, will stagger for long years not only under the burden of poverty but also amid the threat of broken society and the destruction of constitutional government.

I am profoundly convinced that the plain people everywhere in the civilized world today wish to live in peace one with another. And still leaders and Governments resort to war. Truly, if the genius of mankind that has invented the weapons of death cannot discover the means of preserving peace, civilization as we know it lives in an evil day.

But we cannot now, especially in view of our common purpose, accept any defeatist attitude. We have learned by hard experience that peace is not to be had for the mere asking; that peace, like other great privileges, can be obtained only by hard and painstaking effort. We are here to dedicate ourselves and our countries to that work.

You who assemble today carry with you in your deliberations the hopes of millions of human beings in other less fortunate lands. Beyond the ocean we see continents rent asunder by old hatreds and new fanaticisms. We hear the demand that injustice and inequality be corrected by resorting to the sword and not by resorting to reason and peaceful justice. We hear the

cry that new markets can be achieved only through conquest. We read that the sanctity of treaties between Nations is disregarded.

We know, too, that vast armaments are rising on every side and that the work of creating them employs men and women by the millions. It is natural, however, for us to conclude that such employment is false employment; that it builds no permanent structures and creates no consumers' goods for the maintenance of a lasting prosperity. We know that Nations guilty of these follies inevitably face the day when either their weapons of destruction must be used against their neighbors or when an unsound economy, like a house of cards, will fall apart.

In either case, even though the Americas become involved in no war, we must suffer too. The madness of a great war in other parts of the world would affect us and threaten our good in a hundred ways. And the economic collapse of any Nation or Nations must of necessity harm our own prosperity.

Can we, the Republics of the New World, help the Old World to avert the catastrophe which impends? Yes; I am confident that we can.

First, it is our duty by every honorable means to prevent any future war among ourselves. This can best be done through the strengthening of the processes of constitutional democratic government; by making these processes conform to the modern need for unity and efficiency and, at the same time, preserving the individual liberties of our citizens. By so doing, the people of our Nations, unlike the people of many Nations who live under other forms of government, can and will insist on their intention to live in peace. Thus will democratic government be justified throughout the world.

In this determination to live at peace among ourselves we in the Americas make it at the same time clear that we stand shoulder to shoulder in our final determination that others who, driven by war madness or land hunger, might seek to commit acts of aggression against us will find a Hemisphere wholly prepared to consult together for our mutual safety and our mutual good. I repeat what I said in speaking before the Congress and the Supreme Court of Brazil: "Each one of us has learned the glories of independence. Let each one of us learn the glories of interdependence."

Secondly, and in addition to the perfecting of the mechanisms of peace, we can strive even more strongly than in the past to prevent the creation of those conditions which give rise to war. Lack of social or political justice within the borders of any Nation is always cause for concern. Through democratic processes we can strive to achieve for the Americas the highest possible standard of living conditions for all our people. Men and women blessed with political freedom, willing to work and able to find work, rich enough to maintain their families and to educate their children, contented with their lot in life and on terms of friendship with their neighbors, will defend themselves to the utmost, but will never consent to take up arms for a war of conquest.

Interwoven with these problems is the further self-evident fact that the welfare and prosperity of each of our Nations depend in large part on the benefits derived from commerce among ourselves and with other Nations, for our present civilization rests on the basis of an international exchange of commodities. Every Nation of the world has felt the evil effects of recent efforts to erect trade barriers of every known kind. Every individual citizen has suffered from them. It is no accident that the Nations which have carried this process farthest are those which proclaim most loudly that they require war as an instrument of their policy. It is no accident that attempts to be self-sufficient have led to falling standards for their people and to ever-increasing loss of the democratic ideals in a mad race to pile armament on armament. It is no accident that, because of these suicidal policies and the suffering attending them, many of their people have come to believe with despair that the price of war seems less than the price of peace.

This state of affairs we must refuse to accept with every instinct of defense, with every exhortation of enthusiastic hope, with every use of mind and skill.

I cannot refrain here from reiterating my gratification that in this, as in so many other achievements, the American Republics have given a salutary example to the world. The resolution adopted at the Inter-American Conference at Montevideo endorsing the principles of liberal trade policies has shone forth like a beacon in the storm of economic madness which has been sweeping over the entire world during these later years. Truly, if the principles there embodied find still wider application in your deliberations, it will be a notable contribution to the cause of peace. For my own part I have done all in my power to sustain the consistent efforts of my Secretary of State in negotiating agreements for reciprocal trade, and even though the individual results may seem small, the total of them is significant. These policies in recent weeks have received the approval of the people of the United States, and they have, I am sure, the sympathy of the other Nations here assembled.

There are many other causes for war—among them, long-festering feuds, unsettled frontiers, territorial rivalries. But these sources of danger which still exist in the Americas, I am thankful to say, are not only few in number but already on the way to peaceful adjudication. While the settlement of such controversies may necessarily involve adjustments at home or in our relations with our neighbors which may appear to involve material sacrifice, let no man or woman forget that there is no profit in war. Sacrifices in the cause of peace are infinitesimal compared with the holocaust of war.

Peace comes from the spirit and must be grounded in faith. In seeking peace, perhaps we can best begin by proudly affirming the faith of the Americas: the faith in freedom and its fulfillment, which has proved a mighty fortress beyond reach of successful attack in half the world.

That faith arises from a common hope and a common design given us by our fathers in differing form but with a single aim: freedom and security of the individual, which has become the foundation of our peace.

If, then, by making war in our midst impossible, and if within ourselves and among ourselves we can give greater freedom and fulfillment to the individual lives of our citizens, the democratic form of representative government will have justified the high hopes of the liberating fathers. Democracy is still the hope of the world. If we in our generation can continue its successful application in the Americas, it will spread and supersede other methods by which men are governed and which seem to most of us to run counter to our ideals of human liberty and human progress.

Three centuries of history sowed the seeds which grew into our Nations; the fourth century saw those Nations become equal and free and brought us to a common system of constitutional government; the fifth century is giving to us a common meeting ground of mutual help and understanding. Our Hemisphere has at last come of age. We are here assembled to show its unity to the world. We took from our ancestors a great dream. We here offer it back as a great unified reality.

Finally, in expressing our faith of the Western World, let us affirm:

That we maintain and defend the democratic form of constitutional representative government.

That through such government we can more greatly provide a wider distribution of culture, of education, of thought, and of free expression.

That through it we can obtain a greater security of life for our citizens and a more equal opportunity for them to prosper.

That through it we can best foster commerce and the exchange of art and science between Nations.

That through it we can avoid the rivalry of armaments, avert hatreds, and encourage good-will and true justice.

That through it we offer hope for peace and a more abundant life to the peoples of the whole world.

But this faith of the Western World will not be complete if we fail to affirm our faith in God. In the whole history of mankind, far back into the dim past before man knew how to record thoughts or events, the human race has been distinguished from other forms of life by the existence, the fact, of religion. Periodic attempts to deny God have always come and will always come to naught.

In the constitution and in the practice of our Nations is the right of freedom of religion. But this ideal, these words, presuppose a belief and a trust in God.

The faith of the Americas, therefore, lies in the spirit. The system, the sisterhood, of the Americas is impregnable so long as her Nations maintain that spirit.

In that faith and spirit we will have peace over the Western World. In that faith and spirit we will all watch and guard our Hemisphere. In that faith and spirit may we also, with God's help, offer hope to our brethren overseas.

From: B. D. Zevin, ed. *Nothing to Fear: The Selected Addresses of Franklin Delano Roosevelt, 1932–1945.* Boston: Houghton Mifflin, 1946.

ROOSEVELT'S "QUARANTINE" OF AGGRESSOR NATIONS SPEECH, OCTOBER 5, 1937

The "quarantine" speech, as it was called, was the first major policy statement made by President Franklin D. Roosevelt about the recent aggressions conducted by Japan (invasion of China), Italy (war against Ethiopia, intervention in Spain), and Germany (remilitarization, reoccupation of the Rhineland, intervention in Spain). Although Roosevelt mentioned none of the countries by name, he insisted in this 1937 speech that other nations join the United States in quarantining aggressor states. While historically an important milestone in the United State's reinvolvement in world affairs, the speech had little effect at the time, as an isolationist Congress and public largely prevented Roosevelt from acting on the suggestions offered in the speech.

. . . On my trip across the continent and back I have been shown many evidences of the result of common sense cooperation between municipalities and the Federal Government and I have been greeted by tens of thousands of Americans who have told me in every look and word that their material and spiritual well-being has made great strides forward in the past few years.

And yet, as I have seen with my own eyes, the prosperous farms, the thriving factories and the busy railroads, as I have seen the happiness and security and peace which covers our wide land, almost inevitably I have been compelled to contrast our peace with very different scenes being enacted in other parts of the world.

It is because the people of the United States under modern conditions must, for the sake of their own future, give thought to the rest of the world, that I, as the responsible executive head of the Nation, have chosen this great inland city and this gala occasion to speak to you on a subject of definite national importance.

The political situation in the world, which of late has been growing progressively worse, is such as to cause grave concern and anxiety to all the peoples and nations who wish to live in peace and amity with their neighbors.

Some fifteen years ago the hopes of mankind for a continuing era of international peace were raised to great heights when more than sixty nations solemnly pledged themselves not to resort to arms in furtherance of their national aims and policies. The high aspirations expressed in the Briand-Kellogg Peace Pact and the hopes for peace thus raised have of late given way to a haunting fear of calamity. The present reign of terror and international lawlessness began a few years ago.

It began through unjustified interference in the internal affairs of other nations or the invasion of alien territory in violation of treaties; and has now reached a stage where the very foundations of civilization are seriously threatened. The landmarks and traditions which have marked the progress of civilization toward a condition of law, order and justice are being wiped away.

Without a declaration of war and without warning or justification of any kind, civilians, including vast numbers of women and children, are being ruthlessly murdered with bombs from the air. In times of so-called peace, ships are being attacked and sunk by submarines without cause or notice. Nations are fomenting and taking sides in civil warfare in nations that have never done them any harm. Nations claiming freedom for themselves deny it to others.

Innocent peoples, innocent nations, are being cruelly sacrificed to a greed for power and supremacy which is devoid of all sense of justice and humane considerations.

To paraphrase a recent author, "perhaps we foresee a time when men, exultant in the technique of homicide, will rage so hotly over the world that every precious thing will be in danger, every book and picture and harmony, every treasure garnered through two millenniums, the small, the delicate, the defenseless—all will be lost or wrecked or utterly destroyed."

If those things come to pass in other parts of the world, let no one imagine that America will escape, that America may expect mercy, that this Western Hemisphere will not be attacked and that it will continue tranquilly and peacefully to carry on the ethics and the arts of civilization.

If those days come "there will be no safety by arms, no help from authority, no answer in science. The storm will rage till every flower of culture is trampled and all human beings are leveled in a vast chaos."

If those days are not to come to pass—if we are to have a world in which we can breathe freely and live in amity without fear—the peace-loving nations must make a concerted effort to uphold laws and principles on which alone peace can rest secure.

The peace-loving nations must make a concerted effort in opposition to those violations of treaties and those ignorings of humane instincts which today are creating a state of international anarchy and instability from which there is no escape through mere isolation or neutrality.

Those who cherish their freedom and recognize and respect the equal right of their neighbors to be free and live in peace, must work together for the triumph of law and moral principles in order that peace, justice and confidence may prevail in the world. There must be a return to a belief in the pledged word, in the value of a signed treaty. There must be recognition of the fact that national morality is as vital as private morality.

A bishop wrote me the other day: "It seems to me that something greatly needs to be said in behalf of ordinary humanity against the present practice of carrying the horrors of war to helpless civilians, especially women and children. It may be that such a protest might be regarded by many, who claim to be realists, as futile, but may it not be that the heart of mankind is so filled with horror at the present needless suffering that that force could be mobilized in sufficient volume to lessen such cruelty in the days ahead. Even though it may take twenty years, which God forbid, for civilization to make effective its corporate protest against this barbarism, surely strong voices may hasten the day."

There is a solidarity and interdependence about the modern world, both technically and morally, which makes it impossible for any nation completely to isolate itself from economic and political upheavals in the rest of the world, especially when such upheavals appear to be spreading and not declining. There can be no stability or peace either within nations or between nations except under laws and moral standards adhered to by all. International anarchy destroys every foundation for peace. It jeopardizes either the immediate or the future security of every nation, large or small. It is, therefore, a matter of vital interest and concern to the people of the United States that the sanctity of international treaties and the maintenance of international morality be restored.

The overwhelming majority of the peoples and nations of the world today want to live in peace. They seek the removal of barriers against trade. They want to exert themselves in industry, in agriculture and in business, that they may increase their wealth through the production of wealth-producing goods rather than striving to produce military planes and bombs and machine guns and cannon for the destruction of human lives and useful property.

In those nations of the world which seem to be piling armament on armament for purposes of aggression, and those other nations which fear acts of aggression against them and their security, a very high proportion of their national income is being directly for armaments. It runs from thirty to as high as fifty per cent. We are fortunate. The proportion that we in the United States spend is far less—eleven or twelve per cent.

How happy we are that the circumstances of the moment permit us to put our money into bridges and boulevards, dams and reforestation, the conservation of our soil and many other kinds of useful works rather than into huge standing armies and vast supplies of implements of war.

I am compelled and you are compelled, nevertheless, to look ahead. The peace, the freedom and the security of ninety per cent of the population of the world is being jeopardized by the remaining ten per cent who are threatening a breakdown of all international order and law. Surely the ninety per cent who want to live in peace under law and in accordance with moral standards that have received almost universal acceptance through the centuries, can and must find some way to make their will prevail.

The situation is definitely of universal concern. The questions involved relate not merely to violations of specific provisions of particular treaties; they are questions of war and of peace, of international law and especially of principles of humanity. It is true that they involve definite violations of agreements, and especially of the Covenant of the League of Nations, the Briand-Kellogg Pact and the Nine Power Treaty. But they also involve problems of world economy, world security and world humanity.

It is true that the moral consciousness of the world must recognize the importance of removing injustices and well-founded grievances; but at the same time it must be aroused to the cardinal necessity of honoring sanctity of treaties, of respecting the rights and liberties of others and of putting an end to acts of international aggression.

It seems to be unfortunately true that the epidemic of world lawlessness is spreading.

When an epidemic of physical disease starts to spread, the community approves and joins in a quarantine of the patients in order to protect the health of the community against the spread of the disease.

It is my determination to pursue a policy of peace. It is my determination to adopt every practicable measure to avoid involvement in war. It ought to be inconceivable that in this modern era, and in the face of experience, any nation could be so foolish and ruthless as to run the risk of plunging the whole world into war by invading and violating, in contravention of solemn treaties, the territory of other nations that have done them no real harm and are too weak to protect themselves adequately. Yet the peace of the world and the welfare and security of every nation, including our own, is today being threatened by that very thing.

No nation which refuses to exercise forbearance and to respect the freedom and rights of others can long remain strong and retain the confidence and respect of other nations. No nation ever loses its dignity or its good standing by conciliating its differences, and by exercising great patience with, and consideration for, the rights of other nations.

War is a contagion, whether it be declared or undeclared. It can engulf states and peoples remote from the original scene of hostilities. We are determined to keep out of war, yet we cannot insure ourselves against the disastrous effects of war and the dangers of involvement. We are adopting such measures as will minimize our risk of involvement, but we cannot have complete protection in a world of disorder in which confidence and security have broken down.

If civilization is to survive, the principles of the Prince of Peace must be restored. Trust between nations must be revived.

Most important of all, the will for peace on the part of peace-loving nations must express itself to the end that nations that may be tempted to violate their agreements and the rights of others will desist from such a course. There must be positive endeavors to preserve peace.

America hates war. America hopes for peace. Therefore, America actively engages in the search for peace.

From: B. D. Zevin, ed. *Nothing to Fear: The Selected Addresses of Franklin Delano Roosevelt, 1932–1945.* Boston: Houghton Mifflin, 1946.

ROOSEVELT'S FIRESIDE CHAT ON THE EUROPEAN WAR, SEPTEMBER 3, 1939

On September 1, 1939, the armed forces of Nazi Germany invaded Poland, triggering declarations of war by England and France and formally initiating the hostilities of World War II. Two days later, President Franklin D. Roosevelt delivered one of his now-familiar radio chats on the subject. He told the American people that their country would maintain strict neutrality in the conflict. Yet, at the same time, he spoke out strongly against the aggression. This mix of outrage and neutrality was carefully gauged to capture the mood of the American people.

Tonight my single duty is to speak to the whole of America.

Until four-thirty this morning I had hoped against hope that some miracle would prevent a devastating war in Europe and bring to an end the invasion of Poland by Germany.

For four long years a succession of actual wars and constant crises have shaken the entire world and have threatened in each case to bring on the gigantic conflict which is today unhappily a fact.

It is right that I should recall to your minds the consistent and at times successful efforts of your Government in these crises to throw the full weight of the United States into the cause of peace. In spite of spreading wars I think that we have every right and every reason to maintain as a national policy the fundamental moralities, the teachings of religion and the continuation of efforts to restore peace—for some day, though the time may be distant, we can be of even greater help to a crippled humanity.

It is right, too, to point out that the unfortunate events of these recent years have, without question, been based on the use of force and the threat of force. And it seems to me clear, even at the outbreak of this great war, that the influence of America should be consistent in seeking for humanity a final peace which will eliminate, as far as it is possible to do so, the continued use of force between nations.

It is, of course, impossible to predict the future. I have my constant stream of information from American representatives and other sources throughout the world. You, the people of this country, are receiving news through your radios and your newspapers at every hour of the day.

You are, I believe, the most enlightened and the best informed people in all the world at this moment. You are subjected to no censorship of news, and I want to add that your Government has no information which it withholds or which it has any thought of withholding from you.

At the same time, as I told my press conference on Friday, it is of the highest importance that the press and the radio use the utmost caution to discriminate between actual verified fact on the one hand, and mere rumor on the other.

I can add to that by saying that I hope the people of this country will also discriminate most carefully between news and rumor. Do not believe of necessity everything you hear or read. Check up on it first.

You must master at the outset a simple but unalterable fact in modern foreign relations between nations. When peace has been broken anywhere, the peace of all countries everywhere is in danger.

It is easy for you and for me to shrug our shoulders and to say that conflicts taking place thousands of miles from the continental United States, and, indeed, thousands of miles from the whole American Hemisphere, do not seriously affect the Americas—and that all the United States has to do is to ignore them and go about its own business. Passionately though we may desire detachment, we are forced to realize that every word that comes through the air, every ship that sails the sea, every battle that is fought, does affect the American future.

Let no man or woman thoughtlessly or falsely talk of America sending its armies to European fields. At this moment there is being prepared a proclamation of American neutrality. This would have been done even if there had been no neutrality statute on the books, for this proclamation is in accordance with international law and in accordance with American policy.

This will be followed by a Proclamation required by the existing Neutrality Act. And I trust that in the days to come our neutrality can be made a true neutrality.

It is of the utmost importance that the people of

this country, with the best information in the world, think things through. The most dangerous enemies of American peace are those who, without well-rounded information on the whole broad subject of the past, the present and the future, undertake to speak with assumed authority, to talk in terms of glittering generalities, to give to the nation assurances or prophesies which are of little present or future value.

I myself cannot and do not prophesy the course of events abroad—and the reason is that, because I have of necessity such a complete picture of what is going on in every part of the world, I do not dare to do so. And the other reason is that I think it is honest for me to be honest with the people of the United States.

I cannot prophesy the immediate economic effect of this new war on our nation, but I do say that no American has the moral right to profiteer at the expense either of his fellow citizens or of the men, the women and the children who are living and dying in the midst of war in Europe.

Some things we do know. Most of us in the United States believe in spiritual values. Most of us, regardless of what church we belong to, believe in the spirit of the New Testament—a great teaching which opposes itself to the use of force, of armed force, of marching armies and falling bombs. The overwhelming masses of our people seek peace—peace at home, and the kind of peace in other lands which will not jeopardize our peace at home.

We have certain ideas and certain ideals of national safety, and we must act to preserve that safety today, and to preserve the safety of our children in future years.

That safety is and will be bound up with the safety of the Western Hemisphere and of the seas adjacent thereto. We seek to keep war from our own firesides by keeping war from coming to the Americas. For that we have historic precedent that goes back to the days of the Administration of President George Washington. It is serious enough and tragic enough to every American family in every State in the Union to live in a world that is torn by wars on other continents. Those wars today affect every American home. It is our national duty to use every effort to keep them out of the Americas.

And at this time let me make the simple plea that partisanship and selfishness be adjourned; and that national unity be the thought that underlies all others.

This Nation will remain a neutral Nation, but I cannot ask that every American remain neutral in thought as well. Even a neutral has a right to take account of facts. Even a neutral cannot be asked to close his mind or his conscience.

I have said not once, but many times, that I have seen war and that I hate war. I say that again and again.

I hope the United States will keep out of this war. I believe that it will. And I give you assurance and reassurance that every effort of your Government will be directed toward that end.

As long as it remains within my power to prevent, there will be no black-out of peace in the United States.

From: B. D. Zevin, ed. *Nothing to Fear: The Selected Addresses of Franklin Delano Roosevelt, 1932–1945.* Boston: Houghton Mifflin, 1946.

ACT OF HAVANA ON HEMISPHERIC DEFENSE, JULY 29, 1940

Since the mid-1930s, both Nazi Germany and Fascist Italy had made overtures to Latin American countries, promising those nations more favorable terms of trade than those that existed between them and other Western European countries and the United States. With the Nazi conquest of Holland and France in spring 1940 came the threat of Nazi control of these countries' colonies in Latin America. With the Act of Havana of July 29, 1940, the United States and various Latin American governments made it clear that they would not accept Nazi influence in or control of countries or colonies in the Western Hemisphere.

The governments represented in the second consultative meeting of American Foreign Ministers considering:

That, as a consequence of the acts which are developing on the European Continent, there might be produced in territories of possessions which some belligerent nations hold in America situations wherein that sovereignty may be extinguished or essentially affected, or the government suffers acephalism [becomes headless], generating peril for the peace of the Continent and creating a situation wherein the dominion of law and order and respect of life, liberty and property of the inhabitants disappears;

That the American republics would consider any transfer or attempt to transfer sovereignty, jurisdiction, possession or any interest or control in any of these regions to another non-American State as contrary to American sentiments, principles and rights of American States to maintain their security and political independence;

That the American republics would not recognize nor accept such transfer or intent to transfer or acquire interests or rights, direct or indirect, in any of these regions whatever might be the form employed to realize it;

That the American republics reserve the right to judge through their respective organs of government if some transfer or intent to transfer sovereignty, jurisdiction, cession or incorporation of geographical regions in America owned by European countries until Sept. 1, 1939, may impair their political independence even though there has been no formal transfer or change in the status of the regions;

That for this reason it is necessary to establish for unforeseen cases as for any other which may produce acephalism of the government in the said regions a regime of provisional administration, while arriving at the objective for free determination of the peoples;

That the American republics, as an international community which acts integrally and forcefully, supporting itself on political and juridical principles which have been applied for more than a century, have the incontestable right, in order to preserve their unity and security, to take under their administration said regions and to deliberate over their destinies in accordance with their respective degrees of political and economic development;

That the provisional and transitory character of the measures agreed upon does not mean forgetfulness or abrogation of the principle of non-intervention, the regulator of inter-American life, a principle proclaimed by the American Institute, recognized by the celebrated committee of experts on international law which met at Rio de Janeiro and consecrated in all its amplitude in the seventh Pan-American conference held at Montevideo;

That this community therefore has the international juridical capacity to act in such matters;

That in such a case the most adequate regime is that of provisional administration.

Desiring to protect their peace and security and to promote the interests of any of the regions to which this [document] refers and which are understood to be within the foregoing consideration;

Have resolved to conclude the following convention:

First—If a non-American State attempts directly or indirectly to substitute for another non-American State in the sovereignty or control which that [other State] exerted over any territory situated in America, thereby threatening the peace of the continent, said territory automatically will be considered to be within the stipulations of this convention, and will be submitted to a regime of provisional administration.

Second—That administration shall be executed—as it is considered advisable in each case—by one or more American States by virtue of previous consent.

Third—When administration is established over a region it shall be executed in the interest of the security of America and to the benefit of the administered region looking toward its well-being and development, until the region is found to be in condition to administer itself or to return to its former status, so long as this is compatible with the security of the American republics.

Fourth—Administration of the territory shall operate under conditions which guarantee freedom of conscience and faith with the restrictions demanded by the maintenance of public order and good habits.

Fifth—The administration shall apply local laws, coordinating them with the objectives of this convention, but it may adopt in addition those decisions necessary to solve situations concerning which no such local laws exist.

Sixth—In all that concerns commerce and industry the American nations shall enjoy equal conditions and the same benefits and the administrator never shall create a situation of privilege for himself or his compatriots or for any particular nations. Liberty of economic relations with all countries on a basis of reciprocity shall be maintained.

Seventh—The natives of the region shall participate as Citizens in the public administration and tribunals of justice with no other consideration than that of competence.

Eighth—In so far as possible rights of any kind shall be governed by local laws and customs, acquired to be protected in conformity with such laws.

Ninth—Forced labor shall be abolished in regions where it exists.

Tenth—The administration will provide means to diffuse public education in all grades, with the double aim of promoting the wealth of the region and better living conditions of the people, especially in regard to public and individual hygiene, and preparation of the exercise of political autonomy in the shortest time.

Eleventh—The natives of the region under administration shall have their own organic charter, which the administration shall establish, consulting the people in whatever way possible.

Twelfth—The administration shall submit an annual report to the inter-American organization charged with control of the administered regions, on the manner in which it carried out its mission, attaching accounts and measures adopted during the year in said region.

Thirteenth—The organization to which the preceding article refers shall be authorized to take cognizance of petitions which inhabitants of the region transmit through the intermediary of the administration with reference to the operation of the provisional administration. The administration shall remit, along with these petitions such observations as it considers convenient.

Fourteenth—First the administration shall be authorized for a period of three years, at the termination of which, and in case of necessity, it shall be renewed for successive periods of not longer than a decade.

Fifteenth—Expenses incurred in the exercise of the administration shall be covered by revenues from the administered region, but in case these are insufficient the deficit shall be covered by the administering nation or nations.

Sixteenth—There shall be established a commission which shall be called the "Inter-American Commission of Territorial Administration" and shall be composed of one representative for each of the States which ratify this convention, and it shall be the international organization to which the convention refers.

Any country which ratifies it [the convention] may call the first meeting, indicating the most convenient city. The commission shall elect a president, complete its organization and fix a definite headquarters. Two-thirds of its members shall constitute a quorum and two-thirds of the members present may adopt agreements.

Seventeenth—The commission is authorized to establish a provisional administration over regions to which the present convention applies; it also is authorized to install the said administration so that it will be operated by the number of States which will be determined according to the case, and to legalize its execution in terms of the preceding articles.

Eighteenth—The present convention will be opened for signatures of the American republics in Havana and shall be ratified by the high contracting parties in accordance with their constitutional procedures. The Secretary of State of the Republic of Cuba shall transmit, as soon as possible, authentic copies certified to the various governments to obtain ratifications. Instruments of ratification shall be deposited in the archives of the Pan-American Union in Washington, which shall notify the signatory governments of said deposit; such notification shall be considered as exchange of ratifications.

Nineteenth—The present convention shall be effective when two-thirds of the American States shall have deposited their respective instruments of ratification.

From: Reprinted from the *New York Times*, July 30, 1940.

ROOSEVELT'S "FOUR FREEDOMS" SPEECH, JANUARY 6, 1941

In his struggle to wrest aid for Britain from a reluctant, isolationist Congress, President Franklin D. Roosevelt made his famous "four freedoms" speech in January 1941, outlining the purpose of U.S. participation in the war. The four freedoms were freedom of speech and expression, freedom of religion, freedom from want, and freedom from fear. The speech was effective and helped win passage of the Lend-Lease Act, which provided billions of dollars in aid to Britain and other countries fighting the Axis powers of Germany, Italy, and Japan.

I address you, the Members of the Seventy-seventh Congress, at a moment unprecedented in the history of the Union. I use the word "unprecedented," because at no previous time has American security been as seriously threatened from without as it is today.

Since the permanent formation of our government under the Constitution, in 1789, most of the periods of crisis in our history have related to our domestic affairs. Fortunately, only one of these—the four year War between the States—ever threatened our national unity. Today, thank God, one hundred and thirty million Americans, in forty-eight States, have forgotten points of the compass in our national unity.

It is true that prior to 1914 the United States often had been disturbed by events in other Continents. We had even engaged in two wars with European nations and in a number of undeclared wars in the West Indies, in the Mediterranean and in the Pacific for the maintenance of American rights and for the principles of peaceful commerce. In no case, however, had a serious threat been raised against our national safety or our independence.

What I seek to convey is the historic truth that the United States as a Nation has at all times maintained opposition to any attempt to lock us in behind an ancient Chinese wall while the procession of civilization went past. Today, thinking of our children and their children, we oppose enforced isolation for ourselves or for any part of the Americas.

That determination of ours was proved, for example, during the quarter century of wars following the French Revolution.

While the Napoleonic struggles did threaten interests of the United States because of the French foothold in the West Indies and in Louisiana, and while we engaged in the War of 1812 to vindicate our right to peaceful trade, it is, nevertheless, clear that neither France nor Great Britain nor any other nation was aiming at domination of the whole world.

In like fashion from 1815 to 1914—99 years—no single war in Europe or in Asia constituted a real threat against our future or against the future of any other American nation.

Except in the Maximilian interlude in Mexico, no foreign power sought to establish itself in this Hemisphere; and the strength of the British fleet in the Atlantic has been a friendly strength. It is still a friendly strength.

Even when the World War broke out in 1914, it seemed to contain only a small threat of danger to our own American future. But, as time went on, the American people began to visualize what the downfall of democratic nations might mean to our own democracy.

We need not over emphasize imperfections in the Peace of Versailles. We need not harp on failure of the democracies to deal with problems of world reconstruction. We should remember that the Peace of 1919 was far less unjust than the kind of "pacification" which began even before Munich [1938], and which is being carried on under the new order of tyranny that seeks to spread over every continent today. The American

people have unalterably set their faces against that tyranny.

Every realist knows that the democratic way of life is at this moment being directly assailed in every part of the world—assailed either by arms, or by secret spreading of poisonous propaganda by those who seek to destroy unity and promote discord in nations still at peace.

During sixteen months this assault has blotted out the whole pattern of democratic life in an appalling number of independent nations, great and small. The assailants are still on the march, threatening other nations, great and small.

Therefore, as your President, performing my constitutional duty to "give to the Congress information of the state of the Union," I find it necessary to report that the future and the safety of our country and of our democracy are overwhelmingly involved in events far beyond our borders.

Armed defense of democratic existence is now being gallantly waged in four continents. If that defense fails, all the population and all the resources of Europe, Asia, Africa and Australasia will be dominated by the conquerors. The total of those populations and their resources greatly exceeds the sum total of the population and resources of the whole of the Western Hemisphere—many times over.

In times like these it is immature—and incidentally untrue—for anybody to brag that an unprepared America, single-handed, and with one hand tied behind its back, can hold off the whole world.

No realistic American can expect from a dictator's peace international generosity, or return of true independence, or world disarmament, or freedom of expression, or freedom of religion—or even good business.

Such a peace would bring no security for us or for our neighbors. "Those, who would give up essential liberty to purchase a little temporary safety, deserve neither liberty nor safety."

As a Nation we may take pride in the fact that we are softhearted; but we cannot afford to be soft-headed.

We must always be wary of those who with sounding brass and a tinkling cymbal preach the "ism" of appeasement.

We must especially beware of that small group of selfish men who would clip the wings of the American eagle in order to feather their own nests.

I have recently pointed out how quickly the tempo of modern warfare could bring into our very midst the physical attack which we must expect if the dictator nations win this war.

There is much loose talk of our immunity from immediate and direct invasion from across the seas. Obviously, as long as the British Navy retains its power, no such danger exists. Even if there were no British Navy, it is not probable that any enemy would be stupid enough to attack us by landing troops in the United States from across thousands of miles of ocean, until it had acquired strategic bases from which to operate.

But we learn much from the lessons of the past years in Europe—particularly the lesson of Norway, whose essential seaports were captured by treachery and surprise built up over a series of years.

The first phase of the invasion of this Hemisphere would not be the landing of regular troops. The necessary strategic points would be occupied by secret agents and their dupes—and great numbers of them are already here, and in Latin America.

As long as the aggressor nations maintain the offensive, they—not we—will choose the time and the place and the method of their attack.

That is why the future of all American Republics is today in serious danger.

That is why this Annual Message to the Congress is unique in our history.

That is why every member of the Executive Branch of the Government and every member of the Congress faces great responsibility—and great accountability.

The need of the moment is that our actions and our policy should be devoted primarily—almost exclusively—to meeting this foreign peril. For all our domestic problems are now a part of the great emergency.

Just as our national policy in internal affairs has been based upon a decent respect for the rights and dignity of all our fellowmen within our gates, so our national policy in foreign affairs has been based on a decent respect for the rights and dignity of all nations, large and small. And the justice of morality must and will win in the end.

Our national policy is this:

First, by an impressive expression of the public will and without regard to partisanship, we are committed to all-inclusive national defense.

Second, by an impressive expression of the public will and without regard to partisanship, we are committed to full support of all those resolute peoples, everywhere, who are resisting aggression and are thereby keeping war away from our Hemisphere. By this support, we express our determination that the democratic cause shall prevail; and we strengthen the defense and security of our own nation.

Third, by an impressive expression of the public will and without regard to partisanship we are committed to the proposition that principles of morality and considerations for our own security will never permit us to acquiesce in a peace dictated by aggressors and sponsored by appeasers. We know that enduring peace cannot be bought at the cost of other people's freedom.

In the recent national election there was no substantial difference between the two great parties in respect to that national policy. No issue was fought out on this line before the American electorate. Today, it is abundantly evident that American citizens everywhere are demanding and supporting speedy and complete action in recognition of obvious danger.

Therefore, the immediate need is a swift and driving increase in our armament production.

Leaders of industry and labor have responded to our summons. Goals of speed have been set. In some cases these goals are being reached ahead of time; in some cases we are on schedule; in other cases there are slight but not serious delays; and in some cases—and I am sorry to say very important cases—we are all concerned by the slowness of the accomplishment of our plans.

The Army and Navy, however, have made substantial progress during the past year. Actual experience is improving and speeding up our methods of production with every passing day. And today's best is not good enough for tomorrow.

I am not satisfied with the progress thus far made. The men in charge of the program represent the best in training, ability and patriotism. They are not satisfied with the progress thus far made. None of us will be satisfied until the job is done.

No matter whether the original goal was set too high or too low, our objective is quicker and better results.

To give two illustrations:

We are behind schedule in turning out finished airplanes; we are working day and night to solve the innumerable problems and to catch up.

We are ahead of schedule in building warships; but we are working to get even further ahead of schedule.

To change a whole nation from a basis of peace time production of implements of peace to a basis of war time production of implements of war is no small task. And the greatest difficulty comes at the beginning of the program, when new tools and plant facilities and new assembly lines and ship ways must first be constructed before the actual material begins to flow steadily and speedily from them.

The Congress, of course, must rightly keep itself informed at all times of the progress of the program. However, there is certain information, as the Congress itself will readily recognize, which, in the interests of our own security and those of the nations we are supporting, must needs be kept in confidence.

New circumstances are constantly begetting new needs for our safety. I shall ask this Congress for greatly increased new appropriations and authorizations to carry on what we have begun.

I also ask this Congress for authority and for funds sufficient to manufacture additional munitions and war supplies of many kinds, to be turned over to those nations which are now in actual war with aggressor nations.

Our most useful and immediate role is to act as an arsenal for them as well as for ourselves. They do not need man power. They do need billions of dollars worth of the weapons of defense.

The time is near when they will not be able to pay for them in ready cash. We cannot, and will not, tell them they must surrender, merely because of present inability to pay for the weapons which we know they must have.

I do not recommend that we make them a loan of dollars with which to pay for these weapons—a loan to be repaid in dollars.

I recommend that we make it possible for those nations to continue to obtain war materials in the United States, fitting their orders into our own program. Nearly all of their materiel would, if the time ever came, be useful for our own defense.

Taking counsel of expert military and naval authorities, considering what is best for our own security, we are free to decide how much should be kept here and how much should be sent abroad to our friends who by their determined and heroic resistance are giving us time in which to make ready our own defense.

For what we send abroad, we shall be repaid, within a reasonable time following the close of hostilities, in similar materials, or, at our option, in other goods of many kinds which they can produce and which we need.

Let us say to the democracies: "We Americans are vitally concerned in your defense of freedom. We are putting forth our energies, our resources and our organizing powers to give you the strength to regain and maintain a free world. We shall send you, in ever-increasing numbers, ships, planes, tanks, guns. This is our purpose and our pledge."

In fulfillment of this purpose we will not be intimidated by the threats of dictators that they will regard as a breach of international law and as an act of war our aid to the democracies which dare to resist their aggression. Such aid is not an act of war, even if a dictator should unilaterally proclaim it so to be.

When the dictators are ready to make war upon us, they will not wait for an act of war on our part. They did not wait for Norway or Belgium or the Netherlands to commit an act of war.

Their only interest is in a new one-way international law, which lacks mutuality in its observance, and, therefore, becomes an instrument of oppression.

The happiness of future generations of Americans may well depend upon how effective and how immediate we can make our aid felt. No one can tell the exact character of the emergency situations that we may be called upon to meet. The Nation's hands must not be tied when the Nation's life is in danger.

We must all prepare to make the sacrifices that the emergency—as serious as war itself—demands. Whatever stands in the way of speed and efficiency in defense preparations must give way to the national need.

A free nation has the right to expect full cooperation from all groups. A free nation has the right to look to the leaders of business, of labor, and of agriculture to take the lead in stimulating effort, not among other groups but within their own groups.

The best way of dealing with the few slackers or trouble makers in our midst is, first, to shame them by patriotic example, and, if that fails, to use the sovereignty of government to save government.

As men do not live by bread alone, they do not fight by armaments alone. Those who man our defenses, and those behind them who build our defenses, must have the stamina and courage which come from an unshakeable belief in the manner of life which they are defending. The mighty action which we are calling for, cannot be based on a disregard of all things worth fighting for.

The Nation takes great satisfaction and much strength from the things which have been done to make its people conscious of their individual stake in the preservation of democratic life in America. Those things have toughened the fibre of our people, have renewed their faith and strengthened their devotion to the institutions we make ready to protect.

Certainly this is no time to stop thinking about the social and economic problems which are the root cause of the social revolution which is today a supreme factor in the world.

There is nothing mysterious about the foundations of a healthy and strong democracy. The basic things expected by our people of their political and economic systems are simple. They are:

Equality of opportunity for youth and for others.

Jobs for those who can work.

Security for those who need it.

The ending of special privilege for the few.

The preservation of civil liberties for all.

The enjoyment of the fruits of scientific progress in a wider and constantly rising standard of living.

These are the simple and basic things that must never be lost sight of in the turmoil and unbelievable complexity of our modern world. The inner and abiding strength of our economic and political systems is dependent upon the degree to which they fulfill these expectations.

Many subjects connected with our social economy call for immediate improvement.

As examples:

We should bring more citizens under the coverage of old age pensions and unemployment insurance.

We should widen the opportunities for adequate medical care.

We should plan a better system by which persons deserving or needing gainful employment may obtain it.

I have called for personal sacrifice. I am assured of the willingness of almost all Americans to respond to that call.

A part of the sacrifice means the payment of more money in taxes. In my budget message I recommend that a greater portion of this great defense program be paid for from taxation than we are paying today. No person should try, or be allowed, to get rich out of this program; and the principle of tax payments in accordance with ability to pay should be constantly before our eyes to guide our legislation.

If the Congress maintains these principles, the voters, putting patriotism ahead of pocketbooks, will give you their applause.

In the future days, which we seek to make secure, we look forward to a world founded upon four essential human freedoms.

The first is freedom of speech and expression—everywhere in the world.

The second is freedom of every person to worship God in his own way—everywhere in the world.

The third is freedom from want—which, translated into world terms, means economic understandings which will secure to every nation a healthy peace time life for its inhabitants—everywhere in the world.

The fourth is freedom from fear—which, translated into world terms, means a world-wide reduction [in] armaments to such a point and in such a thorough fashion that no nation will be in a position to commit an act of physical aggression against any neighbor—anywhere in the world.

That is no vision of a distant millennium. It is a definite basis for a kind of world attainable in our own time and generation. That kind of world is the very antithesis of the so-called new order of tyranny which the dictators seek to create with the crash of a bomb.

To that new order we oppose the greater conception—the moral order. A good society is able to face schemes of world domination and foreign revolutions alike without fear.

Since the beginning of our American history we have been engaged in change—in a perpetual peaceful revolution—a revolution which goes on steadily, quietly adjusting itself to changing conditions—without the concentration camp or the quick-lime in the ditch. The world order which we seek is the cooperation of free countries, working together in a friendly, civilized society.

This Nation has placed its destiny in the hands and heads and hearts of its millions of free men and women; and its faith in freedom under the guidance of God. Freedom means the supremacy of human rights everywhere. Our support goes to those who struggle to gain those rights or keep them. Our strength is in our unity of purpose.

To that high concept there can be no end save victory.

From: B. D. Zevin, ed. *Nothing to Fear: The Selected Addresses of Franklin Delano Roosevelt, 1932–1945*. Boston: Houghton Mifflin, 1946.

LEND-LEASE ACT, MARCH 11, 1941

The Lend-Lease Act, passed on March 11, 1941, was the most ambitious effort to date to aid Britain and other countries fighting the Axis powers of Nazi Germany, Fascist Italy, and imperial Japan. The argument made by President Franklin D. Roosevelt and other supporters of the legislation was that the defense of these countries was critical to the defense of the United States. Ultimately, the United States provided over $50 billion in military aid, largely to Britain, but also to the Soviet Union, China, and more than forty other nations.

Be it enacted That this Act may be cited as "An Act to Promote the Defense of the United States." . . .

SEC. 3.

(a) notwithstanding the provisions of any other law, the President may, from time to time, when he deems it in the interest of national defense, authorize the Secretary of War, the Secretary of the Navy, or the head of any other department or agency of the Government—

(1) To manufacture in arsenals, factories, and shipyards under their jurisdiction, or otherwise procure, to the extent to which funds are made available therefor, or contracts are authorized from time to time by the Congress, or both, any defense article for the government of any country whose defense the President deems vital to the defense of the United States.

(2) To sell, transfer title to, exchange, lease, lend, or otherwise dispose of, to any such government any defense article, but no defense article not manufactured or procured under paragraph (1) shall in any way be disposed of under this paragraph, except after consultation with the Chief of Staff of the Army or the Chief of Naval Operations of the Navy, or both. The value of defense articles disposed of in any way under authority of this paragraph, and procured from funds heretofore appropriated, shall not exceed $1,300,000,000. The value of such defense articles shall be determined by the head of the department or agency concerned or such other department, agency or officer as shall be designated in the manner provided in the rules and regulations issued hereunder. Defense articles procured from funds hereafter appropriated to any department or agency of the Government, other than from funds authorized to be appropriated under this Act, shall not be disposed of in any way under authority of this paragraph except to the extent hereafter authorized by the Congress in the Acts appropriating such funds or otherwise.

(3) To test, inspect, prove, repair, outfit, recondition, or otherwise to place in good working order, to the extent to which funds are made available therefor, or contracts are authorized from time to time by the Congress, or both, any defense article for any such government, or to procure any or all such services by private contract.

(4) To communicate to any such government any defense information, pertaining to any defense article furnished to such government under paragraph (2) of this subsection.

(5) To release for export any defense article disposed of in any way under this subsection to any such government.

(b) The terms and conditions upon which any such foreign government receives any aid authorized under subsection (a) shall be those which the President deems satisfactory, and the benefit to the United States may be payment or repayment in kind or property, or any other direct or indirect benefit which the President deems satisfactory.

(c) After June 30, 1943, or after the passage of a concurrent resolution by the two Houses before June 30, 1943, which declares that the powers conferred by or pursuant to subsection (a) are no longer necessary to promote the defense of the United States, neither the President nor the head of any department or agency shall exercise any of the powers conferred by or pursuant to subsection (a); except that until July 1, 1946, any of such powers may be exercised to the extent necessary to carry out a contract or agreement with such a foreign government made before July 1, 1943, or before the passage of such concurrent resolution, whichever is the earlier.

(d) Nothing in this Act shall be construed to authorize or to permit the authorization of convoying vessels by naval vessels of the United States.

(e) Nothing in this Act shall be construed to authorize or to permit the authorization of the entry of any American vessel into a combat area in violation of section 3 of the Neutrality Act of 1939. . . .

SEC. 8

The Secretaries of War and of the Navy are hereby authorized to purchase or otherwise acquire arms, ammunition, and implements of war produced within the jurisdiction of any country to which section 3 is applicable, whenever the President deems such purchase or acquisition to be necessary in the interests of the defense of the United States.

SEC. 9

The President may from time to time, promulgate such rules and regulations as may be necessary and proper to carry out any of the provisions of this Act; and he may exercise any power or authority conferred on him by this Act through such department, agency, or officer as he shall direct.

From: *U.S. Statutes at Large.* 1941. Vol. 55, p. 31.

ATLANTIC CHARTER, AUGUST 14, 1941

The Atlantic Charter—signed aboard the British warship HMS Prince of Wales on August 14, 1941, by President Franklin D. Roosevelt and British Prime Minister Winston Churchill—was meant to assure the American people that the country's growing involvement in the anti-Nazi alliance was to serve democratic ideals. The need for such a declaration became essential after communist Russia joined the struggle against Nazi Germany in June 1941.

The President of the United States of America and the Prime Minister, Mr. Churchill, representing His Majesty's Government in the United Kingdom, being met together, deem it right to make known certain common principles in the national policies of their respective countries on which they base their hopes for a better future for the world.

First, their countries seek no aggrandizement, territorial or other;

Second, they desire to see no territorial changes that do not accord with the freely expressed wishes of the peoples concerned;

Third, they respect the right of all peoples to choose the form of government under which they will live; and they wish to see sovereign rights and self government restored to those who have been forcibly deprived of them;

Fourth, they will endeavor, with due respect for their existing obligations, to further the enjoyment by all States, great or small, victor or vanquished, of access, on equal terms, to the trade and to the raw materials of the world which are needed for their economic prosperity;

Fifth, they desire to bring about the fullest collaboration between all nations in the economic field with the object of securing, for all, improved labor standards, economic advancement and social security;

Sixth, after the final destruction of the Nazi tyranny, they hope to see established a peace which will afford to all nations the means of dwelling in safety within their own boundaries, and which will afford assurance that all the men in all the lands may live out their lives in freedom from fear and want;

Seventh, such a peace should enable all men to traverse the high seas and oceans without hindrance;

Eighth, they believe that all of the nations of the world, for realistic as well as spiritual reasons must come to the abandonment of the use of force. Since no future peace can be maintained if land, sea or air armaments continue to be employed by nations which threaten, or may threaten, aggression outside of their frontiers, they believe, pending the establishment of a wider and permanent system of general security, that the disarmament of such nations is essential. They will likewise aid and encourage all other practicable measures which will lighten for peace-loving peoples the crushing burden of armaments.

Franklin D. Roosevelt
Winston Churchill

From: Samuel Rosenman, ed. *The Public Papers and Addresses of Franklin Delano Roosevelt.* Vol. 10, p. 314. New York: Random House, 1938–50.

ROOSEVELT'S WAR MESSAGE TO CONGRESS, DECEMBER 8, 1941

On December 7, 1941, the naval and air forces of Japan attacked the U.S. naval base at Pearl Harbor in the Hawaiian Islands. The assault came after months and years of rising animosity between Japan and the United States and increasing tensions in the Pacific Basin. Whether or not the attack was truly the surprise President Franklin D. Roosevelt made it out to be—America had already broken the Japanese diplomatic code—it galvanized Americans for war in a way that all the speeches about preparedness could not do. Roosevelt's request for a state of war with Japan was followed within a few days by a declaration of war by Germany and Italy against the United States and vice versa. World War II for the United States had begun; the era of the Great Depression was over.

Yesterday, December 7, 1941—a date which will live in infamy—the United States of America was suddenly and deliberately attacked by naval and air forces of the Empire of Japan.

The United States was at peace with that nation and, at the solicitation of Japan, was still in conversation with its Government and its Emperor looking toward the maintenance of peace in the Pacific. Indeed, one hour after Japanese air squadrons had commenced bombing in Oahu, the Japanese Ambassador to the United States and his colleague delivered to the Secretary of State a formal reply to a recent American message. While this reply stated that it seemed useless to continue the existing diplomatic negotiations, it contained no threat or hint of war or armed attack.

It will be recorded that the distance of Hawaii from Japan makes it obvious that the attack was deliberately planned many days or even weeks ago. During the intervening time the Japanese Government has deliberately sought to deceive the United States by false statements and expressions of hope for continued peace.

The attack yesterday on the Hawaiian Islands has caused severe damage to American naval and military forces. Very many American lives have been lost. In addition American ships have been reported torpedoed on the high seas between San Francisco and Honolulu.

Yesterday the Japanese Government also launched an attack against Malaya. Last night Japanese forces attacked Hong Kong. Last night Japanese forces attacked Guam. Last night Japanese forces attacked the Philippine Islands. Last night the Japanese attacked Wake Island. This morning the Japanese attacked Midway Island.

Japan has, therefore, undertaken a surprise offensive extending throughout the Pacific area. The facts of yesterday speak for themselves. The people of the United States have already formed their opinions and well understand the implications to the very life and safety of our nation.

As Commander-in-Chief of the Army and Navy, I have directed that all measures be taken for our defense.

Always will we remember the character of the onslaught against us.

No matter how long it may take us to overcome this premeditated invasion, the American people in their righteous might will win through to absolute victory.

I believe I interpret the will of the Congress and of the people when I assert that we will not only defend ourselves to the uttermost but will make very certain that this form of treachery shall never endanger us again.

Hostilities exist. There is no blinking at the fact that our people, our territory and our interests are in grave danger.

With confidence in our armed forces—with the unbounded determination of our people—we will gain the inevitable triumph—so help us God.

I ask that the Congress declare that since the unprovoked and dastardly attack by Japan on Sunday, December seventh, a state of war has existed between the United States and the Japanese Empire.

From: Samuel Rosenman, ed. *The Public Papers and Addresses of Franklin Delano Roosevelt.* Vol. 10, p. 514. New York: Random House, 1938–50.

GLOSSARY AND ACRONYMS

A

AAA. Agricultural Adjustment Administration.

Action Française. Fascist organization of 1930s-era France.

ADC. Aid to Dependent Children.

AFL. American Federation of Labor.

Agricultural Adjustment Act (1938). Legislation that established a quota system to maintain farm prices and that provided loans to farmers.

ALP. American Labor Party.

American Artists' Congress. Communist Party–affiliated organization of visual artists founded in 1936.

American Negro Labor Congress. Federation of black trade unions.

ANG. American Newspaper Guild.

Anschluss. German for "connection": the absorption of Austria into Nazi Germany in March 1938.

anthracite coal. Also known as hard coal; dug up in open, or strip, mines.

appeasement. Late 1930s policy followed by Britain and France of making concessions to Adolf Hitler and Nazi Germany in the hopes of averting a general war.

art deco. Popular streamlined style of the 1930s, commonly used in architecture and industrial design.

Ashwander v. TVA **(1935)**. Supreme Court case upholding the constitutionality of the Tennessee Valley Authority.

Association Against the Prohibition Amendment. Main organization, largely consisting of wealthy industrialists, calling for an end to the prohibition of alcohol.

Axis. Military alliance of Japan, Italy, and Germany initiated in 1936.

B

BAC. *See* **Business Advisory Council**.

back-to-work groups. Anti-labor organizations of local townspeople, usually organized by companies facing union organizing campaigns.

Bankhead-Jones Farm Tenancy Act (1937). Legislation that replaced the Resettlement Agency with the Farm Security Administration.

Banking Act (1935). Law that replaced the Federal Reserve Board with a board of governors of the Federal Reserve Bank, and also gave the Federal Reserve Bank greater control over the nation's banking.

Battalion of Death. Name used by Franklin D. Roosevelt's supporters for the four conservative Supreme Court justices— Pierce Butler, James McReynolds, George Sutherland, and Willis Van Devanter—who ruled numerous New Deal acts unconstitutional in the early and mid-1930s.

Battle of the Running Bulls. Battle between police and strikers during a sit-down strike at General Motors on January 11, 1937.

"beer bill." Popular name for 1933 legislation that legalized 3.2 percent alcohol content beer, the first alcoholic beverage permitted since passage of Prohibition in 1920.

bituminous coal. Also known as soft coal; generally mined in deep mines in the eastern United States.

Black bill. Measure introduced by Senator Hugo Black (D-AL) in 1933 that would have established a federally mandated thirty-hour workweek in order to save jobs; opposed by Franklin D. Roosevelt, the bill never made it out of Congress.

black Thursday. Popular term for October 24, 1929, the first day in which stock prices plummeted on Wall Street, ushering in the Great Depression.

black Tuesday. Popular term for October 29, 1929, the second day in which stock prices plummeted on Wall Street, ushering in the Great Depression.

Blue Eagle. Logo of the National Recovery Administration, displayed by businesses that participated in the economic recovery program.

B movie. Low-budget Hollywood film of the 1930s.

boll weevil. Parasitic insect that devastated southern cotton fields in the early twentieth century.

bootlegging. Selling illegal alcohol during Prohibition.

breadline. Lines of homeless or jobless people waiting for free or inexpensive food offered by charities.

BSCP. Brotherhood of Sleeping Car Porters.

Business Advisory Council (BAC). Semipublic organization of business leaders established by the Franklin D. Roosevelt administration in 1933 with the aim of getting the business community to back the New Deal.

Butler v. United States **(1936)**. Supreme Court decision that rendered the Agricultural Adjustment Act's provisions for control and processing taxes unconstitutional.

C

CCC. Civilian Conservation Corps; *see also* **Commodity Credit Corporation**.

Chicago Tribune. Newspaper owned by isolationist conservative Robert McCormick and considered among the most influential anti–New Deal periodicals in the 1930s.

CIO. *See* **Congress of Industrial Organizations**.

citizen councils. Anti-labor organizations of local townspeople; usually organized by companies facing union organizing campaigns.

Civil Aeronautics Board. Agency created in 1938 to regulate the civilian airline industry.

Committee for Industrial Organization. *See* **Congress of Industrial Organizations.**

Committee on Economic Security. Convened by labor secretary Frances Perkins; a group of experts who drew up the Social Security Act of 1935.

Committee to Defend America by Aiding the Allies. Most important late Depression group advocating American aid to Britain and other countries fighting Nazi Germany, Fascist Italy, and militarist Japan.

Commodity Credit Corporation. Government-administered corporation established in 1935 to carry out financial activities associated with government loans for farmers.

Communist International. Organization established by the Soviet Union after the Russian revolution to coordinate activities of communist parties around the world.

Congress of Industrial Organizations. Formerly the Committee for Industrial Organization, this association was formed by United Mine Workers president John L. Lewis and Amalgamated Clothing Workers president Sidney Hillman in 1938 to organize industrial workers.

Conservative Manifesto. Issued by Senator Josiah Bailey (D-NC) and other southern senators in 1937; condemned sit-down strikes, high federal taxes, budget deficits, government regulation that encroached on states' rights, and the creation of welfare programs.

Cotton Club. Popular 1920s and 1930s entertainment nightclub in Harlem, New York.

countercyclical spending. Deficit spending by the federal government during times of economic depression in order to pump more money into the economy.

CPUSA. Communist Party of the United States of America.

craft union. Union in which all members of a craft are organized, regardless of what industry they work in, such as the United Brotherhood of Carpenters.

Croix de feu. Fascist organization of 1930s-era France.

CWA. Civil Works Administration.

D

death sentence clause. Clause in the Public Utilities Holding Companies Act of 1935 that outlawed holding companies that were twice removed from their operating subsidiaries.

destroyer deal. Executive order of 1940 exchanging fifty United States World War I–vintage destroyers for leases on British bases in the Western Hemisphere.

"Don't Buy Where You Don't Work." Slogan for national boycott of the 1930s against retail businesses that refused to hire African Americans.

dual unionism. In context of the Great Depression, the Communist Party strategy of establishing separate labor organizations to rival existing noncommunist trade unions.

E

***Electric Bond and Share Company v. Securities and Exchange Commission* (1938).** Supreme Court decision that affirmed the constitutionality of the Public Utilities Holding Company Act.

Emergency Farm Mortgage Act (1933). An act passed in the first days of the Roosevelt administration designed to prevent farm mortgage foreclosures; incorporated into the Farm Relief Act of May 1933, which also included the Agricultural Adjustment Act.

Emergency Relief Appropriations Act (1935). Legislation that created federal job programs.

Employee Representation Board. *See* **Employee Representation Program**.

Employee Representation Program. The more formal name for a company union.

EPIC. End Poverty in California.

ERB. *See* **Employee Representation Board**.

ERP. *See* **Employee Representation Program.**

"Every Man a King." Slogan of Huey P. Long's Share Our Wealth movement.

F

Fannie Mae. *See* **Federal National Mortgage Association**.

FAP. Federal Art Project.

Farm Credit Administration. Created under the Agricultural Adjustment Act of 1933 to provide loans and refinancing for farm mortgages.

Farmers Union. Radical small farmers' group involved in the Farm Holiday movement of the early 1930s.

Farm Relief Act (1933). An act passed in May 1933 that incorporated the Agricultural Adjustment Act and the Emergency Farm Mortgage Act into a single law designed to aid American farmers by providing loans and subsidies.

FBI. Federal Bureau of Investigation.

FCC. Federal Communications Commission.

FDIC. Federal Deposit Insurance Corporation.

Federal Council on Negro Affairs. Association of black officials in the Franklin D. Roosevelt administration that sought to improve civil rights; popularly referred to as the "black cabinet."

Federal Crop Insurance Program. Crop insurance program to protect farmers from natural calamities and falling farm prices; created under the Agricultural Adjustment Act of 1938.

Federal Farm Board. Agency created by the Herbert Hoover administration to buy farm products and keep them off the market, thereby preventing falling prices.

Federal Home Loan Bank Act (1932). Legislation establishing twelve Federal Home Loan Banks to supply credit to troubled savings and loan associations.

Federal Housing Act (1934). Legislation that created the Federal Housing Administration.

Federal National Mortgage Association. Created in 1934; aided lending institutions to resell mortgages, thereby improving lenders' liquidity and increasing the amount of money available for home construction.

Federal One. Division within the Works Progress Administration charged with creating public works projects for the arts; component parts of Federal One included the Federal Art Project, the Federal Music Project, the Federal Theater Project, and the Federal Writers' Project.

Federal Radio Commission. Predecessor agency of the Federal Communications Commission.

Federal Works Administration. Created in 1939, the successor agency to the Works Progress Administration.

FEPC. Fair Employment Practices Committee.

FERA. Federal Emergency Relief Administration.

FHA. Federal Housing Administration.

First Hundred Days. First hundred days of the Franklin D. Roosevelt administration in early 1933; marked by numerous pieces of legislation designed to lift the nation out of the Great Depression.

Fisher Body Plant Number One. General Motors plant in Flint, Michigan, where the sit-down strikes of 1936–37 began.

FMP. Federal Music Project.

Food Stamp Program. Department of Agriculture program created to replace the Federal Surplus Commodities Corporation and designed to buy up farm surpluses and distribute them to poor and hungry people through federal and other food relief programs.

"Four Freedoms." Freedom of speech and religion, as well as freedom from fear and want; enunciated by Franklin D. Roosevelt as the goals of U.S. participation in World War II in January 1941.

"four horsemen." After the biblical four horsemen of the apocalypse, a name used by Franklin D. Roosevelt's supporters for the four conservative Supreme Court justices—Pierce Butler, James McReynolds, George Sutherland, and Willis Van Devanter—who ruled numerous New Deal acts unconstitutional in the early and mid-1930s.

FSA. Farm Security Administration.

FTP. Federal Theater Project.

FWP. Federal Writers' Project.

G

G-Man. Short for "government man," a popular term for an FBI agent.

greenbelt communities. Parkland suburbs created around major urban areas to house industrial workers; promoted by Resettlement Administration head Rexford Tugwell.

Green Shirts. Profascist paramilitary organization in France in the 1930s.

Greer **incident.** September 1941 exchange of fire between the destroyer USS *Greer* and a German submarine.

Guffey-Snyder Stabilization Act (1935). Legislation establishing a federal commission to fix coal prices and allocate production, guaranteeing miners' right to organize, and mandating minimum wages and maximum hours.

H

Helvering v. Davis **(1937).** Supreme Court ruling upholding the constitutionality of the old-age benefits provision of the Social Security Act of 1935.

Historical American Buildings Survey. Authorized under the Civil Works Administration in early 1934 to hire museum curators, architects, and historians to develop a record of all architecture of historical significance in the United States.

Historical Records Survey. Originally part of the Federal Writers' Project and set up as a separate program in 1936 to preserve historical documents; chronicled narratives of the last surviving former slaves in dozens of volumes of interviews.

Home Owners Loan Act (1933). Legislation that established the Home Owners Loan Corporation to provide federal money to prevent home mortgage foreclosures.

Hoovervilles. Popular term for encampments of the homeless in the 1930s; named after the unpopular Republican president Herbert Hoover.

HUAC. House Un-American Activities Committee.

I

ILGWU. International Ladies' Garment Workers' Union.

Indian congresses. Series of meetings organized by Bureau of Indian Affairs head John Collier to confer with Indian leaders and rally support for the Indian Reorganization Act of 1934.

industrial union. Union in which all workers in a given industry—regardless of their specific craft or skill—are organized together, such as the United Automobile Workers.

internationalism. Ideology popular in the late 1930s that emphasized America's critical role in world affairs and the need to support those countries fighting against fascism and Nazism.

International Labor Defense. Communist-led legal organization that defended trade unionists and others; best known for work on the Scottsboro case.

International Longshoreman's Association strike. Dockworker strike that closed most ports on the Pacific Coast during May and June 1934.

International Workers Order. Communist-led organization that offered insurance, cultural activities, and other benefits to worker-members.

isolationism. Ideology popular in the 1930s that called for the United States to stay out of all foreign entanglements.

IWO. *See* **International Workers Order**.

J

jitterbug. Athletic dance style popular at swing music shows.

K

Kearney **incident**. Attack on the USS *Kearney* by a German submarine in October 1941 that left the ship severely damaged.

Kingfish. Popular name for Louisiana senator and radical demagogue Huey P. Long.

Kristallnacht. German for "night of broken glass": the systematic attacks on Jewish homes, businesses, and synagogues in Nazi Germany on the night of November 9–10, 1938.

L

Lindbergh law. As a result of Lindbergh kidnapping, a law that made transporting a kidnapping victim across state lines a federal offense.

Living Newspaper. Dramatizations of current affairs staged by the Federal Theater Project.

Loyalists. Communist and democratic forces backing republican government of Spain in the civil war of the late 1930s.

M

marathon dance. Contest in which couples would dance for as long as possible, with the last couple standing winning a prize.

McCormack-Dickstein Committee. *See* **Special Committee on Un-American Activity**.

MGM. Metro-Goldwyn-Mayer.

Militants. Young, radical members of the Socialist Party who sought alliances with the Communists during the 1930s.

Miller-Tydings Act (1937). Legislation that legalized price-maintenance agreements between wholesalers and their distributors; largely affected nationally sold name brand products.

Monopoly.™ Trademarked board game that involved the buying and selling of real estate; invented by Charles Darrow in 1933 and purchased by Parker Bros. in 1935.

Motor Carrier Act (1935). Legislation designed to regulate the trucking industry.

MOWM. March on Washington Movement.

MPPC. Motion Picture Production Code.

"My Day." Syndicated daily newspaper column written by First Lady Eleanor Roosevelt.

N

National Association of Manufacturers. Main business trade group of the 1930s, still an influential lobbying voice in Washington.

National Highway Users Conference. Trade organization of auto, oil, and rubber industry executives created in 1933 to lobby the federal government for more highway construction.

National Housing Act (1933). Legislation that established the Federal Housing Administration to provide federally insured bank loans to private individuals to purchase homes or make home improvements.

National Housing Act (1934). Legislation that established the Federal Housing Administration.

Nationalists. Fascist antigovernment forces in Spanish civil war of the late 1930s.

National Labor Board. Created in 1933, an agency within the National Recovery Administration designed to mediate employer-employee conflicts and establish rules for union representation.

National Recovery Administration. Economic regulatory agency established by the 1933 National Industrial Recovery Act, which was ruled unconstitutional in the 1935 *Schechter Poultry Corporation v. United States* Supreme Court decision.

National Union for Social Justice. Political advocacy organization led by radio priest Father Charles E. Coughlin.

Natural Gas Act (1938). Legislation regulating natural gas pipelines and industry.

Negro Leagues. African-American baseball leagues prior to the integration of major league baseball in 1947.

NHUC. *See* **National Highway Users Conference**.

NIRA. National Industrial Recovery Act.

NLRA. National Labor Relations Act.

NLRB. National Labor Relations Board.

Non-Intervention Agreement (1935). Pact by Britain and France not to intervene in Spanish civil war of the late 1930s.

Nonpartisan League. Pro-farmer North Dakota political party; predecessor to Minnesota's Farmer-Labor Party.

North American Committee to Aid Spanish Democracy. Communist-led organization to provide American citizens' aid to the Loyalists in the Spanish civil war of the late 1930s.

NRA. National Recovery Administration.

NUL. National Urban League.

Nuremburg laws. Set of laws passed by Nazi Germany in 1935 that put severe restrictions on the rights of Jews.

NUSJ. National Union for Social Justice.

NYA. National Youth Administration.

NYSE. New York Stock Exchange.

O

OARP. *See* **Old Age Revolving Pensions, Incorporated**.

Old Age Revolving Pensions, Incorporated. Official name of the Townsend Clubs, organized in the mid-1930s to support an old-age pension plan by California physician Francis Townsend.

Old Guard. Term for older, conservative members of the Socialist Party who preferred to keep the party out of alliances with the Communists during the 1930s.

On to Ottawa Trek. Canadian protest march of 1935 demanding unemployment relief.

OPM. Office of Production Management.

P

Panay **incident**. The sinking of an American gunboat on the Yangtze River in China by the Japanese military in 1937; although two American sailors died and thirty were wounded, the event did not lead to confrontation between the two countries, as Japan issued an official apology and paid $2 million in reparations.

parity. Price paid to farmers by the government based on the high crop prices of the years immediately preceding World War I.

Pinkertons. Paid anti-union spies and anti-security forces.

Popular Front. Policy of the Communist Party of the United States to work with liberals, Democrats, and Socialists to confront conservative forces during the late 1930s; also, late 1930s policy of the Soviet Union to promote alliances with antifascist regimes in Europe and between communist and liberal parties in western democracies.

POUR. President's Organization on Unemployment Relief.

President's Emergency Committee for Employment. Voluntary group established by President Herbert Hoover in 1930 to combat unemployment; in 1931, the name was changed to the President's Organization on Unemployment Relief.

production for use. Policy set forth by Upton Sinclair in his 1934 End Poverty in California campaign for governor that called for the state to take over idle factories and farms and turn them into farmer- and worker-run cooperatives.

Public Contracts Act (1936). Legislation that mandated an eight-hour day and forty-hour week for companies doing work for the federal government.

"pump priming." Popular expression for government spending designed to stimulate the economy.

PWA. Public Works Administration.

Q

"quarantine" speech. Franklin D. Roosevelt's 1937 speech calling for international "quarantines" to be placed around aggressor nations.

quickie strike. Brief sit-down strike involving a limited number of workers.

R

RA. Resettlement Administration.

Railway Labor Act (1934). Legislation guaranteeing railroad workers the same rights to organize as manufacturing workers received in Section 7 of the National Industrial Recovery Act.

rape of Nanking. Japanese attack on the Chinese city of Nanking that resulted in atrocities, including massacres and mass rape; widely condemned in the United States but resulted in no retaliatory action by the U.S. government.

REA. Rural Electrification Administration.

Reading Formula. A policy under the National Recovery Administration that set up rules in 1933 whereby workers could hold supervised elections to choose leaders and organizations to represent them in collective bargaining with employers.

Re-Employment Agreement. Clause within the National Industrial Recovery Act of 1935 setting a minimum wage of $15 and a maximum workweek of forty hours for companies participating in the National Recovery Administration program.

regionalism. Depression-era genre of art and literature that emphasized stories, characters, language, and imagery associated with various regions of the United States.

Reuben James. U.S. destroyer sunk by German submarines in October 1939 with the loss of 115 sailors.

RFC. Reconstruction Finance Corporation.

River Rouge. In Detroit, Ford Motor Company's largest plant in the 1930s and the scene of a police attack on a hunger march in 1932.

RKO Studios. Major Hollywood studio of the 1930s; produced Orson Welles's *Citizen Kane*.

Robinson-Patman Act (1936). Law that prevented chain stores from discounting prices below profit in order to drive local competitors out of business.

Rome-Berlin Axis. Defensive alliance established between Fascist Italy and Nazi Germany in 1936.

Roosevelt recession. A downturn in the economy in 1937–38 that was, many economic historians argue, triggered by Roosevelt's decision to balance the budget and cut back on government spending on public works.

Route 66. Highway taken by many families fleeing the dust bowl of the Midwest for California (now largely Interstate 40).

S

Savoy Ballroom. Popular entertainment dance club opened in 1929 in Harlem, New York.

screwball comedies. Popular film genre of the Great Depression that featured fast-paced plots and dialogue, usually set in upper-class society.

SEC. Securities and Exchange Commission.

sharecropping. Legal and economic arrangement established between landlord and tenant farmer in which income from the crop is shared between them; predominated in the South from the end of the Civil War through the Great Depression.

"short of war" policy. Informal name for American foreign policy following Nazi conquests of Western Europe in 1940; it called for the United States to provide aid to Britain and other countries fighting Germany but not to get involved in the fighting itself.

"soak-the-rich" tax plan. Informal name for bill introduced by Franklin D. Roosevelt in 1935 to drastically raise taxes on wealthy Americans' income; it was watered down significantly by Congress to become the Wealth Tax Act of that same year.

Social Fascists. Derogatory word used by Communists to describe members of the Socialist Party in the early 1930s.

social realism. Popular international art style of the 1930s that was characterized by bold images of workers, farmers, and ordinary people and was often used in public works murals.

soup kitchen. Popular term for a charity- or church-run kitchen that offered free meals to homeless and jobless persons.

SP. Socialist Party.

Special Areas Act (1935). Law establishing government public works projects for the unemployed in Britain.

Special Committee on Un-American Activity. Also known as the McCormack-Dickstein committee, after its chair, Representative John McCormack (D-MA), and its most outspoken member, Representative Samuel Dickstein (D-NY); organized in 1934 as the forerunner of the House Un-American Activities Committee.

SSA. Social Security Administration.

S.S. *St. Louis*. Ship with 970 Jewish refugees from Germany that was refused the right to dock in the United States in 1939; the refugees were returned to Europe, where most were eventually captured by the Nazis and sent to concentration camps.

stay-in. Alternative name for sit-down strike.

Steel Labor Relations Board. Established under the National Industrial Recovery Act to mediate relations between steel manufacturers and workers; outlawed by the *Schechter Poultry v. United States* Supreme Court decision of 1935.

Steel Mediation Board. Committee established by President Franklin D. Roosevelt in 1937 to mediate relations between steel manufacturers and unions.

Steward Machine Company v. Davis **(1937)**. Supreme Court decision upholding the constitutionality of the federal tax designed to coerce states into providing unemployment insurance under the 1935 Social Security Act.

STFU. Southern Tenant Farmers Union.

Stimson Doctrine. Issued by Secretary of War Henry L. Stimson in 1931, calling for U.S. nonrecognition of the puppet state of Manchukuo established by Japan in Manchuria and Mongolia, but offering little to force Japan out; the doctrine became the core of U.S. policy toward Asian conflict during the rest of the decade.

storm troopers. Paramilitary force used by Adolf Hitler to eliminate internal enemies in Nazi Germany.

studio system. Replaced the "star system" of the 1920s in which major film actors dominated movie production; in the 1930s, studios maintained contracts on major stars and controlled most aspects of film production.

Sudetenland. Predominantly German-speaking area of Czechoslovakia that was given to Nazi Germany at the Munich Conference of 1938.

Surplus Reserve Loan Corporation. Agency created under the Agricultural Adjustment Act of 1938 that provided loans to farmers secured by surplus crops placed in the national food reserve.

swashbuckler. Popular 1930s-era term for an action-adventure film or a star of such a film.

swing. Popular style of jazz pioneered in the 1930s that featured big bands playing danceable compositions.

SWOC. Steel Workers Organizing Committee.

T

Temporary National Economic Committee. Senate committee established in 1938 to investigate corporations and corporate consolidation.

TERA. Temporary Emergency Relief Administration.

Textile Labor Relations Board. Established by Franklin D. Roosevelt after national textile workers' strike of 1934; designed to mediate labor disputes in the textile industry.

Third Period. Period in the early 1930s when Communist Party members were supposed to eschew political connections to all other parties.

TNEC. *See* **Temporary National Economic Committee**.

Transportation Act (1940). Legislation placing most forms of interstate transportation under the jurisdiction of the Interstate Commerce Commission.

Treasury Relief Art Projects. Treasury Department program from 1935 to 1939 that funded art for public buildings.

Trotskyists. Followers of deposed Russian communist leader Leon Trotsky; radical Communists who believed in world revolution.

TUUL. Trade Union Unity League.

TVA. Tennessee Valley Authority.

Twelve Point Crime Program. Series of laws in 1934 that made virtually all kidnappings federal offenses.

Twentieth Amendment. Ratified in 1933; moved the presidential inauguration day from March 4 to January 20 and the beginning of the first congressional term after national elections to January 3; passed in response to the long wait between the end of Herbert Hoover's term in office and the beginning of Franklin D. Roosevelt's, when the nation was mired in the Depression and the government, being in transition, was able to do little to remedy the situation.

Twenty-first Amendment. Ratified in 1933; ended Prohibition by repealing the Eighteenth Amendment to the Constitution, which had given Congress the power to pass legislation to ban the manufacture, sale, or transportation of alcoholic beverages.

Tydings-McDuffie Act (1934). Law that promised to grant the Philippines independence after a ten-year transitional period.

U

UAW. United Automobile Workers.

UMW. United Mine Workers.

Unemployment Relief Camps. Construction camps established by the Canadian government for unemployed youth.

United Rubber Workers. Largest union of tire workers in the United States in the 1930s; among the first unions to engage in sit-down strikes.

United States Housing Authority. Agency established by the Wagner-Steagall Housing Act of 1937 to encourage the building of public and low-cost housing.

URW. *See* **United Rubber Workers.**

USS. United States Steel.

V

Versailles Conference. Post–World War I peace conference of 1919 that established international order of 1920s and 1930s.

Volstead Act (1920). Law that made manufacture, sale, or transportation of intoxicating liquors illegal; repealed in 1933.

W

Wagner Act (1935). Officially the National Labor Relations Act sponsored by Senator Robert Wagner (D-MT).

War Industries Board. World War I agency that regulated the war economy, considered a model for the National Recovery Administration.

Wheeler-Howard Act (1934). Alternate name for Indian Reorganization Act; named after Senators Burton Wheeler (D-MT) and Edgar Howard (D-NE).

wildcat strike. Strike unauthorized by union leadership.

Women's Organization for National Prohibition Reform. Major organization calling for an end to the prohibition of alcohol.

WPA. Works Progress Administration; Work Projects Administration.

Y

yellow-dog contract. Name for a contract in which an employer requires an employee to renounce joining a trade union; rendered illegal under the Norris-La Guardia Anti-Injunction Act of 1932.

BIBLIOGRAPHY

Achenbaum, W. Andrew. *Old Age in a New Land: The American Experiences Since 1790*. Baltimore: Johns Hopkins University Press, 1978.

Ackerman, Bruce. *We the People: Transformations*. Cambridge, MA: Harvard University Press, 1998.

Acuna, Rodolfo. *Occupied America: A History of Chicanos*. 4th ed.. New York: Longman, 2000.

Adamic, Louis. *Laughing in the Jungle*. New York: Arno, 1969 (reprint).

———. *My America, 1928–1938*. New York: Da Capo, 1976 (reprint).

Adams, Grace. *Workers on Relief*. New Haven, CT: Yale University Press, 1939.

Adams, Henry H. *Harry Hopkins: A Biography*. New York: Putnam, 1977.

———. *Thomas Hart Benton: An American Original*. New York: Knopf, 1989.

Agee, James. *Let Us Now Praise Famous Men: Three Tenant Families*. Boston: Houghton Mifflin, 1941.

Agee, William C. *The 1930s: Painting and Sculpture in America*. New York: Whitney Museum of American Art, 1968.

Albini, Joseph. *The American Mafia*. New York: Meredith, 1971.

Allen, James, ed. *Democracy and Finance: The Addresses and Public Statements of William O. Douglas As Member and Chairman of the Securities and Exchange Commission*. Port Washington, NY: Kennikat, 1969.

Allswang, John. *The New Deal and American Politics: A Study in Political Change*. New York: Wiley, 1978.

Alpert, Hollis. *The Life and Times of Porgy and Bess: The Story of an American Classic*. New York: Knopf, 1990.

Alsop, Joseph. *The 168 Days*. New York: Da Capo, 1973.

Amenta, Edwin. *Bold Relief: Institutional Politics and the Origins of Modern American Social Policy*. Princeton, NJ: Princeton University Press, 1998.

Anderson, Marian. *My Lord, What a Morning: An Autobiography*. Madison: University of Wisconsin Press, 1992.

Andrews, Bart, and Ahrgus Juilliard. *Holy Mackerel! The Amos 'n' Andy Story*. New York: Dutton, 1986.

Argersinger, Jo Ann E. *Toward a New Deal in Baltimore: People and Government in the Great Depression*. Chapel Hill: University of North Carolina Press, 1988.

Arkes, Hadley. *The Return of George Sutherland: Restoring a Jurisprudence of Natural Rights*. Princeton, NJ: Princeton University Press, 1994.

Armstrong, Louis. *Satchmo: My Life in New Orleans*. New York: Prentice-Hall, 1954.

Arnold, Thurman. *The Folklore of Capitalism*. New Haven, CT: Yale University Press, 1937.

———. *The Symbols of Government*. New Haven, CT: Yale University Press, 1935.

Arrington, Leonard J. "Western Agriculture and the New Deal." *Agricultural History* 44: 4 (October 1970): 337–54.

Ashby, Joe C. *Organized Labor and the Mexican Revolution Under Lázaro Cárdenas*. Chapel Hill: University of North Carolina Press, 1967.

Asher, Robert, and Ronald Edsforth, eds. *Autowork*. Albany: State University of New York Press, 1995.

Ashwander v. TVA (297 U.S. 288).

Atack, Jeremy, and Peter Passell. *A New Economic View of American History From Colonial Times to 1940*. New York: Norton, 1994.

Auerbach, Jerold S. "New Deal, Old Deal, or Raw Deal: Some Thoughts on New Left Historiography." *Journal of Southern History* 35:1 (February 1969): 18–30.

Autry, Gene, and Michkey Herskowitz. *Back in the Saddle*. Garden City, NY: Doubleday, 1978.

Axinn, June, and Herman Levin. *Social Welfare: A History of the American Response to Need*. New York: Dodd, Mead, 1975.

Badger, Anthony J. *The New Deal: The Depression Years, 1933–1940*. New York: Hill & Wang, 1989.

Baigell, M. *The American Scene: American Painting of the 1930's*. New York: Praeger, 1974.

Baigell, M., and J. Williams, eds. *Artists Against War and Fascism: Papers of the First American Artists' Congress*. New Brunswick, NJ: Rutgers Universtiy Press,1986.

Bailey, Beth L. *From Front Porch to Back Seat: Courtship in Twentieth-Century America*. Baltimore: Johns Hopkins University Press, 1988.

Baker, Leonard. *Back to Back: The Duel between FDR and the Supreme Court*. New York: Macmillan, 1967.

———. *Brandeis and Frankfurter: A Dual Biography*. New York: New York University Press, 1986.

Baker, William J. *Jesse Owens: An American Life*. London: Collier Macmillan, 1986.

———. *Sports in the Western World*. Urbana: University of Illinois Press, 1988.

Barber, James G. *Portraits from the New Deal*. Washington, DC: Smithsonian Institution Press, 1983.

Barfield, Ray E. *Listening to Radio, 1920–1950* Westport, CT: Praeger, 1996.

Barkley, Alben William. *That Reminds Me.* Garden City, NY: Doubleday, 1954.

Barnard, Rita. *The Great Depression and the Culture of Abundance: Kenneth Fearing, Nathanael West and Mass Culture in the 1930s.* New York: Cambridge University Press, 1995.

Barnes, Irston. *The Economics of Public Utility Regulation.* New York: F.S. Crofts, 1942.

Barnhart, Michael. *Japan Prepares for Total War: The Search for Economic Security, 1919–1941.* Ithaca, NY: Cornell University Press, 1987.

Barnouw, Erik. *Documentary: A History of the Non-Fiction Film.* New York: Oxford University Press, 1983.

———. *A History of Broadcasting in the United States.* Vol. 1, "A Tower in Babel," and Vol. 2, "The Golden Web." New York: Oxford University Press, 1966, 1968.

Barrow, Joe Louis and Barbara Munder. *Joe Louis: 50 Years an American Hero.* New York: McGraw-Hill, 1988.

Barry, Dan, and Harvey Kurtzman. *Flash Gordon.* Princeton, NJ: Kitchen Sink, 1988.

Barsam, Richard. *Nonfiction Film: A Critical History.* Bloomington: Indiana University Press, 1973.

Bartlett, Donald L., and James B. Steele. *Empire: The Life, Legend and Madness of Howard Hughes.* New York: Norton, 1979.

Bartlett, John H. *The Bonus March and the New Deal.* New York: M.A. Donohue, 1937.

Baruch, Bernard Mannes. *Baruch: My Own Story.* New York: Holt, 1957–60.

Basie, Count. *Good Morning Blues: The Autobiography of Count Basie.* New York: Random House, 1985.

Baskin, Alex. "The Ford Hunger March—1932." *Labor History* (Summer 1972).

Baughman, James L. *Henry R. Luce and the Rise of the American News Media.* Boston: Twayne, 1987.

Bauman, John F., and Thomas H. Coode. *In the Eye of the Great Depression: New Deal Reporters and the Agony of the American People.* DeKalb: Northern Illinois University Press, 1988.

Baxt, George. *The William Powell and Myrna Loy Murder Case.* New York: St. Martin's, 1996.

Baxter, John. *Hollywood in the Thirties.* New York: A.S. Barnes, 1968.

Beasley, Norman. *Frank Knox, American: A Short Biography.* Garden City, NY: Doubleday, Doran, 1936.

Becker, Marjorie. *Setting the Virgin on Fire: Lázaro Cárdenas, Michoacán Peasants, and the Redemption of the Mexican Revolution.* Berkeley: University of California Press, 1995.

Behlmer, Rudy. "Johnny Weismuller: Olympics to Tarzan." *Films in Review* (July/August 1996): 20–33.

Belknap, Michael R. *Cold War Political Justice: The Smith Act, the Communist Party, and American Civil Liberties.* Westport, CT: Greenwood, 1977.

Bell, Thomas. *Out of This Furnace.* Pittsburgh: University of Pittsburgh Press, 1976.

Bellows, Sidney. *Poverty and Politics: The Rise and Decline of the Farm Security Administration.* Chapel Hill: University of North Carolina Press, 1968.

Bellush, Bernard. *The Failure of the NRA.* New York: Norton, 1975.

Bennett, Davis H. *Demagogues in the Depression: American Radicals and the Union Party, 1932–1936.* New Brunswick, NJ: Rutgers University Press, 1969.

Bennett, Edward M. *Franklin D. Roosevelt and the Search for Security: American-Soviet Relations, 1933–1939.* Wilmington, DE: Scholarly Resources, 1985.

Bennett, Harry. *Ford: We Never Called Him Henry.* New York: Tom Doherty Associates, 1951.

Bentley, Joanne. *Hallie Flanagan: A Life in the American Theatre.* New York: Knopf, 1988.

Benton, Thomas Hart. *An Artist in America.* Columbia: University of Missouri Press, 1983.

Berg, A. Scott. *Goldwyn: A Biography.* New York: Knopf, 1989.

———. *Lindbergh.* New York: Berkley, 1998.

Berger, Arthur Asa. *Li'l Abner: A Study in American Satire.* New York: Twayne, 1969.

Bergreen, Laurence. *As Thousands Cheer: The Life of Irving Berlin.* New York: Viking Penguin, 1990.

———. *Capone: The Man and the Era.* New York: Simon & Schuster, 1994.

———. *James Agee: A Life.* New York: Dutton, 1984.

Berle, Adolf A. *The Modern Corporation and Private Property.* New York: Macmillan, 1933.

Bernstein, Irving. *The Lean Years: A History of the American Worker, 1920–1933.* Boston: Houghton Mifflin, 1960.

———. *The New Deal Collective Bargaining Policy.* Berkeley: University of California Press, 1950.

———. *Turbulent Years: A History of the American Worker, 1933–1941.* Boston: Houghton Mifflin, 1971.

Bernstein, Michael A. *The Great Depression: Delayed Recovery and Economic Change in America, 1929–1939.* New York: Cambridge University Press, 1987.

Bertin, Amy. *Competition and Productivity in the Depression-Era Steel Industry.* Master's thesis, Harvard University, 1994.

Beschloss, Michael R. *Kennedy and Roosevelt: The Uneasy Alliance.* New York: Norton, 1980.

Betts, John Richard. *America's Sporting Heritage: 1850–1950.* Reading, MA: Addison-Wesley, 1974.

Bezner, Lili Corbus. *Photography and Politics in America: From the New Deal into the Cold War.* Baltimore: Johns Hopkins University Press, 1999.

Bickel, Alexander M. *The Least Dangerous Branch: The Supreme Court at the Bar of Politics.* New Haven, CT: Yale University Press, 1986.

Biles, Roger. *A New Deal for the American People.* Dekalb: Northern Illinois University Press, 1991.

———. *The South and the New Deal.* Lexington: University Press of Kentucky, 1994.

Bindas, Kenneth J. *All of This Music Belongs to the Nation: The WPA's Federal Music Project and American Society.* Knoxville: University of Tennessee Press, 1995.

Bird, Caroline. "The Discovery of Poverty." In *The Way We Lived: Essays and Documents in American Social History,* ed. Frederick M. Binder and David M. Reimers, 205–16. Lexington, MA: Heath, 1988.

Black, Allida. *Casting Her Own Shadow: Eleanor Roosevelt and the Shaping of Postwar Liberalism.* New York: Columbia University Press, 1996.

———. *Courage in a Dangerous World: The Political Writings of Eleanor Roosevelt.* New York: Columbia University Press, 1999.

Black, Hugo Lafayette. *A Constitutional Faith.* New York: Knopf, 1969.

Black, Shirley Temple. *Child Star, USA.* New York: Warner, 1989.

Blackford, Mansel G., and K. Austin Kerr. *Business Enterprise in American History*. 3rd ed. Boston: Houghton Mifflin, 1994.

Blackorby, Edward C. *Prairie Rebel*: *The Public Life of William Lemke*. Lincoln: University of Nebraska Press, 1963.

Blake, Nelson Manfred. *A Short History of American Life*. New York: McGraw-Hill, 1952.

Blatz, William E. *The Five Sisters: A Study of Child Psychology*. New York: Morrow, 1938.

Bles, Mark, and Robert Low. *The Kidnap Business*. London: Pelham, 1987.

Bliss, Edward, ed. *In Search of Light: The Broadcasts of Edward R. Murrow, 1938–1964*. New York: Knopf, 1967.

Blotner, Joseph. *Faulkner*: *A Biography*. 2 vols. New York: Random House, 1974.

Blotner, Joseph Leo. *Robert Penn Warren: A Biography*. New York: Random House, 1997.

Blum, John Morton, ed. *Roosevelt and Morgenthau*. Boston: Houghton Mifflin, 1970.

———. *From the Morgenthau Diaries*. 3 vols. Boston: Houghton Mifflin, 1959–1967.

———. ed. *The Price of Vision: The Diary of Henry A. Wallace, 1942–1946*. Boston: Houghton Mifflin, 1973.

Blum, Léon. *For All Mankind*. New York: Viking, 1946.

Bogdanovich, Peter. *John Ford*. Berkeley: University of California Press, 1968.

Bold, Christine. *The WPA Guides: Mapping America*. Jackson: University Press of Mississippi, 1999.

Boller, Paul. *Presidential Campaigns*. Oxford: Oxford University Press, 1984.

Borg, Dorothy. *The United States and the Far Eastern Crisis of 1933–1938*. Cambridge, MA: Harvard University Press, 1964.

Boroff, David, ed. *The Nation One Hundredth Anniversary Issue*. New York: Nation, 1965.

Boswell, Peyton, Jr. *Modern American Painting*. New York: Dodd, Mead, 1939.

Bosworth, R. J. B. *The Italian Dictatorship: Problems and Perspectives in the Interpretation of Mussolini and Fascism*. London: Arnold, 1998.

Bothwell, Robert, et al. *Canada, 1900–1945*. Toronto: University of Toronto Press, 1987.

Bowen, Ezra, ed. *This Fabulous Century*. Vol. 3, 1920–1930, and Vol. 4, 1930–1940. New York: Time-Life Books, 1970.

Boyle, Peter G. *American-Soviet Relations: From the Russian Revolution to the Fall of Communism*. London: Routledge, 1993.

Braeman, John, Robert Bremner, and David Brody. "Introduction," in Braeman et al., eds., *The New Deal: The State and Local Levels*. Vol. 2. Columbus: Ohio State University Press, 1975.

———. *The New Deal*, Vol. 1. Columbus: Ohio State University Press, 1975.

———. *The New Deal: The National Level*. Columbus: Ohio State University Press, 1975.

Branch, Edgar Marquess. *James T. Farrell*. New York: Twayne, 1971.

Brandeis, Louis. *Other People's Money and How Bankers Use It*. Boston: Bedford Books of St. Martin's, 1913.

Brecher, Jeremy. *Strike*. 2nd ed. Boston: South End, 1997.

Bremner, Robert H. *American Philanthropy*. Chicago: University of Chicago Press, 1960.

Brendon, Piers. *The Life and Death of the Press Barons*. New York: Atheneum, 1983.

Brenman-Gibson, Margaret. *Clifford Odets, American Playwright: The Years from 1906 to 1940*. New York: Atheneum, 1981.

Brian, Denis. *Einstein: A Life*. New York: Wiley, 1996.

Bridges, Herb. *Gone with the Wind: The Definitive Illustrated History of the Book, the Movie, and the Legend*. New York: Simon & Schuster, 1989.

Brinkley, Alan. *The End of Reform: New Deal Liberalism in Recession and War*. New York: Knopf, 1995.

———. *Voices of Protest: Huey Long, Father Coughlin, and the Great Depression*. New York: Knopf, 1982.

Brinkley, David. *Washington Goes to War*. New York: Knopf, 1988.

Brinkley, Douglas, and David R. Facey-Crowther, eds. *The Atlantic Charter*. New York: St. Martin's, 1994.

Britton, Andrew. *Katherine Hepburn: Star as Feminist*. New York: Continuum, 1995.

Broadus, Mitchell. *Depression Decade: From New Era Through New Deal, 1929–1941*. New York: Harper & Row, 1947.

Brody, David. *Workers in Industrial America: Essays on the Twentieth Century Struggle*. New York: Oxford University Press, 1980.

Brooks, John. *Once in Golconda*: *A True Drama of Wall Street, 1920–1938*. New York: Harper & Row, 1969.

Brooks, Robert, and Romano Ravi. *As Steel Goes . . . : Unionism in a Basic Industry*. New Haven and London: Oxford University Press, 1940.

Broun, Heywood Hale, ed. *Collected Edition of Heywood Broun*. New York: Harcourt, Brace, 1941.

Browder, Earl. *The People's Front*. New York: International Publishers, 1938.

Brown, Francis Joseph. *The Social and Economic Philosophy of Pierce Butler*. Washington, DC: Catholic University of America Press, 1945.

Brown, Lorraine, and John O'Connor, eds. *Free, Adult, Uncensored: The Living History of the Federal Theatre Project*. Washington, DC: New Republic Books, 1978.

Brown, Peter Harry, and Pat H. Broeskie. *Howard Hughes: The Untold Story*. New York: Dutton, 1996.

Brown, Robert J. *Manipulating the Ether: The Power of Broadcast Radio in Thirties America*. Jefferson, NC: McFarland, 1998.

Brownlee, W. Elliot. *Federal Taxation in America: A Short History*. New York: Cambridge University Press, 1996.

Bryan, Ford R. *Henry's Lieutenants*. Detroit: Wayne State University Press, 1993.

Bryant, Keith L., Jr., ed. *Railroads in the Age of Regulation, 1900–1980*. New York: Bruccoli Clark Layman, 1988.

Buck, Pearl. *My Several Worlds*: A *Personal Record*. New York: Day, 1954.

Buechner, Thomas S. *Norman Rockwell, Artist and Illustrator*. New York: Abradale/Abrams, 1996.

Buhite, Russell D., and David W. Levy, eds. *FDR's Fireside Chats*. Norman: University of Oklahoma Press, 1992.

Bureau of the Census. *Fifteenth Census of the United States: 1930. Population*. Washington, DC: Government Printing Office, 1931–33.

Bureau of the Census. *Historical Statistics of the United States: Colonial Times to 1970*. Washington, DC: Department of Commerce, Bureau of the Census, 1989.

Bureau of the Census. *Historical Statistics of the United States: Colonial Times to 1970, Part 1*. Washington, DC: Government Printing Office, 1970.

———. *Statistical Abstract of the United States*. Washington, DC: Government Printing Office. Various Editions.

Burgess, Anthony. *Ernest Hemingway and His World*. New York: Scribner, 1978.

Burner, David. *Herbert Hoover: A Public Life*. New York: Knopf, 1979.

———. *The Politics of Provincialism: The Democratic Party in Transition, 1918–1932*. New York: Norton, 1967.

Burns, Helen. *The American Banking Community and New Deal Banking Reforms: 1933–1935*. Westport, CT: Greenwood, 1974.

Burns, James MacGregor. *Roosevelt: The Lion and the Fox, 1882–1940*. New York: Harcourt Brace Jovanovich, 1956.

Bustard, Bruce I. *A New Deal for the Arts*. Seattle: University of Washington Press, 1997.

Butler, Michael A. *Cautious Visionary: Cordell Hull and Trade Reform, 1933–1937*. Kent, OH: Kent State University Press, 1998.

Butow, Robert J. C. *Tojo and the Coming of the War*. Stanford, CA: Stanford University Press, 1961.

Byrnes, James F. *All in One Lifetime*. New York: Harper, 1958.

Caldwell, Erskine. *God's Little Acre*. Athens: University of Georgia Press, 1995 (reprint).

———. *Tobacco Road*. Athens: University of Georgia Press, 1995 (reprint).

———. *You Have Seen Their Faces*. Athens: University of Georgia Press, 1995 (reprint).

Callow, Simon. *Orson Welles: The Road to Xanadu*. New York: Viking, 1996.

Calloway, Cab. *Of Minnie the Moocher & Me*. New York: Crowell, 1976.

Canedy, Susan. *America's Nazis: A Democratic Dilemma: A History of the German American Bund*. Menlo Park: Markgraf, 1990.

Cannadine, David, ed. *Blood, Toil, Tears, and Sweat: The Speeches of Winston Churchill*. Boston: Houghton Mifflin, 1989.

Cannistraro, Philip V. *Historical Dictionary of Fascist Italy*. Westport, CT: Greenwood, 1982.

Cantor, Louis. *A Prologue to the Protest Movement: The Missouri Sharecropper Roadside Demonstration of 1939*. Durham, NC: Duke University Press, 1969.

Cantril, Hadley. *The Invasion From Mars: A Study in the Psychology of Panic: With the Complete Script of the Famous Orson Welles Broadcast*. Princeton, NJ: Princeton University Press, 1982.

Capp, Al. *The Best of Li'l Abner*. New York: Holt, Rinehart, and Winston, 1978.

Capra, Frank. *The Name Above the Title: An Autobiography*. New York: Macmillan, 1971.

Carey, Gary. *All the Stars in Heaven: Louis B. Mayer's MGM*. New York: Dutton, 1981.

Carlton, David L., and Peter A. Coclanis, eds. *Confronting Southern Poverty in the Great Depression: The Report on Economic Conditions of the South with Related Documents*. New York: Bedford Books of St. Martin's, 1996.

Carnegie, Dale. *How to Win Friends and Influence People*. New York: Pocket Books, 1982.

Carney, Raymond. *American Vision: The Films of Frank Capra*. New York: Cambridge University Press, 1987.

Carringer, Robert L. *The Making of Citizen Kane*. Berkeley: University of California Press, 1996.

Carter, Dan. *Scottsboro: A Tragedy of the American South*. Baton Rouge: Louisiana State University Press, 1979.

Carter, Joseph H. *Never Met a Man I Didn't Like: The Life and Writings of Will Rogers*. New York: Avon, 1991.

Cash, William M., and R. Daryl Lewis. *The Delta Council: Fifty Years of Service to the Mississippi Delta*. Stoneville, MS: Delta Council, 1986.

Cashman, Sean. *America in the Twenties and Thirties: The Olympian Age of Franklin Delano Roosevelt*. New York: New York University Press, 1989.

Cassels, Alan. *Fascism*. New York: Crowell, 1975.

———. "Fascism for Export: Italy and the United States in the Twenties." *American Historical Review* 69 (April 1964): 707–12.

Caute, David. *The Great Fear: The Anti-Communist Purge Under Truman and Eisenhower*. New York: Simon & Schuster, 1978.

Cayleff, Susan E. *Babe: The Life and Legend of Babe Didrikson Zaharias*. Urbana: University of Illinois Press, 1995.

Chadwin, Dean. *Those Damn Yankees: The Secret Life of America's Greatest Franchise*. New York: Verso, 1999.

Chafe, William H. *The American Woman: Her Changing Social, Economic, and Political Roles, 1920–1970*. New York: Oxford University Press, 1972.

Chan, Sucheng. *Asian Americans: An Interpretive History*. New York: Twayne, 1991.

Chandler, Raymond. *The Big Sleep & Farewell, My Lovely*. New York: Modern Library, 1995 (reprint).

Childs, Marquis. *The Farmer Takes a Hand*. New York: Doubleday, 1952.

Childs, William R. "The Infrastructure." In *Encyclopedia of the United States in the Twentieth Century*, 1331-35. ed. Stanley I. Kutler, New York: Simon & Schuster/Macmillan, 1996.

Chun, Gloria Heyung. *Of Orphans and Warriors: Inventing Chinese American Culture and Identity*. New Brunswick, NJ: Rutgers University Press, 2000.

Churchill, Winston. *While England Slept: A Survey of World Affairs, 1932–1938*. New York: Putnam, 1938.

Clark, Paul F., Peter Gottlieb, and Donald Kennedy, eds. *Forging a Union of Steel: Philip Murray, SWOC, and the United Steelworkers*. Ithaca, NY: International Labor Review Press, 1987.

Clarke, Donald. *Wishing on the Moon: The Life and Times of Billie Holiday*. New York: Viking, 1994.

Clarke, Jeanne N. *Roosevelt's Warrior: Harold L. Ickes and the New Deal*. Baltimore: Johns Hopkins University Press, 1996.

Clausen, John A. *American Lives: Looking Back at the Children of the Great Depression*. New York: Free Press, 1993.

Clements, Cynthia. *George Burns and Gracie Allen: A Bio-Bibliography*. Westport, CT: Greenwood, 1996.

Clurman, Harold. *The Fervent Years: The Story of the Group Theatre and the Thirties*. New York: Harcourt Brace Jovanovich, 1975.

Cochran, Thomas. *The American Business System*. Cambridge, MA: Harvard University Press, 1957.

Coffey, Thomas M. *Lion by the Tail: The Story of the Italian-Ethiopian War*. New York: Viking, 1974.

Cohen, Elizabeth. *Making a New Deal: Industrial Workers in Chicago*. New York: Cambridge University Press, 1990.

Cohn, Jan. *Creating America: George Horace Lorimer and the "Saturday Evening Post."* Pittsburgh, PA: University of Pittsburgh Press, 1989.

Cole, Olen, Jr. *The African-American Experience in the Civilian Conservation Corps*. Gainesville: University Press of Florida, 1999.

Cole, Wayne S. *America First: The Battle Against Intervention, 1940–1941*. New York: Octagon Books, 1971.

————. *Charles A. Lindbergh and the Battle Against American Intervention in World War II.* New York: Harcourt Brace Jovanovich, 1974.

————. *Roosevelt and the Isolationists, 1932–45.* Lincoln: University of Nebraska Press, 1983.

————. *Senator Gerald P. Nye and American Foreign Relations.* Minneapolis: University of Minnesota Press, 1962.

Collier, James Lincoln. *Duke Ellington.* New York: Oxford University Press, 1987.

Collier, Peter. *The Fords: An American Epic.* New York: Summit, 1987.

Collins, Robert. *The Business Response to Keynes, 1929–1964* New York: Columbia University Press, 1981.

Colton, Joel. *Léon Blum: Humanist in Politics.* New York: Knopf, 1966.

Commission to Study the Organization of Peace. *Comment on the Eight-Point Declaration of President Roosevelt and Prime Minister Churchill, August 14, 1941.* New York: Commission to Study the Organization of Peace, 1941.

Congdon, Don, ed. *The 30's: A Time to Remember.* New York: Simon & Schuster, 1962.

Conkin, Paul. *The New Deal.* Arlington Heights, IL: Harlan Davidson, 1975.

Conn, Peter J. *Pearl S. Buck: A Cultural Biography.* New York: Cambridge University Press, 1996.

Conquest, Robert. *The Great Terror: A Reassessment.* New York: Oxford University Press, 1990.

Cook, Blanche Wiesen. *Eleanor Roosevelt: A Life.* Vols. 1 and 2. New York: Viking, 1992.

Cook, Sylvia Jenkins. *Erskine Caldwell and the Fiction of Poverty: The Flesh and the Spirit.* Baton Rouge: Louisiana State University Press, 1991.

Cooke, Morris Llewellyn. "National Plan for the Advancement of Rural Electrification Under Federal Leadership and Control With State and Local Cooperation and As A Wholly Public Enterprise." February 1934. Box 230, Morris Cooke Papers, Franklin and Eleanor Roosevelt Library, Hyde Park, New York.

Copland, Aaron. *Copland on Music.* Garden City, NY: Doubleday, 1960.

Cormier, Frank. *Reuther.* Englewood Cliffs, NJ: Prentice-Hall, 1970.

Coughlin, Charles Edward. *The New Deal in Money.* Royal Oak, MI: The Radio League of the Little Flower, 1933.

Cowan, Ruth Schartz. "Two Washes in the Morning and a Bridge Party At Night: The American Housewife Between the Wars." *Women's Studies* 3: 2 (1976):147–72.

Cowley, Malcolm. *The Dream of the Golden Mountains: Remembering the 1930s.* New York: Penguin, 1981.

Cramer, Richard Ben. *Joe DiMaggio: The Hero's Life.* New York: Simon & Schuster, 2000.

Cray, Ed. *The Chrome Colossus: General Motors and Its Times.* New York: McGraw-Hill, 1980

Creese, Walter L. *TVA's Public Planning: The Vision and the Reality.* Knoxville: University of Tennessee Press, 1990.

Cremin, Lawrence. *American Education: The Metropolitan Experience.* New York: Harper & Row, 1988.

Croce, Arlene. *The Fred Astaire & Ginger Rogers Book.* New York: Vintage, 1977.

Crouse, Joan M. *The Homeless Transient in the Great Depression: New York State, 1929–1941.* Albany: State University of New York Press, 1986.

Crowley, James B. *Japan's Quest for Autonomy: National Security and Foreign Policy, 1930–1938.* Princeton, NJ: Princeton University Press, 1966.

Culbert, David Holbrook. *News for Everyman: Radio and Foreign Affairs in Thirties America.* Westport, CT: Greenwood, 1976.

Culhane, John. *Walt Disney's* Fantasia. New York: Abradale, 1983.

Culver, John C., and John Hyde. *American Dreamer: The Life and Times of Henry A. Wallace.* New York: Norton, 2000.

Currie, David P. "Constitution in the Supreme Court: The New Deal, 1931–1940." *University of Chicago Law Review,* 40 (1987): 504.

Curtis, James. *Mind's Eye, Mind's Truth: FSA Photography Reconsidered.* Philadelphia: Temple University Press, 1989.

Cushman, Barry. *Rethinking the New Deal Court: The Structure of a Constitutional Revolution.* New York: Oxford University Press, 1998.

Dalleck, Robert. *Franklin D. Roosevelt and American Foreign Policy, 1932–45.* New York: Oxford University Press, 1981.

Dance, Stanley. *The World of Count Basie.* New York: Scribner's, 1980.

Danelski, David, and Joseph S. Tulchin, eds. *The Autobiographical Notes of Charles Evans Hughes.* Cambridge, MA: Harvard University Press, 1973.

Danese, Tracy E. *Claude Pepper and Ed Ball: Politics, Purpose, and Power.* Gainesville: University Press of Florida, 2000.

Daniel, Cletus E. *The ACLU and the Wagner Act: An Inquiry into the Depression-Era Crisis of American Liberalism.* Ithaca, NY: Cornell University Press, 1980.

Daniel, Pete, et al. *Official Images: New Deal Photography.* Washington: Smithsonian Institution Press, 1987.

Daniels, Les. *DC Comics: Sixty Years of the World's Favorite Comic Book Heroes.* Boston: Little, Brown, 1995.

Daniels, Roger. *The Bonus March: An Episode of the Great Depression.* Westport, CT: Greenwood, 1971.

Daniels, Roger. "Public Works in the 1930s: A Preliminary Reconnaissance." In *The Relevancy of Public Works History: The 1930s—A Case Study.* Washington, DC: Public Works Historical Society, 1975.

Danish, Max. *The World of David Dubinsky.* Cleveland: World, 1957.

Davidson, Bill. *Spencer Tracy: Tragic Idol.* New York: Dutton, 1987.

Davidson, Eugene. *The Making of Adolf Hitler: The Birth and Rise of Nazism.* Columbia: University of Missouri Press, 1997.

Davis, Audrey B. "Life Insurance and the Physical Examination: A Chapter in the Rise of American Medical Technology." *Bulletin of the History of Medicine,* 55:3 (1981): 392–406.

Davis, Kenneth S. *FDR: The New York Years, 1928–1933.* New York: Random House, 1985.

————. *The Hero.* London: Longmans, 1959.

Davis, Kingsley. *Youth in the Depression.* Chicago: University of Chicago Press, 1935.

Davis, Polly Ann. *Alben W. Barkley: Senate Majority Leader and Vice President.* New York: Garland, 1979.

Davis, Ronald L. *John Ford: Hollywood's Old Master.* Norman: University of Oklahoma Press, 1995.

Dawes, Charles G. *How Long Prosperity?* Chicago: A. N. Marquis, 1937.

Dawson, Robert M. *William Lyon Mackenzie King: A Political Biography.* Toronto: University of Toronto Press, 1958.

Deakin, F.W. *The Brutal Friendship: Mussolini, Hitler, and the Fall of Italian Fascism.* London: Weidenfeld & Nicolson, 1962.

DeDedts, Ralph F. *The New Deal's SEC: The Formative Years.* New York: Columbia University, 1964.

De Grand, Alexander J. *Italian Fascism: Its Origins and Development.* Lincoln: University of Nebraska Press, 1982.

Denning, Michael. *The Cultural Front: The Laboring of American Culture.* London: Verso, 1996.

Dennis, James M. *Grant Wood: A Study in American Art and Culture.* Columbia: University of Missouri Press, 1986.

DeNoon, Christopher. *Posters of the WPA.* Los Angeles: Wheatley, 1987.

Department of Agriculture. *USDA Yearbook of Agriculture. Washington, 1929–1941.*

Department of State. *The United States Senate Committee on Agriculture, Nutrition, and Forestry 1825–1998*, Washington, DC: GPO, 1998.

Derickson, Alan. "Health Security for All? Social Unionism and Universal Health Insurance, 1935–1958." *Journal of American History* 80:4 (1994): 1333–56.

Deschner, Donald. *The Complete Films of W.C. Fields.* Secaucus, NJ: Citadel, 1989.

DeSoto, Clinton B. *200 Meters & Down: The Story of Amateur Radio.* West Hartford, CT: American Radio Relay League, 1936.

Deuss, Jean. *Banking in the U.S.: An Annotated Bibliography.* Metuchen, NJ: Scarecrow, 1990.

Deutsch, Sarah. *No Separate Refuge: Culture, Class and Gender on an Anglo-Hispanic Frontier in the American Southwest, 1880–1940.* New York: Oxford University Press, 1987.

Dewey, Thomas. *The Case Against the New Deal.* New York: Harper, 1940.

Diamond, Sander A. *The Nazi Movement in the United States, 1924–1941.* Ithaca, NY: Cornell University Press, 1974.

Dickens, Homer. *The Films of Gary Cooper.* New York: Citadel, 1970.

———. *The Films of Ginger Rogers.* Secaucus, NJ: Citadel, 1975.

Dies, Martin. *The Trojan Horse in America.* New York: Dodd, Mead, 1940.

Dietrich, Marlene. *Marlene.* New York: Grove, 1989.

Diggins, John P. "American Catholics and Italian Fascism." *Journal of Contemporary History* 2 (October 1967): 51–68.

———. "Flirtation with Fascism: American Pragmatic Liberals and Mussolini's Italy." *American Historical Review* 71 (January 1966): 487–506.

———. "The ItaloAmerican AntiFascist Opposition." *Journal of American History* 54 (June 1967): 579–98.

———. "Mussolini and America: Hero Worship, Charisma, and the 'Vulgar Talent.'" *Historian* 28 (August 1966): 559–85.

Dinwoodie, David H. "Indians, Hispanos and Land Reform: A New Deal Struggle in New Mexico." *Western Historical Quarterly* 17:3 (July 1986): 291–323.

Doan, Edward N. *The La Follettes and the Wisconsin Idea.* New York: Rinehart, 1947.

Doan, Mason C. "State Labor Relations Acts." *Quarterly Journal of Economics* 56:4 (August 1942); 507–59.

Doenecke, Justus D., ed. *In Danger Undaunted: The Anti-interventionist Movement of 1940–1941 as Revealed in the Papers of the America First Committee.* Stanford, CA: Hoover Institution Press, 1990.

Donner, Frank J. *The Un-Americans.* New York: Ballantine, 1961.

Dooley, Dennis, and Gary Engle. *Superman at Fifty: The Persistence of a Legend.* Cleveland: Octavia Press, 1987.

Dos Passos, John. *U S A.* New York: Modern Library, 1937.

Douglas, William O. *Go East, Young Man: The Early Years: The Autobiography of William O. Douglas.* New York: Random House, 1974.

Doyle, Paul A. *Pearl S. Buck.* Boston: Twayne, 1980.

Draper, Theodore. *The Roots of American Communism.* New York: Viking, 1957.

Droze, Wilmon H. *High Dams and Slack Waters: TVA Rebuilds a River.* Baton Rouge: Louisiana University Press, 1965.

Duberman, Martin B. *Paul Robeson.* New York: Knopf, 1989.

Dubinsky, David, and A. H. Raskin. *David Dubinsky: A Life with Labor.* New York: Simon & Schuster, 1977.

Dubofsky, Melvyn. *The State and Labor in Modern America.* Chapel Hill: University of North Carolina Press, 1994.

Dubofsky, Melvyn, ed. *The New Deal: Conflicting Interpretations and Shifting Perspectives.* New York: Garland, 1992.

Dubofsky, Melvyn, and Foster Rhea Dulles. *Labor in America: A History.* Wheeling, IL: Harlan Davidson, 1999.

Dubofsky, Melvyn, and Warren Van Time. *John L. Lewis: A Biography.* Urbana: University of Illinois Press, 1986.

Dubofsky, Melvyn, and Stephen Burwood, eds. *The New Deal: Selected Articles on the Political Response to the Great Depression.* New York: Garland, Inc. 1990.

Dunn, Dennis J. *Caught Between Roosevelt & Stalin: America's Ambassadors to Moscow.* Lexington: University Press of Kentucky, 1998.

Dunning, John. *On the Air: The Encyclopedia of Old-Time Radio* New York: Oxford University Press, 1998.

Durgnat, Raymond. *King Vidor, American.* Berkeley: University of California Press, 1988.

Dykeman, Wilma. *Seeds of Southern Change: The Life of Will Alexander.* New York: Norton, 1976.

Dykstra, Robert R., and David R. Reynolds. "In Search of Wisconsin Progressives, 1904–1952." In *The History of American Electoral Behavior*, Joel Silbey et al., eds. Princeton, NJ: Princeton University Press, 1978.

Eames, John Douglas. *The MGM Story.* New York: Crown, 1976.

Earhart, Amelia. *The Fun of It: Random Records of My Own Flying and of Women in Aviation.* New York: Brewer, Warren & Putnam, 1932.

Eastman, Joel. *Styling vs. Safety: The American Automobile Industry and the Development of Automotive Safety, 1900–1966.* Lanham, MD: University Press of America, 1984.

Eastman, Lloyd E. *The Abortive Revolution: China Under Nationalist Rule, 1927–1937.* Cambridge, MA: Harvard University Press, 1974.

———. *Seeds of Destruction: Nationalist China in War and Revolution, 1937–1949.* Stanford, CA: Stanford University Press, 1984.

Eccles, George. *The Politics of Banking.* Salt Lake City: University of Utah, 1982.

Eccles, Marriner. *Beckoning Frontiers: Public and Personal Recollections.* New York: Knopf, 1951.

Edel, Leon, ed. *The Thirties: From Notebooks and Diaries of the Period: Edmund Wilson.* New York: Farrar, Straus, and Giroux, 1980.

Edsforth, Ronald. *The New Deal: America's Response to the Great Depression.* Malden, MA: Blackwell, 2000.

Edwards, Corwin. "Thurman Arnold and the Anti-Trust Laws." *Political Science Quarterly* 42 (September 1943): 143–55.

Edwards, Jerome E. *The Foreign Policy of Col. McCormick's Tribune, 1929–1941.* Reno: University of Nevada Press, 1971.

Eells, George. *Hedda and Louella.* New York: Putnam, 1972.

Eichengreen, Barry. *Golden Fetters: The Gold Standard and the Great Depression, 1919–1939.* New York: Oxford University Press, 1992.

Eisner, Marc Allen. *From Warfare State to Welfare State.* University Park, PA: Pennsylvania State University Press, 2000.

Ekirch, Arthur A., Jr. *Ideologies and Utopias: The Impact of the New Deal on American Thought.* Chicago: Quadrangle, 1969.

Elder, Glen H., Jr. *Children of the Great Depression: Social Change in Life Experience.* Chicago: University of Chicago Press, 1974.

Ellington, Duke. *Music Is My Mistress.* Garden City, NY: Doubleday, 1973.

Ellington, Mercer. *Duke Ellington in Person: An Intimate Memoir.* New York: Da Capo, 1978.

Elson, Robert T. *Time, Inc.: The Intimate History of a Publishing Enterprise, 1923–1941.* New York: Atheneum, 1968.

Ely, Melvin Patrick. *The Adventures of Amos 'n' Andy: A Social History of an American Phenomenon.* New York: Free Press, 1991.

Evans, Sara M. *Born for Liberty: A History of Women in America.* New York: Free Press/Macmillan, 1989.

Faber, Doris. *The Life of Lorena Hickok: E. R.'s Friend.* New York: Morrow, 1980.

Fabre, Michel. *The Unfinished Quest of Richard Wright.* Urbana: University of Illinois Press, 1993.

Farley, James A. *Jim Farley's Story: The Roosevelt Years.* New York: Whittlesey House, 1948.

Fassett, John D. *New Deal Justice: The Life of Stanley Reed of Kentucky.* New York: Vantage, 1994.

Fausold, Martin L. *The Presidency of Herbert C. Hoover.* Lawrence: University Press of Kansas, 1985.

Fearon, Peter. *War, Prosperity and Depression: The US Economy 1917–1945.* Oxford, England: Philip Alan, 1987.

Federal Trade Commission. *Report on Motor Vehicle Industry.* Washington, DC: Government Printing Office, 1939.

Federal Works Agency. *Final Report on the WPA Program, 1935–1943.* Washington, DC: Government Printing Office, 1946.

Feingold, Henry L. *The Politics of Rescue: The Roosevelt Administration and the Holocaust, 1938–1945.* New York: Holocaust Library, 1970.

Fensch, Thomas, ed. *Conversations with John Steinbeck.* Jackson: University Press of Mississippi, 1988.

Ferrell, Robert H. *American Diplomacy in the Great Depression: Hoover-Stimson Diplomacy, 1929–1933.* New Haven, CT: Yale University Press, 1957.

Fielding, Raymond. *The American Newsreel 1911–1967.* Norman: University of Oklahoma Press, 1972.

Findling, John E., ed. *Historical Dictionary of World's Fairs and Expositions, 1851–1988.* New York: Greenwood, 1990.

Fine, Sidney. *The Automobile Under the Blue Eagle.* Ann Arbor: University of Michigan Press, 1963.

———. *Frank Murphy.* Ann Arbor: University of Michigan Press, 1975.

———. *Sit-Down: The General Motors Strike of 1936–1937.* Ann Arbor: The University of Michigan Press, 1969.

Finegan, T. Aldrich, and Robert A. Margo. "Work Relief and the Labor Force Participation of Married Women in 1940." *Journal of Economic History.* 54:1 (1994): 64–84.

Finkenbine, Roy E. *Sources of the African-American Past.* New York: Longman, 1997.

Finley, Joseph E. *The Corrupt Kingdom: The Rise and Fall of the United Mine Workers.* New York: Simon & Schuster, 1972.

Firestone, Ross. *Swing, Swing, Swing: The Life & Times of Benny Goodman.* New York: Norton, 1939.

Fischer, David Hackett. *Growing Old in America.* New York: Oxford University Press, 1977.

Fite, Gilbert C. *George N. Peek and the Fight for Farm Parity.* Norman: University of Oklahoma Press, 1954.

Fitzgerald, Richard. "New Masses: New York, 1926–1948." In *The American Radical Press, 1880–1960,* Vol. 2, ed. Joseph R. Conlin. Westport, CT: Greenwood, 1974.

Flanagan, Hallie. *Arena.* New York: Duell, Sloan, and Pearce, 1940.

Flannery, Gerald V., ed. *Commissioners of the FCC, 1927–1994.* Lanham, MD: University Press of America, 1995.

Fleischhauer, Carl, and Beverly W. Brannan, eds. *Documenting America, 1935–1943.* Berkeley: University of California Press, 1988.

Fletcher, William Miles. *The Search for a New Order: Intellectuals and Fascism in Prewar Japan.* Chapel Hill: University of North Carolina Press, 1982.

Flynn, Errol. *My Wicked, Wicked Ways.* London: Heinemann, 1960.

Foner, Philip, ed. *Paul Robeson Speaks: Writings, Speeches, Interviews, 1918–1974.* New York: Brunner/Mazel, 1978.

Foner, Philip S., and Ronald L. Lewis, eds. *The Era of Post-War Prosperity and the Great Depression, 1920–1936.* Vol. 6, *The Black Worker.* Philadelphia: Temple University Press, 1981.

Forrest, Suzanne. *The Preservation of the Village: New Mexico Hispanics and the New Deal.* Albuquerque: University of New Mexico Press, 1989.

Foster, William Z. *History of the Communist Party of the United States.* New York: International Publishers, 1952.

Fox, Richard Wrightman. *Reinhold Niebuhr: A Biography.* New York: Pantheon, 1985.

Francisco, Charles. *Gentleman: The William Powell Story.* New York: St. Martin's, 1985.

Franklin, John Hope, and Alfred A. Moss Jr. *From Slavery to Freedom: A History of Negro Americans.* New York: Knopf, 1988.

Fraser, Steve. "The 'Labor Question.'" In *The Rise and Fall of the New Deal Order, 1930–1980,* ed. Steve Fraser and Gary Gerstle, 55–84. Princeton, NJ: Princeton University Press, 1989.

———. *Labor Will Rule: Sidney Hillman and the Rise of American Labor.* Ithaca, NY: Cornell University Press, 1993.

Fraser, Steve, and Gary Gerstle, eds. *The Rise and Fall of the New Deal Order, 1930–80.* Princeton, NJ: Princeton University Press, 1989.

Freedland, Michael. *Irving Berlin.* New York: Stein and Day, 1974.

Freedman, Max, ed. *Roosevelt and Frankfurter: Their Correspondence, 1928–1945.* Boston: Little, Brown, 1967.

Freidel, Frank. "Election of 1932." In *History of American Presidential Elections, 1789–1968,* Vol. 3, ed. Arthur M. Schlesinger Jr. and Fred L. Israel, 2707–2806. New York: McGraw-Hill, 1971.

———. *Franklin D. Roosevelt: Launching the New Deal.* Boston: Little, Brown, 1973.

———. *Franklin D. Roosevelt: A Rendezvous with Destiny.* Boston: Little, Brown, 1990.

Fricke, John, Jay Scarfone, and William Stillman. *The Wizard of Oz: The Official 50th Anniversary Pictorial History.* New York: Warner, 1989.

Fuchser, Larry William. *Neville Chamberlain and Appeasement: A Study in the Politics of History.* New York: Norton, 1982.

Furia, Philip. *Ira Gershwin: The Art of the Lyricist.* New York: Oxford University Press, 1996.

Furuya, Keiji. *Chiang Kai-shek: His Life and Times.* New York: St. John's University Press, 1981.

Fury, David. *Kings of the Jungle: An Illustrated Reference to Tarzan on Screen and Television.* Jefferson, NC: McFarland, 1994.

Gabler, Neal. *Winchell: Gossip, Power, and the Culture of Celebrity*. New York: Knopf, 1994.

Gaddis, John Lewis. *Russia, the Soviet Union and the United States: An Interpretative History*. New York: Wiley, 1978.

Galbraith, John Kenneth, assisted by G. G. Johnson Jr. *The Economic Effects of the Federal Public Works Expenditures, 1933–1938*. Washington, DC: Government Printing Office, 1940.

———. *The Great Crash*. Boston: Houghton Mifflin, 1954.

Galeston, Walter. *The Unionization of the American Steel Industry*. Berkeley: University of California Press, 1956.

Gallagher, Tag. *John Ford: The Man and His Films*. Berkeley: University of California Press, 1986.

Garfinkel, Herbert. *When Negroes March: The March on Washington Movement in the Organizational Politics for FEPC*. New York: Atheneum, 1959.

Garvin, Richard M. *The Midnight Special: The Legend of Leadbelly*. New York: Bernard Geis Associates, 1971.

Garwood, Darrell. *Artist in Iowa: A Life of Grant Wood*. New York: Norton, 1944.

Gaydowski, J.D. "Eight Letters to the Editor: The Genesis of the Townsend National Recovery Plan." *Southern California Quarterly*, 52:4 (1970) p. 365–382.

Gayer, Arthur D. *Public Works in Prosperity and Depression*. New York: National Bureau of Economic Research, 1935.

Gayle, Addison. *Richard Wright: Ordeal of a Native Son*. Garden City, NY: Anchor Press/Doubleday, 1980.

Gellermann, William. *Martin Dies*. New York: John Day, 1944.

Gellman, Irwin. *Good Neighbor Diplomacy: United States Policies in Latin America, 1933–1945*. Baltimore: Johns Hopkins University Press, 1979.

———. *Secret Affairs: Franklin Roosevelt, Cordell Hull, and Sumner Welles*. Baltimore: Johns Hopkins University Press, 1995.

Géraud, André. *The Gravediggers of France: Gamelin, Daladier, Reynaud, Pétain, and Laval: Military Defeat, Armistice, Counter-Revolution*. Indianapolis: Bobbs-Merrill, 1940.

Gieske, Millard. *Minnesota Farmer-Laborism: The Third Party Alternative*. Minneapolis: University of Minnesota Press, 1979.

Gilbert, Jess, and Carolyn Howe. "Beyond 'State vs. Society': Theories of the State and New Deal Agricultural Policies." *American Sociological Review* 56 (1991): 204–20.

Gilbert, Martin. *Churchill: A Life*. New York: Holt, 1991.

Giles, Ray. "A Step Toward Livelier Old Age." *Readers Digest* (August 1937): 26–28.

Gingrich, Arnold. *Nothing But People: The Early Days at Esquire: A Personal History, 1928–1958*. New York: Crown, 1973.

Girardin, G. Russell. *Dillinger: The Untold Story*. Bloomington: Indiana University Press, 1994.

Glassford, Larry A. *Reaction and Reform: The Politics of the Conservative Party Under R. B. Bennett, 1927–1938*. Toronto: University of Toronto Press, 1992.

Glickman, Marty. *The Fastest Kid on the Block*. Syracuse, NY: Syracuse University Press, 1996.

Godfrey, Donald G., and Frederic A. Leigh, eds. *Historical Dictionary of American Radio*. Westport, CT: Greenwood, 1998.

Godfrey, Lionel. *The Life and Crimes of Errol Flynn*. New York: St. Martin's, 1977.

Goldberg, Vicki. *Margaret Bourke-White: A Biography*. New York: Harper & Row, 1986.

Goldner, Orville, and George E. Turner. *The Making of King Kong*. New York: Ballantine, 1976.

Gonzales, Manuel G. *Mexicanos: A History of Mexicans in the United States*. Bloomington: Indiana University Press, 1999.

Goodman, Benny. *The Kingdom of Swing*. New York: Stackpole, 1939.

Goodman, James. *Stories of Scottsboro*. New York: Vintage, 1995.

Goodwin, Doris Kearns. *No Ordinary Time: Franklin and Eleanor Roosevelt: The Home Front in World War II*. New York: Simon & Schuster, 1994.

Gordon, Colin. *New Deals: Business, Labor, and Politics in America, 1920–1935*. Cambridge: Cambridge University Press, 1994.

Gordon, Eric A. *Mark the Music: The Life and Work of Marc Blitzstein*. New York: St. Martin's, 1989.

Gordon, Linda. "Black and White Visions of Welfare: Women's Activism, 1980–1945." In *Unequal Sisters: A Multicultural Reader in U.S. Women's History*, ed. Vicki L. Ruiz and Ellen Carrol DuBois. New York: Routledge, 1994.

Gottesman, Ronald, and Harry Geduld. *The Girl in the Hairy Paw: King Kong as Myth, Movie, and Monster*. New York: Avon, 1976.

Gottfried, Martin. *George Burns and the Hundred-Year Dash*. New York: Simon & Schuster, 1996.

Gould, Jean. *Walter Reuther: Labor's Rugged Individualist*. New York: Dodd, Mead, 1972.

Gower, Calvin W. "The Struggle of Blacks for Leadership Positions in the Civilian Conservation Corps: 1933–1942." *Journal of Negro History* 61:2 (1976): 123–35.

Graebner, William. *A History of Retirement: The Meaning and Function of an American Institution, 1885–1978*. New Haven: Yale University Press, 1980.

Graham, Otis L. *An Encore for Reform: The Old Progressives and the New Deal*. New York: Oxford University Press, 1967.

Green, Adwin Wigfall. *The Man Bilbo*. Baton Rouge: Louisiana State University Press, 1963.

Green, James R. *The World of the Worker: Labor in Twentieth Century America*. 2nd ed. Chicago: University of Illinois Press, 1998.

Green, William. *Labor and Democracy*. Princeton, NJ: Princeton University Press, 1939.

Greenberg, Hank, and Ira Berkow. *Hank Greenberg: The Story of My Life*. New York: Times Books, 1989.

Greenfeld, Howard. *Ben Shahn: An Artist's Life*. New York: Random House, 1998.

Gregor, A. James. *Young Mussolini and the Intellectual Origins of Fascism*. Berkeley: University of California Press, 1979.

Gresset, Michel. *A Faulkner Chronology*. Jackson: University of Mississippi Press, 1985.

Gross, James. *The Making of the National Labor Relations Board*. Albany: State University of New York Press, 1974.

Grossman, Jonathan. "Fair Labor Standards of 1938: Maximum Struggle of a Minimum Wage." *Monthly Labor Review* 101:6 (1978): 22–30.

Grubbs, Donald H. *Cry From the Cotton: The Southern Tenant Farmers' Union and the New Deal*. Chapel Hill: University of North Carolina Press, 1971.

Grubs, Donald. "Jackson, That Socialist Tenant Farmers' Union, and the New Deal." *Agricultural History* 42:2 (April 1968): 125–37.

Guerrant, Edward O. *Roosevelt's Good Neighbor Policy*. Albuquerque: University of New Mexico Press, 1950.

Gurda, John. *The Quiet Company: A Modern History of Northwestern Mutual Life*. Milwaukee: Northwestern Mutual Life Insurance Company, 1983.

Guthrie, Woody. *Bound for Glory.* New York: Dutton, 1943.

Guttmann, Allen. *The Games Must Go On: Avery Brundage and the Olympic Movement.* New York: Columbia University Press, 1984.

———. *The Olympics: A History of the Modern Games.* Urbana: University of Illinois Press, 1992.

———. *The Wound in the Heart: America and the Spanish Civil War.* New York: Free Press of Glencoe, 1962.

Haber, Carole. *Beyond Sixty-five: The Dilemmas of Old Age in America's Past.* Cambridge: Cambridge University Press, 1983.

Haber, Carole, and Brian Gratton. *Old Age and the Search for Security: An American Social History.* Bloomington: Indiana University Press, 1994.

Hacker, Louis. *The Course of American Economic Growth and Development.* New York: Wiley, 1970.

Hahamovitch, Cindy. *The Fruits of Their Labor: Atlantic Coast Farm Workers and the Making of Atlantic Poverty, 1870–1945.* Chapel Hill: University of North Carolina Press, 1997.

Haines, Gerald K. "Under the Eagle's Wing: The Franklin Roosevelt Administration Forges an American Hemisphere." *Diplomatic History* 1 (Fall 1977): 380–87.

Halpern, Martin. *UAW Politics in the Cold War Era.* Albany: State University of New York Press, 1988.

Hamblin, Dora Jane. *That Was the Life.* New York: Norton, 1977.

Hamilton, Alastair. *The Appeal of Fascism: A Study of Intellectuals and Fascism.* With a foreword by Stephen Spender. New York: Macmillan, 1971.

Hamilton, David E. *From New Day to New Deal: American Farm Policy from Hoover to Roosevelt, 1928–1933.* Chapel Hill: University of North Carolina Press, 1991.

Hamilton, Marybeth. *"When I'm Bad, I'm Better": Mae West, Sex, and American Popular Entertainment.* New York: HarperCollins, 1993.

Hargrove, Erwin and Paul Conkin, eds., *TVA: Fifty Years of Grassroots Bureaucracy.* Urbana: University of Illinois Press, 1983.

Harlan, Lebo. Citizen Kane: *The Fiftieth-Anniversary Album.* New York: Doubleday, 1990.

Harmetz, Aljean. *The Making of* The Wizard of Oz. New York: Delta, 1989.

Harris, Brice. *The United States and the Italo-Ethiopian Crisis.* Stanford, CA: Stanford University Press, 1964.

Harris, William Hamilton. *Keeping the Faith: A. Philip Randolph, Milton P. Webster, and the Brotherhood of Sleeping Car Porters, 1925–37.* Urbana: University of Illinois Press, 1991.

Hart, Vivien. "Minimum-Wage Policy and Constitutional Inequality: The Paradox on the Fair Labor Standards Act of 1938." *Journal of Policy History* 1:3 (1999): 319–43.

Harwell, Richard, ed. Gone with the Wind *as Book and Film.* Columbia: University of South Carolina Press, 1992.

Haskins, James. *Always Movin' On: The Life of Langston Hughes.* Trenton, NJ: Africa World Press, 1993.

Hawes, Douglas W. *Utility Holding Companies.* New York: Clark, Boardman, 1987.

Hawley, Ellis W. *The New Deal and the Problem of Monopoly.* Princeton, NJ: Princeton University Press, 1966.

Hay, Peter. *MGM: When the Lion Roars.* Atlanta: Turner, 1991.

Hayes, Richard K. *Kate Smith: A Biography.* Jefferson, NC: McFarland, 1995.

Haynes, John Earl. *Dubious Alliance: The Making of Minnesota's DFL Party.* Minneapolis: University of Minnesota Press, 1984.

Hays, Will H. *Memoirs.* Garden City, NY: Doubleday, 1955.

Head, Sydney W. *Broadcasting in America: A Survey of Radio and Television.* 3rd ed. Boston: Houghton Mifflin, 1976.

Heale, M. J. *American Anticommunism: Combating the Enemy Within, 1830–1970.* Baltimore: Johns Hopkins University Press, 1990.

Heilbroner, Robert L. *The Worldly Philosophers: The Lives and Ideas of the Great Economic Thinkers.* 7th ed. New York: Simon & Schuster, 1999.

Heinemann, Ronald. *Depression and New Deal in Virginia: The Enduring Dominion.* Charlottesville: University Press of Virginia, 1983.

Heller, Nancy, and Julia Williams. *The Regionalists: Painters of the American Scene.* New York: Watson-Guptill, 1976.

Helmbold, Lois Rita. "Downward Occupational Mobility During the Great Depression: Urban Black and White Working Women." *Labor History.* 29:2 (1988):135–72.

———. *Making Choices, Making Do: Black and White Working Class Women's Lives and Work During the Great Depression.* Ph.D. diss., Stanford University, 1983. Ann Arbor, MI: UMI, 1992. 5712–8307166.

Helmbold, Lois Rita, and Ann Schofield. "Women's Labor History, 1790–1945." *Reviews in American History.* 17:4 (1989): 501–18.

Henderson, A. Scott. *Housing and the Democratic Ideal: The Life and Thought of Charles Abrams.* New York: Columbia University Press, 2000.

Hendrickson, Kenneth D., ed. *Hard Times in Oklahoma: The Depression Years.* Oklahoma City: Oklahoma State Historical Society, 1983.

Henie, Sonja. *Wings on My Feet.* New York: Prentice-Hall, 1940.

Hepburn, Katherine. *Me: Stories of My Life.* New York: Knopf, 1991.

Herner de Larrea, Irene. *Diego Rivera's Mural at Rockefeller Center.* Mexico City: Edicupes, S.A. de C.V., 1990.

Hickok, Lorena A. *One-Third of a Nation: Lorena Hickok Reports on the Great Depression.* Urbana: University of Illinois Press, 1981.

Hicks, Granville. *Part of the Truth: An Autobiography.* New York: Harcourt, Brace & World, 1965.

Higham, Charles. *Merchant of Dreams: Louis B. Mayer, M.G.M., and the Secret Hollywood.* New York: D.I. Fine, 1993.

Hill, Edwin G. *In the Shadow of the Mountain: The Spirit of the CCC.* Pullman: Washington State University Press, 1990.

Hillmer, Norman, and J.L. Granatstein. *For Better or For Worse.* Toronto: Copp Clark Pitman, 1991.

Hilmes, Michele. *Radio Voices: American Broadcasting, 1922–1952.* Minneapolis: University of Minnesota Press, 1997.

Himmelberg, Robert. *The Origins of the National Recovery Administration: Business, Government, and the Trade Association Issue, 1921–1933.* New York: Fordham University Press, 1976.

Hirsch, Foster. *Edward G. Robinson.* New York: Pyramid, 1975.

Historical Statistics of the United States: From Colonial Times to 1970. Washington, DC: Department of Commerce, Bureau of the Census, 1975: 723–741.

Hitler, Adolf. *Mein Kampf.* Trans. by Ralph Manheim. Boston: Houghton Mifflin, 1999.

Hobdell, George H. "Frank Knox, 11 July 1940–28 April 1944." In *American Secretaries of the Navy,* Vol. 2, ed. Paolo Coletta. Annapolis, MD: Naval Institute Press, 1980.

Hobson, Archie, ed. *Remembering America: A Sampler of the WPA American Guide Series.* New York: Columbia University Press, 1985.

Hodges, Donald, and Ross Gandy. *Mexico, 1910–1982: Reform or Revolution?* 2nd ed. Westport, CT: Zed, 1983.

Hodgson, Godfrey. *The Colonel: The Life and Wars of Henry Stimson, 1867–1950.* New York: Knopf, 1990.

Hoehlihng, A. A. *Who Destroyed the Hindenburg?* Boston: Little, Brown, 1962.

Hoffman, Abraham. *Unwanted Mexican Americans in the Great Depression.* Tucson: University of Arizona Press, 1974.

Hoff-Wilson, Joan. *Herbert Hoover: Forgotten Progressive.* Boston: Little, Brown, 1975.

Hofstadter, Richard. *The Age of Reform: From Bryan to F.D.R.* New York: Vintage, 1955.

———. *The American Political Tradition.* New York: Vintage, 1948.

Hogan, William Thomas. *Economic History of the Iron and Steel Industry in the United States.* Lexington, MA: Heath, 1971.

Holley, Donald. "The Negro in the New Deal Resettlement Program." *Agricultural History.* 45:3 (July, 1971): 179–95.

Holliday, Billie. *Lady Sings the Blues.* Garden City, NY: Doubleday, 1956.

Hollis, Daniel W. "'Cotton Ed' Smith—Showman or Statesman?" *South Carolina Historical Magazine* 71 (October 1970): 235–56.

Holt, Rackham. *Mary McLeod Bethune: A Biography.* Garden City, NY: Doubleday, 1964.

Holtzman, Abraham. *The Townsend Movement: A Political Study.* New York: Bookman Associates, 1963.

Honig, Donald. *The New York Yankees: An Illustrated History.* New York: Crown, 1987.

Honig, Nathaniel. *The Trade Union Unity League Today: Its Structure, Policy, Program and Growth.* New York: Labor Unity Publishers, 1934.

Hook, Sidney. *Out of Step: An Unquiet Life in the 20th Century.* New York: Harper & Row, 1987.

———. *Towards the Understanding of Karl Marx: A Revolutionary Interpretation.* New York: John Day, 1933.

Hoopes, Roy. *Cain.* New York: Holt, Rinehart & Winston, 1982.

Hoover, Herbert. *The Memoirs of Herbert Hoover: The Cabinet and the Presidency, 1920–1933.* New York: Macmillan, 1952.

———. *The Memoirs of the Great Depression, 1929–1941.* New York: Macmillan, 1952.

Hoover, J. Edgar. *Persons in Hiding.* Boston: Little, Brown, 1938.

Hopkins, Harry Lloyd. *Spending to Save: The Complete Story of Relief.* New York: Norton, 1936.

Hopkins, June. *Harry Hopkins: Sudden Hero, Brash Reformer.* New York: St. Martin's, 1999.

Hopper, Hedda. *From Under My Hat.* Garden City, NY: Doubleday, 1952.

Hosley, David. *As Good as Any Foreign Correspondent on American Radio, 1930–1940.* Contributions to the Study of Mass Media and Communications, 2. Westport, CT: Greenwood, 1984.

Howard, Donald S. *The WPA and Federal Relief Policy.* New York: Russell Sage Foundation, 1943.

Howard, Lillie P. *Zora Neale Hurston.* Boston: Twayne, 1980.

Howard, Moe. *Moe Howard and the Three Stooges.* Secaucus, NJ: Citadel, 1977.

Hoxie, Frederick, ed. *Encyclopedia of North American Indians.* New York: Houghton Mifflin, 1996.

Hoxie, Frederick, and Peter Iverson, *Indians in American History.* New York: Harlan Davidson, 1999.

Hughes, Charles Evans. *The Autobiographical Notes of Charles Evans Hughes.* Cambridge, MA: Harvard University Press, 1973.

———. *The Supreme Court of the United States: Its Foundation, Methods and Achievements: An Interpretation.* New York: Columbia University Press, 1928.

Hughes, H. Stuart. *The United States and Italy.* Cambridge, MA: Harvard University Press, 1965.

Hughes, Langston. *The Big Sea: An Autobiography.* New York: Hill & Wang, 1993 (reprint).

Hull, Cordell. *The Memoirs of Cordell Hull.* New York: Macmillan, 1948.

Hurley, Forrest Jack. *Portrait of a Decade: Roy Stryker and the Development of Documentary Photography in the Thirties.* Baton Rouge: Louisiana State University Press, 1972.

Hurston, Zora Neale. *Dust Tracks on a Road.* New York: Harper Perennial, 1996 (reprint).

———. *Folklore, Memoirs, and Other Writings.* New York: Library of America, 1995.

Huthmacher, J. Joseph. *Senator Robert F. Wagner and the Rise of Urban Liberalism.* New York: Atheneum, 1968.

Hyman, Sidney. *Marriner S. Eccles, Private Entrepreneur and Public Servant.* Stanford, CA: Graduate School of Business, Stanford University, 1976.

Ickes, Harold L. *The Autobiography of a Curmudgeon.* New York: Reynal and Hitchcock, 1943.

———. *Back to Work: The Story of the PWA.* New York: Macmillan, 1935.

Iriye, Akira..*The Cambridge History of American Foreign Relations,* Vol. 3, "The Globalizing of America, 1913–1945." New York: Cambridge University Press, 1993.

Irye, Akira. *Pearl Harbor and the Coming of the Pacific War: A Brief History with Documents and Essays.* Boston: Bedford/ St. Martin's, 1999.

Isakoff, Jack F. *The Public Works Administration.* Urbana: University of Illinois Press, 1938.

Iverson, Peter. *The Navajo Nation.* Albuquerque: University of New Mexico Press, 1981.

Jackson, Donald C. *Great American Bridges and Dams.* New York: Wiley, 1996.

Jackson, Julian. *The Politics of Depression in France, 1932–1936.* New York: Cambridge University Press, 1985.

———. *The Popular Front in France: Defending Democracy 1934–1938.* New York: Cambridge University Press, 1988.

Jackson, Kenneth T. *Crabgrass Frontier: The Suburbanization of the United States.* New York: Oxford University Press, 1985.

Jackson, Peter. "Vito Marcantonio and Ethnic Politics in New York." *Ethnic and Racial Studies* January (1983): 50–72.

Jacobs, Lewis. *The Documentary Tradition.* New York: W.W. Norton, 1979.

James, Dorris Clayton. *The Years of MacArthur.* Vol. 1, *1880–1941.* Boston: Houghton Mifflin, 1970.

Jeansonne, Glen. *Gerald L. K. Smith, Minister of Hate.* New Haven, CT: Yale University Press, 1988.

———. *Messiah of the Masses: Huey P. Long and the Great Depression.* New York: HarperCollins, 1993.

Jenkins, Roy. *Baldwin.* London: Collins, 1987.

Jessup, John K., ed. *The Ideas of Henry Luce.* New York: Atheneum, 1969.

Johanningsmeir, Edward P. *Forging American Communism: The Life of William Z. Foster.* Princeton, NJ: Princeton University Press, 1994.

Johnpoll, Bernard K. *Pacifist's Progress: Norman Thomas and the Decline of American Socialism.* Chicago: Quadrangle, 1970.

Johnson, Charles S., Will Alexander, and Edward R. Embree. *The Collapse of Cotton Tenancy.* Chapel Hill: University of North Carolina Press, 1935.

Johnson, Diane. *Dashiell Hammett: A Life.* New York: Random House, 1983.

Johnson, Donald Bruce. *The Republican Party and Wendell Willkie.* Urbana: University of Illinois Press, 1960.

Johnson, Hugh Samuel. *The Blue Eagle from Egg to Earth.* Garden City, NY: Doubleday, Doran, 1935.

Johnson, Roger T. *Robert M. La Follette, Jr. and the Decline of the Progressive Party in Wisconsin.* New York: Anchor, 1970.

Johnston, Carol Ingalls. *Of Time and the Artist: Thomas Wolfe, His Novels, and the Critics.* Columbia, SC: Camden House, 1995.

Jonas, Manfred. *Isolationism in America.* Ithaca, NY: Cornell University Press, 1966.

———. *The United States and Germany: A Diplomatic History.* Ithaca: Cornell University Press, 1984.

Jones, A.H. "The Search for a Usable American Past in the New Deal Era." *American Quarterly,* 23 (1971): 710–24.

Jones, Harry E. *Railroad Wages and Labor Relations, 1900–1952.* New York: Bureau of Information of the Eastern Railways, 1953.

Jones, Jesse H., with Edward Angly. *Fifty Billion Dollars: My Thirteen Years with the RFC (1932–1945).* New York: Macmillan, 1951.

Jordan, Rene. *Clark Gable.* New York: Galahad, 1973.

Josephson, Matthew. *Sidney Hillman: Statesman of American Labor.* Garden City, NY: Doubleday, 1952.

Kaufman, Andrew L. *Cardozo.* Cambridge, MA: Harvard University Press, 1998.

Kaufman, George G. *Banking Risk in Historical Perspective.* Chicago: Federal Reserve Bank of Chicago, 1986.

Kay, Jane Holtz. *Asphalt Nation: How the Automobile Took Over America and How We Can Take It Back.* New York: Crown, 1997.

Kazakoff, George. *Dangerous Theatre: The Federal Theatre Project As a Forum For New Plays.* New York: Peter Lang, 1989.

Keene, Jennifer. *Doughboys, the Great War, and the Remaking of America.* Baltimore: Johns Hopkins University Press, 2000.

Keiler, Allan. *Marian Anderson: A Singer's Journey.* New York: Scribner, 2000.

Kelley, Robin. *Hammer and Hoe: Alabama Communists During the Great Depression.* Chapel Hill: University of North Carolina Press, 1990.

Kemp, Giles. *Dale Carnegie: The Man Who Influenced Millions.* New York: St. Martin's, 1989.

Kempf, James Michael. *The Early Career of Malcolm Cowley: A Humanist Among the Moderns.* Baton Rouge: Louisiana State University Press, 1985.

Kendall, Alan. *George Gershwin: A Biography.* New York: Universe, 1987.

Kendall, Kathleen. *Communication in the Presidential Primaries: The Candidate and the Media, 1912–2000.* Westport, CT: Praeger, 2000.

Kennedy, David M. *Freedom From Fear: The American People in Depression and War, 1929–1945.* New York: Oxford University Press, 1999.

Kennedy, Ludovic. *The Airman and the Carpenter: The Lindbergh Kidnapping and the Framing of Richard Hauptmann.* New York: Viking, 1985.

———. *Crime of the Century: The Lindbergh Kidnapping and the Framing of Richard Hauptmann.* New York: Penguin Books, 1996.

Kennedy, Susan. *The Banking Crisis of 1933.* Lexington: University Press of Kentucky, 1973.

Kerr, K. Austin. *Organized for Prohibition: A New History of the Anti-Saloon League.* New Haven, CT: Yale University Press, 1985.

Kessler-Harris, Alice. "Gender Ideology in Historical Reconstruction: A Case Study from the 1930s." *Gender and History* 1 (Spring 1989): 31–44.

———. *Out to Work: A History of Wage-Earning Women in the United States.* New York: Oxford University Press, 1983.

Kessner, Thomas. *Fiorello La Guardia and the Making of Modern New York.* New York: McGraw-Hill, 1989.

Kettenman, Andrea. *Diego Rivera (1886–1957): A Revolutionary Spirit in Modern Art.* New York: Taschen, 1997.

Keynes, John Maynard. *The Collected Writings of John Maynard Keynes.* New York: St. Martin's, 1971.

———. *Essays in Persuasion.* Rev. ed. New York: W.W. Norton, 1963.

———. *General Theory of Employment, Interest and Money.* New York: Harcourt Brace, 1936.

———. "Open Letter to the President." *New York Times,* December 31, 1933, sec. 8, page 2.

Khademian, Anne M. *SEC and Capital Market Regulation: The Politics of Expertise.* Pittsburgh: University of Pittsburgh Press, 1992.

Kihlstedt, Folke T. "Utopia Realized: The World's Fairs of the 1930's." In *Imagining Tomorrow: History, Technology, and the American Future,* ed. Joseph J. Corn, 97–118. Cambridge: MIT Press, 1986.

Kimball, Warren. "Baffled Virtue . . . Injured Innocence: The Western Hemisphere as Regional Role Model." In *The Juggler.* Princeton, NJ: Princeton University Press, 1991.

Kimball, Warren F., ed. *Churchill and Roosevelt: The Complete Correspondence.* Princeton, NJ: Princeton University Press, 1984.

Kindleberger, C. *The World in Depression, 1929–1939.* Berkeley: University of California Press, 1986.

Kirby, John B. *Black Americans in the Roosevelt Era: Liberalism and Race.* Knoxville: University of Tennessee Press, 1980.

Kirkendall, Richard S. "The New Deal and Agriculture." In *The New Deal: The National Level,* ed. John Braeman, Robert H. Bremner, and David Brody, 83–109. Columbus: Ohio State University Press, 1975.

Kirkpatrick, Ivone, Sir. *Mussolini: A Study in Power.* New York: Avon, 1964.

Kirkwood, James Trace. "Corporate Profile: The American Life and Accident Insurance Company of Kentucky." *Filson Club History Quarterly* 66:2 (1992): 265–69.

Klebaner, Benjamin Joseph. *American Commercial Banking: A History.* Boston: Twayne, 1990.

Klehr, Harvey. *The Heyday of American Communism: The Depression Decade.* New York: Basic, 1984.

Klehr, Harvey and John Earl Haynes. *The American Communist Movement: Storming Heaven Itself.* New York: Twayne, 1992.

Klein, Joe. *Woody Guthrie: A Life.* New York: Knopf, 1980.

Klurfeld, Herman. *Winchell: His Life and Times.* New York: Praeger, 1976.

Knudson, R. Rozanne. *Babe Didrikson: Athlete of the Century.* New York: Viking Kestrel, 1985.

Kobler, John. *Capone: The Life and World of Al Capone.* New York: Putnam, 1971.

Konefsky, Samuel Joseph. *Chief Justice Stone and the Supreme Court.* New York: Macmillan, 1946.

———. *The Legacy of Holmes and Brandeis: A Study in the Influence of Ideas.* New York: Macmillan, 1956.

Koskoff, David E. *Joseph P. Kennedy: A Life and Times.* Englewood Cliffs, NJ: Prentice-Hall, 1974.

———. *The Mellons: The Chronicle of America's Richest Family.* New York: Crowell, 1978.

Kozol, Wendy. *Life's America.* Philadelphia: Temple University Press, 1994.

Kracauer, Siegfried, and Joseph Lyford. "A Duck Crossed Main Street." *New Republic* 13 (December 1948): 13.

Kraus, Henry. *Heroes of Unwritten Story: The UAW, 1934–1939.* Urbana, IL: University of Illinois Press, 1993.

———. *The Many and the Few: A Chronicle of the Dynamic Auto Workers,* 2d ed. Urbana: University of Illinois Press, 1985.

Kraus, Henry. *Heroes of Unwritten Story: The UAW, 1934–1939.* Urbana: University of Illinois Press, 1993.

Krooss, Herman, ed. *Documentary History of Banking and Currency in the United States.* New York: Chelsea House, 1969.

Kuehl, Warren F. *Keeping the Covenant: American Internationalists and the League of Nations, 1920–1939.* Kent, OH: Kent State University Press, 1997.

Kurian, George Thomas. *Datapedia of the United States, 1790–2000: America Year by Year.* Lanham, MD: Bernan Press, 1994.

Kurson, Robert, and Martin Short. *The Official Three Stooges Encyclopedia: The Ultimate Knucklehead's Guide to Stoogedom.* Lincolnwood, IL: Contemporary Books, 1998.

Kurtz, Ernest. *A.A.: The Story.* San Francisco: Harper & Row, 1988.

Kwolek-Follan, Angel. *Engendering Business: Men and Women in the Corporate Office, 1870–1930.* Baltimore: Johns Hopkins University Press, 1994.

La Guardia, Fiorello. *The Making of an Insurgent.* Philadelphia: Lippincott & Crowell, 1948.

Lacey, Robert. *Ford, the Men and the Machine.* Boston: Little, Brown, 1986.

Lacy, Leslie Alexander. *The Soil Soldiers: The Civilian Conservation Corps in the Great Depression.* Radnor, Pennsylvania: Chilton, 1976.

Lambert, Roger C. "Drought Relief for Cattlemen: The Emergency Purchase Program of 1934–1935." *Panhandle-Plains Historical Review* (1972).

Landis, Arthur H. *Death in the Olive Groves: American Volunteers in the Spanish Civil War, 1936–1939.* New York: Paragon House, 1989.

Landsberg, Melvin. *Dos Passos' Path to U.S.A.: A Political Biography, 1912–1936.* Boulder, CO: Associated University Press, 1972.

Lane, Roger. *Murder in America.* Columbus: Ohio State University Press, 1997.

Lange, Dorothea. *An American Exodus: A Record of Human Erosion in the Thirties.* New Haven, CT: Yale University Press, 1969 (reprint).

Langer, William L., and S. Everett Gleason. *The Undeclared War: 1940–1941.* New York: Harper, 1953.

Larrowe, Charles P. *Harry Bridges: The Rise and Fall of Radical Labor in the United States.* New York: Lawrence Hill, 1972.

Lash, Joseph P. *Dealers and Dreamers: A New Look at the New Deal.* New York: Doubleday, 1988.

Laslett, John H. M., ed. *The United Mine Workers of America: A Model of Industrial Solidarity?* University Park: Pennsylvania State University Press, 1996.

Lawson, Don. *The Abraham Lincoln Brigade: Americans Fighting Fascism in the Spanish Civil War.* New York: Crowell, 1989.

Layman, Richard. *Shadow Man: The Life of Dashiell Hammett.* New York: Bruccoli Clark Layman, 1981.

Leab, Daniel J. *A Union of Individuals: The Formation of the American Newspaper Guild, 1933–1936.* New York: Columbia University Press, 1970.

Lee, Alfred McClung, and Elizabeth Briant Lee, eds. *The Fine Art of Propaganda: A Study of Father Coughlin's Speeches.* New York: Harcourt Brace, 1939.

Lee, Stephen J. *Stalin and the Soviet Union.* New York: Routledge, 1999.

Leff, Mark H. *The Limits of Symbolic Reform: The New Deal and Taxation.* Cambridge: Cambridge University Press, 1984.

Leibovitz, Clement. *In Our Time: The Chamberlain-Hitler Collusion.* New York: Monthly Review, 1998.

Lekachman, Robert. *The Age of Keynes.* New York: Vintage, 1968.

Lender, Mark Edward, and James Kirby Martin. *Drinking in America: A History.* New York: Free Press, 1982.

Leonard, Charles A. *A Search for a Judicial Philosophy: Mr. Justice Roberts and the Constitutional Revolution of 1937.* Port Washington, NY: Kennikat, 1971.

Leuchtenberg, William E. *Franklin D. Roosevelt and the New Deal.* New York: Harper & Row, 1963.

———. *The Supreme Court Reborn: Constitutional Revolution in the Age of Roosevelt.* New York: Oxford University Press, 1995.

Levenson, Leah. *Granville Hicks: The Intellectual in Mass Society.* Philadelphia: Temple University Press, 1993.

Levine, Rhonda F. *Class Struggle and the New Deal: Industrial Labor, Industrial Capital, and the State.* Lawrence: University of Kansas Press, 1988.

Levy, Beryl Harold. *Cardozo and Frontiers of Legal Thinking, with Selected Opinions.* Cleveland: Press of Case Western Reserve University, 1969.

"Lewis, John L." In *Biographical Dictionary of American Labor Leaders,* ed. Gary M. Fink. Westport, CT: Greenwood, 1974.

"Lewis, John L." In *Current Biography 1942,* ed. Maxine Block. New York: Wilson, 1942.

Lewis, Tom. *Empire of the Air: The Men Who Made Radio.* New York: Edward Burlingame, 1991.

Lichtenstein, Nelson. *The Most Dangerous Man in Detroit: Walter Reuther and the Fate of American Labor.* New York: Basic, 1995.

Liebovich, Louis. *Press Reaction to the Bonus March of 1932: A Re-evaluation of the Impact of an American Tragedy.* Columbia, SC: Association for Education in Journalism and Mass Communication, 1990.

Lindbergh, Charles Augustus. *Of Flight and Life.* New York: Scribner's, 1948.

Lindblom, Charles. *Politics and Markets.* New York: Basic, 1977.

Lindley, Betty, and Ernest K. Lindley. *A New Deal for Youth: The Story of the National Youth Administration.* New York: Viking, 1938.

Lippmann, Walter. *An Inquiry into the Principles of the Good Society.* Boston: Little, Brown, 1937.

———. *A New Social Order.* New York: John Day, 1933.

Lipstadt, Deborah E. *Beyond Belief: The American Press and the Coming of the Holocaust, 1933–1945*. New York: Free Press, 1986.

Lisio, Donald J. *The President and Protest: Hoover, Conspiracy, and the Bonus Riot*. Columbia: University of Missouri Press, 1974.

Lorant, Stefan. *The Presidency: A Pictorial History of Presidential Elections From Washington to Truman*. New York: Macmillan, 1951.

Lord, Russell. *The Century of the Common Man, by Henry A. Wallace. Selected from Public Papers*. New York: Reynal & Hitchcock, 1943.

Loss, Louis. *Fundamentals of Securities Regulation*. 2nd ed. Boston: Little, Brown, 1988.

Louchheim, Katie. *The Making of the New Deal: The Insiders Speak*. Cambridge, MA: Harvard University Press, 1983.

Louvish, Simon. *Man on the Flying Trapeze: The Life and Times of W.C. Fields*. New York: Norton, 1997.

———. *Monkey Business: The Lives and Legends of the Marx Brothers: Groucho, Chico, Harpo, Zeppo, with added Gummo*. London: Faber & Faber, 1999.

Lovell, Mary S. *The Sound of Wings: The Life of Amelia Earhart*. New York: St. Martin's, 1989.

Lower, Richard Coke. *A Bloc of One: The Political Career of Hiram W. Johnson*. Stanford, CA: Stanford University Press, 1993.

Lowitt, Richard. *George Norris: The Making of a Progressive, 1861–1912*. Urbana: University of Illinois Press, 1963.

———. *George Norris: The Persistence of a Progressive, 1913–1933*. Urbana: University of Illinois Press, 1971.

———. *George Norris: The Triumph of a Progressive, 1933–1944*. Urbana: University of Illinois Press, 1978.

Lubell, Samuell. "The Roosevelt Coalition." In *The New Deal: Analysis and Interpretation*, ed. Alonzo Hamby. New York: Weybright & Talley, 1969.

Luce, Henry R. *The American Century*. New York: Farrar & Rinehart, 1941.

Luger, Stan. *Corporate Power, American Democracy and the Automobile Industry*. New York: Cambridge University Press, 2000.

Lukacs, John. *The Hitler of History*. New York: Knopf, 1997.

Lunt, Richard D. *The High Ministry of Government: The Political Career of Frank Murphy*. Detroit: Wayne State University Press, 1965.

Lynn, Kenneth Schuyler. *Hemingway*. New York: Simon & Schuster, 1987.

Lyons, Robert. *World War II: A Short History*. Englewood Cliffs, NJ: Prentice-Hall, 1999.

MacArthur, Douglas. *Reminiscences*. New York: McGraw-Hill, 1978.

MacDonald, Lois. "The National Labor Relations Act." *American Economic Review* 26:3 (September 1936): 412–27.

Mack Smith, Denis. *Mussolini*. New York: Vintage, 1982.

MacLeish, Archibald. *A Continuing Journey*. Boston: Houghton Mifflin, 1968.

MacMahon, Arthur W., John D. Millett, and Gladys Ogden. *The Administration of Federal Work Relief*. Chicago: Public Administration Service, 1941.

Maharidge, Dale. *And Their Children After Them: The Legacy of Let Us Now Praise Famous Men: James Agee, Walker Evans, and the Rise and Fall of Cotton in the South*. New York: Pantheon, 1989.

Maland, Charles J. *Frank Capra*. New York: Twayne, 1995.

Mallery, Otto T. "Prosperity Reserves." *Survey*, 62: 1 (April 1, 1929).

Manchester, William Raymond. *American Caesar: Douglas MacArthur, 1880–1964*. Boston: Little, Brown, 1978.

Mandell, Richard D. *The Nazi Olympics*. New York: Macmillan, 1971.

Maney, Patrick J. *"Young Bob" La Follette: A Biography of Robert M. La Follette, Jr., 1895–1953*. Columbia: University of Missouri Press, 1978.

Mangione, Jerre G. *The Dream and the Deal: The Federal Writer's Project, 1935–1943*. Philadelphia: University of Pennsylvania Press, 1983.

Mann, Arthur. *La Guardia: A Fighter Against His Times*. Philadelphia: Lippincott, 1959.

Marcus, Robert D. *Grand Old Party: Political Structure in the Gilded Age, 1880–1896*. New York: Oxford University Press, 1971.

Margo, Robert A. "Labor and the Labor Markets in the 1930s." In *The Economics of the Great Depression*, ed. Mark Wheeler, 9–27. Kalamazoo, MI: W. E. Upjohn Institute for Employment Research, 1998:

Markowitz, Gerald, and David Rosner, eds. *"Slaves of the Depression": Workers' Letters about Life on the Job*. Ithaca, NY: Cornell University Press, 1987.

Marling, Karal Ann. *Wall-to-Wall America: A Cultural History of Post-Office Murals in the Great Depression*. Minneapolis: University of Minnesota Press, 1982.

Marling, William. *Raymond Chandler*. Boston: Twayne, 1986.

Marquand, David. *Ramsay MacDonald*. London: Jonathan Cape, 1977.

Marquis, Alice G. *Hope and Ashes: The Birth of Modern Times 1929–1939*. New York: Free Press, 1986.

Marquis, James. *Mr. Garner of Texas*. Indianapolis: Bobbs-Merrill, 1939.

Martin, Albro. *Railroads Triumphant: The Growth, Rejection, and Rebirth of a Vital American Force*. New York: Oxford University Press, 1992.

Martin, George W. *Madame Secretary: Frances Perkins*. Boston: Houghton Mifflin, 1976.

Marx, Arthur. *Goldwyn: A Biography of the Man Behind the Myth*. New York: Norton, 1976.

Marx, Samuel, and Jan Clayton. *Rodgers and Hart: Bewitched, Bothered, and Bedeviled*. New York: Putnam, 1976.

Mason, Alpheus Thomas. *Harlan Fiske Stone: Pillar of the Law*. New York: Viking, 1956.

"Matinee Idols of the News Reels," *Literary Digest*, September 5, 1931: 32.

Mayer, George H. *The Political Career of Floyd B. Olson*. Minneapolis: University of Minnesota Press, 1951.

McBride, Joseph, ed. *Hawks on Hawks: Discussions*. Berkeley: University of California Press, 1982.

McBrien, William. *Cole Porter: A Biography*. New York: Knopf, 1998.

McCabe, John. *Cagney*. New York: Knopf, 1997.

McCann, Graham. *Cary Grant: A Class Apart*. New York: Columbia University Press, 1996.

McCarthy, Todd. *Howard Hawks: The Grey Fox of Hollywood*. New York: Grove, 1997.

McCarty, Clifford. *The Complete Films of Humphrey Bogart*. Secaucus, NJ: Carol Publishing Group, 1995.

McChesney, Robert W. *Telecommunications, Mass Media, and*

Democracy: The Battle for the Control of U.S. Broadcasting, 1928–1935. New York: Oxford University Press. 1993.

McCluskey, Audrey Thomas, and Elaine M. Smith, eds. *Mary McLeod Bethune: Building a Better World: Essays and Selected Documents.* Bloomington: IN University Press, 1999.

McConnell, Grant. *The Decline of Agrarian Democracy.* New York: Atheneum, 1969.

McCoy, Donald R. *Angry Voices: Left-of-Center Politics in the New Deal Era.* Lawrence: University of Kansas Press, 1958.

———. *Landon of Kansas.* Lincoln: University of Nebraska Press, 1966.

McCraw, Thomas K. *Prophets of Regulation: Charles Francis Adams, Louis D. Brandeis, James M. Landis, Alfred E. Kahn.* Cambridge: Belknap Press of Harvard University Press, 1984.

McCurry, Dan C. *The Farmer-Labor Party: History, Platform, and Programs.* New York: Arno, 1975.

McDonald, Forrest. *Insull.* Chicago: University of Chicago Press, 1962.

McDonald, William F. *Federal Relief Administration and the Arts: The Origins and Administrative History of the Arts Projects of the Works Progress Administration.* Columbus: Ohio State University Press, 1969.

McDonough, Frank. *Neville Chamberlain: Appeasement and the British Road to War.* New York: St. Martin's, 1998.

McElvaine, Robert S. *The Great Depression: America, 1929–1941.* New York: Oxford University Press, 1984.

———. *The Depression and New Deal: A History in Documents.* New York: Oxford University Press, 2000.

McGovern, James R. *And a Time for Hope: Americans in the Great Depression.* Westport, CT: Praeger, 2000.

McKinzie, Richard D. *The New Deal for Artists.* Princeton, NJ: Princeton University Press, 1973.

McMurtry, Larry. *Pretty Boy Floyd: A Novel.* New York: Simon & Schuster, 1994.

McQuaid, Kim. *Big Business and Presidential Power.* New York: Morrow, 1982.

McWilliams, Carey. *Louis Adamic and Shadow-America.* Los Angeles: Whipple, 1935.

Mead, Chris. *Champion—Joe Louis: Black Hero in White America.* New York: Scribner, 1985.

Meltzer, Milton. *Dorothea Lange: A Photographer's Life.* Syracuse, NY: Syracuse University Press, 2000.

Menefee, Selden. "The Movies Join Hearst," *The New Republic,* October 9, 1935: 241.

Merkley, Paul. *Reinhold Niebuhr: A Political Account.* Montreal: McGill-Queen's University Press, 1975.

Merrill, Hugh. *Esky: The Early Years at Esquire.* New Brunswick, NJ: Rutgers University Press, 1995.

Merrill, Perry H. *Roosevelt's Forest Army: A History of the Civilian Conservation Corps.* Barre, VT: Northlight Studio, 1981.

Mettler, Susanne. *Dividing Citizens: Gender and Federalism in New Deal Public Policy.* Ithaca, NY: Cornell University Press, 1998.

Meyer, Gerald. "American Labor Party." In *Encyclopedia of Third Parties in America,* ed. Immanuel Ness and James Ciment. Armonk, NY: Sharpe, 2000.

———. *Vito Marcantonio: Radical Politician, 1902–1954.* Albany: State University of New York, 1989.

Meyers, Jeffrey. *Edmund Wilson: A Biography.* Boston: Houghton Mifflin, 1995.

———. *Gary Cooper: American Hero.* New York: Morrow, 1998.

Michaelis, Meir. *Mussolini and the Jews: German-Italian Relations and the Jewish Question in Italy, 1922–1945.* New York: Oxford University Press, 1978.

Milkis, Sidney. *The President and the Parties: The Transformation of the American Party System Since the New Deal.* New York: Oxford University Press, 1993.

Miller, Dan B. *Erskine Caldwell: The Journey from Tobacco Road: A Biography.* New York: Knopf, 1995.

Miller, John E. *Governor Philip F. La Follette, the Wisconsin Progressives, and the New Deal.* Columbia: University of Missouri Press, 1982.

Milner, E. R. *The Lives and Times of Bonnie and Clyde.* Carbondale: Southern Illinois University Press, 1996.

Minter, David. *William Faulkner: His Life and Work.* Baltimore: Johns Hopkins University Press, 1980.

Mintz, Frank P. *The Liberty Lobby and the American Right: Race, Conspiracy, and Culture.* Westport, CT: Greenwood, 1985.

Mitchell, Broadus. *Depression Decade: From New Era through new Deal, 1929–1941.* New York: Harper & Row, 1947.

Mitchell, Glenn. *The Marx Brothers Encyclopedia.* London: Batsford, 1996.

Mitchell, Greg. *The Campaign of the Century: Upton Sinclair's Race for Governor of California and the Birth of Media Politics.* New York: Random House, 1992.

Mitchell, Richard H. *Thought Control in Prewar Japan.* Ithaca, NY: Cornell University Press, 1976.

Modell, John. *Into One's Own: From Youth to Adulthood in the United States, 1920–1975.* Berkeley: University of California Press, 1989.

Moley, Raymond. *After Seven Years.* New York: Harper, 1939.

———. *The Hays Office.* Indianapolis: Bobbs-Merrill, 1945.

———. *Realities and Illusions, 1886–1931: The Autobiography of Raymond Moley.* New York: Garland, 1980.

Moley, Raymond, and Eliot A. Rosen. *The First New Deal.* New York: Harcourt, Brace & World, 1966.

Monroy, Douglas. *Rebirth: Mexican Los Angeles From the Great Migration to the Great Depression.* Berkeley: University of California Press, 1999.

Montoya, Maria E. "The Roots of Economic and Ethnic Divisions in Northern New Mexico: The Case of the Civilian Conservation Corps." *Western Historical Quarterly* 26:1 (Spring 1995): 14–34.

Mooney, Booth. *Roosevelt and Rayburn: A Political Partnership.* Philadelphia: Lippincott, 1971.

Moore, Clayton, and Frank Thompson. *I Was That Masked Man.* Dallas: Taylor, 1996.

Moore, Jesse Thomas. *A Search for Equality: The National Urban League, 1910–1961.* University Park: Pennsylvania State University Press, 1981.

Moore, John Robert. *Senator Josiah William Bailey of North Carolina.* Durham, NC: Duke University Press, 1968.

Mora, Gilles. *Walker Evans: The Hungry Eye.* New York: Abrams, 1993.

Morehead, Philip D, with Anne MacNeil. *The New International Dictionary of Music.* New York: Penguin, 1992.

Moreo, Dominic W. *Schools in the Great Depression.* New York: Garland, 1996.

Morgan, Austen. *J. Ramsay MacDonald.* Manchester, England: Manchester University Press, 1987.

Morison, Elting Elmore. *Turmoil and Tradition: A Study of the Life and Times of Henry L. Stimson.* New York: Atheneum, 1964.

Morse, Arthur D. *While Six Million Died: A Chronicle of American Apathy*. New York: Random House, 1968.

Morwood, William. *Duel for the Middle Kingdom: The Struggle Between Chiang Kai-shek and Mao Tse-tung for Control of China*. New York: Everest House, 1980.

Mosley, Leonard. *Disney's World: A Biography*. New York: Stein and Day, 1985.

————. *Marshall: Hero for Our Times*. New York: Hearst, 1982.

Moyers, Bill. "*Profile of Edward R. Murrow,*" *American Masters*, PBS, 2/21/91, pt. 2.

Mueller, John E. *Astaire Dancing: The Musical Films*. New York: Knopf, 1985.

Mulcahy, C. Richard. "Working Against the Odds: Josephine Roche, The New Deal, and the Drive for National Health Insurance." *Maryland Historian* 25:2 (1994): 1–21.

Mund, Vernon Arthur. "Prosperity Reserves of Public Works." In *Annals of the American Academy of Political and Social Science* 149, Part II (May 1930): 1–47.

Murray, Edward. *Clifford Odets: The Thirties and After.* New York: Ungar, 1968.

Muscio, Giuliana. "*Film, Industry, and the New Deal*" Ph.D. diss. University of California, Los Angeles, 1992.

Myrdal, Gunnar. *An American Dilemma: The Negro Problem and Modern Democracy*. Vol. 1. New York: Harper & Row, 1962.

Naison, Mark. *Communists in Harlem During the Depression*. New York: Grove, 1983.

Namorato. Michael V. *Rexford G. Tugwell: A Biography*. New York: Praeger, 1988.

Nasaw, David. *The Chief: The Life of William Randolph Hearst*. Boston: Houghton Mifflin, 2000.

Nash, Gerald. *The Great Depression and World War II: Organizing America, 1933–1945*. New York: St. Martin's, 1979.

Nation Associates. *The Best of* The Nation: *A Selection of the Best Articles of Lasting Value to Appear in* The Nation *During the Recent Past*. New York: The Nation Associates, 1952.

National Emergency Council. *Report on Economic Conditions of the South*. Washington, 1938.

National Labor Relations Board. *A Guide to Basic Law and Procedures Under the National Labor Relations Act*. Prepared in the Office of the General Counsel. Washington, DC: Government Printing Office, 1976.

Neatby, H. Blair. *The Politics of Chaos: Canada in the Thirties*. Toronto: Copp Clark Pitman, 1986.

Neimi, Albert W., Jr. *U.S. Economic History: A Survey of the Major Issues*. Chicago: Rand McNally , 1975.

Nelson, Bruce. *Workers on the Waterfront: Seamen, Longshoremen, and Unionism in the 1930s*. Urbana: University of Illinois Press, 1988.

Nelson, Daniel. "The Great Goodyear Strike of 1936." *Ohio History* 92 (1983): 6–36.

————. "Origins of the Sit-Down Era: Worker Militancy and Innovation in the Rubber Industry, 1934–1938," *Labor History* 23:2 (1982): 198–225

Nelson, Nancy, ed. *Evenings with Cary Grant: Recollections in His Own Words and by Those Who Knew Him Best*. New York: Morrow, 1991.

Neumann, Caryn E. "The End of Gender Solidarity: The History of the Women's Organization for National Prohibition Reform in the United States, 1929–1933." *Journal of Women's History* 9:2 (Summer 1997): 31–51.

Newman, Roger K. *Hugo Black: A Biography*. New York: Pantheon, 1994.

Nish, Ian Hill. *Japan's Struggle with Internationalism: Japan, China, and the League of Nations, 1931–33*. New York: K. Paul International, 1993.

Norris, George. *Fighting Liberal: The Autobiography of George W. Norris*. New York: Macmillan, 1945.

North, Joseph, ed. New Masses: *An Anthology of the Rebel Thirties*. New York: International Publishers, 1969.

O'Connor, F.V. ed.: *Art for the Millions: Essays from the 1930s*. Greenwich, CT: New York Graphic Society, 1973.

————. *The New Deal Art Projects: An Anthology of Memoirs*. Washington, DC: Smithsonian Institution Press, 1972.

O'Connor, Harvey. *Mellon's Millions: The Biography of a Fortune: The Life and Times of Andrew W. Mellon*. New York: John Day, 1933.

O'Connor, Richard. *The First Hurrah: A Biography of Alfred E. Smith*. New York: Putnam, 1970.

————. *Heywood Broun: A Biography*. New York: Putnam, 1975.

————. *Sinclair Lewis*. New York: McGraw-Hill, 1971.

Odum, Howard W., and Harry E. Moore. *American Regionalism*. New York: Holt, 1938.

Office of Management and Budget. *Budget of the United States Government, Fiscal Year 2000: Historical Tables*. Washington, DC: Government Printing Office, 2000.

Offner, Arnold A. *American Appeasement: United States Foreign Policy and Germany, 1933–1938*. New York: Norton, 1969.

Ogden, August Raymond. *The Dies Committee: A Study of the Special House Committee for the Investigation of Un-American Activities, 1938–1944*. Washington, DC: The Catholic University of America Press, 1945.

Ohl, John Kennedy. *Hugh Johnson and the New Deal*. Dekalb: Northern Illinois University Press, 1985.

Olson, James S. *Herbert Hoover and the Reconstruction Finance Corporation, 1931–1933*. Ames: Iowa State University Press, 1977.

Olson, James S. *Saving Capitalism: The Reconstruction Finance Corporation and the New Deal, 1933–1940*. Princeton, NJ: Princeton University Press, 1988.

O'Reilly, Kenneth. *Hoover and the Un-Americans: The FBI, HUAC, and the Red Menace*. Philadelphia: Temple University Press, 1983.

————. "A New Deal for the FBI: The Roosevelt Administration, Crime Control, and National Security." *Journal of American History* 69 (December 1982): 683–58.

Ott, Frederick W. *The Films of Carole Lombard*. Secaucus, NJ: Citadel, 1972.

Ottanelli, Fraser. *The Communist Party of the United States: From the Depression to World War II*. New Brunswick, NJ: Rutgers University Press, 1991.

Owens, Jesse, and Paul G. Neimark. *Blackthink: My Life as Black Man and White Man*. New York: Morrow, 1970.

Owens, Louis. *John Steinbeck's Re-vision of America*. Athens: University of Georgia Press, 1985.

Paige, Leroy, and David Lipman. *Maybe I'll Pitch Forever: A Great Baseball Player Tells the Hilarious Story Behind the Legend*. Lincoln: University of Nebraska Press, 1993.

Palmer, Frederick. *This Man Landon: The Record and Career of Governor Alfred M. Landon of Kansas*. New York: Dodd, Mead, 1936.

Papers of the Rural Electrification Administration. *Record Group 221, National Archives and Records Administration*. College Park, MD.

Parini, Jay. *John Steinbeck: A Biography*. New York: Holt, 1995.

Paris, Barry. *Garbo: A Biography*. New York: Random House, 1995.

Parman, Donald L. "The Indian and the Civilian Conservation Corps." In *The American Indian*, ed. Hundley, Norris. Santa Barbara: University of California Press, 1974.

Parrish, Michael E. *Anxious Decades: America in Prosperity and Depression, 1920–1941*. New York: Norton, 1992.

———. *Felix Frankfurter and His Times*. New York: Free Press, 1982.

———. *Securities Regulation and the New Deal*. New Haven, CT: Yale University Press, 1970.

Parsons, Kenneth H., Raymond J. Penn, and Philip M. Raup. *Land Tenure*. Madison: University of Wisconsin Press, 1951.

Parsons, Louella. *The Gay Illiterate*. Garden City, NY: Doubleday, Doran, 1944.

Paschal, Joel Francis. *Mr. Justice Sutherland: A Man Against the State*. Princeton, NJ: Princeton University Press, 1951.

Patrick, Sue Carol. *Reform of the Federal Reserve System in the Early 1930s: The Politics of Money and Banking*. New York: Garland, 1993.

Patterson, Donald O. "Male Retirement Behavior in the United States, 1930–1950." *Journal of Economic History*. 51:3 (September 1991): 657–74.

Patterson, James T. *America's Struggle Against Poverty 1900–1980*. Cambridge: Harvard University Press, 1981.

———. *Congressional Conservatism and the New Deal: The Growth of the Conservative Coalition in Congress, 1933–1939*. Lexington: University of Kentucky Press, 1967.

———. *The New Deal and the States: Federalism in Transition*. Princeton, NJ: Princeton University Press, 1969.

Paulsen, George. "Ghost of the NRA: Drafting National Wage and Hour Legislation in 1937." *Social Science Quarterly* 67:2 (June 1986): 241–54.

———. *A Living Wage for the Forgotten Man: The Quest for Fair Labor Standards, 1933–1941*. Selinsgrove, PA: Susquehanna University Press, 1996.

Payne, Stanley G. *A History of Fascism, 1914–1945*. Madison: University of Wisconsin Press, 1995.

Pecora, Ferdinand. *Wall Street Under Oath; The Story of Our Modern Money Changers*. New York: Simon & Schuster, 1939.

Peek, George N. *Why Quit Our Own*. New York: Van Nostrand, 1936.

Pegram, Thomas R. *Battling Demon Rum: The Struggle for a Dry America, 1800–1933*. Chicago: Ivan R. Dee, 1998

Pepper, Claude. *Pepper: Eyewitness to a Century*. San Diego: Harcourt Brace Jovanovich, 1987.

Perkins, Frances. *The Roosevelt I Knew*. New York: Viking, 1946.

Persico, Joseph E. *Edward R. Murrow: An American Original*. New York: McGraw-Hill, 1988.

Peterson, Merrill D. *Coming of Age with the New Republic, 1938–1950*. Columbia: University of Missouri Press, 1999.

Peterson, Theodore. *Magazines in the Twentieth Century*. Urbana: University of Illinois Press, 1964.

Pfeffer, Paula F. *A. Philip Randolph: Pioneer of the Civil Rights Movement*. Baton Rouge: Louisiana State University Press, 1990.

Phelan, Craig. *William Green: Biography of a Labor Leader*. Albany: State University of New York Press, 1989.

Phelps, Christopher. *Young Sidney Hook: Marxist and Pragmatist*. Ithaca, NY: Cornell University Press, 1997.

Philip, Kenneth. *John Collier's Crusade for Indian Reform, 1920–1954*. Tucson: University of Arizona Press, 1981.

Phillips, Cabell. *The New York Times Chronicle of American Life: From the Crash to the Blitz, 1929–1939*. London: Macmillan, 1969.

Phillips, Susan M., and J. Richard Zecher. *The SEC and the Public Interest*. Cambridge, MA: MIT Press, 1981.

Pike, Bob. *The Genius of Busby Berkeley*. Reseda, CA: CFS Books, 1973.

Pike, Frederick. *FDR's Good Neighbor Policy: Sixty Years of Generally Gentle Chaos*. Austin: University of Texas Press, 1995.

Pitigliani, Fausto. *The Italian Corporative State*. New York: Macmillan, 1934.

Pitts, Michael R. *Kate Smith: A Bio-bibliography*. New York: Greenwood, 1988.

"Play Past Sixty." *Recreation* (September 1936): 301–02.

Plotke, David. *Building a Democratic Order: Reshaping American Liberalism in the 1930s and 1940s*. Princeton, NJ: Princeton University Press, 1996.

Polenberg, Richard. *War and Society: The United States, 1941–1945*. Philadelphia: Lippincott, 1972.

Pollack, Howard. *Aaron Copland: The Life and Work of an Uncommon Man*. New York: Holt, 1999.

Potter, Claire Bond. *War on Crime: Bandits, G-Men, and the Politics of Mass Culture*. New Brunswick, NJ: Rutgers University Press, 1998.

Powers, Richard Gid. *G-Men: Hoover's FBI in American Popular Culture*. Carbondale: Southern Illinois University Press, 1983.

———. *Not Without Honor: The History of American Anticommunism*. New York: Free Press, 1995.

Prange, Gordon. *At Dawn We Slept: The Untold Story of Pearl Harbor*. New York: McGraw-Hill, 1981.

Pratt, Julius William. *Cordell Hull, 1933–1944*. New York: Cooper Square, 1964.

Prescott, Kenneth Wade. *The Complete Graphic Works of Ben Shahn*. New York: Quadrangle, 1973.

"President Roosevelt's March 12, 1933 Fireside Chat." In *Documentary History of Banking and Currency in the United States*, ed. Herman Krooss. New York: Chelsea House, 1969.

Preston, Paul. *The Coming of the Spanish Civil War: Reform, Reaction and Revolution in the Second Republic*. 2nd ed. New York: Routledge, 1994.

———. *Franco: A Biography*. New York: Basic, 1994.

Preston, William. *Aliens and Dissenters: Federal Suppression of Radicals, 1903–1933*. Cambridge: Harvard University Press, 1963.

Pringle, Henry Fowles. *Alfred E. Smith: A Critical Study*. New York: AMS, 1970.

Pryor, Thomas M. "Newsreels for the Home." *New York Times* July 4, 1937: 4.

Public Works Administration. *America Builds: The Record of PWA*. Washington, DC: Government Printing Office, 1939.

Purcell, Carol W., Jr. "The Administration of Science in the Department of Agriculture, 1933–1940." *Agricultural History* 42:3 (July 1968): 231–40.

Pusey, Merlo John. *Charles Evans Hughes*. New York: Macmillan, 1951.

Rader, Benjamin. *American Sports*. Englewood Cliffs, NJ: Prentice-Hall, 1990.

Radford, Gail. *Modern Housing for America: Policy Struggles in the New Deal Era*. Chicago: University of Chicago Press, 1996.

Rae, John. *The American Automobile: A Brief History*. Chicago: University of Chicago Press, 1965.

Rampersad, Arnold. *The Life of Langston Hughes*. 2 vols. New York: Oxford University Press, 1986.

Raper, Arthur Franklin. *The Tragedy of Lynching*. New York: Dover, 1970 (reprint).

Rappoport, Helen. *Joseph Stalin: A Biographical Companion.* Santa Barbara: ABC-CLIO, 1999.

Rauch, Basil, *The History of the New Deal, 1933–1938.* New York: Creative Age Press, 1944.

Raymond, Alex. *Flash Gordon.* Franklin Square, PA: Nostalgia Press, 1967.

Reeves, William D. "PWA and Competitive Administration in the New Deal." *Journal of American History,* 60 (September 1973): 357–72.

Reiman, Richard A. *The New Deal and American Youth: Ideas and Ideals in a Depression Decade.* Athens: University of Georgia Press, 1992.

Rein, Conrad L. *From Southland to Sunbelt: The Legacy of Dependent Development in New Orleans and Louisiana, 1930–1990.* Ann Arbor, MI: UMI, 1998.

Reutter, Mark. *Sparrows Point: Making Steel: The Rise and Ruin of American Industrial Might.* New York: Summit, 1989.

Reynolds, Michael S. *Hemingway: The American Homecoming.* Cambridge, MA: Blackwell, 1992.

Ribowsky, Mark. *Don't Look Back: Satchel Paige in the Shadows of Baseball.* New York: Simon & Schuster, 1994.

Ribuffo, Leo. *The Old Christian Right: The Protestant Far Right from the Great Depression to the Cold War.* Philadelphia: Temple University Press, 1983.

Richardson, R. Dan. *Comintern Army: The International Brigades and the Spanish Civil War.* Lexington: University Press of Kentucky, 1982.

Ridley, Jasper Godwin. *Mussolini.* New York: St. Martin's, 1998.

Riley, Glenda. *Inventing the American Woman: A Perspective on Women's History 1865 to the Present.* Arlington Heights, IL: Harlan Davidson, 1986.

Robbins, Jack Alan, ed. *Granville Hicks in the New Masses.* Port Washington, NY: Kennikat, 1974.

Roberts, Owen J. *The Court and the Constitution.* Cambridge, MA: Harvard University Press, 1951.

Roberts, Ron E. *John L. Lewis: Hard Labor and Wild Justice.* Dubuque, IA: Kendall/Hunt, 1994.

Robertson, David. *Sly and Able: A Political Biography of James F. Byrnes.* New York: Norton, 1994.

Robertson, Nan. *Getting Better: Inside Alcoholics Anonymous.* New York: Morrow, 1988.

Robeson, Paul. *Here I Stand.* Boston: Beacon, 1971 (reprint).

Robeson, Susan. *The Whole World in His Hands: A Pictorial History of Paul Robeson.* Secaucus, NJ: Citadel, 1981.

Robinson, Edward G. *All My Yesterdays: An Autobiography.* New York: Hawthorn, 1973.

Rock, William R. *Chamberlain and Roosevelt: British Foreign Policy and the United States, 1937–1940.* Columbus: Ohio State University Press, 1988.

Rockwell, Norman. *My Adventures As an Illustrator.* New York: Abrams, 1988.

———. *Norman Rockwell and the* Saturday Evening Post*: The Complete Cover Collection, 1916–1971.* New York: MJF Books, 1994.

Roddick, Nick. *A New Deal in Entertainment: Warner Brothers in the 1930s.* London: British Film Institute, 1983.

Rodger Streitmatter, ed. *Empty Without You: The Intimate Letters of Eleanor Roosevelt and Lorena Hickok.* New York: Free Press, 1998.

Rodgers, Richard. *Musical Stages: An Autobiography.* New York: Random House, 1975.

Rogers, Will, and Donald Day. *Autobiography.* Boston: Hougton Mifflin, 1949.

Rollins, Alfred Brooks. *Roosevelt and Howe.* New York: Knopf, 1962.

Rollins, Peter C. "Ideology and Film Rhetoric: Three Documentaries of the New Deal Era (1936–1941)." In *Hollywood as Historian: American Film in a Cultural Context,* ed. Peter C. Rollins. Lexington: University Press of Kentucky, 1983.

Romasco, Albert U. *The Politics of Recovery: Roosevelt's New Deal.* New York: Oxford University Press, 1983.

———. *The Poverty of Abundance: Hoover, the Nation, the Depression.* New York: Oxford University Press, 1965.

Roosevelt, Eleanor. *Autobiography.* New York: Harper & Row, 1961.

Roosevelt, Franklin. *The Public Papers and Addresses of Franklin D. Roosevelt.* Compiled by Samuel I. Rosenman. 13 vols. New York: Random House, 1950.

Rose, Nancy E. *Put to Work: Relief Programs in the Great Depression.* New York: Monthly Review Press, 1994.

Roseboom, Eugene, and Alfred Eckes. *A History of Presidential Elections from George Washington to Jimmy Carter.* New York: Macmillan, 1979.

Rosen, Elliot A. *Hoover, Roosevelt, and the Brains Trust: From Depression to New Deal.* New York: Columbia University Press, 1977.

Rosenberg, Deena. *Fascinating Rhythm: The Collaboration of George and Ira Gershwin.* New York: Dutton, 1991.

Rosenberg, Emily S. *Spreading the American Dream: American Economic and Cultural Expansion, 1890–1945.* New York: Hill & Wang, 1982.

Rosenberg, Rosalind. *Divided Lives: American Women in the Twentieth Century.* New York: Hill & Wang, 1992.

Rosenof, Theodore. *Economics in the Long Run: New Deal Theorists and their Legacies, 1933–1993.* Chapel Hill: University of North Carolina Press, 1997.

Rosenstone, Robert A. *Crusade of the Left: The Lincoln Battalion in the Spanish Civil War.* New York: Pegasus, 1969.

Ross, Barbara Joyce. *J. E. Spingarn and the Rise of the NAACP, 1911–1939.* New York: Atheneum, 1972.

Rothel, David. *The Gene Autry Book.* Madison, WI: Empire, 1988.

Rubin, Martin. *Busby Berkeley and the Tradition of Spectacle.* New York: Columbia University Press, 1993.

Rubinstein, Annette, ed. *I Vote My Conscience: Debates, Speeches, and Writings of Vito Marcantonio.* New York: Vito Marcantonio Memorial, 1956.

Ruth, David E. *Inventing the Public Enemy: The Gangster in American Culture, 1918–1934.* Chicago: University of Chicago Press, 1996.

Ryan, James G. *Earl Browder: The Failure of American Communism.* Tuscaloosa: University of Alabama Press, 1997.

Rydell, Robert W. *World of Fairs: The Century-of-Progress Expositions.* Chicago: University of Chicago Press, 1993.

Rydell, Robert W., and Nancy Gwinn, eds. *Fair Representations: World's Fairs and the Modern World.* Amsterdam: VU University Press, 1994

Sachs, Bernard. "Recreation After Fifty." *Recreation* (August 1937): 308, 332–333.

Salmond, John A. *The Civilian Conservation Corps, 1933–42: A New Deal Case Study.* Durham, NC: Duke University Press, 1967.

———. "The Civilian Conservation Corps and the Negro." *Journal of American History* 52:1 (1965): 75–88.

———. *A Southern Rebel: The Life and Times of Aubrey Willis*

Williams, 1890–1965. Chapel Hill: University of North Carolina Press, 1983.

Saloutos, Theodore, and John D. Hicks. *Agricultural Discontent in the Middle West, 1900–1939*. Madison: University of Wisconsin Press, 1951.

Saloutos, Theodore. *The American Farmer and the New Deal*. Ames: Iowa State University Press, 1982.

———. "The New Deal and Farm Policy in the Great Plains." *Agricultural History* 43:3 (July 1969): 51–74.

Salvemini, Gaetano. "Economic Conditions in Italy, 1919–1922." *Journal of Modern History* 23 (March 1951): 29–37.

———. *Prelude to World War II*. London: Gollancz, 1953.

Sanchez, George J. *Becoming Mexican American: Ethnicity, Culture and Identity in Chicano Los Angeles, 1900–1945*. New York: Oxford University Press, 1993.

Santelli, Robert, and Emily Davidson, eds. *Hard Travelin': The Life and Legacy of Woody Guthrie*. Hanover, NH: University Press of New England, 1999.

Santino, Jack. *Miles of Smiles, Years of Struggle: Stories of Black Pullman Porters*. Urbana: University of Illinois Press, 1989.

Sarti, Roland. *Fascism and the Industrial Leadership in Italy, 1919–1940: A Study in the Expansion of Private Power under Fascism*. Berkeley: University of California Press, 1971.

Sautter, Udo. *Three Cheers for the Unemployed: Government and Unemployment before the New Deal*. Cambridge, England: Cambridge University Press, 1991.

Sauvy, Alfred, *Histoire économique de la France entre les deux guerres*. 3 vols. Paris: Fayard, 1965–72.

Savage, John. *Balanced Budgets and American Politics*. Ithaca: Cornell University Press, 1990.

Savage, Sean. *Roosevelt: The Party Leader, 1932–1945*. Lexington: University Press of Kentucky, 1991.

Schaller, Michael. *The U.S. Crusade in China, 1938–1945*. New York: Columbia University Press, 1979.

Scharf, Lois. *To Work and to Wed: Female Employment, Feminism, and the Great Depression*. Westport, CT: Greenwood, 1980.

Schickel, Richard. *The Disney Version: The Life, Times, Art, and Commerce of Walt Disney*. New York : Simon & Schuster, 1985.

Schlesinger, Arthur A., Jr. *The Age of Roosevelt: The Crisis of the Old Order, 1919–1933*. Boston: Houghton Mifflin, 1957.

———. *The Coming of the New Deal*, Vol. 2. Boston: Houghton Mifflin, 1958.

———. *The Politics of Upheaval*. Boston: Houghton Mifflin, 1959.

Schmidt, Carl T. *The Corporate State in Action: Italy Under Fascism*. New York: Oxford University Press, 1939.

Schonbach, Morris. *Native American Fascism During the 1930s and 1940s*. New York: Garland, 1985.

Schorer, Mark. *Sinclair Lewis: An American Life*. New York: McGraw-Hill, 1961.

Schrecker, Ellen. *Many Were the Crimes: McCarthyism in America*. Princeton, NJ: Princeton University Press, 1998.

Schwantes, Carlos A."We've Got'em on the Run, Brothers: The 1937 Non-Automotive Sit Down Strikes in Detroit." *Michigan History* 56:3 (1972): 179–99.

Schwartz, Benjamin I. *Chinese Communism and the Rise of Mao*. Cambridge, MA: Harvard University Press, 1951.

Schwartz, Charles. *Cole Porter: A Biography*. New York: Dial, 1979.

Schwarz, Jordan A. *The Interregnum of Despair: Hoover, Congress, and the Depression*. Urbana: University of Illinois Press, 1970.

———. *Liberal: Adolf A. Berle and the Vision of an American Era*. New York: Free Press, 1987.

———. *The New Dealers: Power Politics in the Age of Roosevelt*. New York: Knopf, 1993.

———. *The Speculator: Bernard M. Baruch in Washington, 1917–1965*. Chapel Hill: University of North Carolina Press, 1981.

Sealander, Judith. *Private Wealth and Public Life: Foundation Philanthropy and the Reshaping of American Social Policy from the Progressive Era to the New Deal*. Baltimore: John Hopkins University Press, 1997.

Seely, Bruce Edsall. "Iron and Steel in the Twentieth Century." *Encyclopedia of American Business History and Biography*. New York: Facts on File, 1994.

Seideman, David. *The New Republic: A Voice of Modern Liberalism*. New York: Praeger, 1986.

Seidler, Murray B. *Norman Thomas: Respectable Rebel*. 2nd ed. Syracuse: Syracuse University Press, 1967.

Seligman, Joel. *The SEC and the Future of Finance*. New York: Praeger, 1985.

Senate, Committee on the Judiciary. *American Ground Transport: A Proposal for Restructuring the Automobile, Truck, Bus and Rail Industries*. A report by Bradford Snell to the subcommittee on Antitrust and Monopoly. 93rd Cong., 2nd sess., 1974.

Shahn, Ben, and James Thrall Toby. *Paintings*. New York: Braziller, 1963.

Shahn, Ben, and Margaret R. Weiss. *Ben Shahn, Photographer: An Album from the Thirties*. New York: Da Capo, 1973.

Sheldon, Marcus. *Father Coughlin: The Tumultuous Life of the Priest of the Little Flower*. Boston: Little, Brown, 1973.

Sheridan, James E. *China in Disintegration: The Republican Era in Chinese History, 1912–1949*. New York: Free Press, 1975.

Sherrow, Victoria. *Hardship and Hope: America and the Great Depression*. New York: Twenty-First Century Books, 1997.

Sherwood, Robert Emmet. *Roosevelt and Hopkins: An Intimate History*. New York: Harper, 1950.

Shideler, James H. "The Development of the Parity Price formula for Agriculture, 1919–1923." *Agricultural History*, 27:3 (July 1953): 445–55.

Shifflett, Crandall A. *Coal Towns: Life, Work, and Culture in Company Towns of Southern Appalachia, 1880–1960*. Knoxville: University of Tennessee Press,1991.

Shillony, Ben-Ami. *Revolt in Japan: The Young Officers and the February 26, 1936, Incident*. Princeton, NJ: Princeton University Press, 1973.

Shirer, William. *The Rise and Fall of the Third Reich: A History of Nazi Germany*. New York: Simon & Schuster, 1990.

Short, Philip. *Mao: A Life*. New York: Holt, 2000.

Shover, John L. "The Farmers' Holiday Association Strike, August 1932." *Agricultural History* 39:4 (October, 1965): 197–203.

Simon, James F. *Independent Journey: The Life of William O. Douglas*. New York: Harper & Row, 1980.

Sinclair, Andrew. *John Ford*. New York: Dial, 1979.

Sinclair, Upton. *The Autobiography of Upton Sinclair*. New York: Harcourt, Brace & World, 1962.

———. *I, Governor of California, and How I Ended Poverty: A True Story of the Future*. Published by the author, 1933.

Sirgiovanni, George. *An Undercurrent of Suspicion: Anti-Communism in America During World War II*. New Brunswick and London: Transaction Publishers, 1990.

Sitkoff, Harvard. *A New Deal for Blacks: The Emergence of Civil Rights as a National Issue*. Vol. 1, *The Depression Years*. New York: Oxford University Press, 1978.

Skenazy, Paul. *James M. Cain*. New York: Ungar, 1989.

Skidelsky, Robert Jacob Alexander. *John Maynard Keynes: A Biography*. 2 vols. London: Macmillan, 1983.

———. *Keynes*. Oxford, NY: Oxford University Press, 1996.

———. *Politicians and the Slump: The Labour Government of 1929–1931*. London: Macmillan, 1967.

Sklar, Robert. *Movie-Made America: A Cultural History of the American Movies*. New York: Random House, 1975.

Skousen, K. Fred. *An Introduction to the SEC*. Cincinnati: South-Western, 1976.

Sloan, Alfred P., Jr. *My Years with General Motors*. Garden City, NY: Doubleday, 1963.

Smesler, Marshall. *The Life That Ruth Built: A Biography*. New York: Quadrangle, 1975.

Smith, Alfred Emanuel. *The Citizen and His Government*. New York: Harper, 1935.

Smith, Daniel Scott. "Accounting for the Change in the Families of the Elderly in the United States, 1900–Present." In *Old Age in a Bureaucratic Society* ed. David Van Tassel and Peter N. Stearns. New York: Greenwood, 1986.

Smith, Gene. *The Shattered Dream: Herbert Hoover and the Great Depression*. New York: Morrow, 1970.

Smith, Grover Cleveland. *Archibald MacLeish*. Minneapolis: University of Minnesota Press, 1971.

Smith, Richard Norton. *The Colonel: The Life and Legend of Robert R. McCormick, 1880–1955*. Boston: Houghton Mifflin, 1997.

———. *An Uncommon Man: The Triumph of Herbert Hoover*. New York: Simon & Schuster, 1984.

Smith, Rixey. *Carter Glass: A Biography*. New York: Longmans, 1939.

Smith, Wendy. *Real Life: The Group Theatre and America, 1931–1940*. New York: Knopf, 1990.

Snellgrove, Laurence Ernest. *Franco and the Spanish Civil War*. New York: McGraw-Hill, 1968.

Snow, Edgar. *Red Star Over China*. New York: Random House, 1938.

Sobel, Robert. *The Age of Giant Corporations*. Westport, CT: Greenwood, 1972.

———. *AMEX: A History of the American Stock Exchange, 1921–1971*. New York: Weybright & Talley, 1972.

———. *NYSE: A History of the New York Stock Exchange 1935–1975*. New York: Weybright & Talley, 1975.

Sparks, Randy J. "Heavenly Houston or Hellish Houston? Black Unemployment and Relief Efforts, 1929–1936." In *Hope Restored: How the New Deal Worked in Town and Country*. ed. Bernard Sternsher. Chicago: Ivan R. Dee, 1999: 182–195.

Speer, Albert. *Inside the Third Reich: Memoirs*. Trans. Richard Winston and Clara Winston. New York: Simon & Schuster, 1997.

Sperber, Ann M. *Bogart*. New York: Morrow, 1997.

Spoto, Donald. *Blue Angel: The Life of Marlene Dietrich*. New York: Doubleday, 1992.

Stacey, C.P. *Canada in the Age of Conflict: A History of Canadian External Policies, Vol. 2: 1921–1948: The Mackenzie King Era*. Toronto: University of Toronto Press, 1981.

Stacey, Thomas. *The Hindenburg*. San Diego: Lucent, 1990.

Starr, John Bryan. *Continuing the Revolution: The Political Thought of Mao*. Princeton, NJ: Princeton University Press, 1979.

Staub, Michael E. *Voices of Persuasion: Politics of Representation in 1930s America*. New York: Cambridge University Press, 1994.

St. Clair, Jeffrey. *The Motorization of American Cities*. New York: Praeger, 1987.

Steel, Ronald. *Walter Lippman and the American Century*. Boston: Little, Brown, 1980.

Stein, Herbert. *The Fiscal Revolution in America*. Chicago: University of Chicago Press, 1969.

Steinbeck, Elaine, and Robert Wallsten, eds. *Steinbeck: A Life in Letters*. New York: Viking, 1975.

Steinberg, Alfred. *Sam Rayburn: A Biography*. New York: Hawthorn, 1975.

Sterling, Bryan B., and Frances N. Sterling. *A Will Rogers Treasury: Reflections and Observations*. New York: Crown, 1982.

Sternsher, Bernard, ed. *Hitting Home: The Great Depression in Town and Country*. Chicago: Quadrangle, 1970.

Stewart, Maxwell Slutz. *Steel: Problems of a Great Industry*. New York: Public Affairs Committee, 1937.

Stiles, Lela Mae. *The Man Behind Roosevelt: The Story of Louis McHenry Howe*. Cleveland: World, 1954.

Stimson, Henry L. *On Active Service in Peace and War*. New York: Harper, 1948.

Stock, Catherine McNicol. *Main Street in Crisis: The Great Depression and the Old Middle Class on the Northern Plains*. Chapel Hill: University of North Carolina Press, 1992.

Stolberg, Mary M. *Fighting Organized Crime: Politics, Justice, and The Legacy of Thomas E. Dewey*. Boston: Northeastern University Press, 1995.

Stoler, Mark A. *George C. Marshall: Soldier-Statesman of the American Century*. Boston: Twayne, 1989.

Stone, Mildred F. *A Short History of Life Insurance*. Indianapolis: Insurance Research and Review Service, 1942.

Storb, Ilse. *Louis Armstrong: The Definitive Biography*. New York: Peter Lang, 1999.

Storrs, Landon R.Y. *Civilizing Capitalism*. Chapel Hill: University of North Carolina Press, 2000.

Stott, William. *Documentary Expression and Thirties America*. Chicago: University of Chicago Press, 1973.

Stover, John F. *American Railroads*. Chicago: University of Chicago Press, 1961.

———. *The Life and Decline of the American Railroad*. New York: Oxford University Press, 1970.

Stowe, David W. *Swing Changes: Big Band Jazz in New Deal America*. Cambridge, MA: Harvard University Press, 1994.

Strasser, Susan, Charles McGovern, and Matthias Judt, eds. *Getting and Spending: European and American Consumer Societies in the Twentieth Century*. Washington, DC: German Historical Institute, Cambridge University Press, 1998.

Stryker, Roy Emerson. *In This Proud Land: America 1935–1943 As Seen in the FSA Photographs*. Boston: New York Graphic Society, 1973.

Sullivan, Patricia. *Days of Hope: Race and Democracy in the New Deal Era*. Chapel Hill: University of North Carolina Press, 1996.

Sutton, Francis X., Seymour E. Harris, Carl Kaysen, and James Tobin. *The American Business Creed*. Cambridge, MA: Harvard University Press, 1956.

Swain, Martha H. "A New Deal In Libraries: Federal Relief Work and Library Service, 1933–1943." *Libraries & Culture* 30:3 1995: 265–283.

Swanberg, W.A. *Citizen Hearst: A Biography of William Randolph Hearst*. New York: Scribner, 1961.

———. *Norman Thomas: The Last Idealist*. New York: Scribner, 1976.

Swenson, Karen. *Greta Garbo: A Life Apart*. New York: Scribner, 1997.

Swindell, Larry. *Screwball: The Life of Carole Lombard*. New York: Morrow, 1975.

Taft, Philip. *The A.F. of L. From the Death of Gompers to the Merger*. New York: Harper, 1959.

Tasca [Rossi], Angelo. *The Rise of Italian Fascism, 1918–1922*. New York: H. Fertig, 1966.

Tate, Juanita. *Philip Murray as a Labor Leader*. Ann Arbor, MI: University Microfilms, 1970.

Tauianac, John. *The Empire State Building: The Making of a Landmark*. New York: Scribner, 1995.

Taylor, Deems. *Walt Disney's* Fantasia. New York: Simon & Schuster, 1940.

Teatero, William. *Mackenzie King: Man of Mission*. Don Mills, Ontario: T. Nelson, 1979.

Tebbel, John. *The American Magazine: A Compact History*. New York: Hawthorn, 1969.

———. *George Horace Lorimer and the* Saturday Evening Post. Garden City, NY: Doubleday, 1948.

Tebbel, John, and Mary Ellen Zuckerman. *The Compact History of the American Newspaper*. New York: Hawthorn, 1969.

———. *The Magazine in America, 1741–1990*. New York: Oxford University Press, 1991.

Terkel, Studs. *Hard Times: An Oral History of the Great Depression*. New York: Pantheon, 1970.

Terrill, Ross. *Mao: A Biography*. New York: Harper & Row, 1980.

Tesher, Ellie. *The Dionnes*. Toronto: Doubleday Canada, 1999.

Thelan, David P. *Robert M. LaFollette and the Insurgent Spirit*. Boston: Little, Brown, 1976.

Theoharis, Athan, and John Stuart Cox. *The Boss: J. Edgar Hoover and the Great American Inquisition*. New York: Bantam, 1990.

Theoharis, Athan, et al. *The FBI: A Comprehensive Reference Guide*. New York: Checkmark, 2000.

Thomas, Bob. *Bud & Lou: The Abbott & Costello Story*. Philadelphia: Lippincott, 1977.

Thomas, Dorothy Swaine. *Japanese American Evacuation and Resettlement: The Salvage*. Berkeley: University of California Press, 1952.

Thomas, Hugh. *The Spanish Civil War*. 3d ed. London: Hamish Hamilton, 1977.

Thomas, Norman. *Socialism Re-examined*. New York: Norton, 1963.

Thomas, Tony. *The Films of Errol Flynn*. New York: Citadel Press, 1969.

Thomson, David. *Rosebud: The Story of Orson Welles*. New York: Knopf, 1996.

Tidd, James Frances, Jr. "Stitching and Striking: WPA Sewing Rooms and the 1937 Relief Strike in Hillsborough County" In *Hope Restored: How the New Deal Worked in Town and Country*. Bernard Sternsher, 207–220. Chicago: Ivan R. Dee, 1999.

Timberlake, Richard H. *Monetary Policy in the United States: An Intellectual and Institutional History*. Chicago: University of Chicago Press, 1993.

Timmons, Bascom Nolly. *Garner of Texas: A Personal History*. New York: Harper, 1948.

Tindall, George Brown. *The Emergence of the New South 1913–1945*. Baton Rouge: Louisiana University Press, 1967.

Titus, David Anson. *Palace and Politics in Prewar Japan*. New York: Columbia University Press, 1974.

Tomlins, Christopher L. "AFL Unions in the 1930s: Their Performance in Historical Perspective." *Journal of American History* 65:4 (March 1979): 1021–42.

Tornabene, Lyn. *Long Live the King: A Biography of Clark Gable*. New York: Putnam, 1976.

Townsend, Francis. *New Horizons*. Chicago: J.L. Stewart, 1943.

Tozzi, Romano. *Spencer Tracy: 1900–1967*. New York: Galahad, 1973.

Tucker, Robert C. *Stalin in Power: The Revolution from Above, 1928–1941*. New York: Norton, 1990.

Tugwell, Rexford G. *The Brains Trust*. New York: Viking, 1968.

———. *The Diary of Rexford G. Tugwell: The New Deal, 1932–1935*. New York: Greenwood, 1992.

Tull, Charles J. *Father Coughlin and the New Deal*. Syracuse, NY: Syracuse University Press, 1965.

Turner, Jane, ed., *The Dictionary of Art*. New York: Macmillan, 1996.

Tyack, David B. *Great Depression and Recent Years*. Cambridge: Harvard University Press, 1984.

Tyler, Gus. *Look for the Union Label: A History of the International Ladies Garment Workers Union*. Armonk, NY: Sharpe, 1995.

U.S. v Butler (297 U.S. 1).

United States of America. *U.S. Statutes at Large, 74th Congress, 1935–1936*, Volume 49 Washington, DC: Government Printing Office, 1936.

Urofsky, Melvin I. *Louis D. Brandeis and the Progressive Tradition*. Boston: Little, Brown, 1981.

Urofsky, Melvin I., and David M. Levy, eds. *Letters of Louis D. Brandeis*. Albany: State University of New York Press, 1971–1978.

Uys, Errol Lincoln. *Riding the Rails: Teenagers on the Move during the Great Depression*. New York: TV Books, 1999.

Valelly, Richard M. *Radicalism in the States: The Minnesota Farmer-Labor Party and the American Political Economy*. Chicago: University of Chicago Press, 1989.

Vallée, Rudy. *Let the Chips Fall*. Harrisburg, PA: Stackpole, 1975.

Van Hise, James. *Who Was That Masked Man? The Story of the Lone Ranger*. Las Vegas: Pioneer, 1990.

Venkataramani, M.S. "Norman Thomas, Arkansas Sharecroppers, and the Roosevelt Agricultural Policies, 1933–37." *The Mississippi Valley Historical Review*. 47:2 (September 1960): 225–246.

Veysey, Laurence. "A Postmortem on Daniel Bell's Postindustrialism." *American Quarterly* 34:1 (1982) 49–69.

Vickers, Kenneth Wayne. "John Rankin: Democrat and Demagogue." Master's thesis, Mississippi State University, 1993.

Vidor, King. *A Tree Is a Tree*. New York: Harcourt, Brace, 1953.

Vogel, David. "Why Businessmen Distrust Their State: The Political Consciousness of American Corporate Executives." *British Journal of Political Science*. (1978): 45–78.

Wagenheim, Kal. *Babe Ruth: His Life and Legend*. New York: Praeger, 1974.

Wainwright, Loudon. *The Great American Magazine: An Inside History of* Life. New York: Knopf, 1986.

Walters, F. P. *A History of the League of Nations*. Westport, CT: Greenwood, 1986.

Waltzer, Kenneth. "The Party and the Polling Place: American Communism and the American Labor Party in the 1930s." *Radical History Review* (Spring 1980):104–129.

Wandersee Bolin, Winifred D. "The Economics of Middle-Income Family Life: Working Women During the Great Depression." *Journal of American History* 65:1 (1978): 60–74.

Ware, Gilbert. *William Hastie: Grace Under Pressure*. New York: Oxford University Press, 1984.

Ware, Susan. *Beyond Suffrage: Women in the New Deal*. Cambridge: Harvard University Press, 1981.

Ware, Susan. *Holding Their Own: American Women in the 1930's.* Boston: Twayne, 1982.

Warren, Donald I. *Radio Priest: Charles Coughlin, the Father of Hate Radio.* New York: Free Press, 1996.

Warren, Doug. *James Cagney: The Authorized Biography.* New York: St. Martin's, 1983.

Warren, Frank. *An Alternative Vision: The Socialist Party in the 1930's.* Bloomington: University of Indiana Press, 1974.

Warren, Harris G. *Herbert Hoover and the Great Depression.* New York: Oxford University Press, 1959.

Warren, Robert Penn. *A Robert Penn Warren Reader.* New York: Random House, 1987.

Warrick, Richard A. "Drought in the Great Plains: A Case Study of Research on Climate and Society in the USA." In *IIASA Proceedings Series: Climate Constraints and Human Activities.* ed. Jessee Ausubel and Asit K. Biswas. New York: Pergamon, 1980.

Waters, Walter W. *B.E.F.: The Whole Story of the Bonus Army, by W. W. Waters as Told to William C. White.* New York: AMS, 1970.

Watkins, Floyd C., John T. Hiers, and Mary Louise Weaks. *Talking with Robert Penn Warren.* Athens: University of Georgia Press, 1990.

———. *Righteous Pilgrim: The Life and Times of Harold L. Ickes, 1874–1952.* New York: Holt, 1990.

———. *The Great Depression: America in the 1930s.* New York: Back Bay, 1993.

———. *The Hungry Years: A Narrative History of the Great Depression in America.* New York: Holt, 1999.

Watson, Forbes. *American Painting Today.* Washington, DC: The American Federation of Art, 1939.

Watt, Donald Cameron. *How War Came: The Immediate Origins of the Second World War, 1938–1939.* New York: Pantheon, 1989.

Weare, Walter B. *Black Business in the New South: A Social History of the North Carolina Mutual Life Insurance Company.* Urbana: University of Illinois Press, 1973.

Weatherson, Michael A. *Hiram Johnson: A Bio-Bibliography.* New York: Greenwood, 1988.

Weaver, Robert C. *Negro Labor: A National Problem.* New York: Harcourt Brace, 1946.

Weber, Debra. *Dark Sweat, White Gold: California Farm Workers, Cotton and the New Deal.* Berkeley and Los Angeles: University of California Press, 1994.

Weed, Clyde P. *The Nemesis of Reform: The Republican Party During the New Deal.* New York: Columbia University Press, 1994.

Weems, Robert E., Jr. "The Chicago Metropolitan Mutual Assurance Company: A Profile of a Black-Owned Enterprise." *Illinois Historical Journal* 86:1 (1993): 15–26.

Weinberg, Gerhard L. *A World At Arms: A Global History of World War II.* Cambridge, England: Cambridge University Press, 1994.

Weisbrot, Robert. *Father Divine and the Struggle for Racial Equality.* Urbana: University of Illinois Press, 1983.

Weisenberger, Bernard A., ed. *The WPA Guides to America: the Best of 1930s America as Seen by the Federal Writer's Project* New York: Pantheon, 1985.

Weiss, Nancy J. *Farewell to the Party of Lincoln: Black Politics in the Age of FDR.* Princeton, NJ: Princeton University Press, 1983.

———. *The National Urban League, 1910–1940.* New York: Oxford University Press, 1974.

Weller, Cecil Edward. *Joe T. Robinson: Always a Loyal Democrat.* Fayetteville: University of Arkansas Press, 1998.

Welles, Benjamin. *Sumner Welles: FDR's Global Strategist: A Biography.* New York: St. Martin's, 1997.

Welles, Orson. *Orson Welles on Shakespeare: The W.P.A. and Mercury Theatre Playscripts.* New York: Greenwood, 1990.

———. *The Cradle Will Rock: An Original Screenplay.* Santa Barbara, CA: Santa Teresa Press, 1994.

Welles, Orson, and Peter Bogdanovich. *This Is Orson Welles.* New York: HarperCollins, 1992.

Welles, Sumner. *The Time for Decision.* New York: Harper, 1944.

West, Kenneth B. " 'On the Line': Rank and File Reminiscences of Working Conditions and the General Motors Sit-Down Strike of 1936–37." *Michigan Historical Review* 12:1 (1986): 57–82.

West, Mae. *Goodness Had Nothing to Do With It: The Autobiography of Mae West.* New York: Belvedere, 1981 (reprint).

Weyl, Nathaniel. *The Reconquest of Mexico: The Years of Lázaro Cárdenas.* New York: Oxford University Press, 1939.

Whalen, Richard J. *The Founding Father: The Story of Joseph P. Kennedy.* New York: New American Library, 1964.

Whealey, Robert H. *Hitler and Spain: The Nazi Role in the Spanish Civil War 1936–1939.* Lexington, KY: University Press of Kentucky, 1989.

———. Mussolini's Ideological Diplomacy: An Unpublished Document." *Journal of Modern History* 39 (December 1967): 432–37.

Wheeler, Burton K., and Paul F. Healy. *Yankee from the West: The Candid, Turbulent Life Story of the Yankee-born U.S. Senator from Montana.* Garden City, NY: Doubleday, 1962.

White, Graham. *FDR and the Press.* Chicago: University of Chicago Press, 1979.

White, Michael, and John Gribbin. *Einstein: A Life in Science.* New York: Dutton, 1994.

White, Walter Francis. *A Man Called White: The Autobiography of Walter White.* New York: Viking Press, 1948.

Whitney, Simon. *Antitrust Policies.* Vol. 1. New York: The Twentieth Century Fund, 1958.

Wicker, Elmus. *The Banking Panics of the Great Depression.* New York: Cambridge University Press, 1996.

Williams, J. Kerwin. *Grants-In-Aid under the Public Works Administration: A Study in Federal-State-Local Relations.* New York: Columbia University Press, 1939.

Williams, Thomas Harry. *Huey Long.* New York: Random House, 1981.

Williamson, Philip. *Stanley Baldwin: Conservative Leadership and National Values.* New York: Cambridge University Press, 1999.

Willis, Carol. "Empire State Building." In *The Encyclopedia of New York City* ed. Kenneth Jackson. New Haven, CT: Yale University Press, 1995.

Willis, Donald C. *The Films of Howard Hawks.* Metuchen, NJ: Scarecrow, 1975.

Willkie, Wendell. *This Is Wendell Willkie; a Collection of Speeches and Writings on Present-Day Issues.* New York: Dodd, Mead, 1940.

Wilson, Joan Hoff. *Herbert Hoover: Forgotten Progressive.* New York: HarperCollins, 1975.

Windeler, Robert. *The Films of Shirley Temple.* New York: Citadel, 1995.

Winters, Donald L. "The Persistence of Progressivism: Henry Cantwell Wallace and the Movement For Agricultural Economics." *Agricultural History,* 41:2 (April 1967): 109–120.

Wise, Rebecca, ed. *Rural Electric Fact Book*. Washington, DC: National Rural Electric Cooperative Association, 1964.

Witte, Edwin E. *The Development of the Social Security Act* Madison: University of Wisconsin Press, 1962.

Wolfe, Charles K. *The Life and Legend of Leadbelly*. New York: HarperCollins, 1992.

Wolseley, Roland E. *The Changing Magazine*. New York: Hasting House, 1973.

Wolters, Raymond. *Negroes and the Great Depression: The Problem of Economic Recovery*. Westport, CT: Greenwood, 1970.

Wood, Bryce. *The Making of the Good Neighbor Policy*. New York: Columbia University Press, 1961.

Worster, Donald. *Dust Bowl: The Southern Plains in the 1930's*. New York: Oxford University Press, 1979.

Wright, Gavin. *The Political Economy of the Cotton South: Households, Markets an*d *Wealth in the Nineteenth Century*. New York: Norton, 1978.

Yates, JoAnne. "Information Technology and Business Processes in the Twentieth Century Insurance Industry." *Business and Economic History* 21 (1992): 317–25.

Yoshihake Takehiko. *Conspiracy in Manchuria: The Rise of the Japanese Military*. New Haven, CT: Yale University, 1963.

Young, Donald, ed. *Adventure in Politics: The Memoirs of Philip LaFollette*. New York: Holt, Rinehart, and Winston, 1970.

Young, Louise. *Japan's Total Empire: Manchuria and the Culture of Wartime Imperialism*. Berkeley: University of California Press, 1998.

Yu, Renqiu. *To Save China, To Save Ourselves: The Chinese Hand Laundry Alliance of New York*. Philadelphia: Temple University Press, 1992.

Zangrando, Robert L. *The NAACP Crusade Against Lynching, 1909–1950*. Philadelphia: Temple University Press, 1980.

Zelman, Donald L. "Alazan-Apache Courts: A New Deal Response to Mexican American Housing Conditions in San Antonio." *Southwestern Historical Quarterly* 87:2 (October 1983): 123–150.

Zevin, B. D. *Nothing to Fear: The Selected Addresses of Franklin Delano Roosevelt, 1932–1945*. Boston: Houghton Mifflin, 1946.

Zieger, Robert H. *American Workers, American Unions, 1920–1985*. Baltimore: Johns Hopkins University Press, 1986.

———. *John L. Lewis: Labor Leader*. New York: Macmillan, 1988.

———. "Toward a History of the CIO: A Bibliographic Report" in *Labor History* 26: 4 (Fall 1985): 487–516.

———. *The CIO: 1935–1955*. Chapel Hill: University of North Carolina Press, 1995.

SUBJECT INDEX

Numbers in bold indicate volume.

Numbers in bold indicate volume.

Numbers in bold indicate volume.

Numbers in bold indicate volume.

BIOGRAPHICAL INDEX

Numbers in bold indicate volume.

Numbers in bold indicate volume.

Numbers in bold indicate volume.

Numbers in bold indicate volume.

Numbers in bold indicate volume.

LEGAL INDEX

Numbers in bold indicate volume.

Numbers in bold indicate volume.

Numbers in bold indicate volume.